Standard
COMMENTARY®

ENGLISH STANDARD VERSION®

Jim Eichenberger
Senior Editor

Ronald L. Nickelson
Commentary Editor

Margaret K. Williams
Activities Editor

Volume 2

Standard®
PUBLISHING
part of the David C Cook family

IN THIS VOLUME

Standard Lesson Commentary is published annually by Standard Publishing, www.standardpub.com. Copyright © 2016 by Standard Publishing, part of the David C Cook family, Colorado Springs, Colorado 80918. All rights reserved. Printed in the United States of America. Unless otherwise indicated, all Scripture quotations are from The ESV® Bible (The Holy Bible, English Standard Version®), copyright 2001 by Crossway, a publishing ministry of Good News Publishers. Used by permission. All rights reserved. Lessons and/or readings based on *International Sunday School Lessons for Christian Teaching*; copyright © 2013, by the Committee on the Uniform Series.

INDEX OF PRINTED TEXTS

The printed texts for 2016–2017 are arranged here in the order in which they appear in the Bible.

LOGOS DOWNLOAD AVAILABLE!

You can purchase the Standard Lesson eCommentary as a download from www.logos.com/standard. This purchase is separate from that of the print edition.

DON'T FORGET THE VISUALS!

The visuals pictured in the lessons are small reproductions of large, full-color posters included in the *Adult Resources* packet for each quarter. These visuals include maps, charts, Bible art, photography, and calligraphy that will engage the visual learners in your class. Also included is a *Presentation Tools* CD featuring digital images of all the printed posters, PowerPoint® presentations for the lessons, and reproducible student activity pages.

From your supplier, order numbers 1629116 (fall 2016), 2629117 (winter 2016–2017), 3629117 (spring 2017), and 4629117 (summer 2017). Call 1-800-323-7543 or go to www.standardlesson.com/standard-lesson-resources/ .

STANDARD LESSON COMMENTARY

An effective study for ANY type of group starts here!

For over six decades, *Standard Lesson Commentary* (SLC) has been a trusted resource for Bible teachers. Those decades have seen new educational structures and technologies emerge. During that time, Standard Lesson products have been developed to help teachers in nearly any Bible teaching environment.

Classic Midweek Study

OUR CONGREGATION HAS A VIBRANT WEDNESDAY NIGHT STUDY. ABOUT 50 OF US GATHER IN THE CHURCH AUDITORIUM FOR A LECTURE-ORIENTED LESSON. HOW DO I USE STANDARD LESSON COMMENTARY IN THIS "PULPIT TO PEW" SETTING?

What you need:
- *Standard Lesson Commentary*
- **CD from Adult Resources**

The outline on the second page of each SLC lesson is designed to structure a lecture presentation. Use the two verbal illustrations in the lesson at the appropriate points in the outline. Close with the "Thought to Remember" and prayer from the seventh page of the lesson.

A word of caution: Don't think that a traditional setting cannot benefit from modern technology! The CD in Adult Resources contains a PowerPoint® presentation for each session. For this environment, remove all slides except for the teaching outline, "Thought to Remember," and the visual for the lesson. As you teach, click through the slides to keep your group on task and engaged.

Mobile Mania

MY GROUP COULD NOT BE MORE DIFFERENT THAN THE PRECEEDING EXAMPLE! WE ARE A SMALL CLASS OF TWENTY-SOMETHINGS WHO ARE SERIOUS ABOUT BIBLE STUDY. BUT EVERYONE IN THE GROUP USES A SMARTPHONE OR TABLET TO ACCESS THE BIBLE. HOW CAN STANDARD LESSON COMMENTARY HELP ME WITH MY MOBILE-MANIACS?

What you need:
- *Standard Lesson Commentary*
- **Free memberships to StandardLesson.com**

Smartphones and tablets have changed the way we access information. This technology can be a great asset to serious Bible study.

Have students access www.standardlesson.com during your next class. Then have them click on the "Members" tab on the right-hand side of their menu bars and sign up for a free membership. A few clicks and they're connected!

Your copy of the SLC will still be your go-to resource, but your students will participate through the resources they now have access to as members of Standardlesson.com.

Start your class by having members download the latest edition of In the World. This is a current events discussion activity to introduce the lesson of the week. Have them read the article and discuss the accompanying questions.

Your lesson structure will come from the eighth page of the lesson, titled Involvement Learning.

Note the sections of that lesson plan that refer to using the reproducible pages.

Your students have access to those free reproducible pages with their Standardlesson.com memberships. Have them open the page for that lesson as directed in your lesson place on the Involvement learning page. You are leading the class from the wealth of resources in your SLC, and your group is participating with the free resources accessible with their mobile devices.

Traditional Classroom Setting

I TEACH IN A VERY TYPICAL SUNDAY SCHOOL SETTING. WE HAVE A CLASSROOM, TABLES, AND CHAIRS. WHAT TOOLS DO I NEED TO USE STANDARD LESSON COMMENTARY IN THIS SETTING?

What you need:
- *Standard Lesson Commentary*
- *Adult Resources*
- **Student books**
  (*KJV* & *NIV* only)

Display the colorful posters from Adult Resources in your classroom to pique interest in each lesson. There is one poster designed for each session. The SLC will tell you how and when to refer to it.

You will use your copy of the SLC to structure the lesson. Your students will have copies of the Bible text and an abbreviated version of the commentary in their student books. This will aid in presentation and understanding of the main points of the lesson.

Your students will be able to analyze and apply the content with written exercises in their student books. These exercises will help them gain a deeper understanding and application of the Bible lesson of the day.

Deep Thinkers, Big Talkers

MY GROUP NOT ONLY LOVES TO STUDY THE BIBLE, THEY CAN'T STOP TALKING ABOUT IT! HOW CAN THE STANDARD LESSON COMMENTARY HELP ME LEAD DISCUSSION-ORIENTED CLASSES EFFECTIVELY?

What you need:
- *Standard Lesson Commentary*
- **Free memberships to StandardLesson.com**

Bible study is not complete without a commitment to apply what has been studied. Certainly strong, informed discussion is a great way to do just that.

A free membership to Standardlesson.com will give you access to In the World, a perfect way to open a discussion-oriented class. Each week our writer looks at the top news stories and seeks to apply the current week's Bible lesson to one of them. Before class, download this article with discussion questions and make copies for every member of your group. Begin the session by distributing this activity and discussing it.

The commentary in the SLC will help you unpack the Bible content, verse by verse. Note that interspersed in the Bible commentary are What Do You Think? discussion questions. As you encounter these questions during your lesson presentation, open discussion by using them. This will allow your class to think deeply about the Bible content and encourage members to apply it while it is fresh in their minds.

Please note that these questions do not have pat answers! They are meant to *get* your group to think, not *tell* them what to think. These challenging questions are just what your group of deep thinkers and big talkers need for engaging, meaningful Bible study!

(continued next page)

Getting Down to Business

OUR MEN'S BIBLE CLASS IS FILLED WITH BUSINESS PROFESSIONALS. I CAN'T HELP BUT THINK THAT THEY FEEL MORE AT HOME IN THE COMPANY BOARDROOM THAN IN THE CHURCH'S CLASSROOM! HOW CAN THE STANDARD LESSON COMMENTARY HELP ME HELP THEM?

What you need:
- *Standard Lesson Commentary*
- *Adult Resources* CD

Few things are more ubiquitous in the business world than PowerPoint® slide presentations. This means of communicating ideas is sure to be familiar to a class such as yours.

The *Adult Resources* CD contains a PowerPoint presentation for every lesson. Each slide presentation includes the lesson outline, the visual for that lesson, What Do You Think? discussion questions, and learning activities that will help the group discover and apply lesson content.

The SLC comments will help you present the Bible content while you project the slides to your class. A great advantage of PowerPoint is that the group is engaged visually while you control the pace and content of the lesson.

For Personal Growth

I HAVE USED THE STANDARD LESSON COMMENTARY IN SUNDAY SCHOOL FOR YEARS. I AM IN A DIFFERENT CONGREGATION NOW, AND MY GROUP USES SOMETHING ELSE. I MISS MY STANDARD LESSON COMMENTARY! WHAT WOULD BE A WAY THAT I CAN USE THIS TREASURED BOOK ON MY OWN DURING MY DAILY QUIET TIMES?

What you need:
- *Standard Lesson Commentary*
- *Copies of 365 Devotions* or our quarterly *Devotions* books.

The *Standard Lesson Commentary* is designed specifically to help a Bible teacher. But there is nothing stopping you from being both the teacher and a classroom of one!.

Both *365 Devotions* and our quarterly *Devotions* books contain the same devotional reading for any given date. Both also coordinate to the topics covered in the *Standard Lesson Commentary*. You will find that every Sunday's devotion uses Scripture from the weekly lesson.

Our devotional readings are designed to begin with the topic for the week on Monday, and then build to a climax with our Sunday lesson. We suggest that each day you study a part of the lesson for the coming week, ending with your devotion.

There are any number of ways to divide the lesson commentary throughout the week, and we encourage you to find one that works best for you. To get you started, however, here is a suggestion.
Monday: Lesson introduction and background
Tuesday–Thursday: Verse-by-verse commentary
Friday: Lesson illustrations
Saturday: Discussion ("What Do You Think?" questions)
Sunday: Conclusion, Prayer, and Thought to Remember.

• •

For more than six decades, *Standard Lesson Commentary* has been "that Sunday school book"—a trusted resource for adult education in the church. But Standard Lesson adds to this resource with helps for a wide variety of Bible study contexts. Effective study for any group starts here!

PRICELESS RESOURCES

At no cost!

SIGN UP TODAY!

Every month our newsletter delivers content designed to help you in your teaching ministry. Each issue contains:

- The latest product news about the Standard Lesson line

- Monthly special offers to get you valuable resources at special prices

- A monthly article from respected Bible teachers that will help you be more effective as you teach God's Word

Go to this link to start receiving this helpful newsletter:

http://www.standardlesson.com/standard-lesson-enews-form/

Home Standard Lesson Commentary® Standard Lesson Quarterly® Standard Lesson Resources® Standard Lesson Teacher's Study Bible Members

Standard LESSON™

Sign up for our eNewsletter

Standard LESSON RESOURCES® | ENHANCE LEARNING

DEVOTIONS® In the World
Adult Resources
THE LOOKOUT® SEEK® TEACHER TIPS

MEMBERSHIP HAS ITS PRIVILEGES!

Your place for the latest resources for effective Bible teaching is www.standardlesson.com.

With a FREE membership you get:

• **In the World**—Help your students see the relevance of this week's lesson for life today. In the World connects each lesson with a related current news story. Use In the World to introduce or to wrap up your lesson.

• **Reproducible student activity pages**—Engage your students in the Involvement Learning plan suggested on the final page of each lesson. One page is available for every lesson throughout the year! (These pages are also available in print with the *Standard Lesson Commentary Deluxe Edition*s and digitally on the *Adult Resources* CD.)

• **Sample downloads**—Review some of what is available from Standard Lesson before you buy.

With a PAID membership you get all of the above plus:

• Weekly teacher tips to help you present the current lesson with variety and creativity

• An archive of our helpful Classroom Tips articles

• A new devotion each day from *365 Devotions*

StandardLesson.com

THE SOVEREIGNTY OF GOD

Special Features

Lessons

Unit 1: The Sovereignty of the Father

Unit 2: The Sovereignty of Jesus

Unit 3: Alpha and Omega

QUARTERLY QUIZ

Use these questions as a pretest or as a review. The answers are on page iv of This Quarter in the Word.

Lesson 1

1. The Messiah is prophesied to be able to kill the wicked with his breath. T/F. *Isaiah 11:4*

2. In the coming peace, the wolf will dwell with the what? (lamb, owl, snake?) *Isaiah 11:6*

Lesson 2

1. Isaiah believed future blessings of the Lord would fall only on Israel. T/F. *Isaiah 25:6*

2. Isaiah foresaw a time when the Lord will wipe away _____. *Isaiah 25:8*

Lesson 3

1. From God's perspective, people are like what? (grasshoppers, sparrows, roses?) *Isaiah 40:22*

2. Isaiah teaches that those who hope in God will soar on wings like _____. *Isaiah 40:31*

Lesson 4

1. The "year of the Lord's favor" will include a "day of vengeance." T/F. *Isaiah 61:2*

2. God will give the garment of _____ for the spirit of despair. *Isaiah 61:3*

Lesson 5

1. In Old Testament times, God spoke to "our fathers" by the _____. *Hebrews 1:1*

2. What has the Son inherited that is much superior to that of the angels? (mission, people, name?) *Hebrews 1:4*

Lesson 6

1. Biblically, Jesus can be called what? (pick two: dove, apostle, high priest, shaman?) *Hebrews 3:1*

2. The wise man builds his house on _____. *Matthew 7:24*

Lesson 7

1. What did Jesus experience that is just like what we experience? (commission of sin, failures of faith, temptations?) *Hebrews 4:15*

2. The Jewish high priest had to offer sacrifices for his own sins. T/F. *Hebrews 5:3*

Lesson 8

1. Melchizedek was the king of what city? (Salem, Ai, Tyre?) *Hebrews 7:1*

2. Who gave Melchizedek a tenth of the spoils from battle? (Noah, Abraham, Saul?) *Hebrews 7:2*

Lesson 9

1. Jesus is the founder and perfecter of our faith. T/F. *Hebrews 12:2*

2. The first readers of Hebrews had resisted to the point of bloodshed. T/F. *Hebrews 12:4*

Lesson 10

1. When John sees the new heaven and earth, there is no more _____. *Revelation 21:1*

2. The "lake that burns with fire and sulfur" is called "the second _____." *Revelation 21:8*

Lesson 11

1. How many gates will the new Jerusalem have? (3, 7, 12?) *Revelation 21:12*

2. The new Jerusalem will have an extraordinarily large temple. T/F. *Revelation 21:22*

Lesson 12

1. The tree of life in the new Jerusalem will produce healing leaves. T/F. *Revelation 22:2*

2. John was assured that the sayings were trustworthy and what? (profound, honorable, true?) *Revelation 22:6*

Lesson 13

1. When Christ returns, he will bring what? (recompense, crown, leaves?) *Revelation 22:12*

2. Jesus is the bright morning _____. *Revelation 22:16*

3. Adding things to the book of Revelation will bring plagues. T/F. *Revelation 22:18*

QUARTER AT A GLANCE

by Douglas Redford

THE BIBLE clearly teaches the sovereignty of God, the theme of this quarter's lessons. Believing in that sovereignty is not difficult when life is going well. What often leaves us perplexed (and sometimes annoyed or even angry) are the turmoils and tragedies of daily life. These can cause us to wonder, "Is God really sovereign? If so, then why do nations wage genocide? Why do people flaunt wickedness with impunity? Why do families continue to disintegrate?"

Troubling Times

We take care to note that many portions of the Bible that proclaim God's sovereignty were recorded during periods of great turmoil and tragedy. The prophet Isaiah, for example, carried out his ministry during a time when God's people were confronted by the seemingly invincible Assyrian empire. God's sovereignty? Nice in theory, perhaps; but that idea can be hard to embrace when Assyrian troops are overrunning your territory! As if that were not enough to discourage God's people, Isaiah also looked ahead to the time when Babylon would pose a similar threat. Can God be truly sovereign amidst all this chaos?

The Scripture texts for our first unit of lessons boldly assert the Lord's plans for his kingdom. That kingdom is to be characterized by true and lasting peace (lesson 1), freedom from grief and want (lesson 2), and the riches of an everlasting covenant (lesson 4). No enemy can limit what the Lord's sovereign purpose intends to accomplish. Foes such as Assyria and Babylon may have their day in the sun, but the Lord is the one who brings their "princes to nothing, and makes the rulers of the earth as emptiness" (Isaiah 40:23, lesson 3).

Our third unit of lessons also considers daunting threats to the people of God—in this case, his church. These four lessons from Revelation concentrate on the grand finale of God's sovereign plan to bring his people to a place where the bro-

kenness of a sin-cursed world exists no more. All of "the former things have passed away" (Revelation 21:4). Isaiah's vision in lesson 2 is fulfilled in the establishment of "a new heaven and a new earth" (Revelation 21:1, lesson 10).

Sovereign Savior

What Revelation describes is possible only through the all-sufficient work of Jesus. His sovereignty is the primary message of the book of Hebrews. From that book come the lessons of our second unit of study. The unsurpassed excellence of Jesus is proclaimed right from the book's opening words (lesson 5). Jesus is "over God's house as a son," the house to which we belong "if indeed we hold fast our confidence and our boasting in our hope" (Hebrews 3:6, lesson 6).

In exercising his sovereignty, Jesus has become the "founder and perfecter" of our faith (Hebrews 12:2, lesson 9). His suffering at the cross earned him these designations as well as that of "great high priest" (Hebrews 4:14, lesson 7).

With a similar spirit of endurance, Christians today proclaim Christ to a sin-soaked world, the very existence of which causes people to challenge the concept of a sovereign God. As we endure and

> *"Come, Lord Jesus!"*
> *—Revelation 22:20*

respond to these challenges, we must not forget that his sovereignty has been questioned before—during the onslaught of the Assyrians in Old Testament times, amidst the shame of the cross in New Testament times, etc. Yet God's promises and purposes have remained steadfast.

They remain so for us—during whatever today's times may bring. We acknowledge that sovereignty when we pray "Come, Lord Jesus" (Revelation 22:20, lesson 13).

GET THE SETTING

by Mark S. Krause

IN THE GAME Rock-Paper-Scissors, no position is all-powerful. Rock breaks scissors; scissors cut paper; paper covers rock. The pagan nations in Bible times had a similar view of their gods.

Less Than All-Powerful Gods

Pagans did not see any one deity as being almighty. Take for example Baal, worshipped by the Canaanites. Baal was understood to be the god of weather and therefore of agricultural abundance. Although seen as very powerful, there were checks on his abilities. Canaanites believed that Baal was subservient to the creator god, named El. They did not worship El as much, though, seeing him as distant and uninvolved in the world. Baal had consorts (goddess wives) who wielded great influence over him. Furthermore, Canaanite priests and priestesses supposedly knew the weaknesses of the gods and how to curry their favor. In this sense, people had limited power over their deities.

Competitive Gods

The various pantheons of pagan deities were not places of harmony! The Greeks pictured Mt. Olympus (the home of many gods) as a place of plots, intrigues, and rivalries. Such gods could be jealous, petty, and vain. Although the gods had great power, humans could challenge and trick them at times, a favorite theme of the myths.

Other ancient cultures saw their gods as needy beings who competed for human worship and devotion. For example, the Gilgamesh flood myth relates the story of a certain man named Utnapishtim who builds a giant boat and survives the deluge. When the waters subside, he leaves the boat, offers animal sacrifice, and burns incense. The story says the gods, who apparently were starved for human adoration while Utnapishtim and his people were afloat, "swarmed like flies" over the smell of the sacrifice and the incense.

Changing Gods

Ancient peoples created new deities when agendas called for it. Pharaoh Akhenaten, of the fourteenth-century BC, is an example. He abandoned the gods of his ancestors to focus on Aten, his version of the sun god. Seen by some historians as a shift toward a "one god" doctrine, Akhenaten's ideas did not last. Egyptians quickly reverted to their "many gods" outlook after his death.

Students of ancient history know of a set of Greek gods and a parallel set of Roman gods. For example, the Greek Zeus is the Roman Jupiter and the Greek Hermes is the Roman Mercury. It wasn't quite as simple as different names for the same gods, though. As the Romans occupied Greek-speaking lands, they imposed their own view of deities. For example, the city of Ephesus had a famous temple dedicated to Artemis, the Greek goddess of hunting, that the Romans aligned with their goddess Diana. Although these goddesses were similar, they were not identical (see Acts 19).

God of the Bible

In contrast with these pagan deities, the Bible presents a singular, all-powerful God. He alone sustains the world that he alone created. He doesn't compete with other gods, because there are no other gods. It doesn't matter if kings change allegiance among various false gods, because the God of the Bible remains the true God. He is not needy for our worship, but has created us to worship him. In this, worship is about our fulfilling our purpose, not about fulfilling God's needs. The God of the Bible is not a mix of various national deities and their myths, but is the true God who has revealed himself to us through his Word.

Our God, the sovereign Lord of the universe, is unlike any pagan god of the ancient world or any false god of the modern one. "All the gods of the peoples are worthless idols, but the Lord made the heavens" (Psalm 96:5).

· 4 ·

THIS QUARTER IN THE WORD

Mon, Aug. 29	God's Offer to Solomon	1 Kings 3:3-9
Tue, Aug. 30	God Pleased with Solomon's Requests	1 Kings 3:10-15
Wed, Aug. 31	Live Together in Harmony	1 Peter 3:8-13
Thu, Sep. 1	Build a Peaceful Lifestyle	2 Peter 1:3-11
Fri, Sep. 2	Support the Interests of Others	Philippians 2:1-11
Sat, Sep. 3	Build a Just and Righteous Community	Psalm 72:1-7
Sun, Sep. 4	Presiding Over a Peaceful Community	Isaiah 11:1-9
Mon, Sep. 5	Praise for Deliverance from Oppression	Isaiah 25:1-5
Tue, Sep. 6	Healing Can't Wait!	Luke 14:1-6
Wed, Sep. 7	Wait to Be Seated	Luke 14:7-11
Thu, Sep. 8	Invite the Needy to Your Table	Luke 14:12-14
Fri, Sep. 9	Dinner Will Be Served!	Luke 14:15-23
Sat, Sep. 10	Christ Died for Our Sins	1 Corinthians 15:1-11
Sun, Sep. 11	Attending God's Banquet Feast	Isaiah 25:6-10a
Mon, Sep. 12	See God's Saving Power	Luke 3:2-6
Tue, Sep. 13	Power to Overcome Illness	Isaiah 38:9-20
Wed, Sep. 14	God's Word Stands Forever	Isaiah 40:1-8
Thu, Sep. 15	God Leads like a Shepherd	Isaiah 40:9-11
Fri, Sep. 16	God's Wisdom Is Unmatched	Isaiah 40:12-14
Sat, Sep. 17	God Unlike the Nations and Idols	Isaiah 40:15-20
Sun, Sep. 18	Our Powerful and Everlasting God	Isaiah 40:21-31
Mon, Sep. 19	A Light to the Nations	Isaiah 42:5-9
Tue, Sep. 20	Anointed for Ministry	Luke 4:16-21

Thu, Nov. 10	Missing from the Holy City	Revelation 21:1-4
Fri, Nov. 11	City of the Alpha and Omega	Revelation 21:5-8
Sat, Nov. 12	The Architectural Splendor of the New Jerusalem	Revelation 21:15-21
Sun, Nov. 13	Vision of the New Jerusalem	Revelation 21:9-14, 22-27
Mon, Nov. 14	Wash and Be Healed	2 Kings 5:10-14
Tue, Nov. 15	Healing River Flows from the Temple	Ezekiel 47:1, 2, 12
Wed, Nov. 16	God Is Present and City Is Secure	Psalm 46
Thu, Nov. 17	The Sustaining, Healing Water of Life	Isaiah 41:17-20
Fri, Nov. 18	The Lord Acts with Passion	Isaiah 42:10-17
Sat, Nov. 19	The Paralytic Walks Again	Matthew 9:2-8
Sun, Nov. 20	Ready for the Lord's Return	Revelation 22:1-7
Mon, Nov. 21	You Will Not Find Me	John 7:32-36
Tue, Nov. 22	This Is the Messiah	John 7:37-43
Wed, Nov. 23	The Lord God, the Almighty	Revelation 1:4b-8
Thu, Nov. 24	Your First Work Rewarded	Revelation 2:1-7
Fri, Nov. 25	Worship Without End	Revelation 7:9-12
Sat, Nov. 26	Promised Redemption Fulfilled	Isaiah 43:1-7
Sun, Nov. 27	Yes, I Am Coming Soon!	Revelation 22:12-21

Answers to the Quarterly Quiz on page 2

Lesson 1—1. true. 2. lamb. **Lesson 2**—1. false. 2. rears. **Lesson 3**—1. grasshoppers. 2. eagles. **Lesson 4**—1. true. 2. praise. **Lesson 5**—1. prophets. 2. name. **Lesson 6**—1. apostle, high priest. 2. rock. **Lesson 7**—1. temptations. 2. true. **Lesson 8**—1. Salem. 2. Abraham. **Lesson 9**—1. true. 2. false. **Lesson 10**—1. sea. 2. death. **Lesson 11**—1. 12. 2. false. **Lesson 12**—1. true. 2. true. **Lesson 13**—1. recompense. 2. star. 3. true.

LESSON CYCLE CHART

International Sunday School Lesson Cycle, September 2016–August 2022

Year	Fall Quarter (Sep, Oct, Nov)	Winter Quarter (Dec, Jan, Feb)	Spring Quarter (Mar, Apr, May)	Summer Quarter (Jun, Jul, Aug)
2016–2017	The Sovereignty of God (Isaiah, Matthew, Hebrews, Revelation)	Creation: A Divine Cycle (Psalms, Luke, Galatians)	God Loves Us (Psalms, Joel, Jonah, John, Romans, Ephesians, 1 Peter, 1 John)	God's Urgent Call (Exodus, Judges, Prophets, Acts)
2017–2018	Covenant with God (Pentateuch, 1 & 2 Samuel, Nehemiah, Jeremiah, Ezekiel, 1 Corinthians, Hebrews)	Faith in Action (Daniel, Matthew, Acts, Ephesians, 1 Timothy, James)	Acknowledging God (Pentateuch, 2 Chronicles, Psalms, Luke, John, 2 Corinthians, Hebrews, Revelation)	Justice in the New Testament (Matthew, Mark, Romans, 2 Corinthians, Colossians)
2018–2019	God's World and God's People (Genesis)	Our Love for God (Exodus, Deuteronomy, Joshua, Psalms, Matthew, Luke, Epistles)	Discipleship and Mission (Matthew, Luke, Acts, Romans)	Covenant in God (Ruth, 1 Samuel, Matthew, Mark, Ephesians, Colossians, Hebrews)
2019–2020	Responding to God's Grace (Pentateuch, 1 Samuel, 1 Kings, Luke, Epistles)	Honoring God (1 Kings, 1 Chronicles, Matthew, Luke)	Justice and the Prophets (Esther, Prophets, 1 Corinthians)	Many Faces of Wisdom (Proverbs, Ecclesiastes, Gospels, James)
2020–2021	Love for One Another (Genesis, 1 Samuel, Luke, John, Acts, Epistles)	Call in the New Testament (Isaiah, Gospels, Acts, Romans, 1 Corinthians, Hebrews, 2 Timothy)	Prophets Faithful to God's Covenant (Exodus, Joshua, 1 & 2 Kings, Ezra, Nehemiah, Prophets)	Confident Hope (Leviticus, Matthew, Luke, Romans, 2 Corinthians, Hebrews, 1 John)
2021–2022	Celebrating God (Exodus, 2 Samuel, Psalms, Mark, Acts, Revelation)	Justice, Law, History (Pentateuch, 2 Samuel, Ezra, Job, Isaiah, Nahum)	God Frees and Redeems (Deuteronomy, Ezra, Matthew, John, Romans, Galatians)	Partners in a New Creation (Isaiah, John, Revelation)

God	Creation	Love	Call	Covenant	Faith	Worship	Justice

NO BAD SINGERS

Teacher Tips by Ronald L. Nickelson

MANY YEARS AGO, I was watching a TV program about people who were learning to sing. Family and friends considered them to be hopeless cases—people who couldn't carry a tune in the proverbial bucket. Their attempts to sing were truly cringeworthy.

But the instructor had a positive outlook. Her philosophy was that there are no bad singers; there are only untrained singers. And her training method worked!

I have adopted the same outlook regarding teachers of the Bible: there are no bad teachers; there are only untrained teachers. Take my father, for instance. When I was in high school in the early 1970s, he was thrust into the role of teacher of my Sunday school class. So with *Standard Lesson Commentary* in hand, he stood and read it to us. Head down. No eye contact. Bored students. My father was not a bad teacher, merely an untrained one.

Broadly speaking, there are two aspects to becoming an able teacher: (1) developing a certain level of subject-matter expertise and (2) developing skills in the teaching craft itself. Both can involve self-training and training by others.

You, the Subject-Matter Expert

The most important thing you can do to improve your teaching is to work toward subject-matter expertise on the Bible as a whole. How can you teach something you don't know (compare Hebrews 5:12-14)? Don't merely *read* the Bible in your private times; *study* it. There is a difference (2 Timothy 2:15).

Even so, self-study usually can take one only so far. A person desiring to learn about medicine can study medical textbooks personally, but the highest levels of learning will come through the guidance of those who are already physicians. That's why people go to medical school. Not everyone is able to attend Bible college in residence, of course.

But many such colleges offer online courses. Avail yourself of these! To prepare yourself and others for deeper levels of study, your church can offer the Bible overview in Standard Publishing's *Training for Service* 26-session certification program.

Today, I have considerable skills in carpentry and auto mechanics. One reason is that my father's subject-matter expertise in those areas went a long way in enabling him to teach them to me in his one-on-one "classroom" at home. Even so, subject-matter expertise does not automatically translate into good teaching skills. We have all encountered (or heard others complain of) teachers who "know it, but can't teach it." Subject-matter expertise must be accompanied by teaching skills.

You, the Skilled

Teaching is a spiritual gift (see Romans 12:7; 1 Corinthians 12:28; compare 1 Timothy 3:2). But having been so gifted by the Holy Spirit doesn't mean there's nothing to learn about the teaching craft! All teachers can grow in techniques and skills.

A good place to start is self-directed study of the methods of skilled teachers. I do that every time I look back over the years at my father's one-on-one classroom at home. He knew how much to expect from me at my age. He knew when to be "hands on" in directing my learning and when to be "hands off" so I could make my own mistakes. He knew my learning style. He knew how to handle me when I became a "problem" student.

I learned a lot about teaching when I had the privilege of attending the Air Force's *Academic Instructor School*. Eye-opening it was! If you are not in a position to receive formal instruction regarding the teaching craft, invite a mentor to attend your class for the express purpose of evaluating how you can improve. Search YouTube® videos on the teaching craft. And if you ask for feedback from your learners, they will oblige!

THE PEACEFUL KINGDOM

DEVOTIONAL READING: Psalm 72:1-7

BACKGROUND SCRIPTURE: Isaiah 11:1-9

ISAIAH 11:1-9

1 There shall come forth a shoot from the
stump of Jesse,
and a branch from his roots shall bear
fruit.

2 And the Spirit of the LORD shall rest upon
him,
the Spirit of wisdom and understanding,
the Spirit of counsel and might,
the Spirit of knowledge and the fear of
the LORD.

3 And his delight shall be in the fear of the
LORD.
He shall not judge by what his eyes see,
or decide disputes by what his ears hear,

4 but with righteousness
he shall judge the
poor,
and decide with
equity for the
meek of the earth;
and he shall strike the
earth with the rod
of his mouth,

and with the breath of his lips he shall
kill the wicked.

5 Righteousness shall be the belt of his
waist,
and faithfulness the belt of his loins.

6 The wolf shall dwell with the lamb,
and the leopard shall lie down with the
young goat,
and the calf and the lion and the fattened
calf together;
and a little child shall lead them.

7 The cow and the bear shall graze;
their young shall lie down together;
and the lion shall eat straw like the ox.

8 The nursing child shall play over the hole
of the cobra,
and the weaned child shall put his hand
on the adder's den.

9 They shall not hurt or destroy
in all my holy mountain;
for the earth shall be full of the knowledge of the LORD
as the waters cover the sea.

KEY VERSE

*They shall not hurt or destroy in all my holy mountain; for the earth shall be full of the knowledge of the
LORD as the waters cover the sea.* —**Isaiah 11:9**

THE SOVEREIGNTY OF GOD

Unit 1: The Sovereignty of the Father

LESSONS 1–4

LESSON AIMS

After participating in this lesson, each learner will be able to:

1. Summarize the impact that the promised branch was prophesied to have.

2. Contrast the peace that the branch inaugurates with modern understandings of peace.

3. Suggest one way he or she can promote the peace that the branch inaugurates and make a plan to do so.

LESSON OUTLINE

Introduction

A. Searching for Peace

Before there were GPS (Global Positioning System) devices, I used the set of maps in the back of the telephone book to find a location in my city. First, I had to look up the street name in the index. Then I had to find the correct map by referring to the code that accompanied the index entry. I had to make sure I ended up looking at the right map, otherwise I could find myself "running out of room" as the street trailed off the edge of the (wrong) map before I found the desired location.

Our world seeks many of the positive qualities described in today's lesson text from the prophet Isaiah. Who in his or her right mind does not desire righteousness, equity, and peace? The problem is that the ethical maps that the world consults are too small—they are limited to this world's sinful perspective, and they do not reflect God's point of view. We will find righteousness, equity, and peace (along with many other blessings) only when we humble ourselves enough to consult Heaven's GPS: God's Promised Son. It is he who is at the heart of today's study.

B. Lesson Background

The book of Isaiah appears in our Bibles as the first of the group known as the Major Prophets —so-called because of their length (the Minor Prophets are shorter books). Isaiah is known for his numerous prophecies of Jesus, many of which are quoted in the New Testament. Some of these prophecies will be highlighted in the first four lessons of this quarter, a unit titled, "The Sovereignty of the Father."

The issue of God's sovereignty likely was a hot-button topic in Isaiah's day, since that was one of the more chaotic times in the history of God's people. Isaiah's call to prophetic service came "in the year that King Uzziah died" (Isaiah 6:1). That was about 738 BC, not quite two hundred years after God's people had split into the two kingdoms of Israel to the north and Judah to the south. Uzziah (or Azariah; see 2 Kings 15:1, 13) was one of Judah's better kings, though he finished poorly as a result of pride (2 Chronicles 26:16-21).

Isaiah 7 records the prophet's confrontation with one of Judah's worst kings, Ahaz (grandson of Uzziah). At the time, Judah was facing the rising threat of Assyria to the northeast. Ahaz rejected the counsel of Isaiah to trust in the Lord (Isaiah 7:1-12). The prophet warned the defiant king of the folly of this course of action (or inaction) and declared that Assyria would indeed wreak havoc on Judah (7:17-20; 10:5, 6).

It is always a mistake, though, to underestimate God in the midst of a seemingly hopeless situation. Often that is when he does his best work! Isaiah 10:10, 11, 22, 23 predicted that God's judgment on his people would not leave much. But it would leave something: a remnant sufficient for God to carry out his sovereign purpose (10:20, 21).

God had informed Isaiah that his ministry would not appear to be that successful. The prophet was to proclaim God's message "until cities lie waste and without inhabitant, . . . and the land is a desolate waste" (Isaiah 6:11). The population of Judah would go into exile (6:12). Although God compared the people with a tree stripped of its leaves, "the holy seed" would remain from which new growth would come (6:13).

I. The Just Ruler
(ISAIAH 11:1-5)
A. His Humanity (v. 1)
1a. There shall come forth a shoot from the stump of Jesse,

Isaiah provides another picture of life emerging from unpromising conditions. Hindsight establishes that Jesus is the subject of the unfolding prophecy. But why would *Jesse*, the father of King David, be mentioned rather than David himself?

HOW TO SAY IT

Ahaz	*Ay*-haz.
Assyria	Uh-*sear*-ee-uh.
Azariah	Az-uh-*rye*-uh.
Beatitudes	Bee-*a*-tuh-toods (*a* as in *mat*).
Hosea	Ho-*zay*-uh.
Uzziah	Uh-*zye*-uh.
Zechariah	Zek-uh-**rye**-uh.

In the case at hand, Isaiah is not prophesying the coming of a successor of David; Isaiah is announcing, rather, that another David will come. This is in keeping with prophecies such as those found in Jeremiah 30:8, 9; Ezekiel 34:23, 24; and Hosea 3:5. About 270 years before Isaiah's day, God raised up a shepherd boy (David) to become king over Israel; about 740 years after Isaiah, Jesus will come as the good shepherd who will "lay down [his] life for the sheep" (John 10:14, 15). The idea of humble origins suggested by the verse before us applies to both David and Jesus.

1b. and a branch from his roots shall bear fruit.

The word *branch* is used elsewhere in the Old Testament as a title for the coming Messiah (Jeremiah 23:5; 33:15; Zechariah 3:8; 6:12). The Hebrew word for branch is *netzer,* a point that may help to illuminate a passage in the Gospels. Matthew 2:23 states that Jesus "went and lived in a city called Nazareth, so that what was spoken by the prophets might be fulfilled, that he would be called a Nazarene." Noticing how close in sound are the words *Nazareth* and *netzer,* perhaps Matthew has in mind the promise concerning the branch. Jesus' living in Nazareth ("Branchville") fulfills Isaiah's prophecy as it describes the lowly nature of the village (compare John 1:45, 46) where Jesus grew up.

◆ OUT OF THE ASHES ◆

Peter Gladwin was barely a year old when his family's house caught fire, leaving him scarred and disabled. Growing up in a rough neighborhood, he was frequently in trouble with the police. He lost the use of an arm in a knife fight. He eventually descended into a life of substance abuse.

Then Peter found the Lord. Peter eventually became a probation officer, working in dangerous communities, drug rehabilitation centers, and prisons. He founded a ministry called *Out of Ashes,* which uses the transforming power of the gospel to rescue people from the consequences of their poor, sinful decisions.

Isaiah predicted that the Messiah would come in the midst of a seemingly hopeless situation. But the Lord specializes in bringing hope out of hopelessness! When all options seem exhausted, he has ways of making the impossible happen. Gladwin discovered that the Lord remains our first and final hope. Have you?   —D. C. S.

B. His Divinity (vv. 2, 3a)

2.   And the Spirit of the LORD shall rest
        upon him,
     the Spirit of wisdom and
        understanding,
     the Spirit of counsel and might,
     the Spirit of knowledge and the fear of
        the LORD.

The Spirit of the Lord refers to the Holy Spirit, who came upon Jesus at his baptism (Matthew 3:16). The word *rest* implies a constant dwelling. John 3:34 tells us that Jesus possessed the Spirit "without measure," or limitation. That is implied here as well, given that the Holy Spirit abounds in *wisdom . . . understanding . . . counsel . . . might . . . knowledge . . .* and *fear of the Lord.*

The qualities Isaiah lists call to mind passages that highlight their presence in Jesus. For example, Paul notes Jesus' wisdom in 1 Corinthians 1:24 and Colossians 2:2, 3. The word *counsel* suggests the prophecy of a "Counselor" in Isaiah 9:6. *Might* could be linked to the title "Mighty God," also in Isaiah 9:6, since the words *might* and *mighty* come from the same Hebrew word.

> ### What Do You Think?
> What steps can we take to ensure that church plans, programs, and projects enhance rather than hinder the work of the Branch (Jesus)?
> *Talking Points for Your Discussion*
> - Regarding the individual Christian
> - Regarding the church as a body

3a. And his delight shall be in the fear of the LORD.

The Hebrew verb translated *delight* occurs only 11 times in the Old Testament, with an aromatic sense in 8 of the other 10. If the same is intended here, the idea would be to perceive something in a positive sense (compare Genesis 8:21). This implies the promised branch's high degree of commitment to pleasing *the Lord.*

C. His Righteousness (vv. 3b-5)

3b. He shall not judge by what his eyes see, or decide disputes by what his ears hear,

The remainder of verse 3 refers to two other senses of perception: seeing and hearing. The promised branch will not be guided by visual, physical appearances or by opinions voiced by others. *His eyes* and *his ears* are to be governed by the will of his Father. Centuries hence, Jesus (the branch) will say, "I can do nothing on my own. As I hear, I judge, and my judgment is just, because I seek not my own will but the will of him who sent me" (John 5:30).

4a. but with righteousness he shall judge the poor, and decide with equity for the meek of the earth;

The branch will be guided by God's unchanging standards of right and wrong, not by the shifting whims of culture. The branch will display the qualities of *righteousness* and *equity* on behalf of groups that are often neglected or mistreated: *the poor* and *the meek.* God requires his people in both Old and New Testament times to care for the poor and not become callous toward them (Leviticus 23:22; Deuteronomy 15:7, 8; Psalm 41:1; Galatians 2:10; James 2:1-4).

Isaiah's words may be intended to acknowledge those who recognize their spiritual poverty and humbly admit that they depend on God for help. One should note Jesus' language about the "poor in spirit" and "the meek" in the Beatitudes (Matthew 5:3, 5).

> ### What Do You Think?
> How can Christians model both the "judge not" (Matthew 7:1; etc.) and "judge" (1 Corinthians 5:12, 13; etc.) attributes that Jesus expects?
> *Talking Points for Your Discussion*
> - Considering correct and incorrect ideas about judging
> - Considering context
> - Other

4b. and he shall strike the earth with the rod of his mouth, and with the breath of his lips he shall kill the wicked.

This half-verse goes on to describe an aspect of the branch's judgment that is far more severe. Such language calls to mind the picture given elsewhere in the New Testament of Jesus' final judgment (2 Thessalonians 1:7-9; Hebrews 10:26-31; Revelation 19:11-15, 21). We may note that during his earthly ministry, Jesus demonstrates both sides of judgment described by Isaiah. Jesus deals compassionately with the outcasts of his day, but some of his harshest words are reserved for those religious leaders who look at the "sinners" around them with great contempt. Such leaders frequently feel the sting of *the rod of his mouth*. Jesus does not mince words with them!

5. Righteousness shall be the belt of his waist,
and faithfulness the belt of his loins.

This verse offers another way of picturing what is to characterize the conduct of the promised branch. *Belt* refers to the sash that is worn around an individual's *waist* in biblical times. It holds clothing in place. Thus the qualities of *righteousness* and *faithfulness* will support or sustain the promised branch's character and conduct, specifically the judgment highlighted in verse 4a, above.

Loins points more to the inner organs where emotions and motives are believed to originate (Psalm 7:9; 26:2; 73:21; Jeremiah 20:12; Revelation 2:23). For faithfulness to be the belt of the branch's loins implies that this quality is to be the prime motivation behind every phase of his conduct.

II. The Peaceful Rule
(ISAIAH 11:6-9)

A. Radical Change (vv. 6-8)

6a. The wolf shall dwell with the lamb,
and the leopard shall lie down with the young goat,
and the calf and the lion and the fattened calf together;

This verse begins a very striking series of portrayals of the impact of the promised branch's ministry. The changes described are radical—in fact, miraculous—in nature. Only the Creator himself can bring about the kind of transformation among

his created beings that we see here. The *wolf,* the *leopard,* and the *lion* are predatory animals. The *lamb,* the *young goat,* the *calf,* and the *fattened calf* (a cow being raised or "fattened" for meat) do not stand a chance of survival before any of them under normal conditions. Here, however, are these creatures living at peace with one another, with no violence or aggressiveness whatsoever!

> **What Do You Think?**
> ▶ What can you do to address the causes of strife that result in people preying on (rather than praying for) others?
> **Talking Points for Your Discussion**
> ▪ Regarding strife resulting from differing religious convictions
> ▪ Regarding strife between social classes
> ▪ Other

6b. and a little child shall lead them.

As if the unusual pairings of verse 6a were not remarkable enough, the leader of the menagerie is to be *a little child*! We would never place animals like wolves, leopards, or lions in a petting zoo for young children to touch them. Yet that is the picture Isaiah paints.

7. The cow and the bear shall graze;
their young shall lie down together;
and the lion shall eat straw like the ox.

The prophet continues his depiction of peaceful surroundings. Again we see animals acting quite contrary to what we expect of them. A *cow*, with no worry of being attacked, shares a meal with a *bear*. Meanwhile, *their young* ones nap together. The carnivorous *lion* switches to a vegetarian diet (see parallel expressions in Isaiah 65:25a).

> **What Do You Think?**
> ▶ How can your church help move a fallen world toward the ideal picture painted by Isaiah?
> **Talking Points for Your Discussion**
> ▪ Concerning evangelism and benevolence (outreach)
> ▪ Concerning spiritual maturity of her members (inreach)
> ▪ Concerning worship practices (upreach)

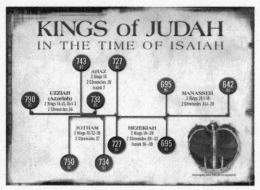

KINGS of JUDAH
IN THE TIME OF ISAIAH

Visual for Lesson 1. *Keep this chart on display for the first four Sundays of this quarter to give your learners a chronological perspective.*

8. The nursing child shall play over the hole of the cobra,
    and the weaned child shall put his hand on the adder's den.

Once more, the degree of human interaction with deadly creatures is amazing: a *nursing child,* or infant, need not be protected from *the cobra.* The last phrase offers parallel elements. The (different) child in view here is no longer in the nursing stage, but is *weaned* (weaning normally occurs at around three years of age). Like the first child, this one is seen to do something that no conscientious parent would allow: explore an area known to be infested with deadly snakes, for that is what an adder is. See Proverbs 23:32, where the same Hebrew word is translated "adder" as well and stands parallel with the word *serpent.* The serpent was humanity's first enemy (Genesis 3).

◆   *Getting Along*   ◆

A cheetah kitten and a puppy grew up together in the Cincinnati Zoo and became good friends. They maintained their playful relationship even a decade later. Perhaps you have seen YouTube® videos of house cats and parakeets, etc., lounging around together. Such "odd couples" amaze us because their behavior is not the norm.

Isaiah describes a time of peace where everything seems unnatural: lions eating grass; cows and bears grazing together; leopards and goats, wolves and sheep, babies and snakes—all get-

ting along. Such peace will characterize humanity when Jesus returns to reign in all fullness. This peace will not just be a state of harmony between people, but also between people and God.

This kind of peace is not as the world gives, but as only God's Son can provide (compare John 14:27). The curse of sin will be lifted fully, never to return. How do we prepare for the great day when Jesus brings that final peace?   —D. C. S.

B. Global Change (v. 9)
9a. They shall not hurt or destroy in all my holy mountain;

The phrase *holy mountain* occurs 21 times in the Hebrew Old Testament, with differing English translations (example: Daniel 9:20). The book of Isaiah features 6 of these 21, and this is the first. Of particular note among the others is Isaiah 65:25b, which features identical wording in both English and Hebrew to what we see in the verse before us (compare Isaiah 56:7; 57:13; 65:11; 66:20).

9b. for the earth shall be full of the knowledge of the Lord as the waters cover the sea.

The conjunction *for* points us to the cause of the marvelous picture of peace that Isaiah paints up to this point. The fact that *the earth shall be full of the knowledge of the Lord* is quite a positive thing (Habakkuk 2:14 is very similar; compare Jeremiah 31:34). Two ways are suggested for understanding the fulfillment of this prophetic portrait of peace, each with biblical support.

One way is to view Isaiah's description as that of the literal "new heavens" and "new earth," mentioned in Isaiah 65:17; 66:22. Between those two texts, 65:25a is quite similar to 11:6, 7, and 9 in today's lesson. All this is seen to imply Isaiah to be depicting the complete elimination of the curse of sin (compare Revelation 21:1). According to Paul, the "whole creation has been groaning together in the pains of childbirth" (Romans 8:22) as it longs for the day of deliverance from the "bondage to corruption" (8:21). The pain that we see in the created world—the violence that animals inflict on one another (and on humans)—will no longer be present when God re-creates the universe "in which righteousness dwells" (2 Peter 3:13).

The other potential interpretation is to see the prophecies fulfilled in a more figurative sense, with the animals representing humans who clash with one another. In the Bible, human enemies are often compared with animals (Psalm 22:12, 13, 16, 20, 21; Acts 20:29; etc.). But because of the branch's impact and the forgiveness and peace he brings about (through Jesus' death and resurrection), hatred and bitterness are no more.

Possibly Isaiah's words are intended to be understood both ways. Just as the words of Isaiah 11:4 are descriptive both of Jesus' earthly ministry and what will occur at his return, so verses 6–9 may be picturing the impact of the church's ministry as it takes the gospel to the world as well as what Jesus himself will bring to pass when he returns to usher in the new heavens and the new earth.

> *What Do You Think?*
> How does verse 9 challenge you today?
> *Talking Points for Your Discussion*
> • Regarding short-term goals of your life in Christ
> • Regarding long-term goals of your life in Christ

Conclusion

A. Two Pictures of Peace

The story is told of two artists who were commissioned to paint a picture that conveyed the theme of peace. One painted a quiet rural scene featuring a beautiful country home in the center. Next to the home were fields with crops awaiting harvest. Contented cows loitered under trees. The sun was setting in the distance, with the skies tinted at just the right colors. The other artist drew an entirely different picture. In his, a storm was raging. Trees swayed on the mountainside and in the valley below. Flashes of lightning punctuated the dark and gloomy sky.

At first glance, the second painting seemed to depict the very opposite of a peaceful setting. But on a rock projecting from a cliff protected by an overhang, a small bird sat calmly on her nest. She remained at peace in spite of the storm.

In a day to come, everything that is destructive, harmful, painful, and sorrowful will be eliminated without exception. That is God's clear promise to us. Until then, we reside in a world that still suffers the brutal effects of sin. The circumstances of many Christians are especially stormy. Some are persecuted because of their faith; many are in anguish as they, family members, and/or close friends wrestle with intense pain, wondering how they can make it through another day.

Under such conditions, the peace that God promises becomes a cherished anchor for the soul. Pointing to the unceasing strife in the world, cynics note the lack of peace that Jesus came to bring (see Luke 2:14). But until Jesus returns, peace is not found in the *absence* of life's storms, but rather in the *midst* of life's storms. Jesus was very clear: "In the world you will have tribulation" (John 16:33b). Anyone could say that, of course, but only Jesus could say what follows: "But take heart; I have overcome the world" (16:33c). And only Jesus could say, "I have said these things to you, that in me you may have peace" (16:33a).

That peace is not of this world (John 14:27) just as Jesus' kingdom is not of this world (18:36). Jesus' peace sustains us when the world around us is coming to pieces. The way we model that peace can be a compelling witness to the stormy, broken world around us. There is a peaceful kingdom here and now. It is the church, whose Lord is the Prince of Peace.

B. Prayer

Father, we thank you that we are part of Jesus' unshakable kingdom of peace, a kingdom not of this world. Embolden us to invite others in as well. We pray this in the name of the Prince of Peace. Amen.

C. Thought to Remember
We have the peace of Jesus now,
with more to come.

VISUALS FOR THESE LESSONS

The visual pictured in each lesson (example: page 14) is a small reproduction of a large, full-color poster included in the *Adult Resources* packet for the Fall Quarter. That packet also contains the very useful *Presentation Tools* CD for teacher use. Order No. 1629116 from your supplier.

INVOLVEMENT LEARNING

Enhance your lesson presentation with the reproducible activity page,
available as a free download at www.standardlesson.com.

Into the Lesson

Edward Hicks (1780–1849), American Quaker minister and folk painter, illustrated today's text more than 50 times. Most are labeled *Peaceable Kingdom*. Download one of these images from the Internet for use as an introduction to the lesson. Ask learners if they recognize the image and which Bible verse it relates to. After discussion, say "Hicks's view of the peaceable kingdom is different from the image of the peaceable kingdom described in today's text."

Alternative. Read the first two paragraphs of *War and Peace* by Tolstoy. Ask, "Can anyone identify what story this is?" If no one does, identify the title, with the comment, "Tolstoy knew of war and peace. The Napoleonic incursions into his beloved Russia had begun a long, hard period of oppression and then freedom, war, and peace. Isaiah, the author of today's text, knew also of war and peace." Use the Lesson Background on the conflicts of Isaiah's day between God's people and pagan conquerors and oppressors.

Into the Word

Ask your class to name qualities of the perfect monarch or ruler from an earthly, political perspective. Write the list on a board. Have someone read Isaiah 11:1-5. Ask, "What attributes do you see in Isaiah's description of the ideal monarch?" Add this second list beside your initial list for comparison and contrast.

Such descriptors as the following may find their way into either or both lists: fears and reverences God; has and resembles the Spirit of God; is fully perceptive of the behaviors and motives of others; will condemn and punish wickedness; judges others with righteousness and fairness; will preside over a people who live in harmony in every way. Your list(s) may include elements such as: he tells the truth, she is well-informed on all matters of necessity, and others. Relate entries to the text.

Display these two words: *UTOPIA* and *SHANGRI-LA*. Note that these are writers' designations for fictional ideal kingdoms in which people and other creatures live in marvelous harmony and unity. Have someone read Isaiah 11:6-9. Ask, "How does this picture of a fully harmonious existence of God's creatures reflect a sense of an ideal existence, an ideal kingdom?" The absolute absence of fear and death is at the heart of the desired answer.

Ask, "How do you see the absence of these elements in government leaders' and in species' interrelationships as reflective of the fact that sin is at work in the world?" Note the different concepts of peace as reflected in today's text and in today's world.

Emphasize that Isaiah is describing a "peaceable kingdom" that does not exist on the earth and will not. Have someone read John 16:33; the emphasized truth is that peace is in Christ, who has overcome this world and its curse of sin. Say, "That is the peaceable kingdom we are looking forward to."

Option. Make copies of "The Family Tree" activity from the reproducible page, which you can download. Assign half of the class to answer the first question by referring to the Matthew genealogy, and the other half to answer with the Luke genealogy. Complete the rest of the activity together.

Into Life

The Spirit's picture of the peaceful kingdom wherein animals and children get along regardless of what we consider to be "natural tendencies" reveals much about God's plan and the future. It is obvious that God's Spirit and the Branch can create an idyllic existence such as today's text and general biblical revelation suggest. Ask, "What can you do to bring about the peaceable kingdom?"

Alternative. Distribute copies of the "An Odd Zoo" activity from the reproducible page. Have students work in pairs. Ask for ideas on how to be a peacemaker.

THE MOUNTAIN OF GOD

DEVOTIONAL READING: 1 Corinthians 15:1-11
BACKGROUND SCRIPTURE: Isaiah 25

ISAIAH 25:6-10

6 On this mountain the LORD of hosts will
    make for all peoples
    a feast of rich food, a feast of well-aged
    wine,
    of rich food full of marrow, of aged
    wine well refined.
7 And he will swallow up on this mountain
    the covering that is cast over all peoples,
    the veil that is spread over all nations.
8   He will swallow up death forever;
and the Lord GOD will wipe away tears
    from all faces,
    and the reproach of his people he will
    take away from all the earth,
for the LORD has spoken.
9 It will be said on that day,
    "Behold, this is our God; we have waited
    for him, that he might save us.
    This is the LORD; we have waited for him;
    let us be glad and rejoice in his
    salvation."

10 For the hand of the LORD will rest on this
    mountain,
    and Moab shall be trampled down in
    his place,
    as straw is trampled down in a dunghill.

KEY VERSE

He will swallow up death forever; and the Lord GOD will wipe away tears from all faces, and the reproach of his people he will take away from all the earth, for the LORD has spoken. —**Isaiah 25:8**

The Sovereignty of God

Unit 1: The Sovereignty of the Father

Lessons 1–4

Lesson Aims

After participating in this lesson, each learner will be able to:

1. List some characteristics of our final deliverance by God from oppression.

2. Compare and contrast Isaiah 25:6-10a with 1 Corinthians 15:54 and Revelation 7:17; 21:4.

3. Identify an oppressive situation in his or her community and suggest a way to bring the love of Christ to bear on it.

Lesson Outline

Introduction

A. Memories in the Mountains

One weekend during the fall of 2013, our daughter and daughter-in-law planned a weekend getaway for our family at a cabin up in the Smoky Mountains near Gatlinburg, Tennessee. The cabin turned out to be much farther up in the mountains than we first had thought; once we turned off the main highway, it was still another 30 or 40 minutes of curving and swerving our way up the road until we finally arrived at the cabin.

Our family had never gone on an excursion like this, but it became one of our most memorable experiences. For my wife and me, having our children and grandchildren together in one place for three days created an array of truly precious memories. Of course, the day came when we had to come down from the mountaintop and face life back in the real world. That is typical of any "mountaintop experience"; eventually one has to return to the valley below.

Many mountains are mentioned in the Bible, including Mounts Horeb, Gerizim, Ebal, Sinai, Nebo, Zion, Carmel, and Hermon (which may have been the mount of Jesus' transfiguration). Some of the most significant events in Scripture occurred on those mountains. In today's text Isaiah describes a mountain where some truly memorable events will take place in the future.

B. Lesson Background

Our lesson title ties nicely into last week's text from Isaiah 11:1-9. That passage concluded with the statement that nothing harmful or destructive is to have any place in God's "holy mountain." Today's text comes from a section of the book that is often called "The Isaiah Apocalypse" (chapters 24–27). This is because the scenes pictured are similar to the apocalyptic language (which is imagery describing the end of the world) found in the book of Revelation (compare Zechariah 9–14; Mark 13:24-27).

Using the kind of vivid symbolism found there, the prophet pictures the whole earth coming under the judgment of God. Isaiah 24 in particular uses such language, illustrated quite well by verse 20. There Isaiah's apocalypse opens with a description of the Lord's plans to devastate utterly.

The tone shifts rather abruptly with Isaiah 25, moving from somber words of judgment to words of praise to God. (Such a shift is not unusual in Isaiah or in other prophetic books.) God is praised for the "wonderful things" he has done (25:1), including being a source of strength to his people and bringing judgment on their enemies (vv. 2-5). The language at the conclusion of verse 5 is especially noteworthy: "The song of the ruthless is put down." Last week's lesson highlighted the marvelous things that God's Branch would accomplish. "The branch" of chapter 25 has a very different future from the one of chapter 24!

Isaiah previously described "the mountain of the Lord" as a place where noteworthy events in God's sovereign plan are to unfold. Isaiah 2:2-4 pictures the place as "established as the highest of the mountains," a place to which "all the nations shall flow." They will do so because that is where the house of the Lord is located, a place where his Word is taught. The reference suggests Jerusalem, or Zion; indeed, both Jerusalem and Zion are mentioned in Isaiah 2:3. This sets a backdrop for today's study.

I. God's Graciousness
(ISAIAH 25:6-8)
A. Offering a Feast (v. 6)

6a. On this mountain the LORD of hosts will make for all peoples a feast of rich food,

HOW TO SAY IT

apocalypse	uh-*pock*-uh-lips.
Carmel	*Kar*-mul.
Ebal	*Ee*-bull.
Gerizim	*Gair*-ih-zeem or Guh-*rye*-zim.
Hermon	*Her*-mun.
Horeb	*Ho*-reb.
Lazarus	*Laz*-uh-rus.
Nebo	*Nee*-bo.
Sinai	*Sigh*-nye or *Sigh*-nay-eye.
Zechariah	*Zek*-uh-**rye**-uh.
Zion	*Zi*-un.

Isaiah describes what is to happen on the holy mountain (see the Lesson Background). The depiction is that of a place of joyful fellowship. A banquet will be prepared by the ultimate master chef—*the Lord of hosts* himself!

What is to come is first of all depicted as available *for all peoples*. That phrase refers to all people groups, since the word *peoples* is plural. The guest list is limitless. No one is meant to be excluded, "on the outside looking in."

What is to happen is then described: it will be *a feast of rich food*. This signifies that God, as the host on his holy mountain, intends to provide only the finest of menu offerings. In Old Testament times, rich food includes the fatty portions of meat, which are considered to be the best; this is why the fat portions of sacrifices are to be offered to the Lord (Leviticus 3:12-16). Such a banquet menu may not seem very appealing in our health-conscious era. But we can be assured that God will provide his best.

> **What Do You Think?**
> What are some ways your church can foster, if not create, "mountaintop experiences"? Why is it important to do so?
> *Talking Points for Your Discussion*
> - For its worship services
> - For its social gatherings

6b. a feast of well-aged wine,

Well-aged wine is of the highest quality. As Jesus will say centuries later, "No one after drinking old wine desires new, for he says, 'The old is good'" (Luke 5:39). Clearly God will be serving only the best to those who attend this very special banquet (compare John 2:10). No shortcuts here!

6c. of rich food full of marrow, of aged wine well refined.

These two phrases reinforce the description of the banquet to come. The *rich food* includes the *marrow*, which is the innermost part of the bone; it symbolizes prosperity (Job 21:24b). Given the more spiritual significance attached to the mountain of the Lord elsewhere in this book (Isaiah 2:2-4; 11:9; 65:25), some propose that the menu items should be understood in spiritual terms.

Because Australia is in the southern hemisphere, Christmas Day comes during its summer. The temperature can be quite high on this festive day! But despite the heat, all of the Christmas paraphernalia is still snow related, with icicles, snowflakes, etc. And although the cyclone season is well underway in northern Australia at the time, that threat does not seem to dampen the celebration of Christmas. Australian Christians go all out to celebrate the birth of Jesus. It is a great time of feasting, with "shrimp-on-the-barby" being a big hit, along with other grilled delicacies.

Isaiah prophesies that the coming of the Messiah will also bring a time of celebration that is marked by a great feast. "The marriage supper of the Lamb" (Revelation 19:6-9) will be the greatest banquet in all history! It will celebrate the fact that God has completed his plan for the world. It is in that light we wait and watch with great anticipation for the second coming of the Lord and Savior, Jesus Christ. To fail to be ready for his return would be the gravest of errors (see Matthew 22:1-14; 25:13).　　　　　—D. C. S.

B. Overcoming Death (vv. 7, 8)

7. And he will swallow up on this mountain the covering that is cast over all peoples, the veil that is spread over all nations.

God will take the steps necessary to make certain that nothing hinders the enjoyment of the feast that he will prepare. The Hebrew verb translated *swallow up* is repeated in verse 8, next, and translated the same way. This suggests a complete, overwhelming victory.

That victory is over *the covering that is cast over all peoples*. The Hebrew word translated *covering* is used only here in the Old Testament, and the exact meaning is unclear. But since *the covering* stands in parallel with *the veil,* we logically conclude that it is something that hinders *all peoples* and *all nations*.

Some students propose that reference to a veil is similar to Paul's use of that word in 2 Corinthians 3:12-18. There the apostle describes how the truth about Jesus remains hidden (veiled) from unbelievers. However, given the reference in our next

verse to death being swallowed up, it is preferable to interpret the covering and veil in that light instead. Since death is what is being destroyed, the idea of a covering for a corpse (a shroud) seems to capture the intent. Death shows no partiality toward peoples and nations. When God removes this covering, he will do it completely for all who reside on his mountain.

> *What Do You Think?*
> When was a time you sensed God destroying something that threatened your security in him? How did you grow spiritually from this?
> *Talking Points for Your Discussion*
> - Regarding a time when you were alone
> - Regarding a time when you were part of a group

8a. He will swallow up death forever;

Here we see stated more clearly the impact of Jesus' death and resurrection, and the language of verse 8 appears in two New Testament passages. First, in 1 Corinthians 15:54 the apostle Paul draws on the majestic phrase before us to celebrate the results of Jesus' triumph over death: "When the perishable puts on the imperishable, and the mortal puts on immortality, then shall come to pass the saying that is written: 'Death is swallowed up in victory.'"

Death is itself dealt the death blow when "the one who holds the power of death, that is, the devil," is destroyed by Christ (Hebrews 2:14).

8b. and the Lord GOD will wipe away tears from all faces,

Second, verse 8 is also found in Revelation 7:17; 21:4. The latter verse is part of the apostle John's view of "a new heaven and a new earth," which begins at 21:1 (lesson 10). John mentions no mountain in his description, but that should not be allowed to diminish the wonder of what life will be like in that far better place. The most important thing to note in John's testimony is that "the former things have passed away" (21:4). Anything that causes weeping in this world will have no place in the one to come. The punishment linked to the first sin ("you shall surely die," Genesis 2:17) is removed.

8c. **and the reproach of his people he will take away from all the earth,**

While living in a sinful world, God's people often face rebuke and shameful treatment from scoffers and opponents of their faith. Peter writes of such scoffers who question whether the return of Jesus will ever occur (2 Peter 3:3, 4). But when he does return and when death is swallowed up in victory, all cynics and critics will have to acknowledge that Jesus Christ is Lord (Philippians 2:9-11). Those who have poked fun at, harassed, or persecuted Christians will be silenced. God's sovereignty will no longer be denied.

◆ *FORGIVEN AND FREE* ◆

"We're married in God's eyes." That was the line Donna's boyfriend used to convince her to have intimate relations with him. Then Donna got pregnant, and everything changed.

Donna's father was a well-known businessman and a leader in their church. In his mind, news of Donna's out-of-wedlock pregnancy would damage his business and tarnish his reputation in the church. So at the insistence of her parents and in spite of her own better instincts, Donna got an abortion.

Years later, Donna found herself involved in a program called "Forgiven and Set Free." As she moved through the healing and grieving process, she gave the name *Doug* to the little boy she never held, and she wrote a loving letter to him. She then held a small memorial service for her baby and put up a figurine to remind her of his presence in Heaven. Donna eventually coauthored a book on abortion recovery to help other young women who had made the same regrettable decision as she had. As Donna explains, "Our prayer is that younger women will find healing so they can become the women God desires of them."

Isaiah tells us the Messiah will swallow up death and wipe away the tears of those who have borne rebuke. God calls us to show compassion to the spiritually injured (compare 2 Corinthians 2:6-8 following 1 Corinthians 5:11-13); doing so will keep us from "shooting the wounded" regarding our fellow Christians. We can and should help wipe away tears in the here and now even as we

Visual for Lessons 2 & 10. *As you discuss verse 8, point to this visual and ask, "What causes the most tears? Why?"*

anticipate the day when God dries the tears of his people for all eternity. —D. C. S.

8d. **for the LORD has spoken.**

This is the ultimate assurance that the prophecy will come true. Isaiah is not engaging in wishful thinking! The Lord can do the things described. He will do them because he has said he will. After being privileged to view the new Jerusalem, John's words of assurance are similar: "Write this down, for these words are trustworthy and true" (Revelation 21:5). And they are.

II. People's Gratitude
(ISAIAH 25:9, 10a)
A. Words of Testimony (v. 9)

9. **It will be said on that day,**
"Behold, this is our God; we have waited for him, that he might save us. This is the LORD; we have waited for him; let us be glad and rejoice in his salvation."

Isaiah 25 begins with Isaiah's personal tribute of praise, "O Lord, you are my God; I will exalt you; I will praise your name." Now the praise extends to the lips of all who will come to the mountain of the Lord to share in all the "wonderful things" (again, 25:1) provided there. Note the use of the pronouns *our, we* (twice), and *us* (twice). The language is similar to the familiar and often sung words of Psalm 118:24: "This is the day which the Lord hath made; we will rejoice and be glad in it" *(King James Version)*.

We should note that the Hebrew name *Isaiah* means "the Lord saves" or "the Lord is salvation." Both *save* and *salvation* appear in this verse. Consider also that the name *Jesus* means the same thing (Matthew 1:21). He will be the one who accomplishes the wonders that Isaiah is describing.

> **What Do You Think?**
> What tends to rob you of joy as you serve Christ? How do you overcome this problem?
> *Talking Points for Your Discussion*
> - In a work or school context
> - In social contexts
> - In family life
> - Other

B. Words of Truth (v. 10a)

10a. For the hand of the LORD will rest on this mountain.

The hand of the Lord is active throughout the Bible. Sometimes it is associated with blessing (Joshua 4:23, 24; Ezra 7:6; Luke 1:66; Acts 11:21); at other times it is extended for discipline or punishment (Exodus 9:3; Judges 2:15; Ruth 1:13; 1 Samuel 5:6).

Here, however, the focus is on the hand being at rest (contrast Isaiah 5:25; 9:21; 11:15; 19:16; 23:11). God *will rest* after he ushers in his new creation—the new Heaven and the new earth. Before that rest occurs, "The last enemy to be destroyed is death" (1 Corinthians 15:26). When death is defeated for good at the return of Jesus, it will be cast into the lake of fire (Revelation 20:14), never again to cause pain and tears.

> **What Do You Think?**
> How is the hand of the Lord active in your life right now? Why do you think so?
> *Talking Points for Your Discussion*
> - In your family relationships
> - In your personal service to Jesus
> - Other

It is important at this point to add a couple of other New Testament passages that aid in our understanding of the fulfillment of Isaiah's prophecy. One is Hebrews 12:22, where the inspired writer tells Christians that "you have come to Mount Zion and to the city of the living God, the heavenly Jerusalem, and to innumerable angels in festal gathering." According to the writer, Christians are *now* at that mount!

Christians have arrived at the mountain Isaiah describes. For those who claim Jesus as Lord, death is a beaten foe. Our trust in Jesus means we need not fear death (see John 11:25). When death comes to fellow Christians, the ideal is not to "grieve as others do who have no hope" (1 Thessalonians 4:13). We await the day when death is fully and completely vanquished, never again to cause sorrow or tears.

> **What Do You Think?**
> How should a Christian's expression of grief differ from that of unbelievers? Why?
> *Talking Points for Your Discussion*
> - In reaction to acts of violence perpetrated by humans
> - In reaction to forces of nature that result in death and destruction
> - Other

The feast language in today's passage is also used by John in Revelation to picture the great gathering at the "marriage supper of the Lamb" (Revelation 19:9). Anyone can have a close fellowship with Jesus here on earth, if he or she "opens the door" (Revelation 3:20). The ultimate realization of that will come about when the church—the bride of Christ—joins him in his dwelling place in feasting eternally on the best God has to offer.

Conclusion

A. A Somber Anniversary

The news programs will not let anyone go unreminded that today marks the fifteenth anniversary of the 9/11 terrorist attacks. Many can recall exactly where they were or what they were doing on that dreadful morning in 2001 when news of the attacks began to roll in.

Death is difficult in any circumstance, but especially so when it involves a tragedy like the attacks of 9/11, when 2,977 victims lost their lives. Yet death occurs regularly; about 7,000 people die each day in the U.S. alone. You can be sure that people are dealing with death's bitter sting everywhere in the world at the very moment you are reading this. They are planning or taking part in funeral services, visiting gravesites of loved ones, going through the belongings of deceased family members, and taking all the other difficult steps that accompany death's unwelcome presence.

It can be hard in the face of death (particularly an unexpected or tragic death) to think of promises such as those in today's text from Isaiah. We should not try to hide or mask our grief or act as if all is well. The presence of death in this world is a sign that all is not well. This world is still suffering the effects of sin's terrible curse. Yes, in Christ there is personal victory and peace in all circumstances (as we noted in last week's study); but Christians still reside in this broken world and are not immune to its heartaches.

Jesus' weeping at the grave of Lazarus was evidence of the Son of God's distress regarding death (John 11:35). Yet the resurrection of Lazarus that followed was indisputable proof of Jesus' claim to be the resurrection and the life (11:25). Jesus' enemies could not deny what he had done (11:45, 46); consequently, they plotted his death to put a stop to his growing influence (11:47-53). Their efforts proved futile, however, when Jesus himself arose from the dead. That was the ultimate validation of all his claims (Romans 1:4).

Death can leave us shaken and staggering. But the historical certainty of Jesus' resurrection gives ultimate credibility to his many promises, including this one: "Because I live, you also will live" (John 14:19). Rest assured that Jesus will have the last and best word regarding death. At his return he will put death to death—forever.

B. A Song of Hope

Bill Gaither and his wife, Gloria, have written numerous popular Christian songs over the last five decades. One of their most beloved is "Because He Lives." Bill once recounted the story behind this particular song:

> We wrote "Because He Lives" after a period of time when we had had a kind of dry spell and hadn't written any songs for a while. . . . Also at the end of the 1960s, our country was going through some great turmoil with the height of the drug culture, and the whole "God is Dead" theory was running wild in our country. Also it was the peak of the Vietnam War.
>
> During that time our little son was born. . . . I can remember at the time we thought, "Brother, this is really a poor time to bring a child into the world." At times we were even quite discouraged by the whole thing. And then Benjy did come. We had two little girls whom we love very much, but this was our first son, and so that lyric came to us, "How sweet to hold our newborn baby and feel the pride and joy he gives; but better still the calm assurance that this child can face uncertain days because Christ lives." And it gave us the courage to say, "Because Christ lives we can face tomorrow" and keep our heads high.
>
> (Taken from *Amazing Grace: 366 Inspiring Hymn Stories for Daily Devotions,* © 1990 by Kenneth W. Osbeck. Published by Kregel Publications, Grand Rapids, MI. Used by permission of the publisher. All rights reserved.)

In some respects, little has changed in the world since the Gaithers composed "Because He Lives" over 40 years ago. There is still much turmoil. Wars are still fought. Skepticism and doubt about the existence or relevance of God are still voiced, sometimes with great boldness. People still become discouraged by their circumstances. Anniversaries such as today's, remembering what occurred 15 years ago, can be very painful. But in the midst of all of this, Jesus still lives and his promises are still true.

C. Prayer

Father, help us to take heart from Jesus' conquest of death and the many precious promises that we know will come to pass because he lives. Especially in times of tragedy and great loss, may his words provide a hope that the world can never offer. We pray this in Jesus' name. Amen.

D. Thought to Remember

When discouraged, think of the mountain!

INVOLVEMENT LEARNING

Enhance your lesson presentation with the reproducible activity page,
available as a free download at www.standardlesson.com.

Into the Lesson

Display pictures of various famous mountains such as the Matterhorn, Everest, Denali, Vesuvius, Yosemite's Half Dome, the Smokies, Rushmore. As class begins, say, "Look around and guess what today's lesson theme object might be." Next, display this question: "How many biblical mountains can you name?" Let the group make a list.

Alternative. Distribute copies of the "God on the Mountain" activity from the reproducible page, which you can download. Have students pair off and share their answers to the last question.

Into the Word

Prepare copies of today's text divided into segments for responsive reading. For example, verse 6 can be divided after "for all peoples." Look for similarly obvious dividing places in each verse through verse 9. Save verse 10a to be read by all in unison. Divide your group into two smaller groups and have them read aloud the responsive reading.

Have learners flip this responsive reading sheet over for the second text activity. Ask learners to write in large letters, *THE LORD WILL . . .* across the top. Direct your students to look at the text and write as many conclusions to that statement as they can find. For example, from verse 6, "The Lord will make a feast" is obvious.

As you solicit entries from the lists made, be prepared to ask, "Where else in Scripture do you find an example of God doing the same essential thing?" For example, for God making a feast, one might refer to the marriage supper of the Lamb in Revelation 19:9. From Isaiah 25:8, a second example would be, "The Lord will wipe away tears." Learners might note such occasions as Jesus raising the widow of Nain's son or raising Lazarus or even the second citation of this "wipe away tears" phenomenon in Revelation 7:17 or the third time in Revelation 21:4.

What should God's people do in response to what God has done? The obvious answer is in the end of verse 9: rejoicing, being glad in our salvation accomplished in him. Ask, "How should we demonstrate that internal attitude of gladness and that external demonstration in rejoicing?" One obvious answer is in singing the songs of gladness. Ask your class to identify hymns, choruses, and gospel songs that express such affirmations. If response is slow, have two or three class members ready to "break into song" with such songs as "Sing Praise to God Who Reigns Above" or "I've Got the Joy, Joy, Joy, Joy Down in My Heart" or others of your choosing from selections your class may know from your worship assemblies.

Option. Distribute copies of "Sound Familiar?" from the reproducible page, and ask students to form groups of three or four to complete the activity. It allows your learners to look at key ideas of the text and relate them to other biblical revelations of God's plan for his people.

Into Life

Say, "Oppression is everywhere. Such matters as schoolyard bullying, spousal abuse, abandonment of the elderly, taking advantage of workers on job sites—all are, at their core, matters of oppression. Whereas Isaiah writes of God's plan to lift the oppression of his people (from enemies and from sin), we are in a position, to and need to, deal with the oppression of those near us. How do we do that?"

Note that the world is filled with oppressed groups, many of whom are refugees forced from their homes and country. Ask the class, "Can you name a Christian agency active in helping such oppressed groups?" Then, "Is there some way our class or you individually could help?" In the closing prayer time, be certain to include a call for God's protection of those being oppressed, in any way.

FOUNDATIONS OF THE EARTH

DEVOTIONAL READING: Isaiah 40:1-8
BACKGROUND SCRIPTURE: Isaiah 40

ISAIAH 40:21-31

21 Do you not know? Do you not hear?
   Has it not been told you from the
      beginning?
   Have you not understood from the
      foundations of the earth?
22 It is he who sits above the circle of the earth,
   and its inhabitants are like grasshoppers;
   who stretches out the heavens like a
      curtain,
   and spreads them like a tent to dwell in;
23 who brings princes to nothing,
   and makes the rulers of the earth as
      emptiness.
24 Scarcely are they planted, scarcely sown,
   scarcely has their stem taken root in the
      earth,
   when he blows on them, and they wither,
   and the tempest carries them off like
      stubble.
25 To whom then will you compare me,
   that I should be like him? says the Holy
      One.
26 Lift up your eyes on high and see:
   who created these?

He who brings out their host by number,
   calling them all by name,
by the greatness of his might,
   and because he is strong in power
   not one is missing.
27 Why do you say, O Jacob,
   and speak, O Israel,
"My way is hidden from the LORD,
   and my right is disregarded by my God"?
28 Have you not known? Have you not heard?
The LORD is the everlasting God,
   the Creator of the ends of the earth.
He does not faint or grow weary;
   his understanding is unsearchable.
29 He gives power to the faint,
   and to him who has no might he
      increases strength.
30 Even youths shall faint and be weary,
   and young men shall fall exhausted;
31 but they who wait for the LORD shall renew
      their strength;
   they shall mount up with wings like
      eagles;
   they shall run and not be weary;
   they shall walk and not faint.

KEY VERSE

Have you not known? Have you not heard? The Lord is the everlasting God, the Creator of the ends of the earth. He does not faint or grow weary; his understanding is unsearchable. —**Isaiah 40:28**

The Sovereignty of God

Unit 1: The Sovereignty of the Father

Lessons 1–4

Lesson Aims

After participating in this lesson, each learner will be able to:

1. List characteristics of the Creator that are uniquely his.

2. Contrast the life of an individual who acknowledges God as Creator with the life of one who does not.

3. Help plan a worship service that focuses on God as Creator.

Lesson Outline

Introduction

A. One Isaiah or Two?

Over the years, some students of the Bible have proposed that someone other than the prophet Isaiah wrote chapters 40–66. This position is taken because the tone and focus shift significantly in Isaiah 40. Assyria, so prominent in the first 39 chapters, is no longer a threat to God's people; Babylon is the new menace (Isaiah 47:1-7; 48:14-22). There is also a greater emphasis in chapters 40–66 on promises of hope and a brighter future for God's people in contrast with the theme of judgment that is so prevalent in the previous chapters.

The book's focus does shift somewhat in the later chapters, but that does not require a different author. C. S. Lewis wrote books that differed markedly from one another in style and content (compare *Mere Christianity* with The Chronicles of Narnia series). But no one seriously suggests that these materials could not have been written by the same person.

Furthermore, the New Testament cites passages from throughout the book of Isaiah and never attributes authorship to anyone other than Isaiah. Note especially John 12:37-41, where two passages from Isaiah are quoted, one from chapter 6 and the other from the supposedly different section in chapter 53. Yet John attributed both to the prophet Isaiah. The testimony of Scripture itself is clear: the book of Isaiah is singular in nature, and one prophet is its author.

B. Lesson Background

Isaiah 40 begins with words of comfort to God's people, specifically to Jerusalem. The "hard service" that "has been completed" (v. 2) likely describes the captivity predicted in 39:5-7. God's people are to be released to return home. That will show that "her sin has been paid for" (40:2).

But there is more in the future than just that homecoming. Isaiah 40:3 speaks of a voice in the wilderness crying "prepare the way of the Lord." This is fulfilled in the person and work of John the Baptist (Matthew 3:1-3), whose ministry prepared for the coming of Jesus. Isaiah, who spoke prophetically of Jesus (example: the text from lesson 1), then continued his Spirit-guided fore-shadowings across the rest of his book. Some are the most stirring messianic prophecies in the Old Testament. Isaiah 53 is a prime example, and another will be seen in next week's lesson.

As though responding to skeptics about whether his words would come to pass, the prophet offered in Isaiah 40 a passionate defense of God's uniqueness and power. If Isaiah's predictions seemed too good to be true, then perhaps his hearers needed to reevaluate their view of the God for whom Isaiah spoke. God was more than capable of doing everything his prophet said he would do.

I. Sovereign Power
(ISAIAH 40:21-26)

A. Over Earth and the Heavens (vv. 21, 22)

21. Do you not know? Do you not hear?
Has it not been told you from the beginning?
Have you not understood from the foundations of the earth?

This verse continues a series of penetrating questions that begin in Isaiah 40:12-14 and resume in verse 18. They challenge Isaiah's audience to ponder the greatness and uniqueness of their God. He needs no one to advise or counsel him. He is the Creator, and he stands alone as infinitely superior to any other so-called god.

Isaiah's words in the verse before us appear to be chiding God's people. It is as if the prophet is saying, "You should not have to be reminded of what I am telling you. You should already know this." Yet these words can also be aimed at all people everywhere. As Paul says, "For his invisible attributes, namely, his eternal power and divine nature, have been clearly perceived, ever since the creation of the world, in the things that have been made. So they are without excuse" (Romans 1:20). From the time of the creation itself—*from the beginning* as Isaiah says—this message has been communicated. The Hebrew word translated *beginning* is very similar to the same word used to "begin" the Bible in Genesis 1:1.

A form of the Hebrew word for *foundations* is also used elsewhere in this book to describe God's creative activity (Isaiah 28:16; 48:13). He is pictured as the master builder, one who does all the proper work that is preliminary to construction of *the earth* (compare Psalms 102:25; 104:5). This fact should serve as a basis for human knowledge.

22a. It is he who sits above the circle of the earth,

This observation is in keeping with the understanding that *the earth* is round, though some suggest that *the circle* refers more to the domed shape of the horizon. Of greater importance to Isaiah's point is that the Lord sits as a ruler on his throne, in this case as sovereign of the earth.

22b. and its inhabitants are like grasshoppers;

This statement reminds us of how the Israelites viewed themselves in contrast with the inhabitants of the land of Canaan (Numbers 13:33, same Hebrew word). This does not appear to be a very flattering description! This is especially so when one considers that human beings are created in the image of God and given dignity and special responsibility as the crowning glory of God's creative activity (Genesis 1:26-28). But Isaiah's use of the word *grasshoppers* is meant to impress upon the readers how they measure up against the Creator. He is the potter, and we are the clay. We get in serious trouble when we try to reverse the roles (see Isaiah 29:15, 16; 41:25; 64:8; Jeremiah 18:1-6; Romans 9:19-21).

◆ *WHAT GOD SEES, WHAT WE SEE* ◆

E. O. Wilson enjoyed the great outdoors as a youngster. He was born in 1929, and this meant that there were no electronic gadgets to tempt him away from exploring nature! But pleasure turned to pain one day when he injured his right eye while fishing. He did not tell anyone what had

HOW TO SAY IT

adrenaline	uh-*dreh*-nuh-lin.
Amos	*Ay*-mus.
Canaan	*Kay*-nun.
entomologist	en-tuh-*maw*-luh-jist.
epinephrine	eh-puh-*neh*-frin.
Isaiah	Eye-*zay*-uh.
Israelite	*Iz*-ray-el-ite.

happened, but his parents took him for surgery when the pupil clouded over with a cataract.

Wilson ended up with full vision in his left eye only, but the sight in that eye tested at a sharp 20/10 on the eye chart. His ability to see intricate details of the smallest kind opened his eyes, so to speak, to the wonders of nature—specifically butterflies and ants. Wilson became one of the world's foremost entomologists.

Isaiah describes the Lord as one who sits high above and observes us almost as an entomologist studies grasshoppers. But unlike insects, we are made in the image of God—and so his surveillance is anything but mere dispassionate science. He is sovereign over all of creation.

Sadly, Wilson has declared that "for the sake of human progress, the best thing we could possibly do would be to diminish, to the point of eliminating, religious faiths." Perhaps Jeremiah has the best response: "Hear this, O foolish and senseless people, who have eyes, but see not" (Jeremiah 5:21; compare Matthew 13:13). How do we get skeptics to lift their "eyes on high and see" to ponder the Creator (Isaiah 40:26, below)?   —D. C. S.

22c. who stretches out the heavens like a curtain,
   and spreads them like a tent to dwell in;

The Hebrew word translated *curtain* is quite rare in its noun form, occurring only here in the Old Testament. But the parallel phrase *tent to dwell in* helps us get the meaning: the idea is that of a place of habitation (contrast Psalm 69:25). This is in keeping with similar language elsewhere (see Psalm 19:4; Isaiah 54:2).

B. Over Earthly Rulers (vv. 23, 24)

23. who brings princes to nothing,
   and makes the rulers of this earth as emptiness.

A further statement of God's sovereign power is given in parallel thoughts:

Action	Object	Result
brings	princes	to nothing
makes	rulers	as emptiness

Earthly rulers are often prone to think of themselves far more highly than warranted. But God has ways of correcting such arrogance (examples: Daniel 4; Acts 12:19b-23).

The Hebrew words for *nothing* and *emptiness* are both used earlier: "All the nations are as nothing before him, they are accounted by him as less than nothing and emptiness" (Isaiah 40:17). What is true of earthly rulers is true of nations. Isaiah is not saying that the nations and their rulers mean nothing to God or that he has no concern for them. He desires the "ends of the earth" to be saved (Isaiah 45:22). But without God, both nations and rulers are destined to come to nothing (though in the world's eyes they may become quite renowned).

When compared with the sovereign God, the idea that humans can create a "sovereign nation" or designate a "sovereign ruler" becomes absurd. There is only one true sovereign, and he is the Lord.

What Do You Think?
   How can we help one another appreciate our insignificance when compared with God? Why is it important to do so?
Talking Points for Your Discussion
   ▪ Regarding personal independence
   ▪ Regarding our impact on the universe
   ▪ Other

24. Scarcely are they planted, scarcely sown, scarcely has their stem taken root in the earth,
   when he blows on them, and they wither, and the tempest carries them off like stubble.

Earthly rulers in their arrogance sometimes act as if they are indestructible, as though they will always be in power. Even those who harbor no such illusion may view their nations as permanent. But all earthly rulers and nations are subject to ending up in the proverbial "dustbin of history" (compare Daniel 7, 8, 11).

The Hebrew word translated *taken root* is a verb form of the noun translated "roots" in Isaiah 11:1, which describes the nature of the promised Branch (see lesson 1). His roots will be firmly planted under God's blessing, unlike earthly rulers in view here. All it takes is but one breath from the sovereign God for them to *wither* to nothing. When that happens, they are worth no more than *stubble* or chaff to be discarded (compare Job 21:18; Isaiah 41:2; Daniel 2:35; Luke 3:17). Would that earthly rulers today viewed themselves as subjects of the one, true sovereign! What a difference it would make in how they carry out their responsibilities!

◆ **RISE AND FALL** ◆

Frank Reed has put together a fascinating animation (available on YouTube®) that depicts the changing of European borders over the course of 1,000 years. Viewers are treated to the rise and fall of empires in less than three minutes!

In light of God's sovereignty, Isaiah does not seem to take political power all that seriously. Kingdoms rise and fall. Emperors conquer great lands only to be conquered themselves. Many powerful people from history have only a few paragraphs dedicated to them in textbooks. Hitler's twisted dream of a "thousand-year reich" lasted only 12 years.

Sometimes earthly power is used in ways that honor God; more often it is not. In all cases, however, earthly power and authority are always temporary. As the tenure of one leader ends, another steps up to take his or her place—a cycle repeated thousands of times throughout history. If nothing else, let us remind ourselves that our time on earth is limited, regardless of our status or the power we wield. What matters is whether or not we use our positions of influence to glorify God.
—D. C. S.

C. Over the Stars (vv. 25, 26)

25. To whom then will you compare me, that I should be like him? says the Holy One.

This verse raises a question in two forms. Of course, the Scriptures themselves compare God with various objects as a way to express certain of his characteristics. Psalm 18:2 alone uses five such comparisons: God as a "rock," a "fortress," a "shield," a "horn," and a "stronghold." These imply strength and security. Psalm 91:4 mentions "his

pinions" and "his wings" to call attention to God's ability to shelter his people. The point of Isaiah's question is that no other so-called god is like the Lord, none is his equal.

The title *Holy One* is used by Isaiah far more than any other Old Testament writer, with more than half the occurrences in his book. This feature may be linked to Isaiah's personal experience of God's holiness during the prophet's own call to ministry, as recorded in Isaiah 6 (note v. 3).

> *What Do You Think?*
> Based on your own experiences with God, what adjectives would you use to describe him?
> *Talking Points for Your Discussion*
> - When reflecting on spiritually "up" times
> - When reflecting on spiritually "down" times

26. Lift up your eyes on high and see: who created these?
    He brings out their host by number, calling them all by name.
    by the greatness of his might, and because he is strong in power not one is missing.

Isaiah now challenges his audience to consider an example of God's supremacy. The prophet specifically calls attention to *the host,* indicating that the Lord takes a personal interest in them, *calling them all by name, by the greatness of his might.* The awe-inspiring nature of the heavenly array serves a profound purpose in reminding observers of the Creator (compare Job 9:7-9; 38:31, 32; Psalm 19:1; Amos 5:8).

Modern science establishes that stars can die as they explode (supernova) then fade out, which may make us wonder about the phrase *not one is missing.* We should realize that a supernova is an extremely rare sight, particularly in times that lack telescopes. Indeed, the first record of an observed supernova is not until AD 185. People's regular experience is that the stars are always there, the same ones night after night. God is in control. He is the one who sustains the stars, just as he is the one who will bring their existence to an end on the last day (Mark 13:24-29 [quoting Isaiah 13:10; 34:4]; 2 Peter 3:10-12).

II. Sustaining Power
(ISAIAH 40:27-31)
A. Shortsighted Israel (v. 27)

27. Why do you say, O Jacob?
and speak, O Israel,
"My way is hidden from the LORD,
and my right is disregarded by my
God"?

Isaiah offers us more parallel expressions, with *say* equivalent to *speak,* and *Jacob* equivalent to *Israel* (compare Genesis 32:28; 35:10; 46:2). These direct the question that follows (which is also in the form of two parallel expressions) right at the covenant people: How can they possibly claim that their *way is hidden from the Lord* and their *right is disregarded by . . . God?*

Perhaps Isaiah is looking ahead to the time of the Babylonian captivity (Isaiah 39:5-7) and anticipating the doubts that some will entertain as time drags on. Is God really going to bring his people home? Does he even care about bringing the punishment to an end? Isaiah questions why the people should ever think this way, given what he has just stated to be true about God. In effect, Isaiah is asking rhetorically, "If God has counted the stars and given them names, will he not also care for his people and keep his promises to them?"

B. Never-Failing God (v. 28)

28. Have you not known? Have you not heard?
The LORD is the everlasting God,
the Creator of the ends of the earth.
He does not faint or grow weary;
his understanding is unsearchable.

The two phrases that begin this verse are similar to the two that open verse 21, above. The questions in verse 21, however, are written in the plural in Hebrew, while the phrases here are singular. It is as if Isaiah is making his appeal more personal at this point. The God who cares about each and every star (v. 26) also cares about each and every person.

The questions in verse 21 lead to a declaration of God as the sovereign ruler over creation and earthly rulers. The questions here lead to a reassurance of God's strength and power, which never weakens. The Israelite people in their (future)

captivity—or for that matter, people in any kind of crisis—may *grow weary,* but *the everlasting God* is not subject to such limitation.

> **What Do You Think?**
> What experiences have you had with the fact that God does not grow weary? How do these relate to Isaiah 1:14 and Malachi 2:17, if at all?
> *Talking Points for Your Discussion*
> - Regarding non-sinful mistakes
> - Regarding sin

Later the prophet will make a statement similar to *his understanding is unsearchable* when he relays the Lord's declaration that "As the heavens are higher than the earth, so are my ways higher than your ways and my thoughts than your thoughts" (Isaiah 55:9). We cannot be educated to understand or be able to explain the ways of the Lord in every circumstance. That is not possible for finite humans (compare Job 38–41). What is required of us is simple, trusting faith (Luke 18:17; Hebrews 11:6).

C. Never-Ending Strength (vv. 29-31)

29. He gives power to the faint,
and to him who has no might he
increases strength.

Among the wonders of Israel's (and our) God is that his power is evident not only in creation in general but is also available to humans personally. But it is not given to those who are proud and self-sufficient (compare Proverbs 3:34, which is quoted in James 4:6; 1 Peter 5:5). It is in *the faint* and *him who has no might* where God's power is seen most clearly. This is a lesson the apostle Paul learned personally (see 2 Corinthians 12:7-10).

30. Even youths shall faint and be weary,
and young men shall fall exhausted;

Younger people often are the ones who most think themselves able to handle or do just about anything on their own. But they too can reach a point where struggles and disappointments leave them "gasping for air" in a spiritual sense. Without a genuine relationship with God, their resources are limited to those of this world—resources inadequate to cope with the brokenness that we inevitably encounter on this sin-cursed planet.

31. but they who wait for the LORD shall renew their strength;
they shall mount up with wings like eagles;
they shall run and not be weary;
they shall walk and not faint.

Here is the grand climax to the chapter. Those who *wait for the Lord*—the ones who look expectantly to him and find hope in his steadfast promises—are the ones who will find *their strength* renewed. The reference to *wings like eagles* suggests soaring far above the earth below. Whether the pace demanded of us is fast (running) or slow (walking), the Lord's strength provides the resources to do so. It is he, not the world, who empowers us through life.

Conclusion
A. Spiritual Adrenaline

Adrenaline (also called *epinephrine*) is a hormone and a neurotransmitter produced by the body in response to stressful situations. Adrenaline production results in an additional burst of energy. Occasionally we hear of a person who lifts a car off of someone pinned beneath it, and adrenaline is the key to being able to do so. The rescuer, though not very big or strong, suddenly finds a rush of strength to accomplish the rescue.

Today's lesson highlights what might be called spiritual adrenaline—the strength God provides to those who become weary and overwhelmed by circumstances. We all suffer the repercussions of life in a fallen world. Some suffer these more personally and painfully than others. But to all who become faint of heart and who feel they have no strength to continue, there is a strength available that is not their own. It is a strength that cannot be found in this world's resources. It is a strength that does not require any kind of self-help manual, surgical procedure, or dietary supplement. The requirement is merely to wait for the Lord. Those who do, promised Isaiah, find the help they need.

Whenever we study the book of Isaiah, we often focus on what he has to say about the messianic future, as in our first two lessons. But the prophet also has much to say about the messy present that people experience daily. Never forget that everything Isaiah says about the Lord in today's passage is still true.

B. Prayer

Father, thank you for strength to carry us through! May we witness that strength to others so that they too may "walk and not faint." We pray in Jesus' name. Amen.

C. Thought to Remember
The God of Isaiah 40 is our God as well.

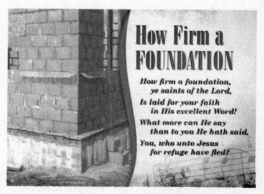

How Firm a FOUNDATION

How firm a foundation,
ye saints of the Lord,
Is laid for your faith
in His excellent Word!
What more can He say
than to you He hath said,
You, who unto Jesus
for refuge have fled?

Visual for Lesson 3. *For deeper discussion, point to this visual as you highlight other "firm foundation" passages in Isaiah 28:16; 48:13; 51:13, 16; 54:11, 12.*

INVOLVEMENT LEARNING

Enhance your lesson presentation with the reproducible activity page,
available as a free download at www.standardlesson.com.

Into the Lesson

Consider showing a video of an eagle in flight. The Internet offers many choices. Let the class be fascinated by the majesty and freedom of the bird, and then comment, "Wouldn't we all like to be able to do that? Today's text makes us that promise."

Alternative. Come to class wearing a set of fake wings or simply have a set on prominent display. Respond to learner reactions.

Into the Word

Distribute copies of this word-find puzzle with these directions: "Look at this puzzle to find 12 attributes of God. Once you find them, relate each to today's text in Isaiah 40."

```
H A D V E Y O U N O T K N O
W I E N ? R O T A E R C H A
V U N E Q U A L E D E I Y O
U N O C O T Y H E A R T D ?
H A R S O L I T N O T S B E
E N H O O M N I S C I E N T
P B T H V I P O U S T J F R
O O N M T H E A B E E A G R
W R E L A E V E R I N M E N
E I N G ? H A N V A E L Y O
R G U N O T A U N D B E R S
F T D O O L D ? G A O L D I
U S O U N H I S N T H R E O
L N E I J N H E E A V E N !
```

The attributes to be found are *CREATOR, ENABLER, ENTHRONED, ETERNAL, HOLY, INCOMPARABLE, JUDGE, MAJESTIC, OMNISCIENT, POWERFUL, REVEALER, UNEQUALED.* Say, "The filler letters reveal four rhetorical questions and a resounding affirmation, based on today's text. Write the letters in sequence —with the question marks and exclamation mark —to reveal a grand truth." The questions are "Have you not known?"; "Have you not heard?"; "Has it

not been obvious from the beginning?"; and "Have you not understood?" The grand affirmation is "God is on his throne in Heaven!"

Alternative: Make copies of the "Why Are You Complaining?" activity from the reproducible page, which you can download. It can easily be related to the simple truth in the preceding sentence.

Say, "Now let's look back at the list of God's attributes. What will be different for the person who accepts the truth of these from one who rejects or denies them?" Consider flash cards with each of the words. As you hold up a card, ask, "How does this attribute of God affect the way you live?" For example, display *REVEALER* and note that regular attention will be given to God's revelation in the Scriptures; also, a believer will have a curious intentional attitude toward what God has revealed in his creation, an interest in various disciplines such as science and the arts. For *JUDGE,* a believer will be content to leave the judgment of sin in others to God; the believer will live knowing that ultimately he or she will be judged by God.

Alternative: Distribute copies of the "What God Does" activity from the reproducible page. It is closely related to these same truths.

Into Life

Assign groups to make brainstorming decisions in the four following categories of planning a worship assembly centering on God as Creator: (1) key Bible texts to be read by individuals or in groups responsively; (2) songs and hymns to be played instrumentally in prelude and postlude, during offering and Communion, and as solos and congregational singing; (3) prayer elements to be emphasized in various prayer times; (4) Bible texts to be studied and developed in the assembly's sermon/teaching segment.

Allow about five minutes for groups to decide. Collect the ideas to pass along to the congregation's worship planners/leaders.

EVERLASTING
COVENANT

DEVOTIONAL READING: Isaiah 42:5-9
BACKGROUND SCRIPTURE: Isaiah 61

ISAIAH 61:1-4, 8-11

1 The Spirit of the Lord GOD is upon me,
  because the LORD has anointed me
to bring good news to the poor;
  he has sent me to bind up the
  broken-hearted,
to proclaim liberty to the captives,
  and the opening of the prison to those
  who are bound;
2 to proclaim the year of the LORD's favor,
  and the day of vengeance of our God;
  to comfort all who mourn;
3 to grant to those who mourn in Zion—
  to give them a beautiful headdress
  instead of ashes,
the oil of gladness instead of mourning,
  the garment of praise instead of a faint
  spirit;
that they may be called oaks of
  righteousness,
  the planting of the LORD, that he may
  be glorified.
4 They shall build up the ancient ruins;
  they shall raise up the former
  devastations;
they shall repair the ruined cities,
  the devastations of many generations.

. . . .

8 For I the LORD love justice;
  I hate robbery and wrong;
I will faithfully give them their recompense,
  and I will make an everlasting covenant
  with them.
9 Their offspring shall be known among the
  nations,
  and their descendants in the midst of
  the peoples;
all who see them shall acknowledge them,
  that they are an offspring the LORD has
  blessed.
10 I will greatly rejoice in the LORD;
  my soul shall exult in my God,
for he has clothed me with the garments of
  salvation;
  he has covered me with the robe of
  righteousness,
as a bridegroom decks himself like a priest
  with a beautiful headdress,
  and as a bride adorns herself with her
  jewels.
11 For as the earth brings forth its sprouts,
  and as a garden causes what is sown in
  it to sprout up,
so the Lord GOD will cause righteousness
  and praise
  to sprout up before all the nations.

KEY VERSE

I the LORD love justice; I hate robbery and wrong; I will faithfully give them their recompense, and I will make an everlasting covenant with them. —**Isaiah 61:8**

THE SOVEREIGNTY OF GOD

Unit 1: The Sovereignty of the Father

LESSONS 1–4

LESSON AIMS

After participating in this lesson, each learner will be able to:

1. Describe the nature and range of God's promised blessings.

2. Explain Jesus' use of Isaiah 61:1, 2 in Luke 4:18, 19.

3. Write a prayer of thanks for God's faithfulness in keeping his promises.

LESSON OUTLINE

Introduction
    A. "My Name's in the Bible!"
    B. Lesson Background
 I. Future Blessings (ISAIAH 61:1-4)
    A. The Person (v. 1a)
    B. The Message (vv. 1b, 1c)
    C. The Time (vv. 2a, 2b)
    D. The Impact (vv. 2c-4)
      Mighty Trees, Small Acorns
II. Faithful God (ISAIAH 61:8-11)
    A. Covenant's Endurance (v. 8)
    B. Israelites' Reputation (v. 9)
      Reputations: Ours and God's
    C. Special Clothing (v. 10)
    D. Global Witness (v. 11)
Conclusion
    A. It's Our Move
    B. Prayer
    C. Thought to Remember

Introduction

A. "My Name's in the Bible!"

One summer found my future wife helping with a church in the Boston area during her college years. Among her responsibilities was working with Vacation Bible School, which the church conducted yearly.

During that VBS, she became acquainted with a teenage girl of Asian descent whose first name was Yi (pronounced *Ye*). One of the Scriptures covered was Jesus' Great Commission, which is recorded in Matthew 28:18-20. Verse 19, as worded in the *King James Version,* begins with his command to "Go ye therefore, and teach all nations."

When young Yi heard that verse, she became very excited. "Jesus is talking to me!" she exclaimed. "He wants Yi to go and tell others about him!" Yi was quite thrilled to think that her name was in the Bible.

Names are important, none more so than that of *Jesus,* found throughout the New Testament. Although Jesus is not mentioned in the Old Testament specifically by that name, numerous prophecies there highlight various aspects of his life and ministry that were to come. Today's text includes a passage that Jesus specifically cited and declared as "fulfilled" in himself (Luke 4:21).

B. Lesson Background

Today's study is the final one in this unit of lessons, "The Sovereignty of the Father," drawn from the book of Isaiah. Our passage under consideration, like those of lessons 1 and 2, includes an important messianic thrust.

Isaiah 61 appears in the closing section of the book of Isaiah, a section typically delineated as being chapters 60–66. Bryan Beyer rightly refers to these chapters as "the grand finale of God's restoration." Their content was intended to give great hope to God's people in Isaiah's day. Their purpose may be compared with the closing chapters of the book of Revelation. Those chapters offer hope to Christians in any age, particularly those suffering persecution. In fact, there are numerous similarities between the closing chapters of the two books, as this listing makes clear:

Isaiah	Revelation
60:3, 5, 11	21:24-26
60:19, 20	21:23; 22:5
61:6	1:6; 5:10
61:10	19:8; 21:2
62:2	2:17
62:11	22:12
63:1-3	14:20; 19:13, 15
65:17; 66:22	21:1
65:19	21:4
66:6	16:1
66:7	12:2, 5

I. Future Blessings
(ISAIAH 61:1-4)

Traditionally, the book of Isaiah is seen to feature four "servant songs": Isaiah 42:1-4; 49:1-6; 50:4-9; and 52:13–53:12. Scholars do not agree on the passage boundaries, and some see 61:1-3 as a fifth servant song, building especially on the fourth.

A. The Person (v. 1a)
1a. The Spirit of the Lord GOD is upon me,

In lesson 1 we saw Isaiah foretell the branch promised to come "from the stump of Jesse" (Isaiah 11:1). The prophet declared, in wording similar to the half verse before us, "The Spirit of the Lord shall rest upon him" (11:2). The New Testament records that "the Holy Spirit descended on [Jesus] in bodily form, like a dove" (Luke 3:22). Jesus, "full of the Holy Spirit," then "was led by the Spirit in the wilderness," where he was tempted (4:1). Later, "Jesus returned in the power of the Spirit to Galilee" (4:14). Then, in the Nazareth synagogue, he quotes from our passage in Isaiah (Luke 4:16-19).

Without the witness of the completed New Testament, we may wonder who the *me* refers to. But Luke leaves no doubt.

B. The Message (vv. 1b, 1c)
1b. because the LORD has anointed me
to bring good news to the poor;
he has sent me to bind up the
brokenhearted,

Per the above, Jesus is clearly the one who is *anointed* to do all the things listed here. The words *good news* are directed in this case *to the poor*. The prophet sets "the meek" parallel with "the poor" in Isaiah 11:4; 29:19; such people are the ones who humble themselves and acknowledge their destitution apart from God's aid.

Their poverty may include both material and spiritual aspects (compare Matthew 11:4, 5; 5:3). The reference to *the brokenhearted* calls to mind a portion of David's words of repentance: "The sacrifices of God are a broken spirit; a broken and contrite heart, O God, you will not despise" (Psalm 51:17; compare 34:18; 143:7).

1c. to proclaim liberty to the captives,
and the opening of the prison to those
who are bound;

The task *to proclaim liberty* is rooted in the regulations of the year of jubilee, described in Leviticus 25:8-55. Specifically, verse 10 describes the return of and to land that had been sold during the previous 49 years, as it reverts back to original owners. *To proclaim liberty* in Luke 4:18, 19 foreshadows what Jesus will do by means of his death and resurrection. In those acts he makes possible the return of human beings to their rightful owner (the Lord) by freeing them from *the prison* of sin, death, and Satan (Hebrews 2:14, 15; 9:15; see also Romans 6:18; 8:2; Revelation 1:5b, 18).

> ### What Do You Think?
> What has God equipped you to do for the advancement of his kingdom? How can you better accept this challenge?
> #### Talking Points for Your Discussion
> - Considering "lessons learned" from lost opportunities
> - Considering your mentor and/or protégé role in relation to others similarly equipped
> - Other

C. The Time (vv. 2a, 2b)
2a. to proclaim the year of the LORD's favor,

This task may again reflect an aspect of the year of jubilee, mentioned above. However, one should not think in this case of a specific 12-month period, but of a general extent of time (compare "day of salvation" in 2 Corinthians 6:2).

2b.   and the day of vengeance of our God;

When Jesus reads Isaiah 61:1, 2 in the Nazareth synagogue, it is noteworthy that he stops just before this phrase (Luke 4:18-20). Jesus does not come to earth the first time to condemn, as he himself says (John 3:17). *The day of vengeance* will occur when Jesus returns (2 Thessalonians 1:7-9).

D. The Impact (vv. 2c-4)

2c.   to comfort all who mourn;
3a. to grant to those who mourn in Zion—
         to give them a beautiful headdress
            instead of ashes,
         the oil of gladness instead of mourning,
            the garment of praise instead of a faint
               spirit;

The prophecy returns to a more encouraging tone. The words *mourn* and *mourning* call to mind Jesus' promise in the Beatitudes that those who mourn shall be comforted (Matthew 5:4; compare Luke 6:21). The opportunity to exchange *ashes* (used along with sackcloth in Old Testament times to express mourning; see Esther 4:1, 3; Jeremiah 6:26) for *something beautiful* emphasizes the transformation that will take place.

Receiving *the oil of gladness* in place of *mourning* adds further emphasis. Oil (olive oil in this case) is associated in Scripture with prosperous surroundings (Deuteronomy 8:7, 8; Jeremiah 31:12). It is used in anointing ceremonies (Psalm 45:7) and in welcoming guests into one's home (Luke 7:46).

Furthermore, a completely new wardrobe is provided: *the garment of praise* in exchange for *a faint spirit*. All of this amounts to quite a "makeover"!

> ▶ **What Do You Think?**
> What spiritual impact should we hope to have on those within our sphere of influence?
> *Talking Points for Your Discussion*
> • In terms of new things embraced
> • In terms of old things discarded

3b. that they may be called oaks of
         righteousness,

the planting of the LORD, that he may
   be glorified.

The prophet's imagery changes. In an earlier description of coming judgment, Isaiah had said of God's people, "You shall be like an oak whose leaf withers, and like a garden without water" (Isaiah 1:30). Things are different, however, thanks to the work of the master arborist (compare Isaiah 60:21; contrast Matthew 15:13).

◆   *MIGHTY TREES, SMALL ACORNS*   ◆

When I was a child, it was a treat to get away from the daily routine of the farm and go shopping in the nearby city. Along the way, the intriguing message on a certain roadside billboard would always catch my attention.

And just why was it so intriguing? I suppose the odd phrasing of its message was one reason: "Tall oaks from little acorns grow." People did not talk that way; it sounded like something out of a poetry book. But that phrase stayed with me as I thought about what it could mean. My childhood mind wondered why it was significant enough to warrant a billboard.

To adults, its message is obvious: even the largest trees start small. That message has countless applications. For one, it applies to God's people. The beginning of our Christian journey of faith may not be marked by an emotional avalanche (compare Isaiah 6; Acts 9:1-19). We may simply wonder what this new life in Christ will mean to us, where it will take us, how we will succeed in pleasing God and enduring the trials we are told will come. But when we allow God to have his way with us, our "acorn faith" will grow into a "big-tree witness," tall and strong for all to see (compare Psalms 1:3; 52:8; 92:12).   —C. M. W.

4.   They shall build up the ancient ruins;
         they shall raise up the former
            devastations;
         they shall repair the ruined cities,
            the devastations of many generations.

This promise seems to apply to what transpires when God's people return from captivity in Babylon. However, one must note how this kind of language is used elsewhere in Scripture. For example, the prophet Amos speaks of a time when God will "raise up the booth of David" and "repair its breaches" and "rebuild it as in the days of old" (Amos 9:11). This too sounds like the prophet is foreseeing a major stone-and-wood building program. But according to James in his address to the Jerusalem Conference, Amos's words are fulfilled through the inclusion of Gentiles into the church (Acts 15:13-19). Isaiah uses the language of topographical transformation in Isaiah 40:4, but this is fulfilled in a spiritual sense in the ministry of John the Baptist (Luke 3:2-6).

Since Isaiah 61 begins with words that Jesus declares fulfilled in himself, it seems best to see the verse before us as describing the impact of his ministry. Just as verse 3 uses word pictures of clothing and tree planting to portray the spiritual transformation accomplished by Jesus, the present verse uses the language of urban renewal to make a similar point. The New Testament describes the growth of the church as a "building" program (1 Corinthians 3:10, 11; Ephesians 2:19-22; 1 Peter 2:5). Further, Paul uses the terminology of planting and building consecutively in 1 Corinthians 3:5-11 to explain how the church is to grow.

II. Faithful God
(ISAIAH 61:8-11)

In verses 5-7 (not in today's text), Isaiah continues his stirring account of the coming changes. Instead of serving "strangers" and "foreigners" (v. 5), as God's people are to do during the Babylonian captivity, the reverse will happen. However, their relationship toward the "nations" (v. 6) will not be one of domination as payback. Rather, God's people are described as becoming "priests of the Lord" and "ministers of our God" (v. 6). Their exalted position is not one of privilege, but

HOW TO SAY IT

Beatitudes	Bee-*a*-tuh-toods (*a* as in *mat*).
Canaan	*Kay*-nun.
Galilee	*Gal*-uh-lee.
Nazareth	*Naz*-uh-reth.
synagogue	*sin*-uh-gog.

of responsibility to teach the "strangers" the Lord's way (compare Isaiah 2:2-4). Thus this portion of the chapter also highlights the future "makeover" of God's people.

A. Covenant's Endurance (v. 8)
8a. For I the LORD love justice;
I hate robbery and wrong;

The word *justice* carries the idea of *righteousness*. Indeed, the two words often occur together as synonyms or near synonyms (examples: Isaiah 9:7; 59:9, 14). The Lord himself is just (Deuteronomy 32:4), and he requires the same of his people (Proverbs 21:3), especially of their leaders (2 Samuel 23:3). As the Lord hates *robbery and wrong,* so must his people.

God makes clear that acts of worship from those who do not follow him wholeheartedly are repulsive, with hypocritical offerings mentioned (examples: Isaiah 1:10-17; Amos 5:21-24). The Lord intends to bring about dramatic changes in his people; his righteous standards do not change.

> *What Do You Think?*
> When considering our response to injustice, how do we make sure not to tread in areas that God has reserved for himself to handle?
> *Talking Points for Your Discussion*
> - Regarding initiatives as individuals
> - Regarding initiatives as a church

8b. I will faithfully give them their recompense,
and I will make an everlasting covenant with them.

These two promises are linked. With the use of the word *faithfully*, it is clear that God is firmly committed to keeping the promise he is making. The covenant foreshadowed here has been established by the one who affirmed, "I am the way, and the truth, and the life. No one comes to the Father except through me" (John 14:6). The writer of Hebrews does not quote Isaiah's prophecy, but does quote Jeremiah's lengthy promise of a new covenant (Jeremiah 31:31-34; Hebrews 8:8-12). Jeremiah's "new covenant" is the same as Isaiah's *everlasting covenant.*

B. Israelites' Reputation (v. 9)

9. **Their offspring shall be known among the nations,**
   and their descendants in the midst of the peoples;
   all who see them shall acknowledge them,
   that they are an offspring the LORD has blessed.

Again we see poetic repetition, with *their offspring* parallel with *their descendants* and *the nations* parallel with *the peoples* (plural in the Hebrew— "the people groups"). This verse therefore highlights another aspect of the dramatic transformation concerning the ancient Israelites' reputation.

In their future captivity, the Israelites will be derided by foreigners (Deuteronomy 28:36, 37); God's covenant people will become "a reproach" (example: Jeremiah 29:17-19). But Isaiah pictures a time when that reputation changes to *an offspring the Lord has blessed.* An important aspect of that state of blessing will be inclusion of the Gentiles. They will be part of the everlasting covenant.

◆ *REPUTATIONS: OURS AND GOD'S* ◆

Nathaniel Hawthorne's classic book *The Scarlet Letter* tells the story of a young woman forced to wear a large letter *A*, scarlet in color, on the front of her blouse. Its purpose was to shame publicly the adulterous woman. The punishment revealed the attitude of seventeenth-century Boston toward the woman and her unknown paramour. Once ruined, a reputation was not easily restored in that Puritan context. One might be banished from town.

The Bible reveals varied reactions to sinfully shameful behavior. Stonings, by nature, were public (Leviticus 24:14; etc.). By contrast, the "very great" sins of Eli's sons, which included adultery, went unchallenged except for a weak, private rebuke from their father (1 Samuel 2:12-17, 22-25) until God himself intervened (2:34; 4:11).

We dare not forget that our reputations communicate something about God to the unbelieving world (see Matthew 5:16; Romans 2:24; 1 Peter 2:12; etc.). Christians are blessed because of God's promises to restore his covenant people. We are blessings to others as we model principles that glorify God (1 Peter 3:13-17). —C. M. W.

> **What Do You Think?**
> What do others see in you that causes them to realize that you are blessed by God?
> *Talking Points for Your Discussion*
> - What family members see
> - What friends and acquaintances see
> - What strangers see

C. Special Clothing (v. 10)

10. **I will greatly rejoice in the LORD;**
    my soul shall exult in my God,
    for he has clothed me with garments of salvation;
    he has covered me with the robe of righteousness,
    as a bridegroom decks himself like a priest with a beautiful headdress,
    and as a bride adorns herself with her jewels.

Who is the *I* speaking in this verse? The Lord is speaking in verse 8, but the individual in view here says *I will greatly rejoice in the Lord.* To resolve this question, we return to the opening verse of this chapter: "The Spirit of the Lord God is upon me." This individual is Jesus, as we have already noted in our comparison with Luke 4:16-21. The reason he finds great joy in the Lord is that he has been *clothed . . . with garments of salvation* and *covered . . . with a robe of righteousness.*

Thus let us picture Jesus, having surveyed the impact of his ministry in Isaiah 61:2-9, now concluding his assessment by expressing satisfaction. As God looked on the original creation and declared it to be "very good" (Genesis 1:31), so Jesus looks at the "re-creation"—the new creation made possible through his everlasting covenant— and concludes likewise.

The analogy involving *a bridegroom* and *a bride* brings to mind the relationship between Jesus and his church (Ephesians 5:22-33). We may wonder what kind of *headdress* a bridegroom wears. The Hebrew word may refer to some type of turban, as the word is used in Ezekiel 24:17, 23; 44:18. A bridegroom in biblical times usually wears a headpiece that resembles a turban.

While recognizing that the language of the verse before us applies to Jesus, we also note that the blessings described are blessings he shares with his followers. Revelation 19:7-9 informs us of the special clothing that awaits those who are part of the "Bride" of the Lamb; he prepares us to join him at his "marriage" (compare 21:2).

What Do You Think?

What most influences your level of joy in the Lord? Why?

Talking Points for Your Discussion
- Regarding positive influences
- Regarding negative influences

D. Global Witness (v. 11)

11. For as the earth brings forth its sprouts,
 and as a garden causes what is sown in
 it to sprout up,
 so the Lord GOD will cause righteousness
 and praise
 to sprout up before all the nations.

The imagery of a fruitful and abundant *garden* echoes language of "the planting" in verse 3. Isaiah previously had pictured the word of the Lord as producing results similar to what we see in the verse before us (Isaiah 55:10, 11). Paul uses agricultural language in 1 Corinthians 3:7 to acknowledge that the Lord is the ultimate source of church growth. As the church continues to carry out the Great Commission (Matthew 28:19, 20), *righteousness and praise* will *sprout up before all nations.*

Conclusion

A. It's Our Move

Following the Israelites' conquest of Canaan and allotment of the land, we read this summary: "Thus the Lord gave to Israel all the land that he swore to give to their father. And they took possession of it, and they settled there. . . . Not one word of all the good promises that the Lord had made to the house of Israel had failed" (Joshua 21:43, 45). Yet we read earlier that various locations in the promised land had not been conquered by the Israelites; such areas remained in the hands of the peoples who lived there (13:13; 15:63; 16:10). We reconcile these passages by recognizing that God had done all he promised to provide victory for his people, but they were responsible to finish the task. The promised land would be fully theirs only as they exerted the effort and trust required by the Lord.

Today's text records some profound blessings on God's people. Yet we may look around us and wonder, "How can this ever happen? When will it take place?" In many nations, followers of Jesus are persecuted intensely, even to death. Why does "righteousness and praise" not "sprout up before all the nations" (Isaiah 61:11)?

It's at this point that the church should take a close and painful look in the mirror. Are we dedicated to fulfilling the Great Commission, or has it become the Great Omission? God has done his part in giving his Son to establish his "everlasting covenant" (Isaiah 61:8), but are we failing on our end like Israel of old? The fields are still "white for harvest" (John 4:35). It's our move.

B. Prayer

Father, help us see the tasks in our Scripture today as our service in a broken world so that righteousness and praise may "sprout up before all the nations." We pray in Jesus' name. Amen.

C. Thought to Remember

We are partners with God
in the greatest undertaking in history.

Visual for Lesson 4. *Point to this visual as you ask, "In what ways do you find this image to be a good representation of your new life in Christ?"*

INVOLVEMENT LEARNING

Enhance your lesson presentation with the reproducible activity page,
available as a free download at www.standardlesson.com.

Into the Lesson

On the board write the following words: *Contracts, Agreements, Promises*. Ask students to think about a time when someone disappointed them in one of these areas. Encourage students to share their stories, but without mentioning anyone by name. Ask, "What excuses did the person or company make for not fulfilling their commitment?" Then say, "Today's lesson is about an 'everlasting covenant' that God has made with his people. And with God we can be absolutely sure that he will do what he has promised."

Alternative. Write the following quote on the board: "A promise means everything; but once it is broken, *sorry* means nothing" (author unknown). Direct learners' attention to the quote, and ask, "What is the person trying to convey about the importance of promises? Do you agree with the sentiment expressed?" After a few minutes of discussion, state, "Today's lesson contains many promises that God made to his people. We will see how all of them were kept through his Son, Jesus Christ."

Into the Word

Have your students open their Bibles to Isaiah 61. Introduce this passage by saying, "Today's text from Isaiah is a messianic prophecy, which was fulfilled 700 years later. Listen to the account of the day Jesus read from this passage." Have someone read Luke 4:16-19 aloud, and then ask, "How were the words of Isaiah fulfilled in Jesus' life?" Learners may mention such things as Jesus' bringing the good news of salvation, comforting those that mourn with hope for the future, and setting free those who were captives to sin.

Divide the class into two groups. The first group will work on the *God's Promises* assignment. Use Isaiah 61:1-4 to answer the following questions: "When God's 'anointed' one came, what were some of the good things he would do for God's people? Make a list of them." "In what way would

the promises to 'those who mourn' be especially comforting?" "When the Israelites were later carried off into Babylonian captivity, how might these promises encourage them?" The second group will work on *God's Faithfulness*. "Hebrews 8:6 states, 'The covenant [Jesus] mediates is better.' In what ways was the old covenant inferior to the new covenant?" "Why would the garments provided by God make his people 'greatly rejoice'?" "According to verses 9 and 11, how will the attitude of the nations toward Israel change because of God's blessings?" Allow time for groups to answer the questions; then ask for volunteers to share their answers. Make the point that because of God's true and faithful nature, we can be assured that he will keep all the promises in his eternal covenant.

Option. Distribute copies of the "Promises Fulfilled" activity from the reproducible page, which can be downloaded. Encourage students to give reasons for their Scripture matches. Put the emphasis on how Jesus fulfilled these promises in his ministry and through his death and resurrection.

Into Life

Write the following scenarios on index cards: (1) Parents are brokenhearted because their son is a drug addict; (2) a young woman struggles with clinical depression and anxiety; (3) a middle-aged man has endured months of unemployment; (4) an elderly woman has had money stolen by a relative. Give one card to each of four small groups, and ask them to select one or more verses from today's text that they could use to counsel the people described. Encourage them to remind the people that Jesus is the source of help and comfort as promised in these verses.

Option. Distribute copies of the "Praise Expressed" activity from the reproducible page. Ask for volunteers to share how some of those promises have been fulfilled in their lives.

THE RADIANCE OF GOD'S GLORY

DEVOTIONAL READING: John 1:1-5, 10-14
BACKGROUND SCRIPTURE: Hebrews 1

HEBREWS 1:1-9

1 Long ago, at many times and in many ways, God spoke to our fathers by the prophets, 2 but in these last days he has spoken to us by his Son, whom he appointed the heir of all things, through whom also he created the world. 3 He is the radiance of the glory of God and the exact imprint of his nature, and he upholds the universe by the word of his power. After making purification for sins, he sat down at the right hand of the Majesty on high, 4 having become as much superior to angels as the name he has inherited is more excellent than theirs.

5 For to which of the angels did God ever say,

"You are my Son,
  today I have begotten you"?

Or again,

"I will be to him a father,
  and he shall be to me a son"?

6 And again, when he brings the firstborn into the world, he says,

"Let all God's angels worship him."

7 Of the angels he says,

"He makes his angels winds,
  and his ministers a flame of fire."

8 But of the Son he says,

"Your throne, O God, is forever and ever,
  the scepter of uprightness is the scepter
    of your kingdom.
9   You have loved righteousness and hated
      wickedness;
  therefore God, your God, has anointed you
    with the oil of gladness beyond your
      companions."

KEY VERSE

He is the radiance of the glory of God and the exact imprint of his nature, and he upholds the universe by the word of his power. —**Hebrews 1:3**

THE SOVEREIGNTY OF GOD

Unit 2: The Sovereignty of Jesus

LESSONS 5–9

LESSON AIMS

After participating in this lesson, each learner will be able to:

1. Identify key terms that set forth Jesus' identity and status.

2. Explain Jesus' position as the climax of God's saving plan.

3. Describe one way he or she can exhibit greater submission to Jesus as supreme king and make a plan to do so.

LESSON OUTLINE

Introduction

A. Who Is the Greatest?

A good way to start a lively discussion is to ask people who is the all-time greatest in a particular field. The greatest athlete, the greatest artist, the greatest political leader, the greatest singer, the greatest writer—everyone who has an interest in the activity will have an opinion. And most of those interested will have opinions that differ.

Our text for today begins to make a case for the greatest. It states that Jesus is the climax of all that God has done in history, that he is the greatest in God's plan because he is the divine Son of God. Those who wonder who is greatest in God's plan have their answer; and on this question, no one can afford to be indifferent. Everything in life is at stake in this most important matter.

B. Lesson Background

The letter to the Hebrews is a book with an origin shrouded in mystery but with a message of enormous influence. Hebrews does not name its author, unlike other New Testament letters. In the early centuries of the church, some believed that it was written by Paul. But although it does show a connection with Paul's circle (his associate Timothy is mentioned in Hebrews 13:23), the treatise is written in a style very different from that normally seen in Paul's letters.

In fact, the style of Hebrews is different from all other books of the New Testament. We can say with some confidence that the letter was written by someone who was influenced by Paul or his associates, but who wrote no other book that survives to the present. Some have suggested Apollos, Barnabas, or Priscilla as possible authors, but these remain mere speculation.

Even so, we can infer much about the circumstances that this letter addresses. Hebrews emphasizes Christ's supremacy, his fulfillment of the Old Testament, and the utter necessity of continuing in faith in him. Thus it seems likely that Hebrews was written to Jews who had put faith in Jesus when they heard the gospel, but who then faced intense social pressure to renounce that faith and return to the practice of Judaism.

Conversations between these Christians and their Jewish families and friends are easy to imagine. Perhaps the unbelievers had said that while Jesus may have been an important person, perhaps even an angel, he simply did not fit the prophecies about God's promised king. Returning to the old ways would mean continuing to be part of God's "chosen people" while no longer experiencing the ostracism that faith in Jesus prompted.

Hebrews offers a sharp correction to that line of thinking. Yes, God had been at work in Israel to fulfill his promises. But those promises were indeed fulfilled—in a deep, thorough, and unexpected way—by Jesus. Because God's divine Son, Jesus, is the greatest in God's plan, then to reject Jesus is to reject God and his plan. But to hold to Jesus is to experience the fullness of God's promises and the inauguration of God's eternal blessings.

I. Revealer of Truth
(Hebrews 1:1, 2)
A. That Was Then (v. 1)

1. Long ago, at many times and in many ways, God spoke to our fathers by the prophets,

Many people view the long-ago events of the Bible as having little connection with them personally today. But for the original recipients of this letter, the distant past of biblical history is their own past. God had communicated with the patriarchs Abraham, Isaac, and Jacob, who came before *the prophets.* That communication continued through centuries that spanned the conquest of the promised land and the eras of the judges and the kings, during the exile, and into the restoration after exile.

Over those periods God made promises, protected the helpless, orchestrated victories,

HOW TO SAY IT

aeons (or eons)	*ee*-unz.
Apollos	Uh-*pahl*-us.
Barnabas	*Bar*-nuh-bus.
patriarchs	*pay*-tree-arks.
Priscilla	Prih-*sil*-uh.

appointed leaders, gave laws, and issued warnings. How God was at work and what it meant was declared by his prophets. They were empowered by his Spirit to speak authoritatively for him.

The words of the prophets and the inspired history of God's dealings that they provided was Israel's heritage. In these the people of Israel could truly say that they had heard God's voice and understood his will. The book of Hebrews affirms that God had indeed been at work through Israel's prophets. But now a page of that history turns to one who brings about the intended fulfillment.

> **What Do You Think?**
> What stories of God's work in Old Testament times are especially meaningful to you? Why?
> *Talking Points for Your Discussion*
> - Stories of deliverance
> - Stories of judgment
> - Stories of transformation
> - Stories of promise
> - Other

B. This Is Now (v. 2)

2a. but in these last days he has spoken to us by his Son,

The past holds the story of God's work, but recent days hold something more. The phrase *in these last days* indicates the recent past, but it also implies that in such days God has been bringing his plan to its climax. What the past has promised, these last days have seen fulfilled. God had indeed spoken through many prophets, but in these last days he has spoken through one who is greater than a prophet.

As the book unfolds, Hebrews will paint a detailed portrait of what it means to be God's *Son.* Here at the beginning, the book's Jewish-Christian readers understand the term against its Old Testament background. God's "son" in Israel's Scriptures is sometimes Israel itself (Hosea 11:1, quoted in Matthew 2:15 to apply to Jesus). But more often the "son" was God's appointed king (1 Chronicles 22:6-10). The idea of a promised king is a keystone in the foundation on which Hebrews builds its case for the superiority of Jesus.

2b. whom he appointed the heir of all things, through whom also he created the world.

The appearance of this kingly Son is indeed the high point of all that God has done. As God's king of fulfillment, he is God's *heir,* figuratively inheriting all of creation as God appoints him ruler. The king whom God promised through the prophets is described as the one to exercise God's righteous rule over all things (Isaiah 9:6, 7). This Son of the last days fulfills that promise.

But this Son is not king simply by God's recent appointment. The Son assumes the throne by right of his very nature. In affirming that God *created the world* through the Son, the writer uses an expression that suggests all of time and space (literally *aeons* or *eons*). All creation, including humanity, is subject to the rule of this Son because he is the Creator of all (compare John 1:3; Colossians 1:16).

Already we hear an unmistakable, emphatic declaration. The writer and the readers agree that the world was created by the one true God. Now the writer says that God created the world through his Son. This can mean only that God's Son is indeed divine, by nature God. He is by appointment and by nature God's greatest spokesman because he is God. To submit to him is to submit to God; to reject him is to reject God.

II. Revealer of Glory
(Hebrews 1:3, 4)
A. Person and Work (v. 3)
3a. He is the radiance of the glory of God

Because of his divine identity, the Son, who came in the flesh (John 1:14), has revealed God as he has never before been revealed. It is the Son who brings the prophets' revelations to the high point of completeness and fulfillment. *The glory of God* is the full expression and revelation of his being. Everything that God is, his glory expresses. The divine Son was able to bring *the radiance* of his glory because the divine Son is that radiance. God's glory was revealed to a certain extent in Israel's history (Exodus 16:6, 10; 24:15-17; 33:18-23; etc.). In Jesus it has been revealed as fully as it can be until he returns (1 Thessalonians 4:16, 17; Titus 2:13; Revelation 1:7).

3b. and the exact imprint of his nature,

This phrase makes a point similar to the above. The word *imprint,* like radiance, does not refer to a revelation of God's physical appearance, of course, since God has no physical body. Rather, it means the making clear of God's true nature or essence (compare 2 Corinthians 4:4 and Colossians 1:15, where a different Greek word is translated "image"). In the Son, God's nature is fully revealed. He shows us fully who God is (John 14:9).

◆ Jesus Is Nice; God Is Mean? ◆

"Oh, I just love Jesus. Jesus is nice. But God—now he's mean." My acquaintance must have read the confusion on my face because she elaborated as she continued: "Oh, you know—he's always destroying nations and sending plagues and all of that stuff."

So that was it. To her, God the Father—the God of the Old Testament description—is the punishing deity. Jesus, on the other hand, is the God of mercy—the one who forgives and heals.

Those who think that the God of the Old Testament is all about wrath have apparently never read the book of Jonah! The book of Hebrews is also a lens through which to see the true nature of God—the one God of both the Old and New Testaments. If we want to have the best, clearest picture of God that has ever been given, we need to look at Jesus (compare John 14:9).

People of the first century encountered God in Jesus. When they did, he blew up their preconceived notions. They watched him shock the experts, melt hard hearts, restore hope, and touch those considered "the least" of humanity. What a clear, beautiful picture of God! What held true in the first century still holds true today: if you want to understand God, look to Jesus.   —V. E.

3c. and he upholds the universe by the word of his power.

The Son—the radiating, revealing image-bearer —is central to all that exists. His sovereign *word* carries the created world to its God-appointed destiny. In all ways Jesus is God's king who fulfills his purpose.

3d. After making purification for sins, he sat down at the right hand of the Majesty on high,

But simply ruling is not the entirety of God's purpose. The sovereign God seeks to forgive rebellious humans. So the Son who is king is also the Son who is high priest (Hebrews 4:14–5:10, lesson 7). His work, what Hebrews reveals as his offering of his own life as a sacrifice, is to cleanse the rebels of their guilt. He reconciles as well as rules.

Having accomplished his work of reconciliation, Christ assumed the position of authority on the throne of divine power. So the alternatives for humanity are clear: (1) acknowledge the Son as king and receive the cleansing that his death offers or (2) reject his offer and his authority, thereby persisting as his enemies and being subject to his punishment.

B. Status and Name (v. 4)

4. having become as much superior to angels as the name he has inherited is more excellent than theirs.

Angels are of great interest to Jews of the first century. Such spirit-beings, who appear occasionally in the Old Testament as God's messengers, had become the subject of much well-intended speculation. But the Son of God is fundamentally greater than any angel. For one thing, he has an inheritance, bearing the authority of God himself. The Son's *name*—how he is to be known to all—is superior to that of any angel because he has acted to bring God's plan to its intended fulfillment (compare Philippians 2:8, 9).

The text does not tell us how the original readers viewed Jesus in relation to angels. But the author slams the door on any attempt to equate them.

III. Worthy of Worship
(Hebrews 1:5-9)
A. Status of Angels (vv. 5-7)

5a. For to which of the angels did God ever say,

> **"You are my Son,**
> **today I have begotten you"?**

At this point, the letter begins a series of quotations from the Old Testament. As the writer quotes these texts, he expects the readers to remember the contexts from which the quotes are taken and to think of how those contexts put the kingly Son's role in perspective. It is a role greater than that of any angel or other created being.

The first text quoted is Psalm 2:7 (also in Acts 13:33; Hebrews 5:5). This psalm asserts that God's king will bring righteous peace to a world overwhelmed with arrogant human rebellion. With verse 7, God pronounces that his Son will rule with all the power and authority of God himself.

5b. Or again,

> **"I will be to him a father,**
> **and he shall be to me a son"?**

Now the writer draws on 2 Samuel 7:14 (retold in 1 Chronicles 17:13), which is part of God's promise to David that the Son—the king to build God's true temple and whose throne God would establish forever—would be of David's "offspring." Hebrews goes on to state that as God's Son, Jesus' death constituted the true sacrifice; and as high priest, he carried his own blood to the true tabernacle (the temple's precursor) of Heaven (Hebrews 9:11, 12). Neither is ever said of angels.

6. And again, when he brings the firstborn into the world, he says,

> **"Let all God's angels worship him."**

Visual for Lesson 5. *Start a discussion by turning this statement into a question: "In what ways does Jesus reflect God's glory?"*

The last six words translate a phrase from the old Greek version of Deuteronomy 32:43. This phrase does not appear in English translations of the Old Testament that are not based on that Greek version. Psalm 97:7 is similar.

The writer of Hebrews applies the action of this phrase to the Son as God's *firstborn*. This term in context means not "first one created" but "authoritative one" (compare Colossians 1:15, 18). So, argues the writer, God's designated authoritative one, who himself is fully divine, holds the authority of God and deserves worship as God. The implication is clear: if this Son receives worship from angels, surely he must receive worship from us as well.

7. Of the angels he says,
"He makes his angels winds,
and his ministers a flame of fire."

This is a quotation of Psalm 104:4, but if you turn there you will discover that it reads differently. One issue is that the ancient Hebrew word for *wind* is also the word for *spirit*. Also, both the Hebrew and Greek words for *angels* can refer either to heavenly or earthly messengers (examples: Genesis 32:3; Exodus 3:2; Luke 7:27; 22:43). The inspired author of the book of Hebrews, who quotes from the old Greek version of Psalm 104:4, therefore has to make choices. Modern translators of English versions also must choose! But no matter how great God's servants are—be they angelic or otherwise—there is one who is greater.

◆ **THE GREAT AND POWERFUL** ◆

A memorable scene in the classic film *The Wizard of Oz* takes place in the basilica-like hall where the great and powerful wizard holds audience. Billowing smoke and terrifying sounds accompany his thunderous voice and larger-than-life visage. Who could stand in that hall without being in awe of the wizard's manifest powers?

Angelic appearances result in similar reactions in the pages of Scripture. Angels sometimes must help humans overcome terror before completing the task of delivering God's message to them (examples: Daniel 10; Luke 1:11-17; 2:8-12). We may be tempted to smirk at ancient believers for being overly impressed by these celestial beings when we remember that humans are the ones created in God's image (Genesis 1:27) and that we will judge angels (1 Corinthians 6:3). But we must not overlook the need to humble ourselves before the Creator of all: Jesus the Christ.

Which impresses you more as you read the Bible: angelic appearances that inspire awe and fright or the lowly appearance of the baby Jesus in a manger? Although he could have come to earth in radiance and power far outshining that of angels, he chose not to. Jesus did not come to terrify us into submission by means of his mighty power. He came, rather, to die for us. How will you model this humility before others this week?

—V. E.

B. Status of the Son (vv. 8, 9)
8. But of the Son he says,
"Your throne, O God, is forever and ever,
the scepter of uprightness is the scepter
of your kingdom.

To contrast the Son with angels, the writer quotes from Psalm 45:6, 7 in this verse and the next. This psalm appears to have been written as a celebration of the wedding of Israel's king. As the psalm invites those gathered to admire and congratulate the king as he appears for the ceremony, it reminds the audience that Israel's king rules under the authority of God. It is God's *throne* that endures *forever and ever*. His authority, symbolized by *the scepter*, enforces his right way, not the personal interests of a selfish king.

9a. "You have loved righteousness and hated wickedness;

To love *righteousness* and hate *wickedness* are two sides of the same coin. The king's commitment in this regard must be absolute. The ideal king who rules under the true God will never reverse that love/hate outlook, no matter what the situation. And Jesus never has, does, or will.

9b. "therefore God, your God, has anointed you

with the oil of gladness beyond your companions."

Kings in ancient Israel were recognized as such by being anointed with oil (examples: 2 Samuel 2:4; 5:3). Since Jesus was anointed with the Holy Spirit instead of oil (Acts 10:38), the expression *the oil of gladness* is used figuratively to signify the fulfillment of God's promise to bless his people with a worthy king (compare Isaiah 61:3, lesson 4).

The quoted psalm describes the ideal king, and that ideal is fulfilled in Jesus. Even the best of Israel's ancient kings failed in various ways at times. But Jesus is the king whose throne God establishes forever (2 Samuel 7:13). Jesus, the only one without sin (Hebrews 4:15, lesson 7) in Israel's line of kings, is the only one who can bring about God's righteous rule. He stands apart as unique.

Conclusion
A. The Crucified King

The letter's opening connects Jesus with the great history of God's dealings with his people. Jesus does not break with that history but brings it to God's intended climax. Today's passage begins an extended explanation of Jesus' fulfillment of every aspect of God's promises. Yet remarkably, Jesus is not mentioned by name in today's text; he will not be mentioned by name until Hebrews 2:9. But our author knows that the first-century readers are quite familiar with the story of Jesus' life, death, and resurrection. He wants to make sure that they understand its implications.

The familiarity of this story should give us pause. The one whom Hebrews proclaims as the greatest figure in God's plan is the divine Son who experienced all the tests to which humans are subject. He is the one who died a tortuous, humiliating death on a Roman cross. The king who is exalted above even angels is the crucified one, raised again to triumphant life as he bears the marks of his death (John 20:27; Revelation 5:6).

The subjects of this king suffer rejection and persecution as he did. They are pressured to give up the path of submission to God as was Jesus when challenged to come down from the cross (Matthew 27:40-42). But the stakes are too high ever to give in to such pressure. The Son stands above angels and earthly kings in authority, exalted to the very throne of God. To belong to Jesus is to belong to God and gain eternal life; to reject him is to reject God and forfeit that life.

B. Prayer

Father, along with all creation we bow before your Son as our king. May he lead us to submit to your supreme authority in every aspect of our lives. We pray this in his name. Amen.

C. Thought to Remember

Seek the guidance of the Son.

INVOLVEMENT LEARNING

Enhance your lesson presentation with the reproducible activity page,
available as a free download at www.standardlesson.com.

Into the Lesson

Ask learners to identify some Old Testament figures who heard the voice of God or witnessed miracles. Then ask learners to name some Old Testament kings who received God's divine appointment.

Say, "The Jews of Jesus' day were no strangers to miracles. Their history was full of accounts of God's chosen prophets and leaders, as well as encounters with angels. When Jesus came, many recognized that he was different from any prophet or king who had come before him. Yet keeping that conviction proved challenging for some when they experienced pressure to dismiss Jesus as a mere prophet. Today's lesson text reaffirms for us who Jesus is and where he stands in relationship to God, the angels, and mankind."

Alternative. Before learners arrive, place in chairs copies of the "Identity of Jesus" activity from the reproducible page, which you can download. Allow learners several minutes to work individually on the activity. Then say, "In today's culture, there is sometimes pressure to dismiss Jesus as a mere philosopher, prophet, or role model. Early Jews who became followers of Jesus experienced a similar pressure, but in today's text we are reminded of the true nature of Jesus and encouraged to worship and serve him appropriately."

Into the Word

Divide learners into three groups. Give the first group an index card labeled *God (Hebrews 1:1-3)*, the second group an index card labeled *Angels (Hebrews 1:4-7)*, and the third group an index card labeled *Kings (Hebrews 1:8, 9)*.

Have the groups read together the portion of the lesson text indicated on their cards, then discuss where the writer of Hebrews says Jesus, referred to in the text as "the Son," stands in relation to God, angels, or kings, as indicated by the groups' index cards.

Allow time for small-group discussion. Then ask a speaker from each group to read aloud their assigned verses and to share with the class their findings. Jot the responses on the board. (Possible responses: *God*—God speaks through Jesus, he appointed Jesus as heir of all things, Jesus is the glory of God, Jesus is the express image of God, Jesus sits at God's right hand; *Angels*—Jesus is so much better than the angels, all the angels of God worship Jesus, none of the angels is called God's begotten Son and Jesus is; *Kings*—Jesus sits on the throne of God forever, Jesus is above all other kings. Ask, "What do all these phrases and comparisons tell us about the identity of Jesus?" (Possible responses: Jesus is the Son of God, Jesus is God, Jesus is the king of all, Jesus is the way to salvation.)

Into Life

Pair learners to discuss this question: "In light of everything Hebrews tells us about Jesus' identity, what are some ways we can exhibit greater submission to him?" Ask for volunteers to share thoughts with the class. Possible responses: Bible study (2 Timothy 3:14-17; etc.), prayer (Matthew 6:9-15; Luke 18:1; etc.), confession (James 5:16; 1 John 1:9; etc.), stewardship (2 Corinthians 9:7; Philippians 4:14-16; etc.), serving others (Matthew 25:31-40; 2 Corinthians 8:1-5; etc.), forgiving one another (Matthew 18:21, 22; Colossians 3:13; etc.), sharing the gospel (Matthew 28:19, 20; Romans 10:12-15; etc.), emulating Christ (1 John 2:6; etc.).

Use this discussion to note that Jesus' identity as the Son of God reveals God's glory and teaches us how we should live, while his identity as the supreme king merits our submission in all aspects of our lives.

Option. Distribute copies of the "At the King's Throne" activity from the reproducible page. Have learners complete the activity on their own.

Say, "It is important we remember Jesus is not only our loving Savior but also our righteous king."

BUILDER OF
THE HOUSE

DEVOTIONAL READING: Hebrews 10:19-25
BACKGROUND SCRIPTURE: Hebrews 3:1-6; Matthew 7:19-29

HEBREWS 3:1-6

[1] Therefore, holy brothers, you who share in a heavenly calling, consider Jesus, the apostle and high priest of our confession, [2] who was faithful to him who appointed him, just as Moses also was faithful in all God's house. [3] For Jesus has been counted worthy of more glory than Moses—as much more glory as the builder of a house has more honor than the house itself. [4] (For every house is built by someone, but the builder of all things is God.) [5] Now Moses was faithful in all God's house as a servant, to testify to the things that were to be spoken later, [6] but Christ is faithful over God's house as a son. And we are his house if indeed we hold fast our confidence and our boasting in our hope.

MATTHEW 7:24-29

[24] "Everyone then who hears these words of mine and does them will be like a wise man who built his house on the rock. [25] And the rain fell, and the floods came, and the winds blew and beat on that house, but it did not fall, because it had been founded on the rock. [26] And everyone who hears these words of mine and does not do them will be like a foolish man who built his house on the sand. [27] And the rain fell, and the floods came, and the winds blew and beat against that house, and it fell, and great was the fall of it."

[28] And when Jesus finished these sayings, the crowds were astonished at his teaching, [29] for he was teaching them as one who had authority, and not as their scribes.

KEY VERSE

Jesus has been counted worthy of more glory than Moses—as much more glory as the builder of a house has more honor than the house itself. —**Hebrews 3:3**

The Sovereignty of God

Unit 2: The Sovereignty of Jesus
Lessons 5–9

Lesson Aims

After participating in this lesson, each learner will be able to:

1. List some implications of the fact that Jesus is the greatest and final authority because of his identity as God's divine Son.

2. Compare and contrast the significance of the word *house* in the Matthew and Hebrews segments of the lesson text.

3. Identify the part of Christ's spiritual house(hold) that is most in need of repair and commit to helping to correct the problem.

Lesson Outline

Introduction
  A. The Presence of Greatness
  B. Lesson Background
 I. Faithful Builder (HEBREWS 3:1-6)
  A. Like Moses (vv. 1, 2)
  B. Greater than Moses (vv. 3-6)
    Side-by-Side Comparisons
 II. Faithful Teacher (MATTHEW 7:24-29)
  A. Wise Plan (vv. 24, 25)
  B. Foolish Plan (vv. 26, 27)
  C. Ultimate Authority (vv. 28, 29)
    Cite the Highest Source
Conclusion
  A. The Greatness of Jesus
  B. Prayer
  C. Thought to Remember

Introduction
A. The Presence of Greatness

Some people are fortunate to observe exceptional talent before it is widely recognized. They see a young athlete perform, hear a budding musician play, or listen to an emerging leader deliver a speech. The discerning recognize that they are experiencing something remarkable. When the talented individual later rises to prominence, the early witnesses are able to say, "I knew I was in the presence of greatness even way back when."

In some ways, Jesus appeared as an unexceptional person (Isaiah 53:2b). Yet in ways that some perceived at the time, he was unlike any other. In his resurrection from the dead, God confirmed that Jesus was indeed like no other! No mere prophet or wise man, he was God's divine Son, the one who fulfilled all of God's great promises.

In our lesson today, we will consider two texts that emphasize this. The first will show us how Jesus compared and contrasted with God's leaders who came before, thereby demonstrating him to be fundamentally greater than all others. The second will remind us how Jesus demonstrated greatness by the authority with which he taught, even before his resurrection.

B. Lesson Background

Our first segment of our lesson text is from the book of Hebrews. The background is therefore the same as that of last week's lesson, and that information need not be repeated here.

Our second text is from the end of Jesus' famous Sermon on the Mount as Matthew 5:1–7:29 records it. The lowly son of a carpenter from the lowly town of Nazareth was in the first of his three years of earthly ministry. He was on his first general tour of Galilee (4:23–11:30) as he taught what it means to be subjects of God's kingdom. He spoke with an authority that could only belong to God. To listen to Jesus and obey meant blessing; to ignore him meant ruin.

Hebrews explains how Jesus, the divine, authoritative Son of God, fulfilled God's promises. Matthew shows how Jesus' one-of-a-kind greatness was revealed in what he said and did. Together they declare that to follow Jesus is to be in the presence of greatness.

I. Faithful Builder
(HEBREWS 3:1-6)

In Hebrews 1:10–2:18, which comprises the 23 verses between last week's lesson and today's first segment, the author uses six Old Testament passages to establish facts regarding the nature and work of Jesus. The opening "therefore" of today's text indicates that conclusions and implications in this regard are in store.

A. Like Moses (vv. 1, 2)

1. Therefore, holy brothers, you who share in a heavenly calling, consider Jesus, the apostle and high priest of our confession,

The readers are addressed as *brothers* not because they necessarily share the same Jewish heritage but because together they belong to God and so are *holy.* Together they *share in a heavenly calling*—a calling that is the solemn, authoritative invitation that comes from the most authoritative source of all: God himself.

The holy brothers have this identity because they share a *confession,* something that together they proclaim, profess, or confess to be true. That, of course, is the good news of Jesus. It is time for the readers to think carefully yet again about the one who is the center of that message, the very one who has brought them God's calling.

What Do You Think?
What are some ways to live out our own calling from God, which comes from faith in Jesus?
Talking Points for Your Discussion
- In general ways, as modeled in the first century by Jesus himself
- In specific ways that are especially appropriate to culture of the twenty-first century

---

Jesus—God's promised, chosen king—is *the apostle* of what the readers profess. We know of this designation as it is used for leaders of the first-century church, especially the 12 disciples plus Paul. The word *apostle* indicates one who car-

ries an authoritative message from an authoritative figure. Applied to Jesus, it describes him as God's most authoritative messenger (Hebrews 1:1-4, last week's lesson). His message is God's climactic message, the fulfillment of every message that God has delivered in the past.

Jesus is also *high priest,* a designation used often in this letter (Hebrews 2:17; 4:14; 5:5, 10; 6:20; 7:26; 8:1; 9:11). Israel's high priest offered the once yearly sacrifice in the tabernacle or temple on the Day of Atonement. Carrying blood of a sacrificial animal into the Most Holy Place, he sprinkled it on the "mercy seat," which is the top of the ark of the covenant. This act was payment for the sins of all Israel (Leviticus 16; Hebrews 9:7). What God promised in that office and rite, Jesus fulfilled by his death, resurrection, and ascension to the most holy place of Heaven. Jesus both proclaimed the fulfillment of God's promise as apostle and accomplished it as high priest.

2. who was faithful to him who appointed him, just as Moses also was faithful in all God's house.

Before developing further the idea of Jesus' greatness, the author of the book of Hebrews focuses on Jesus' faithfulness. Moses was a preliminary example of that trait. Privileged to speak with God directly (Numbers 12:8), Moses was declared by God to be his faithful servant (12:7). Moses demonstrated his faithfulness when he was challenged in his leadership role. In meekness, he did not speak for himself; he let God vindicate him instead (12:3).

HOW TO SAY IT

Colossians	Kuh-*losh*-unz.
Deuteronomy	Due-ter-*ahn*-uh-me.
Ephesians	Ee-*fee*-zhunz.
Ezekiel	Ee-*zeek*-ee-ul or Ee-*zeek*-yul.
Galilee	*Gal*-uh-lee.
Hebrews	*Hee*-brews.
Isaiah	Eye-*zay*-uh.
Levitical	Leh-*vit*-ih-kul.
Leviticus	Leh-*vit*-ih-kus.
Mosaic	Mo-*zay*-ik.
Nazareth	*Naz*-uh-reth.

Jesus' faithfulness is of a similar kind. Submitting to the will of God the Father, he allowed himself to be arrested, beaten, and crucified. He suffered as his people suffered (Hebrews 2:10, 14). He did not defend himself but let God speak for him by raising him from the dead.

As the original readers consider Jesus, they are to remember afresh that his faithfulness should be reflected in their own faithfulness. Like Moses, Jesus has shown what faithfulness to God is. In so doing, Jesus has issued the heavenly calling that urges his followers to the same faithfulness.

What Do You Think?

What aspects of Jesus' faithfulness most challenge you personally to be faithful? Explain.

Talking Points for Your Discussion

- Regarding temptation
- In dealing with the flaws of others
- In service
- Other

B. Greater than Moses (vv. 3-6)

3. For Jesus has been counted worthy of more glory than Moses—as much more glory as the builder of a house has more honor than the house itself.

The writer could compare Jesus with Moses to show that while both were faithful, Jesus was more faithful. But instead he moves to a different comparison: as *the builder of a house,* Jesus is logically greater *than the house itself.*

Two aspects of Bible-era culture will help us understand the significance of this. The first concerns the term *house.* As used here, this word refers not to a structure but to people who reside together (family members, servants, etc.). We use the term *household* for this concept, and Acts 16:15 translates the same Greek word used here that way. Jesus is the one who builds the spiritual household of faith (see Ephesians 2:19-22).

The second aspect is the role of the son in such a household. As the father's heir, the firstborn son has a status in the household greater than that of his siblings (compare Deuteronomy 21:15-17). Jesus has the position of firstborn Son (Hebrews

1:6, last week's lesson; compare Colossians 1:15). Faithful in lowly submission to the Father's will, obedient in waiting for the Father's vindication, Jesus as firstborn held and holds for all eternity the highest status possible. He lived as God's servant; he exists as God's authoritative Son.

4. (For every house is built by someone, but the builder of all things is God.)

The existence of a house in any sense—whether that of a physical structure or of relationships (as in "household")—presupposes a builder, whether human or divine. God is the greatest builder, as he is the Creator of all that exists. Whatever authority and honor there are in the world, God is supremely worthy of them as the ultimate builder and sustainer.

5. Now Moses was faithful in all God's house as a servant, to testify to the things that were to be spoken later,

The writer cites God's pronouncement in Numbers 12:7 to establish the faithfulness of Moses. Deuteronomy moves to its conclusion with the statement that "there has not arisen a prophet since in Israel like Moses, whom the Lord knew face to face" (Deuteronomy 34:10). For the people of Israel, including the original Jewish-Christian readers of Hebrews, Moses-the-prophet is a defining figure of their history.

But God had spoken to Moses of a prophet to come after him, a prophet who would be like him (Deuteronomy 18:15, 18; compare Acts 3:22, 23; 7:37). In relation to that promised figure, Moses' life served as a witness—an indicator or sample of what was yet to come in God's plan. Moses was great among God's servants, but he was a servant who served the greater one to come after him.

6. but Christ is faithful over God's house as a son. And we are his house if indeed we hold fast our confidence and our boasting in our hope.

Despite the greatness that may be attributed to Moses, Jesus stands alone as the Servant-Son. *Christ,* as *a son,* participated with the Father in the very creation of the world (Hebrews 1:2). Christ claims rule over the household of God's people by means of the redemption purchased at the cross. He is the one promised by God, like the servant Moses but greater in all respects.

That conclusion leads the writer back to where he started in this passage. We who follow Christ, who have received his message at God's authoritative invitation (Hebrews 3:1), now belong to his household. As his unworthy servants, we are graciously blessed as God's children. We belong to this household only by what Christ has done. Our remaining in the household is God's gift to us, but it is conditioned on our bold allegiance to Christ and what God promises through him (compare Colossians 1:23; Hebrews 3:14). How foolish it would be to neglect or reject God's greatest!

◆　*Side-by-Side Comparisons*　◆

Side-by-side comparisons have been an effective marketing tool since . . . well as long as there has been marketing. Today, many Internet sites offer tools that invite visitors to see various features of products in a simple side-by-side tabular format. I have used these tools for evaluating cell phone plans, selecting area rugs, etc. Between the photographs, product details, and pricing and shipping information, comparison tools make choosing the best option easier, if not outright obvious.

The book of Hebrews in general and today's passage in particular address issues the Jewish Christians of the first-century church were facing. These issues centered on how to view Jesus in light of established practices and doctrines of the Jewish people—practices and doctrines that had come from God himself.

The methodology of Hebrews in this regard is that of comparing and contrasting the person and work of Jesus with those of angels, Moses, the Levitical priesthood, etc. The result demonstrates that the new covenant is built on a better sacrifice, a single one that is eternal as contrasted with the many that were temporary; is delivered through a better priest, one who is eternal and sinless as contrasted with the many that were mortal and committed sin; and offers a fuller revelation, of God through his Son in contrast with the old piecemeal communications via prophets.

The logic is airtight, and the conclusion is inescapable. In the end, the reader is left with only two choices: either (1) make the decision that pleases God and results in eternity with him, or (2) make

Visual for Lesson 6. *Start a discussion by pointing to this visual as you ask, "What are some of our duties as caretakers of God's household of faith?"*

a different, shortsighted decision to please those around us. This choice confronts us yet today.

—V. E.

II. Faithful Teacher
(Matthew 7:24-29)

Hebrews speaks of Jesus' preeminence as divine Son; Matthew demonstrates it with examples of Jesus' authoritative teaching. In the Sermon on the Mount, Jesus speaks on sacred topics as he makes assertions without appeal to anyone's authority but his own. Jesus ends the sermon by illustrating repeatedly that those who listen to him and do what he says will experience God's blessing, while those who do not do so will experience God's judgment. The parable that begins the next part of our lesson is Jesus' final statement of those alternatives in the sermon. (Luke 6:47-49 is parallel.)

A. Wise Plan (vv. 24, 25)

24. "Everyone then who hears these words of mine and does them will be like a wise man who built his house on the rock.

The opening *everyone then* links what Jesus is about to say with what he has just said in Matthew 7:21-23. Those verses set forth a radical choice to make, and so will the verses that follow.

Jesus' story begins by inviting the mental image of a certain *wise man* who chooses a *rock* as the location for his building project. Such a place is a relatively difficult one on which to establish the foundation of a *house,* but one that offers security from seasonal flooding. In connecting the wisdom of such a plan with hearing Jesus' *words* and doing them, Jesus echoes Psalm 111:10: "The fear of the Lord is the beginning of wisdom." (Compare Proverbs 1:7; 9:10; 15:33.)

25. "And the rain fell, and the floods came, and the winds blew and beat on that house, but it did not fall, because it had been founded on the rock.

The land of Israel has many seasonal rivers that flow from hills and mountains. Between rains, the riverbeds can be completely dry. But when rains fall in the higher elevations of Palestine, water rushes down those riverbeds in torrents. Thus Jesus' illustration draws on what is familiar to the people of his time and place.

A house built on a secure foundation can endure a crisis of *floods* and accompanying *winds.* The storm in this story suggests not merely the hardships of life but the final judgment of God (compare Isaiah 28:16, 17). In the previous story, Jesus spoke of those who would stand and speak to him "on that day," the Day of Judgment (Matthew 7:22). The wise, Jesus now implies, will be secure on the Day of Judgment because they have heard and done what he teaches. Jesus, the divine Son, is the one who will judge.

> **What Do You Think?**
> What will you do to continue to build the house of your life on the rock of Christ?
> *Talking Points for Your Discussion*
> - Regarding values assessment
> - Regarding the identification of rivals
> - Regarding Bible study
> - Regarding the choosing of mentors
> - Other

B. Foolish Plan (vv. 26, 27)

26. "And everyone who hears these words of mine and does not do them will be like a foolish man who built his house on the sand.

Jesus now draws the contrast between the wise man and the fool. A sandy area is an easier place to build a house, since such a surface yields easily to the shovel. But everyone in Jesus' audience knows that no *house* built *on the sand* will last long. A person who builds on sand is an obvious fool.

Jesus' words again echo the Psalms, which twice say, "The fool says in his heart, 'There is no God'" (Psalms 14:1; 53:1). This is the position of the person who hears Jesus' *words* but *does not do them.* No one who is listening to Jesus can miss the implication: Jesus is asserting himself to be God.

27. "And the rain fell, and the floods came, and the winds blew and beat against that house, and it fell, and great was the fall of it."

The same situation confronts the foolish man as confronts the wise: *rain, floods,* and *winds* threaten the house. Lacking a secure foundation, the house of the fool collapses (compare Ezekiel 13:10-13). Jesus emphasizes the magnitude of the loss: *great was the fall of it.* To have lived life and not heeded the word of one's Creator means the greatest loss that can be.

> **What Do You Think?**
> How can we better help others realize the recklessness of living without regard to Christ's authority?
> *Talking Points for Your Discussion*
> - In our attitudes toward those who so live
> - In our actions toward those who so live
> - In our speech toward those who so live

C. Ultimate Authority (vv. 28, 29)

28. And when Jesus finished these sayings, the crowds were astonished at his teaching,

Matthew occasionally notes people's *astonished* reactions to Jesus' words and actions (compare Matthew 9:33; 13:54; 22:33). *His teaching,* which here refers both to what he teaches and how he teaches it, surprises and amazes them. We can infer that they are unsure whether to heed or reject it.

29. for he was teaching them as one who had authority, and not as their scribes.

In some respects, Jesus teaches ideas that are common among Jewish religious teachers of his time. For instance, his saying about treating others as we would like to be treated (Matthew 7:12) is very similar to the sayings of other rabbis. What makes Jesus different, astonishingly so, is the *authority* of his teaching. The *scribes,* the ones who are experts in Israel's Scriptures, often cite the authority of earlier teachers for their views. Jesus, on the other hand, asserts everything on his own authority. He does so by beginning his correction of common views with "But I say to you" (examples: Matthew 5:22, 28, 32, 34, 39, 44).

Much of what Jesus teaches is about himself in claiming to fulfill the Mosaic law (Matthew 5:17), to stand in the place of final judgment (7:21-23), etc. He now boldly asserts that final judgment depends entirely on hearing and doing his teaching. This is a claim to authority like no other!

What Do You Think?
What did Jesus do or teach that demonstrates most vividly to you his supreme authority?
Talking Points for Your Discussion
- Acts and words of power or authority
- Acts and words of weakness or service

◆   CITE THE HIGHEST SOURCE   ◆

While in journalism school, we students were constantly challenged to evaluate when our writing was objective (referring to established facts) and when it had slipped into editorializing (containing some slant or opinion). We were trained to make statements only when they could be attributed to a credible source, such as a recognized expert in the subject area being addressed.

We would justify our sources by noting their accomplishments in their field. On a topic of great importance or great controversy, it was best to cite the highest authority possible on the topic at hand in order to establish credibility for the information in the article.

The common folk of the first century recognized something different about Jesus' teaching. Unlike their own teachers, who would refer to the interpretive opinions of other teachers for support, Jesus simply spoke the truth. In modern journalism, a writer does have license to state facts and conclusions without referring to other sources under one condition: if he or she is a subject-matter expert. Jesus was just such a one—the ultimate one. His expertise resulted in condemnation of self-serving and hypocritical teaching (examples: Matthew 23; Mark 7:1-13), recognition of false choices intended to ensnare (examples: Luke 20:20-26; John 8:2-11), etc.

Jesus did not need to justify his interpretations or teachings by referring to a higher source because he was the highest source. He still is.

—V. E.

Conclusion
A. The Greatness of Jesus

Was Jesus' claim to divine authority a true claim? After all, he *was* arrested, convicted, and crucified on a Roman cross! Some who were there said the crucifixion itself proved that Jesus was disfavored by God (Matthew 27:43; Luke 23:35-39); others reached a different conclusion (Matthew 27:54; Luke 23:40-43).

God settled the question when he raised Jesus from the dead. The Gospel of Matthew, the letter to the Hebrews, and the rest of the New Testament show us that many moved from astonishment to faith as a result.

Will we accept the authority of Jesus, or will we not? This has remained the most vital of decisions for nearly 2,000 years. If Jesus is indeed the fulfillment of God's plans and purposes, if he is indeed the exalted Creator and self-sacrificing Redeemer, then he must be heard and obeyed. All of life, now and forever, depends on doing so.

B. Prayer

Heavenly Father, we stand astonished and amazed in the presence of your Son. May our lives reflect that amazement as we glorify him by faithfully hearing and doing that which he asks of us. We pray for this in his name, the one who did all you asked of him. Amen.

C. Thought to Remember

"The fear of the Lord is the beginning of wisdom" (Psalm 111:10).

INVOLVEMENT LEARNING

Enhance your lesson presentation with the reproducible activity page,
available as a free download at www.standardlesson.com.

Into the Lesson

Distribute four strips of paper on which you have written the following statements: 1. Frank Lloyd Wright was recognized in 1991 by the American Institute of Architects as "the greatest American architect of all time." 2. His hundreds of completed structures, in addition to many homes, included churches, offices, skyscrapers, hotels, and museums. 3. He also designed many interior elements of his buildings, including furniture and stained glass. 4. Only 300 of the buildings still survive. As the statements are read in order, display pictures you have found of Wright's constructions. Ask for comments from those who have seen any Frank Lloyd Wright buildings. Then say, "Today we are going to look at an even more famous builder, whose house is eternal and will never be destroyed, since it's built on solid rock."

Alternative. Distribute copies of the "Jesus Is Greater Than . . ." activity from the reproducible page, which you can download. Have your students work in pairs to complete the matching activity. As they give their answers, also ask for a brief explanation of why Jesus is superior to each item. Then say, "Today, we'll be looking at why Jesus is a superior builder because of the house he built."

Into the Word

Hold up a photo of your house along with a picture of your family as you give the following explanation. "I want to show you two pictures of a house. The first is a place of residence, and the second is of the house of _____ [insert your last name]. The Greek word for *house* is used with both meanings several times in today's texts. In some verses it refers to a building, but in others it refers to God's house, meaning his people—as in *household*."

Divide your class in half, and ask one half to find the two verses in Hebrews 3:1-6 that use *house* to refer to a structure, and the other half to find the three verses that use *house* to mean God's

people. After receiving the answers of verses 3 and 4 (building) and verses 2, 5, and 6 (people), ask them to do the same for Matthew 7:24-27. They should conclude that all uses in Matthew refer to a building. Then say, "Hebrews presents the image of Jesus as a builder who is superior to Moses because he is the Son who is over God's house. The Matthew text has Jesus giving a valuable lesson on the importance of building our houses—and our lives—on a firm foundation."

Have students break into two groups to discuss either the Hebrews or the Matthew text. Distribute a sheet of paper with the appropriate exercise for each group. *Hebrews Group:* 1. List all the reasons why Jesus is worthy of great honor. 2. As part of Jesus' house, what can we do to show him the honor he deserves? *Matthew Group:* 1. List all the ways a person could benefit from putting Jesus' teaching here into practice. 2. What was it about Jesus' teaching that so amazed the people? Allow time for both groups to share.

Into Life

Ask, "Have any of you been involved in repairs to your living space lately? If so, did you do it yourself or hire someone to do it? What led to that decision?" After brief discussion, stress "As hard as it is to do building repairs, making repairs to God's household, our church family, can be even more difficult. What ministry areas of our church family need to be repaired or built up?" Have students discuss this question in their small groups. Encourage them not only to identify the problem but also come up with ways that they can be part of the solution. Ask for volunteers to share what they have discussed, being careful to keep it from becoming a personal attack on anyone.

Option. Distribute copies of the "Master Builder, Master Teacher" activity from the reproducible page. Have students discuss these scenarios within their small groups.

THE GREAT HIGH PRIEST

DEVOTIONAL READING: Ephesians 4:7-13
BACKGROUND SCRIPTURE: Hebrews 4:14–5:10

HEBREWS 4:14-16

[14] Since then we have a great high priest who has passed through the heavens, Jesus, the Son of God, let us hold fast our confession. [15] For we do not have a high priest who is unable to sympathize with our weaknesses, but one who in every respect has been tempted as we are, yet without sin. [16] Let us then with confidence draw near to the throne of grace, that we may receive mercy and find grace to help in time of need.

HEBREWS 5:1-10

[1] For every high priest chosen from among men is appointed to act on behalf of men in relation to God, to offer gifts and sacrifices for sins.

[2] He can deal gently with the ignorant and wayward, since he himself is beset with weakness. [3] Because of this he is obligated to offer sacrifice for his own sins just as he does for those of the people. [4] And no one takes this honor for himself, but only when called by God, just as Aaron was.

[5] So also Christ did not exalt himself to be made a high priest, but was appointed by him who said to him,

"You are my Son,
today I have begotten you";

[6] as he says also in another place,

"You are a priest forever,
after the order of Melchizedek."

[7] In the days of his flesh, Jesus offered up prayers and supplications, with loud cries and tears, to him who was able to save him from death, and he was heard because of his reverence. [8] Although he was a son, he learned obedience through what he suffered. [9] And being made perfect, he became the source of eternal salvation to all who obey him, [10] being designated by God a high priest after the order of Melchizedek.

KEY VERSE

Since then we have a great high priest who has passed through the heavens, Jesus, the Son of God, let us hold fast our confession. —**Hebrews 4:14**

The Sovereignty of God

Unit 2: The Sovereignty of Jesus
Lessons 5–9

Lesson Aims

After participating in this lesson, each learner will be able to:

1. List ways that Jesus fulfills the role of great high priest.

2. Compare and contrast the priesthoods of Jesus, Aaron, and Melchizedek.

3. Praise God for giving us the perfect high priest.

Lesson Outline

Introduction
  A. Power That Listens
  B. Lesson Background
  I. Sinless High Priest (Hebrews 4:14-16)
  A. His Greatness (v. 14)
  B. His Temptations (v. 15)
  C. His Mercy (v. 16)
    Entitled
 II. Human High Priests (Hebrews 5:1-3)
  A. Nature and Role (v. 1)
  B. Weakness and Sin (vv. 2, 3)
III. Appointed High Priest (Hebrews 5:4-6)
  A. God-Given Honor (vv. 4, 5)
  B. Eternal Order (v. 6)
IV. Obedient High Priest (Hebrews 5:7-10)
  A. Suffering Son (vv. 7, 8)
    Been There, Done That
  B. Perfected Founder (vv. 9, 10)
Conclusion
  A. Jesus Understands
  B. Prayer
  C. Thought to Remember

Introduction

A. Power That Listens

Watch closely the next time you see video of a successful politician greeting voters. Even though politicians meet thousands, the best campaigners know how to connect with individuals one by one (or at least appear to do so). Meeting person after person, the candidate takes a moment to shake hands, make substantial eye contact, and listen. After such encounters, many voters will say, "I believe that candidate is listening to people like me and understands our problems."

All of us crave a listening ear. When we are in pain, in need, or in trouble, we especially want to be heard. When someone has the power to help us, we desperately want that person to listen.

Today's text reminds us of how God has given his listening ear for our deepest needs. If God in his glory seems distant, in Christ we have proof of something else. Christ, our divine high priest, has the power to meet our needs. Christ, the human who suffered like us, hears us as one who knows our problems firsthand.

B. Lesson Background

As the letter to the Hebrews urges readers to continue in their faith in Jesus, it focuses heavily on the concept of the high priesthood. This ancient office plays a crucial role in today's lesson and in the letter as a whole. The Law of Moses decreed that a high priest preside over worship, both in the tabernacle and in the temple that superseded it. Aaron was the first high priest, and all members of Israel's priesthood were required to be descended from him (Exodus 28:1; 29:9; 40:12-15).

Israel's high priest was one of many priests who offered sacrifices of various kinds on the sacred altar. But once a year, on the Day of Atonement, only the high priest officiated at the special sacrifices. *Atonement* translates a word meaning "covering over"; sacrifices were made on the Day of Atonement to cover over the sins of all Israel.

On that occasion the high priest first offered the sacrifice of a bullock. That animal's life was offered as a substitute, taking the punishment in place of the lives of the high priest and his household for their sins (Leviticus 16:6). The high priest also cast lots to determine which of two goats would be sacrificed and which would be sent away (alive) as a scapegoat (16:7-10). The high priest sprinkled blood of the sacrificed bull and goat on "the mercy seat," which was the top of the ark of the covenant (16:2, 14, 15). This was located in the inner room, called "the Most Holy Place," of the tabernacle or temple (Exodus 26:34). Only on this one day of the year did anyone enter that room.

The essence of the Day of Atonement therefore was that of substitutionary sacrifice: the lives of animals were given in place of the lives of human sinners. But equally important was God's ordaining the high priest to this ministry. Only the one who occupied the office that God created could preside over this sacred rite. As do other New Testament writers, the author of Hebrews explains Jesus' death as the fulfillment of Israel's system of sacrifices.

I. Sinless High Priest
(HEBREWS 4:14-16)
A. His Greatness (v. 14)

14. Since then we have a great high priest who has passed through the heavens, Jesus, the Son of God, let us hold fast our confession.

The writer of Hebrews begins the description of Jesus as not just an eligible high priest but as *a great high priest* (see also Hebrews 3:1, lesson 6; 6:20; 7:26, lesson 8; 8:1; 9:11). Unlike others, he has gone not into the Most Holy Place of the earthly tabernacle (see the Lesson Background), but *through the heavens,* the true presence of God. That observation underlines how crucial it is to *hold fast our confession,* continuing faithfully to

HOW TO SAY IT

Aaron	*Air*-un.
Gethsemane	Geth-*sem*-uh-nee (*G* as in *get*).
Levi	*Lee*-vye.
Leviticus	Leh-*vit*-ih-kus.
Melchizedek	Mel-*kiz*-eh-dek.
Moses	*Mo*-zes or *Mo*-zez.
Nazareth	*Naz*-uh-reth.

confess that Jesus is God's promised one (compare 10:23).

B. His Temptations (v. 15)

15. For we do not have a high priest who is unable to sympathize with our weaknesses, but one who in every respect has been tempted as we are, yet without sin.

Jesus' supreme magnitude as the divine Son of God may seem to imply that he is distant and unapproachable. But the writer reminds us immediately that there is another aspect to his person: he *has been tempted as we are.* This was part of what it meant for the divine Son of God to become a human of lowly birth in the person of Jesus of Nazareth.

The story of Jesus includes the account of his temptation in the wilderness (Matthew 4:1-11), which echoes Israel's wilderness experience. Jesus' story includes his agony in the Garden of Gethsemane. There he expressed his desire not to die, but he ultimately submitted to the will of the Father (Matthew 26:36-42). He went on to experience horrific suffering on the cross (27:26-50).

These experiences show that Jesus' humanity was just as lowly as ours, just as tested as ours, if not more so. In his exaltation, he is not distant. He has suffered what we suffer.

> **What Do You Think?**
> How does the fact that Jesus underwent temptation as everyone else affect you personally?
> *Talking Points for Your Discussion*
> - In the way you pray
> - In the example you set
> - Other

Yet in his testing as a human, Jesus remained *without sin* (John 8:46; 2 Corinthians 5:21; 1 Peter 1:19; 2:22; 1 John 3:5). Unlike Aaron and the high priests after him, Jesus had no need to make sacrifice for his own sins because he had none.

C. His Mercy (v. 16)

16. Let us then with confidence draw near to the throne of grace, that we may receive mercy and find grace to help in time of need.

JESUS

Access to the throne of God

Tempted on earth;
Interceding
in Heaven

Visual for Lesson 7. *Start a discussion by pointing to this visual as you ask, "Exactly how does Jesus function as a key to unlock access to God's throne?"*

Jesus the high priest who entered the heavenly most holy place is also Jesus the king who is enthroned in Heaven at God's right hand (Hebrews 1:3, lesson 5; 8:1; 10:12; 12:2, lesson 9). His people know him as high priest and king, the one who has made atonement for their sins and who rules the world.

Approaching a mighty king to seek mercy can be dangerous (compare Esther 4:11). The king holds absolute power. A plea for mercy may draw a harsh reaction (compare 1 Kings 12:13, 14). But the king in view is also the high priest who has experienced in his lowliness what we experience. He is ready to give just the help we need, just when we need it. We approach him confidently, able to speak whatever our need may be (compare Hebrews 10:19-22).

◆ *ENTITLED* ◆

There she was, leaning on the horn of her SUV in the mall parking lot. How could that other driver have had the nerve to zip into the coveted parking space ahead of her? Surely that driver had seen that her blinking turn signal entitled her to that spot!

The verb *entitle* and its associated noun *entitlement* have taken on a negative ring over the years. The reason for this is that these words are often uttered in contexts of demanding what one thinks is owed. People use these words as justification for behaving as though they deserve honor,

acknowledgment, and other considerations. This is reflected in one particular dictionary definition that *entitlement* is a "belief that one is deserving of . . . certain privileges."

But that same dictionary also offers this definition of the verb *entitle*: "to furnish with proper grounds for seeking or claiming something." Today's text and others in Hebrews address a legal right that was purchased when God's Son died in our place: his death furnishes the proper grounds for us to have eternal life (compare Hebrews 9:15). But let us be quick to add that the entitlement created is God's not ours. He is entitled to us, not we to him. Jesus is the one who has "the keys of Death and Hades" (Revelation 1:18), not us.

Even so, God's entitlement yields astonishing benefits. One is his invitation to confidently "draw near to the throne of grace, that we may receive mercy and find grace to help in time of need." May we do so out of a sense of gratitude, not entitlement.   —V. E.

II. Human High Priests
(HEBREWS 5:1-3)
A. Nature and Role (v. 1)

1a. For every high priest chosen from among men is appointed to act on behalf of men in relation to God,

Developing Jesus' priestly identity, the writer of Hebrews now lays out what *every high priest* is and does. First among these is that the high priest comes from the people for whom he ministers. He is taken from humanity to serve on behalf of humanity. Fully human, Jesus fulfills that role.

The high priest's ministry for people is directed to God. As God's eternal Son, ordained and sent by the Father for this role, Christ fulfills it like no other.

1b. to offer gifts and sacrifices for sins.

The work of the high priest is to make offerings at the altar to atone for the sins of the people (see the Lesson Background). Jesus stands supreme in that role, having offered himself—not an animal but a human being innocent of sin—for the sins of others. Again, he fulfills the priesthood as no other can.

B. Weakness and Sin (vv. 2, 3)

2. He can deal gently with the ignorant and wayward, since he himself is beset with weakness.

A high priest must have empathy, able to understand the experiences of people who do not know God (the *ignorant*) or who have been deceived into abandoning the truth (the *wayward*). That is, the true high priest must minister not out of strength but *weakness*.

> **What Do You Think?**
> How can we better communicate that Christ shared and understands our weaknesses?
> *Talking Points for Your Discussion*
> • In worship (upreach)
> • In evangelism and benevolence (outreach)
> • In teaching (inreach)

3. Because of this he is obligated to offer sacrifice for his own sins just as he does for those of the people.

One similarity between Jesus as high priest and the high priests who came before him is the fact that they all offered sacrifices for *the people*. (In Jesus' case, it was just one sacrifice—himself.) A crucial difference, however, is that every high priest who came before Jesus was required first to make a sacrifice *for his own sins*. But the sinless Jesus can approach God without the need first to be purified. Being without sin, Jesus himself was a suitable offering—the atoning sacrifice—for the sins of others. There is no sacrifice greater or more fitting.

III. Appointed High Priest
(Hebrews 5:4-6)
A. God-Given Honor (vv. 4, 5)

4. And no one takes this honor for himself, but only when called by God, just as Aaron was.

The writer addresses another possible objection to Jesus' high priesthood. Even if Jesus is fitting in all the ways already noted, the high priest must be appointed by God himself to be valid. Clearly God had authorized Aaron and his descendants of the tribe of Levi to hold the priesthood (Exo-

dus 28:1; 40:12-15; Numbers 26:58, 59). But how can Jesus, standing outside that ancient line as he does (Matthew 1:1-16; Hebrews 7:13, 14), have any claim to divine appointment to priesthood? Are Christians being absurdly presumptuous in declaring Jesus to be the great high priest?

5. So also Christ did not exalt himself to be made a high priest, but was appointed by him who said to him,
> **"You are my Son;**
>   **today I have begotten you";**

The writer next begins to show that God had planned and promised for generations to provide his Son as the great *high priest*. Two Old Testament texts demonstrate how God made that promise.

The first text the writer of Hebrews offers is Psalm 2:7, quoted in the verse before us (see also Hebrews 1:5, lesson 1). This psalm celebrates God's rule over his people through the king whom he has appointed. In verse 7, God addresses the king as "my Son," indicating the Son's special, unique place in God's plan. For God to say *today I have begotten you* indicates not the Son's creation or physical birth. Rather, it is a figure of speech for his being appointed king by God.

While Israel used this psalm for generations to celebrate its kings, the faithful knew that none of those kings was what this psalm ideally described. So they looked forward with hope to the fulfillment of God's promise to send a greater king, a Son of David, who would build God's house and whose throne God would establish forever (1 Chronicles 17:11-14).

Jesus, says the writer of Hebrews, is that promised king. At both his baptism and transfiguration, Jesus was addressed by God with words that echoed Psalm 2:7 (see Matthew 3:17; 17:5). But wait—what does all this discussion about Jesus-as-king have to do with Jesus-as-priest? The answer to that unfolds as the writer of Hebrews brings to bear the analogy of Melchizedek (next verse).

B. Eternal Order (v. 6)

6. as he says also in another place,
> **"You are a priest forever,**
>   **after the order of Melchizedek."**

The author now quotes Psalm 110:4, which is the second of the two Old Testament texts that demonstrate God's promise to send his Son as priest. This psalm, like Psalm 2, celebrates and expresses hope for Israel's king. The first verse of Psalm 110, quoted eight times in the New Testament, is God's invitation to his appointed king to sit at God's right hand while God subdues the king's enemies (compare Hebrews 1:13). Yet amazingly, here is a statement right in the middle of the seven verses of Psalm 110 that discusses being a priest! This is startling because kings did not serve as priests in ancient Israel (2 Chronicles 19:11; 26:18). Although there were seemingly rare occasions when a king performed priestly functions (2 Samuel 6:16-18; 1 Kings 8:62-64), the two offices were distinct.

Even so, the writer of Hebrews sees the two roles of king and priest come together in an enigmatic individual named *Melchizedek.* Several hundred years before the formation of Israel as a nation, this man was both "king of Salem" and the "priest of God Most High" (Genesis 14:18). He was a king and priest so great that even the patriarch Abraham paid tithes to him (Genesis 14:20b; Hebrews 7:1-4, lesson 8).

For the ministry of the promised Messiah to be *after the order of Melchizedek* therefore announces that the promised king of fulfilled prophecy will also be a priest. Two offices will come together in one person, Jesus, as foreshadowed by the ancient Melchizedek.

IV. Obedient High Priest
(Hebrews 5:7-10)
A. Suffering Son (vv. 7, 8)

7. In the days of his flesh, Jesus offered up prayers and supplications, with loud cries and tears, to him who was able to save him from death, and he was heard because of his reverence.

Having established Christ's divine appointment as great high priest, the writer now returns to Jesus' lowly position in that regard. That lowliness was seen *in the days of his flesh,* an expression that emphasizes how he shared the weakness and vulnerability of physical existence with the rest of humanity during his life on earth.

Jesus' *prayers and supplications, with loud cries and tears* certainly suggest his struggle when he prayed that God would let the "cup" of death pass from him. How then was Jesus *heard because of his reverence* since he went to his death anyway? A vital part of his prayer is "nevertheless, not as I will, but as you will" followed by "your will be done" (Matthew 26:39, 42). Exalted though he was, Jesus experienced every aspect of human weakness. It was in that weakness he submitted utterly to the will of God the Father.

8. Although he was a son, he learned obedience through what he suffered.

We may wonder how the divine Son of God *learned* anything. After all, God already knows everything, right? And as the divine Son of God, eternal with the Father and sharing in creation, Christ enjoyed the most exalted position: the very position of God (John 1:1-3).

Yet the Scripture affirms that "Jesus increased in wisdom" (Luke 2:52) and that the Father had some knowledge that the Son did not have (Matthew 24:36; Mark 13:32). Therefore what the Son was able to learn seems to be tied closely to his experience in becoming human (John 1:14).

In becoming one with humanity, Jesus established no boundaries to his submission to the Father (compare Philippians 2:6-8). This included accepting the limitations of the flesh. As a result, he suffered in the worst that humanity can suffer.

Some things can be learned only by experience. Solomon was "wiser than all other men" (1 Kings 4:31), but it took the personal experience of disobedience for him to learn to obey (1 Kings 11:4-6; Ecclesiastes 4:13). Jesus was never disobedient to the Father, but he too learned by personal experience.

◆ BEEN THERE, DONE THAT ◆

Celebrate Recovery® is a Christ-centered program that helps free people from addictions. The program is used in thousands of churches worldwide. Broader in scope than other multistep programs, Celebrate Recovery recognizes that everyone has hurts and habits that must be addressed. While one person may not struggle with a certain type of temptation as another would, we all face temptation.

One temptation for everyone to beware of is a periodic desire to shake our fists toward Heaven and cry, "You don't know what it's like down here!" But God *does* know what it's like. He has never been an absentee God. In Jesus we see clearly what has always been reality: God's willingness to suffer alongside of, and on behalf of, those created in his image. Jesus never sinned, but he certainly felt the stress of every temptation.

Celebrate Recovery offers the healing freedom of being accepted as a fellow struggler. That's valuable, but there is something more valuable yet: as Jesus "learned obedience through what he suffered," so can we.   —V. E.

B. Perfected Founder (vv. 9, 10)

9, 10. And being made perfect, he became the source of eternal salvation to all who obey him, being designated by God a high priest after the order of Melchizedek.

Christ's humble obedience fulfills God's eternal purpose. By his obedient suffering he can exalt forever those who suffer for their own obedience to God. For sinners (and all are sinners) he makes God's mercy possible by taking the sinner's punishment on himself. For God's suffering people (and everyone suffers) he dignifies and exalts their suffering, providing the model for their obedience.

The *eternal salvation* he brings refers not only to the blessed life beyond death but also to God's blessing in the present. Fulfilling every divine promise of the past, Christ brings God's victorious salvation forward through eternity without end.

These observations help us understand what it means for Christ to be *made perfect*. This expression in this context means not the correcting of an imperfection but the attaining of a goal or purpose. It echoes Jesus' words from the cross, "It is finished" (John 19:30). God's plan from the beginning, even before the time of *Melchizedek* some 2,000 years before Christ, was for the Son to bring salvation as he would learn obedience by submitting to the Father.

> **What Do You Think?**
> What can we do to model our priesthood of 1 Peter 2:5, 9 after that of Jesus?
> *Talking Points for Your Discussion*
> - In terms of service to others
> - In terms of pursuing personal holiness
> - Other

Conclusion
A. Jesus Understands

People often ask, "Where is God when I hurt?" In hard times, we ask God, "Why?" The Bible does not answer that *Why?* with the clarity we crave. But it provides something more powerful: Christ says he understands what we are going through. He understands it personally. He invites us to trust him again. When we do, our *Why?* question can become the better question *What's next?*

B. Prayer

Father, may the obedience of your Son become the pattern of our own lives as your grateful, forgiven people. We pray in Jesus' name. Amen.

C. Thought to Remember

As Jesus learned from suffering, so may we.

INVOLVEMENT LEARNING

Enhance your lesson presentation with the reproducible activity page,
available as a free download at www.standardlesson.com.

Into the Lesson

Say, "The following statement was made by the son of a famous businessman. Can you guess whom he was describing?"

> By the time Sunday came, . . . he was just worn out. . . . So he was closed that first Sunday, and we've been closed ever since. He figured if he didn't like working on Sundays, that other people didn't either. He said, "I don't want to ask people to do that [which] I am not willing to do myself."

Accept either of the following answers: the founder of Chik-fil-A or S. Truett Cathy. Then say, "Cathy was willing to suffer a potential loss of income out of compassion for his employees. Have you ever worked for that kind of a boss? What was it like?"

After a few people have shared, say, "One reason Jesus was such a 'great high priest' was because he knew what it was to suffer. As a result he was able to have compassion for the people he came to save. As we read Hebrews, we'll learn other reasons why Jesus was so great."

Alternative. Distribute copies of the "What Do You Know?" activity from the reproducible page, which you can download. Have volunteers share their answers. Then ask, "How is it possible for Jesus to be our 'great high priest' since he was not descended from Aaron? If you don't know the answer, you will find it out in today's lesson."

Into the Word

Assign half of your class to be in the *Aaron Group*, and the other half to be the *Jesus Group*. Ask for a volunteer from the Aaron group to read aloud Hebrews 4:14–5:3; then have someone from the Jesus group read Hebrews 5:4-10. Instruct both groups to listen for verses that seem to apply best to either Aaron's priesthood or that of Jesus.

Distribute copies of the following "High Priest Checklist," which you have prepared in advance: 1. Sacrifices a bull for own sin. 2. Was tempted but didn't sin. 3. Was called by God to the office of high priest. 4. Comes from the people for whom he ministers. 5. Offered a sacrifice in Heaven. 6. Has compassion for the ignorant and the wayward. 7. Is part of a superior priesthood. 8. Learned obedience through intense suffering. 9. Presides over worship in the temple. 10. Is considered "perfect."

Distribute copies of the checklist. Within the larger groups have students form small groups of three or four, and tell them to check off the characteristics for their group. When most groups are done, go down the list and have them identify the items they checked. Both groups will have chosen some items. The suggested answers for Aaron are 1, 3, 4, 6, 9; the items for Jesus are 2, 3, 4, 5, 6, 7, 8, 10.

Use the following questions to lead a discussion about the similarities and differences between the two priesthoods. 1. In what ways were the priesthoods of Aaron and Jesus similar? 2. How were they different? 3. In what way did Jesus offer a superior sacrifice? 4. Since Jesus wasn't from the tribe of Levi, how could he be a priest? 5. Why was the priesthood of Melchizedek superior to that of Aaron? Which came first? (See Genesis 14:18-20.)

Into Life

Write the heading "Our Great High Priest" on the board. Then ask students to suggest why Jesus deserves that title. Encourage students to come up with as many short, pithy statements as they can. Then distribute strips of poster board and markers. Assign each pair of students one of the statements, and encourage them to draw it on the poster board in a colorful and creative way. Post the statements around the room. Close with prayer, praising God for sending us Jesus to serve as our mediator, Savior, and great high priest.

Option. Hand out copies of the "Whom Do You Tell?" activity from the reproducible page for students to take home for self-evaluation.

THE HIGH PRIEST FOREVER

DEVOTIONAL READING: Psalm 110

BACKGROUND SCRIPTURE: Hebrews 7

HEBREWS 7:1-3, 18-28

[1] For this Melchizedek, king of Salem, priest of the Most High God, met Abraham returning from the slaughter of the kings and blessed him, [2] and to him Abraham apportioned a tenth part of everything. He is first, by translation of his name, king of righteousness, and then he is also king of Salem, that is, king of peace. [3] He is without father or mother or genealogy, having neither beginning of days nor end of life, but resembling the Son of God he continues a priest forever.

. . . .

[18] For on the one hand, a former commandment is set aside because of its weakness and uselessness [19] (for the law made nothing perfect); but on the other hand, a better hope is introduced, through which we draw near to God.

[20] And it was not without an oath. For those who formerly became priests were made such without an oath, [21] but this one was made a priest with an oath by the one who said to him:

"The Lord has sworn
 and will not change his mind,
'You are a priest forever.'"

[22] This makes Jesus the guarantor of a better covenant.

[23] The former priests were many in number, because they were prevented by death from continuing in office, [24] but he holds his priesthood permanently, because he continues forever. [25] Consequently, he is able to save to the uttermost those who draw near to God through him, since he always lives to make intercession for them.

[26] For it was indeed fitting that we should have such a high priest, holy, innocent, unstained, separated from sinners, and exalted above the heavens. [27] He has no need, like those high priests, to offer sacrifices daily, first for his own sins and then for those of the people, since he did this once for all when he offered up himself. [28] For the law appoints men in their weakness as high priests, but the word of the oath, which came later than the law, appoints a Son who has been made perfect forever.

KEY VERSE

He holds his priesthood permanently, because he continues forever. —**Hebrews 7:24**

THE SOVEREIGNTY OF GOD

Unit 2: The Sovereignty of Jesus
LESSONS 5–9

LESSON AIMS

After participating in this lesson, each learner will be able to:

1. Identify the one whose priesthood is eternal.

2. Compare and contrast the priesthoods of Jesus, Melchizedek, and those descended from Levi.

3. Explain to a new Christian or an unbeliever the concept of priesthood and Jesus' role therein.

LESSON OUTLINE

Introduction

A. Unexpected Support

The Lord of the Rings trilogy, published in the mid-1950s, is a classic story of the victory of virtue and providence over the power of evil. A mysterious ring, which proves to be an instrument of evil, falls into the possession of a humble hobbit named Frodo. He learns that the ring must be destroyed at the mountain where it was forged, and he sets out with friends on a journey that proves to be momentous and dangerous.

Early in their journey, the travelers are rescued by Tom Bombadil. He is a powerful and enigmatic character, but he shows the weary hobbits rich hospitality and provides wise counsel for their perilous journey. Similarly, the enigmatic Melchizedek appears on the scene of Old Testament history to render aid to a virtuous person who is on a journey, namely Abraham (Genesis 14:18-24). Tom Bombadil is fictional, but Melchizedek was real.

B. Lesson Background: Mysterious Priest

Melchizedek appears in the Old Testament only in Genesis 14 and Psalm 110. These passages note his considerable status, but otherwise give very little information about him.

As a result, his identity has been the subject of speculation. Some Jewish scholars propose that he was a visitation of Enoch, a man who had "walked with God" (Genesis 5:22, 24). Others suggest that Melchizedek was the angel Michael, the defender of God's people (Daniel 12:1).

Some Christian scholars, for their part, propose that Melchizedek was actually a theophany (a visual manifestation of God). But if Melchizedek's presence and ministry in Canaan as "priest of God Most High" (14:18) was part of why God called Abraham to settle in that land (12:1), then such theories should be set aside.

The opening "for this Melchizedek" of today's text picks up on the closing verses of chapter 6. There the writer focuses (1) on the oath by which God confirmed his promise to Abraham as support for our hope of salvation and (2) on the work of Jesus as our "high priest forever after the order of Melchizedek." By this the writer is not indicating the existence of a continuing priestly order led by Melchizedek. The idea is that of a special category rather than of an established institution.

C. Lesson Background: Messianic Psalm

Psalm 110 looks forward to the Messiah and the deliverance he will bring about. The importance the New Testament writers assign to this psalm is revealed by its 10 quotations and 14 allusions in the Gospels, Acts, the letters of Paul, and the letter to the Hebrews.

Psalm 110:4 affirms that "The Lord has sworn and will not change his mind: 'You are a priest forever after the order of Melchizedek.'" The writer of Hebrews repeatedly points to this divine decree in calling the reader to remain faithful to Christ (Hebrews 5:6, 10; 6:17-20; 7:11-17, 21). Melchizedek, whose genealogy and death are not recorded in Scripture, is a type of Christ—Christ who continues to minister to us as king and high priest by "the power of an indestructible life" (7:16). The phrase *type of Christ* recognizes that the New Testament writers use a technique known as *typology* to draw on patterns from the Old Testament to understand aspects of the era of the new covenant. One example is that of Adam, described by Paul as "a type of the one who was to come" (Romans 5:14).

I. Priest of God
(Hebrews 7:1-3)
A. Lesser and Greater (vv. 1, 2)

1, 2. For this Melchizedek, king of Salem, priest of the Most High God, met Abraham returning from the slaughter of the kings and blessed him, and to him Abraham apportioned a tenth part of everything. He is first, by translation of his name, king of righteousness, then he is also king of Salem, that is, king of peace.

The fact that *Melchizedek* was *king of Salem* points decisively to the man as a historical figure, not an angel or a theophany (see the Lesson Background). According to the first-century Jewish historian Josephus, *Salem* refers to *Jerusalem*; the latter designation is merely a longer form of the city's name (compare Psalm 76:2). *Salem*, from the Hebrew word *shalom*, means "peace."

Melchizedek was not only king there but also *priest of the Most High God*, a status of extraordinary honor. The man's greatness is shown in the fact that even Abraham, who is held in the highest regard in the history of Israel, paid tithes (*a tenth part of everything*) to him (Genesis 14:17-20). The implication (hinted at here and clearly affirmed in Hebrews 7:4-17, not in today's text) is that there is no scriptural basis for maintaining allegiance to the old Levitical priesthood in preference to the high priest of the new covenant, Jesus Christ.

B. Out of Nowhere (v. 3)

3. He is without father or mother or genealogy, having neither beginning of days nor end of life, but resembling the Son of God he continues a priest forever.

A primary question concerning the identity of Melchizedek is whether the writer to the Hebrews is intending to present him as more than human. A literalistic reading of the verse before us could lead us to say *yes,* but a broader look at Hebrews 5–7 will restrain us from doing so.

That broader look reveals that the writer's main purpose across those three chapters is to establish the superiority of Jesus over the Levitical priesthood. For this purpose, comparisons between the natures of Jesus and Melchizedek themselves are unnecessary. Instead, it is sufficient to note parallels between their respective priesthoods, contrasting them along the way with elements of the Levitical priesthood.

HOW TO SAY IT

Apocrypha	Uh-*paw*-kruh-fuh.
Enoch	*E*-nock.
Levi	*Lee*-vye.
Levitical	Leh-*vit*-ih-kul.
Melchizedek	Mel-*kiz*-eh-dek.
Messiah	Meh-*sigh*-uh.
shalom (*Hebrew*)	shah-*lome*.
Sirach	*Sigh*-rak.
theophany	the-*ah*-fuh-nee.

The priesthoods of both Jesus and Melchizedek are outside the genealogical boundaries of the Levitical priesthood, boundaries grounded in the Law of Moses (Exodus 28:1-4; 29:44; Leviticus 8; etc.). Melchizedek and Jesus were appointed by God to priesthoods that do not base their validity on having Levi as an ancestor. Melchizedek was appointed "priest of the Most High God" apart from recorded genealogical credentials, and Jesus has been appointed our great high priest "not on the basis of a legal requirement concerning bodily descent, but by the power of an indestructible life" (Hebrews 7:16).

Jesus was from the tribe of Judah, not Levi (Matthew 1:1-17; Hebrews 7:14). Yet it was God's purpose, as promised in Psalm 110, that a descendant of King David would, as Messiah, be both king and priest. The readers of Hebrews can have no greater king or priest, and they would be foolish to forsake Jesus to return to the old covenant. Equally foolish would be to compromise submission to Christ by attempting to combine new-covenant faith with old-covenant practices that are "ready to vanish away" (Hebrews 8:13).

II. Priest by Divine Oath
(Hebrews 7:18-22)
A. Better Hope (vv. 18, 19)

18, 19. For on the one hand, a former commandment is set aside because of its weakness and uselessness (for the law made nothing perfect); but on the other hand, a better hope is introduced, through which we draw near to God.

The priestly ministry established by the Law of Moses could not bring people to sinlessness and complete spiritual maturity. The priests themselves were not without sin and were subject to mortality. The law by itself could point to, but could not provide for, the redemption of sinners; only the work of Christ on the cross could accomplish that. As Paul explained, "So then, the law was our guardian until Christ came, in order that we might be justified by faith" (Galatians 3:24).

The death and resurrection of Jesus brought into history *a better hope.* Jesus is the high priest of

the new covenant. He is the one who offered the perfect sacrifice for our sin: the sacrifice of himself. He now mediates between us and the Father so that we may *draw near to God* with confidence (Hebrews 4:16).

> **What Do You Think?**
> How do we keep a healthy balance between respect for law and reliance on grace? Or is *balance* even the right word? Explain.
> *Talking Points for Your Discussion*
> - Regarding our salvation
> - Regarding our personal holiness
> - Regarding the laws of society
> - Other

◆ PROTECTIVE BOUNDARIES ◆

Throughout elementary school, my daughter did her homework on her own without any prodding from me. During the first week of junior high, she forgot to do her homework twice. The new schedule—which featured a greater variety of classes and social engagements, combined with more responsibility and less teacher supervision—was taking its toll on her. Consequently, I told her that I would have to check her homework at night to make sure she had finished it before she could do fun activities.

Shocked, she said that this had never happened before. I replied that she had never needed it before, but the previously unnecessary rule came into effect when she did need it. The boundary of "finish your homework in a timely manner" had existed since she had begun to be assigned homework. It was only when the boundary was violated that a corrective procedure was enforced.

God's law drew the behavioral boundaries for the Old Testament era. When people crossed those boundaries, he enacted corrective procedures. The people of that day were not ready for the freedom that we in the New Testament era enjoy (Galatians 5:1; Ephesians 3:12; James 2:12). This freedom is available because of the better hope that Jesus' life, death, and resurrection bring (compare Colossians 2:14). Even so, we are not to use our "freedom as a cover-up for evil, but living as servants of God"

(1 Peter 2:16). Our place in God's story is one of relationship with his Son rather than keeping of rules. But there are still boundaries. —L. M. W.

B. Sworn Declaration (vv. 20-22)

20, 21. And it was not without an oath. For those who formerly became priests were made such without an oath, but this one was made a priest with an oath by the one who said to him:
"The Lord has sworn
and will not change his mind,
'You are a priest forever.'"

The contrast between the priesthood of Jesus and the Levitical priesthood continues. Levites were appointed to be priests according to stipulations of the Law of Moses; such priests could be appointed *without an oath*. But Jesus' appointment was accompanied by an oath, recorded here as being Psalm 110:4.

What Do You Think?
Under what circumstances, if any, does the oath God affirmed serve as a model for swearing oaths or taking vows on our part?
Talking Points for Your Discussion
- Considering positive view in Hebrews 6:16, 17
- Considering negative views in Matthew 5:33-37; 23:16-22; James 5:12
- Relevance of 1 Thessalonians 5:27?

The idea of the Lord swearing an oath is not a new one (see Genesis 24:7; Psalm 89:49; Ezekiel 16:8; etc.). The fact that *the Lord has sworn and will not change his mind* means that he will never rescind his decision that the Messiah will forever serve as the high priest of his people. Jesus' authority to fulfill this office is grounded not in the temporary Law of Moses but in the everlasting oath of the Creator. **22. This makes Jesus the guarantor of a better covenant.**

The noun in the original language that is translated *guarantor* is quite rare, occurring only here in the New Testament. For Jesus to become *the guarantor* means that he is something like a bondsman or underwriter, who provide a guarantee. A nonbiblical text from the Apocrypha, written before the time of Christ, is intriguing in this regard:

"Do not forget the kindness of your guarantor, for he has given his life for you" (Wisdom of Jesus the Son of Sirach 29:15).

The *better covenant* Jesus guarantees is the new covenant, a point further developed in Hebrews 8:6-13. The old covenant served well its purposes of revealing the holiness of God and the holiness he expected of his people (compare 1 Peter 1:16, which quotes Leviticus 19:2). However, the old covenant was promissory rather than complete. It was not faultless as an instrument of salvation (Hebrews 8:7), and it served as "our guardian" as it demonstrated our need for the Messiah (Galatians 3:24). He alone fulfills the righteous requirements of the law, first for himself by his sinless life and then for us by his death and resurrection.

◆ SUBSTITUTES ◆

When parents leave their child for a short time, they trust a babysitter in their place. The babysitter provides for the child's care, and the two may enjoy a close relationship. But despite any mutual affection, the care of the child reverts back to the parents when they return. The nature of the relationship between parent and child is of a wholly different order than a bond between babysitter and child. The babysitter is a temporary substitute.

The Old Testament law was something like a babysitter. It served to care for humanity until Jesus could come to renew the bond between heavenly Father and earthly children. As a babysitter is temporarily responsible for enforcing the parents' desires for their child, the Old Testament law enforced God's desires by pointing out sin.

The roles of Melchizedek, Abraham, Moses, Aaron, etc., can remind us that the old covenant law was never intended to be permanent. It was established as "our guardian" (again, Galatians 3:24) until Jesus came to do all that the law itself could not (3:25–4:7). —L. M. W.

Jesus became "the founder and perfecter of our faith" (Hebrews 12:2, next week's lesson) by accepting upon himself the justice of God that we deserve for our sins and by his resurrection to life beyond death. That resurrection foreshadows our own and is the basis for it; God promises that we too will be raised to everlasting life (1 Corinthians 15). In light of this, how is there any advantage in turning away from Jesus or attempting to combine faith in him with faith in someone or something else? Those who consider abandoning or modifying their faith in Christ in order to be less offensive to others need to think again!

III. Priests Contrasted
(HEBREWS 7:23-28)

A. Permanence and Intercession (vv. 23-25)

23, 24. The former priests were many in number, because they were prevented by death from continuing in office, but he holds his priesthood permanently, because he continues forever.

The writer begins sketching contrasts between Jesus and the Levitical priests. The latter were necessarily *many in number* because of their mortality, a fact patently obvious to anyone. But Jesus holds a *priesthood permanently* by "the power of an indestructible life" (Hebrews 7:16).

25. Consequently, he is able to save to the uttermost those who draw near to God through him, since he always lives to make intercession for them.

The fact that the priestly ministry of Jesus saves *to the uttermost* means that salvation through him continues forever. It includes the sanctification in this life and glorification for eternity. We walk in assurance that our high priest will bring us into the very presence of God. Jesus will transform our lowly natural bodies into glorious spiritual ones when he returns (1 Corinthians 15:44); we will be beyond the reach of death permanently.

The assurance of eternity in Heaven is what sets our present lives in this fallen world in proper perspective. As Paul stressed, "If in Christ we have hope in this life only, we are of all people most to be pitied" (1 Corinthians 15:19). The Christian faith is rightly weighed on its own terms, not on those of a secular understanding of life that can see no farther than the moment of physical death.

The phrase *those who draw near to God through him* reminds us of Jesus' own declaration "I am the way, and the truth, and the life. No one comes to

the Father except through me" (John 14:6). Only Jesus can *make intercession* for us with the Father—and he does (compare Romans 8:34; 1 John 2:1).

> **What Do You Think?**
> What more can you do to show appreciation for and reliance on the one interceding for you?
> **Talking Points for Your Discussion**
> - In your prayer life
> - In your public witness
> - In how you manage money
> - Other

B. Character and Exaltation (v. 26)

26. For it was indeed fitting that we should have such a high priest, holy, innocent, unstained, separated from sinners, and exalted above the heavens.

The contrasts between Jesus and those of the Levitical priesthood continue. Only Jesus can be characterized fully by the descriptions we see in the verse before us. Only he has been *exalted above the heavens*.

> **What Do You Think?**
> What are some ways to model Jesus' separateness from sinners while still engaging with them for purposes of evangelism?
> **Talking Points for Your Discussion**
> - Regarding you as an individual
> - Regarding your congregation as a whole

C. Sacrifice and Consecration (vv. 27, 28)

27, 28. He has no need, like those high priests, to offer sacrifices daily, first for his own sins and then for those of the people, since he did this once for all when he offered up himself. For the law appoints men in their weakness as high priests, but the word of the oath, which came later than the law, appoints a Son, who has been made perfect forever.

Verse 27 presents us with a slight problem, because the phrasing of the high priest's sacrifice as *first for his own sins and then for those of the people* seems to refer to the yearly (rather than *daily*) sacrifice on the Day of Atonement (Leviticus 16). A solution presents itself when we realize that it was possible for high priests, like anyone else, to sin daily without meaning to do so. And daily sin required daily sacrifice (Leviticus 4:1-3).

But Jesus sinned neither intentionally nor unintentionally. Thus he was able to be the perfect sacrifice "without blemish or spot" (1 Peter 1:19) for the sins of the world. *Those high priests* who served under the Law of Moses were weak toward sin, but the Son of God was perfected by living a life without sin. He lived out daily the holiness that was never lacking in his character.

The final point of contrast concerns the divine oath revealed in Psalm 110:4, sworn by God during the life of King David. That was four centuries after the Law of Moses had been given, so there is no doubt that God himself intended the Levitical priesthood to be superseded by the everlasting ministry of Christ as high priest of his people.

The distinctive qualities of Melchizedek noted in Genesis 14:18-20 combine with the promise of Psalm 110 to point to the singular, superlative high priesthood of Jesus Christ. The writer of Hebrews will reiterate later the decisive contrast: "For Christ has entered, not into holy places made with hands, which are copies of the true things, but into heaven itself, now to appear in the presence of God on our behalf" (Hebrews 9:24). Our high priest lives, our king reigns, forever and ever.

Visual for Lesson 8. *Test comprehension by pointing to this visual as you ask, "How do the ideas of* priest *and* sacrifice *come together in Jesus?"*

What Do You Think?
How can trust in our high priest be reflected in our Christian priesthood of 1 Peter 2:5, 9?
Talking Points for Your Discussion
- Regarding your graciousness toward and prayer intercession for fellow Christians
- Regarding your graciousness toward and prayer intercession for unbelievers
- Other

Conclusion
A. Faithful Mediator

Surely there was no one in Abraham's day (about 2000 BC) who anticipated that Melchizedek's dual positions as king and priest foreshad-

owed those two roles of the Messiah to come! But that foreshadowing and its implications are precisely what the book of Hebrews establishes.

Times of affliction and the discouragement they bring may make us feel far from God, unable to communicate with him. Job certainly felt this way during his time of suffering as he lamented, "[God] is not a man, as I am, that I might answer him, that we should come to trial together. There is no arbiter between us, who might lay his hand on us both" (Job 9:32, 33).

Job describes someone who stands between two others to reconcile them. Job longed for a such a person in his day, for someone who was able to speak directly to God on Job's behalf. God has answered that longing in Christ, our high priest who offered the once-for-all-time sacrifice and who always intercedes for us with God. As Paul reminded Timothy, "There is one God, and there is one mediator between God and men, the man Christ Jesus" (1 Timothy 2:5).

B. Prayer

Father, may we never embrace any savior other than Jesus! Only he could offer the perfect sacrifice of self to pay the penalty for our sins—and he did. It is with gratitude that we pray to you in his name. Amen.

C. Thought to Remember
Rely completely and only on Jesus for salvation.

INVOLVEMENT LEARNING

Enhance your lesson presentation with the reproducible activity page,
available as a free download at www.standardlesson.com.

Into the Lesson

Challenge your class to see how few clues it takes to identify the Mystery Man according to clues you will give. After you read each clue aloud, allow about 30 seconds for guessing the name of the Bible character. Give the following clues: 1–He had no children. 2–He blessed a major Bible character after that person killed some kings. 3–He is a perpetual priest. 4–He was King of Salem. 5–He received a tithe from Abraham. 6–He was made like the Son of God. 7–Jesus is a priest forever after his order.

Congratulate the team that first comes up with the name *Melchizedek*. Then say, "Melchizedek is certainly one of the most mysterious characters in the Bible. We're going to learn more about him today and how his priestly order makes Jesus' eternal priesthood far superior to that of Aaron."

Alternative. Write the following question on the board: *Who was the greatest baseball player of all time?* Underneath it list these names: Hank Aaron, Ty Cobb, Lou Gehrig, Babe Ruth, Ted Williams. Encourage your students to give their opinions. Then say, "Most listings rank Babe Ruth as the best overall player, but there are others who would debate it. However, when it comes to the best order of high priest, that honor goes to Melchizedek, whose priesthood serves as a model for that of Jesus."

Into the Word

Early in the week, ask one of your students to give a brief lecture about Melchizedek, based on the information provided in the introduction under "Lesson Background: Mysterious Priest."

On index cards write the following words, one per card: *appointed, death, intercession, king, oath, sacrifice, sinful, covenant.* Distribute all the cards to individuals or pairs of students. Instruct them to search the lesson text to see how their word(s) could be used to make the case that Jesus as high priest in the order of Melchizedek is superior to the priesthood of Aaron. After allowing for study time, ask for volunteers to reveal their words and tell how they relate to the two priesthoods.

Here are some possible responses: *appointed*—the law appointed weak men as high priests, but God appointed Jesus as our perfect high priest; *death*—mortality prevented high priests from continuing in office, but Jesus lives forever; *intercession*—Jesus always lives to make intercession for us; *king*—Aaron's successors were only priests, but Melchizedek was both priest and king, as is Jesus; *oath*—no oath is involved in the human priesthood, but Jesus' was established by God's oath; *sacrifice*—human priests have to offer continual sacrifices for themselves and the people, but Jesus sacrificed himself only once; *sinful*—humans are sinful and weak, but Jesus is "holy . . . exalted above the heavens" (Hebrews 7:26); *covenant*—Jesus is the guarantor of a much superior covenant, which gives us hope, rather than the one based on the law.

Option. Distribute copies of the "How Do They Compare?" activity from the reproducible page, which you can download. Have students work in pairs to complete it; then discuss their answers.

Into Life

Say, "Help me list the things that the high priest did for the Israelites." Jot responses on the board, expecting the following: offered sacrifices, entered God's presence on the Day of Atonement, set high standards of conduct, represented them to God, etc. Then say, "If you had to explain to a new believer what it means for Jesus to be our high priest, what would you say?" Responses could use the answers given before to state that Jesus offered one sacrifice—himself—for all our sins, he is daily in God's presence interceding for us, he is the perfect example for how we are to live, etc.

Option. Have students discuss possible responses to the "What Would Jesus Say?" activity from the reproducible page.

MODEL OF ENDURANCE

DEVOTIONAL READING: Isaiah 53:1-6
BACKGROUND SCRIPTURE: Hebrews 12

HEBREWS 12:1-13

[1] Therefore, since we are surrounded by so great a cloud of witnesses, let us also lay aside every weight, and sin which clings so closely, and let us run with endurance the race that is set before us, [2] looking to Jesus, the founder and perfecter of our faith, who for the joy that was set before him endured the cross, despising the shame, and is seated at the right hand of the throne of God.

[3] Consider him who endured from sinners such hostility against himself, so that you may not grow weary or fainthearted. [4] In your struggle against sin you have not yet resisted to the point of shedding your blood. [5] And have you forgotten the exhortation that addresses you as sons?

> "My son, do not regard lightly the discipline of the Lord,
>   nor be weary when reproved by him.
> [6] For the Lord disciplines the one he loves,
>   and chastises every son whom he receives."

[7] It is for discipline that you have to endure. God is treating you as sons. For what son is there whom his father does not discipline? [8] If you are left without discipline, in which all have participated, then you are illegitimate children and not sons. [9] Besides this, we have had earthly fathers who disciplined us and we respected them. Shall we not much more be subject to the Father of spirits and live? [10] For they disciplined us for a short time as it seemed best to them, but he disciplines us for our good, that we may share his holiness. [11] For the moment all discipline seems painful rather than pleasant, but later it yields the peaceful fruit of righteousness to those who have been trained by it.

[12] Therefore lift your drooping hands and strengthen your weak knees, [13] and make straight paths for your feet, so that what is lame may not be put out of joint but rather be healed.

KEY VERSES

Let us run with endurance the race that is set before us, looking to Jesus, the founder and perfecter of our faith. —**Hebrews 12:1, 2**

THE SOVEREIGNTY OF GOD

Unit 2: The Sovereignty of Jesus

LESSONS 5–9

LESSON AIMS

After participating in this lesson, each learner will be able to:

1. List some features of God's discipline.

2. Explain the connection between discipline and righteousness.

3. Identify the verbs in the lesson text and describe how these will serve as "action words" in his or her life.

LESSON OUTLINE

Introduction

A. Classic Stories

Some stories we read, hear, or watch don't stick with us for long, even if they have great appeal at the time. Other stories, however, may cause us to ponder and deliberate over the course of months and years. Why the difference? What is it that sets enduring, classic stories apart from the many that are soon forgotten, even though the latter may feature many exciting elements of action and adventure?

A story is *classic* to the degree it resonates with the moral order that God has established in creation and written on our hearts. The classic stories reflect in some way the broader human story of creation, fall, and redemption. And as they do, such stories lead us to deeper truths about ourselves and about life under God. The Chronicles of Narnia series is an example.

The hero in classic stories is one who, by struggle and sacrifice, restores a right moral order for self and others. This is the direction taken in Hebrews 11, sometimes referred to as "Faith's Hall of Fame." There, faith as trust in the character and promises of God is illustrated in the lives of numerous named individuals of Israel's past. As the writer moves into what we designate as chapter 12, the heroic stories of the lives of patriarchal and other old-covenant believers are connected with ours.

B. Lesson Background

Those who have virtuously endured severe suffering display a certain seriousness of character that sets them apart. Yet such suffering also enables them better to understand and relate to others. Foremost among such individuals is Jesus, of whom the writer to the Hebrews notes, "Although he was a son, he learned obedience through what he suffered" (Hebrews 5:8, lesson 7; compare 2:18; 4:15). The writer's point is not that Jesus moved from a state of disobedience to a state of obedience. Rather, he learned obedience in the sense of living out experientially the capacity for complete obedience that was at all times part of his character.

When we think of the character of Jesus, we usually think first of his love, and we rightly want to be able to love others as he has loved us (1 John 4:11). Our ability to love is the outcome of our development in the basic virtues. If we want to love well, we seek the virtues of humility, integrity, wisdom, and holiness, because these virtues are grounded in who God is. They lead us to become like him and enable us to love more as he loves.

We develop these virtues largely through pursuing them intentionally as we experience the adversities of life in a fallen world. As the discipline of physical exercise strengthens the body, so too the discipline of spiritual exercise strengthens the soul (sanctification). God's intent is that Christ be formed in us (Galatians 4:19). Discipline through suffering develops and refines our hearts as we mature in Christlike holiness.

A goal of the writer of Hebrews is to encourage suffering Christians of Jewish background to persevere as followers of Jesus (see the Lesson Background of lesson 5). The pain of being ostracized seemed to be taking its toll. As tragic as that was, a return to a Judaism-without-Christ would be a case of "the cure is worse than the disease."

The writer argues against this course of action by establishing the superiority of Jesus over the old covenant and its priesthood. Although Israel's history had many heroes of faith, "[they] did not receive what was promised, since God had provided something better for us, that apart from us they should not be made perfect" (Hebrews 11:39, 40). With the opening *therefore* of today's lesson, the writer begins summarizing why all this is important to the reader.

I. Preparing for the Race
(Hebrews 12:1-4)
A. What to Do (v. 1)

1. Therefore, since we are surrounded by so great a cloud of witnesses, let us also lay aside every weight, and sin which clings so closely, and let us run with endurance the race that is set before us,

The writer calls the readers to follow the examples of the heroes of faith just listed in Hebrews 11.

Together, these heroes constitute *so great a cloud of witnesses.* They are witnesses first by their own testimony of faith—some by what they accomplished and some by what they suffered. They are also witnesses as they in some way observe those of us in later generations of believers who are running *the race that is set before us.*

An important part of running to win is to lay aside anything that hinders us in the race (compare 1 Corinthians 9:24). Our race is not a 100-yard sprint but a lifelong marathon. Hindrances once set aside may have ways of reattaching themselves to us over the years of our race. The Old Testament heroes of faith became sad examples of this at various times. Thus we *run with perseverance* as we are ever alert in this regard.

◆   **The Race of Life**   ◆

Every two years, police officers and firefighters from around the world gather at a host city to compete in the World Police & Fire Games. The games include typical athletic competitions, but also events tailored specifically to participants' jobs.

For firefighters, abilities to carry and use various pieces of equipment while being burdened with heavy attire characterize the timed events. Participants appear to complete the competitions effortlessly, and this is due to hours of hard work in training. Firefighters practice the same actions repeatedly so that they will be ready and able to save lives when an emergency comes. Preparedness is their goal, and they are careful to keep it in sight.

The equipment and attire that firefighters use in the games and in real life are burdensome but necessary. As such, these items cannot be cast off in the interest of greater speed. Similarly, Christians throughout the centuries have practiced their faith with an eye toward what should be cast off as a

HOW TO SAY IT

Deuteronomy	Due-ter-*ahn*-uh-me.
Hebrews	*Hee*-brews.
patriarchal	pay-tree-*are*-kul.
sanctification	*sank*-tuh-fuh-**kay**-shun.

hindrance and what must be retained as necessary for remaining faithful in the race of life. We can look at their successes and failures in that regard for help in keeping our focus on the end, on Jesus. His is the ultimate example of faithfulness that should inspire us daily. See the next verse.

—L. M. W.

B. Where to Look (vv. 2-4)

2. looking to Jesus, the founder and perfecter of our faith, who for the joy that was set before him endured the cross, despising the shame, and is seated at the right hand of the throne of God.

Our faith is the Christian faith, which replaces the faith the readers have left (or should have left) behind. By his sinless life and atoning death, Jesus is *the founder* of the Christian faith. He is also the one who will bring faith to its complete fulfillment when he returns as *perfecter*.

By mentioning Christ's endurance of *the cross*, the writer may intend to show that Jesus' willingness to suffer human brutality and divine wrath makes him the ideal example of faith as trust in the promises of God. As he suffered, Jesus held fast to the everlasting *joy that was set before him*. As the promise of Heaven fortified his resolve to endure, so it can strengthen us to pursue righteousness in whatever temptation, injustice, and suffering come our way.

In *despising the shame* of an undeserved public crucifixion, Jesus saw the injustice in its right measure: it was of such little weight and brief duration as to be "not worth comparing with the glory" that was to follow (Romans 8:18). As a result, he was seated *at the right hand of the throne of God*. We do well to consider our trials of faith and sufferings in this life as Jesus did!

3, 4. Consider him who endured from sinners such hostility against himself, so that you may not grow weary or fainthearted. In your struggle against sin you have not yet resisted to the point of shedding your blood.

The writer understands that at least some readers are in danger of losing the will to continue enduring the animosity directed against them. But those who follow Christ should contemplate not just the end-result of what Jesus accomplished but also the process as he accomplished it. Jesus "set his face to go to Jerusalem" (Luke 9:51), knowing what would happen to him there. He understood clearly and was dedicated fully to his purpose. Jesus knew there would be hostility, deceit, and fury directed against him. His death was assured and drawing nearer by the hour—yet he set his face toward it.

This is our example; this is our master; *consider him*. Have we as his followers been pressed to the point of personal harm or loss of life? If we ever are so pressed, will it be too much to ask of us? Do we not trust that eternal life awaits, and that the Lord will continue to rule over the world we leave behind? Thus we are called to (re)consider him lest we cease our *struggle against sin* and come to presume as ours the blessings of grace without the cost or discipline of discipleship.

II. Nature of the Race
(HEBREWS 12:5-11)

A. What to Remember (vv. 5, 6)

5, 6. And have you forgotten the exhortation that addresses you as sons?

"My son, do not regard lightly the discipline of the Lord,
nor be weary when reproved by him.

For the Lord disciplines the one he loves, and chastises every son whom he receives."

The phrase *have you forgotten* is written so that it may be understood either as a statement or as a rhetorical question. Either way, the writer warns readers that they are in spiritual danger if they forget who they are in Christ: children of God. Proverbs 3:11, 12, quoted here, culminates a passage that calls the believer to a life of wisdom grounded in trust in, fear of, and honor toward the Lord. This exhortation brings a mild rebuke. But it is also a word of encouragement in that *the discipline of the Lord* is itself evidence of the believers' status and value as children of the loving Father.

Jewish teachers like to set Proverbs 3:11, 12 alongside Lamentations 3:40 ("Let us test and examine our ways, and return to the Lord") and Psalm 94:12 ("Blessed is the man whom you discipline, O Lord, and whom you teach out of your law"). Just as old-covenant believers were called to discern the Lord's discipline, faithfulness, and love in the hardships of life, so also are new-covenant believers. His chastening springs from love that seeks our highest good; the purpose is to lead us to be like his Son in our virtues.

In drawing the relation between discipline and sonship, the writer recalls a theme highlighted earlier: "For it was fitting that he, for whom and by whom all things exist, in bringing many sons to glory, should make the founder of their salvation perfect through suffering" (Hebrews 2:10; compare also "founder" in 12:2). Jesus was made perfect by remaining faithful throughout the course of his sinless life and especially by his sacrificial suffering and death on the cross. The writer's point in both Hebrews 2:10 and 12:5, 6 is that if Jesus was made perfect through sufferings, then we should not think that we will reach the completeness that God desires of us apart from sufferings.

B. What to Expect (vv. 7-11)

7, 8. It is for discipline that you have to endure. God is treating you as sons. For what son is there whom his father does not discipline? If you are left without discipline, in

Visual for Lesson 9. *Start a discussion by pointing to the compass as you ask, "What other images can illustrate the truths you read on the right?"*

which all have participated, then you are illegitimate children and not sons.

The writer draws out clearly the application of Proverbs 3:11, 12: discipline is part of a father's responsibility toward and relationship with his children. The child that is *without discipline* is a child that is not loved well. Thus the writer is pressing the readers to accept that the divine discipline they have endured and will endure is to be expected and indeed welcomed. Such discipline speaks to the legitimacy of their relationship with their heavenly Father (compare Deuteronomy 8:5; 2 Samuel 7:14).

The writer's point that *all have participated* in discipline parallels the reminder Paul offers in 1 Corinthians 10:13 that "No temptation has overtaken you that is not common to man." As creatures who bear the image of God, we are intelligent, free, and therefore morally responsible. We know the difference between good and evil, between right and wrong. Even if the most ethical choice is not immediately clear in certain situations, still we are granted the gift and burden of responsibility for our actions.

We live in a morally ordered world (at least in original design, if not in everyday practice). The moral order of creation is grounded in the moral character of God himself. We may at times be tempted to complain that our punishment is greater than we can bear (compare Genesis 4:13). But the reality that God grants us the power to make decisions—some with eternal consequences—means that we must accept our responsibility for those decisions. This is true not only for Christians but for humanity as a whole (not including children who are yet to reach their age of moral accountability before God).

It is appropriate also to note that Paul's assertion in 1 Corinthians 10:13 regarding temptation as a universal experience is joined with the encouragement that "God is faithful, and he will not let you be tempted beyond your ability, but with the temptation he will provide the way of escape, that you may be able to endure it." We who are children of God are called to endure suffering, resist temptation, and prove ourselves in testing. We can do so when we recall our status in Christ, God's love as it desires our highest good, and his faithfulness toward us in every situation in life.

9. Besides, this, we have had earthly fathers who disciplined us and we respected them. Shall we not much more be subject to the Father of spirits and live?

The Bible speaks to the subject of parental discipline of children in several places (examples: Proverbs 13:24; 22:6, 15; 23:13, 14; 29:15, 17; Ephesians 6:4). If we respectfully received the training by which our human fathers sought to prepare us to live effective and responsible lives, then so much more we should respectfully receive the training for life from *the Father of spirits*! The Creator is investing himself in us for our good.

◆ *Discipline with a Goal* ◆

My preteen son angrily stomped down the hallway after I sent him to his room for misbehavior.

I heard a thump and then silence. When I went to investigate, I saw a foot-sized hole in the door to his sister's room. His face registered my own surprise: he had not realized that he was strong enough to produce a hole in the door by kicking it.

I sat down on the bed next to him and told him that he would have to pay for a new door and help his dad install it. He nodded in agreement. I said, "I'm not angry at you. I know people get mad sometimes. I just want you to learn how to control that anger and frustration because someday you probably will be a husband and a father. Someday you will be so frustrated with your wife or your children that if you have not learned how to tame your anger and deal with it in a healthy way, you may hurt them."

I allowed him to experience the consequences of his out-of-control anger when he was young and the stakes were low so that he will not falter after he grows up and the stakes are very high. I discipline him out of love.

God's discipline is also rooted in love. He desires that we live holy lives that point others to him. Do you accept his discipline in that regard, or do you resist it?

—L. M. W.

10. For they disciplined us for a short time as it seemed best to them, but he disciplines us for our good, that we may share his holiness.

The Lord, through the writer of the book of Hebrews, clearly states his objective in our discipline: *that we may share his holiness* (compare 1 Peter 1:15, 16). Whether God is making use of the hardships of life in a fallen world or is himself bringing testing or correction upon us, he does so out of love for us as sons or daughters; he does so for our maturing in Christlike holiness; he does so in his faithfulness to us; and he does so for our highest good and his greatest glory.

To refuse to subject ourselves to his discipline is to demonstrate a prideful distrust in his character and wisdom. We are called instead to trust his character and promises (Hebrews 11), to humble ourselves before him (James 4:7-10), and to obey his Word (John 14:23).

11. For the moment all discipline seems painful rather than pleasant, but later it yields

the peaceful fruit of righteousness to those who have been trained by it.

Divine discipline is never pleasant as one undergoes it. The way it confronts the presumptions of our hearts can create intensely difficult internal conflicts. But if we work honestly through those hard conversations between our will and our conscience, then the Lord promises us *the peaceful fruit of righteousness.* The goal of God's discipline is the purity of a self-disciplined heart. The Lord is more interested in our character than in our comfort, and we do well to align our priorities with his. May we resolve to discern and be faithful to his purposes in us and for us; this is the path of true, abundant life.

> *What Do You Think?*
> How would you convince a new Christian that life in Christ is worth the pain that comes with it?
> *Talking Points for Your Discussion*
> - Regarding the necessary discipline from the heavenly Father
> - Regarding earthly opposition from unbelievers
> - Regarding spiritual opposition from Satan

III. Recharging in the Race
(HEBREWS 12:12, 13)

12, 13. Therefore lift your drooping hands and strengthen your weak knees, and make straight paths for your feet, so that what is lame may not be put out of joint but rather be healed.

The word *therefore* indicates that we have arrived at the author's summary of this unit of thought. The summary is based in exhortations from Isaiah 35:3 and the old Greek version of Proverbs 4:26.

The writer draws from these Old Testament passages to show the better way. To succumb to discouragement is to weaken in faith and turn aside from the right and good path of following Christ. The first-century Christian readers of Jewish background are already *lame* in their faith; if they do not now place their feet carefully, they will soon be farther off course and in even worse spiritual health.

By contrast, if the readers will heed this warning and commit themselves again to the discipline of following Christ, they will find their souls *healed.* The promise of Jesus will then be fulfilled once again: "Come to me, all who labor and are heavy laden, and I will give you rest. Take my yoke upon you, and learn from me, for I am gentle and lowly in heart, and you will find rest for your souls. For my yoke is easy, and my burden is light" (Matthew 11:28-30). This is the promise of discipleship.

> *What Do You Think?*
> How can our church do better at encouraging people to get back on the right path?
> *Talking Points for Your Discussion*
> - Concerning those beginning to stray
> - Concerning those whose straying has been lengthy

Conclusion
A. To Seek His Will

We live in a fallen world, and we ourselves are not without sin. The hardships and sufferings of life can bring intense discouragement, even times of despair. But there is a truth that can lift us above discouragement and draw us ever closer to Jesus. That truth is that God can and does work through the hardships of life in a fallen world. He also works directly in his ministry of discipline to lead us to maturity. That maturity, which is Christlike holiness, is for our highest good and for his greatest glory. Seek it!

B. Prayer

Heavenly Father, we confess that we find it difficult to thank you for your discipline. But when that discipline comes, may we see it as the best expression of your love. May we never try to sidestep your discipline. Let us instead look ever to your Son as our model for a spiritually disciplined life. We pray for this in his name. Amen.

C. Thought to Remember
If God is not disciplining you,
then something is wrong!

INVOLVEMENT LEARNING

Enhance your lesson presentation with the reproducible activity page,
available as a free download at www.standardlesson.com.

Into the Lesson

If anyone in your congregation runs regularly or has competed in a marathon, invite that person to your class to be interviewed about these experiences. Mention that bringing samples of running clothes and shoes would be helpful. Give the interviewee a list of possible questions, such as the following: What are some of your most memorable experiences as a runner? What challenges have you had to overcome in preparing for a race? How does what you wear influence how well you run? Do you have techniques that help you if you become discouraged and want to quit? What are some characteristics of successful runners? Allow students also to ask questions. Then say, "The writer of Hebrews also has some good advice for us on how we are to run life's race."

Alternative. Make two copies of the skit, "The Unready Runner," activity from the reproducible page, which you can download. Early in the week, enlist two people to present the skit at the start of class. Ask the person who is the Runner to bring the clothes and items mentioned in the skit. After it is completed, ask, "What do you think the chances are of this runner's completing the race? Which of the runner's choices might prevent a successful race?" After a brief discussion, say, "The writer of Hebrews compares our lives to running a race, and he has some good advice on what we can do to complete the race successfully."

Into the Word

Divide your class into three groups, and give each of them one of the following assignments to complete. *Group 1: Christ's Example.* Read Hebrews 12:1-4. Discuss these questions: What advice does the writer give on how to run the race of life? What can we learn about endurance from Jesus? Why should Jesus' life inspire us to give total commitment to our discipleship? What can cause us to become weary and discouraged? *Group 2: God's*

Discipline. Read Hebrews 12:5-11. Discuss these questions: When God disciplines us, what does it show us about how he feels about us? In what way does discipline confirm that we are God's children? How is God's discipline superior to what we receive from our human fathers? What are some of the benefits of God's discipline? *Group 3: God's Children.* Read Hebrews 12:9-13. Discuss these questions: Since we accept the discipline of human parents, what should our response be when God corrects us? When we are suffering, why is it so hard for us to see any benefit from it? When tempted to complain, what should we do instead? What are some of the benefits of having a proper attitude toward God's discipline of us? Allow time for sharing.

On the board write the question, "Why is God allowing me to suffer in this way?" Then inquire, "Have any of you ever asked this question? From what we've discussed today, what are some possible answers?" The responses may include: God allows us to suffer the consequences for our disobedience; he uses the bad things in our lives to teach us to trust him more; he wants to make us more like Christ as we learn to endure hardship; he wants to develop the "peaceful fruit of righteousness" in our lives.

Into Life

Hand each student a card with the following words: *RUN, LOOK, RESIST, STRIVE, ENDURE, SUBMIT, DO RIGHT.* Then say, "There were a lot of verbs in today's text. Read through this list. Do any of them inspire you to want to do something different in your life? If you had to pick just one to live by this week, which one would it be? Encourage the class to share with each other which word they've chosen and why."

Option. Distribute copies of the "Runner's Checklist" activity from the reproducible page. Encourage students to complete these at home to help them evaluate how well prepared they are for the race of life.

BRAND NEW

DEVOTIONAL READING: Revelation 7:13-17
BACKGROUND SCRIPTURE: Revelation 21:1-8

REVELATION 21:1-8

¹ Then I saw a new heaven and a new earth, for the first heaven and the first earth had passed away, and the sea was no more. ² And I saw the holy city, new Jerusalem, coming down out of heaven from God, prepared as a bride adorned for her husband. ³ And I heard a loud voice from the throne saying, "Behold, the dwelling place of God is with man. He will dwell with them, and they will be his people, and God himself will be with them as their God. ⁴ He will wipe away every tear from their eyes, and death shall be no more, neither shall there be mourning, nor crying, nor pain anymore, for the former things have passed away."

⁵ And he who was seated on the throne said, "Behold, I am making all things new." Also he said, "Write this down, for these words are trustworthy and true." ⁶ And he said to me, "It is done! I am the Alpha and the Omega, the beginning and the end. To the thirsty I will give from the spring of the water of life without payment. ⁷ The one who conquers will have this heritage, and I will be his God and he will be my son. ⁸ But as for the cowardly, the faithless, the detestable, as for murderers, the sexually immoral, sorcerers, idolaters, and all liars, their portion will be in the lake that burns with fire and sulfur, which is the second death."

KEY VERSE

"He will wipe away every tear from their eyes, and death shall be no more, neither shall there be mourning, nor crying, nor pain anymore, for the former things have passed away." —**Revelation 21:4**

Graphic: pialhovik / iStock / Thinkstock

THE SOVEREIGNTY OF GOD

Unit 3: Alpha and Omega

LESSONS 10–13

LESSON AIMS

After participating in this lesson, each learner will be able to:

1. Identify those who escape "the second death" and those who do not.

2. Contrast aspects of the old creation with those of the new creation.

3. Identify one way to shift his or her focus from the current world to the new heaven and earth, and make a plan to do so.

LESSON OUTLINE

Introduction

A. New City

My family and I have lived in several large cities, including Seattle, Los Angeles, and Chicago. A few years ago, we took a trip to interview for my current job in Omaha, a midsized city. We were excited to visit a city of which we knew nothing.

We arrived at night. Our host drove us past a shimmering lake, gleaming tall buildings, a new ballpark where the College World Series is played, and other intriguing sights. We were impressed. Omaha seemed like a clean, vibrant city.

And it is. But having lived in Omaha for several years now, we have seen the other sights too: the scruffy neighborhoods of substandard housing; the once proud mall that is now nearly abandoned; the vacant lots of former gas stations that await environmental cleanup. Omaha is a great city, but it is a mix of the new and the old, the shining and the tarnished, the well-maintained and the dilapidated.

In that regard, Omaha is like most all cities. While Omaha is home to many strong churches and faithful Christians, it is also home to many social problems: gangs, prostitution, homelessness, and drugs. Were someone able to establish a new city that had just the "good" parts, it wouldn't stay that way for long. An Internet search on the subject of *utopian movements* is telling in this regard.

By contrast, John's vision in today's lesson is that of a genuine, eternal utopia. The new Jerusalem is the perfect place, for it is the dwelling place of God and of the Lamb. It is a place of spiritual wholeness, where there will be no more tears and where those who despise God are denied entrance. It is the ultimate, eternally new city, the city of God for all time—the focus of our lesson.

B. Lesson Background

The book of Revelation (not "Revelations") is fittingly the last book in the Bible. It is likely the final book that was written, penned by the apostle John near the end of his life. Very early tradition places the writing in about AD 96. That was the final year of Roman Emperor Domitian's 15-year reign, the year he was assassinated.

John was on the island of Patmos in the Aegean Sea (Revelation 1:9). The island was a barren, rocky place of less than 14 square miles in area. We think that John had been exiled there as punishment for conducting forbidden evangelistic work in the city of Ephesus.

The book of Revelation has three parts. The first chapter relates an appearance of the risen Christ to John on Patmos. This occurred "on the Lord's day" (Revelation 1:10), the day of worship for John. Christ told John that he (John) was to receive visions of glorious and mysterious things. John was to write them down for sending to the churches of seven nearby cities (1:11).

The second part of the book consists of personalized messages to those churches (Revelation 2, 3). We sometimes refer to these as "letters to the seven churches," but they are more than that. Each serves as an introduction to the book as a whole for the named congregations. The third part, chapters 4–22, is John's record of the series of visions he experiences. These are visions of Heaven and its activities, along with prophetic words delivered to John by angels who serve as his guides.

The book of Revelation features a type of literature known as *apocalypse*. That word does not mean "worldwide catastrophe" (as the word is often used in popular media today), but "uncovering of the hidden" and thus "revelation." This book reveals the hidden workings and plans of the Lord God Almighty in the midst of the church's trials and tribulations to give hope to the persecuted. It has been serving this function for nearly 2,000 years, showing readers that evil will not triumph. God has a plan for ending the power of evil emperors and of Satan and his allies.

I. United
(REVELATION 21:1-4)
A. Bride and Groom (vv. 1, 2)

1. Then I saw a new heaven and a new earth, for the first heaven and the first earth had passed away, and the sea was no more.

What John sees as a future reality should be understood in the context of the creation story in Genesis. There we are told that, "In the beginning, God created the heavens and the earth" (Genesis 1:1). The account goes on to tell of a chaotic watery void at the beginning. A primary act of creation was separation of dry land from the seas on the third day (1:9).

John's vision of a new creation differs from the first creation story in a significant way: *the sea was no more*. The seas are hostile places to ancient peoples; the seas seem almost in rebellion against God. But there will be no such terror in the new heaven and earth.

> *What Do You Think?*
> How does the Lord help you cope with the rough seas of life?
> *Talking Points for Your Discussion*
> - When waves take you to undesired places
> - When a riptide undertow threatens your safety
> - When weary from fighting the current
> - Other

The prediction that *the sea was no more* is not new, since it repeats a longstanding prophecy in the Bible (see Isaiah 65:17; 66:22; compare 2 Peter 3:13). Sin has spoiled creation, and God's promised solution is to re-create. This is not simply a "makeover," for the current heaven and earth are to be *passed away*.

◆ FIRST, OUT WITH THE OLD ... ◆

We once lived near a restaurant that was absolutely nasty. We went there a few times because it was cheap and we were poor, but every time we

HOW TO SAY IT

Aegean	A-*jee*-un.
Alpha	*Al*-fa.
apocalypse	uh-*pock*-uh-lips.
Artemis	*Ar*-teh-miss.
Domitian	Duh-*mish*-un.
Ephesus	*Ef*-uh-sus.
Omega	O-*may*-guh or O-*mee*-guh.
Patmos	*Pat*-muss.
utopian	you-*toe*-pea-un.
Zechariah	*Zek*-uh-*rye*-uh.

Visual for Lessons 2 & 10. *Start a discussion by pointing to this visual as you pose the question associated with Revelation 21:4.*

left, I wanted to run home and wash my hands. A thin film of grease, ketchup, and unrecognizable grime seemed to cover everything.

One day, I drove by and saw bulldozers demolishing that restaurant; afterward, a new one was built in its place. The first time I visited it, I felt like I had stepped into a different world. The counters gleamed, the décor looked high class, and the equipment shone. Everyone working there wore smiles and new uniforms. I sighed with relief.

God does his work of reconstruction like that: before the new can come, the old must go. This is just as true for the "old self" of sin (Romans 6:6) as it is for the new Heaven and earth to come. "If anyone is in Christ, he is a new creation. The old has passed away; behold, the new has come" (2 Corinthians 5:17). Which do others most see in you—the old creation or the new?   —L. M. W.

2. And I saw the holy city, new Jerusalem, coming down out of heaven from God, prepared as a bride adorned for her husband.

A major feature of the new heaven and earth now presents itself. The descent of *new Jerusalem* to settle on the earth indicates that Heaven and earth are to be together. God will not dwell in a place that is separated from his people. He will dwell with his people utterly, completely, eternally.

Jerusalem is referred to as *the holy city* six times outside the book of Revelation (see Nehemiah 11:1, 18; Isaiah 48:2; 52:1; Matthew 4:5; 27:53).

Those are idealized descriptions since there always seems to be unholiness present (examples: 2 Kings 21:16; Lamentations 1:8; Micah 1:5). By contrast, the new Jerusalem is holy in all ways and at all times because of the very presence of God.

Isaiah foresaw a time when many would desire to "go up to the mountain of the Lord" to worship him (Isaiah 2:3). "Go up" is a natural thing to say since earthly Jerusalem is at a higher elevation than the surrounding terrain (compare: 1 Kings 12:27, 28; Psalm 24:3; Zechariah 14:16, 17; Matthew 20:17, 18). How surprised Isaiah might be with John's clarifying vision! The mountain of God becomes a city, and it is coming to meet us! This is further clarified in Revelation 21:10, where we are given the impression that the holy city is descending to rest on the top of a mountain. Isaiah 52:1 and 61:10 prefigure the images of the phrase *as a bride adorned for her husband.*

◆ A BEAUTIFUL BRIDE ◆

I remember shopping for a wedding dress. I lived overseas at the time, working as a teacher for a missionary family. Since I loved them like my own family, I asked them to go with me to look at dresses. I preferred a simple, elegant look, but decided to try on an elaborate dress with a hoop skirt and a lot of lace.

When my kindergartner student saw me in it, his eyes grew wide as he said with awe, "You look like a princess!" Everyone chuckled. I didn't like the dress, but his reaction made me feel so beautiful that I was tempted to choose it anyway!

What woman doesn't want to be seen as a beautiful princess on her wedding day? We spend a lot of time and money preparing for it: beauty treatments, manicures, hair styling, and purchase of a dress we will wear once all are part of the process. Even for an inexpensive wedding, we do everything we can to look our best. We want our groom to see us at our finest. What can you do to help the church look her finest for her husband, Jesus, as the great day approaches?   —L. M. W.

B. God and His People (vv. 3, 4)
3a. And I heard a loud voice from the throne saying,

We naturally may think any *voice from the throne* would be that of deity. But that is not necessarily the case, since Revelation 19:5 tells us that "from the throne came a voice saying, 'Praise our God, all you his servants.'" We scarcely can imagine that God would refer to himself as "our God"! It's quite possible that the voice in the verse before us is that of an angel. Elsewhere in this book (especially in chapter 14) they speak in loud voices to make great pronouncements.

3b. "Behold, the dwelling place of God is with man. He will dwell with them, and they will be his people, and God himself will be with them as their God.

The voice announces the significance of the new city. In Old Testament times, *the dwelling place of God* was the portable tabernacle (2 Samuel 7:6) before the temple was built. The tabernacle was actually a tent; the Hebrew word is translated that way in hundreds of places (example: Genesis 4:20). We may struggle to comprehend God as dwelling in a tent inside a city, no matter how perfect and glorious either might be!

But that is not the point here. John's vision is revealing to us a future time when all the things that separate us from perfect fellowship with God will be removed. Will this seem like city-dwelling to us? Perhaps (see Revelation 21:10-27), but it will also have the features of the great throne and the worship room of God, pictured in previous chapters of Revelation. That room is where uncounted multitudes of the saved will be present (see 7:9).

We will be his people and he will be our God, and there will be no physical or spiritual barrier separating us. This is an absolute and eternal future, not a temporary situation like the current separation of Heaven and earth. "And so we will always be with the Lord" (see 1 Thessalonians 4:17).

4. "He will wipe away every tear from their eyes, and death shall be no more, neither shall there be mourning, nor crying, nor pain anymore, for the former things have passed away."

The voice now describes some of the spiritual and emotional aspects of this new situation. The future with God will be a time when death and every other cause of pain and suffering will be no more. This is surely one of the greatest promise-

verses in all the Bible, a verse that we can hold dearly (compare Isaiah 25:8; 35:10; 65:19; Revelation 7:17). Life brings us sorrow, sometimes in an unrelenting fashion. We tell ourselves, "It can't get any worse," and then it does. Sometimes it is the headline news of great tragedies. Often it is the personal news of our families. Christians are not immune from pain and tears.

Imagine this: no more *death . . . mourning . . . crying . . . pain*! No more cause for weeping! The emotional body blows we suffer will cease forever! Just as the old creation is passed away, so are our lives of pain and hardship. How can this be? Won't we remember the past and its pain? John goes on to explain some of the aspects of this in the remainder of the book.

> *What Do You Think?*
> Given that pain is a present reality, how can we use it to grow spiritually?
> *Talking Points for Your Discussion*
> ▪ Regarding physical pain
> ▪ Regarding emotional pain
> ▪ Considering last week's lesson (Hebrews 12)

II. Separated
(REVELATION 21:5-8)
A. New Creation (vv. 5, 6a)

5, 6a. And he who was seated on the throne said, "Behold, I am making all things new." Also he said, "Write this down, for these words are trustworthy and true." And he said to me: "It is done! I am the Alpha and the Omega, the beginning and the end.

If an angel has been speaking in verses 3 and 4, John now hears a different voice that addresses him in a direct and personal way. Twelve times in this book John is told to *write*, and this is the final one. The command comes from the one *seated on the throne*. Combining the image of a throne of authority with other *the Alpha and the Omega* self-designations in this book, we conclude the voice to be that of "the Lord God . . . the Almighty" (1:8).

The *trustworthy and true* fact that the Lord will be *making all things new* is certainly a commentary on all that John is seeing. But there is more here. This is a promise for the readers, a promise so important that John is reminded he must write it down. *I am making all things new*! This promise is needed in John's day as his readers deal with the dark specter of persecution and martyrdom. *I am making all things new*! This promise is needed today for believers struggling to live faithfully for Christ. The pain and heartaches we experience are not the final chapter of our stories. There is a future that has no more pain or tears, a time when all is new and perfect and does not grow old or corrupt.

The Alpha and the Omega (also 22:13) are the first and last letters of the Greek alphabet. So in English, this is like the voice saying, "I am the A and the Z." The concept is repeated when the voice identifies the one speaking as *the beginning and the end*. We take care to note that this is not an attempt to establish beginning and ending points for God's existence or reign. It is saying, rather, that he is the source and the goal of all things.

God was there at the beginning of history with the first creation, and he will there at the end of history as well—at the re-creation of Heaven and earth. He is "the Lord our God the Almighty" who reigns forever (Revelation 19:6; compare Isaiah 44:6; 48:12).

B. Life Water (vv. 6b, 7)

6b. "To the thirsty I will give from the spring of the water of life without payment.

We are not to understand this promise merely to mean that the new Jerusalem will have a safe and abundant water supply. Rather, this is a fulfillment of a promise from the prophet Isaiah, who prophesied spiritual satisfaction for those who seek the Lord (Isaiah 55:1).

We sometimes understand this image to be that of eternal life, and rightly so (John 4:14). But there is more here: in the language of John, the living water is also the Holy Spirit (7:38, 39). No spiritual thirst will go unquenched in the new Heaven and earth. Just as there is direct access to the Lord God and to Christ the Lamb, there will be a lavish abundance of the Holy Spirit to all residents of the new Jerusalem (compare Revelation 22:17).

7. "The one who conquers will have this heritage, and I will be his God and he will be my son.

The theme of overcoming or being victorious is pervasive in the book of Revelation and elsewhere in John's writings (see John 16:33; 1 John 2:13, 14; 4:4; 5:4, 5). It is based on the Greek word *nike* which derives from *Nike*, the name of the Greek winged goddess of victory. (It's also the same word trademarked today as a line of athletic apparel.) To overcome is to conquer and be victorious.

Each of the greetings to the seven churches in chapters 2 and 3 ends with a promise to the one who overcomes: permission to eat from the tree of life (Revelation 2:7), immunity from the second death (2:11), a new name (2:17), authority to rule the nations (2:26), a white robe (3:5), a part in the new Jerusalem (3:12), and even an invitation to share the great throne of authority (3:21; compare 2:26). All these are summed up in the verse before us, for the one who overcomes is promised *this heritage*.

This is a climactic, all-inclusive promise to the readers, to us. God promises to be our God, and we can consider ourselves his sons and daughters. In this we are "co-heirs with Christ" (Romans 8:17), God's beloved Son.

C. Fire Lake (v. 8)

8. "But as for the cowardly, the faithless, the detestable, as for murderers, the sexually immoral, sorcerers, idolaters, and all liars, their portion will be in the lake that burns with fire and sulfur, which is the second death."

The picture here is that of cosmic housecleaning. Those listed are the opposite of the overcomers, the antithesis of the victorious who have lived faithfully. *The cowardly* are those who have been afraid to commit fully to Jesus and thereby overcome. Similarly, *the faithless* are those who refuse to trust Jesus and follow him.

The word translated *detestable* includes the sense of stench, those who stink of sin. It also has the sense of being polluted and may be inclusive of those who "rob temples" (Romans 2:22). *Murderers* is a category especially pointed to those who have killed the faithful, who cry "O Sovereign Lord, holy and true, how long before you will judge and avenge our blood on those who dwell on the earth?" (Revelation 6:10). Martyrs (those who die for the faith) will not share eternity with their unrepentant killers.

The sexually immoral are especially men who engage in prostitution. They violate God's standards for sexual purity as they perpetrate such degradation. *Sorcerers* seek power through the spiritual forces of evil and are thus completely opposed to God. *Idolaters* constitute an ongoing threat to the church. This problem is underlined by the book's connection with Ephesus (Revelation 2:1-7), for that city is the home of the great temple of the pagan goddess Artemis, also known as Diana (Acts 19:23-41).

The list concludes with a group we might think would be a lesser threat: *liars*. The idea behind this designation is only partly covered by saying that these are people who tell lies. More directly, these are false brothers and sisters, imposters in the church (see 2 Corinthians 11:13; Galatians 2:4; 2 Peter 2:1; Jude 4; Revelation 2:2). God, who knows the hearts of all, will see through any pretense; such frauds will not be allowed into the holy city.

Rather than be admitted into the city, those listed go to a lake of fire as their just punishment. There they will join their true masters: the devil and his associates (Revelation 19:20; 20:10). While even the thought of this eternal abode is unpleasant, its further description is the more chilling: it is *the second death*. To be consigned to *the lake that burns with fire and sulfur* is to be cut off from God and Christ for eternity.

Conclusion
A. One Life

Life seems to gallop by at ever-increasing speed as we age. We cannot slow it down. I have a plaque in my office to remind me of this. It reads:

> *Only one life, 'twill soon be past,*
> *Only what's done for Christ will last.*
> *To me to live is Christ.*

What does the future hold for us, then? John's vision of the new Jerusalem helps us answer this question. We have confidence, for we believe the promises of Revelation "are trustworthy and true" (Revelation 21:5). We have a reward, for we believe we are heirs of the riches of God (v. 7a). Most of all we have an assured hope, for we will have perfect, eternal fellowship with him (v. 7b).

B. Prayer

Eternal God, may we remain true and faithful through all difficulties. May we never forget your promise that you are our God and we are your sons and daughters. May we not fear death, for we know what eternity holds for us. We praise the Son, who makes all this possible and in whose name we pray. Amen.

C. Thought to Remember

Trust the promises of Revelation!

INVOLVEMENT LEARNING

Enhance your lesson presentation with the reproducible activity page,
available as a free download at www.standardlesson.com.

Into the Lesson

Display the first and last letters of the alphabets of English, Greek, Hebrew, and other languages (easy to find on the Internet). Ask, "What do these represent?" After responses, ask, "What do they have to do with today's study?"

Alternative. Distribute copies of the "Old Becomes New" activity from the reproducible page, which you can download. Students can work alone or in pairs.

Into the Word

Call the following activity "The Great Escape." Give each person a card with *ESCAPE* in large letters on the front, *NO ESCAPE* on the back. Say, "I am going to name some groups that are included or implied in today's text. When I mention each one, hold up the correct side of your card to show me whether that group escapes the second death or does not." Use the following list: the one who thirsts spiritually; the one who is cowardly; the one who overcomes; the one who lies; the one who lives in the Holy City; the one who is detestable; the one who is made new; the one who is a murderer; the people of God; the one who practices sorcery; the one who is sexually immoral; the one who practices idolatry.

Then ask the class, "What is something that you consider better in its old form, of which you would say 'Old is better!'?" Allow several answers. Then ask, "What is something that you consider better in its new form, of which you would say 'New is better!'?" Allow several answers. Ask three class members to find and read: 2 Corinthians 5:17; Ephesians 2:11-14; Revelation 2:17 in sequence, without comment. Then affirm, "Wow! Those are some significant new things that are better than the old. Today's text pictures a new creation that is better than the old. How is that true?" Allow learners to examine the text and offer answers. Write the list in full view of the group.

At the end, exclaim, "Now that is a new that is better!"

Option. The "Something New" activity from the reproducible page could be effectively worked into this old vs. new study.

Show a picture of the items below, one at a time, and mention the verse listed with it. Ask how the picture relates to that verse. Mix up the cards so they don't appear in verse order. For verse 1, a card with these letters: *A B D E F G H* ("the C/sea was no more"); for verse 2, a wedding dress ("a bride adorned for her husband"); for verse 3, a CD album of a great singer ("a loud voice"); for verse 4, a box of facial tissues ("wipe away every tear"); for verse 5, a chair ("seated on the throne"); for verse 6, a large book with the first page and the final page marked to be shown ("the beginning and the end"); for verse 6, a bottle of water ("water of life"); for verse 7, a document clearly marked "Last Will and Testament" ("this heritage"); for verse 8, a picture of lava flow ("lake that burns with fire and sulfur").

Into Life

Suggest your learners add these letters and exclamation mark to this month's calendar: *H, E, A, V, E, N, !,* respectively to the days of the week. Propose this as a devotional guide for the month: "On each Sunday, under the *H*, write an idea beginning with *H* that will help you focus on the new creation God has in store. Do the same for Monday through Friday, with their assigned letters. On Saturdays, write a grand truth about the new creation that is worthy of an exclamation mark." Example: Sunday—*H*—Hear God's Word about the future, such as John 14:1-3; Monday—*E*—End! All the troubles of this life will end; Tuesday—*A*—Ask for nothing unless it has eternal value; Wednesday—*V*—Victory in sight; Thursday—*E*—Encourage others to think of God's promises; Friday—*N*—No more mourning, for there is no more death; Saturday—!—Tears will never fall there!

NEW JERUSALEM

DEVOTIONAL READING: Genesis 1:28–2:3
BACKGROUND SCRIPTURE: Revelation 21:9-27

REVELATION 21:9-14, 22-27

⁹ Then came one of the seven angels who had the seven bowls full of the seven last plagues and spoke to me, saying, "Come, I will show you the Bride, the wife of the Lamb." ¹⁰ And he carried me away in the Spirit to a great, high mountain, and showed me the holy city Jerusalem coming down out of heaven from God, ¹¹ having the glory of God, its radiance like a most rare jewel, like a jasper, clear as crystal. ¹² It had a great, high wall, with twelve gates, and at the gates twelve angels, and on the gates the names of the twelve tribes of the sons of Israel were inscribed— ¹³ on the east three gates, on the north three gates, on the south three gates, and on the west three gates. ¹⁴ And the wall of the city had twelve foundations, and on them were the twelve names of the twelve apostles of the Lamb.

· ·

²² And I saw no temple in the city, for its temple is the Lord God the Almighty and the Lamb. ²³ And the city has no need of sun or moon to shine on it, for the glory of God gives it light, and its lamp is the Lamb. ²⁴ By its light will the nations walk, and the kings of the earth will bring their glory into it, ²⁵ and its gates will never be shut by day—and there will be no night there. ²⁶ They will bring into it the glory and the honor of the nations. ²⁷ But nothing unclean will ever enter it, nor anyone who does what is detestable or false, but only those who are written in the Lamb's book of life.

KEY VERSES

I saw no temple in the city, for its temple is the Lord God the Almighty and the Lamb. And the city has no need of sun or moon to shine on it, for the glory of God gives it light, and its lamp is the Lamb.

—Revelation 21:22, 23

Photo: papparaffie / iStock / Thinkstock

The Sovereignty of God

Unit 3: Alpha and Omega
LESSONS 10–13

LESSON AIMS

After participating in this lesson, each learner will be able to:

1. List features of the Jerusalem that descends "out of heaven from God."

2. Describe the function of "the Lamb's book of life" and locate other references to it.

3. Describe one way that the lesson text should change one's attitude or behavior, and make a plan to implement that change.

LESSON OUTLINE

Introduction
  A. Firm Foundations
  B. Lesson Background
I. Holy City from the Outside (REVELATION 21:9-14)
  A. Angel and Bride (v. 9)
  B. Spirit and Glory (vv. 10, 11)
  C. Wall and Gates (vv. 12-14)
II. Holy City from the Inside (REVELATION 21:22-27)
  A. No Need for a Temple (v. 22)
  B. No Need for Sun or Moon (vv. 23, 24)
    Life Without Light
  C. No Need for Closed Gates (vv. 25-27)
    Parade of Nations
Conclusion
  A. Eternal Temple
  B. Prayer
  C. Thought to Remember

Introduction

A. Firm Foundations

Houses are built on many types of foundations. A very old house we owned in Tennessee was built on a brick foundation. This did not prove to be durable, for part of it collapsed, causing the front of the house to sag. Our house in Seattle was built on a hill that was actually debris from an ancient glacier. This was prone to washing away, and several houses on our cul-de-sac had ongoing foundation issues. Our home in Nebraska is apparently built on dirt fill that was used to level the lots in the subdivision. This makes these homes susceptible to settling, something that has cracked and distorted our driveway but not damaged the house itself (so far).

Jesus used the idea of a firm foundation in his great parable of houses built on rock and sand (Matthew 7:24-27). The analogy explained why lives must be founded on obedience to Jesus. The strength of a foundation and the ground on which it is built are huge factors in a house's longevity. Crumbling brick, eroding dirt, or settling fill are not the best choices for a house intended to last.

Today's lesson describes the new Jerusalem and some features of its construction. It has massive walls, and it is built on the rock of a mountain. We expect nothing less for a city intended to last forever.

B. Lesson Background

Cities of the ancient world were established with three primary concerns: access to water, access to trade routes, and defensibility. Regarding the last, cities were usually built on high ground. Combined with the added height of the city's walls, this gave a strong tactical advantage to the defenders of the city. Attackers had to advance uphill, making them easier targets for city defenders to shoot arrows and hurl stone from atop the ramparts (compare 2 Chronicles 26:15).

A strong wall and gate system not only permitted an able defense, they deterred many would-be attackers from even considering an attempt to conquer a city. Walls defined the city's fortified footprint, and the walls' gates controlled access.

The walls could be massive. Excavations reveal that the rampart walls of Nebuchadnezzar's Babylon were some 300 feet high and as much as 80 feet thick at the base. Supposedly there was enough width at the top to allow chariot races up there! Such walls made the city virtually impregnable to direct attack and contributed to the city's grandeur and prestige.

All this helps us understand why John's vision reveals the new Jerusalem to be a city with tremendous walls and gates. For John and his first-century readers, the greatest city imaginable would have an imposing outward appearance. The new Jerusalem of his vision was not a figment of his imagination. Even so, we should not take every detail of its description as a physical characteristic, since the Bible does contain figurative or symbolic language (examples: Galatians 4:24-26; Hebrews 9:9).

Using words describing ultimates (entirely pure gold; Revelation 21:18) and perfection (cube shaped; 21:16), John's vision is of the unimaginable dwelling place of God to be available to humanity. With its tree of life (22:2), the city is something of an "Eden restored," but not as a pristine garden. It is a city, a place with plenty of room for the great multitudes of the saved (7:9).

I. Holy City from the Outside

(Revelation 21:9-14)

Revelation 19:9 records the blessing on those "invited to the marriage supper of the Lamb." In that context, the Bride of Christ is ready to be revealed, clothed in "fine linen, bright and pure" (19:8). But we do not see her then. Instead, the bridegroom (Christ the Lamb) is delayed, for he is called to fight a great heavenly battle (19:11-19).

The battle results in the capture of the beast and the defeat of his allies, followed by their judgment. The sentence of the beast and his companion, the false prophet, is to be thrown into the lake of fire (Revelation 19:20). They are later to be joined there by the devil (20:10) and by others who are not among the saved (20:15; 21:8). With the delay caused by the need for the Lamb to lead a victorious heavenly army now over, the Bride is revealed.

A. Angel and Bride (v. 9)

9. Then came one of the seven angels who had the seven bowls full of the seven last plagues and spoke to me, saying, "Come, I will show you the Bride, the wife of the Lamb."

This book features three cycles of sevens: breaking of seals (Revelation 6:1–8:5), blowing of trumpets (8:6–11:19), and pouring out of *bowls* (15:1–16:21). The breaking, blowing, and pouring trigger events that John then sees in his visions. The third of the three series concerns *plagues* that symbolize the wrath of God (15:1; 16:1).

When these plagues are poured out, this judgmental wrath of God is finished (Revelation 15:1; 16:17). The final plague is a catastrophic earthquake accompanied by massive hailstones; the result is the destruction of Babylon, the city in rebellion against God (16:19). Babylon is very likely symbolic of the city of Rome (compare 1 Peter 5:13), the greatest city the world has seen to John's time. It is the seat of a government that persecutes God's people. It is fitting, then, for one of the angels who assists in that city's demise to be John's guide to reveal the new Jerusalem, *the Bride.*

What Do You Think?

If an angel said to your community "I will show you the bride" while pointing to your congregation, what would you want people to see?

Talking Points for Your Discussion

- With regard to purity
- With regard to devotion to the bridegroom
- Other

B. Spirit and Glory (vv. 10, 11)

10. And he carried me away in the Spirit to a great, high mountain, and showed me the holy city Jerusalem coming down out of heaven from God.

For John to be *in the Spirit* indicates the beginning of a new visionary event (see also Revelation 1:10; 4:2; 17:3; compare 2 Corinthians 12:1-4). To be *carried . . . away* gives him the experience of moving to a different location so he can see what is next to be revealed. This is something of a repeat of John's encounter with the new Jerusalem as related in Revelation 21:2, last week's lesson. The emphasis there is on hearing things that are said. Now the emphasis is visual.

The vision begins with John's locating the scene on *a great, high mountain.* This gives the impression of a lofty peak that tops the immense bulk of a mountain that covers many square miles of land (compare Ezekiel 40:2; Matthew 4:8). This towering mountain is met by *the holy city Jerusalem* as the latter descends. Heaven and earth are meeting, a central feature of the new Heaven and the new earth (compare Revelation 21:1, 2, last week's lesson).

> **What Do You Think?**
> How can we make our "mountaintop experiences" have lasting spiritual impact?
> *Talking Points for Your Discussion*
> - In the context of the natural world (real mountains)
> - In the context of church endeavors
> - In the context of family activities
> - Considering Matthew 17:1-13; Hebrews 12:22-24; 2 Peter 1:18

11. having the glory of God, its radiance like a most rare jewel, like a jasper, clear as crystal.

It's hard to imagine the detailed description of the new city beginning on a higher note! Above all, the city shines with *the glory of God,* a divine *radiance* caused by the Lord's presence (compare Isaiah 60:1, 2, 19).

John tries to describe this for the readers, who have never experienced God's glory (compare Isaiah 66:18; John 17:24). John can only say that it is like seeing the brilliance of one of the most beautiful of gems, *a most rare jewel.*

He chooses *jasper* (a variety of chalcedony) to embody this description. This stone is well known and beloved in the ancient world (compare Exodus 28:20; 39:13; Ezekiel 28:13; Revelation 4:3; 21:18, 19). But this particular stone is unlike any jasper that John's readers have ever seen, for it is *clear as crystal,* not veined or speckled. This implies shining luminosity, helping to explain the radiance and light of the city.

C. Wall and Gates (vv. 12-14)

12, 13. It had a great, high wall, with twelve gates, and at the gates twelve angels, and on the gates the names of the twelve tribes of the sons of Israel were inscribed—on the east three gates, on the north three gates, on the south three gates, and on the west three gates.

Combined with Revelation 21:16 (not in today's text), these two verses tell us that John is seeing a cube-shaped city. Three similar gates on each of the four walls indicates symmetry. The gates may be spaced evenly along the length of the walls.

An alternative arrangement is for the gates to be grouped together, perhaps as a three-fold gate at the center of each wall. Such a triple gate has been found on the southern wall of the temple mount in Jerusalem, still visible today. These gates represent a later rebuilding, but it is likely that such a triple gate was used to enter the city during the time of Jesus. If so, John's vision may be for him a certain déjà vu experience, as in "I've seen this pattern before!"

As with many things in John's description, the gates have symbolic meaning. *The twelve tribes of the sons of Israel* (another name for the patriarch Jacob, see Genesis 49:1-28) are scattered in John's day (compare James 1:1). That has been the case for hundreds of years. But now he sees the perfect city with the gathered and reunited tribes (compare Exodus 28:17-21; 39:10-14; Revelation 7:4-8). The dispersion is ended, and everyone is invited to come home. Each tribe will even find a special gate with its name on it. There is no service entrance or back gate here. All who are admitted are of equal dignity.

14. And the wall of the city had twelve foundations, and on them were the twelve names of the twelve apostles of the Lamb.

Ancient city walls have huge stones at their base. These are *foundations,* chiseled to precise shapes to anchor the wall for stability. Here, such stones form symbolic counterparts to the gates of verse 12 above, for they bear *the twelve names of the twelve apostles of the Lamb.* The city is thus made up of the Old Testament people of God (signified by the 12 tribes) and the New Testament people of God (signified by the 12 apostles).

II. Holy City from the Inside

(Revelation 21:22-27)

John next watches an angel measure the city's walls to be 12,000 stadia in length (Revelation 21:15, 16, not in today's text). Just short of 1,400 miles, that is approximately the straight-line distance from New York City to Dallas, Texas! The dimensions of the new Jerusalem point to its divine origin. The further description of the city's gates as being each carved from a gigantic pearl (21:21) is the reason we commonly refer to the gates of Heaven as "the pearly gates."

A. No Need for a Temple (v. 22)

22. And I saw no temple in the city, for its temple is the Lord God the Almighty and the Lamb.

Our lesson text now takes us to what John sees within the city. His first observation is striking if we have been reading the previous chapters of the book: there is *no temple in the city*. In earlier visions, John saw the temple of Heaven several times (example: Revelation 15:5), and even was told to measure it (11:1). But that was in "old" Heaven. In the "new" Heaven, there is no need for a place for people to go to worship God. The permanent and immediate presence of *the Lord God the Almighty and the Lamb* make this unnecessary. In this way, they themselves are *its temple*.

The most important feature of the earthly Jerusalem's temple was (past tense, since it lies in ruins as John writes) its inner sanctuary, the holy of holies. But there are no "levels" of holiness here, for the holiness of God makes the entire city a temple or tabernacle (Revelation 21:3).

HOW TO SAY IT

Babylon	*Bab*-uh-lun.
chalcedony	kal-*suh*-din-ee
	or **kal**-sah-**doe**-nee.
Corinthians	Ko-*rin*-thee-unz (*th* as in *thin*).
Ezekiel	Ee-*zeek*-ee-ul or Ee-*zeek*-yul.
Isaiah	Eye-*zay*-uh.
Jerusalem	Juh-*roo*-suh-lem.
Nebuchadnezzar	*Neb*-yuh-kud-**nez**-er.
Zechariah	Zek-uh-**rye**-uh.

What Do You Think?

How can we relate the future fact of God as the temple with the current reality that we as the church are God's temple (2 Corinthians 6:14–7:1; Ephesians 2:21, 22; etc.)?

Talking Points for Your Discussion

- As a witness for fellow believers to see
- As a witness for unbelievers to see

B. No Need for Sun or Moon (vv. 23, 24)

23. And the city has no need of sun or moon to shine on it, for the glory of God gives it light, and its lamp is the Lamb.

John's old-creation cosmology must change! He is familiar, of course, with the account of God's creation of the *sun* to be the dominant light source and the *moon* to serve a similar but lesser role (Genesis 1:16-18). This arrangement is no more.

Even so, the absence of sun and moon do not result in a darkened city. The reasons seem to be two in number at first glance. But looking at the text closely leads us to conclude that the two reasons are really one and the same. *The glory of God* is the idea of his presence being experienced as brilliant illumination (compare: Isaiah 60:1-3, 19, 20; Luke 2:9). The same thing in different words is the fact that *its lamp is the Lamb*. The word translated *lamp* is the word used for the flame of an oil lamp (compare Mark 4:21; John 5:35; Revelation 18:23). The Lamb is pictured as such an overpowering flame that the entire city is illuminated.

◆ Life Without Light ◆

My husband and I spent our first year of marriage living in Ukraine. Because of energy shortages, the local government rationed electricity by turning it off every evening. The lights would go out just about the time the sun had set completely, so we kept on hand candles, a lighter, etc.

At first, complete darkness was an adventure. But before long we felt imprisoned inside our apartment, since leaving the house meant navigating a completely darkened city. I was in a stairwell without a flashlight on one occasion, and I sensed someone on the landing above me. So I stuck close

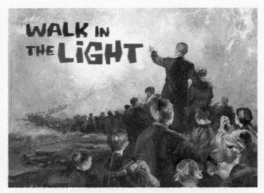

Visual for Lesson 11. *Start a discussion by pointing to this imperative as you ask, "How do we know when we're doing this and when we are not?"*

to the right side and listened to his (or her) breathing and footsteps as we passed in pitch black.

Living where electricity was a precious commodity taught me the importance of light by its absence. But we will not have to depend on electricity or sun or moon in the new Jerusalem. Jesus himself will be the eternal light! But isn't he that right now, even when (or especially when) earthly darkness surrounds us? See John 8:12.

—L. M. W.

24. By its light will the nations walk, and the kings of the earth will bring their glory into it,

John now describes fulfillment of Isaiah 60:3-5, which foresees a time when more than just the people of Israel will stream to the city of God. Peoples from *the nations* are coming, and their rulers contribute to the city's majesty by bringing and yielding their own *glory*. We get the sense here that this action is irresistible. *The kings of the earth* are drawn to the city even though they realize that they themselves will neither rule nor receive adoration. Their status pales in comparison with the glory of God and the Lamb.

We are reminded of Revelation 4:10, 11, where the elders "cast their crowns before the throne." The kings are doing something similar, for their authority counts for nothing in this city. They will be grouped with all the rest of the city's servants—no higher, no lower (22:3).

C. No Need for Closed Gates (vv. 25-27)

25. and its gates will never be shut by day—and there will be no night there.

The *gates* of ancient cities are normally open during daylight hours and closed when darkness falls. Since there is to be *no night* in the new city, the old practice of gate closure will not apply (Isaiah 60:11; Zechariah 14:7; Revelation 22:5). We should remember, though, that each gate is guarded by an angel (Revelation 21:12; compare Genesis 3:24), so this is not a case of uncontrolled access. Later we will be told about those who "may enter the city by the gates" (Revelation 22:14) in contrast with those who are left "outside" (22:15).

Some students claim that the image of gates that are eternally open means that, in the end, all people will enter—all will somehow come to repentance and be saved. But this is not the image we are given in the last chapters of this book, where some are in the city and others are outside and in the lake of fire (Revelation 21:8, lesson 10).

> **What Do You Think?**
> In what ways can we make sure the doors of our church are not shut in a welcoming sense?
> *Talking Points for Your Discussion*
> - To those seeking God
> - To those seeking acceptance
> - To those needing help
> - Considering Romans 16:17-19; 1 Corinthians 5

26. They will bring into it the glory and the honor of the nations.

John repeats his assertion that the rulers of the earth will bring *the glory and the honor of the nations* with them, since *they* refers to the kings of Revelation 21:24, above. This creates a mental image of a public parade of royalty who are attired in their best garb that is reserved for official occasions.

They do not come to be admired, however, but to offer their best to the ruler of the new city and acknowledge him as God and king (compare Psalm 72:10, 11). We are given the impression that this is the fullest expression of worship they can offer. Perhaps we see the visit of the foreign wise men to worship the newborn King Jesus as prefiguring this (Matthew 2:11). John does not make this connection, however.

◆ *Parade of Nations* ◆

The Games of the XXXI Olympiad will be history by the time of this lesson. If it is like previous games, it will have featured a Parade of Nations in the opening ceremony, when smiling athletes from every corner of the globe marched into the arena. The ceremony proclaims camaraderie as athletes from countries hostile to one another converge peacefully. The feeling of goodwill displayed tends to be infectious.

What a wonderful opening ceremony it will be when the glory and honor of the nations parades into the new Jerusalem! As the rulers of the earth enter, we can imagine that they are accompanied by those who have been redeemed from "every tribe and language and people and nation" (Revelation 5:9). Believers from every place on earth will gather, their cultural finery giving glory to the creativity of God.

Unlike the Olympics, though, the Parade of Nations during Heaven's opening ceremony will not be a prelude to competition and disappointment. There will be no disgruntled athletes and commentators to tweet about substandard lodging or mistakes in judging as in every Olympics. The beauty of the nations will glorify God, for he has created that beauty.   —L. M. W.

27. But nothing unclean will ever enter it, nor anyone who does what is detestable or false, but only those who are written in the Lamb's book of life.

Having celebrated the glory of those entering the city, John now gives a general summary of the characteristics of those to be denied entrance. Fuller descriptions may be found in 1 Corinthians 6:9, 10; Revelation 21:8 (lesson 10); and 22:15 (lesson 13). The unrepentant, morally filthy noncitizens are identical with those not listed in *the Lamb's book of life* and therefore forbidden from entering the city. This vitally important book is mentioned also in Exodus 32:32, 33; Psalm 69:28; Daniel 12:1; Philippians 4:3; Revelation 3:5; 13:8; 17:8; 20:12, 15. The names in it have been written

there "from the foundation of the world" (Revelation 17:8). The holy city will be just that—holy.

> *What Do You Think?*
> How can we use various familiar listings to illustrate to others the importance of being named in the Lamb's book of life?
> *Talking Points for Your Discussion*
> - Immigration records at Ellis Island
> - A *Who's Who* publication
> - A preferred guest list
> - Voting rolls for a community
> - Other

Conclusion
A. Eternal Temple

A church in my city is disbanding. For many reasons and for many years, its numbers have dwindled and its finances deteriorated. Another church is buying the building to establish a satellite campus. But the building needs a lot of work before that can happen. It looks great on the outside, but close inspection reveals years of delayed maintenance and neglect. The shell of the building is impressive, but the insides are rotten.

Delayed maintenance, crumbling infrastructures, etc., are ongoing problems in our realm of existence. We build great things, but they don't last forever. But the picture John gives is of a worship reality that will never grow old. It needs no building to house services, because the Lord is its temple. It needs no electrical upgrade, because the Lord is its light. It is a place prepared for us, where we will never grow old either. When we have been there 10,000 years, we will be just beginning!

B. Prayer

Holy God, we thank you for giving us great hope through John's great vision! Give us strength to endure as we await the day when we join you in the eternal, holy city. We pray this in the name of the Lamb who makes this possible. Amen.

C. Thought to Remember

Make sure your name
is in the Lamb's book of life.

INVOLVEMENT LEARNING

Enhance your lesson presentation with the reproducible activity page,
available as a free download at www.standardlesson.com.

Into the Lesson

If you have computer projection capabilities, show video segments from National Geographic's Jerusalemthemovie.com or from vimeo.com/15034110. If you do, say, "Now you have seen old Jerusalem as you came down upon it; now let's see New Jerusalem from John's perspective, as it comes down upon us from Heaven!"

Alternative. Distribute copies of the "Old Jerusalem" activity from the reproducible page, which you can download to use as an introductory study.

Into the Word

Search online for a printable cube pattern, which will look something like the illustration below. Prepare a copy for each learner.

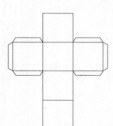

Then distribute the following attributes of John's description in Revelation 21 of the new Jerusalem, on separate slips randomly to learners:

1. the Lamb's wife; 2. coming down out of Heaven; 3. surrounded by a great, high wall; 4. with 12 gates; 5. with inscriptions of the names of the 12 tribes of Israel; 6. each gate is pearly, as if carved from a giant pearl; 7. characterized by a shining luminosity; 8. has three gates on each wall facing the four directions; 9. wall sits on 12 foundation stones; 10. names of the 12 apostles are on the 12 foundation stones; 11. has no temple structure; 12. needs no external light sources; 13. has citizens from all nations; 14. kings will bring their glory to it, but will give that glory to God; 15. each side of the "cube" city is 12,000 furlongs in length; 16. the Lamb himself provides all the light needed; 17. no evil thing or deed is found therein; 18. the gates are never closed; 19. the residents are all those named in the Lamb's book of life; 20. the streets are made of transparent golden glass.

Say, "We are going to have read several attributes of the new Jerusalem, as described by John in Revelation 21. As they are read, I may have a comment or question, but for each one I want you to identify in which verse or verses these descriptions can be found. Then I want you to choose up to 12 statements you will add to your squares on your sheet, two per square. Write them in as we go. Decide which of the attributes are impressive to you; make your choices."

Call on learners randomly to read their phrases or sentences. Ask any questions; make any explanatory commentary as needed. Be certain to pin each descriptor to a verse or verses, noting that some of the elements are not in verses of the printed text. At the end, suggest, "Sometime later today, cut out and fold your shape into a cube and tape it. Keep the cube close by for a few days as a reminder."

Ask, "What does the cube-shaped sheet you have been using have to do with today's text?" The answer, of course, relates to the "foursquare," cubic shape of the new Jerusalem as John sees it.

Option. Ask learners to relate the list and the image on the reproducible page under "New Jerusalem." They will easily see the difficulty John has in describing the new city, even as the artist had in preparing his image.

Into Life

Point out that the concept of *bringing glory/glory and honor* is included twice in today's text, in verses 24 and 26. Then ask, "What are some ways to demonstrate the glory of Christ by honoring him in such ways that others will see him in us?"

Encourage free discussion as your learners suggest ideas. Jot ideas on the board. Challenge learners to pick one idea each to work into their lives in the week ahead.

LIVING
WATERS

DEVOTIONAL READING: Psalm 46
BACKGROUND SCRIPTURE: Revelation 22:1-7

REVELATION 22:1-7

¹ Then the angel showed me the river of the water of life, bright as crystal, flowing from the throne of God and of the Lamb ² through the middle of the street of the city; also, on either side of the river, the tree of life with its twelve kinds of fruit, yielding its fruit each month. The leaves of the tree were for the healing of the nations. ³ No longer will there be anything accursed, but the throne of God and of the Lamb will be in it, and his servants will worship him. ⁴ They will see his face, and his name will be on their foreheads. ⁵ And night will be no more. They will need no light of lamp or sun, for the Lord God will be their light, and they will reign forever and ever.

⁶ And he said to me, "These words are trustworthy and true. And the Lord, the God of the spir-

its of the prophets, has sent his angel to show his servants what must soon take place."

⁷ "And behold, I am coming soon. Blessed is the one who keeps the words of the prophecy of this book."

KEY VERSE

Then the angel showed me the river of the water of life, bright as crystal, flowing from the throne of God and of the Lamb. —**Revelation 22:1**

THE SOVEREIGNTY OF GOD

Unit 3: Alpha and Omega
LESSONS 10–13

LESSON AIMS

After participating in this lesson, each learner will be able to:

1. State characteristics and function of the river of life.

2. Compare and contrast Revelation 22:1-7 with Genesis 2:8-10 and Ezekiel 47:1-12.

3. Prepare a devotional of hope based on Revelation 22:1-7, and submit it for publication in his or her church's newsletter.

LESSON OUTLINE

Introduction
  A. Life Extenders
  B. Lesson Background
 I. What John Sees (REVELATION 22:1-5)
  A. Water of Life (v. 1)
    Consider the Source
  B. Tree of Life (vv. 2a, b)
  C. Leaves of Healing (v. 2c)
  D. Absence of Curse (v. 3a)
  E. Servants of God (vv. 3b-5)
    The Problem of Night
 II. What John Hears (REVELATION 22:6, 7)
  A. Angel Speaks (v. 6)
  B. Jesus Speaks (v. 7)
Conclusion
  A. The Beginning and the End
  B. Prayer
  C. Thought to Remember

Introduction

A. Life Extenders

How long do you expect to live? A person born in 1850 in America had an average life expectancy of less than 40 years. That statistic is skewed, however, by a high infant mortality rate. Those born in 1850 who managed to live to be 5 years old (thus avoiding the many deadly illnesses that claimed young children) could expect to live to their mid-50s.

Today's life expectancy is between 75 and 82 years, depending on race and gender. The sharp increase is due to better medical treatment, chlorination of drinking water, etc. Yet some people want to extend their lives even further. They work hard to eat healthy food, maintain high fitness levels, etc. Predictions are that we will continue to see a greater percentage of our fellow citizens in their 90s and 100s than ever before.

The Bible tells the story of the paradise of Eden that was lost to humanity because of sin. In this garden was the tree of life, and eating its fruit would allow men and women to live forever (see Genesis 2:9, 3:22). When Adam and Eve sinned, they were expelled from the garden and denied access to this tree (2:17; 3:22-24). Death has been a certainty for every child born ever since (with the two exceptions in Genesis 5:24 and 2 Kings 2:11). What if we could have that life-giving fruit? Today's lesson pictures just such an opportunity in John's vision of the new Jerusalem.

B. Lesson Background

The image of *water* is used in both physical and spiritual senses in the Bible. In a physical sense, fresh (sweet) water has as its opposite water that is brackish (bitter). Fresh water sustains life (Judges 15:18, 19; Job 38:25-27); water that is brackish or absent altogether yields the opposite (Deuteronomy 8:15; 2 Kings 2:19-22). The ultra-salty Dead Sea is aptly named!

The prophets Ezekiel and Zechariah had visions that bear similarities to John's vision of the new Jerusalem. A feature of the city foreseen by Ezekiel and Zechariah was that of a river flowing out of it. The water of this river is so refreshing that it not only nourishes life, it changes the ultra-salty Dead Sea into a freshwater lake (Ezekiel 47:8; Zechariah 14:8; compare Joel 3:18). In Revelation, the idea of spiritual water includes the property of eternal life. Such water is seen as a divine gift, an ever-flowing fountain that provides life to those who drink of it (see Revelation 7:17; 22:17).

Another feature of the new Jerusalem drawn from the Old Testament is a *tree of life*. This mysterious tree is referred to in three books in the Bible. It first appears as an important part of the Garden of Eden (Genesis 2:9). A (but not "the") tree of life is also mentioned four times in the book of Proverbs as metaphors for divine wisdom (Proverbs 3:18), the fruit of righteousness (11:30), desire fulfilled (13:12), and a properly used tongue (15:4).

Finally, *the tree of life* is mentioned in Revelation as a primary feature of "the paradise of God" (Revelation 2:7). We might call this paradise *Eden restored* as people eat the fruit of the tree with God's blessing.

I. What John Sees
(REVELATION 22:1-5)
A. Water of Life (v. 1)

1a. Then the angel showed me the river of the water of life, bright as crystal,

As we pick up where last week's lesson ended, John is still inside the holy city, the new Jerusalem of his vision. He is still being guided by an angel of the seven bowls of Revelation 21:9.

John sees a river, and his descriptions of it signify two things. First, the river's purity and clarity indicate that anything that might pollute it has been banished from the city. This water is not muddy or cloudy. It does not have the greenish tinge of algae, as stagnant water might have. We can imagine that it gives off no bad smell (contrast Exodus 7:21). The city of pure gold (Revelation 21:21) features a river of pure water.

Second, the river's designation as *the water of life* implies much more than a refreshing source of water for a parched throat. The water has divine qualities, and we do not sense that John is surprised by this. He seems to expect to find this river of life in the new city. His vision is that of a great

urban complex combined with a garden paradise. No garden would be lush and inviting without a proper water source.

◆ CONSIDER THE SOURCE ◆

We live in a time of merchandising exaggeration —but you already know that. Like you, I have seen health products advertised to add 10 years to one's life. Marketing hype for a diet pill claims you will lose 42 pounds in two weeks. (That's three pounds a day!) As the list grows ever longer, there seems to be more and more wisdom in the old Roman adage *caveat emptor* ("buyer, beware").

Advertising for bottled water seems particularly bold considering the nature of the product. A typical claim is that a certain brand comes from a mountain spring or some other emotionally satisfying source. A mountain spring may indeed be the source, but there is no certificate that says the water from there is purer than the water from your own well or municipal supply.

Bottled water in sizes smaller than one gallon did not exist in the U.S. prior to 1976. But that was the year that single-serve bottled water began to be marketed successfully. Since then, bottled water has become the $12 billion industry that it is today in the U.S.

It's amazing that people will spend so much money to ensure they drink the best water but at the same time will be rather careless about the quality of the "spiritual water" they consume. In our next half verse, John tells us about the only proper source for that kind of water. And we won't have to worry about recycling plastic bottles!   —J. B. N.

1b. flowing from the throne of God and of the Lamb

The river streams from the central feature of the city. In so doing, the vision again defies our expectations, which are grounded in the daily experiences of life. A cube-shaped city is hard to

HOW TO SAY IT

caveat emptor *(Latin)*   **ka**-vee-*ought* emp-ter.

Ezekiel   Ee-*zeek*-ee-ul or Ee-*zeek*-yul.

Zechariah   *Zek*-uh-**rye**-uh.

imagine (Revelation 21:16). Pearls large enough to be carved as city gates are unknown to us (21:21a). Streets of transparent gold have never been seen (21:21b). Likewise, a spring on a mountaintop city that results in a river that flows from a seat of authority is something we can only wonder at. As we do, we acknowledge that in the new Jerusalem there may be new laws of physics that defy current textbook science.

> **What Do You Think?**
>   What are some ways to be a conduit of the "water of life" to others on a daily basis?
> *Talking Points for Your Discussion*
>   - To unbelievers who are spiritually thirsty
>   - To unbelievers who are skeptical of the church
>   - To believers who have backslidden
>   - Other

B. Tree of Life (vv. 2a, b)

2a. through the middle of the street of the city; also, on either side of the river, the tree of life

This verse also describes something difficult for us to visualize: the river of life, which comes from the throne, is in *the middle of the* primary *street of the city*. We need to think of an immense street here, a boulevard or parkway so broad that a river with lush, fertile banks divides its lanes.

To propose dimensions is speculative. But perhaps we can imagine a street that is 200 yards wide (double football-field length) with a tree-lined river taking up the middle 100 yards of it (single football field), and golden lanes (Revelation 21:21) that are 50 yards wide each on each side of the river. This may give an idea of proportions, but it is likely that the scene John witnesses is much grander than this.

This river of living water leads to *the tree of life*, known to us from Genesis 2:9 (see the Lesson Background). This is similar to Ezekiel's vision of a great river flowing from a restored Jerusalem temple to transform the Dead Sea (Ezekiel 47:1-12). The prophet saw this river lined on both sides with many trees (47:7, 12). Some scholars believe that is what John is seeing here, and that we should take *tree* in a plural sense as being a forest or grove of trees. But that is not what John describes.

Somehow, the tree of life is on both sides of the river, perhaps spanning it and towering over it. This is a gigantic tree, not a dwarf variety. Its powerful roots spring up from each side of the river and support a mighty trunk with branches that droop to the banks on each side of the river. This makes its fruit and leaves easily accessible to the residents of the city. No tree can grow like this naturally, and we do not need to expect such growth here. This is a supernatural tree planted by the Lord.

2b. with its twelve kinds of fruit, yielding its fruit each month.

The tree is fruit bearing, but in a way unlike that of any fruit tree of our experience. We might know of different months for picking various fruits (cherries in June, peaches in July, apples in September), but we know of no tree that bears 12 varieties of fruit with a different one ripening each month!

Even so, an ever-bearing multi-fruit tree is one more feature of the new Jerusalem that exceeds anything in our experience. The practical aspect of this is that the life-giving fruit will be available to citizens of the city daily without interruption or times of shortage. The eternal city has an eternal tree that provides eternal life.

C. Leaves of Healing (v. 2c)

2c. The leaves of the tree were for the healing of the nations.

In modern city life, we do not associate tree leaves with healing. The closest we may come is using the gel of aloe vera leaves to treat burns. But aloe vera is a plant, not a tree.

Yet consider that tea leaves are dried and boiled to obtain a liquid with healthful properties. Tea leaves come from the tea shrub, which is considered by some to be a small tree. The idea presented in the verse before us seems to be that the leaves of the wondrous tree of life can be used to produce a healing elixir of some sort.

This healing is not stated to be for curing of wounds, viruses, etc. Rather, it is for *the healing of the nations*. A key idea is that of spiritual healing for all the peoples from many nations, for Revelation 21:24 (last week's lesson) depicts the kings of the earth streaming into the new city. This indicates, among other things, a final and lasting peace among all nations. In this light, the city is truly the new Jerusalem as we recall that *salem* means "peace" (see lesson 8).

D. Absence of Curse (v. 3a)

3a. No longer will there be anything accursed, but the throne of God and of the Lamb will be in it,

The holy city is just that—utterly holy. It admits neither anything that is *accursed* nor anything that needs to be cursed (compare 1 Corinthians 12:3; 16:22; Galatians 1:8, 9). The curses of humanity are gone.

We often think that the first curse resulting from the first sin was the cursing of Adam and Eve. But the first two curses were on the serpent (Genesis 3:14) and on the ground itself (3:17; compare 5:29; 8:21). There is no Satan-serpent in this city, for he has been consigned to the lake of fire (see Revelation 20:2, 10). There is no cursed ground, for the fertile soil and water of life allow the tree of life to thrive with its year-round fruit and healing leaves.

Proverbs 3:33 tells us that "The Lord's curse is on the house of the wicked, but he blesses the dwelling of the righteous." Yet there will be no wicked people in this city! Any and all things that might bring divine condemnation are absent, for the city is overwhelmed by God's throne and inhabited by his righteous servants. At long last, humanity will be freed from the stain of sin that ended residence in the original garden.

> *What Do You Think?*
> What practices have you found most useful in helping you live beyond the sin-curse daily?
> *Talking Points for Your Discussion*
> - Practices for achieving a positive outcome
> - Practices for avoiding a negative outcome

E. Servants of God (vv. 3b-5)

3b, 4. and his servants will worship him. They will see his face, and his name will be on their foreheads.

The psalmist asks "My soul thirsts for God, for the living God. When shall I come and appear before God?" (Psalm 42:2). The answer is right here! Everyone living in the city will have access to the throne.

All residents of the city are God's servants, and John describes them in three ways: what they do, what they see, and how they are marked. What they do is *worship him*. The Greek verb behind this can be translated "worship" or "serve" (Acts 24:14; Philippians 3:3; compare Revelation 7:15). The servants are engaged in acts of worship before the throne of God.

What they see is *his face*, which John does not describe. (We will have to wait to see for ourselves; 1 John 3:2.) To see the face of a king in the ancient world is a gift of fellowship (compare Esther 1:14; contrast Exodus 10:28). This is a fulfillment of Jesus' promise to those with pure hearts (Matthew 5:8; compare Psalm 17:14, 15).

How they are marked is with God's *name . . . on their foreheads*. This is a divine marking placed by either Jesus (Revelation 3:12) or God's angels (7:1-3). It is a beautiful image of acceptance and possession by God. It is the opposite of the mark of the beast that is placed on unbelievers (see 13:15-17; 14:9-11; 16:2; 19:20; 20:4).

> *What Do You Think?*
> What are some positive and negative aspects of the various ways that believers attempt to "mark" themselves as Christians?
> *Talking Points for Your Discussion*
> - Regarding Christianized bumper stickers
> - Regarding Christianized clothing accessories
> - By keeping a Bible prominently visible at work
> - Other

5. And night will be no more. They will need no light of lamp or sun, for the Lord God will be their light, and they will reign forever and ever.

We encountered this *no more* night description in last week's lesson concerning Revelation 21:23, 25. There as here, light given off by God himself illuminates the city. But now we see an important addition: the never-ending light is accompanied by the never-ending reign of God's people.

Shall we gather at the RIVER

Shall we gather at the river,
where bright angel feet
have trod,
with its crystal tide forever,
flowing by the throne of God?

Visual for Lesson 12. *Give each learner a copy of all stanzas of this hymn (public domain) to compare and contrast with today's text.*

This fulfills the prophecies and promises of Daniel 7:18, 27 and Revelation 1:6; 5:10. As Christ will "reign forever and ever" (Revelation 11:15), so shall we with him!

◆ *The Problem of Night* ◆

"It was a dark and stormy night" is the opening line of the novel *Paul Clifford,* written by Edward Bulwer-Lytton in 1830. Although often parodied, that line fairly represents a sense of pending doom. The darkness of nighttime is often symbolic of evil—of bad tidings, forebodings, and disasters. Night is a time of fear, and there is even a scientific word to identify fear of the dark: *achluophobia.* Children can feel threatened with the "bogeyman," a nocturnal prowler. Prolonged darkness can lead to psychological problems.

The fact that the writers of the New Testament view *night* and *darkness* also in negative terms tells us that human nature doesn't change in this regard (examples: Luke 1:79; 11:33-36; John 12:35; Romans 13:12; 1 Thessalonians 5:4-8; 1 Peter 2:9). God's solution is to banish night forever!

When that happens, all the fears and disorders associated with darkness will be no more. As children of light, we will be with the eternal light, the one in whom "is no darkness at all" (1 John 1:5). Until that time, let us have an urgency for the work of the kingdom as Jesus did when he said "We must work the works of him who sent me

while it is day; night is coming, when no one can work" (John 9:4).   —J. B. N.

II. What John Hears
(Revelation 22:6, 7)
A. Angel Speaks (v. 6)

6. And he said to me, "These words are trustworthy and true. And the Lord, the God of the spirits of the prophets, has sent his angel to show his servants what must soon take place."

The *he* speaking is still the angel of the bowls (Revelation 21:9), John's guide to the holy city. The angel's statement touches on several things we have read previously. First, the emphasis that what John hears being *trustworthy* and *true* are the same two affirmations made by him "who was seated on the throne" at the beginning of the vision of new Jerusalem (21:5; compare 3:14; 19:11).

Second, the reliability and importance of *these words* are underlined by reference to their source as being *the Lord, the God of the spirits of the prophets.* This fact serves to (1) include John in the ranks of earlier prophets and (2) emphasize the nature of the book of Revelation as prophecy (Revelation 1:3; see 19:10; 22:19).

Third, the visions are described as God's showing to *his servants what must soon take place.* The wording in the Greek is precisely the same as that found in the book's opening lines (Revelation 1:1). There are 15 verses left in the book as we come to the verse before us, but the final mention of showing—which is that of the holy city—is right here. Thus the initial showing of Revelation 1:1 and the final showing of Revelation 22:6 serve as book ends to the showings in between them (compare 4:1; 17:1; 21:9, 10).

We may wonder why the angel promises that the events will happen *soon* when, from our perspective of some 2,000 years hence, they are yet to occur. Many explanations have been proposed. One idea is that all the events of Revelation happen "invisibly" and are known only to a spiritually elite group. Another theory is that these events are symbolic ways of describing the destruction of Jerusalem in AD 70 as the new era of the church began. A more likely explanation is that these events will happen "quickly" when they do come, but they are being delayed for reasons we understand only partially (compare 2 Peter 3:9).

God is not controlled by time in the ways we are (2 Peter 3:8), and we are wise to use that reality to temper our desire to know details of the future. The message of Revelation is trustworthy and true even if we are inadequate to comprehend all of it. Let us believe that when these events do take place, those who are witnesses and have read Revelation will think, "Of course! Now it all makes sense."

> *What Do You Think?*
>   What should others see in us that demonstrates we believe Jesus may return at any time?
> *Talking Points for Your Discussion*
>   - In how we conduct relationships
>   - In what we value
>   - By the topics of our casual conversation
>   - Other

B. Jesus Speaks (v. 7)

7. "And behold, I am coming soon. Blessed is the one who keeps the words of the prophecy of this book."

The voice of the Lamb breaks through to deliver a promise and a blessing. He will return. He has not abandoned his people. In the midst of suffering, whether from the ancient Roman government or modern persecutors, he is with us. The initial blessing of Revelation 1:3 is repeated—directed to those who keep *the words of the prophecy.* That leads to the great question prompted by Revelation: What does keeping these sayings entail?

The book does not hide the answers to this question. Faithfulness is the primary answer, and that concept includes repentance (Revelation 2:5, 16; 3:3, 19; 9:20, 21; 16:9, 11) and patient endurance in the face of opposition (2:10; 13:10; 14:12).

> *To be faithful is to keep the words of the prophecy!*
> *To repent is to keep the words of the prophecy!*
> *To endure is to keep the words of the prophecy!*

There is an abiding message here that transcends any confusion we might have about the details of Christ's second coming. When he comes, may he find us faithful (compare Luke 18:8).

> *What Do You Think?*
>   Which specific Scriptures help you most to remain faithful and not give up? Why?
> *Talking Points for Your Discussion*
>   - Scriptures that promise
>   - Scriptures that comfort
>   - Scriptures that encourage
>   - Scriptures that warn
>   - Other

Conclusion

A. The Beginning and the End

Many things have clearly defined beginnings and ends. We begin reading a book, then we finish it. We buy a house, then we sell it. We begin a job, then the job ends. Transcending all our starts and stops of life is the timelessness of God, who was there at all the beginnings and will be there at all the ends. He is the Alpha and Omega, the A and Z, but with an enduring nature that stretches beyond the range of any human alphabet.

All this is illustrated by the new Jerusalem, a city to feature a physical size that is beyond our comprehension. It will be a city with unending day, an ever-flowing river of life, an ever-bearing fruit tree of life, ceaseless worship, and priceless building materials. It will be ever new.

Such will be our relationship with the Lord. That relationship will be eternally consistent, pure, and true. Yet this description fails to describe the relationship fully, for there is a limitlessness on God's side. Nonetheless, we are blessed by John's revelation to us of his visions. May we be faithful in keeping the lessons we learn.

B. Prayer

Father, we barely understand the marvels of your promised holy city, a place where you will provide all the light we need for both eyes and hearts. May we hold these promises tightly, so that when your Son returns, he will find us faithful and ready. We pray this in his name. Amen.

C. Thought to Remember

Seek the living water now!

INVOLVEMENT LEARNING

Enhance your lesson presentation with the reproducible activity page,
available as a free download at www.standardlesson.com.

Into the Lesson

If finances allow, provide a bottle of water for each learner, being sure that somewhere on the label is the word *pure*. (If you choose, provide one bottle to a single learner, and ask that learner to read the whole label aloud.) Note other words on the label that imply the unadulterated quality of the water within.

Alternative. Show a wrapped bar of Ivory soap and ask, "Does anyone here remember or know the original advertising for this soap product?" The original ad touted Ivory as "99 44/100% pure. It floats!" Note: A product "99 44/100% pure" is *not* pure, by definition, for it obviously contains 56/100% of contaminants.

For either example used, comment, "Aah, purity! It is a thing to be desired. Today's study begins with absolute purity and then describes a place and consequence of such purity. Let's take a look."

Option. Distribute copies of the "There Is a River" activity from the reproducible page, which you can download. Use it as a way to introduce the theme of the river of life.

Into the Word

Give to each learner a sheet divided into three columns with the headings *Revelation 22:1-7, Genesis 2:8-10*, and *Ezekiel 47:1-12*. Give these directions: "Find all three of these texts, and write into the three columns appropriate elements you find in at least two. Match them up side by side to see God's pictures of the ideal place God wants for his children." Allow five to eight minutes for work. You might choose to put your learners into groups of three and give one of the texts to each learner in each group so they can read back and forth to make their decisions and entries. After the allotted time, ask each to identify a parallel discovered among the three texts. Comment on the consistency with which the biblical revelation proceeds.

Before class have one of your artistic class members prepare a simple sketch of a tree (Revelation 22:2a) with leaves and conspicuous fruit, 12 different kinds if possible, with each piece of fruit large enough to write a word or two on it. Have it labeled "Golden Blessing Tree." Copy and distribute this image to each learner. Give these directions: "Look once again at today's text. Identify 12 golden blessings we will receive in Heaven. Abbreviate each one enough to write it onto one of the fruit images on The Tree of Life. On several of the leaves, write in the medical prescription symbol, Rx, to indicate the truth of verse 2b."

Entries such as "no night" and "life-giving tree" are obvious. Such entries as "no hunger" and "no scars of sin" may not be as obvious, but will be legitimate entries, because of the consistent supply of life-giving fruit and the spiritual healing effects of the leaves. As learners identify their entries, commend both the obvious and the not-so-obvious suggestions.

Option. Use the "Just the Opposite" activity from the reproducible page to allow a close look at the text to identify elements of the new heavens and earth pictured therein.

Into Life

Give your learners the following list of devotional titles. "Put Away the Handkerchiefs"; "A River with an Interesting Source"; "What an Odd Fruit Tree"; "Forget the Flashlights"; "Can You Believe It?"; "How to Be One of the Blessed."

Say, "Examine this list of titles connected to our study text today. Relate each one to a verse or an idea there. Choose one that you will develop in writing. Consider two ways to let your thoughts encourage and bless others: (1) send it by e-mail to all other class members, or (2) submit it to the church office for consideration for publication in the church newsletter or bulletin. Everyone needs to think about the glories of our heavenly home."

FIRST AND LAST

DEVOTIONAL READING: Revelation 1:4b-8
BACKGROUND SCRIPTURE: Revelation 22:8-21

REVELATION 22:11-21

¹¹ Let the evildoer still do evil, and the filthy still be filthy, and the righteous still do right, and the holy still be holy."

¹² "Behold, I am coming soon, bringing my recompense with me, to repay each one for what he has done. ¹³ I am the Alpha and the Omega, the first and the last, the beginning and the end."

¹⁴ Blessed are those who wash their robes, so that they may have the right to the tree of life and that they may enter the city by the gates.

¹⁵ Outside are the dogs and sorcerers and the sexually immoral and murderers and idolaters, and everyone who loves and practices falsehood.

¹⁶ "I, Jesus, have sent my angel to testify to you about these things for the churches. I am the root and the descendant of David, the bright morning star."

¹⁷ The Spirit and the Bride say, "Come." And let the one who hears say, "Come." And let the one who is thirsty come; let the one who desires take the water of life without price.

¹⁸ I warn everyone who hears the words of the prophecy of this book: if anyone adds to them, God will add to him the plagues described in this book, ¹⁹ and if anyone takes away from the words of the book of this prophecy, God will take away his share in the tree of life and in the holy city, which are described in this book.

²⁰ He who testifies to these things says, "Surely I am coming soon." Amen. Come, Lord Jesus!

²¹ The grace of the Lord Jesus be with all. Amen.

KEY VERSE

I am the Alpha and the Omega, the first and the last, the beginning and the end. —**Revelation 22:13**

Photo: Wavebreak Media / Thinkstock

THE SOVEREIGNTY OF GOD

Unit 3: Alpha and Omega

LESSONS 10–13

LESSON AIMS

After participating in this lesson, each learner will be able to:

1. Identify the descriptions that are intended to apply to Jesus.

2. Explain the descriptions of Jesus.

3. Sing a praise chorus, song, or traditional hymn that expresses the hope of Jesus' promised return.

LESSON OUTLINE

Introduction

A. Delays

Your flight has been delayed. These words are distressing to the air traveler. In an environment of tight connections and few direct flights, a flight delay can result in disrupted plans and great inconvenience. It is a mark of our impatience as a society how traumatic a few hours' delay can be.

Yet delays are part of our everyday life. Car repairs take longer than expected. That package with promised two-day delivery actually takes three. Our food at the restaurant takes 10 minutes longer than we think it should. Delays are a frustratingly common element of life.

But what if the delay is for hundreds of years? Thousands? Christians must balance their expectation of Christ's "could be at anytime" return with the awareness that his return has yet to happen after nearly 2,000 years. How do we live expectantly for Christ's return while simultaneously being in an "expect delays" mode? This quandary has faced the church since the first generation of believers.

B. Lesson Background

The Old Testament teaches in many places that God will send a deliverer for his people. The people of Israel in the first century thought such a person would be a political and military rescuer. God's anointed leader, they thought, would be empowered to defeat their nation's enemies, bringing peace and independence in the process (compare Acts 1:6; etc.). Jerusalem and its temple would be freed from Gentile influence, and pure worship of the Lord could then take place.

But two unexpected things happened. First, the Messiah that God sent did not come to be a leader of armies and defeat pagan invaders (John 6:15). He came, rather, to save his people from their sins (Matthew 1:21). His mission ultimately was for all humanity, for all are sinners. His death was a sacrifice for sins, intended to be effective for all people for all time, for he was the sacrificial Lamb who took away the sin of the world (John 1:29). Most first-century Jews rejected Jesus as the Messiah because he did not meet their expectations.

Second, the Jerusalem temple was destroyed by the Romans in AD 70 during the horrific War of the Jews. This was something that no Israelite of the time expected. Jewish faith, based as it was on the sacrifices of the temple, went into a downward spiral. Expectations of a military messiah to defeat the Romans were crushed.

Some, perhaps most, Christians of the same century found their own hopes under distress as Jesus' return did not materialize as they thought it should (compare 2 Peter 3:3, 4). But Jesus himself promised that he would indeed return. His return is to be "with power and great glory" (Matthew 24:30). His return will usher in the final judgment of both the living and the dead (Acts 10:42; 2 Thessalonians 1:5-10). Christians and some Jews both look for the Messiah to come, but their expectations are very different.

As today's text opens, the apostle John is still being addressed by the angel of the bowls of plagues, his guide to the new Jerusalem (Revelation 21:9; 22:1, 8-10). The angel has just told him that the prophecies he is to write are not to be sealed up "for the time is near" (22:10). This gives a heightened sense of the necessary fulfillment of these prophecies. It causes us to focus anew on the greatest of all of Revelation's prophecies: Christ will return.

I. Paths, Advent, Separation
(REVELATION 22:11-15)
A. Two Types (v. 11)

11. "Let the evildoer still do evil, and the filthy still be filthy, and the righteous still do right, and the holy still be holy."

The angel sums up the state of things for John by noting the paths taken by *the evildoer,* the *filthy,* the *righteous,* and the *holy.* There are really just two categories here, and the contrast is strong: the unrepentant, who continue to walk the wide path of sin, and the repentant, who take the narrow way (Matthew 7:13, 14). In contrast with Revelation 2:5, 16; 3:3, 19, there is no call for repentance here, for it is as if the judgment has already been cast. The obedient will continue to obey. The disobedient are not listening (see also Revelation

9:20, 21; 16:8-11). Only those with ears to hear will listen (2:7), the ones whose hearts are attuned to God's words.

B. Second Coming (vv. 12, 13)

12. "Behold, I am coming soon, bringing my recompense with me to repay each one for what he has done.

As in Revelation 22:7 (last week's lesson), the voice of the Lamb (Jesus) breaks through. He does so to restate his promise *I am coming soon* (see 2:16; 3:11). Previously a blessing was given to the ones who kept the words of the prophecy (1:3). Here, however, we might interpret the Lamb's pronouncement as both a blessing and a curse, for he promises to reward *each one for what he has done.* The two sets of rewards are set forth in verse 14, below.

13. "I am the Alpha and the Omega, the first and the last, the beginning and the end.

For the final time in Revelation, we hear a voice asserting the speaker to be *the Alpha and the Omega* (compare Revelation 1:8; 21:6). The first time we hear this self-designation, it is clearly "the Lord God . . . the Almighty" speaking (1:8). Now the speaker is the one who is coming, Jesus the Lamb. We should not be troubled by this apparent blurring of the distinction between the Lord God Almighty and the conquering Lamb, which is a feature of this book. They are seated on the throne together (Revelation 22:1) to rule the new Jerusalem as one. While our Bible teaches us that there are three persons in the Trinity—Father, Son, and Holy Spirit (and all three are in Revelation)—we should not forget that there is only one God. We do not worship three gods, but one God. While this unity of persons might be mysterious, it is true (Matthew 28:19; 1 Peter 1:2; etc.).

In this final case of Alpha and Omega self-designation, the two letters of the Greek alphabet letters are doubly explained. That alphabet has 24 letters, with Alpha standing at the beginning and Omega at the end. To be the Alpha and the Omega is therefore another way of saying *the first and the last, the beginning and the end* of all things (compare Isaiah 44:6; 48:12; Revelation 1:17; 2:8).

C. Two Outcomes (vv. 14, 15)

14. "Blessed are those who wash their robes, so that they may have the right to the tree of life and that they may enter the city by the gates.

The only way to enter the city is *by the gates* of pearl (Revelation 21:21). There is no secret passageway. No one can sneak over the walls at night, because there is no night (21:25; 22:5). The gates are guarded by powerful angels (21:12, lesson 11), and only those who have lived victorious, obedient lives will be allowed into the city. These are granted eternal life, as signified by their access to *the tree of life* (compare 22:2, last week's lesson). They have overcome (2:7).

What Do You Think?
In what ways has Christ made you an overcomer?
Talking Points for Your Discussion
- Over your own past
- Over opposition in the present

---

15. "Outside are the dogs and sorcerers and the sexually immoral and murderers and idolaters, and everyone who loves and practices falsehood.

Comparing this listing with the one in Revelation 21:8 (see lesson 10), we note the latter designates eight categories of evildoers, while the verse before us has six. Five of these six are duplicates of those in 21:8, while one is new: *dogs*. It is unlikely that John would include a literal reference to an animal group in listing categories of human transgressors, so something else must be meant here.

There are several possibilities. The word *dog*, in singular or plural, is a metaphor for a male prosti-tute (Deuteronomy 23:18, see ESV footnote), for those who mocked Jesus at his crucifixion (Psalm 22:16-18; Matthew 27:35-44), for the enemies of David (Psalm 59:1-7, 14), for Israel's greedy watchmen (Isaiah 56:9-12), for profane people who are incapable of receiving what is holy (Matthew 7:6), for Gentiles (Matthew 15:21-26), for Judaizers (Philippians 3:2), and for false teachers (2 Peter 2:1, 22).

There seems to be no decisive textual basis for selecting any one of these as the singular reference over all the others. But a common thread is that the above categories refer to people who reject God's authority. As seen in lesson 10, those to be denied access to "the water of life" (Revelation 21:6) are designated for housing in the lake of fire (21:8). These are the evildoers who are left outside the city in the text before us.

◆ WHEN GOD FINALLY GIVES UP ◆

We normally picture God as one who never gives up on people. But there are times when God does seem to give up, times when he releases people fully to their own wicked desires and lusts (examples: Jeremiah 44:24-28; Psalm 81:11, 12; Acts 7:42, 43; Romans 1:18-32). When that happens, it is almost as if God is saying, "You want to live like that? Fine. I'll let you live like that."

As we look at all the evil in our world today, we may wonder why God tolerates it. Why doesn't he just wipe everything out, as in the days of Noah (Genesis 6:5-7)? The reason he does not do so is stated in 2 Peter 3:9: God "is patient toward you, not wishing that any should perish, but that all should reach repentance."

HOW TO SAY IT

Alpha	*Al*-fa.
Gentile	*Jen*-tile.
Isaiah	Eye-*zay*-uh.
Jeremiah	Jair-uh-*my*-uh.
Maranatha (Aramaic)	Mare-ah-*nath*-ah (*nath* as in *math*).
Messiah	Meh-*sigh*-uh.
Omega	O-*may*-guh or O-*mee*-guh.
Sirius	*Sir*-ee-oss.
Zechariah	Zek-uh-*rye*-uh.

But make no mistake: there will come a day when God does indeed give up on the unrepentant —for all eternity. Those who do evil and are filthy will be separated from those who do right and are holy. The former are left outside, while the latter are admitted to the city. It's a dangerous thing to test the patience of God!   —J. B. N.

II. Testimony, Offer, Warning
(REVELATION 22:16-19)
A. Jesus (v. 16)

16. "I, Jesus, have sent my angel to testify to you about these things for the churches. I am the root and the descendant of David, the bright morning star."

Jesus includes more self-designations that help us understand the importance of the book of Revelation. To be *the descendant of David* is easy to grasp: Jesus is from the line of David by the earthly genealogy traced to Joseph (Matthew 1:1-17; Romans 1:3). The imagery of *the root* is a little more complicated, though. Prophecy spoke of the coming Messiah as a "branch" to grow from "roots" (see Isaiah 11:1, see lesson 1; compare Jeremiah 23:5; 33:15; Zechariah 6:12). For Jesus himself to be that root in an ultimate sense is quite a strong claim! He is Messiah in all its fullness. Any status that David has ultimately flows from Jesus Christ, not the other way around.

The final self-identifier, *the bright morning star,* has resulted in Bible students searching the Old Testament for various "star" prophecies or tie-ins to the star of Bethlehem. But that is unnecessary. Early risers have seen the phenomenon called "the morning star," which is a reference to Venus as it is visible in the eastern sky before sunrise.

At its brightest, Venus (a planet in our terminology, not a literal star) can be up to 16 times brighter than Sirius, the brightest actual star (not counting the sun). One who observes the rising of bright Venus knows one thing for certain: night is almost over, since the appearance of the sun is imminent. This is another way for Jesus to say that he is coming soon. The eternal day of the holy city and of the everlasting reign of the Lord and the Lamb is near (compare 2 Peter 1:19).

B. Water (v. 17)

17. The Spirit and the Bride say, "Come." And let the one who hears say, "Come." And let the one who is thirsty come; let the one who desires take the water of life without price.

We do not have to wait for Christ to come again to respond to the invitation given in this verse. *The Spirit* is the Holy Spirit, the promised divine presence on earth after Christ's ascension (see John 16:7-13). *The Bride* is the church, the embodiment of Christ in his followers on earth. These representatives of Christ are present now, and they invite all who hear their message to *come* and drink of the eternal *water of life* now. This is a call to faith and obedience, a call to join Christ before he comes again. It is a choice available to all!

> *What Do You Think?*
> What are some ways churches hinder themselves from issuing clear "come to the water" invitations? How can this problem be fixed?
> *Talking Points for Your Discussion*
> - In terms of ministry priorities
> - In terms of staffing priorities
> - Considering cultural contexts and differences
> - Considering reputation in the community
> - Other

C. Tampering (vv. 18, 19)

18. I warn everyone who hears the words of the prophecy of this book: if anyone adds to them, God will add to him the plagues described in this book,

The voice of the book now switches to that of the one who records it, John himself. Two stern warnings are in order at this point, and the first one is that hearers of this book must not add content. The penalty of *plagues* on anyone foolish enough to do so is described in Revelation 16.

19. and if anyone takes away from the words of the book of this prophecy, God will take away his share in the tree of life and in the holy city, which are described in this book.

Deletions from the book are also warned against. All the book's messages are to be taken to heart! Taking out parts we don't like will have consequences. Persons unwise to the point of making such subtractions will not be part of the citizenry of the new Jerusalem. Deuteronomy 4:2; 12:32 inform us that neither this prohibition nor the one just before it is anything new!

All this should give us something to think about in studying Revelation, because we tend to be selective. We avoid chapters that seem too violent, too disturbing, or too hard to understand. A good strategy is to read the entire book in one sitting, to allow its full message to speak to our hearts. This is how we will gain the full blessings of its prophecies. This will be true even if we do not comprehend everything. This book promises blessings for the future, but also for today (Revelation 1:3). It is the grandest story of all time. It is the promise that God will defeat the forces of evil in our world and reign in victory forever from his golden, eternal city.

◆   THE DANGER OF DELETION   ◆

In the world of quotations, citations, and references, there are rules about how all this is to be done. The "fair use" concept, for example, allows the use of someone else's copyrighted material with certain restrictions. Fairness implies that cited material must be quoted accurately; this is true with regard to the words used as well as the intent. For example, consider a hypothetical critic by the name of John Smith whose review of a play reads like this:

> This presentation was terrible. The acting was poor, the dialogue was inane, and the plot superficial. It was about as riveting as watching grass grow. The plot was well developed if written by a preschooler. The acting was wonderful if these people were reading their lines for the first time.

Then imagine the producers of the play quoting the critic this way:

> John Smith described the play as "riveting," noting that "the plot was well developed" and "the acting was wonderful.'"

Obviously the exact quotations do not give the sense that the original critic intended! That is blatant dishonesty; that's why a quotation must give a fair sense of the original. Leaving out words may give a very wrong impression.

God feels the same way about his book. Adding to the original is bad; leaving things out can be just as bad if not worse. God does not want his masterpiece tampered with. One must wonder if Thomas Jefferson read Revelation 22:19 before he decided to create his own cut-and-paste version of the Bible!   —J. B. N.

> **What Do You Think?**
> In what ways do people minimize or dilute the authority of God's Word? How do we guard ourselves against this danger?
> *Talking Points for Your Discussion*
> - Regarding the way we live
> - Regarding how we speak
> - Regarding financial priorities
> - Other

III. Promising, Longing, Closing
(REVELATION 22:20, 21)
A. Reaffirmation (v. 20a)

20a. He who testifies to these things says, "Surely I am coming soon."

One last time John reminds us of Jesus' promise that he is *coming soon*. This promise embraces both the presence of Christ in his church today (compare Revelation 2:5, 16; 3:11) and the promise of Christ's return in the future (compare 22:7, 12).

There will be only two reactions when Christ returns: joy and fear. Christ is coming the second time in glory and judgment, and he will vanquish all the evil that seems so powerful now. Who can stand before the wrath of the Lamb? No one (Revelation 6:17). The intent of this book as a whole is to bring readers to repentance, faithfulness, and endurance so that we will greet the return of Christ with joy.

B. Desire (v. 20b)

20b. Amen. Come, Lord Jesus!

Lack of fear is the position of John as he ends the book with a short prayer. *Amen* means, "It is true." This is a loaded, powerful word in this context, for John is in effect saying, "Everything I just told you—all the visions, all the prophecies, all the warnings, all the blessings—is absolutely true." If this were not the case, then John would not dare express a desire for Jesus to return, lest John's falsehood be exposed!

But John is telling the truth, and his *Amen. Come, Lord Jesus!* is similar to Paul's expressed desire in 1 Corinthians 16:22. Perhaps the greatest faith prayer a Christian can utter is to ask sincerely for Christ to come, for that means the one praying is ready to meet the Lord, master, and judge face to face (compare 2 Timothy 4:8).

What Do You Think?
What will be your part in helping fellow Christians be better prepared to meet the Lord face to face?
Talking Points for Your Discussion
- In terms of knowledge (Colossians 1:10)
- In terms of faith (2 Corinthians 10:15)
- In terms of service (Ephesians 4:16)
- Other (2 Peter 1:5-9)

C. Benediction (v. 21)

21. The grace of the Lord Jesus be with all. Amen.

John offers a final blessing to the readers. This is comforting for the persecuted and fearful readers of the seven churches of Revelation 2 and 3, for they are in sore need of God's grace and mercy in their difficult situations. Likewise for us, this is a blessed word of calming peace, assuring us that God's marvelous grace toward us is not just past or future. It is present and available right now.

Conclusion

A. Praying Maranatha

The return of Christ is a key theme of the book of Revelation. We joyously celebrate his first coming, his first "advent," in the Christmas season. But daily we should also anticipate and pray for his return, his second "advent," to take us home to be with him forever.

This morning I did so by praying "Maranatha," an Aramaic word meaning "Come, Lord" (see the ESV footnote on 1 Corinthians 16:22). I am ready for Christ to come again. When I read the news of another mass shooting, of another suicide bomber, of another outrage to my Christian conscience, I am ready for Christ to come again. Despite the efforts of people of good faith, the dark side of humanity seems an unquenchable source of evil. I am ready for Christ to come again.

I don't know exactly how his coming or our residence in the new Jerusalem will work. The closing chapters of Revelation give answers, but in all honestly they raise questions as well. Yet I don't need to know everything, and I am at peace with that. I am ready for Christ to come again.

Are you ready as well, or does part of your heart fear that you will be among those excluded from the holy city? Being able and willing to pray for Christ to return right now is a great test of one's spiritual health, a test of one's relationship with the Lord Jesus.

Practice the Maranatha prayer for a week. Pray it sincerely, in true faith. If you take this seriously, it will make a difference.

B. Prayer

Maranatha! Come, Lord Jesus! Come now, we pray. Amen.

C. Thought to Remember

Make the Alpha and Omega
first and last in your life.

Visual for Lesson 13. *Start a discussion by pointing to this visual as you ask, "How else can we illustrate 'the first and the last' nature of Jesus?"*

INVOLVEMENT LEARNING

Enhance your lesson presentation with the reproducible activity page,
available as a free download at www.standardlesson.com.

Into the Lesson

As class begins, have a learner with a strong, emphatic voice stand abruptly and read Revelation 1:7. After the reading, note, "That is the theme from beginning to end of our book of study: Jesus is coming again! From that verse just read in chapter 1 to our text in chapter 22, that is the key truth: Jesus is coming again."

Use the gospel song "Coming Again" by Mosie Lister to begin class today, either being sung by a soloist or as a group activity. You will need to provide the words, and you may want to recruit a leader and/or accompanist. The words about his coming again will be sung 12 times, a fitting emphasis for today's text.

Alternative. Download and distribute copies of the "I Know He's Coming" activity from the reproducible page to consider others who believed in Jesus' coming.

Into the Word

Say, "A key question to be asked always is 'Why?'" Then distribute these why questions to your learners randomly: 1. Why is there no call to repentance in verse 11? 2. Why would Jesus have said he is coming soon when he has been gone 2,000 years? 3. Why is reward to be based on what one has done? I thought works were irrelevant and only grace matters. 4. Why would Jesus call himself the beginning and the end? Isn't he eternal? 5. Why are some given access to the tree of life? 6. Why would practitioners of the magic arts be singled out as banned from Heaven? Isn't it just harmless fun? 7. Why does Jesus use intermediary angels to give his revelation to John and us? 8. Why is the invitation to "Come" repeated in verse 17? 9. Why is the one who adds to or subtracts from the message of this book given such a drastic punishment? 10. Why would John feel compelled to pray for Jesus to come when Jesus has just repeated his promise to do so?

Let learners ask and answer the questions freely. Jot ideas on the board as appropriate. Add clarity from the commentary as necessary.

Since Revelation 22 has been a rich source for hymns, gospel songs, and choruses through the ages, use a musical activity to draw attention to key ideas and phrases in the text. Perhaps have an instrumentalist play melody lines from the following songs/hymns, and ask to name the song: (1) "Come, Every One Who Is Thirsty" by Lucy J. Rider; (2) "He the Pearly Gates Will Open" by Fredrick A. Blom; (3) "O Morning Star, How Fair and Bright" by Philip Nicolai; (4) "The King Is Coming" by Bill and Gloria Gaither; (5) "Of the Father's Love Begotten" by Aurelius Prudentius (includes "He is Alpha and Omega").

Many contemporary songs also issue from Revelation 22 and its beauty; you may well want to choose some of those for your class. Web pages such as hymnal.net and songandpraise.org can provide choices and sound tracks.

Into Life

Distribute copies of the well-known hymn, "O Come, O Come Emmanuel," which you have prepared in advance. Say, "Though traditionally used at Christmas, this hymn is an appropriate conclusion to today's study. It is a prayer petitioning God for a prompt resolution of all things, similar to John's joyous, anticipatory cry at the end of Revelation: 'Come, Lord Jesus.'"

If group singing is inappropriate, invite a soloist to prepare and sing the song. Be sure to ask the group to add a rousing "Amen" at the end, to parallel the way the Spirit ends John's book.

Option. Distribute copies of the "So Be It!" activity from the reproducible page. Either have students complete it individually or read it together as a class and voice the "Amens" heartily.

CREATION:
A DIVINE CYCLE

Special Features

Lessons
Unit 1: The Savior Has Been Born

Unit 2: Praise from and for God's Creation

Unit 3: The Birthing of a New Community

QUARTERLY QUIZ

Use these questions as a pretest or as a review. The answers are on page iv of This Quarter in the Word.

Lesson 1

1. When the angel first spoke to Mary, her reaction was one of great joy. T/F. *Luke 1:29*
2. In Luke, what relative of Mary was pregnant at the same time she was? (Hannah, Susanna, Elizabeth?) *Luke 1:36*

Lesson 2

1. Mary predicted that future generations would call her blessed. T/F. *Luke 1:48*
2. Mary said that the Lord had scattered the _____. *Luke 1:51*

Lesson 3

1. An angel appeared to Zechariah while he was in the _____. *Luke 1:9, 11*
2. The failure of Zechariah to believe resulted in what? (inability to speak, blindness, leprosy?) *Luke 1:20*

Lesson 4

1. The angel told the shepherds that the Christ had been born in the city of _____. *Luke 2:11*
2. The shepherds found the infant Jesus where? (mother's lap, manger, in a palace?) *Luke 2:16*

Lesson 5

1. What kind of song did the psalmist encourage be sung? (new, old, repetitious?) *Psalm 33:3*
2. What attitude should all the earth have toward the Lord? (mystery, joy, fear?) *Psalm 33:8*

Lesson 6

1. The gods of the nations are what? (demons, angels, idols?) *Psalm 96:5*
2. The Lord is to be worshipped in the splendor of what? (holiness, awe, spirit?) *Psalm 96:9*

Lesson 7

1. The psalmist predicted that all _____ will come to God. *Psalm 65:2*

2. The psalmist affirmed the Lord's capability to still the _____ of the sea and its waves. *Psalm 65:7*

Lesson 8

1. The psalmist saw the Lord clothed with splendor and _____. *Psalm 104:1*
2. When sea creatures die, they return to dust. T/F. *Psalm 104:25, 29*

Lesson 9

1. Hail and snow are elements that are to praise the Lord. T/F. *Psalm 148:7, 8*
2. The name of the Lord is unique in being _____. *Psalm 148:13*

Lesson 10

1. A person who has been baptized into Christ has put on Christ. T/F. *Galatians 3:27*
2. Even in Christ, there is still a sharp division between Jew and Greek. T/F. *Galatians 3:28*

Lesson 11

1. Paul had preached to the Galatians while he was ill. T/F. *Galatians 4:13*
2. How had the Galatians received Paul? (as a prophet, as a rabbi, as an angel?) *Galatians 4:14*

Lesson 12

1. Faith and love have no inherent connection with one another. T/F. *Galatians 5:6*
2. The desires of the flesh are in harmony with the desires of the Spirit. T/F. *Galatians 5:17*

Lesson 13

1. Sorcery is a work of the flesh. T/F. *Galatians 5:19, 20*
2. There is no _____ against the fruit of the Spirit. *Galatians 5:22, 23*
3. We are to do good to all when we have what? (enough rest, opportunity, money?) *Galatians 6:10*

QUARTER AT A GLANCE

by Walter D. Zorn

CREATE—that's just what God does! And he does it for our benefit as he invites us to experience his goodness in the whole cycle of creation and re-creation. This quarter explores various aspects of the great works of our Creator.

Creator of the Universe

God created the universe by his powerful word (lesson 5). He reveals himself as the sustainer of his creation as he renews the earth season by season (lesson 8). The way God cares for us in these acts should inspire "a new song" on our part (lesson 6). Since creation by its very existence acknowledges the Creator, should we not join our praise with that unspoken tribute?

Many people see the universe as a result of random chance. In so doing, they fail to praise, or even acknowledge the existence of, the one who created and sustains all that is. But the songs of ancient Israel teach us to praise God for creation continually and to recognize creation itself as sounding God's praise!

Author of Salvation

Sadly, God eventually saw the created order spoiled by human rebellion. But he had a plan. From the beginning, he intended to send his Son to save humanity and re-create the cosmos.

The promise of a Savior was certain and divinely accomplished. Two of God's willing servants in this climactic event were young Mary and her older relative Elizabeth (lessons 1 and 2). Both women experienced God's miracle of a humanly impossible conception.

Mary's conception was virginal, brought about by the overshadowing of the Holy Spirit (Luke 1:35). Elizabeth's miracle was that of an elderly, postmenopausal woman's being enabled to conceive the forerunner of the Savior (lesson 3). Elizabeth's testimony affirmed to Mary that God had even greater plans for Mary's own son. Zechariah, husband of Elizabeth and initially skeptical of the angel's incredible news, named their son *John* as instructed; he grew to become the man the Bible calls *John the Baptist*.

God's announcement of salvation did not come first to kings or religious authorities. The ones to hear first of the Messiah's birth were simple shepherds when their nightly routine was interrupted by the divine announcement (lesson 4).

Lord of the Re-Created

Jesus came to give his life for us by paying sin's penalty on the cross. The result is new birth for those accepting the gospel's offer of salvation. Those who accept this new birth are collectively known as *the church*.

The church has been described in many ways, but one apt description you may not have thought of is "the community of the re-created." The church is indeed God's ultimate act of re-creation. Everyone—whether Jew or Greek, in bondage or free, male or female—can be re-created by having sins forgiven. Because of Christ, everyone has

> *From the beginning, [God] intended to send his Son to save humanity and re-create the cosmos.*

equal access to salvation; everyone can be part of the church (lesson 10).

We the re-created walk in faith by the power of the Holy Spirit. The result is that we bear the fruit of the Spirit (lesson 13). We "do good to everyone, and especially to those who are of the household of faith" (Galatians 6:10). How can we do otherwise, given what the Son of God has done for us?

May this quarter's studies result in ever-greater humility before him, the one who not only creates, but also re-creates!

GET THE SETTING

by Tom Thatcher

IN STARK CONTRAST with pagan views of the ancient world, the biblical view portrays God as the loving Creator and Sustainer of the universe. It further depicts him acting to reconcile and redeem his creation. This contrast invites scrutiny!

The Selfish Creators in Paganism

Pagans explained the origins of the universe and the human race with fanciful creation stories. The stories vary in details, but overall are remarkably similar. Common themes relate to the nature of gods, the manner of creation, and the purposes of human life.

Both the ancient near east and the Roman world recognized multiple gods—beings who essentially acted like humans. These gods were depicted eating, hunting, wearing clothes, playing instruments, and living in houses. Like humans, they were viewed as sexual beings who created other gods, humans, and natural phenomena through physical reproduction, sometimes even through mating with humans. An example is the Canaanite god Baal of the Old Testament. He was a male fertility deity who brought rain to nourish the earth by means of sexual relations with his consort, Asherah. Greek and Roman gods were viewed as literal parents of the human race.

Pagan religions also generally explained the creation of the physical universe in terms of the gods' manipulation of existing physical materials, or even their own bodies, to form the earth and its various physical features. Rather than being transcendent—different in essence from the physical and human worlds—such gods were merely magnified humans. Human attributes of wrath, greed, and lust were magnified in them as well.

These pagan views shaped (and were shaped by) perceptions of human life and religious obligation. Seeing gods as very similar to human patrons and enemies, ancient religions were dedicated to appeasing them and earning divine favors. Pagan religion focused on rituals, sacrifices, and magical formulas and objects that would protect people from harmful deities or force the gods to bestow blessings.

The notion that the gods "loved" individual human beings, except perhaps in the human sexual sense noted above, was not widespread. Most ancient religions did not teach that the gods would bless or even encourage virtuous behavior. Many taught that humans were created to be slaves to the gods who made them.

Religion and politics were often inseparable. Both the Egyptian Pharaohs of Moses' day and the Roman Emperors in the time of Jesus and Paul were seen as semidivine beings who served as all-powerful rulers and sustainers of human society. In these settings, failure to honor the divine rights of kings was viewed as both treason and impiety.

The Selfless Creator in the Bible

The Bible's view of God and creation is radically different. Yahweh did not create from existing material as would a potter or carpenter. Rather, he spoke the universe into being, sustaining it even now by his power.

Rather than being a spiteful overseer of creation, the God of the Bible is a loving Father who cares for his people while remaining separate from them in essence and holiness. His love is unmerited and entirely pure—it cannot be bought by any action on humanity's part. God's selfless nature is reflected in Israel's history and poetry.

Most distinctive is the biblical doctrine of God's physical entry into the world to give, not to take: he sent his Son to redeem by dying for sin. The New Testament records this to be the Creator's ultimate selfless act. A result of Jesus' death and resurrection is empowerment to be holy as God is holy. This is no less than the re-creation of those who accept the gospel.

THIS QUARTER IN THE WORD

Answers to the Quarterly Quiz on page 114

Lesson 1—1. false. 2. Elizabeth. Lesson 2—1. true. 2. proud. Lesson 3—1. temple. 2. inability to speak. Lesson 4—1. David. 2. manger. Lesson 5—1. new. 2. fear. Lesson 6—1. idols. 2. holiness. Lesson 7—1. flesh. 2. roaring. Lesson 8—1. majesty. 2. true. Lesson 9—1. true. 2. exalted. Lesson 10—1. true. 2. false. Lesson 11—1. true. 2. as an angel. Lesson 12—1. false. 2. false. Lesson 13—1. true. 2. law. 3. opportunity.

Galatia in Paul's Day

Cappadocia

Galatia

Cilicia

Tarsus

Deribe

Iconium

Lystra

Phrygia

Pamphylia

Perga

Attalia

Antioch

Mediterranean Sea

Salamis

Cyprus

Paphos

miles

0   25   50   75

PAPER-BOAT SURPRISE

Teacher Tips by Ronald L. Nickelson

Rhonda* teaches fifth-graders in her church's Sunday school program. Her husband, Luke,* is gifted in other areas of service, so he leaves children's ministry solely to her. As a result, they part ways for a time after stepping inside the church building on Sunday morning: he to an adult-level ministry and she to KidZone* —their church's name for the area of the building devoted to classrooms for children.

On the drive home after services on one particular Sunday, Rhonda had a startling announcement for Luke: he had single-handedly, inadvertently, and unknowingly "saved" the lesson that morning for all the children in KidZone! Luke, having never taken part in children's ministry, was surprised, and Rhonda couldn't wait to tell the story.

Problem Discovered

She began by reminding Luke of a request she had made of him the previous day. He had been watching TV while she sat at the dining-room table preparing the next day's Bible lesson for her class. The lesson was to be on Noah's ark, and the activity segment of the lesson called for students to make a paper boat. Instructional steps were provided, but Rhonda discovered that four steps were missing. Not good!

Rhonda had no experience making paper boats, so she had asked Luke for help. Having made paper airplanes and boats often as a youngster, Luke filled in the rest of the steps easily, walking Rhonda through the process a few times as he did.

Storm Brews

Even given Rhonda's new insight in the making of paper boats, a larger problem existed because (1) the lessons of the curriculum being used were designed to be picked up on Sunday morning and taught without advance preparation by the teachers and (2) children of all age-levels in the church would be studying the same lesson. In a church

averaging more that 500 in attendance, a perfect storm was thus waiting to happen in KidZone.

Storm Hits

Sunday morning came, classes commenced, and teaching began. But it wasn't long before cries of exasperation were heard throughout KidZone. Lo and behold, no teacher save one had looked through the lesson in advance to test the activity. No teacher except Rhonda knew how to fold a piece of paper in such a way that a boat resulted. Springing into action, she immediately made the rounds to guide her fellow teachers through the boat-making process. A lesson that was in danger of sinking (pun intended) throughout KidZone was saved by one teacher's advance preparation.

Rhonda as You?

Rhonda was thoughtful enough to credit Luke for his help. But it was her own understanding of the responsibilities of teaching that made the difference. Here are some key elements evident in her teaching philosophy:

1. No curriculum is perfect. Even the best teaching material has flaws. The worst time to discover a flaw is when facing a roomful of students. Rhonda knew that "instant lesson" is a fantasy, so she prepared in advance.

2. No teacher knows it all. Rhonda has many years of experience teaching children, and she has great expertise in children's ministry as a whole. But when she realized her lack of knowledge about something, she asked for help. Don't let embarrassment keep you from doing likewise!

3. No teammate is unimportant. The teachers in your church are a team, not just a collection of individuals. Rhonda did not find fault when her fellow teachers needed help. Instead, she left her own class in capable hands to come to their rescue. Are you a Rhonda-kind of teacher?

Situation is real; names of people and place changed.

GOD PROMISES A SAVIOR

DEVOTIONAL READING: Isaiah 6:1-8
BACKGROUND SCRIPTURE: Luke 1:26-38

LUKE 1:26-38

²⁶ In the sixth month the angel Gabriel was sent from God to a city of Galilee named Nazareth, ²⁷ to a virgin betrothed to a man whose name was Joseph, of the house of David. And the virgin's name was Mary. ²⁸ And he came to her and said, "Greetings, O favored one, the Lord is with you!" ²⁹ But she was greatly troubled at the saying, and tried to discern what sort of greeting this might be. ³⁰ And the angel said to her, "Do not be afraid, Mary, for you have found favor with God. ³¹ And behold, you will conceive in your womb and bear a son, and you shall call his name Jesus. ³² He will be great and will be called the Son of the Most High. And the Lord God will give to him the throne of his father David, ³³ and he will reign over the house of Jacob forever, and of his kingdom there will be no end."

³⁴ And Mary said to the angel, "How will this be, since I am a virgin?"

³⁵ And the angel answered her, "The Holy Spirit will come upon you, and the power of the Most High will overshadow you; therefore the child to be born will be called holy—the Son of God. ³⁶ And behold, your relative Elizabeth in her old age has also conceived a son, and this is the sixth month with her who was called barren. ³⁷ For nothing will be impossible with God." ³⁸ And Mary said, "Behold, I am the servant of the Lord; let it be to me according to your word." And the angel departed from her.

KEY VERSE

And behold, you will conceive in your womb and bear a son, and you shall call his name Jesus.

—Luke 1:31

CREATION: A DIVINE CYCLE

Unit 1: The Savior Has Been Born
LESSONS 1–4

LESSON AIMS

After participating in this lesson, each learner will be able to:

1. Retell the incident of the angel Gabriel's announcement to Mary.

2. Explain how Gabriel's message prepared Mary to accept God's plan to be the mother of the Messiah.

3. Write a prayer of submission to be God's servant in the Christmas season.

LESSON OUTLINE

Introduction

A. On an Adventure

I am the kind of person who likes to follow a plan. When our family goes on vacation, I want to know the distance and time between each day's destination. I do my homework about where we will stay and how much it will cost. Realizing this tendency may not always make a vacation as enjoyable as it should be for others, I have asked my family to plan daily activities once we get to where we're going.

Whether my plans or theirs, sometimes plans need to change. When this happens, my wife will often say, "It just means we're going on an adventure!" It's her way of saying, "Changing our plans isn't a bad thing, because we're facing the unknown together."

In today's lesson Mary learns that God wants her to be a part of his plan to bring salvation. Her part in his plan is one that will change the plans she and Joseph were making for their life together. As each was visited by an angel, they found their plans being adjusted by God's extraordinary plan to put on human flesh. Joseph and Mary were about to begin an adventure unlike anything either of them could have imagined. It was an adventure that changed their lives, and ours, forever.

B. Lesson Background

Today's lesson examines a vital segment in a sequence of bigger stories. On a personal level, it is Mary's story. At the time of Gabriel's visit, she was a virgin and betrothed to be married to Joseph (see Matthew 1:18).

The path modern couples take to marriage can cloud our understanding of Mary's circumstances. In the ancient Near East, couples might become married through a variety of arrangements. These customs involved various levels of freedom and consent on the part of one or both persons to be married. The betrothal custom was one in which a man and woman became legally bound to one another before the actual marriage ceremony. Betrothal was much more binding than today's custom of "being engaged."

The betrothal period usually lasted about a year. A betrothed couple was committed to see each other but did not live together or engage in sexual intimacy. During that time, a couple made preparations to live together as husband and wife. Since a betrothal was legally binding, ending the relationship required a divorce. Indeed, Joseph considered such action (Matthew 1:18, 19).

The text of today's lesson is part of the larger story of God's relationship with his covenant people. The era in which Gabriel appeared to Mary was a time of subjugation for the Jews. Although Jerusalem and the temple had been rebuilt after the Babylonian exile, the Jewish people remained under the control of various pagan powers over the centuries that followed. The Roman Empire was the occupying power at the time of Jesus' birth. Oppression by those Gentiles fueled hope and expectation that God would send his Messiah to liberate and lead his people.

I. Hearing God's Plan
(LUKE 1:26-33)
A. Mary Greeted (vv. 26-28)

26. In the sixth month the angel Gabriel was sent from God to a city of Galilee named Nazareth,

This verse connects Gabriel's visit to Mary with his visit to the priest Zechariah. In the verses just prior to this one, Gabriel told Zechariah that his wife, Elizabeth, was to give birth to a son. *The sixth month* Luke mentions refers to the progress of Elizabeth's pregnancy (compare Luke 1:36).

HOW TO SAY IT

Cornelius	Cor-*neel*-yus.
Davidic	Duh-*vid*-ick.
Gabriel	*Gay*-bree-ul.
Galilee	*Gal*-uh-lee.
Messiah	Meh-*sigh*-uh.
messianic	mess-ee-*an*-ick.
Nathanael	Nuh-*than*-yull (*th* as in *thin*).
Nazareth	*Naz*-uh-reth.
Theophilus	Thee-*ahf*-ih-luss (*th* as in *thin*).
Zechariah	Zack-uh-*rye*-uh.

Luke may have in mind readers of non-Jewish background as he makes a transition from Jerusalem (where Gabriel encountered Zechariah) *to a city of Galilee named Nazareth.* While most such readers have heard of Jerusalem, it is unlikely they know anything about Nazareth (about 64 miles north of Jerusalem as the crow flies, and perhaps 90 miles by road). Nazareth is a small, insignificant village like so many others in the region of Galilee. This seems to have been the way Nathanael thought of Nazareth (see John 1:46).

27. to a virgin betrothed to a man whose name was Joseph, of the house of David. And the virgin's name was Mary.

After Luke tells us the when and where of God's sending Gabriel to announce the Messiah's arrival, he reveals the circumstances and identity of the recipient of Gabriel's visit: a certain *Mary.* The fact that she is *a virgin* (mentioned twice) is consistent with the betrothal stage of her relationship with *Joseph* (see the Lesson Background). Her virginal status is also significant for understanding how she reacts to the angelic message (v. 34, below).

The fact that Joseph is *of the house of David* is the first suggestion in this Gospel of a messianic significance for what is to happen. The reason this is so is because of the prophecy that the Messiah is to be a descendant of King David (compare Isaiah 11:1, 10; Jeremiah 23:5; Matthew 22:42).

> *What Do You Think?*
> What role should awareness of personal heritage play, if any, in preparing for marriage? Why?
> *Talking Points for Your Discussion*
> - Regarding differing cultural values
> - Regarding expectations of extended family
> - Regarding boundaries within the immediate family of origin
> - Other

28. And he came to her and said, "Greetings, O favored one, the Lord is with you!"

Gabriel initiates the verbal interchange with a greeting that is certainly more than an ordinary "hello"! We may wonder what it is about Mary's character that results in the angel's declaring her to be the *favored one*. The text does not tell us, but elsewhere the Lord's favor is said to be granted to those who seek and find wisdom (Proverbs 8:1, 35) and who pursue a "good" lifestyle (12:2).

This raises the question of whether God's favor toward Mary is a result of merit on her part. Some think the case of Noah is a precedent for an affirmative answer in this regard, since the declaration that he "found favor in the eyes of the Lord" is followed by the analysis that "Noah was a righteous man, blameless in his generation" (Genesis 6:8, 9). On the other hand, evidence for a negative answer might be the case of God's favor on the Israelites as a whole. They proved time and time again that they merited no such favor (Deuteronomy 7:6-8; Nehemiah 9:16-31).

We are safe to assume that Mary's character in some way makes her eligible to receive the great honor of being chosen to give birth to the Messiah (Luke 1:30, 31, below). Even so, there are doubtless many other young Jewish virgins of similar character in Mary's day. Why she receives the honor of being the mother of the Messiah instead of any of them is, in the final analysis, a matter of speculation.

The affirmation *the Lord is with you!* mirrors similar statements found elsewhere (Joshua 1:5; Judges 6:12; etc.). His presence is also part of Matthew's account of an angelic visit to Joseph, although stated in a different way (Matthew 1:20-24).

B. Mary Comforted (vv. 29-33)

29, 30. But she was greatly troubled at the saying, and tried to discern what sort of greeting this might be. And the angel said to her, "Do not be afraid, Mary, for you have found favor with God.

Angelic appearances can be disturbing (compare Matthew 28:5; Luke 1:11, 12; 2:8-10; Acts 10:1-4), and that is the case here. Luke doesn't tell us specifically that Mary is afraid, but it is not hard to imagine that she is!

Gabriel calms any fears by repeating that Mary has *found favor with God*. This reaffirmation lets her know that regardless of any uncertainty that arises and regardless of how others might view her circumstances, she doesn't need to be afraid. She has God's approval.

What Do You Think?

How should we react when we recognize God's favor at work in our lives in various ways?

Talking Points for Your Discussion
- Regarding an opportunity being presented
- Regarding material blessings we already have
- Regarding a change of financial status
- Regarding a change in position of authority
- Other

---

31. "And behold, you will conceive in your womb and bear a son, and you shall call his name Jesus.

There is no small talk or get-acquainted session here! Rather, Gabriel proceeds immediately to deliver the message that is his task to do. Divine initiative is suggested in the promise that Mary will name her forthcoming son *Jesus*. Unlike today, biblical names are loaded with meaning and significance (compare Hosea 1:4-9). The Old Testament origin of Jesus' name is found in the name *Joshua*. In turn, that name is derived from a Hebrew verb that means "to save." When Joseph is told what the name of Mary's baby is to be, the angel leaves no question that the name has prophetic significance (Matthew 1:21).

What Do You Think?

What sequence of steps have you found to be useful when receiving life-changing news?

Talking Points for Your Discussion
- Concerning positive news (job promotion, news of a birth, etc.)
- Concerning negative news (layoff notice, news of a death, etc.)

32a. "He will be great

While most parents think their children are special, Mary has the best reason to think so. Since the Bible refers to God as *great* (Deuteronomy 10:17; Nehemiah 8:6; 9:32; Psalm 95:3; 104:1), the statement *he will be great* seems to highlight the forthcoming child's divine status.

32b. "and will be called the Son of the Most High.

This title, which Gabriel uses to predict the child's exalted status, is reflected in both Old and New Testaments (Genesis 14:18-22; Deuteronomy 32:8; Mark 5:7; Acts 16:17). This divine designation conveys the sense of God's authority over all things. God identifies Jesus as his Son at his baptism (Luke 3:21, 22). Jesus' status as God's Son is also recognized by demons (Matthew 8:29), by Simon Peter (Matthew 16:16), etc.

32c. "And the Lord God will give to him the throne of his father David,

This partial verse helps us understand why Luke mentions Joseph's ancestry in verse 27, above. At this point, Mary should be realizing that Gabriel is saying Jesus will be the Messiah (compare 2 Samuel 7:12, 13, 16; Isaiah 9:7).

33. "and he will reign over the house of Jacob forever, and of his kingdom there will be no end."

Jesus' messianic identity is further confirmed. In the Old Testament, the expression *the house of Jacob* is synonymous with Israel (Exodus 19:3; Isaiah 46:3; Jeremiah 2:4; Ezekiel 20:5), the people over whom the Messiah is expected to reign.

But Gabriel reveals that the nature of Jesus' rule will diverge from expectations. If some believe the Messiah's rule will be limited in duration, Gabriel makes clear that it will be eternal. There will be no line of succession as is customary with earthly kings. Neither Jesus' reign nor his kingdom will ever cease to be.

While nothing is said about when Jesus' rule is to begin, Jesus will speak of his kingdom as present while he is on earth (Luke 17:20, 21). He will speak of it in future terms as well (22:16, 18). The fact that Jesus describes the kingdom of God in both ways indicates that he doesn't see his messianic role being limited to his time on earth.

II. Trusting God's Plan
(LUKE 1:34-38)
A. Mary's Question (v. 34)

34. "And Mary said to the angel, "How will this be, since I am a virgin?"

It's not hard to imagine that Mary's mind is filled with the normal *who, what, where, when,* and *why* questions. But the question she chooses to ask is that of how. Her question suggests she is thinking Gabriel's prediction of her conceiving a child will come to pass sooner rather than later. If she is thinking that Gabriel is talking about Joseph and her having a baby after they consummate their marriage, then her virginity (*I am a virgin*) would be a nonissue, and her how question would not be on her mind.

Zechariah also questioned Gabriel—questioning that resulted in the skeptical priest's being made mute! But no penalty results from Mary's question. The difference seems to be that Zechariah questioned from a standpoint of doubt. The elderly, experienced priest (Luke 1:5-7) should know of the power of God to make things happen. In the history of God's people, barren wives had indeed become pregnant (Genesis 18:10-14; 21:1-7; Judges 13:2, 3, 24; 1 Samuel 1:1-20).

Mary's question, on the other hand, stems from the fact that virgins do not have babies. There is no Old Testament instance of a virginal conception. If there were, her question could make her guilty of undue skepticism. Her question is reasonable.

> **What Do You Think?**
> How do we know when questions to God cross the line from being appropriate (as in Luke 1:34) to being inappropriate or even sinful (as in Luke 1:18)?
> *Talking Points for Your Discussion*
> - In times of national distress
> - In times of personal distress
> - When faced with an opportunity
> - Other

◆ UNIQUE, BUT NOT ALONE ◆

When I used to express concern about being able to do something that seemed too difficult, my husband would reply, "How do you think the pioneers did it?" That response always made me realize that life wasn't as hard as it could be. It also made me wonder how I would have fared in an earlier era—that is, until one day when I had

Visual for Lesson 1. *Use this visual to start a discussion that contrast Mary's reaction to "impossible" news (Luke 1:34, 38) with that of Zacharias (1:18).*

an epiphany. None of my ancestors crossed the mighty Mississippi River until after an interstate highway was built across it! My takeaway lesson was clear: not everyone need be a trailblazer.

At one level, God's plans are the same for every Christian: we are to "walk in a manner worthy of the Lord, fully pleasing to him, bearing fruit in every good work and increasing in the knowledge of God" (Colossians 1:10). Above and beyond that, it seems that God reserves specific plans for relatively few people. All of us are to travel the "highway . . . called the Way of Holiness" in a general sense (Isaiah 35:8), while relatively few are called specifically to go to foreign countries as missionaries with the Word of God in hand as the spiritual machete for hacking a trail.

Mary's call was unique to her, never to be repeated. She had neither podcast sermons nor Christian books to help prepare her for all that the call entailed. Even so, God met her needs—usually, it seems, through interactions with other people (Matthew 2:11; Luke 1:39-45, 56; 2:16-19, 22-38; John 19:25-27; Acts 1:14).

We need not fear what God's plans entail. He has unlimited resources. He is able to provide comfort in any situation. He is faithful to help us succeed in what he entrusts to us. "He who supplies seed to the sower and bread for food will supply and multiply your seed for sowing and increase the harvest of your righteousness" (2 Corinthians 9:10). Expect it!   —V. E.

B. Gabriel's Answer (vv. 35-37)

35. And the angel answered her, "The Holy Spirit will come upon you, and the power of the Most High will overshadow you; therefore the child to be born will be called holy—the Son of God.

The nature of Gabriel's words may leave modern readers with the impression that he is using euphemisms to describe how Mary will become pregnant. On the contrary, Gabriel's descriptions rule out the type of divine-human mating found in some pagan religions. His language describing *The Holy Spirit* at work is similar to what Jesus will later say in Acts 1:8 to prepare the disciples for Pentecost. Gabriel's description of God's overshadowing of Mary is similar to how God is said to be present to protect his people (Psalm 91:4).

36, 37. "And behold, your relative Elizabeth in her old age has also conceived a son, and this is the sixth month with her who was called barren. For nothing will be impossible with God."

Even though Mary doesn't ask for confirmation of Gabriel's words, it is given nonetheless. The confirmation is the startling pregnancy of Elizabeth, a relative of Mary. Mary seems not to know about Elizabeth's pregnancy before Gabriel mentions it, since Elizabeth has hidden it (Luke 1:24).

Gabriel's words are reminiscent of the Lord's words to Abraham in Genesis 18:13, 14. Elizabeth's pregnancy serves as an example to Mary that things that are humanly impossible are not impossible for God. The conceptions of John the Baptist and Jesus are manifestations of this truth.

Luke 1:56 says that Mary stays with Elizabeth "about three months." Since 6 + 3 = 9, some students think Mary is with Elizabeth when John the Baptist is born. However, Luke 1:57 indicates that Mary's departure occurs just prior to John's birth.

C. Mary's Faith (v. 38)

38. And Mary said, "Behold, I am the servant of the Lord; let it be to me according to your word." And the angel departed from her.

There is nothing in Gabriel's words to suggest God's plan is contingent on Mary's agreement. Even so, her statement of submission is important. In describing herself as *servant,* Mary uses a term that refers to slaves. By doing so she expresses her immediate and forthcoming obedience—she is God's, and he is *the Lord*.

While no details are given as to when Mary becomes pregnant, Elizabeth realizes that her younger relative is with child when the two meet (Luke 1:41-45). This suggests Mary becomes pregnant shortly after Gabriel's visit, since she *went with haste* to visit Elizabeth (1:39, 40).

> **What Do You Think?**
> Which Bible passages help you most to distinguish between the Lord's leading and your own personal desires?
>
> *Talking Points for Your Discussion*
> - Regarding Bible commands intended for all
> - Regarding successes and failings of Bible characters
> - Other

◆ *Favorite Quotes* ◆

It seems to be somewhat chic to be called a *nerd* these days. I'm glad, because I suspect I am one. Not the science- or genius-type, mind you. I'm more of a word-nerd in that I love to collect quotes. Consider these treasures from my personal trove:

I have a point of view. You have a point of view. God has view. —Madeleine L'Engle

Time sneaks up on you like a windshield on a bug. —John Lithgow

What comes into our minds when we think about God is the most important thing about us.
—A. W. Tozer

Many of my favorites are verses from the Bible. These favorites pierce the dullness of doubt and my own "analysis paralysis," inspiring me to (quoting Nike®) "Just do it."

You come to me with a sword and with a spear and with a javelin, but I come to you in the name of the Lord of hosts. —David (1 Samuel 17:45)

Here am I. Send me! —Isaiah (Isaiah 6:8)

And at the top of my list is the terse, no-nonsense affirmation by a young lady with no literary credentials: "Let it be to me according to your word" (Luke 1:38). May we too be open to his leading. —V. E.

Conclusion
A. A Change of Plans

Mary's life was already changing by the time of Gabriel's visit: she was betrothed to Joseph, legally committed to becoming his wife. But when God chose her to be the earthly mother of the Messiah, his plan changed her plans. Even given Gabriel's answer to her question, "How will this be?" there was still much she didn't understand about God's plan. Yet Joseph and Mary didn't need to understand everything about that plan to be part of it. What they needed to do—and did do—was trust God.

Before Jesus was born, both Joseph and Mary understood at some level that he would be the promised Messiah. Both Joseph and Mary accepted the "adventure" of the divine plan, even though it meant changing their own plans. At different times, we all need to trust God's promises and plan. When such times come our way, there will be some things we understand and there will be some things we don't. The challenge is to trust when our understanding is incomplete.

When we do so, we change forever. When we agree to be part of God's "adventure," we won't be taking the journey alone. He will be with us every step of the way!

B. Prayer

Heavenly Father, grant us the wisdom to know your will for our lives as you strengthen our faith in your promises. May we realize that your Word has your plan: we are to bear fruit for your kingdom. Grant that we may say yes to every chance to do so. We pray this in the name of Jesus. Amen.

C. Thought to Remember

Trust that depends on full understanding—isn't.

VISUALS FOR THESE LESSONS

The visual pictured in each lesson (example: page 126) is a small reproduction of a large, full-color poster included in the *Adult Resources* packet for the Winter Quarter. That packet also contains the very useful *Presentation Tools* CD for teacher use. Order No. 2629117 from your supplier.

INVOLVEMENT LEARNING

Enhance your lesson presentation with the reproducible activity page,
available as a free download at www.standardlesson.com.

Into the Lesson

Before class, write each of the following phrases on separate index cards: *cross my heart, pinky swear, scout's honor, hand to God, you have my word.*

Start class with a quick game of charades. Hand the cards to volunteers. One at a time, ask the volunteers to communicate their phrase without using words.

Discuss the activity briefly by noting that all the phrases deal with making promises. Ask students to identify the most important promises they have ever made or have been given.

Alternative. Distribute copies of the "Presidential Promises" activity from the reproducible page, which you can download. Have students work individually or in pairs.

After either activity, lead into the Bible study saying, "Promises are important. Those making a promise want us to give them our trust that they plan to make good on the pledge they have given. Today we will look at a very specific promise God gave more than 2,000 years ago."

Into the Word

Before class, make a copy of the lesson text and cut it apart, verse by verse.

Take four envelopes, write one of the following phrases on each envelope, and insert the corresponding verses into the envelope:

Envelope 1—Promises about Mary (vv. 28-30)
Envelope 2—Promises about Jesus (vv. 31-33)
Envelope 3—How the promise would be fulfilled (vv. 27, 34, 35, 37)
Envelope 4—Evidence that the promise would be fulfilled (vv. 26, 36)

(Note that the final verse of the lesson text will be dealt with at the end of the lesson.)

Tell the class that you have cut the lesson text apart, and it will be their job to put it back together. Divide the class into four groups, giving each an envelope. Ask the groups to read their verses and to be prepared to report as to how the verses relate to the phrase on the outside of their envelope.

When groups have completed the activity, allow time for each group to share. Comment on each report, referring to relevant portions of the commentary as necessary.

Into Life

Have a volunteer read verse 38 aloud. Help the class come up with questions that may have been in Mary's mind after Gabriel's visit. These may include:

Is Elizabeth really going to have a baby?
Am I really going to have a child?
How is all this possible?
What will Joseph think?
How can I explain this to others?

Then instruct the class to list reasons Mary accepted the message and submitted herself to the Lord. These may include:

God has promised to save his people.
Great heroes of the past have trusted God in impossible situations.
God has always been faithful to me and my family.

Discuss as a class what it means to be a servant of the Lord today. As a class, list how God's people could be more obedient to his plan.

Encourage the class to consider not only how individuals might submit to God's desires, but also how the class or church together could follow the example of Mary in becoming a servant of the Lord.

Option. Distribute copies of "A Servant's Prayer" from the reproducible page. Ask students to write a prayer of submission to be God's servant. Have volunteers share their prayers as time allows.

Close with a prayer thanking God for the promises fulfilled in Christ.

THE AFFIRMATION
OF THE PROMISE

DEVOTIONAL READING: Psalm 111
BACKGROUND SCRIPTURE: Luke 1:39-56

LUKE 1:39-56

³⁹ In those days Mary arose and went with haste into the hill country, to a town in Judah, ⁴⁰ and she entered the house of Zechariah and greeted Elizabeth. ⁴¹ And when Elizabeth heard the greeting of Mary, the baby leaped in her womb. And Elizabeth was filled with the Holy Spirit, ⁴² and she exclaimed with a loud cry, "Blessed are you among women, and blessed is the fruit of your womb! ⁴³ And why is this granted to me that the mother of my Lord should come to me? ⁴⁴ For behold, when the sound of your greeting came to my ears, the baby in my womb leaped for joy. ⁴⁵ And blessed is she who believed that there would be a fulfillment of what was spoken to her from the Lord."

⁴⁶ And Mary said,

"My soul magnifies the Lord,
⁴⁷   and my spirit rejoices in God my Savior,
⁴⁸ for he has looked on the humble estate of
      his servant.

For behold, from now on all generations
      will call me blessed;
⁴⁹   for he who is mighty has done great things
      for me,
      and holy is his name.
⁵⁰   And his mercy is for those who fear him
      from generation to generation.
⁵¹   He has shown strength with his arm;
      he has scattered the proud in the
         thoughts of their hearts;
⁵²   he has brought down the mighty from
         their thrones
      and exalted those of humble estate;
⁵³   he has filled the hungry with good things,
      and the rich he has sent away empty.
⁵⁴   He has helped his servant Israel,
      in remembrance of his mercy,
⁵⁵   as he spoke to our fathers,
      to Abraham and to his offspring
         forever."

⁵⁶ And Mary remained with her about three months and returned to her home.

KEY VERSES

Mary said, "My soul magnifies the Lord, and my spirit rejoices in God my Savior." —Luke 1:46, 47

CREATION: A DIVINE CYCLE

Unit 1: The Savior Has Been Born
LESSONS 1–4

LESSON AIMS

After participating in this lesson, each learner will be able to:

1. Identify Old Testament themes in Mary's Song ("Magnificat").

2. Explain how themes in Mary's song inform the Christian understanding of God's providential care.

3. Share with a classmate personal experiences of unexpected blessing.

LESSON OUTLINE

Introduction

A. The Joy of Being Chosen

Nothing feels better than being chosen. The childhood joy of receiving an invitation to a party is unforgettable. Being asked on a date (or getting a *yes* when doing the asking) builds self-esteem. Being offered a job, especially after we've lost one, enhances self-confidence. The good feeling that results from such situations may stem from a sense of deserving or having earned the choosing.

On the other hand, things that are unearned can be difficult to receive. We easily imagine Mary to have felt this way after being told that she was God's choice to bear his Son (Luke 1:26-37, last week's lesson). All of us feel awed at times by the depth of God's grace. But to be chosen for no apparent reason to be the earthly mother of the Christ—how overwhelming, especially considering that Mary was likely still a teenager at the time! Today's lesson gives us a glimpse into Mary's joy at being chosen to fill this marvelous role.

B. Lesson Background

Last week's lesson reviewed Gabriel's announcement that Mary was to give birth to the Messiah. Since that announcement forms the immediate background for the lesson at hand, that information need not be repeated here. But against the broader backdrop of salvation-history, the unexpected, miraculous pregnancies of Mary and Elizabeth meant that the two women stood at the very threshold of prophetic fulfillment.

Neither one knew the details of how God would use their unborn sons to fulfill the promises in Luke 1:16, 17, 32, 33. Even so, it is almost certain that at least elderly Elizabeth, wife of a priest, was aware of past incidents of miraculous, old-age pregnancies like hers; such awareness would have undergirded her faith for the days ahead (Genesis 17:19; 25:21; Judges 13:3-5; 1 Samuel 1:5, 20).

The much younger Mary, for her part, may have been aware that her unprecedented virginal conception was fulfilling the prophecy of Isaiah 7:14. Further, her declarations in this week's lesson, traditionally referred to as "Mary's Song," reflect Old Testament passages that praise God for caring for the helpless. For example, scholars often observe that the imagery of Luke 1:46-55 is very similar to that of 1 Samuel 2:1-10, the prayer of Hannah. She, like Mary's relative Elizabeth, had been unable to conceive (1 Samuel 1:2, 5; Luke 1:7), but each was miraculously blessed to bear a son (1 Samuel 1:20; Luke 1:24). Mary and Elizabeth had good reason to celebrate God's faithfulness as the saints before them had.

I. Mary's Visit
(LUKE 1:39-45)
A. Hasty Trip (vv. 39, 40)

39. In those days Mary arose and went with haste into the hill country, to a town in Judah,

Mary lives in "a city of Galilee named Nazareth" (Luke 1:26), while Elizabeth and husband Zechariah (a priest, 1:5) live in an unnamed *town in Judah*. The two villages are located in different areas that later will have different rulers (Matthew 2:22; Luke 3:1), but for now Herod the Great rules both. Hilly Judea is the district that includes Jerusalem.

Most priests do not live in Jerusalem. Instead, they live on property inherited through ancestral lineage (compare Nehemiah 11:20). They serve in Jerusalem on occasion, according to a system of casting lots (Luke 1:8, 9; next week's lesson). Rural priests, as Zechariah seems to be, work on farms as most people do in preindustrial economies.

Mary *arose and went with haste* to visit Elizabeth. Some speculate the haste is from a sense of duty to assist an expectant mother with household chores. This could be especially so given that Elizabeth, "advanced in years" as she is, is now in the sixth month of her pregnancy (Luke 1:7, 36). The

HOW TO SAY IT

Bethlehem	*Beth*-lih-hem.
Gabriel	*Gay*-bree-ul.
Judah	*Joo*-duh.
Judea	Joo-*dee*-uh.
Magnificat	Mag-*nif*-ih-cot.
Nazareth	*Naz*-uh-reth.
Zechariah	Zack-uh-*rye*-uh.

better answer is that Mary's trip is in reaction to what we might call "the sign element" in Gabriel's announcement (1:36). Elizabeth's miraculous pregnancy will be a sign—although the text does not use that word—to Mary, and she wishes to confirm it without delay (compare 2:12, 15, 16).

> **What Do You Think?**
> How can we do better at knowing when haste is called for versus the opposite?
> *Talking Points for Your Discussion*
> - In normal, day-to-day routines
> - In dealing with a crisis
> - When considering a ministry opportunity
> - Comparing and contrasting Proverbs 19:2; 21:5; 29:20; Ecclesiastes 5:2; 7:9; 8:3; Matthew 5:25; 28:8; Luke 2:16; Acts 22:18; 1 Timothy 5:22; and James 1:19

40. and she entered the house of Zechariah and greeted Elizabeth.

The trip must be exhausting for Mary. The minimum distance for the trip is 35 miles, assuming that *Zechariah's home* is at the northernmost tip of Judean territory. But Luke makes no mention either of distance or exhaustion. Instead, he focuses on the interactions of those present.

On entering the house, Mary begins a normal exchange of greetings with Elizabeth; the verb translated *greeted* also is translated elsewhere in terms of greeting (Romans 16:3-11; etc.).

B. Exuberant Reactions (vv. 41-45)

41. And when Elizabeth heard the greeting of Mary, the baby leaped in her womb. And Elizabeth was filled with the Holy Spirit,

Mary's arrival provokes a startling response! There is nothing inherently unusual about a baby moving about in the womb, of course. But the timing of that reaction is significant in view of the relationship that later emerges between Jesus (Mary's child) and John the Baptist (Elizabeth's child). The latter is *"filled with the Holy Spirit, even from his mother's womb"* as empowerment "to make ready for the Lord a people prepared" (Luke 1:15-17; see next week's lesson). Even before his birth, John begins to fulfill his role by signaling to

Visual for Lesson 2. *Start a discussion by pointing to this visual as you ask learners how they will do this and why it is important.*

his mother that the anticipated Christ, himself yet unborn, is present. At the same time, Elizabeth is filled with the Spirit to confirm the message Mary has received from the angel (next verse).

42. and she exclaimed with a loud cry, "Blessed are you among women, and blessed is the fruit of your womb!

The word *blessed* occurs four times in today's text: twice here and once each in verses 45 and 48b. However, different Greek words are behind these translations.

The word behind the two translations of *blessed* here in verse 42 is also our English word *eulogy*. As we use that word today, we refer to statements spoken or written in honor of someone who has died. But we should not take the modern way we use this word and "read it back" into the Bible! There it means "to speak well of," "to praise," "to celebrate with praises," or "to extol" someone, but not just at funerals. Elizabeth is speaking well of Mary while the latter is still very much alive!

In view of the significance attached to this verse in some religious circles, it is important to point out that these two pronouncements do not say why Mary is blessed. That will wait until we encounter different uses of *blessed* in verses 45 and 48, below.

43. "And why is this granted to me that the mother of my Lord should come to me?

Elizabeth is surprised and honored to see her younger relative. In turn, Mary must be very sur-

prised to hear Elizabeth's knowledge of something that Mary herself has only recently learned from an angel! Mary is not visibly pregnant at this time (see 1:26, 35, 36, 39), and time factors make it extremely doubtful that Elizabeth has been informed by any normal mode of communication that Mary has conceived. The greatest likelihood is that Elizabeth has been informed supernaturally by being "filled with the Holy Spirit" (v. 41, above).

44. "For behold, when the sound of your greeting came to my ears, the baby in my womb leaped for joy.

This verse repeats information of verse 41, above, and adds *for joy*. John the Baptist's prenatal reaction seems somehow to reflect his own sense of anticipation of the coming of the one who will give meaning to John's mission.

45. "And blessed is she who believed that there would be a fulfillment of what was spoken to her from the Lord."

The word translated *blessed* here and in verse 48b is the one Jesus will later use in the Beatitudes (Matthew 5:3-11). This word has a range of meanings of something like "enjoying favorable circumstances," "well off," "happy," and/or "fortunate." Use of this word normally includes a reason or explanation for someone to be regarded as blessed.

We see such a reason here in the phrase *that there would be a fulfillment of what was spoken to her from the Lord*. That's why Mary is blessed. She is not said to be blessed because she is particularly outstanding or worthy of merit (see more on v. 48, below).

Elizabeth's declarations provide a transition to Mary's Song that follows by highlighting two themes: (1) God's blessings are for the faithful, and (2) God fulfills his promises.

II. Mary's Song
(LUKE 1:46-55)
A. Joy and Blessing (vv. 46-49)

46, 47. And Mary said:
"My soul magnifies the Lord,
    and my spirit rejoices in God my
        Savior,

The praise Mary expresses reveals that she views Elizabeth's blessing as a confirmation of Gabriel's message of Luke 1:35. If Mary has wondered whether her encounter with the angel were merely a hallucination, her elderly relative's awareness is verification of fact. The terms *rejoices* and *God my Savior* anchor major themes of what follows.

◆ THE GOD WHO CONFIRMS ◆

When the characters in a science-fiction story encounter things typically thought of as unreal, which violate the laws of physics, etc., the writer must find ways to make such things believable to both the characters and the readers. The writer's task is to help suspend disbelief.

But how can you help people believe that the impossible just happened? How can they be assured that they are not hallucinating or otherwise losing their faculties? The more outlandish the literary scenario, the more the author must work to create a realistic response from the characters and thereby keep the reader engaged.

The Bible is not fiction, but its characters are confronted with things outside mind-sets formed by life experiences. Consider the angelic communication to Mary of last week's lesson. This visit carried the risk that she would be left tragically confused—*Did I hallucinate? Am I losing my mind?*—until the passage of weeks and months proved the physical reality of her pregnancy. (Compare Peter's mistaken impression in Acts 12:9-11.) How gracious of God to provide Mary the confirmation we see in today's text!

We serve a God who confirms his Word and his calls (Romans 15:8; 1 Corinthians 1:5, 6; etc.). He does not leave us uncertain. For this may we be filled with the joy of the Lord!   —V. E.

> **What Do You Think?**
> How do you expect God to confirm callings on your life? What if those sources conflict?
> *Talking Points for Your Discussion*
> - The role of Scripture
> - The role of counsel by fellow Christians
> - How we expect God to answer prayer
> - Open and closed doors of opportunity

48a. "for he has looked on the humble estate of his servant.

This is the reason for the praise expressed in verse 47. Clearly, Mary is not chosen for her special role because she is a special person—quite the opposite! The fact that she is of *humble estate* is critical to Luke's account of Jesus' birth: God's Son came from and for such as these (compare Luke 2:8-20; 1 Corinthians 1:26–2:5).

48b. "For behold, from now on all generations will call me blessed;

This prediction we now know to be a matter of established historical fact, and Mary's fame throughout the world and over millennia (*all generations*) is indeed remarkable. Yet if not handled carefully, the prominence of this fact in the history of Christian doctrine may distract from its true significance. Verse 49 (next) clarifies.

◆ FIFTEEN MINUTES OF FAME ◆

In a world with more than seven billion people, attempts to distinguish oneself can be daunting. Even so, video-sharing websites, televised talent competitions, and so-called reality TV have kept alive the concept of "15 minutes of fame," an expression traceable to the late 1960s. Fame seems to be something many would like to achieve.

Fame, whether fleeting or lasting, can bring benefits. A famous person may get special treatment. He or she may even get a platform to influence the world in a positive way. But when God singles out someone for his kind of fame, that person's legacy ends up being eternally significant (see Hebrews 11). Mary was correct in noting that all generations would call her blessed. Selected by God from obscurity, Mary is remembered by Christians every Christmas season for her faithfulness.

Most of us will live our earthly lives in obscurity, as the world defines that concept. But God sees our actions and knows the motives behind them. Loving obedience pleases him (2 John 6); humility results in his grace (1 Peter 5:5). While we may never receive an exalted title, be elected to high office, or be offered an invitation to host a TV show, God makes note of those who serve him faithfully. They are the ones to be called blessed forever. See Revelation 20:6; 22:14.   —V. E.

**49. "for he who is mighty has done great
things for me,
and holy is his name.**

As before, a reason is given why Mary is considered blessed. We should note that the focus is on God, not on Mary. God is the one who does *great things* to her, not the reverse. God is the one whose *name* is *holy* (Psalm 103:1; 105:3; etc.). Despite her lowly status—or perhaps because of it—the mighty Creator of the universe sees fit to include her in his plans. Hannah's prayer in 1 Samuel 2:1-10 is parallel in also affirming God's power and holiness at the outset (see the Lesson Background).

What Do You Think?

Is it possible to overstate God's role in circumstances that change? Why, or why not?

Talking Points for Your Discussion
- Regarding circumstances of blessing
- Regarding circumstances of distress
- Considering Ecclesiastes 9:11

B. Mercy and Retribution (vv. 50-55)

**50. "And his mercy is for those who fear him
from generation to generation.**

Many psalms connect God's mercy and/or love with *those who fear him* (see Psalms 33:18; 103:11, 17; 118:4; 147:11). Mary's point is not that God is never merciful to those who do not fear him, but rather that he is always merciful to those who do —regardless of their circumstances.

What Do You Think?

How do we know when we fear the Lord properly? How do we correct problems here?

Talking Points for Your Discussion
- In attitudes about ourselves
- In interacting with the secular world in general
- In attitudes toward and interactions with others in particular
- In personal habits and disciplines
- Other

**51. "He has shown strength with his arm;
he has scattered the proud in the
thoughts of their hearts;**

The imagery of God's *arm* as an indication of his *strength* or power is a vivid Old Testament theme (Psalm 89:10, 13; Isaiah 40:10; Jeremiah 21:5; etc.). *The proud* refers not so much to those who merely think too highly of themselves (which, of course, is not good; see Romans 12:3), but more to those who actively oppose God and intend harm for his people (Psalm 94:1-6; 123:3, 4). Those controlled by *the thoughts of their hearts* do not allow God's Word to direct their behavior (Ezekiel 13:1-3, 17; Romans 1:21-23).

Old Testament references to God's might or strength are often accompanied by accounts of what he has done to deliver his people from proud schemers (Exodus 15:1-18; etc.). Such passages highlight Israel's lowly state and unworthiness in order to emphasize God's graciousness and power—he overcomes enemies that his people cannot. The verse before us connects Mary's personal experiences with great acts of past deliverance: God exalts the faithful regardless of their status otherwise. He is once again choosing the lowly (Mary) to fill an important role in his plan.

**52. "he has brought down the mighty from
their thrones
and exalted those of humble estate;**

Mary's summarizes much of Israel's history: God *exalted those of humble estate* (Genesis 41:41; Psalm 78:70, 71; 113:7, 8; etc.) while dethroning *the mighty* (Job 12:19; Isaiah 10:12-19; Jeremiah 28:15-17; etc.). The latter theme is especially prominent in terms of foreign powers that oppressed or conspired to destroy Israel. God laughs at such schemes (Psalm 2:1-4).

Mary's statements also anticipate Jesus' later teachings regarding position reversals of the powerful and the weak (Luke 14:7-11; 18:9-14; etc.). He himself will be the ultimate example, as Mary and others will find out (Acts 2:32, 33; 2 Corinthians 8:9; Philippians 2:5-11).

**53. "he has filled the hungry with good
things,
and the rich he has sent away empty.**

This verse parallels the language of Hannah's prayer at 1 Samuel 2:5. *The rich* is usually a derogatory term for those who gain wealth by exploiting the innocent (Proverbs 22:7; James 2:6, 7;

etc.). Although wealthy landowners and officials manipulate the economy and the justice system to their advantage (Ezekiel 22:27-29; Amos 5:11, 12; etc.), God can't be bought. He blesses those who are faithful, and Mary seems to be identifying herself with *the hungry* whom God fills *with good things*. God certainly did not choose the richest woman in the world (as the world counts being rich) to be the earthly mother of Jesus!

**54. "He has helped his servant Israel,
    in remembrance of his mercy,**

Mary's words again echo an Old Testament theme of deliverance (compare Psalm 98:3; Isaiah 41:8-10). Various psalms and prophecies express desire for and prediction of God's deliverance of Israel from dire threats (example: Psalm 79). These were traceable to apostasy (2 Chronicles 6:36-39).

More narrowly, this verse may also focus on Mary's own experience. God had promised to deliver his people through the coming of a certain servant (Isaiah 52:13–53:12; etc.), and Mary recognizes her role in God's fulfillment of that promise. Surely all this is taking place *because he is remembering to be merciful*! God is doing what he said he would do (compare 2 Samuel 7:16; Isaiah 7:14).

**55. "as he spoke to our fathers,
    to Abraham and to his offspring
    forever."**

Deliverance validates God's promises to *our fathers and to Abraham and to his offspring*. God's people are protected if they remain, or return to being, faithful (example: Genesis 17:7; Psalm 105:42-45). Mary connects those promises with her child, but more than 30 years will elapse before she knows all the details. The promises and details are ours as well, since "those who are of faith are blessed along with Abraham, the man of faith" (Galatians 3:9).

III. Mary's Return
(LUKE 1:56)

56. And Mary remained with her about three months and returned to her home.

The fact that six months (Luke 1:36) plus *three months* equals nine months could indicate that Mary stays until John is born. But verse 57 offers

evidence that Mary departs just prior to the birth. *Her home* in Nazareth will be the point of departure for Bethlehem (2:1-5).

Conclusion
A. Ordinary People

In 1984, Helen Ashe of Knoxville, Tennessee, saw a local news story about a church that sponsored a soup kitchen for the needy. Her heart was stirred, and she and her twin sister, Ellen, sensed a call to start a food ministry to "help feed God's children." So on Valentine's Day 1986, the 58-year-old sisters launched The Love Kitchen at a small church, serving 22 people on that first day.

The Love Kitchen today operates out of its own facilities as it serves more than 3,000 meals weekly. Remarkably, it is an all-volunteer organization, with no paid staff.

God still calls ordinary people to do extraordinary things. At age 80, Moses was called from self-imposed exile to lead the Israelites from Egypt (Exodus 3:10; 7:7); elderly Elizabeth suffered infertility (Luke 1:7, 13-25); Mary and Joseph probably had no earthly status above that of any other working-class resident of Galilee. The church today is filled with people who should identify with Mary's statement in Luke 1:48a. Do you?

B. Prayer

Father, we thank you for your works of deliverance! Help us recognize occasions when you call us to participate in your plan. May you strengthen us as we do. In Jesus' name we pray. Amen.

C. Thought to Remember

God uses people we might not expect
in ways we might not imagine.

INVOLVEMENT LEARNING

Enhance your lesson presentation with the reproducible activity page,
available as a free download at www.standardlesson.com.

Into the Lesson

In advance ask one of your musical students to lead the class in singing a familiar hymn about singing. Some possible hymns include:

"I Will Sing the Wondrous Story"
"I Will Sing of My Redeemer"
"Wonderful Words of Life"
"When We All Get to Heaven"

After singing, ask members to share how singing that song made them feel. In what day-to-day situations might humming or singing that song help them? Brainstorm with the class to create a list of situations in which listening to music or singing changes moods or energizes someone. A few of those times might be while exercising, when celebrating, when needing to get out of a sad mood, etc.

Alternative. Before class begins, place in chairs copies of the "Perfect Playlist" activity from the reproducible page, which you can download. Allow students to work individually or in small groups to choose a mood or situation and construct a playlist of songs that would be perfect for it.

Lead into Bible study by saying, "Singing, humming, whistling, and listening to music are powerful tools. There is nothing like a song to motivate, to comfort, or to express feelings that words alone cannot. Today we will look at a time when Mary reacted to her deep joy by singing."

Into the Word

Read through the text as a class to get a feel for the overall flow of events. Briefly, the verses tell that after Mary received the message from Gabriel (last week's lesson), she packed and quickly made her way to her relative Elizabeth. When Mary arrived, the Holy Spirit revealed the significance of Mary's pregnancy to Elizabeth, who greeted her enthusiastically. Mary responded with a song of praise. Mary stayed with Elizabeth for most of the last three months of Elizabeth's pregnancy and the first three months of her own.

Divide the class into three groups, giving each group pen and paper. Each group is to read their assigned portion of the text and to create a diary entry based on the text and personal speculation.

Group 1—Elizabeth's diary (Luke 1:39-45). "I couldn't believe it! No sooner had Mary entered the house than I . . ."

Group 2—Mary's diary (vv. 46-55). "After Elizabeth greeted me, I nearly exploded in song, singing about . . ."

Group 3—The next three months (v. 56). "How the next three months flew by! We had so much to talk about . . ."

After 10–15 minutes, allow groups to share their entries.

Alternative. Distribute copies of the "Mary and Hannah" activity from the reproducible page. Allow students to work individually or in groups. This will allow students to find the common themes between the song of Hannah in the Old Testament and Mary's song in Luke.

Into Life

Today's Bible text tells of two relatives whose lives would not be the same from that day forward. Elizabeth had spent most of her adult lifetime wanting a child, but was unable to conceive —until God stepped in! Mary grew up with her nation in captivity and the future looking bleak— until God stepped in!

Close in prayer, asking class members to consider how they would complete these two sentences:

I felt hopeless because _____
_____

Then God stepped in by _____
_____

THE FORERUNNER
OF THE SAVIOR

DEVOTIONAL READING: John 1:19-23
BACKGROUND SCRIPTURE: Luke 1:1-25, 57-80

LUKE 1:8-20

8 Now while he was serving as priest before God when his division was on duty, 9 according to the custom of the priesthood, he was chosen by lot to enter the temple of the Lord and burn incense. 10 And the whole multitude of the people were praying outside at the hour of incense. 11 And there appeared to him an angel of the Lord standing on the right side of the altar of incense. 12 And Zechariah was troubled when he saw him, and fear fell upon him. 13 But the angel said to him, "Do not be afraid, Zechariah, for your prayer has been heard, and your wife Elizabeth will bear you a son, and you shall call his name John. 14 And you will

have joy and gladness, and many will rejoice at his birth, 15 for he will be great before the Lord. And he must not drink wine or strong drink,

and he will be filled with the Holy Spirit, even from his mother's womb. 16 And he will turn many of the children of Israel to the Lord their God, 17 and he will go before him in the spirit and power of Elijah, to turn the hearts of the fathers to the children, and the disobedient to the wisdom of the just, to make ready for the Lord a people prepared."

18 And Zechariah said to the angel, "How shall I know this? For I am an old man, and my wife is advanced in years." 19 And the angel answered him, "I am Gabriel. I stand in the presence of God, and I was sent to speak to you and to bring you this good news. 20 And behold, you will be silent and unable to speak until the day that these things take place, because you did not believe my words, which will be fulfilled in their time."

KEY VERSES

The angel said to him, "Do not be afraid, Zechariah, for your prayer has been heard, and your wife Elizabeth will bear you a son, and you shall call his name John. And you will have joy and gladness, and many will rejoice at his birth." —**Luke 1:13, 14**

CREATION: A DIVINE CYCLE

Unit 1: The Savior Has Been Born

LESSONS 1–4

LESSON AIMS

After participating in this lesson, each learner will be able to:

1. Summarize the circumstances of John the Baptist's miraculous conception.

2. Identify points where the angel's pronouncement draws on Old Testament themes to depict John's future ministry.

3. Identify times when his or her faith is more like that of Zacharias than that of Mary, and make a plan for change.

LESSON OUTLINE

Introduction

A. When We Least Expect It

Once when I had just quit a bad job, I was driving through my neighborhood thinking that a particular type of work would be ideal for me. Almost at that moment, I looked up and saw a "help wanted" sign in the window of a local business for that very type of job. I applied and was hired the next day.

During my college years, my wife and I prayed that God would lead us to friends who would share and affirm our faith. Within a week, we had met another Christian couple who have remained dear friends for 25 years.

Perhaps most dramatically, and related to today's Scripture passage, my wife became pregnant only two weeks after we had resigned ourselves to never having a second child. That was after several years of infertility following a miscarriage and having received no clear medical explanation after numerous tests. God is known for coming through when we most need it!

B. Lesson Background

Luke 1 provides the only detailed account of John the Baptist's origins, revealing the miraculous circumstances of his birth. In certain respects, the story of Jesus' life and the founding of the church begins with John the Baptist (who is not to be confused with the apostle John). John the Baptist was predicted to be the voice crying "In the wilderness prepare the way of the Lord; make straight in the desert a highway for our God" (Isaiah 40:3; compare Luke 3:4-6); John was to be the messenger to prepare that way (Malachi 3:1; compare Luke 7:27); and John was to be an Elijah in correcting wayward hearts (Malachi 4:5, 6; compare Luke 1:17).

The comparison with the prophet Elijah is telling. Elijah's ministry was one of dramatic confrontation (see 1 Kings 17:1–21:29; 2 Kings 1:3-17; 2 Chronicles 21:12-15), much of it occurring during the reign of King Ahab (about 874–853 BC). He was the infamous monarch who married a pagan and promoted idolatry among the northern tribes of Israel (1 Kings 16:29-33).

The circumstances of Elijah's departure from this life were well known: as his disciple Elisha watched, "behold, chariots of fire and horses of fire separated the two of them. And Elijah went up by a whirlwind into heaven" (2 Kings 2:11).

Some years later, a conclusion was reached that Elijah had not in fact died, but was instead alive with God in Heaven, waiting for a command to return to earth and resume his preaching of repentance. As Malachi 4:5 reveals, Elijah's return is associated with the coming of a great day of judgment.

After introductory remarks, Luke begins his Gospel by sketching the time frame of his first narrative: it was "in the days of Herod, king of Judea," who reigned 37–4 BC (Luke 1:5). The focus then shifts immediately to the situation of a priest named Zechariah and his wife, Elizabeth. Three further facts set the stage: (1) both were righteous, (2) the couple was childless, and (3) no child was expected because of advanced age (1:6, 7).

I. Unsuspecting Priest
(LUKE 1:8-10)
A. Special Honor (vv. 8, 9)
8. Now while he was serving as priest before God when his division was on duty,

The temple in Jerusalem is where a priest carries out the duties of *serving . . . before God*. The temple itself is managed by powerful aristocratic families. Although these individuals are wealthy, most priests live as peasants in the villages and countryside of Judea (compare Luke 1:39, 40). There they

HOW TO SAY IT

Ahab	*Ay*-hab.
Elijah	Ee-*lye*-juh.
Gabriel	*Gay*-bree-uhl.
Herod	*Hair*-ud.
Judea	Joo-*dee*-uh.
Malachi	*Mal*-uh-kye.
Nazirite	*Naz*-ih-rite.
patriarch	*pay*-tree-ark.
Zechariah	Zack-uh-*rye*-us.

support themselves by their own work and perhaps by occasional gifts from neighbors.

Following precedent established under King David, each priest is assigned to 1 of 24 divisions according to family lineage (1 Chronicles 24:1-4). Each division is tasked with staffing operations in the temple for two weeks every year according to a specific *order* (24:3, 19). The order had been established by casting lots to keep things impartial (24:5-18; compare 24:31; 25:8; 26:12-16).

9. according to the custom of the priesthood, he was chosen by lot to enter the temple of the Lord and burn incense.

Assignment of duties inside *the temple of the Lord* are determined by casting lots among the priests within the division on duty. This custom allows God to select the appropriate person for the occasion (see Proverbs 16:33).

With so many priests desiring *to burn incense*—a high honor—none is allowed to do so more than once in a lifetime. For Zechariah, then, the opportunity to serve in this manner has not come before nor will it come again. Incense is offered at the temple of the Lord twice daily (Exodus 30:7, 8).

◆ LOTS OF LUCK? ◆

Some years ago, I was reading about missions to the American Indians. The account was that of a denomination in eastern Pennsylvania deciding in about 1800 to send two men as missionaries to frontier Indiana. The group also decided that at least one of the men should be married. One man agreed. Then the group asked the young women of the community for a volunteer to marry the man. Of several volunteers, one was chosen by lot. This was not the method I used to select a wife, but apparently it worked for them!

Choosing by lot was a common form of selection in the ancient world and remains so today in certain situations. The leaders of ancient Athens were chosen by lot from among the citizens. Modern jury pools are chosen at random from among registered voters. References to assigning "by lot" the various portions of Canaan to the tribes of Israel are numerous in the Old Testament.

When we use Proverbs 16:33 as a lens through which to view the seemingly random selection of

Zechariah for incense-burning duty, the choice doesn't seem so random: "The lot is cast into the lap, but its every decision is from the Lord." The discussion question that comes next seems therefore to be an obvious one to ask!   —J. B. N.

B. Typical Crowd (v. 10)

10. And the whole multitude of the people were praying outside at the hour of incense.

All the assembled worshipers wait prayerfully in the outer courts as Zechariah goes about the duties assigned to him. *The time for the burning of incense* probably is "at three in the afternoon" (Acts 3:1). At this time the priest is near the altar of incense (next verse) to perform his tasks there.

While his duties are profoundly significant for Zechariah personally, the day probably seems quite ordinary to everyone else. Luke does not indicate the setting to be that of a major feast such as Passover. Therefore it is likely that the gathered crowd consists largely of local residents who come to pray because it is their normal practice to do so. On this occasion, however, God interrupts that routine in a remarkable way.

II. Unexpected Announcement
(Luke 1:11-17)

A. Startling Appearance (vv. 11, 12)

11. And there appeared to him an angel of the Lord standing on the right side of the altar of incense.

Zechariah is interrupted—by *an angel of the Lord*, no less! Such a designation occurs dozens of times in the Old Testament (usually fronted with

the instead of *an*). Sometimes this phrase seems to refer to God himself (example: Genesis 16:7-13; 22:15-18). But Luke uses the designation here to refer to a divine envoy, as Luke 1:19 (below) makes clear. The transliterated Greek word *angel* is that language's ordinary word for "messenger," and it is translated that way in Luke 7:24, 27; 9:52.

The choice the translators made in this regard is seen in the Old Testament as well. Particularly interesting is 2 Kings 1:3, where two occurrences of a certain Hebrew word are translated first "angel" then "messengers" in the same sentence.

The structure, use, and placement of *the altar of incense* are described in Exodus 30:1-10; 37:25-28; and 40:26, 27.

12. And Zechariah was troubled when he saw him, and fear fell upon him.

While we do not know what angels look like, Zechariah's response of *fear* is consistent with that of others who encounter them (examples: Judges 13:20-22; Matthew 28:5; Acts 10:1-4).

B. Incredible Promise (vv. 13, 14)

13. But the angel said to him, "Do not be afraid, Zechariah, for your prayer has been heard, and your wife Elizabeth will bear you a son, and you shall call his name John.

As noted in the Lesson Background, *Zechariah* and *wife Elizabeth* have been unable to have children, and now she is past menopause. Infertility is a particular source of grief at the time: aside from the emotional pain of being childless, parents normally are supported in old age by their adult children (compare Mark 7:9-13).

From a cultural perspective, the fact that "children are a heritage from the Lord" (Psalm 127:3) implies God's blessing; on the flip side, however, childlessness may indicate unrighteousness (see Leviticus 20:20, 21; Jeremiah 22:30). Childbearing is seen by Jews as fulfilling the command to Adam and Eve to "be fruitful and increase in number" (Genesis 1:28) as continued through Abraham (15:5; 17:5, 6). Zechariah and Elizabeth must have prayed over this issue many times. But with the passing of years, they eventually must have concluded that their prayer will go unanswered.

> *What Do You Think?*
>
> How can the prayer experience of Zacharias influence your own prayer life?
>
> *Talking Points for Your Discussion*
> - Concerning what you do while waiting on God
> - Dealing biblically with the tension between being satisfied with what you have and the disappointment with what you lack
> - Other

But the absence of a *yes* answer does not mean that God has not heard a person's prayer! In the case at hand, God's answer has not been *no*, but *wait* (compare Daniel 10:12-14). The angel's promise implies that the forthcoming birth will result from a miraculous conception (compare Genesis 17:15-17; 18:10-12). The child's name further speaks to divine purpose: the word translated *John* combines the name of God with a Hebrew verb that means "to be gracious."

> *What Do You Think?*
>
> How would you counsel expectant parents who ask your advice on naming their child?
>
> *Talking Points for Your Discussion*
> - Positive name-associations to consider
> - Negative name-associations to consider
> - Regarding expectations of extended family

14. "And you will have joy and gladness, and many will rejoice at his birth,

What we see predicted in the verse before us indeed comes to pass nine months later, per Luke 1:57-66. Even so, the angel likely refers more broadly to the effect of John's life and ministry. That life will cause *many* to *rejoice* at what John's having come on the scene signifies: the imminent arrival of the Savior (compare Luke 3:1-18).

C. Unique Ministry (vv. 15-17)

15. "for he will be great before the Lord. And he must not drink wine or strong drink, and he will be filled with the Holy Spirit, even from his mother's womb.

The angel's description is reminiscent of conditions for taking a Nazirite vow, the whole of which is set forth in Numbers 6:1-21. Verse 3 in particular addresses one's decision to *not drink wine or strong drink* (see also Judges 13:2-7, 14; compare with priests in Leviticus 10:8-11; Ezekiel 44:21). Those temporarily taking the Nazirite vow do so for a time of spiritual reflection as they "separate [themselves] to the Lord" (Numbers 6:2).

> *What Do You Think?*
>
> What can your church do to help expectant parents prepare to rear their children?
>
> *Talking Points for Your Discussion*
> - In study of scriptural precepts
> - In evaluating secular sources of parenting wisdom
> - In evaluating parental role models
> - Other

Later descriptions of John the Baptist seem to indicate that his life is one of permanent self-denial (Mark 1:6; compare 2 Kings 1:8). Such a lifestyle will help ensure his purity, which is vital for one *filled with the Holy Spirit, even from his mother's womb.* This, in turn, alludes to John's prophetic giftedness. John's greatness in the Lord's sight emphasizes the significance of his work as the Messiah's forerunner (compare Luke 7:28).

16. "And he will turn many of the children of Israel to the Lord their God,

The angel describes John's forthcoming ministry in terms of its scope and effect. Regarding the former, the phrase *the children of Israel* occurs multiple times in the Old Testament to refer to God's covenant people of that era (example: 1 Kings 6:13). They will be John's intended audience, and he will preach to them "a baptism of repentance for the forgiveness of sins" (Luke 3:3) in preparation for the mightier one to come (3:16).

While John apparently will not be empowered to perform miracles (see John 10:41), the four Gospels stress the widespread impact of his preaching. *Many* people will travel to hear his message and receive baptism (Mark 1:5), and a band of disciples eventually gathers around him (Luke 7:18; etc.). Most revealing about John's popularity will be the nature of those who are hostile toward, or at least suspicious about, John and his message (John 1:19-25). That boldness ultimately results in his demise (Mark 6:14-29).

17. "and he will go before him in the spirit and power of Elijah, to turn the hearts of the fathers to the children, and the disobedient to the wisdom of the just, to make ready for the Lord a people prepared."

The angel closes his pronouncement by quoting from the last two verses of the Old Testament, namely Malachi 4:5, 6. This should be a clear signal to Zechariah, a priest knowledgeable in the Scriptures, that his yet-to-be-born son is the one *to make ready for the Lord a people prepared.*

It is important to stress that the angel is referring to John the Baptist's ministry, not his identity. This is seen in the phrase *in the spirit and power of Elijah.* John the Baptist will not be the historical Elijah who has returned, as John himself will confirm (John 1:21). Immediately after that statement, he will describe himself as "the voice of one crying in the wilderness, 'Make straight the way of the Lord'" (John 1:23; quoting Isaiah 40:3; see the Lesson Background).

Jesus, also alluding to Malachi 4:5, eventually will compare John the Baptist with Elijah in order to correct a misconception. Certain elements of the religious establishment of the day hold to a literalistic view that the actual, historic Elijah "first . . . must come" (Matthew 17:10). Jesus' response makes clear that the reference is to John the Baptist (17:11-13), who ends up being what we might refer to as "a type of Elijah."

III. Unwanted Proof
(LUKE 1:18-20)
A. Skeptical Question (v. 18)

18. And Zechariah said to the angel, "How shall I know this? For I am an old man, and my wife is advanced in years."

Surprise turns to skepticism as Zechariah listens to the angel. He and his wife have been unable to have children because "Elizabeth was barren, and both were advanced in years" (Luke 1:7). Aside from the fact that the Jews have been waiting 400 years for the appearance of another prophet, what the angel describes is physically impossible. With the query *How shall I know this?* Zechariah is therefore requesting a sign that will validate the angel's words (compare Judges 6:37).

B. Indignant Response (vv. 19, 20)

19. And the angel answered him, "I am Gabriel. I stand in the presence of God, and I was sent to speak to you and to bring you this good news.

Now we know the identity of the angel: he is *Gabriel,* the one who will appear to Mary as well (Luke 1:26; compare Daniel 8:16; 9:21). His response suggests that Zechariah should not be skeptical of the prophecy, given that priest's presumed Scripture knowledge of children being miraculously conceived in circumstances including old age (example: Genesis 17:15-17; 21:1-7). Gabriel's tone is stern. To be skeptical of a divine message of *good news* delivered by one who stands *in the presence of God* is an outrage!

Behind the indignant response, however, perhaps we see God's patience being illustrated in that Gabriel does not simply withdraw his offer immediately. God certainly can find another couple to bring John the Baptist into the world. But God graciously sticks with Zechariah and even grants the man's request for a sign. It's just not the one Zechariah himself would choose! See the next verse.

20. "And behold, you will be silent and unable to speak until the day that these things take place, because you did not believe my words, which will be fulfilled in their time."

The request of Zechariah for a sign is born of skepticism. The divine reaction to that skeptical request supports the old caution, "Be careful what you ask for; you may just get it!"

Being *silent and unable to speak* throughout the nine months of Elizabeth's pregnancy (Luke 1:21, 22, 57-64) is quite appropriate when we realize the lack of faith that *you did not believe my words* implies. The angel's promise concerns the birth of one who will proclaim God's message to Israel; since Zechariah's doubt about a promised son includes doubt of that son's being God's spokesman, then Zechariah himself is now rendered unable to speak *until the day that these things take place*. This means that Zechariah will be unable to voice what has happened in the temple, the nature of his wife's pregnancy, etc. The elderly priest is therefore being punished with a kind of "time out," and he will have nine months to reflect on his lack of faith.

> **What Do You Think?**
> What are some ways to make the most of a time of temporary disability?
> *Talking Points for Your Discussion*
> • Considering our own culpability (if any) in causing the problem
> • Considering impact on church ministries
> • Considering impact on family members

◆ *On Being Speechless* ◆

Various creatures have a rudimentary ability to communicate with one another. By a series of chirps, mother birds can alert their young ones to danger, food, etc. Scientists study the noises emitted by sea creatures to determine what level of communication passes between them. But no such communication approaches the level of complexity and usefulness enjoyed by humans.

The ability to speak is one of the greatest gifts God has given us. We can talk about physical things as well as abstract ideas. We can describe the varied colors of a sunset. We can talk about deep doctrinal subjects. We can speak at a level for children to understand. Amazing!

Those who temporarily lose the ability to speak due to laryngitis gain an inkling of the frustration Zechariah must have felt at not being able to talk about what he had seen and heard. What can be even worse, however, is (1) when someone asks you a question, (2) you have the ability to speak, but (3) you have nothing to say. Matthew 22:12 is the ultimate warning in that regard.   —J. B. N.

Conclusion
A. Too Good to Be True?

We've all been told to be wary of deals that "seem too good to be true." Even so, scams con-tinue to take in many people, and there are now websites dedicated to exposing the cons. Such sites may include testimonies from those who fell victim to opportunities that seemed too good to be true—and were. If you receive an offer of an unexpected tax return, don't share your bank account number! If a "businessman" from central Africa wants to transfer money to your account before it's seized by the corrupt, collapsing government of his nation, don't reply!

Is it too good to be true? is an important question to ask when evaluating promises from other people. But real-life experiences along this line can make us hesitate to believe and act on God's promises. When we reflect on the hardships of life in general, on our own unmet needs in particular, and on seeming failures of prayer in the past, we may become as skeptical as Zechariah. If that begins to happen, we should quickly read the rest of the account of Zechariah and his family. That account is one more proof that God always keeps his promises.

B. Prayer

Heavenly Father, thank you for being patient in our times of doubt! Grant that our doubt be replaced by faith as we wait for your plan to unfold on your schedule. We pray in Jesus' name. Amen.

C. Thought to Remember

God's timing is always perfect.

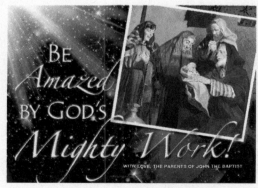

Visual for Lesson 3. *Start a discussion by pointing to this visual as you ask, "What causes us to lose our sense of amazement at God's mighty works?"*

INVOLVEMENT LEARNING

Enhance your lesson presentation with the reproducible activity page,
available as a free download at www.standardlesson.com.

Into the Lesson

Write the following words and phrases on the board:

understudy	second fiddle
sidekick	assistant
helper	subordinate
junior partner	second banana
aide	staffer
supporter	deputy

Lead a discussion about these words, asking how they are similar. Chose one or two from the list and give another word or phrase that it seems to imply. (Example: an understudy would imply a lead actor or actress, a deputy would imply there is a sheriff.) Why is each of these roles important?

Alternative. Distribute copies of the "Supporting Roles" activity from the reproducible page, which you can download. Allow students to work individually or in small groups to pair famous associates with their more prominent partners.

Lead into the Bible study by saying, "While being a sidekick or helper is a secondary role, it is a very important one! Without a secondary, the one in the primary position lacks valuable support. Today we will discuss one of the most important supporting roles in history—the forerunner to the Savior, John the Baptist."

Into the Word

Prepare ahead three copies of the commentary for this lesson and one copy each of the research assignments below. Divide the class into three groups and allow 10–15 minutes to complete the activity.

Group 1—Another Day at the Temple (vv. 8-10)
1. How was Zechariah chosen for his task that day?
2. Explain the significance of incense.
3. Why was Zechariah supposed to be alone in the temple?

Group 2—An Unexpected Announcement (vv. 11-17)
1. How was Zechariah's reaction to an angel a typical one?
2. What phrases in the angel's message indicate John's role as a prophet?
3. Why might it be significant that Gabriel's message quotes Malachi 4:5, 6?

Group 3—A Sign of the Promise (vv. 18-20)
1. Why might you think Zechariah's response to Gabriel's news to be justified?
2. Why might you think Zechariah's response to Gabriel's news to be unjustified?
3. Why was the sign given to him appropriate?

Allow groups to share their research. Comment as necessary to ensure that all questions are answered completely.

Alternative. Distribute copies of the "Forerunner Foretold" activity from the reproducible page. Allow students to work individually or in small groups. Students will see how Gabriel's description of John came to fulfillment later.

Into Life

Before class, write the names of teens or young adults from your congregation on index cards (one name per card).

Close this lesson by saying, "John the Baptist would go on and prepare the way for Jesus. Have we ever considered ourselves to be forerunners? Who will come after us, and how can we prepare the world for that person?

"On these cards, I have written the names of younger individuals in this congregation—people who may well be members of this congregation long after we leave this life.

"Take one card if you will promise to pray for the person whose name is on it. Pray that he or she will prepare for a role in Christ's church, and pray for those who will serve with that person in the future."

The Savior Has Arrived

DEVOTIONAL READING: Luke 2:1-7
BACKGROUND SCRIPTURE: Luke 2:1-21

LUKE 2:8-20

8 And in the same region there were shepherds out in the field, keeping watch over their flock by night. 9 And an angel of the Lord appeared to them, and the glory of the Lord shone around them, and they were filled with great fear. 10 And the angel said to them, "Fear not, for behold, I bring you good news of great joy that will be for all the people. 11 For unto you is born this day in the city of David a Savior, who is Christ the Lord. 12 And this will be a sign for you: you will find a baby wrapped in swaddling cloths and lying in a manger." 13 And suddenly there was with the angel a multitude of the heavenly host praising God and saying,

14 "Glory to God in the highest,
   and on earth peace among those with
      whom he is pleased!"

15 When the angels went away from them into heaven, the shepherds said to one another, "Let us go over to Bethlehem and see this thing that has happened, which the Lord has made known to us." 16 And they went with haste and found Mary and Joseph, and the baby lying in a manger. 17 And when they saw it, they made known the saying that had been told them concerning this child. 18 And all who heard it wondered at what the shepherds told them. 19 But Mary treasured up all these things, pondering them in her heart. 20 And the shepherds returned, glorifying and praising God for all they had heard and seen, as it had been told them.

KEY VERSE

For unto you is born this day in the city of David a Savior, who is Christ the Lord. —**Luke 2:11**

Photo: liquidlibrary / Thinkstock

CREATION: A DIVINE CYCLE

Unit 1: The Savior Has Been Born

LESSONS 1–4

LESSON AIMS

After participating in this lesson, each learner will be able to:

1. Retell the account of the announcement to the shepherds of Jesus' birth.

2. Explain how the angel's announcement and the shepherds' reaction fit within the larger picture of the arrival of Jesus.

3. Identify one or more elements to emulate in the shepherds' reaction and make a plan to do so.

LESSON OUTLINE

Introduction

A. Celebration of Good News

New parents are eager to announce the arrival of their precious newborn. They want to shout from the housetops "It's a boy!" or "It's a girl!" Whether by telephone, e-mail, social media, written letters, or word of mouth, the news travels. The news of Jesus' birth also spread rapidly, but with a difference: it did not travel at the initiative of parents Mary and Joseph. Rather, the news traveled first at God's initiative, then at the initiative of shepherds.

The news of Christ's birth is indeed news to be celebrated in our hearts today! But doing so is only half the task. The other half is to spread this news to "all nations" (Matthew 28:19) from generation to generation.

This is news that never grows old. This Christmas season we can choose to respond in awe and wonder yet again to the fact that God's Son took on flesh to live among us, beginning his earthly life as an ordinary baby. He did so that he might offer the extraordinary gift of salvation to all who are willing to receive it. "Thanks be to God for his inexpressible gift!" (2 Corinthians 9:15), the gift of "surpassing grace" (9:14b) that is made available by the arrival of Jesus!

Today's text paints the scene in which the news of Christ's birth first begins to spread. As we consider reactions and responses on that long-ago night, we are reminded that we have the privilege of evaluating our own at this time each year.

B. Lesson Background

God brought about the birth of Christ by perfect and completed timing (Galatians 4:4, 5). The timing related closely with God's decision regarding the ideal place. Perfect time and perfect place intersected in the context of the Roman Empire during the reign of Caesar Augustus (Luke 2:1), originally known as Gaius Octavius, who was emperor from 27 BC until his death in AD 14.

The reign of Augustus saw the beginning of the so-called *Pax Romana*, or Roman Peace. Since the empire was largely free of military conflict during this time, the good news of Jesus the Christ could spread more rapidly.

Little did anyone at the time know, however, that in Jesus' birth God was inaugurating a kingdom not only of peace but a kingdom never to be destroyed; this was to fulfill Daniel 2:44 (compare Daniel 7:27; Luke 1:33). God even used Roman taxation policy to fulfill prophecy regarding the perfect place for Jesus' birth: Bethlehem (Micah 5:2; compare Matthew 2:3-6; Luke 2:1-5). The fact that the Hebrew word *Bethlehem* means "house of bread" adds power to the imagery of the one sent to be "the bread of life" (John 6:35). The life he brought was deliverance from sin (Matthew 1:21).

The Son arrived in one of the most humble ways possible: by being born to a young peasant woman who had to give birth in less than ideal surroundings. Most of us cannot imagine any newborn child—let alone the Son of God—being placed "in a manger" (Luke 2:7a), which is a feeding trough for animals! Since "there was no place for them in the inn" (2:7b), the Plan B of Joseph and Mary has resulted in the popular depictions of Jesus' birth in a stable. It was in such a context that "the Word became flesh" (John 1:14). What a lowly beginning for the Son of God's ministry!

I. Announcing the Savior
(LUKE 2:8-14)

A. Lowly Shepherds (v. 8)

8. And in the same region there were shepherds out in the field, keeping watch over their flock by night.

The phrase *in the same region* refers to the area around Bethlehem (see Luke 2:4 and the Lesson Background). This area has pasture suitable for livestock (compare 1 Samuel 16:4, 11). Therefore it is not unusual for *shepherds* to be here as they keep *watch over their flock by night* to guard against predators and thieves. "Humble" is a good description of this setting. The nighttime scene also suggests tranquility, but that is about to change (next verse).

B. Heavenly Glory (v. 9)

9. And an angel of the Lord appeared to them, and the glory of the Lord shone around them, and they were filled with great fear.

An ordinary setting is transformed into something extraordinary with the arrival of *an angel of the Lord.* His appearing illuminates the night with *the glory of the Lord* (compare 2 Chronicles 7:1-3). Some think this angel is Gabriel, who has appeared twice already in this Gospel (Luke 1:11-20 [lesson 3]; 1:26-38 [lesson 1]). Ultimately, however, that is speculation since the angel is unnamed.

For the shepherds to be *filled with great fear* is understandable, since fear is a typical reaction in angelic encounters (compare Judges 6:22, 23; 13:21, 22; Luke 1:11, 12; Acts 10:3, 4). If there is such a thing as a once-in-a-lifetime experience for these shepherds, this is it!

C. Stunning News (vv. 10, 11)

10. And the angel said to them, "Fear not, for behold, I bring you good news of great joy that will be for all the people.

The shepherds' fears must be calmed before they will be able to comprehend the message *the angel* is bringing. The angel's declaration that he brings *good news that of great joy* establishes that the shepherds need fear neither the messenger nor the message. The message is not one of judgment and condemnation (contrast Genesis 19:15; Psalm 78:49)—quite the opposite!

> *What Do You Think?*
> ▶ How can we ensure that potentially counter-productive emotional reactions are minimized when launching a new ministry?
> *Talking Points for Your Discussion*
> • With regard to our words
> • With regard to our actions

What should amaze us yet today is that the forthcoming message that is intended *for all the people* is given first to lowly shepherds. We may naturally think that a message from God that is for everyone would be given first to the learned religious leaders. A Jewish commentary on Psalm 23 says, "There is no more disreputable occupation than that of shepherd," and the religious leaders of the day undoubtedly hold shepherds in low regard. Yet the first ones to receive this most-important news are shepherds!

11. "For unto you is born this day in the city of David a Savior, who is Christ the Lord.

The angelic message unfolds in terms of **how** (*is born*), **when** (*this day*), **where** (*in the city of David*), and **who** (*a Savior, who is Christ the Lord*). These elements interact in important ways. The Greek word *Christ* and its Hebrew equivalent *Messiah* (John 1:41, which has both words) each mean "anointed one." This refers to the action that designates someone's being appointed (consecrated, ordained) to an important office (examples: Numbers 3:3; 1 Samuel 15:1). *The Lord* is a title of authority. The helpless newborn is not predicted to be someone who will bear such designations in the future (compare Isaiah 9:6). Rather, this tiny infant has them now! He is worthy of these titles even though he is less than 24 hours old.

The elements of *where* and *who* interact in terms of fulfilled prophecy of Micah 5:2. The phrase *city of David* occurs dozens of times in the Old Testament to refer to Jerusalem after its conquest by David (2 Samuel 5:6-9). But in the verse before us, the reference is to Bethlehem, as the author has already made clear in Luke 2:4. In this sense, *the city of David* refers to where that man grew up and was anointed to be king (1 Samuel 16:4-13; 20:6).The prophecy of Bethlehem as the birthplace of the Christ is apparently well known in this era, as Matthew 2:4-6 and John 7:42 attest.

The message the shepherds should understand is that God is not sending another human-only judge, prophet, priest, or king. Jesus is much more, even as a newborn infant! In the Roman Empire, the word *savior* usually refers to a prominent political or military ruler. Yet the Savior in Luke's narrative is neither. Christ the Lord is being revealed as God himself, entering the world as a human.

D. Visible Sign (v. 12)

12. "And this will be a sign for you: you will find a baby wrapped in swaddling cloths and lying in a manger."

God knows that the shepherds need a way to identify *the baby* in question, since there may be several newborns in Bethlehem when they arrive. The *sign* revealed here allows not only correct identification, but also indicates partially what kind of Christ is come.

To be *wrapped in swaddling cloths* is to be encircled with long strips of material that are intended to retain warmth and provide a sense of security. This is ordinary care for newborns. Indeed, an ancient nonbiblical work notes that the baby who later became King Solomon "was nursed in swaddling clothes, and that with cares. For there is no king that had any other beginning of birth" (Wisdom of Solomon 7:4, *KJV*; the opposite of such care is seen in Ezekiel 16:4). In that regard, *to be wrapped in swaddling cloths* is a sign only in the sense of what the shepherds should not expect: a kingly baby identified by royal clothing.

Of greater value as a sign is the fact that the baby is *lying in a manger*. Since a manger is a feed trough for animals (see the Lesson Background), the implication is that the baby is to be found in a stable! One ancient Christian tradition suggests that this stable is a cave. Such a cave in this context may be a makeshift root cellar in a natural crevice below or near a house. These small caves are used for storage and to shelter domestic animals at night. A stable of any configuration would be unusual for any baby to be born in, much less

HOW TO SAY IT

Augustus Caesar	Aw-*gus*-tus *See*-zer.
Bethlehem	*Beth*-lih-hem.
Gaius Octavius	*Gay*-us Awk-tay-vee-us.
Messiah	Meh-*sigh*-uh.
Micah	*My*-kuh.
Nazareth	*Naz*-uh-reth.
Pax Romana *(Latin)*	Pahks Ro-*mah*-nah.

Christ the Lord, sent by God himself! This element of the sign is therefore unique.

◆ MANGER ◆

When I was a little boy, I had no idea what a manger was. From the context of the Christmas story, I assumed it was a bed of some sort. All the nativity scenes I saw had an X-shaped thing with slats for the sides. Eventually, I learned that a manger is a feeding trough for animals. Our word *manger* comes from the French word *mange*—"to eat."

When we consider how Jesus' life unfolded, we are humbled to conclude how appropriate it was for the one who became the "bread of life" (John 6:35, 48) to be laid in a feeding trough! It may sound a bit crude to refer to Jesus as our feeding trough, but he spoke of the need to eat his flesh and drink his blood (John 6:53-56). He is the spiritual food that gives sustenance to our spirits!

If bread is the staff of life, then Jesus is certainly the staff of spiritual life. The meaning of *Bethlehem* as "house of bread" enhances the imagery: the one born in the house of bread, the one who revealed himself to be the bread of life, had a feeding trough as his first place of earthly rest.   — J. B. N.

E. Angelic Praise (vv. 13, 14)

13. And suddenly there was with the angel a multitude of the heavenly host praising God and saying,

God provides the welcoming party for his Son: *the heavenly host*. This happens *suddenly*, as the singular angel of the previous three verses is joined by this *multitude*. Such phrasing in Old Testament contexts typically identifies an army of angels (compare Psalm 148:2). Whether the multitude fills the sky or stands on the surrounding hillside is unstated; perhaps it's both. What's more important is the fact that the multitude voices praise to God, the content of which praise is described next.

**14. "Glory to God in the highest,
    and on earth peace among those with
        whom he is pleased!"**

The praise is for what God is doing. What God had planned from the beginning is taking place. What the prophets had prophesied is being fulfilled. And what the angels have longed to look into (see 1 Peter 1:10-12) is coming to pass. No wonder the heavenly host praises God! Even those (or especially those) who reside *in the highest* parts of Heaven give *glory to God* for what he is now doing (compare Luke 19:38).

As glory is given to God in the heavenly realms, *peace* and *God's favor* is extended to humanity *on earth*. God is the ultimate peacemaker as he takes the initiative in sending his Son to reclaim hostile, sinful people as his own. The Son is the promised "Prince of Peace" of Isaiah 9:6. In biblical usage, *peace* often signifies security and harmony over and above the mere absence of hostilities (examples: Isaiah 26:3; Philippians 4:7).

Some perceive a progressive movement of God's glory from tabernacle (Exodus 40:34) to temple (1 Kings 8:11) to Bethlehem. Thus the latter is figuratively seen as a new "Most Holy Place" (compare 1 Kings 8:6). But we should be cautious about making connections where the text does not.

II. Meeting the Savior
(LUKE 2:15, 16)
A. Quick Decision (v. 15)

15. When the angels went away from them into heaven, the shepherds said to one another, "Let's go to Bethlehem and see this thing that has happened, which the Lord has made known to us."

The focus shifts back to the shepherds *when the angels* depart, having completed their assignment. The shepherds reveal no confusion regarding "the city of David" (Luke 2:11, above); they know it is *Bethlehem*, not Jerusalem. They embrace the message by immediately expressing their intent to go *and see this thing that has happened*, which the angelic message implies they should do.

What Do You Think?
What would have to happen for you to "drop everything" and react to a ministry opportunity on a moment's notice?
Talking Points for Your Discussion
- Concerning ministry to unbelievers
- Concerning ministry to believers

B. Personal Discovery (v. 16)

16. And they went with haste and found Mary and Joseph, and the baby lying in a manger.

The shepherds do not waste any time! They are eager to see the reality of God's message. What and whom they find are just as the angel promised.

It's easy to imagine that the shepherds share with *Mary and Joseph* the story of their angelic encounter and the content of the angelic message. The parents (Mary in a biological sense, Joseph in a legal sense), would have no trouble believing this account, having had angelic encounters of their own (Matthew 1:20, 21; Luke 1:26-38)! It's also easy to imagine a joyous time of fellowship and worship as all gather around *the baby lying in a manger.*

III. Proclaiming the Savior
(Luke 2:17-20)

A. Exuberant Testimony (v. 17)

17. And when they saw it, they made known the saying that had been told them concerning this child.

The shepherds do not have the message of the entire gospel, but what they do have they are eager to share. The prophecies of a Christ, now hundreds of years old, are coming to pass! What news could be more exciting than this?

> *What Do You Think?*
> What are some ways to regain the excitement we had when we first understood the gospel?
> *Talking Points for Your Discussion*
> - During times alone (personal devotions, etc.)
> - During fellowship with other believers
> - Other

B. Wondrous Reaction (v. 18)

18. And all who heard it wondered at what the shepherds told them.

When God is at work, he gives credibility to his messengers. The word *wondered* (or *marveled, amazed*) is used frequently by this Gospel writer to indicate reaction, often with an element of doubt or confusion, to a divine initiative (examples: Luke 8:25; 9:43; 24:41). Part of the astonishment *at what the shepherds told them* may be that of why God would choose shepherds over religious leaders to receive a message from angels. Further, the people may find it difficult to believe that the Messiah has been born in a stable rather than a palace. As those who witnessed the return of speech to Zechariah, they may have no answer to the question they ask of themselves, "What then will this child be?" (Luke 1:66).

> *What Do You Think?*
> What reactions to our witness can we expect?
> What responses can we prepare in advance?
> *Talking Points for Your Discussion*
> - Regarding witnessing to strangers
> - Regarding witnessing to friends

All people in all eras do well to remind themselves that God's thoughts and ways are not the same as ours (Isaiah 55:8, 9). He does not always operate according to our own thinking processes. Whenever we conclude how God "must" or "is bound to" act in any given situation, danger looms (compare Job 38:1, 2; Micah 4:11, 12; etc.).

C. Silent Pondering (v. 19)

19. But Mary treasured up all these things, pondering them in her heart.

Mary has much to ponder: being favored to be the mother of "the Son of the Most High" (Luke 1:31, 32), her special time with Elizabeth (1:39-45), the (likely) whispers and doubts of the people of Nazareth, the long trip to Bethlehem, the smelly stable, the excited shepherds, etc. She gathers all these memories in the treasure chest of *her heart*, undoubtedly to sort through many times as the years pass (compare 2:51). We easily imagine her verbal celebration of wonder in Luke 1:46-55 now giving way to a silent celebration in amazement of all God has done through her thus far. Mary knows that her child is no ordinary baby!

◆ Keepsakes ◆

Merriam-Webster's defines *hope chest* as "a young woman's accumulation of clothes and domestic furnishings . . . kept in anticipation of her marriage; *also*: a chest for such an accumulation." She may decide she wants her hope chest (whether a physical or a figurative one) to be filled with clothes, dishes, linens, quilts, etc., that she expects to use once she is married and sets up house. As "the big day" approaches, she may check the inventory frequently as she ponders life ahead, thinking of the usefulness of each item.

The passing years may see her reexamining these same items periodically, either by physical touch or in her heart. Doing so may bring back memories of especially good times in her marriage. She may even remember who gave her each item, fondly experiencing again the joyous moment of opening the gift.

What we might call "Mary's hope chest of the heart" was not one she asked for, but one given her by God at his decision and initiative. She did not avoid reflecting on its contents, but actively pondered them. Over the three decades that followed, she could reflect periodically on her experiences and consider how they fit into the working out of God's plans—and not all the hope chest's contents were pleasant to recall (Luke 2:35; John 19:25-27; etc.). When was the last time you examined the contents of your own "spiritual hope chest"?

—J. B. N.

D. Glorious Praise (v. 20)

20. And the shepherds returned, glorifying and praising God for all they had heard and seen, as it had been told them.

The shepherds are changed forever by the dramatic message that they in turn deliver to others. The lowliness of Christ has connected with their own lowly (in the eyes of the world) status. The Son of God has found a place not only in a manger but also in their hearts. While Mary quietly ponders, the shepherds shout from the rooftops.

The shepherds can never again view their lives as they have before. We have no record that any of them gave up his vocation as shepherd to become a full-time herald of the gospel. But ultimately that is irrelevant. They can be gospel messengers in their own families and towns without changing their means of livelihood.

Conclusion
A. Glorious Interruption

We too can become messengers of the gospel without changing our earthly vocations. Although we have not had the experience of the shepherds who were privileged to talk about what they witnessed personally, we should recall Jesus' words to Thomas: "Blessed are those who have not seen and yet have believed" (John 20:29).

We do not wait for a glorious interruption on the order of the one experienced by the shepherds before getting started. God can indeed provide an interruption of such a magnitude yet today, but it's much more likely he will try to get our attention in ways more subtle. For instance, an open door of opportunity to bring the comfort of Christ to a depressed colleague may present itself suddenly during the course of an otherwise ordinary day. God can and does interrupt ordinary days with glorious opportunities. Expect them!

B. Prayer

Almighty God, we invite you to interrupt our routines! As you do, grant that we will recognize your interruptions that we might better share the news of Christ's arrival in a world desperately in need of it. We pray this in Jesus' name. Amen.

C. Thought to Remember
Celebrate Jesus' arrival again for the first time.

Let God disrupt your routine!

WITH LOVE, THE SHEPHERDS

Visual for Lesson 4. *Point to this visual as you ask, "Would you be willing to invite God to disrupt your remaining plans for the season? Why, or why not?"*

INVOLVEMENT LEARNING

Enhance your lesson presentation with the reproducible activity page,
available as a free download at www.standardlesson.com.

Into the Lesson

To begin, help the class participate in a story collaboration exercise about being interrupted during work. You will begin the story. Then one volunteer at a time will add to the story, making it more outrageous as it goes. Start by saying, "I was sitting at my desk working when . . ."

Ask for a volunteer to add the next line, another to add a subsequent line, and so forth. Each line should end with an incomplete statement and the next person should continue. A story might develop like this:

I was sitting at my desk working when . . .
. . . the phone rang. It was . . .
. . . a wrong number. So I . . .
. . . slammed down the receiver, and I . . .
. . . smashed my thumb! I immediately . . .
. . . ran to the first-aid kit. I discovered . . .

Continue for a while, allowing anyone wanting to add to your fractured tale to do so.

Alternative. Distribute copies of the "Corruption by Interruption" activity from the reproducible page, which you can download. Allow students to work individually to guess the extent of time wasted because of interruptions at work.

After either activity, lead into Bible study by saying, "We all have been interrupted at work. The results may not be as dramatic as these, but we do not look forward to work interruptions. Today we will look at a group of men who were interrupted at work and what resulted."

Into the Word

Say, "Haiku is a Japanese poetry form. A haiku uses just a few words to capture a moment and create a picture in the reader's mind. Traditionally, haiku is written in three lines, with five syllables in the first line, seven syllables in the second line, and five syllables in the third line."

Divide your class into groups of three to five. Give each group pen, paper, and one of the following haiku writing assignments. Each group is to write a haiku based on the content of the portion of the lesson text assigned.

Assignment 1—Reception. The shepherds were interrupted by receiving a great message (Luke 2:8-14).

Assignment 2—Research. The shepherds were interrupted by checking out what they had heard (Luke 2:15, 16).

Assignment 3—Reporting. The shepherds were interrupted by telling others what they learned (Luke 2:17-20).

Here are some sample poems:
(vv. 8-14)
　　Poor social outcasts
　　Met by heavenly heralds
　　Salvation has come!
(vv. 15, 16)
　　The sheep forgotten
　　They were off to Bethlehem
　　To find God's shepherd
(vv. 17-20)
　　Finding the Savior
　　They kept silent no longer
　　While mother pondered

Alternative. Write out three sample poems on the board in any order. Read the text, one section at a time, with your class. Match the text with the poem and discuss the content.

Into Life

As the birth of Jesus interrupted the routine of the shepherds, should it not interrupt our Christmas Day routines as well?

Brainstorm with the group and create a list of Jesus-centered activities that could be done in their homes after the gifts are opened.

Alternative. Distribute copies of the "Name That Carol" activity from the reproducible page to each student. Encourage them to break the routine of Christmas afternoon by using this activity with their families.

PRAISE GOD FOR CREATION

DEVOTIONAL READING: Psalm 146
BACKGROUND SCRIPTURE: Psalm 33:1-9

PSALM 33:1-9

1 Shout for joy in the LORD, O you righteous!
   Praise befits the upright.
2 Give thanks to the LORD with the lyre;
   make melody to him with the harp of
   ten strings!
3 Sing to him a new song;
   play skillfully on the strings, with loud
   shouts.
4 For the word of the LORD is upright,
   and all his work is done in faithfulness.
5 He loves righteousness and justice;
   the earth is full of the steadfast love of
   the LORD.
6 By the word of the LORD the heavens were
   made,
   and by the breath of his mouth all their
   host.
7 He gathers the waters of the sea as a heap;
   he puts the deeps in storehouses.

8 Let all the earth fear the LORD;
   let all the inhabitants of the world stand
   in awe of him!
9 For he spoke, and it came to be;
   he commanded, and it stood firm.

KEY VERSE

By the word of the Lord the heavens were made, and by the breath of his mouth all their host.
—**Psalm 33:6**

CREATION: A DIVINE CYCLE

Unit 2: Praise from and for God's Creation

LESSONS 5–9

LESSON AIMS

After participating in this lesson, each learner will be able to:

1. List some reasons to praise the Lord and rejoice in him.

2. Describe worship as a function of God's creation.

3. Suggest one way that his or her church can improve the worship experience.

LESSON OUTLINE

Introduction

A. Call to Worship

Traditional worship services begin with a "call to worship." This may simply be a Scripture (often from the Psalms) read from the pulpit. Or it may take the form of a short responsive reading. Typical of the latter is this:

Leader: *Our soul waits for the LORD; he is our help and our shield.*
People: *For our heart is glad in him, because we trust in his holy name.*
All: *Let your steadfast love, O LORD, be upon us, even as we hope in you.*

These lines, which are Psalm 33:20-22, include the elements of waiting on the Lord, acknowledging his protection, rejoicing and trusting in him, and anticipating his love and mercy. All such elements can play an important part in unifying the congregation to the purpose of worship. We must not forget that we have come to worship, and skilled worship leaders issue this call clearly.

Our lesson today is from the first nine verses of this same psalm. Although the words were penned over 2,000 years ago, the purposes of and necessity for worship have not changed. If we let it, Psalm 33 can enliven and focus both our corporate and personal worship.

B. Lesson Background

The psalmists composed their works for specific purposes, and sometimes the purpose and identity of the author is revealed in a psalm's superscription. For example, the superscription of Psalm 51 refers to that psalm as "of David, when Nathan the prophet went to him, after he had gone in to Bathsheba." What follows is David's repentance for that sinful episode.

If you have a Bible in an electronic format, you may find it interesting to discover these superscriptions to be tagged as "verse zero" of the psalm that follows. Many psalms, however, lack a superscription, and Psalm 33 is one of those. In these cases, we must look within the psalm itself to get an idea of how the Israelites originally used it.

Psalm 33 bears no statement of authorship, but a reasonable guess is David. One piece of evidence to support this theory is that the last verse of Psalm 32 and the first verse of Psalm 33 are worded very similarly, with the superscription of Psalm 32 attributing that composition to David.

Regarding purpose, one theory is that Psalm 33 was used in public assemblies to thank God for a good harvest. In an era when 98 percent of the people made their living by agrarian means in rural settings, the effects of good and bad harvests were felt immediately by nearly everyone. While a national celebration of a good harvest may seem odd to those of the modern Western world, where only 2 percent of people live on farms, such a celebration was quite fitting for the ancients (compare Psalm 65:9; 67:6; 85:12; contrast Jeremiah 8:13).

Giving thanks to God is the essence of worship. When we are aware of and grateful for the blessings of adequate provisions for life, it should be natural to direct our gratitude to God.

I. Praise by the Upright
(Psalm 33:1-5)
A. Use Every Means (vv. 1-3)

1. Sing for joy in the LORD, O you righteous! Praise befits the upright.

The original wording behind the exhortation *sing for joy* is translated similarly in Psalm 81:1 as "sing aloud" and in Psalm 98:4b as "break forth into joyous song." Those two passages include references to loudness, so that is likely implied here as well. We cannot know how the worship of the ancient Israelites sounded, but loud congregational singing seems to be in view.

Such rejoicing must be done *in the Lord,* for he and nothing else is to be the focus in worship. Appropriate worship celebrates God, but that will happen only as we recognize our proper position in the order of creation, our relationship with God, and our dependence on him.

HOW TO SAY IT

Ecclesiastes   Ik-*leez*-ee-*as*-teez.

The rest of the verse before us reveals the feature of *parallelism* for which ancient Hebrew poetry is noted. One form of parallelism involves two lines saying the same thing (or nearly so) with different words. We see this here in that those who are *righteous* and those who are *upright* are actually the same people. Their rejoicing is *praise.*

People are not made righteous by their praise of God, but praising him is the right and proper thing to do. We cannot consider ourselves to be upright if we refuse or neglect worship.

What Do You Think?
What steps can we take to ensure we rejoice in the Lord rather than in "things"?
Talking Points for Your Discussion
- Steps to recognize the problem
- Steps toward a solution that also witnesses to others
- Distinguishing between *joy* and *happiness*

---

2. Give thanks to the LORD with the lyre; make melody to him with the harp of ten strings!

The psalmist (possibly a worship leader) turns his attention to include instrumentalists. As we are on the alert for more parallelism, in light of what we just saw in verse 1, we may be tempted to conclude that only one musical instrument is in view here, with *lyre* and *harp* being merely different words for the same thing (synonyms). But the fact that lyre and harp are listed together in several nonpoetic passages requires that they be seen as distinct instruments (example: 1 Chronicles 15:16).

The fact that the two instruments are different does not mean that parallelism is absent, however. There is more than one kind of parallelism, and the one we see here is a parallel of category: *lyre* and *harp* are both stringed musical instruments, mentioned dozens of times in the Old Testament. David played at least one of these instruments, perhaps both, with skill (see 1 Samuel 16:23).

Lyres can vary widely in size. Some are small enough to be portable (compare Psalm 137:2: "On the willows there we hung up our lyres"). On the other hand, lyres used for worship may be very large, thus capable of producing great volume at the cost of portability. Perhaps the larger ones are played while standing.

Archaeologists have found inscriptions depicting ancient harps, as well as a few actual harps themselves. These reveal configurations of two posts extending from a sound box, with a connecting bar at the top. The strings that connect the sound box with the bar are tuned to specific musical notes. The strings, made from prepared goat or sheep intestines, can be plucked or perhaps played with a bow.

Evidence from ancient drawings indicates curved yokes and jar-shaped sounding boxes to be features of harps. An instrument featuring 10 strings, whether to be plucked or played with a bow, can be enormous if designed for use in large worship gatherings (Psalm 144:9).

3. Sing to him a new song;
    play skillfully on the strings, with loud shouts.

The fact that singers are to *sing . . . a new song* doesn't necessarily mean a newly composed tune, but a song that is fresh and renewing rather than stale and tired (compare Psalm 98:1; Revelation 5:9). And as they sing such a song, the instrumentalists are to hold nothing back in terms of skill, volume, or joyous exuberance.

There is a place for contemplation, stillness, and silence, but not in the worship service envisioned by this psalmist. How wonderful it would be if we discovered a 3,000-year-old video that showed us such a worship service in progress! Our notions of stately, dignified worship in ancient Israel might be turned on their head if we could witness the exuberance of the joyful, loud praise that seems to be sketched here. This psalm offers no words of caution on restraint for worship.

Over-the-top exuberance is not the same as uncontrolled chaos, however. For the musical expressions of singers and notes to blend harmoniously implies the skill that comes from rehearsal. But the motive behind rehearsal is important. Wrong motives put the professionalism of the musicians first. Right motives put the meaningfulness of the worship experience first. And we do well to remember that what is meaningful to us may not be meaningful to God (see Isaiah 1:13; Amos 5:21).

What Do You Think?
How do we keep musical expressions of praise from becoming mere performance?
Talking Points for Your Discussion
- Considering personal spiritual disciplines
- Considering leadership example
- Other

◆   *WHAT ABOUT UNSKILLFUL PRAISE?*   ◆

One Sunday before worship began, our youngest daughter asked to sit with members of our small group in the row behind us. We agreed, and during the service I kept hearing her little-girl voice singing above all others. I don't know whether that was because she sang loudly or I was tuned in to her because she was my child.

Either way, her sweet soprano voice stood out to me as her innocence shone through. Her voice wasn't perfect, and she missed some words. But I imagined that God must have smiled at that little voice praising him.

It's all too easy to get caught up in personal preferences and showmanship in musical expressions of worship. Is the volume according to my taste? Is the worship team properly attired for being on stage? Is each song timed perfectly with no dead space?

That Sunday when I saw my daughter's sweet expression as she sang her heart out to God, I did not notice anything about the quality of the music. Skillful praise is the ideal to aim for, but heartfelt praise also counts (in Isaiah 29:13 we see what God thinks of the opposite). What a blessing it must be to God to hear the sincere praise of his children!   —L. M. W.

B. Acknowledge His Attributes (vv. 4, 5)
4a. For the word of the LORD is upright,

Having primed the singers and the musicians for worship, the psalmist now begins to give content to their praise. What we say in worship is important, and it should not be approached carelessly. It is not profitable for the church to sing words that contain unbiblical sentiments or misleading doctrinal statements.

We guard against such errors by careful study of Scripture in order to derive song lyrics from the Bible itself. No matter how catchy or popular a worship song might be, it should have no place in a church service if it detracts from biblical truth. Music makes words memorable, and church leaders must insist that the worship words in their services glorify and praise the Lord appropriately.

In the half verse before us and the next three, the psalmist celebrates four attributes of the Lord. First, the Lord's word *is upright,* meaning what God has communicated to mankind is true and without error. We can depend on the reliability and authenticity of God's Word. God's Word is truth, always and forever ("your word is truth," John 17:17).

4b.   and all his work is done in faithfulness.

For *all his work* to be *done in faithfulness* means that just as God's words are always trustworthy, his actions are as well. God is consistent in the ways he deals with humanity. He has sent his messengers to proclaim his ways and call people to repent. But in spite of human sin and an all-too-often unwillingness to repent, God loves us deeply. His works are consistent with and speak of both his love for us and his holy insistence that we abandon sinful ways.

This combination of trustworthy words and faithful works means that God always keeps his promises, whether of judgment or of blessing. This is a great lesson of the Old Testament. What God promises Israel, God delivers—even when (or especially when) it is not to their liking. This is true for us also; we can always depend on God's promises.

5a.   He loves righteousness and justice;

Psalm 97:2 tells us that "*righteousness and justice* are the foundation of [God's] throne." Since this is so, it is no wonder that God expects and loves to see righteousness and justice exhibited by his people. *Righteousness* refers to "doing the right thing," while *justice* refers to treating others fairly.

The two ideas are so close in meaning that they are practically synonyms. This indicates one rather than two attributes of God (notice how they are parallel in Psalm 9:8). It's virtually impossible to think of God or anyone else who does the right thing yet is unjust!

God is unrelenting in his calls for the people of Israel to do the right thing in maintaining justice in their society. As righteousness and justice undergird the throne of God, so are they to be the foundation of human society as well.

5b.   the earth is full of the steadfast love of the LORD.

The psalmist looks to creation to find a fourth attribute of God: his provision of good things within our world. God pronounced the goodness of his creation at the beginning (Genesis 1:31), and we should celebrate the one who has provided such bounty for us.

The word translated *steadfast love* is very common in the Old Testament. (See Psalms 33:18, 22; 36:7, 10; 117:2; 119:76.) In any case, the psalmist is saying that creation itself is a testimony of God's constant love toward us. The goodness evidenced in his world should stimulate ongoing praise and worship.

> *What Do You Think?*
> What are some ways to ensure that worship addresses the attributes of God?
> *Talking Points for Your Discussion*
> - Regarding corporate worship
> - Regarding times of personal worship

II. Praise for His Works
(PSALM 33:6, 7)

A. Heavens and Their Host (v. 6)

6.   By the word of the LORD the heavens were made,
and by the breath of his mouth all their host.

The psalmist now steps backward in time to consider the initial creative acts of God. The emphasis is the method of creation found in Genesis 1: God spoke the universe into being. The psalmist's angle is to consider first the realm beyond the earth: *the heavens* and the beings that inhabit them. *Their host* may refer to stars of the night sky or to the angels who reside in Heaven as God's servants. In ancient Israelite thinking, the two may be one and the same (compare Judges 5:20; Job 38:7; Isaiah 40:26).

Modern science has expanded our knowledge of the physical aspects of the universe far beyond that of the psalmist. The number of stars by one estimate is 3×10^{23}—an almost incomprehensible number. The ever-growing list of scientific discoveries tests the faith of some. But how much better it is to allow those awe-inspiring discoveries to drive us to our knees in worship of their Creator!

What Do You Think?
What best helps you appreciate God's creative power? Why?
Talking Points for Your Discussion
- Considering the witness of Scripture
- Considering the witness of creation itself
- Considering your own life experiences
- Other

For creation to come about by the *breath* of God's *mouth* is not to imply that he has physical lungs, mouth, tongue, etc. Rather, the psalmist is emphasizing creation by means of God's words. This is difficult for us to understand, but we might say it this way: God imagines it, speaks it, and it is created.

Interesting to consider at this point is 2 Timothy 3:16: "All Scripture is breathed out by God." Behind the translation of the last four words is a combination of two Greek words, one meaning "God" and the other "breathed."

B. Waters of the Sea (v. 7)

7. He gathers the waters of the sea as a heap; he puts the deeps in storehouses.

The psalmist turns his attention to another realm of great wonder and mystery: the oceans. The fact that God is able to gather *the waters of the sea as a heap* is demonstrated in the facts of history noted in Exodus 14:21, 22; 15:8; Joshua 3:13-16; and Psalm 78:13.

The imagery of the forces of nature being kept in *storehouses* is also reflected in Job 38:22; Psalm 135:7; and Jeremiah 10:13; 51:16, where the trans-

lation of the same Hebrew word is "treasures" or "treasuries." The Creator is the master of the mighty oceans and all other forces of nature.

We manage water supplies, with varying degrees of success, by building colossal dams, levees, and waterways. As we do, we should not allow hubris to cause us to forget that it was God who created the self-renewing water system of the earth in the first place.

◆ GOD'S UNSEEN CREATIVITY ◆

As a result of its extreme depth and pressure, the Mariana Trench in the Pacific Ocean features some unusual life-forms. Food is scarce in the deepest levels, and some organisms there survive on chemicals that emerge from the sea floor. Some such organisms are in the form of giant, single-celled amoebas.

At levels in the trench where no light filters down from the surface, certain creatures have tiny luminescent lures for attracting prey. The fish and other sea creatures found at these levels look very different from those in other parts of the ocean. It is almost as if they don't need to worry about their appearance since no one can see them in the dark that far underwater anyway!

Relatively few people ever think about such forms of life or even know they exist. But keep in mind that the more we learn about creation, the more we learn about the Creator.   —L. M. W.

III. Duties of the Created
(PSALM 33:8, 9)
A. Who (v. 8)

8. Let all the earth fear the LORD; let all the inhabitants of the world stand in awe of him!

The two lines of this verse are saying the same thing (again, parallelism). The contemplation of God's great creative acts prompts the psalmist to call for a proper response: jaw-dropping *fear* and *awe*. There are many aspects to worship, including remembering God's grace, celebrating his love, and expressing our gratitude to him. But what about fear and awe? Have we lost these elements of worship?

A proper fear will strip us of high-minded pride (Romans 11:20) as it humbles our hearts. Any pretense or delusion of our own greatness or worthiness is swallowed up in recognition of the vast superiority of God's eternal power.

B. Why (v. 9)

9. For he spoke, and it came to be; he commanded, and it stood firm.

The psalmist finishes this section with a return to the most baffling and amazing consideration in all of this: God's ability to speak creation into existence. Nothing thwarts God's creative intentions. God speaks, it happens, and it happens in a permanent way. It stands *firm*. This is not digital creation, but hard and fast reality. We are not independent players in this cosmic drama, but part of God's plans and purposes. Our role is to recognize, marvel, and submit.

> *What Do You Think?*
> What are some ways to use verses 8 and 9 in worship?
> *Talking Points for Your Discussion*
> - In various elements of corporate worship
> - In personal worship daily for a week
> - Other

Conclusion

A. Worship Time

Churches today carefully plan and rehearse their worship times. This is designed to bring believers before the throne of God in a spirit of praise. Such elements undergird today's text as well. The psalmist's desire for skill as various elements of musical expression interact implies planning for a large community's time of worship.

Underlying this focus, however, is a broader picture of what worship is. God is not to be awe-inspiring only for an hour or two on Sunday morning; he is eternally and always so. A weekend gathering of believers might be a high point in our worship, but it should not be the only worship experience. We can worship when we see God's activity in a gentle rain or a thundering storm. We can worship him when we view a glorious sunset or a clear, starry

Visual for Lessons 5 & 6. *Start an activity by pointing to this visual and challenging learners to write a prayer using all the words.*

night. We can worship when we gaze into the eyes of a newborn baby. We can worship when we calm our hearts for sleep or when we awaken fresh for a new day. We can worship when we remember the many blessings God has laid in the pathways of our lives, or when we consider the many things he has for us in the future (see Ecclesiastes 3:11).

One implication of all these possibilities is that our worship should not be confined to a sanctuary or worship center in a building. By lifting our "worship awareness" to a higher level, we find endless things that point our hearts to the Lord, the maker of the heavens and the earth and the provider of our daily needs.

Look for small worship opportunities as they present themselves to you in the week ahead. When you recognize one, give a smile as an act of joy directed to the Lord, for he alone is worthy of worship. Mouth this simple prayer, "Thank you, Lord, for letting this remind me of you." When you fill your heart with worship, you will not be disappointed.

B. Prayer

O God, as your great power causes us to stand in proper fear of you, may we also remember your great love for us. We pray this in the name of Jesus, who in that love went to the cross. Amen.

C. Thought to Remember

As you praise God, don't forget why.

INVOLVEMENT LEARNING

Enhance your lesson presentation with the reproducible activity page,
available as a free download at www.standardlesson.com.

Into the Lesson

Begin by asking students to form small groups of four or five people each. You then will go to the first person in each group and say either *land*, *air*, or *water*. That person has 10 seconds to name either a land animal, a type of bird or flying insect, or a type of fish or other creature that lives in the water. If the person is able to supply an appropriate name, he or she then turns to the next person in the group and says either *land*, *air*, or *water*. If the person is unable to supply a name, then he or she is eliminated. Make sure to mention that no creature can be named twice. Allow play to continue for five minutes or so or until a winner emerges.

Alternative. Distribute copies of the "In the Watery Deep" activity from the reproducible page, which you can download. Have students work individually or in pairs.

After either activity, lead into the Bible study saying, "It is hard to look at the created world without acknowledging the Creator. Today we will talk about praising God for his marvelous creation."

Into the Word

Before getting into a study of today's text, write these words from Luke 19:40 on the board (near the top) in this fashion:

"I tell you," he replied, "if they [disciples] keep quiet,

[move down to the middle of the board and write]

the stones will cry out."

Have the class paraphrase this rather strange statement made by Jesus during his triumphal entry into Jerusalem. They may respond with something like, "If God's followers do not praise him, then praise will come from the rest of his creation."

Divide the class into two groups. *Group 1* should read Psalm 33:1-5, looking at the responsibility the righteous followers of God have to praise him. Ask the group to write as many rel-

evant phrases from those verses under the first phrase from Luke 19:40 on the board.

Group 2 should read Psalm 33:6-9, looking for the interaction between God and the rest of his creation. Ask the group to write relevant phrases from those verses under the second phrase from Luke 19:40 on the board.

Reassemble the class and have a spokesperson from each group share what they discovered from the text. Refer to relevant portions of the commentary to support discussion as necessary.

Alternative. Distribute copies of the "Reporter's Notebook" activity from the reproducible page. Have students work in pairs or small groups to complete this exercise.

Into Life

If you did not use the "In the Watery Deep" activity for the first part of the lesson, distribute it now. Allow students to work in small groups to complete it.

If you used the activity earlier, have your class turn to it once more. Close the lesson by having students cite content from that exercise to substantiate these statements about God's nature and power:

- *Even the most powerful earth-moving equipment can't accomplish what God constructed in creation.*
- *Even the most compassionate urban planners can't construct a living environment as hospitable as that which God has created for humankind.*
- *Even the most just of all rulers can't show fairness to the greatest and smallest in his domain as God has.*
- *Even the largest food bank in the world cannot hold a fraction of the provisions God has stored for those he created.*

Read Romans 1:20, Paul's affirmation that God's power and nature are obvious in the world he created. Close with a prayer thanking God for revealing his power and nature in that way.

PRAISE GOD WITH A NEW SONG

DEVOTIONAL READING: 1 Chronicles 16:23, 24
BACKGROUND SCRIPTURE: Psalm 96

PSALM 96

1 Oh sing to the LORD a new song;
   sing to the LORD, all the earth!
2 Sing to the LORD, bless his name;
   tell of his salvation from day to day.
3 Declare his glory among the nations,
   his marvelous works among all the
   peoples!
4 For great is the LORD, and greatly to be
   praised;
   he is to be feared above all gods.
5 For all the gods of the peoples are worthless idols,
   but the LORD made the heavens.
6 Splendor and majesty are before him;
   strength and beauty are in his
   sanctuary.
7 Ascribe to the LORD, O families of the
   peoples,
   ascribe to the LORD glory and strength!
8 Ascribe to the LORD the glory due his
   name;
   bring an offering, and come into his
   courts!

9 Worship the LORD in the splendor of
   holiness;
   tremble before him, all the earth!
10 Say among the nations, "The LORD reigns!
    Yes, the world is established; it shall
    never be moved;
    he will judge the peoples with equity."
11 Let the heavens be glad, and let the earth
    rejoice;
    let the sea roar, and all that fills it;
12   let the field exult, and everything in it!
   Then shall all the trees of the forest sing
    for joy
13   before the LORD, for he comes,
    for he comes to judge the earth.
   He will judge the world in righteousness,
    and the peoples in his faithfulness.

KEY VERSE

Oh sing to the Lord a new song; sing to the Lord, all the earth! —**Psalm 96:1**

Photo: iStock / Thinkstock

CREATION: A DIVINE CYCLE

Unit 2: Praise from and for God's Creation

LESSONS 5–9

LESSON AIMS

After participating in this lesson, each learner will be able to:

1. Summarize the implications of believing in one Creator God.

2. Explain the relationship between creation and worship.

3. Recount an experience when he or she was overawed by the majesty of God's good creation.

LESSON OUTLINE

Introduction

A. God's Awesome Creation

In the summer of 2014, my wife and I decided to go to Yellowstone National Park for a vacation and to celebrate our wedding anniversary. Many friends had recommended the trip, so we took a flight and rented a car.

After seeing several geysers and enjoying the burst of Old Faithful, we left the park and went south toward the Tetons. As we emerged from the high country and forest, a blue silvery lake appeared in the valley as anticipated. But we were not expecting the sudden view of the series of mountains that seemed to jut straight up from the western edge of the lake.

The view was overwhelming. To see the beauty of the Tetons from different angles and various locations around a series of lakes borders on being indescribable. At one point while taking in the view, my wife exclaimed, "This makes me want to sing 'How Great Is Our God' or 'How Great Thou Art'!" We wanted to praise God with all our might at that moment. The beauty of creation reminded us to praise the Creator.

B. Lesson Background

The Bible's collection of 150 psalms is commonly seen in terms of five "books." You can see these book divisions listed just before Psalms 1, 42, 73, 90, and 107 in your Bible. Psalm 96 falls in Book IV, where it is part of a subgroup called "enthronement psalms" (Psalms 93, 96–99).

The enthronement psalms are seen to provide an answer to the question concerning the downfall of David's throne, as recounted in Book III (Psalm 89 in particular). The problem was that the Davidic dynasty had been suspended, if not outright destroyed, in the defeat that resulted in the Babylonian exile (see Psalm 89:38-51). To this the psalmist cried out, "How long, O Lord?" (Psalm 89:46). The enthronement psalms that follow in Book IV provide the answer: "The Lord reigns" (Psalm 93:1; 96:10; 97:1; 99:1).

We can note in passing that Psalm 96 is reproduced, with slight variations and transposition of lines, in 1 Chronicles 16:23-33. Also there is Psalm

105:1-15 (1 Chronicles 16:8-22) and Psalm 106:47, 48 (1 Chronicles 16:35, 36). These are presented as *typical* psalms sung for the accompanying of the ark into Jerusalem by David (1 Chronicles 15; 2 Samuel 6). This is in line with the old Greek version (Septuagint), which adds this as the psalm's title: "When the house was built after the captivity; a song of David." However, Psalm 96 bears no statement of authorship in the Hebrew, so its author is unknown to us. (See discussion of superscriptions in last week's Lesson Background.)

Psalm 96 divides itself into three parts. The thrice-repeated imperative *sing* marks the beginning of the first part (vv. 1, 2), while the similarly constructed *ascribe* marks the beginning of the second (vv. 7, 8). The third part breaks this pattern by beginning with the once-used *say* (v. 10). For this reason, some commentators propose that verse 10 ends the second part rather than beginning the third (see commentary on this below).

I. Necessary Praise
(PSALM 96:1-6)
A. What to Do (vv. 1-3)

**1, 2a. Oh sing to the LORD a new song;
sing to the LORD, all the earth!
Sing to the LORD, bless his name;**

The author uses numerous imperatives (or words that have the force of imperatives) to stress what must be done. He first implores the reader to *sing*. This isn't merely a desire on the part of the psalmist; it's a command! Urgency presents itself in the threefold repetition. The Hebrew Old Testament features 14 imperatives to sing, and three occur right here. Singing is important!

The phrase *new song* is found in eight other passages: Psalms 33:3; 40:3; 98:1; 144:9; 149:1; Isaiah 42:10; and Revelation 5:9; 14:3. Their common element is an accompanying redemptive act. From

HOW TO SAY IT

Babylonian	Bab-ih-*low*-nee-un.
Davidic	Duh-*vid*-ick.
Septuagint	Sep-*too*-ih-jent.
Yahweh *(Hebrew)*	*Yah*-weh.

the discussion of Psalm 33:3 (last week's lesson), we recall that the new song in view doesn't necessarily mean a newly composed tune, but a song that is fresh and renewing. On the other hand, some students believe that the new song that *all the earth* is exhorted to sing is Psalm 96 itself—a new composition.

The one to receive the earth's new song is, of course, *the Lord*. The reason your Bible renders this with small capitals, as LORD, is to indicate that the underlying Hebrew is *Yahweh*. That is God's personal name, as distinguished from other names for him. This feature is explained more fully in the front matter of many Bibles.

The third exhortation to sing has the added imperative *bless his name*. The word *bless* may be a curious word to modern ears, but an examination of its use in psalms similar to the one at hand sheds light. In the clearest parallels, we see encouragements to "let the sound of his praise be heard" (Psalm 66:8), "give thanks" (100:4), "lift up your to the holy place" (134:2). Thus the requirement to bless speaks of a need to worship. (See discussion of parallelism in last week's lesson.)

2b. tell of his salvation from day to day.

To *tell of his salvation* is to be the bearer of "good news" (Isaiah 40:9; 41:27; 61:1). The good news is that of God's deliverance, although the nature of the salvation in view is not stated. But however much the mandate of this half verse applies to the ancient Israelites' rescue from earthly enemies, it must apply to an immeasurably greater degree to salvation from eternal death! The message all the earth is to proclaim is also the message the earth is to receive (see Matthew 28:19, 20; Luke 1:19; 2:10; Romans 10:15; Revelation 14:6; etc.). The news of God's redemptive acts must go forth *from day to day,* never ceasing.

3. Declare his glory among the nations, his marvelous works among all the peoples!

Parallelism presents itself twice in this verse, with the pair *his glory* and *his marvelous works* as the first instance (compare 1 Chronicles 16:24). Although God's glory and wonders are not the same thing, he often reveals his glory by doing things only he can do. Example: since only God could have created the heavens, then "the heavens declare the glory of God" (Psalm 19:1).

We see the second parallel in the phrases *among the nations* and *among all the peoples*. The references reflect one another in stressing that humanity is to be made aware of God's glory and wonders. But the phrases are not quite identical in meaning, since *all the peoples* includes both those of the covenant and those who are not, while *the nations* refers only to those outside the covenant (2 Kings 17:15; etc.).

If the imperatives that open the first three verses of Psalm 96 are parallel with one another, then the reader is to declare the things of God through songs of praise. See further discussion below.

◆ *THE POWER OF SONG* ◆

The fall of the Soviet Union in the early 1990s resulted in a flood of missionaries to Ukraine and other former Soviet republics. On arrival, the missionaries found churches that had met secretly during the Communist era, when being caught at such gatherings or even talking about the gospel could land one in a Siberian work camp.

As a result, the Ukrainian Christians did not have much experience in evangelism. Also, many of the short-term missionaries did not speak much Russian and therefore had trouble communicating the gospel in depth.

Ukrainian church leaders suggested a solution: public singing by the Americans to draw attention. Finding the idea agreeable, the missionaries learned Russian words to familiar praise songs and proceeded to sing them in public. The Ukrainian Christians who accompanied the singers talked with the curious and invited them to church services. Many attended revival meetings because of the Americans' public songs of praise!

Think about it: songs sung in imperfect Russian by Americans who barely knew that language sparked a harvest for Christ and his kingdom! The lesson to be learned is . . . what?   —L. M. W.

B. Why to Do It (vv. 4-6)

4. For great is the LORD, and greatly to be praised; he is to be feared above all gods.

Now we are given reasons why all the earth should worship God: *great is the Lord*! Declarations of people to be great leaders, statesmen, athletes, entertainers, etc., are comparatively rare. And even those who may deserve such an accolade in an earthly sense are not great all the time. But God is!

Only he is worthy of worshipful praise (Revelation 19:4, 5, 10) and reverent fear (Matthew 10:28). The Bible uses the word *gods* (plural and lowercase *g*) more than 240 times. But none of those instances imply that such deities actually exist as supernatural beings. Rather, the word *gods* is used hypothetically (compare Jeremiah 2:11) to demonstrate the worthless nature of idols in contrast with the only true God (Exodus 12:12; 18:11; Galatians 4:8, 9). Such idols might not have a physical representation (example: Ezekiel 14:3, 4, 7), but usually do.

5. For all the gods of the peoples are worthless idols, but the LORD made the heavens.

The word translated *gods* here and in verse 4 above occurs more than 2,600 times in the Hebrew Old Testament. It is used to refer to "the Lord God" (example: Genesis 2:15), "heavenly beings" (example: Psalm 8:5), fictitious deities (example: Isaiah 37:19), and others. Context determines the proper translation.

The word in the original language is plural in form and can convey a sense of power, as in "mighty ones." But the mighty ones here, namely *the gods of the peoples,* are nothing but *worthless idols.* As such, they are nonentities—useless and insignificant fiction (compare Isaiah 44:9-20). There is irony here in that the so-called mighty ones are anything but! By contrast, the real and ultimate mighty one *made the heavens.*

◆   THE ONE ABOVE ALL   ◆

Pagans observe solstices and perform rituals in worship of the gods of nature; pilgrimages to Stonehenge still witness to such practices. Cities in India feature shrines dedicated to Hindu deities, the number of which seems uncountable. Many Japanese practice the rituals of Shinto, Japan's dominant religion, which also reveres a multitude of gods.

All this is nothing new (see Acts 17:16). Indeed, humans seem to have an innate drive to worship (compare Acts 14:11-13). In Western culture today, many seem less inclined to worship nature spirits, etc., and more inclined to pursue self-fulfillment via fame and fortune as their personal god. But this too is nothing new; Paul in his day noted those for whom "their God is their belly" (Philippians 3:19).

The need to worship something seems inescapable. Today's text points us to the only valid worship there is or can be: worship of the one true God. "For great is the Lord, and greatly to be praised" (Psalm 96:4).   —L. M. W.

> *What Do You Think?*
> What are some ways to point out the idols of secular culture to unbelievers? To believers?
> *Talking Points for Your Discussion*
> - Regarding idolatrous things
> - Regarding idolatrous attitudes
> - Regarding idolized people
> - Other

6.   Splendor and majesty are before him; strength and beauty are in his sanctuary.

This verse reinforces the reasons to worship God as the psalmist lists attributes of *splendor,* *majesty, strength,* and *beauty.* The implication is that these personified attributes are always in God's presence, surrounding his throne in Heaven (compare 1 Chronicles 16:27). Such attributes are to be spoken of (see Psalm 145:5).

II. Informed Worship
(PSALM 96:7-9)
A. Glory and Strength (vv. 7, 8a)

7, 8a. Ascribe to the LORD, O families of the peoples,
ascribe to the LORD glory and strength!
Ascribe to the LORD the glory due his name;

The tripled imperative that characterizes the beginning of this psalm is now duplicated, but with *ascribe* instead of *sing.* Most often we use the word *ascribe* in the sense of "lay something to the account of a person." The sense of *ascribe* as used here, however, is along the lines of "attribute to."

Attributing to God *glory and strength* is something all *families of the peoples* who inhabit the world can and should do (compare Revelation 5:9). Psalm 29:1, 2 features an almost exact replication of the triple imperative *ascribe* as used here, except that the ones being addressed there are angels or heavenly beings.

B. Bring and Come (v. 8b)

8b.   bring an offering, and come into his courts!

Words of praise are to be backed up with *an offering.* Under the old covenant, this refers to sacrifices God has specified (see Psalm 20:3; compare Leviticus 1–7). Eventually, only one offering is to be acceptable to God: the sacrifice of his Son (see Psalm 40:6; Hebrews 10:5-10), provided by God himself.

C. Holiness and Fear (v. 9)

9.   Worship the LORD in the splendor of holiness;
tremble before him, all the earth!

The mandate to *worship the Lord in the splendor of holiness* has more than one possible meaning. One is that the word *holiness* refers to the innocent deeds and dispositions of those who approach God in worship. In other words, worshippers must approach God with holy lives (see Psalm 24:3-6).

Other students think, however, that it is God's own holiness that is in view. This proposal is supported by the old Greek version of the Old Testament, which has "his holy court." Either view could be the intended interpretation. It is impossible for God not to be holy, and his holiness is a model for our own (1 Peter 1:15, 16).

What Do You Think?

What can you do this week to understand better the relevance of God's holiness in worship?

Talking Points for Your Discussion

- Scriptures you will read
- Prayers you will pray
- Mentors you will consult
- Other

The phrase *all the earth* is an identical twin to the one at the beginning of this psalm. They serve as bookends for verses 1-9, locking them together. Indeed they are, for their theme is the proper worship of the one who has created all the earth.

III. Ruling Lord
(PSALM 96:10-13)
A. What to Say (v. 10)

10. Say among the nations, "The LORD reigns!"
   Yes, the world is established; it shall never be moved;
   he will judge the peoples with equity."

We have moved from singing a new song to attribute to God glory as offerings are brought, to now exulting in the fact that the Lord is the one who is ruling. The context of the psalmist's instruction to exult in the fact that *the Lord reigns* has been debated. Essentially, there are three time-perspectives that are proposed for the ancient Israelite who sings this psalm in worship.

The past perspective sees this psalm as having been composed and sung in remembrance of a historical triumph, such as return from the Babylonian captivity. Isaiah 42:10 is thought to sup-

port this viewpoint as it enjoins the reader to "sing to the Lord a new song" in response to deliverance (compare Psalm 96:1).

The present perspective sees this psalm as being sung on a regular basis (at least annually) as a reminder to worshippers of the ongoing reality of God's reign. Thought to support this viewpoint is the fact that Psalm 96 also appears, with some variations, in 1 Chronicles 16:23-33, which recounts David's celebration of bringing the ark to Jerusalem. The supposition here is that an annual feast of some kind is in view, a feast where worshippers proclaim again their recognition of God's continuing reign.

The future perspective sees the praise mostly focused on what God is going to do later. Support for this is seen in the future orientation of the phrase *he will judge* in both the verse before us and verse 13 (below). The stress is that everyone, all *peoples,* should be aware of the judgment to come. Unrighteous *nations* and individuals perish under God's righteous judgment (Jeremiah 18:7-10; Hosea 10:8; Revelation 6:15-17; etc.). But what will cause many to fear will ultimately be the reason for universal celebration (next verse).

The three perspectives are not mutually exclusive. Elements of each may be intended.

What Do You Think?

Which Scriptures do you find helpful for needed reminders that God is still in control? Why?

Talking Points for Your Discussion

- In "good times" (productive witness, job promotion, etc.)
- In "bad times" (failed witness, job loss, etc.)

B. What Must Happen (vv. 11, 12)

11, 12. Let the heavens be glad, and let the earth rejoice;
   let the sea roar, and all that fills it;
   let the field exult, and everything in it!
   Then shall all the trees of the forest sing for joy

Although the four verbs *let . . . be glad / rejoice / roar / exult* are technically not stated as imperatives in the original language, they nonetheless express the psalmist's desire. The entirety of the universe is in view given the tandem pairing of *the heavens* and *the earth* (Genesis 1:1–2:1).

The references to various features of the earth complete the picture: the entirety of personified creation rejoices because the Lord reigns. Although not mentioned specifically, animals are in view as well, since the phrasing *the field . . . and everything in it* logically includes them.

Animals, trees, etc., suffer because of human unrighteousness, an unrighteousness that God judges (compare Deuteronomy 20:19; Isaiah 24; Jeremiah 6:6; Zechariah 11:2; Romans 8:22; etc.). But the judgment to come is a cause for celebration! The reason why was mentioned in Psalm 96:10; it is reemphasized in our next verse.

C. Why It Must Happen (v. 13)

**13. before the LORD, for he comes,
for he comes to judge the earth.
He will judge the world in righteousness
and the peoples in his faithfulness.**

The double *he comes* is a literary device to underline the Lord's intent *to judge*. Although not apparent in English, different Hebrew words are translated *judge* in this verse and in verse 10. This is another instance of the parallelism so often found in Hebrew poetry, and the words should be viewed as meaning the same in this context. Psalm 9:8 uses these same two words in similar fashion.

Some form of the words *judge, righteousness,* and *faithfulness* or the concepts they stand for are found together also in Psalm 33:4, 5 (last week's lesson); Isaiah 16:5; Jeremiah 4:2; and John 16:7-13 (contrast Romans 1:18-25). The king is responsible for bringing righteousness to the kingdom (see Psalms 72:1, 2; 99:4). God himself is the ultimate model of righteousness, able and willing to judge the world by his own moral character.

Conclusion

A. All Creation Praise the Lord!

The beauty of nature testifies to its Creator. The only appropriate response is for creation to bow in worship, awe, and wonder. Every avenue of communication must be used to attribute glory to the

Visual for Lessons 5 & 6. *Alternative discussion: substitute "Which of these words" for "Which Scriptures" when you get to the question for verse 10.*

Creator; emotions, declarations, and songs all have a part to play.

We anticipate singing a new song after Jesus returns (Revelation 5:9; 14:3). Even so, there is a sense in which we can sing that new song now, for our salvation can be said to be "now, but not yet." Judgment Day and our final deliverance are yet to come, but come they will (Daniel 12:2; Romans 14:10; 1 Corinthians 15:51-57; Hebrews 9:27; Revelation 6:15-17; etc.). The church prepares for that day by inviting all to learn about and know the Creator, Jesus Christ (John 1:3; Colossians 1:15, 16), the one who now reigns at the Father's right hand (Acts 2:32-36; compare Psalm 110:1).

Until Jesus returns, an important task is to "say among the nations, 'The Lord reigns!'" (Psalm 96:10). That can be said to be a starting point to fulfilling the Great Commission (Matthew 28:19, 20). May we glorify our Creator both as we do and as we invite others to do so as well.

B. Prayer

O God, please remove idols from our lives so that we may see your fingerprint on every good aspect of creation. Help us join all creation in proclaiming your unending reign. We pray in Jesus' name. Amen.

C. Thought to Remember

Praise the Creator when you look at creation.

INVOLVEMENT LEARNING

Enhance your lesson presentation with the reproducible activity page,
available as a free download at www.standardlesson.com.

Into the Lesson

Before class, obtain a book of optical illusions or print out a few illusions that you discover from a search of the Internet.

Say, "In typical optical illusions, our eyes are fooled when we take only a superficial look. When we take a second look, however, we obtain a deeper understanding of what we see."

Alternative. Distribute copies of the "On Second Thought" activity from the reproducible page, which you can download. Have students work individually or in pairs. This exercise contrasts how we viewed things when we were immature compared to how we view the same things as adults.

After either activity, lead into the Bible study saying, "The important matters of life are worthy of more than just a passing glance. Today we will look at a psalm that says just that about our God. When we gain a deeper understanding of who he is, we see him in a new way and respond with a new song."

Into the Word

The key words and phrases of Psalm 96 are echoed throughout the Old Testament. Divide your class into three groups. Say, "Each group will look at a portion of today's text, then look at related verses in the Old Testament that use the same key word or phrase." Prepare the group assignments before class.

Group 1—Sing a new song.
What should we be singing about and telling each other when we see God for who he is?
Compare Psalm 96:1-6 with Psalms 33:3-5; 40:3-5; 98:1-3.
Group 2—Surrender to God.
When we see God for who he is, what do we give/ ascribe to him?
Compare Psalm 96:7-9 with Deuteronomy 32:1-4; 1 Chronicles 16:28-30; Psalm 29:1-4.

Group 3—Celebrate God's presence.
Why do we rejoice when we recognize that God is present?
Compare Psalm 96:10-13 with Psalms 5:11, 12; 33:20-22; 97:10-12.

After groups have finished, reassemble the class and have groups report on their findings.

Alternative. Distribute copies of the "Words of Worship" activity from the reproducible page. Have students work in pairs to complete the matches.

Discuss either activity with questions such as these: "Which of these ideas do you most associate with the Sunday worship service? Which are part of your everyday life? What are some ways we can include the Sunday morning actions into our daily lives?"

Into Life

Ask students to tell what they think about singing new songs versus singing old songs. "Are you less likely to pay attention to what you are singing with familiar songs versus those that are new to you?"

Before class, make copies of familiar hymns that are in the public domain, such as "How Great Thou Art" or "Holy, Holy, Holy." Distribute copies to each class member. Say, "Read through the words of the hymns slowly, underlining phrases that you have overlooked or not thoroughly considered before. Be especially aware of themes common both to these hymns and to Psalm 96."

After a few minutes, ask students to tell what they underlined. Ask, "Why might these words be easily overlooked when we sing them often? How can singing praise while carefully giving attention to the words make an old song a new song being sung to the Lord?"

Close with a prayer asking God to help us give him a second look in all we do, never being complacent in our worship.

PRAISE GOD THE PROVIDER

DEVOTIONAL READING: Psalm 66:1-5
BACKGROUND SCRIPTURE: Psalms 65; 67:6, 7

PSALM 65

1 Praise is due to you, O God, in Zion,
   and to you shall vows be performed.
2 O you who hear prayer,
   to you shall all flesh come.
3 When iniquities prevail against me,
   you atone for our transgressions.
4 Blessed is the one you choose and bring
      near,
   to dwell in your courts!
We shall be satisfied with the goodness of
      your house,
   the holiness of your temple!
5 By awesome deeds you answer us with
      righteousness,
   O God of our salvation,
the hope of all the ends of the earth
   and of the farthest seas;
6 the one who by his strength established the
      mountains,
   being girded with might;
7 who stills the roaring of the seas,
   the roaring of their waves,
   the tumult of the peoples,

8 so that those who dwell at the ends of the
      earth are in awe at your signs.
You make the going out of the morning
   and the evening to shout for joy.
9 You visit the earth and water it;
   you greatly enrich it;
the river of God is full of water;
   you provide their grain,
   for so you have prepared it.
10 You water its furrows abundantly,
   settling its ridges,
softening it with showers,
   and blessing its growth.
11 You crown the year with your bounty;
   your wagon tracks overflow with
      abundance.
12 The pastures of the wilderness overflow,
   the hills gird themselves with joy,
13 the meadows clothe themselves with
      flocks,
   the valleys deck themselves with grain,
   they shout and sing together for joy.

KEY VERSE

By awesome deeds you answer us with righteousness, O God of our salvation, the hope of all the ends of the earth and of the farthest seas. —**Psalm 65:5**

CREATION: A DIVINE CYCLE

Unit 2: Praise from and for God's Creation

LESSONS 5–9

LESSON AIMS

After participating in this lesson, each learner will be able to:

1. List ways the earth is a testimony to God's creative power.

2. Compare and contrast the perceived source of material bounty from the viewpoints of the psalmist and today's culture.

3. Sing a hymn or worship song that praises God as provider and sustainer.

LESSON OUTLINE

Introduction

A. Waiting for Rain

My state of Nebraska is an agricultural power-house. Rich soil, flat land, and sufficient rain make this possible. There has been plenty of rain this year, and record harvests are predicted. But this was not the case two years ago. The usual summer rains did not come. Fields languished in drought conditions. The harvest was a disaster for many farmers.

Science can explain how the cycle of precipitation works, even predict rain with some accuracy, but no technology exists to bring rain reliably. So we wait and pray. We don't understand how God controls the rain, but we believe that he does—so we ask for his help. When we pray for rain, we are not asking Mother Nature to provide it!

Psalm 65 presents God as the Creator of the systems of the earth, and the one in control of these systems. The psalmist surely knew of years when Israel suffered drought, and crops were meager. Yet his confidence remained in God. If God is powerful enough to create the earth, surely he is powerful enough to control the earth and its weather. God did not create something bigger than he!

Some religions of antiquity had separate gods for creation and weather. For example, Canaanite religion featured an ancient creator god who had withdrawn from human affairs. By contrast, their most worshipped deity was the weather or storm god, the one whom they sought to appease and please with their sacrifices. No such nonsense for the psalmist! There is only one God, and he has never withdrawn from his creation.

B. Lesson Background

Many psalms have superscriptions (see discussion on these in the Lesson Background of lesson 5). The superscription of Psalm 65 introduces what follows as being "A Psalm of David. A Song." Both the music and the lyrics evidently came from "the sweet psalmist of Israel" (2 Samuel 23:1).

The superscribed introduction also indicates it was "to the choirmaster." This is more than a dedication. It serves as permission for the composition to be used by those who orchestrated the musical praise for Israel's national celebrations. The psalm serves to reveal the heart of the man whom the Lord selected to be king of his chosen nation, a man after God's own heart (Acts 13:22).

The Israel of David's era seems to have been a nation of singers and instrumentalists (1 Chronicles 13:8; etc.). They had no electronic amplification. They had no technology to allow projection of words on a screen. And Israelite worship did not feature songs that people had been listening to all week on personal devices. Instead, worship featured heartfelt songs sung from memory, sung with passion and conviction.

Psalm 65 seems to have been one those.

I. People's Praise
(Psalm 65:1-4)
A. Because God Hears (vv. 1, 2)

1. Praise is due to you, O God, in Zion, and to you shall vows be performed.

The psalm begins dramatically by addressing the Lord. The address is an invitation for the Lord to be the audience for the upcoming service of *praise*. The people will not be there *in Zion* to celebrate themselves. Since the praise service is for God, it cannot begin without his presence.

A further clarification of purpose presents itself in the mention of vows. The vows to *be fulfilled* are, in various ways, dedications of loyalty to the Lord (compare Numbers 6:21; 30:2; Deuteronomy 23:21; Psalm 116:18; etc.). This helps us understand the reference to *Zion*. There is no temple in Jerusalem in David's day, but Zion is the designated place of worship for the people of Israel. It is the hill upon which the city of David has been built (see 2 Samuel 5:7). It was the holy place for the king's residence (see Psalm 2:6). And now the Lord, the great king, is being invited to join the celebrants in his beloved place (see Psalm 78:68). Worship includes dedicating oneself to God.

◆ Taking Vows Seriously ◆

Did you make any vows for the new year of 2017? Or do you consider New Year's resolutions a tradition that has outworn its welcome? Many people still take the idea seriously (at least for a few days into the new year) as they vow to do better in setting goals, changing habits, etc.

Various kinds of vows, how they are made, and how they are fulfilled or broken are familiar. For example, marriage vows at their finest express God's ideals by which a man and a woman agree to order their marriage henceforth. Given the high percentage of divorce among Christians, one wonders why the vow was not kept.

The New Testament has important things to say about the taking of oaths or vows (see Matthew 5:33-37; 23:16-22; Acts 18:18; James 5:12). While studying those, we may arrive at different conclusions regarding the form, content, and context of oaths/vows appropriate for the New Testament era. But who can doubt that promises—whether made to God or others—should be taken seriously? A vague resolution to "be more faithful" to God in the coming year will not be nearly as motivating as a vow tied to a specific carry through. That's what the psalmist has in mind. —C. R. B.

2. O you who hear prayer, to you shall all flesh come.

The fact that God does *answer prayer* means more than just listening. He hears and answers prayer. With notable exceptions (Proverbs 28:9; Isaiah 1:15; Jeremiah 7:16; Lamentations 3:44; etc.), prayers receive his full attention (compare Proverbs 15:8, 29; Isaiah 38:5; Jeremiah 29:12;

HOW TO SAY IT

Canaanite	*Kay*-nun-ite.
iniquities	in-*ik*-wu-teez.
panentheism	pah-***nen(t)***-thee-*izum*.
pantheism	***pan(t)***-thee-*ih*-zum.
Zion	*Zi*-un.

1 Peter 3:12; etc.). His ability to pay attention to millions of prayers simultaneously teaches us something important about his power!

How can this be? How can God attend to millions of prayers at the same time? The psalmist does not explain here, but consider that time as we experience it does not limit or bind God (see 2 Peter 3:8). Our timeless, ageless Lord does not need to hurry through the prayers that come to him. In ways that are beyond our understanding, God is able to give all the attention he desires to each prayer, whether that prayer be a word of praise, thanksgiving, or request (compare Daniel 9:23; Acts 10:4).

All people are to come only before the Lord with prayer. When the pagan neighbors of Israel pray to their fictitious gods of mountains, rivers, the sun, etc., they miss the only valid prayer destination in the universe.

B. Because God Purges (v. 3)

3. When iniquities prevail against me, you atone for our transgressions.

The psalmist wastes no time in addressing the biggest barrier to worship: *sins* and *transgressions* (compare Psalm 32:5). The fact that God is the one who forgives is what makes worship possible. The word translated *forgave* is the vitally important Old Testament word that is rendered "make atonement" in many other places. Only God in his mercy and grace can grant the forgiveness the worshipper needs—and he does! See Micah 7:18.

What Do You Think?
What can we do to ensure that sin does not hinder worship?
Talking Points for Your Discussion
- Considering the seriousness of sin
- Considering how sin is conquered
- Regarding sins committed against you
- Other

C. Because God Blesses (v. 4)

4. Blessed is the one you choose and bring near, to dwell in your courts!

We shall be satisfied with the goodness of your house, the holiness of your temple!

Those who are forgiven (v. 3) are the ones God chooses. Everyone is eligible to be forgiven, but forgiveness by the Almighty is not earned. Nor is it some kind of inalienable right. Rather, it is a deliberate act of the willing God on the repentant.

Being forgiven and chosen has the immediate privilege of being allowed to come *near to* the Lord. The psalmist continues this figurative depiction in terms of being admitted to the Lord's *holy temple*; this implies close fellowship. The presence of the Lord is signified by viewing his *house* and his *holy temple* as one and the same (see Ezra 3:10, 11; Zechariah 8:9).

There is value in having a dedicated place for corporate praise and prayer. It is true that we can worship the Lord even while driving in heavy freeway traffic, but that will not be without distractions. Nor will it have the sense of holiness of which the psalmist speaks. Although God does not live in our church buildings (compare Acts 17:24), efforts to create appropriate space for worship will not go unrewarded.

II. Psalmist's Analysis
(Psalm 65:5-8)
A. How God Answers (vv. 5-7)

5a. By awesome deeds you answer us with righteousness, O God of our salvation,

The psalmist now begins to consider the vast scope of God's power. The word *awesome* carries the older sense of "terrifying" (compare Psalm 45:4).

The terrifying *things* that God does as *righteous deeds* when he answers *us* are things that should result in awe and reverential fear on our part. The fact that he is *God our Savior* removes any reason for either us or the psalmist to cower in dread (compare Isaiah 41:10).

5b. the hope of all the ends of the earth and of the farthest seas;

The fact stated in verse 5a leads the psalmist to proclaim the universal, worldwide reach of human appreciation for God's mighty acts. He and he alone is the one in whom to place *hope* for salvation. This is true even in the most remote location the psalmist can imagine. Since God has created everything, he is not merely the national God of Israel. All people must look to him (compare Psalm 22:27; Jeremiah 32:27).

**6, 7. the one who by his strength established
      the mountains,
   being girded with might;
who stills the roaring of the seas,
   the roaring of their waves,
   the tumult of the peoples,**

How did *the mountains* get here? Who had a wagon big enough to transport them to the right place? Why does *the roaring of the seas* and *waves* eventually become calm and quiet instead of continuing indefinitely? For the psalmist, the answer is inescapable: only God is powerful enough to bring about such things, for he is the master of that which he has created.

What Do You Think?

What would you say to someone for whom relief from a violent force of nature came about only after his or her house was destroyed?

Talking Points for Your Discussion

- If victim reasons that God is evil or powerless
- If victim reasons that randomly destructive forces of nature prove there is no God
- If victim says the loss is punishment for sin

The psalmist extends this last illustration into human affairs. We know all too well of the warlike propensities of humans, their *turmoil* (Psalm 2:1). Someone rises to power and wants to gain prestige and wealth, so armies march, battles wage, and chaos ensues.

We understand (and hate) the impulse to violence and war, but do we understand peace? Why is there ever any peace and not continual war? The psalmist teaches us that peace between nations, even temporary peace, is brought about only by the intention and power of the Lord. The God who calms the seas also calms the nations, for he is master of both (Psalm 22:28; Isaiah 17:12, 13).

B. What God Reveals (v. 8)

**8a. so that those who dwell at the ends of the
      earth are in awe at your signs.**

We need not picture our psalmist as a world traveler or a master of world geography to appreciate what he says here. He knows that every part of the earth has evidence of God's *signs*, a word frequently found alongside the word "wonders" (example: Jeremiah 32:21).

The psalmist makes this affirmation not because he's personally seen the *awe* of the people who live *at the ends of the earth*. The statement comes from faith. He is completely convinced that each and every part of the earth testifies to its residents concerning the power of God the Creator. How could it be otherwise?

**8b. You make the going out of the morning
      and the evening to shout for joy.**

The psalmist uses another aspect of creation that everyone has experienced: the cycle of the days. Creation passages such as Psalm 104:19-23 reflect this enduring feature of life.

Whether from today's vantage point or that of the psalmist, the rising and the setting of the sun is the most dependable aspect of our natural world we can imagine. We expect that when night falls, daybreak will follow within a few hours. Weather has varying degrees of predictability, but not the daily cycle of sunrise and sunset (compare Joshua 10:12-14; Psalm 72:5; exception: Zechariah 14:6, 7).

The psalmist further pictures this cycle as a way in which nature rejoices. Such witness testifies to the power and faithfulness of God (compare Psalm 148:3).

III. God's Blessings
(Psalm 65:9-13)
A. On the Land (vv. 9, 10)

**9.   You visit the earth and water it;
   you greatly enrich it;
the river of God is full of water;
   you provide their grain,
   for so you have prepared it.**

The psalm now moves into territory that makes it fitting for use at the time of a harvest celebration. While we may rightly bemoan either too little or too much rain, the psalmist chooses not to complain. All waters are blessings from God, who provides the necessities of life.

This is expressed in terms we might miss if we are not careful. *The streams of God* of which the psalmist speaks contrast with the religions of the ancient world that believe in a god for every river or stream. The pagans sacrifice to and serve these local gods so that rivers will be full. The Israelites do not see their Lord as such a dinky deity. He is the Lord of all rivers; he is the master of all water. The psalmist is grateful.

What Do You Think?

In what ways can our stewardship of the environment be a witness for the Creator?

Talking Points for Your Discussion
- Concerning conservation initiatives
- Concerning reactions to natural disasters
- Regarding personal, everyday practices
- Other

---

10. You water its furrows abundantly,
    settling its ridges,
  softening it with showers,
    and blessing its growth.

This is a beautiful picture of gentle rain coming at just the right time. The fact that such rain brings needed moisture to *the furrows* and *the ridges* of a plowed field speaks to the graciousness of the one who "sends rain on the righteous and the unrighteous" (Matthew 5:45).

◆ *Prayer Tendencies* ◆

Many people who don't ordinarily pray did so as a drought extended itself across the southern U.S. from 2010 to 2013. According to the U.S. Drought Monitor, drought affected about 60 percent of the lower 48 states by January 2013, with Canada and Mexico affected to varying degrees.

Human nature is such that we tend not to credit God with blessings received. But when things go badly, even people who don't ordinarily pray may seek divine relief. The psalmist observes that the earth itself praises God for his bounty. Christians more than anyone should be praising

God continually for the necessities of life that he provides daily through his creation.

Try the following experiment. First, think back on your prayers for the past three days and add up the number of requests in those prayers. Then add up the number of praises offered for what you already have. When you compare the two tallies, do you see a problem?   —C. R. B.

B. On the Flocks (vv. 11-13)

11, 12. You crown the year with your bounty;
      your wagon tracks overflow with
        abundance.
    The pastures of the wilderness overflow,
      the hills gird themselves with joy,

These are words of harvest celebration. Well-stocked supermarkets have isolated most of us from the wonder and joy of harvest time. We might sing "Come, ye thankful people, come" in our Thanksgiving service, but we might not see much need to "raise the song of harvest home."

Not so with our psalmist! He has experienced God's *bounty* in a successful harvest. The phrase *carts overflow with abundance* sketches a picture of a harvest so great that some of its produce is falling off the wagons onto the farm roadways! But no one is concerned because there is plenty.

Even the *grasslands of the wilderness* are lush, so the grazing animals will fatten nicely and provide milk and meat. The richness of God's creation at harvest time is so marvelous that it is as if the earth itself is involved in worship, for the *hills* themselves are said to be glad.

What Do You Think?

How do the coronation passages Psalms 8:5; 103:4; Song of Solomon 3:11; and Isaiah 23:8 enrich your understanding of this one? How will this influence your life in the week ahead?

Talking Points for Your Discussion
- Regarding passages where God performs the coronation
- Passages where something or someone other than God performs the coronation

---

13. the meadows clothe themselves with
     flocks,

**the valleys deck themselves with grain,
they shout and sing together for joy.**

Agricultural abundance is the result of God's blessing and providential grace. The *flocks,* meaning primarily sheep and goats, are thriving. The flocks are so abundant it is almost as if the *meadows* themselves are clothed in sheep's wool! This word-picture is extended to *the valleys,* now fully clothed with waves of *grain* ready to be harvested.

The psalmist ends by concluding that this great, rich harvest is an expression of *joy* by the earth. The land is said to *sing* as it produces our food, for that is its purpose in God's created order (see Genesis 1:29, 30). If the earth itself is praising its Creator for using it to the full, can we do any less?

Conclusion

A. Wrong Path

Pantheism is the false belief that all things are God. Closely related is the belief that God is in all things (pan*en*theism). These beliefs are popular today among some people who want to be "spiritual" but reject "religions." Sometimes, pantheists point to Bible texts like Psalm 65 to justify their views, claiming the psalmist extols creation itself as being worthy of worship. The psalmist's depictions of the earth's singing for joy, etc., are thereby misinterpreted to signify that the world is a living entity, capable of offering praise to God just as humans do.

Make no mistake: a pantheistic reading of this psalm is incorrect. The psalmist does indeed marvel as he looks around at creation, but he does not pause to worship created things. He sees creation as evidence of the greatness and kindness of the one who stands behind it: the Creator.

God the Creator is a person in Psalm 65, worthy to be praised and worshipped. Part of the created order is that we are persons too. Our personhood in no way makes us equal to God, but reflects the intention in his design that we are capable of having a personal relationship with him.

We should respect God's creation, but we should never worship it. Pantheists are looking in the right direction, but they stop before they

Visual for Lesson 7. *Start a discussion by pointing to each of the four words in turn as you ask, "Why is this word important in our application of Psalm 65?"*

get to the mighty Creator of the universe. He is the uncreated God who loves, forgives, and cares for us.

B. Right Path

The contents of Psalm 65 suggest praise during a harvest celebration. These community gatherings may have been where the people of Israel learned the words and music of the psalm. But a psalm such as this would also have lent itself to home worship, to be taught to children and sung as a praise and thanksgiving song before the weekly minifeast of Sabbath day.

Psalm 65 still serves us well today, whether as a personal expression of praise or for lending words to corporate worship. May we honor the Lord with our hearts full of thanksgiving. May our voices of joy join with the witness of earth as we lift our praises to the Lord, the Creator of all.

C. Prayer

Holy God, we praise you for providing for our needs. May we focus on our blessings, not on what we think we lack. We pray this in the name of the one who created us all, the one who was and is your greatest blessing: your divine Son, Jesus. Amen.

D. Thought to Remember

May praise for the Lord
always be waiting in our hearts.

INVOLVEMENT LEARNING

Enhance your lesson presentation with the reproducible activity page,
available as a free download at www.standardlesson.com.

Into the Lesson

Before class begins, write the following quotation on the board. Include the underlining that we have added.

My main goal is to be a <u>self-made</u> man and have <u>control</u> over what's <u>mine</u>.
—Actor Kevin Hart

Discuss the quote. Ask, "In what ways do you agree with the attitudes expressed in this quote? In what ways do you disagree? Why are the underlined words significant?"

Alternative. Distribute copies of the "Self-Made" activity from the reproducible page, which you can download. Have students work individually or in pairs.

After either activity, lead into the Bible study saying, "We rightly recognize that some people were born into situations that were difficult. We rightly salute those people who showed extraordinary effort to rise above those circumstances and to succeed. But is it accurate to label such people as self-made? Let's look at Psalm 65, which addresses that very issue."

Into the Word

Divide the class into three groups. Give each group one of the following self-made arguments to refute by using their assigned portion of Psalm 65. Expected responses are in italics, but do not distribute those.

Group 1—I am a self-made believer. I follow my own path to God (vv. 1-4).
  Whom do you praise and to whom do you pray—a god you imagine? (vv. 1, 2).
  Who forgives your sins? Or do you believe that you sin at all? (v. 3)
  With whom do you share your faith? Isn't it lonely not meeting with those who follow a God-made path to him? (v. 4)

Group 2—I am a self-made seeker. I just want to rise above this world and connect to the great life force (vv. 5-8).
  Is this world a meaningless accident, or is it God's response to us, telling us that he is there? (v. 5)
  How do you explain how the earth came to be? (v. 6).
  To whom do you turn when this world is a hostile place? (vv. 7, 8)

Group 3—The earth is our mother. She came into being by herself and birthed us as well (vv. 9-13).
  Doesn't that make nature a god rather than something created and sustained by God? (vv. 9, 10)
  Can the earth take care of itself? Can't we see in our own lives that anything not cared for falls apart? (vv. 10-13).

After groups have finished, reassemble the class and have groups report their findings.

Into Life

Several years ago, a Christian band called NewSong released a song called "God Made Man." Obtain that song from a CD or purchase it inexpensively from a reputable music-download website.

Play the song and compare it to the ideas found in Psalm 65. Ask, "In what ways does the world's view of a self-made man contrast with the biblical view of being made and sustained by God?"

Alternative. Distribute copies of the "God-Made" activity from the reproducible page. Have students work in pairs to look up Scriptures and unscramble the statements.

Follow either activity with a closing prayer asking God to help us look to him and not ourselves to provide all that we need. If time permits, sing some hymns or choruses of worshipful praise.

PRAISE GOD
THE CREATOR

DEVOTIONAL READING: Psalm 8
BACKGROUND SCRIPTURE: Psalm 104

PSALM 104:1-4, 24-30

1 Bless the LORD, O my soul!
  O LORD my God, you are very great!
You are clothed with splendor and majesty,
2   covering yourself with light as with a
    garment,
  stretching out the heavens like a tent.
3 He lays the beams of his chambers on the
    waters;
  he makes the clouds his chariot;
    he rides on the wings of the wind;
4   he makes his messengers winds,
    his ministers a flaming fire.
. . . .
24 O LORD, how manifold are your works!
    In wisdom have you made them all;
    the earth is full of your creatures.
25 Here is the sea, great and wide,
    which teems with creatures innumerable,
    living things both small and great.
26 There go the ships,
    and Leviathan, which you formed to
    play in it.
27 These all look to you,
    to give them their food in due season.

28 When you give it to them, they gather it up;
    when you open your hand, they are
    filled with good things.
29 When you hide your face, they are
    dismayed;
    when you take away their breath, they die
    and return to their dust.
30 When you send forth your Spirit, they are
    created,
    and you renew the face of the ground.

KEY VERSE

O Lord, how manifold are your works! In wisdom have you made them all; the earth is full of your creatures.
—**Psalm 104:24**

CREATION: A DIVINE CYCLE

Unit 2: Praise from and for God's Creation

LESSONS 5–9

LESSON AIMS

After participating in this lesson, each learner will be able to:

1. List some diverse elements of God's creation.

2. Explain the connection between the first segment of the lesson text (vv. 1-4) and the second (vv. 24-30).

3. Write a statement of respect and commitment to care for God's creation.

LESSON OUTLINE

Introduction

A. Recycle vs. Renew

Do you recycle? No one asked this question 40 years ago, but now it is common—and frequently accompanied by moral judgment. In certain ways, ecological awareness and practice has become the new morality. We are urged not to judge people regarding just about everything, but this seems to be a big exception. Filling the Internet with moral filth is OK, but filling our landfills when we could be recycling is deemed unacceptable.

Recycling programs in some cities have gone from voluntary to mandatory, and efforts have expanded far beyond the mere saving of aluminum cans and glass jars. Manufacturers are now very conscious of the packaging they use, designing such materials to be easily recyclable.

The point at which this "green" emphasis does more harm than good (if ever) is a debate best conducted elsewhere. And whether or not we choose to participate in those debates, we must keep in mind that God planned his creation to be capable of more than recycling. He intended it to be continually renewing.

There is no word in the Bible for *recycle*, but *renew* is an important theme. Renewing, from the Bible's perspective, is both part of the plan of God and a process that is dependent on God. Whether it is a renewal of the earth or a renewal of the human spirit, it cannot happen without God's blessing and power. The God who renews is the focus of the celebration that makes up our lesson this week from Psalm 104.

B. Lesson Background

Psalm 104 falls within the Psalms Book IV, the bookends of which are Psalms 90 and 106. At least one scholar sees enough similarity among Psalms 8, 33 (see lesson 5), 104, and 145 to categorize the four as "Songs of Creation."

Psalm 104 also is often paired with Psalm 103, since both feature material drawn from Genesis and both are hymns of praise (note their similar beginnings and endings in that regard). Because of these similarities, some scholars propose that the named author of Psalm 103, who is David, is also the author of Psalm 104, which bears no designation of authorship.

Whether or not David wrote Psalm 104, its original concept apparently came from a pagan source: Pharaoh Akhenaton's Great Hymn to the Sun. This praise of a fictitious sun god is traced to Egyptian mythology of the fourteenth century BC. The fact that the pagan sun-hymn came first means that the writer of Psalm 104 would be the borrower. Yet the two are different in vital ways! Their conclusions, the focus of their tribute, and Psalm 104's dependence on Genesis 1 assured the ancient Hebrew that there would be no confusion between the two compositions.

Even so, we may wonder why the psalmist would borrow from the Egyptian sun-hymn in the first place. Perhaps it was because his culture was already familiar with it. That possibility may lead us to theorize further that Psalm 104's praise of the Creator is an intentional jab at the Egyptian hymn's praise of a part of creation. We should not find such a procedure surprising. The apostle Paul, for his part, used pagan sources in his sermons and letters to uphold Christ (see Acts 17:28; 1 Corinthians 15:33; and Titus 1:12).

Regarding tone, Psalm 104 has more of the personal element than other praise psalms. The fact that it switches in speaking of the Lord with personal address ("You") and narrative ("He") makes it seem suited for both public worship and personal reflection. Vividness is enhanced by the psalmist's use of the technique called *parallelism*. That feature, common in Hebrew poetry, involves saying the same thing (or nearly the same thing) with different words (see discussion in lesson 5).

Our lesson today focuses on verses from the beginning and the end of this great psalm, but students should read the whole thing. In so doing, many phrases used in our worship songs will be detected. This testifies to the richness and the eternal value of this hymn of praise.

HOW TO SAY IT

Akhenaton	Ock-*naw*-tun.
Leviathan	Luh-*vye*-uh-thun.
Pharaoh	*Fair*-o (or *Fay*-roe).

I. Greatness of God
(Psalm 104:1-4)
A. Clothed in Majesty (v. 1)
1a. Bless the LORD, O my soul!

The psalmist begins with a command. The soul is the essence of a person. Is he telling himself to do something? Yes! His comments serve as a reminder not to forget to give *the Lord* his deserved praise and blessing. This is a great start to a time of worship, whether group or private. Let's focus on God, not ourselves.

The books of Genesis and Psalms feature the highest relative occurrences of the Hebrew word translated *bless*. But while the blessing statements in Genesis most often refer to God's blessing a person, those in the Psalms speak of people's blessing the Lord. The latter happens when people offer deserved and appropriate praise to God.

1b. O LORD my God, you are very great!
You are clothed with splendor and
majesty,

We give the Lord the praise due him as we recognize his exceeding greatness. The psalmist's word picture for this is God's clothing as *splendor and majesty*. This describes a glorious king. In Psalm 21:5, these qualities are bestowed on a human king by God; it is as if God lends the man a share of divine glory temporarily. But in the verse before us, we see far more than a tiny derivative of glory, for God wears his majesty like a robe. We are reminded of words of the cherished hymn "How Great Thou Art."

> *What Do You Think?*
> How can we make sure our praise comes from the depths of our souls?
> *Talking Points for Your Discussion*
> - In light of Matthew 15:8
> - In light of Matthew 21:16
> - In light of James 3:10
> - Other

B. Served by Angels (vv. 2-4)
2. covering yourself with light as with a
garment,
stretching out the heavens like a tent.

The word picture is extended. The Lord not only wears a robe of majesty, but this *garment* is made of pure *light*. It is as if God takes the light of the sun and bends its rays to serve as a glorious cloak for himself (compare Revelation 12:1).

This idea of God's using the mighty elements of his creation as fabric goes one stage further when the psalmist sees God *stretching out the heavens like a tent*. This is an insight into the immensity of God, as if he covers the entire sky from the eastern to the western horizon with a stupendous bolt of heavenly cloth. God wraps himself in glory, and he brings his glorious touch to earth itself for us to experience.

◆ GOD'S "CLOTHING" AND OURS ◆

Current culture is less formal today than it was a few generations ago. One way this is seen is in the attire worn on various occasions. An older generation of men still wear coat and tie to weddings and funerals, while younger adults may prefer jeans.

A generational divide is also seen in what people wear to church. The senior saints, who often prefer the traditional worship service, will wear their "Sunday best." It is not uncommon to hear them complain that wearing anything less would fail to show proper respect for God.

The younger folks, on the other hand, may wear cutoffs and sandals to their preferred contemporary worship service. When concerns are voiced about their attire, they might respond that God is more interested in what is in their hearts than what they are wearing.

When we read how God is "clothed," is anything being implied regarding our own attire in approaching him? And does our choice of attire for worship say anything about the level of our regard for him? Perhaps the broader question includes the issue of attire and many other issues as well: *How can we demonstrate our highest regard for God at all times and on all occasions?* —C. R. B.

3. He lays the beams of his chambers on the waters;
he makes the clouds his chariot;
he rides on the wings of the wind;

The psalmist continues his praise of God's wonders by expanding the idea of the skyward presence of the Lord. This imagines *the beams of his chambers* to be posted in the deep waters of the earth. This is a picture of gigantic pillars driven into the seabed to support the structure of Heaven.

In his sky abode, God rides *clouds* as his personal, kingly *chariot* and walks or rides around by using the *wind* as we would the earth's ground (compare Isaiah 66:15). These powerful, poetic expressions of God are saying, "He is not like us. His ways are far above ours. He is glorious beyond our comprehension."

What Do You Think?

What word pictures have you found to be effective when explaining the nature of God?

Talking Points for Your Discussion
- When conversing with a child
- When conversing with an unbeliever

4. he makes his messengers winds, his ministers a flaming fire.

The proper understanding of this verse is difficult, since some words have more than one possible meaning. First, the Hebrew word for *messengers* (see also Numbers 24:12) can also be translated "angels," as it is in Genesis 32:1. Indeed, a function of angels is to bring God's messages to humans. Hebrews 1:7 clearly identifies Psalm 104:4 as speaking "of the angels." Thus angels are to be identified with both *his messengers* and *his ministers,* since the latter two stand parallel to one another (compare Hebrews 1:14).

The Hebrew word for *wind* also presents an issue of dual rendering, since it can be translated "spirit," as it is 2 Chronicles 18:20. The psalmist may be using this fact to depict the heavenly servants as being like winds (compare Revelation 7:1). If so, a couple of things are implied.

First, angels are powerful, for the wording here does not describe light breezes. This is a description of moving weather at its extreme, which can be violent and destructive. Second, these powerful beings are, like the wind, invisible to us (unless God chooses to make them visible). The psalmist truly understands and believes there are angels among us, and this is a humbling and comforting thing for him. We see him awestruck in his description of these heavenly beings as *a flaming fire,* another way of indicating the power of God's angels (compare Psalm 97:3).

II. Greatness of God's Works
(Psalm 104:24-26)
A. The Abundant Earth (v. 24)
24. O Lord, how manifold are your works! In wisdom have you made them all; the earth is full of your creatures.

We see parallelism here as the phrases *your works* and *your creatures* reflect one another. The word *creatures* carries the idea of many different animals and the diversity of the earth's biosphere. Passages such as Psalms 8:3, 4; 66:3; and 92:5 also marvel at the complexity and scope of God's creation.

The psalmist also introduces here a concept that may be less familiar to us: that creation itself is a testimony to the *wisdom* of God. Our universe is not self-explanatory or self-ordering. Its beauty and balance are the result of God's perfect wisdom. We are best able to appreciate the value of our natural world when we rely on the wisdom of God. This comes full circle when we realize that our awe or fear of the Lord is the beginning of our own pathway to wisdom (Psalm 111:10). Human reverence for God and human wisdom are two sides of the same coin.

> *What Do You Think?*
> How can our congregation best use God's great works in nature to bring people closer to him?
> *Talking Points for Your Discussion*
> - For the spiritual growth of fellow Christians
> - For evangelistic outreach to unbelievers

B. The Expansive Sea (vv. 25, 26)
25. Here is the sea, great and wide, which teems with creatures innumerable, living things both small and great.

In turning his attention from the dry land to *the sea, vast and spacious,* the psalmist speaks as one who has spent time on ships personally. Or perhaps he has conversed with others who have. Those who have spent time at sea have the greater appreciation of how vast the oceans are. The experience of sailing out far enough to lose sight of all land can be overwhelming. When no landmarks are visible, the rolling seas seem endless.

The psalmist is also knowledgeable regarding creatures of the sea. He knows that the sea has many *living things both large and small.* All this contributes mightily to the author's spirit of amazement and appreciation for the Creator.

26. There go the ships, and Leviathan, which you formed to play in it.

The psalmist continues expressing wonder at the size of the oceans. There is plenty of room for all *ships,* works of humans that seem puny by comparison to the works of God.

The vastness of the ocean means that even the *Leviathan* is not cramped for space. *Leviathan* is a transliterated Hebrew term, and Isaiah 27:1 describes it as a "serpent" of some kind. This may refer to an eel-like sea creature that is able to curl and contort itself.

The lengthy treatment of *Leviathan* in Job 41 has led to different conclusions, however. Some see a reference to a mythological dragon that no longer exists. Others identify the Leviathan variously as a crocodile, a seagoing dinosaur, or a whale. At any rate, the Leviathan was a huge animal of the sea (see Job 41:1). We should not get so distracted by trying to figure out Leviathan that we lose sight of the psalmist's main point: that of an ocean so spacious that even a creature such as Leviathan seems like a minnow within it.

III. Goodness of God's Works
(Psalm 104:27-30)
A. Feeding the World (vv. 27, 28)
27. These all look to you, to give them their food in due season.

The phrase *all creatures* refers to animal life, including the sea creatures just mentioned. The psalmist solemnly notes that every single creature, from humans to fish, depend on the Lord himself to feed them. The Lord does this indirectly through the earth's systems of production, systems he created. Both humans and sharks may catch fish to eat, but ultimately all food comes from the self-renewing system that continues to operate by God's power. The earth God created in the first place, he continues to sustain to this day.

28. When you give it to them, they gather it up;
    when you open your hand, they are filled with good things.

The fact of our dependence on God's provision for daily food is put in beautiful, basic terms. We *gather* at harvest because God gives. We are *satisfied* (nourished) because of the Lord's open *hand*.

Since most of us purchase our food in a store or a restaurant, we are far removed from the basic elements of food production. Farming takes work, to be sure, but we should still marvel that an empty field of dirt can fill with tall stalks of corn in a few weeks. We should pause in wonder that nets can be dipped into the vast sea and come up full of fish. We should never take our daily bread for granted.

> *What Do You Think?*
> What more can our church do to demonstrate the open hand of God? How will you help?
> *Talking Points for Your Discussion*
> - In meeting physical needs
> - In giving spiritual and emotional support
> - Other

B. Allowing Death (v. 29)

29. When you hide your face, they are dismayed;
    when you take away their breath, they die
    and return to the dust.

As the psalmist considers the cycle of animal life, we see parallel thoughts that interpret each other. When the Lord hides his *face,* the creatures *are terrified*. What does this mean? The next line explains: when the Lord takes *away their breath, they die*. Thus the poetic expression of God's hidden face is a way of saying that the time of death has come.

Animals are *terrified* when death looms because of their instinct for survival, an instinct placed in them by God himself. We too have such an instinct, but he does not abandon us at the time of our death. Our relationship with him helps us overcome the fear of death. It gives us the courage to "walk through the darkest valley" (Psalm 23:4).

> *What Do You Think?*
> At what times other than death does God seem to be hiding? How do we cope?
> *Talking Points for Your Discussion*
> - When things seems centered on one person (example: Job)
> - When a wider group is affected (example: Joshua 7:1)
> - Other

To *return to the dust* is the common result of death. All living things—from trees to tigers to toddlers—are largely composed of the same foundational ingredients of hydrogen, oxygen, nitrogen, carbon, and phosphorus. When organisms die, they begin to decompose almost immediately. Eventually the components of what once was a living body become part (again) of the earth's elements—*dust* in Bible language.

The temporary nature of our current physical existence is a reminder of our mortality (see Genesis 3:19). We are not gods, and our bodies are not invincible or immortal (see Psalm 103:14). As we traditionally say at funerals, "Ashes to ashes, dust to dust."

C. Renewing Life (v. 30)

30. When you send forth your Spirit, they are created,
    and you renew the face of the ground.

This is not the end of the story, however. God continually renews the life of his earth. He never intended the animal or plant life to be a single generation. All plants and animals are created with the capability of reproduction, but that does not happen without God's life-giving spirit. This is one of the wonders in the Genesis 1 account of creation: that each order of plant and animal reproduces according to its kind. In this way, God's creatures multiply and renew *the face of the ground* continually (see Genesis 1:22).

◆ CIRCLE OR CYCLE? ◆

The Lion King is the popular 1994 animated film from Disney studios. The song "Circle of Life" sets the tone for the presentation of a newborn lion cub to the pride's rulers. The scene is reprised at the end of the film as a cub from the next generation is presented.

Some think the phrase *circle of life* is useful to describe what happens in human families as well: as those of the older generation die off, members of the next generation step up to take their place as leaders. Infants are born to keep the circle going.

We should be cautious, however, about haphazardly grabbing phrases from culture and using them uncritically in Christianity. A close look at the lyrics of the "Circle of Life" song reveals elements that are at odds with Scripture.

The self-renewing feature of life on planet Earth, as designed by the Creator, might better be called the *cycle of life*. The self-renewal is not endless, however. The power God uses to create and sustain, he will use again to destroy and create anew (2 Peter 3:10-13). In the meantime, we remember that what we do with our portion of the cycle of life will influence the generations that follow. We are at our best when we embrace fully and firmly the service to which God calls us. It starts with our praise.   —C. R. B.

Conclusion
A. It Didn't Just Happen

Many Christians believe that science is an enemy of faith. This does not need to be so. Some elements of Psalm 104 are the ancient version of scientific observations, but these observations drive the psalmist and the reader to greater faith in God, not less. Science has done a fantastic job of documenting the intricacies and interrelated nature of things. Science increases our knowledge of our world daily. As the ancient psalmist marveled at what he could see on the ocean's surface, today we look in awe at the life-forms on the deepest ocean floor.

As with the psalmist, however, a modern person should pause and ask, "Just how did all of this happen?" The explanation that our complex earth

satisfieS with good things
protects innUmerable creatures
renewS the earth
clothed wiTh majesty
opens His hAnd
created wIth wisdom
rides oN the wind
sends thE Spirit
gives nouRishment

Visual for Lesson 8. *After discussing this visual, write the word CREATOR on the board similarly and ask for learners' suggestions in completing it.*

and its ecosystems simply developed through random chance over billions of years just doesn't ring true or seem plausible to most people. For example, why do plants and animals reproduce? Science can help us see how this happens, but cannot answer the basic question of why. Even if just one single-celled life form developed from unplanned processes, why did it develop with the capability of reproduction, which even amoebas have?

Since scientific observations offer no answer to this question, we are driven to the conclusion that there must be intentionality undergirding our world. We cannot help but see the hand of the transcendent Creator, who is greater than and distinct from his creation. May we, like the psalmist, recognize God in his mighty power to create as we offer praise and thanks of his care for us.

B. Prayer

O Lord, you created us, each and every one. You know us better than we know ourselves, from the number of hairs on our heads to the many memories of our hearts. We owe our existence to you. We owe our daily sustenance to you. May we never forget how truly dependent we are on you, on your grace and mercy. We pray this in the name of your Son, Jesus. Amen.

C. Thought to Remember
Before God was Redeemer,
he was Creator.

INVOLVEMENT LEARNING

Enhance your lesson presentation with the reproducible activity page,
available as a free download at www.standardlesson.com.

Into the Lesson

Before class, invite a member of your congregation who excels at a certain craft to demonstrate that craft or display examples of his or her work.

Give the class a few minutes to examine any displayed work and to ask questions about the process of creating this work.

Alternative. Distribute copies of the "Craftsmen Chaos" activity from the reproducible page, which can be downloaded. Have students work individually or in pairs.

After either activity, lead into Bible study saying, "Beautiful items do not come about by accident. They are the products of a person's skill, effort, and passion. We can know quite a bit about an artist by examining his or her handiwork. The same is true of God. The psalmist tells us that we can understand more about God's nature when we examine the vastness and goodness of his creation."

Into the Word

Divide the class into three groups. Give each group pen and paper, and one of the following sections of the Bible text. Have each group summarize their portion of the text so a preschool child could understand it. Our suggested responses are in italics.

Group 1—God is the king of the world (vv. 1-4).
God is like a king. But he is so big, no royal robes will fit him! The only house big enough for him is the sky! Even the biggest cloud in the sky is too small to be his car!

Group 2—God makes everything (vv. 24-26).
God makes things. But he does not make just a few things. He makes everything there is! Everything he makes is just right. The big things he makes are not too big. The small things he makes are not too small. He gives everything he makes just the right home.

Group 3—God takes care of everything (vv. 27-30).

The animals God makes get hungry sometimes. But they do not have to worry. God will always give them food to eat and water to drink! Animals do not live forever. When the weather gets cold, leaves fall off the trees. But they are not gone forever! God makes fresh, green leaves again in the spring.

After groups have finished, reassemble the class and have groups share their preschool paraphrases.

Alternative. Distribute copies of the "Crafty Creator" activity from the reproducible page. Have students work individually or in pairs.

Close either activity by saying, "While God is the great king, he is not a harsh ruler. While he creates everything, he does not step back and let creation fend for itself. The greatness of God is matched by his goodness. How should we respond to such a powerful, loving Creator?"

Into Life

At the turn of the twenty-first century, author Peter Huber coined the term *hard green* in reference to environmentalism. His focus was to move away from "save the planet" rhetoric that seems to predict immediate destruction of the earth, barring government intervention. In its place he proposed taking a "respect the planet" approach that focused on personal responsibility for conservation, efficiency, and waste disposal.

In light of God's ownership of the world described in Psalm 104, have the class devise personal "hard green" action plans. Write the following headings and questions on the board, and follow them with discussion:

REVIEW—Considering your own possessions and sphere of influence, where might you show better stewardship of God's creation?

RECYCLE—How could you better implement the old Great Depression rhyme: "Use it up, wear it out, make it do, or do without"?

REFRESH—How can your excess be used to help those who have less?

PRAISE GOD WITH ALL CREATION

DEVOTIONAL READING: Psalm 150
BACKGROUND SCRIPTURE: Psalm 148

PSALM 148

1 Praise the LORD!
Praise the LORD from the heavens;
    praise him in the heights!
2 Praise him, all his angels;
    praise him, all his hosts!
3 Praise him, sun and moon,
    praise him, all you shining stars!
4 Praise him, you highest heavens,
    and you waters above the heavens!
5 Let them praise the name of the LORD!
    For he commanded and they were
        created.
6 And he established them forever and ever;
    he gave a decree, and it shall not pass
        away.
7 Praise the LORD from the earth,
    you great sea creatures and all deeps,
8 fire and hail, snow and mist,
    stormy wind fulfilling his word!
9 Mountains and all hills,
    fruit trees and all cedars!
10 Beasts and all livestock,
    creeping things and flying birds!
11 Kings of the earth and all peoples,
    princes and all rulers of the earth!

12 Young men and maidens together,
    old men and children!
13 Let them praise the name of the LORD,
    for his name alone is exalted;
    his majesty is above earth and heaven.
14 He has raised up a horn for his people,
    praise for all his saints,
    for the people of Israel who are near to
        him.
Praise the LORD!

KEY VERSE

Let them praise the name of the Lord! For he commanded and they were created. —**Psalm 148:5**

CREATION: A DIVINE CYCLE

Unit 2: Praise from and for God's Creation

LESSONS 5–9

LESSON AIMS

After participating in this lesson, each learner will be able to:

1. Identify the basis for praising God as Creator as set forth in Psalm 148:13, 14.

2. Explain the significance of creation's praise of its Creator.

3. Write a brief ecological manifesto and note how it differs from a secular one.

LESSON OUTLINE

Introduction
    A. Compliments That Complement
    B. Lesson Background
 I. Praise from the Heavens (PSALM 148:1-6)
    A. Sources (vv. 1-4)
    B. Reasons (vv. 5, 6)
II. Praise from the Earth (PSALM 148:7-12)
    A. Nonhuman Elements (vv. 7-10)
      Ultimate Climate Change
    B. Human Spectrum (vv. 11, 12)
      Nones and Dones
III. Praise from God's Chosen (PSALM 148: 13, 14)
    A. Excellence of Name (v. 13)
    B. People of Israel (v. 14)
Conclusion
    A. The Amazing Creator
    B. Prayer
    C. Thought to Remember

Introduction

A. Compliments That Complement

How can we ensure that a compliment is well received? We do so (or at least have more of a chance of doing so) by offering the type of compliment the receiver appreciates most.

Social observers tell us that women and men are not the same in this regard. Women generally like compliments about *who they are*—words that affirm their personality, etc. Therefore, a compliment such as "You are so easy to talk to" is usually appreciated. Men, on the other hand, prefer to be complimented for *what they do*—words that affirm their skills and accomplishments. A compliment such as "You are so handy" can be counted on to stroke the male ego.

The psalms offer both kinds of praise to God, but he is not praised because of any ego need on his part. Praise of God is mainly for our benefit, since lifting our praise to him reminds us that we are not God. Our praise confesses our dependence on him—that we are not self-sufficient. For these reasons and others, Psalm 148 invites us to join the rest of creation in praising God.

B. Lesson Background

The Lesson Background for lesson 6 introduced the psalms as a whole to be a collection of five books. When examining these five, one notices the predominance of lament in Books I and II. David wrote about three-quarters of their 72 psalms, and he had much to reflect on regarding the conduct of his life.

Moving beyond the problem of exile in Book III, we begin to notice more expressions of praise in Books IV and V. No matter what the problem, God is king (Psalms 96–99, in Book IV), and he will one day make all things right (Psalm 145, in Book V). These facts called for praise on the part of the psalmists.

Psalm 148, today's text, is one of the five chapters known collectively as "the praise conclusion" to the book of Psalms as a whole. Each of the five (that is, Psalms 146–150) begins and ends with the phrase "Praise the Lord," translated from the Hebrew word *hallelujah*. The five chapters of

Psalms 146–150 offer different emphases in regard to praise that should be offered.

I. Praise from the Heavens
(PSALM 148:1-6)
A. Sources (vv. 1-4)

1. Praise the LORD!
Praise the LORD from the heavens;
praise him in the heights!

In a doubled expression, the psalmist makes clear who is to be praised: it is *the Lord*. He is the one who revealed himself to Moses as Yahweh, the great "I AM" (Exodus 3:13-16).

Thinking back to discussions of parallelism in previous lessons, we see that feature here as well: the praise that is to come *from the heavens* will be occurring *in the heights* as well. The nouns *heavens* and *heights* in this context both refer to God's dwelling place (see also Psalm 102:19). Thus, the psalm establishes the very presence of God as the appropriate place where praise is to begin.

The phrase *Praise the Lord* is translated from the Hebrew word *hallelujah*. This word is used in Revelation 19:1, 3, 4, 6. There it is transliterated (not translated) twice in moving from Hebrew to Greek to English.

2. Praise him, all his angels;
praise him, all his hosts!

The first heavenly entities that are commanded to praise the Lord are the supernatural beings known as *angels*. We may wonder if the word *angels* stands parallel with the word *hosts,* since the latter can refer to stars (examples: Deuteronomy 4:19; 2 Kings 17:16) as well to angels (examples: 1 Kings 22:19, 20; Psalm 103:20, 21).

Since (1) parallelism seems intended given its use in this psalm's opening verse and (2) a distinct word for stars occurs within its own parallel in verse 3 (next), then (3) we conclude that the words *angels* and *hosts* are parallel here in verse 2 in expressing the same idea. Both words refer to the heavenly servants who are "all ministering spirits sent out to serve for the sake of those who are to inherit salvation" (Hebrews 1:13, 14).

3. Praise him, sun and moon,
praise him, all you shining stars!

Genesis 1:14-19 describes God's intent for *sun and moon* as he established on the fourth day of creation: they are "for signs and for seasons, and for days and years," "to give light upon the earth," "to rule the day," and "to rule the night" (see also Jeremiah 31:35).

Genesis 1:16 further says, "God made . . . the stars." It does not state a specific function for them, but God's knowing all their names indicates their importance (Psalm 147:4; Isaiah 40:26).

As the revelation of Scripture progresses, we see developed the idea that the heavenly bodies serve as witnesses to the Creator (compare Psalm 19:1-6; etc.), and that is what we see in the verse before us. The fact that they continue functioning daily without fail speaks to the faithfulness of the Creator (compare Psalm 89:36, 37; Jeremiah 33:20, 21). That's praise!

Sadly, we see the opposite in ancient and modern cultures where the heavenly bodies are themselves deemed worthy of receiving worship rather than obligated to give it. The Israelites were strictly forbidden from worshipping elements of creation (Deuteronomy 5:8, 9), with *sun, moon,* and *stars* receiving specific mention (4:15-19; 17:2-5). Israel's history is one of failure in this regard (see 2 Kings 17:16; 21:3; Jeremiah 8:2; Ezekiel 8:16; compare Jeremiah 7:18; 44:16-26; Zephaniah 1:4, 5; Acts 7:42).

4. Praise him, you highest heavens,
and you waters above the heavens!

Ancient cultures are aware that that which is above the earth has a vertical aspect (compare Romans 10:6; Ephesians 4:8-10). Thus they speculate about the various levels regarding the dwelling places of their gods and deceased loved ones. The superlative *highest heavens* indicates the psalmist's

HOW TO SAY IT

Deuteronomy	Due-ter-*ahn*-uh-me.
Ezekiel	Ee-*zeek*-ee-ul or Ee-*zeek*-yul.
hallelujah	*ha*-leh-**loo**-yuh (*a* as in *map*).
Isaiah	Eye-*zay*-uh.
Jeremiah	Jair-uh-*my*-uh.
Yahweh *(Hebrew)*	*Yah*-weh.
Zephaniah	Zef-uh-*nye*-uh.

desire for praise of God to emanate from the highest possible location! This exhortation therefore parallels that of Psalm 148:1, above.

The psalmist's concept of *waters above the heavens* seems to come from Genesis 1:6-8. There "an expanse" is positioned in such a way as to divide "the waters that were under the expanse from the waters that were above the expanse." If the latter refers to the rain that God sends upon the earth as called for (see Genesis 7:11; Deuteronomy 28:12; Isaiah 55:10; Jeremiah 14:22), then we have another location that is spatially "above" humanity that must praise the Lord.

B. Reasons (vv. 5, 6)
5. Let them praise the name of the LORD! For he commanded and they were created.

The small word *for* reveals the first of two reasons to *praise the name of the Lord:* it is because that which is to offer the praise has been *created* by the one who is to receive the praise.

In contrast with complicated pagan myths of creation, the presentation of the biblical account of creation in Genesis 1 is marvelously straightforward: God merely spoke the word and the universe came into being (compare Psalm 33:9, lesson 5). The simple phrase "God said," used numerous times in Genesis 1, indicates that the speaking was complete, perfect, and effective.

6. And he established them forever and ever; he gave a decree, and it shall not pass away.

The psalmist now offers the second reason to praise the Creator. This reason speaks to the enduring nature of the cosmos. We see parallelism once again, with *established them forever and ever* as saying about the same thing as *gave a decree, and it shall not pass away.* Since those last three words sound a bit strange to modern ears, we can note that other occurrences of the underlying Hebrew refer to something that is not violated or transgressed (examples: Numbers 20:17-20; Job 14:5).

What we see here is the utter sovereignty of God. What God has put into motion by fiat in speaking commands will continue to be sustained by him the same way. When someone asks why, a common response is that it simply was and is God's will. That's true enough, of course, but not as helpful as it could be. Better is to view God's will manifested in three ways.

First is God's *purposive will*, referring to actions he takes by his own decision and initiative; these are things he causes. The second is God's *prescriptive will*, referring to things that he desires to happen, but grants human freedom to do otherwise. An example is to say that God's will is for everyone to be saved, even though not all shall be. The third is God's *permissive will*, referring to things he does not want to happen, but grants human freedom otherwise. The premier example here is, of course, sin.

To create and sustain are actions of God's purposive will. His purpose in creation is that humans may glorify him and enjoy his goodness. The praise called for in this psalm comes under the umbrella of God's prescriptive will. A thunderous chorus of praise for the Creator should be offered in the heavenly realm. The same should come from the earth, but it is our choice to offer it or not.

II. Praise from the Earth
(PSALM 148:7-12)
A. Nonhuman Elements (vv. 7-10)
7. Praise the LORD from the earth, you great sea creatures and all deeps,

The "them" of the previous verse refers only to entities in and of the heavens mentioned to that point in this psalm. The author is not about to stop there!

The praise to come "from the heavens" (v. 1) moved from high to low in a spatial sense. The psalmist now starts from the opposite direction as he begins to urge praise *from the earth,* starting with the depths of the sea.

The *great sea creatures* are those who live in the *deeps.* These images in the verse before us seem to refer to "the deep" of Genesis 1:2 and to its residents of "great sea creatures" as recorded in Genesis 1:20, 21. Indeed, the word translated *great sea creatures* in the verse before us is the same word translated "sea monster" in Job 7:12 and "dragon" in Ezekiel 32:2. Another translation is "serpent[s]" in Exodus 7:9, 10, 12. The same word is found in Isaiah 27:1, translated "twisting serpent," where parallelism may indicate its identity as that of Leviathan (see discussion in lesson 8). The very existence of such creatures and their abode testifies to their Creator!

8. fire and hail, snow and mist, stormy wind fulfilling his word!

Meteorological phenomena is next (compare Psalm 147:16-18). *Fire* in this context refers to lightning (compare 2 Kings 1:12; Job 1:16). Lightning *and hail* go together, both in experience and Scripture (Exodus 9:24; Psalm 105:32; Isaiah 30:30).

Snow is not common in Israel except at higher elevations. The Hebrew behind *clouds* is rendered "smoke" in Genesis 19:28 and Psalm 119:83, but in this context it may refer to a thick fog or mist. The latter seems to be better for understanding its relationship with snow. The *stormy wind* is *fulfilling his word,* as the others do, in its function as a general force of nature. But God also reserves his right to use such forces to intervene personally at times; Job 38:22-30 is particularly insightful in this regard.

What Do You Think?

What are some ways to counsel a person who blames "the randomness of the world" for his or her own problems?

Talking Points for Your Discussion

- If the person accepts the authority of the Bible
- If the person does not accept the authority of the Bible

Visual for Lesson 9. *Use this visual to launch a discussion on the various forms that praise can take. Jot responses on the board.*

◆ **ULTIMATE CLIMATE CHANGE** ◆

Debates about climate change ("global warming") just don't seem to get resolved! Discussions go on for years as one side blames humans for climate changes, while the other either denies human culpability or denies that change is even occurring. The talk itself can cause the climate in a room to become quite "heated" at times!

Regardless of which side is right, Christians know that the ultimate change in climate will happen when "the heavenly bodies will be burned up and dissolved, and the earth and the works that are done on it will be exposed" (2 Peter 3:10). Now *that's* global warming!

God granted humans dominion over the earth he created (Genesis 1:28), so we should sense a responsibility to not defile it. Honorable, sincere people may disagree on the extent to which our actions affect our planet's physical environment, if at all, but the effects of our actions and inactions on the world's spiritual environment should never be in doubt. Some are headed to a place where the "warming" never ceases (Revelation 20:15). We must warn them now!   —C. R. B.

9. Mountains and all hills, fruit trees and all cedars!

Given the parallelism seen so far, one might expect "mountains and valleys" instead of the text's *mountains and all hills.* But in order to have mountains and hills, there must be valleys and lowlands presupposed.

The phrasing *fruit trees and all cedars* indicates the presence of a literary device known as a *merism*: two extremes that indicate inclusion of everything in between. The two extremes here are those of cultivated and uncultivated trees. The merism indicates that the psalmist intends the reader to think not only of the specific trees mentioned, but also of all other trees. The natural beauty of majestic mountains, rolling hills, and trees of every kind praise their Creator by being what they are.

> **What Do You Think?**
> What is your reaction to the claim "The more you learn about creation, the more you learn about the Creator"?
> *Talking Points for Your Discussion*
> - Why you agree with it
> - Why you disagree with it
> - Why you are uncertain about it

10. Beasts and all livestock, creeping things and flying birds!

Signifying wild and domesticated animals respectively, the words *beasts* and *all livestock* form another merism. The same goes for *creeping things* and *flying birds*. These praise their Creator by performing all kinds of activities that add beauty, wonder, and variety to the land and sky.

B. Human Spectrum (vv. 11, 12)

11. Kings of the earth and all peoples, princes and all rulers of the earth!

In calling out praise "from the earth" (v. 7), the psalmist has moved from the deep oceans to forces of the atmosphere, to the land itself with its foliage, to all animal forms of land and sky, to those created in the image of God himself: human beings. Thus the psalm as a whole is coming full circle, from rational heavenly beings praising the Creator to rational earthly beings doing the same.

From those in highest positions to those in lowest, both average citizen and those in authority over them must recognize the complete sovereignty of their Creator (see Psalm 2:1, 2, 10-12).

12. Young men and maidens together, old men and children!

Again we see merism, as extremes of age indicate that all humanity is in view. Mention of both sexes cements the all-inclusiveness the psalmist intends.

> **What Do You Think?**
> What are some appropriate ways for God's image-bearers to witness to that fact in various settings?
> *Talking Points for Your Discussion*
> - In a secular work environment
> - While participating in sporting events
> - While watching sporting events
> - While in the company of other Christians
> - Other

◆ NONES *AND* DONES ◆

Western culture was once nominally Christian, but that is no longer the case. The majorities in Western countries who had at least a passing acquaintance with the church and the Christian faith are now the minority.

These days we are hearing about the *Nones*, the one-in-five Americans who have no religious affiliation of any kind. The figure is one-in-three among those under 30. If that weren't sad enough, the latest grouping of the irreligious to emerge in survey is the *Dones*. These are people who were church members at one time, but have decided they want no more of organized religion. The emergence of the *Nones* and *Dones* has some observers predicting the death of the church as we know it.

Without doubt, Western culture as a whole is not praising God in numbers as great as in times past. Even so, God's creation continues to do so. How can the heavens not declare the glory of God? How can the skies not proclaim the work of his hands? (Psalm 19:1). The call of the Bible to us all—whether young, old, or anywhere in between—is to recognize God as God, thereby praising him with lips and lives. How can the church get this message to the world while it is not too late to do so?

—C. R. B.

III. Praise from God's Chosen

(PSALM 148:13, 14)

A. Excellence of Name (v. 13)

13. Let them praise the name of the LORD,
for his name alone is exalted;
his majesty is above earth and heaven.

The phrase *let them praise the name of the Lord* as used in verse 5a summarizes the call for praise "from the heavens" (vv. 1-6). Now the phrase is repeated to summarize the call for praise "from the earth" (vv. 7-12).

All the praise in this psalm has been directed toward the Lord, *for his name alone is exalted.* When people try to make a name for themselves, they fail (see Genesis 11:1-9). When God makes a name for a person, it sticks (see 1 Chronicles 17:8). In both cases, the deciding factor is God, given the enduring excellence of his own name.

> *What Do You Think?*
> If an average Christian accepted the challenge to exhibit praise as a lifestyle, what should others see in him or her? Why?
> *Talking Points for Your Discussion*
> - In attitudes and behaviors adopted
> - In attitudes and behaviors abandoned
> - In attitudes and behaviors unchanged

B. People of Israel (v. 14)

14. He has raised up a horn for his people,
praise for all his saints,
for the people of Israel who are near to
him.
Praise the LORD!

Horn refers to "power" (see 1 Samuel 2:1, 10; Psalms 18:2; 75:10; 112:9; 132:17; etc.). It indicates God's bestowal of strength to his people having returned from exile. The Creator is also the God *for the people of Israel who are near to him.*

What a powerful twist with which to end this psalm! When we ponder God's great creation, we naturally think of his transcendence, his "out there-ness." But after 13 verses of viewing God in such a way, the psalmist concludes by focusing on God's immanence, his "right here-ness"!

Conclusion

A. The Amazing Creator

How unbelievers can study the cosmos and not see the Creator behind it is amazing. The sad tendency instead is to rejoice and celebrate human achievement in unlocking the mysteries of the universe. That is otherwise known as human arrogance or pride—a form of idolatry. The price of arrogance can be quite high, as at least one ancient king found out the hard way (Daniel 4).

Psalm 148 teaches a better way: there is a Creator of the universe, and he is worthy of praise by *all*, a word occurring 10 times in the psalm's 14 verses. The Creator has revealed himself in both creation (general revelation) and Scripture (special revelation). Jesus Christ is God's ultimate revealing of himself (John 1:1-14; 14:9; Hebrews 1:1-4).

How sad it is when the only part of creation that does not acknowledge its Creator is the part created in the image of God! How startling to resist Jesus, the one who "chose us in him before the foundation of the world" (Ephesians 1:4), the one by whom "all things were created, in heaven and on earth, visible and invisible" (Colossians 1:16)!

Before we begin an evangelistic task of Matthew 28:19, 20, we do well to ponder what unbelievers see in us. Do they see lives "filled with the fruit of righteousness that comes through Jesus Christ, to the glory and praise of God" (Philippians 1:11)? Or do they see lives lived in praise of self? Only a people near to God can convince a fallen world that it needs to repent as it returns to its Creator, Jesus Christ. Our task to praise is also our witness.

B. Prayer

O God, Creator of Heaven and earth, we praise your name above all names. We worship not the sun but the Son, in whom all things were created and by whom we are new creations. May we by your strength live our very lives in praise of these facts. We pray in the name of Jesus. Amen.

C. Thought to Remember

All creation praises its Creator.

INVOLVEMENT LEARNING

Enhance your lesson presentation with the reproducible activity page,
available as a free download at www.standardlesson.com.

Into the Lesson

Begin class with a game of Compliment Tag. Start by having the group stand in a circle, facing each other. This works best for a group of 10 or fewer, so you may choose to have multiple groups. Either you or someone you designate should start by "tagging" a member of the group and by saying something you admire about him or her. That person continues the game by complimenting another person in the group.

Alternative. Distribute copies of the "It's Complimentary" activity from the reproducible page, which can be downloaded. Have students work on it individually.

After either activity, lead into Bible study saying, "There is just something about a compliment. Having someone else note something positive about us can really make our day. It also builds the relationship between the one giving the compliment and the one receiving it. While God does not need our praise, we benefit by offering it."

Into the Word

Divide the class into three groups as follows. Give each group a section of the Bible text, and have them try to answer these questions: (1) What do their assigned verses describe as praising the Lord? (2) How might the things mentioned praise the Lord? (3) Why might they praise the Lord?

Suggested responses are in italics, but do not distribute these.

Group 1—All the Heavens (Psalm 148:1-6).

(1) Angels, hosts, celestial bodies, highest heavens, waters above the heavens. (2) By doing God's work. (3) Because God made them.

Group 2—All the Earth (Psalm 148:7-12).

(1) Oceans and deep sea creatures, weather, landscapes, plant life, all animals, rulers, all people. (2) By doing what God made them to do. (3) Because God made them.

Group 3—All the People (Psalm 148:13, 14).

(1) Israel and all God's people. (2) Living as he made us to, caring for creation, worshipping him and praying, giving, etc. (3) Because he made and saved us, because our praise will bring the world closer to him.

Allow several minutes for group discussion; then ask groups to share their findings. Refer to the commentary to correct misconceptions and fill in any gaps.

Alternative. Distribute copies of the "Worthy of Praise" activity from the reproducible page. Have students work individually or in pairs.

Close either activity by saying, "God's creation praises him simply by doing exactly what he created it to do, and in verse 14 the psalmist writes that God has given his people, referred to as Israel, a special horn, meaning power or strength. The psalmist is telling us that through our praise—living as God intended—the world will come to know God."

Into Life

To conclude the class, review these two popular acronyms for structuring personal prayer:

Adoration
    Confession
        Thanksgiving
            Supplication

Praise
    Repent
        Ask
            Yield

Review this briefly, noting that adoring and praising God come first in each one.

End with a prayer time focusing totally on praising God. Allow class members to pray, offering only a single word at a time. That word should be an attribute of God that is worthy of praise.

RE-CREATED TO LIVE IN HARMONY

DEVOTIONAL READING: Colossians 3:12-17
BACKGROUND SCRIPTURE: Galatians 3:26–4:7

GALATIANS 3:26-29

26 [F]or in Christ Jesus you are all sons of God, through faith. 27 For as many of you as were baptized into Christ have put on Christ. 28 There is neither Jew nor Greek, there is neither slave nor free, there is no male and female, for you are all one in Christ Jesus. 29 And if you are Christ's, then you are Abraham's offspring, heirs according to promise.

GALATIANS 4:1-7

4 I mean that the heir, as long as he is a child, is no different from a slave, though he is the owner of everything, 2 but he is under guardians and managers until the date set by his father. 3 In the same way we also, when we were children, were enslaved to the elementary principles of the world. 4 But when the fullness of time had come, God sent forth his Son, born of woman, born under the law, 5 to redeem those who were under the law, so that we might receive adoption as sons. 6 And because you are sons, God has sent the Spirit of his Son into our hearts, crying, "Abba! Father!" 7 So you are no longer a slave, but a son, and if a son, then an heir through God.

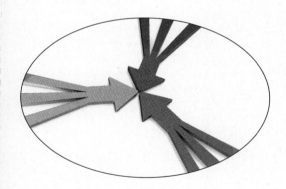

KEY VERSE

There is neither Jew nor Greek, there is neither slave nor free, there is no male and female, for you are all one in Christ Jesus. —**Galatians 3:28**

CREATION: A DIVINE CYCLE

Unit 3: The Birthing of a New Community

LESSONS 10–13

LESSON AIMS

After participating in this lesson, each learner will be able to:

1. Describe the means by which God's grace makes all his people to be of equal standing before him.

2. Explain the connection between faith in Christ and being of Abraham's seed.

3. Articulate one way his or her church can better demonstrate its commitment to the equal standing of all Christians before God.

LESSON OUTLINE

Introduction
  A. The Boundless Variety of Humanity
  B. Lesson Background
I. Foundation of Equality (GALATIANS 3:26-29)
  A. Role of Faith (v. 26)
  B. Role of Baptism (v. 27)
  C. Result of Oneness (vv. 28, 29)
    Inheritance Fiasco
II. Establishment of Equality (GALATIANS 4: 1-5)
  A. That Was Then (vv. 1-3)
  B. This Is Now (vv. 4, 5)
    Adoption Turbulence
III. Outcome of Equality (GALATIANS 4:6, 7)
  A. No Longer Alone (v. 6)
  B. No More a Servant (v. 7)
Conclusion
  A. The Great Sameness of Status
  B. Prayer
  C. Thought to Remember

Introduction

A. The Boundless Variety of Humanity

The next time you are out in a public place, take note of the variety of people. They are tall and short; thin and plump; female and male; with many shades of skin, hair, and eye color. When you get to know people, you find that they are quiet or talkative, funny or serious, trusting or wary—and often a fascinating mixture of several traits!

Each of us feels a closer connection to certain kinds of people. Often they are people who share our life experiences and outlook. Sometimes they may be people who differ from us in intriguing ways. We enjoy building friendships with such people. Our lives are richer because we build bonds with them.

But by the same token, sometimes we feel a barrier between us and others. We find it hard to make a connection with some people. We may even experience fear when we come across people who are different from us in certain ways. With these, we find it hard to build relationships.

God clearly intended to create human beings with infinite variety. We bear God's image regardless of individual characteristics. The God who created each person loves us enough to send Christ to the cross to pay the price for our sins. That is the basis for our mutual fellowship. But if we view the variety of people as a threat, we may add to the gospel additional requirements for mutual acceptance. That was a problem Paul confronted in his letter to the Galatians, and it remains a problem (with different issues) yet today.

B. Lesson Background

We are not certain exactly when Paul wrote his letter to the Galatians. Research proposes dates as early as AD 48 or as late as AD 58. The arguments and the evidence are tedious to sort through, but a date of about AD 57 seems best.

Despite uncertainty regarding *when* the letter was written, the general contours of *why* are quite clear: some individuals in the churches were teaching that Christians of Gentile heritage needed to be circumcised according to the Law of Moses.

Such converts could not belong to God's people until they did so. (See discussion of Paul's opponents in next week's lesson.)

The reasoning for such a position was that Israel had always been distinct as the people of God. It was to Israel that God had revealed himself, given his law, and specified circumcision as the sign of his covenant (Genesis 17:7-14). So if God were making himself known through the gospel to the nations, then people from the nations who come to God in Christ should be circumcised.

To this reasoning Paul had already answered *no* in text preceding that of today's lesson (Galatians 2:3, 11, 12). The numerous verses between that reaction and today's text serve to ramp up the intensity of Paul's line of thought. The preaching and acceptance of the gospel repairs the sin-broken relationship between God and humans. As a happy side effect, the gospel also repairs human-to-human relationships. Both happen because of Christ and his work. Paul wrote to correct the wrong doctrine that the bond provided by Christ had to be accompanied by a certain kind of human law-keeping.

I. Foundation of Equality
(GALATIANS 3:26-29)
A. Role of Faith (v. 26)

26. [F]or in Christ Jesus you are all sons of God, through faith.

Paul writes this statement as a firm assertion of the equal standing of all Christians before God. Those who *through faith* are *in Christ Jesus* are in a family that has no class distinctions. Paul uses the word for male offspring because inheritance generally goes from fathers to *sons* in the ancient world.

Paul has much more to say about faith as it relates to salvation. But right now the summary statement we see here is sufficient for the line of argument he is establishing.

B. Role of Baptism (v. 27)

27. For as many of you as were baptized into Christ have put on Christ.

Paul now appeals to baptism as a common experience of all believers, whether their back-

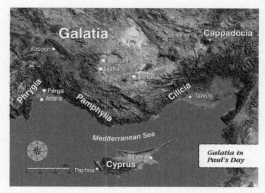

Visual for Lesson 10. *Keep this visual posted throughout the final four lessons of the quarter to give your learners a geographical perspective.*

ground is Jewish (circumcised) or Gentile (uncircumcised). For Paul to say that those who *were baptized into Christ have put on Christ* may strike us as odd, so a bit of investigative work is in order.

Baptism is the ritual of being dipped in water, first practiced by John the Baptist. In the Jewish culture of the day, people purified themselves ceremonially by dipping themselves in water. John's actions, however, were different in procedure and significance. Regarding procedure, the person receiving baptism did not dip herself or himself. Rather, another performed the dipping action on the recipient.

Regarding significance, John's baptism was one "of repentance for the forgiveness of sins" (Mark 1:4; compare Acts 19:4). Repentance remained as a key element of Christian baptism, which superseded John's baptism.

Furthermore, baptism was administered in the name of Jesus for receiving the Holy Spirit. We see all three elements in Peter's exhortation on the Day of Pentecost that followed Jesus' resurrection: "Repent and be baptized every one of you in the name of Jesus Christ for the forgiveness of your sins, and you will receive the gift of the Holy Spirit" (Acts 2:38).

This reorientation of baptism as being toward Jesus shows how new Christians understood that they were forgiven. Jesus—who died, rose, and ascended to God's right hand—is the one who gives God's cleansing forgiveness and fulfills God's promises. To be *baptized into Christ* is to be baptized asking Christ that the forgiveness and fulfilled promises be applied to oneself by Christ's power.

Baptism thus is a powerful expression of the equality and unity of Christ's followers. None are able to cleanse themselves, even those who had grown up following God's law. All rely utterly on Christ's cleansing. None can look to previous Israelite identity as credentials for inheriting eternal life. Rather, all must look to Christ's death and resurrection.

Perhaps we are now better able to see what Paul means when he declares that those who *were baptized into Christ have put on Christ.* The expression speaks of Christ as being like the fresh garment a person dons after being baptized. Christians are not defined by ancestral heritage or former practices, but by Christ's gracious forgiveness and gift of new life. Though we may look and act differently from one another, we all wear the same spiritual clothing. It is the uniform of the gospel that speaks of Christ alone (compare Isaiah 61:10; Romans 13:14).

C. Result of Oneness (vv. 28, 29)
28a. There is neither Jew nor Greek,

Having summarized the equalizing results of the good news of Jesus, Paul begins to note distinctives that serve to categorize and alienate people in his day. The first such is that of *Jew* and *Greek,* the primary division troubling the churches of Galatia.

We should note that the people classified as *Greek(s)* are the same as those classified *Gentile(s)* elsewhere. We see that Paul uses the terms interchangeably as we examine his writings, although he prefers the designation *Gentile(s)*—with the word in the original language sometimes translated *nations*—by a ratio of about three to one. The English word *ethnic* derives from the word translated *Gentile(s)*.

Paul's other letters reveal that he has more to say about the positions of Jews and Gentiles relative to each other (see Romans 3:1-9; 11:11-24; etc.). But here the stark and succinct *there is nei-*

ther Jew nor Greek suffices. Neither group should be saying that the other is lesser, for the gospel of Jesus indicts the sin of both groups as it freely offers forgiveness to all.

Paul, "a Hebrew of Hebrews; . . . a Pharisee" (Philippians 3:5), fights hard for this point in the letter to the Galatians. Gentiles do not need to become Jews to belong to God's people, and Jews do not need to live as Gentiles either. Both have equal standing before the cross (compare Romans 10:12; Colossians 3:11).

28b. there is neither slave nor free,

The enslavement of humans is a common practice in the Roman world. Slaves perform a variety of tasks, from manual labor to highly skilled, technical tasks such as those required in the fields of education and document production.

Most slaves of the first century AD do not suffer the extremes of physical abuse that we associate with slavery as practiced more recently. Even so, no slave is accorded full human dignity, and no slave can live life as the slave chooses. People who are *free* are used to thinking of slaves as lesser beings.

But in Christ, there is no difference between the two in their standing before God. One who is enslaved may be accorded pastoral responsibilities in the church, and that slave's master may submit to the slave's instruction and care. A few years later, Paul will remind a slave master to treat as a brother a runaway slave who has become a Christian (Philemon 16). The entire institution of slavery is undermined as the radical equality of the gospel is brought to bear.

> **What Do You Think?**
> What responsibilities do Christians have to confront the injustices of inequality that exist outside the church? Why?
> *Talking Points for Your Discussion*
> - Responsibilities of Christians as individuals
> - Responsibilities of the church as a body

28c. there is no male and female,

The third distinction echoes the biblical account of human creation (Genesis 1:27). While we can easily exaggerate the inequality between the sexes in the ancient world, that inequality was nevertheless real.

Indeed, in most cultures the vulnerability of women becomes a basis for men to take positions of privilege. Such inequality includes, among other things, the customs of inheritance: women typically do not inherit property in the Greco-Roman world of the first century AD. Inheritance in terms of having access to salvation is in view in the text at hand (see v. 29, below). The fact that *there is neither male nor female* means no inequality exists in that regard in Christ.

Both male and female inherit the fulfillment of God's promises of salvation in Christ. While they remain male and female individuals as God created them to be, they have no difference in status before God.

28d. for you are all one in Christ Jesus.

Divisions that result from living in a fallen world, including those that vex us yet today, are overcome by the gospel. Oneness in Christ means we treat each other with absolute love and respect as equal heirs of salvation.

> **What Do You Think?**
> In what ways can we put into visible action the six affirmations of Galatians 3:26-28?
> *Talking Points for Your Discussion*
> - Regarding the three positive affirmations of verses 26, 27, and 28d
> - Regarding the three negative affirmations of verses 28a, 28b, and 28c

29. And if you are Christ's, then you are Abraham's offspring, heirs according to promise.

The promise to Abraham was that through his *offspring, or seed,* God would bless all nations. Abraham's descendants would be like the sand on the seashore (Genesis 22:17, 18).

Christ himself fulfills this promise, with the word *seed* stressed as singular in Galatians 3:16. So those in Christ become part of Abraham's family, sharing in the inheritance of God's promise given to him. Jews are therefore heirs not because of circumcision, but because of Christ. Gentiles therefore do not need circumcision, for they are

already members of God's people with full status as heirs, equal to Jewish Christians in every way. There are not separate inheritance qualifiers for men and women.

◆ **INHERITANCE FIASCO** ◆

The Queen of Mean was the unflattering title for Leona Helmsley. Her infamous temper was the reason for the derogatory moniker. But she wasn't mean to her dog, Trouble. When Helmsley died in 2007, her will excluded several relatives, but Trouble was left $12 million! A court later cut that to "only" $2 million.

By one estimate, 70 percent of families experience inheritance problems, but most of them are not as strange as those surrounding Leona Helmsley's estate. Sometimes the issue isn't monetary, but emotional. These may be seen in fights over possessions that have only sentimental value.

Judaizers of Paul's day taught that Gentiles couldn't be heirs of salvation through Christ unless they became "members of the family" as those Judaizers saw the admission requirements to be. Paul had to remind his flocks otherwise. Do we put requirements on people today that the gospel does not?   —C. R. B.

II. Establishment of Equality
(GALATIANS 4:1-5)
A. That Was Then (vv. 1-3)

1. I mean that the heir, as long as he is a child, is no different from a slave, though he is the owner of everything,

To explain the sweep of God's plan in history, Paul extends the comparison with inheritance practices in ancient cultures. He does so by picturing a son who will inherit the father's property when the son comes of age. The son has already been designated as *the heir,* who will control the property. The son is therefore always *the owner of everything.*

But until the son is granted control of the property, he has no power at all! In that respect he is like *a slave* in the father's household.

2. but he is under guardians and managers until the date set by his father.

In Roman custom, the heir of the father's estate is under the supervision of a tutor, someone who both teaches and protects the son until age 14. After that age, his life is under the control of another, who supervises him and restricts his decisions until age 25. Only after that age does the son receive full rights as heir.

3. In the same way we also, when we were children, were enslaved to the elementary principles of the world.

Paul now makes the comparison: like *children*, the Galatian Christians had lived not as heirs but as slaves *to the elementary principles of the world*. What exactly Paul is referring to as he uses that phrase is difficult to determine (see also Galatians 4:9; Colossians 2:8, 20; compare Hebrews 5:12; 2 Peter 3:10, 12). It's fairly safe to conclude that the *elementary principles* in this context means "something that is basic or elementary," such as learning one's ABCs.

Some students think that the elementary thing in view here is the Law of Moses. If so, Paul's point would be that the law functioned as teacher and protector to prepare the world for the fulfillment of God's promises. Now that Christ has come, the Galatians should look to him instead of that law.

> *What Do You Think?*
> Which Scriptures help you best resist the lure of returning to the life you led as an unbeliever?
> *Talking Points for Your Discussion*
> - Passages featuring direct commands
> - Indirect commands through parables, etc.

B. This Is Now (vv. 4, 5)

4. But when the fullness of time had come, God sent forth his Son, born of woman, born under the law,

As a father has a plan for his son to become his heir, so God has a plan for all people to become his people. *The fullness of time* was the point at which God acted decisively to fulfill his promises. That decisive act was to send *his Son*.

Christ entered the world with the full status as God's Son, the one who truly was and is heir to the world (Hebrews 1:2). Although he possessed privilege as Lord, he took instead the lowly position of those who lived under the custodianship of God's law. In emptying himself of privilege, he identified completely with the servitude of humanity (Philippians 2:6, 7).

> *What Do You Think?*
> In what ways can Christ's lowliness be a model in helping you overcome barriers to equality among Christians?
> *Talking Points for Your Discussion*
> - Considering one or more specific examples of something Jesus said or did
> - Considering one or more specific examples of something Jesus did not say or do

5. to redeem those who were under the law, so that we might receive adoption as sons.

Becoming human yet living without sin, Jesus was able to take the curse of sin on himself (Galatians 3:13, 14). In so doing, he paid the price that bought for humanity freedom from bondage to sin, a bondage illustrated by Israel's continual failure to keep *the law*. *To redeem* is to pay a price that gives freedom, the very thing Christ did on the cross. Having been freed from the curse, people can join God's family as heirs. Unlike Christ's sonship, our status is not one that we have by nature. Rather, it is granted to us by God as a gift, like an *adoption* (also Romans 8:15).

◆ ADOPTION TURBULENCE ◆

Jesse was adopted at age 4 from a Bulgarian orphanage by an American family. It wasn't long, however, before his adoptive mother thought she had "ruined her family's life." She was overwhelmed by Jesse's behavior as he adapted to his new life. Whenever she tried to leave the house, he would throw tantrums, a behavior pattern exhibiting what is called *separation anxiety disorder*.

According to experts who work with such adoptees, other common problems are attention deficit/hyperactivity, oppositional defiance, and autism. Many problems are traceable to years of institutional neglect. But counseling, medication, and time may bring healing.

Jesse eventually became a straight-A student and a star player on his high school's basketball team. Even so, his mother says of the experience, "It's misleading to think it's a pathway covered with rose petals. . . . It [was] hard and serious work."

Our adoption into God's family may also result in "separation anxiety" behavioral problems as we distance ourselves from past ways or beliefs. If you see someone in such a state this week, be sure to bring him or her the patient love of the Father as you act as his hands and feet.   —C. R. B.

III. Outcome of Equality
(Galatians 4:6, 7)
A. No Longer Alone (v. 6)

6. And because you are sons, God has sent the Spirit of his Son into our hearts, crying, "Abba! Father!"

Paul again reminds his readers of their equality as he notes that they *are sons*. In addition to their baptisms (Galatians 3:27), their common experience of having *the Spirit of his Son* in their *hearts* affirms their equality. They had received the Holy Spirit by faith in Christ (3:26), not by undergoing circumcision. In turn, the Holy Spirit empowers Christians to address God with confidence as *Father*. This is not a timid expression, but is the deep cry of the heart in dependence and joy.

> #### What Do You Think?
> What can and should Christians do in order to experience more deeply the Spirit-filled joy of their adoption in Christ?
> #### Talking Points for Your Discussion
> - In times of corporate worship
> - In times of private worship
> - Other

Paul, writing in Greek, uses a word from the Aramaic language to express this heartfelt address to God: *Abba*. This is the warm, familiar word used in the household for a father. It is not equivalent to *Daddy*, as young children might say today. Rather, it is a term of endearment and closeness. Jesus distinctively addressed God with this word (Mark 14:36), a different expression than the one commonly used for God as Israel's Father. So, Paul says, we who have the Spirit can address God with the same confidence as did Jesus. All Christians share this relationship with God through Christ. None in Christ has a lesser or greater position.

B. No More a Servant (v. 7)

7. So you are no longer a slave, but a son, and if a son, then an heir through God.

The Spirit's presence is proof of one's new status as *heir*. As full members of God's family, we all receive God's promises fulfilled in Christ. Thus Paul concludes the argument begun in verse 1.

Conclusion
A. The Great Sameness of Status

Jewish Christians of the first century were accustomed to seeing themselves as insiders and Gentiles as outsiders. But the gospel teaches something different: neither group could claim the better status. Both had their deficiencies, deficiencies canceled by Christ. Everyone was to be welcomed into God's family not by markers of past identity, but by faith in Christ as they put on Christ in baptism (Galatians 3:26, 27).

None of this has changed. We dare not think of ourselves as insiders because of economic status, etc. As we understand one another in our differences, let us remember how we came to God's people: not by our own doing, but by Christ's.

B. Prayer

Father, forgive us when we think of ourselves as entitled. When we begin to dwell on differences among people, help us to see everyone's need of Jesus as Savior. In Jesus' name we pray. Amen.

C. Thought to Remember

"The ground is level at the foot of the cross."
—Author unknown

HOW TO SAY IT

Abba	*Ab*-buh.
Aramaic	*Air*-uh-**may**-ik.
Judaizers	**Joo**-duh-*ize*-ers.

INVOLVEMENT LEARNING

Enhance your lesson presentation with the reproducible activity page,
available as a free download at www.standardlesson.com.

Into the Lesson

Display this statement prominently as learners assemble: "All people are created *UNequal*," with a little extra space before the word *created*. Have the *U* and *N* of *UNequal* stuck on as separate squares. Have on the reverse of the *U* an *R*; on the reverse of the *N* an *E*. Ask, "In what ways are we as class members unequal?"

Allow the class to suggest 10 to 12 attributes of learner inequalities (examples: age, weight, size, vocation, education, financial status, length of service to Christ, and others may be offered). Now remove the *U* and the *N*, turn them over, and stick the *R* and *E* before the word *created*. The sentence will now read, "All people are re-created equal."

Alternative. Distribute copies of the "Taking It Personally" activity from the reproducible page, which you can download. Have students work in small groups.

After either activity, lead into the Bible study saying, "No, we are not all alike! But we *can* get along. All who are re-created in Christ have equal standing before God."

Into the Word

To help your class study today's text, you will create a graffiti wall. Attach a large sheet of newsprint to the wall and have a supply of washable markers nearby. Write, "It's Time!" as a heading on the newsprint. Read Galatians 4:4 aloud, pointing out that God's plan for salvation took place at just the right time.

Divide the class into three groups. Give each group a section of the Bible text. Instruct the groups to read their text and create "It's time" statements based on the content of their verses. When they discover one, a member of that group can write it on the graffiti wall.

The verse divisions and a few sample statements follow:

Group 1—Galatians 3:26-29.

It's time to affirm that we are God's children. It's time to put on Christ like clothing. It's time to be unified with others who are in Christ.

Group 2—Galatians 4:1-5.

It's time to leave the slavery of sin behind. It's time to be adopted as God's children. It's time to grow up.

Group 3—Galatians 4:6, 7.

It's time to reach up our arms and cry for our Father. It's time to prepare to receive an inheritance.

Close by saying, "This is the grand truth we celebrate: When the time was right, God sent his Son. His work allows people born in unequal circumstances to be one people before him."

Into Life

Have a volunteer read James 2:1-4, a text citing a possible sense of inequality because of unequal treatment by those assembled for worship and fellowship.

Ask, "What are some differences that separate people in a congregation? Are there any ways in which you see division in our own congregation or in the daily living we as individual Christians experience? What steps can be taken to move toward a genuine sense of equality?"

Alternative. Distribute copies of the "Dovetailed Differences" activity and allow students to work on it individually.

After either activity, review lists of differences you have found. Ask students to select one set of differences and suggest something that can be done to promote unity. For example, the gap between young and old might be bridged with a Paul and Timothy club, a pairing of adults and teens so one may pray daily for the other.

If you wish, you may close the class by handing out snack-size packages of candy-coated chocolate. Note that while the pieces differ on the outside, they are all the same inside!

NEW BIRTH
BRINGS FREEDOM

DEVOTIONAL READING: Romans 8:1-11
BACKGROUND SCRIPTURE: Galatians 4

GALATIANS 4:8-20

8 Formerly, when you did not know God, you were enslaved to those that by nature are not gods. 9 But now that you have come to know God, or rather to be known by God, how can you turn back again to the weak and worthless elementary principles of the world, whose slaves you want to be once more? 10 You observe days and months and seasons and years! 11 I am afraid I may have labored over you in vain.

12 Brothers, I entreat you, become as I am, for I also have become as you are. You did me no wrong. 13 You know it was because of a bodily ailment that I preached the gospel to you at first, 14 and though my condition was a trial to you, you did not scorn or despise me, but received me as an angel of God, as Christ Jesus. 15 What then has become of your blessedness? For I testify to you that, if possible, you would have gouged out your eyes and given them to me. 16 Have I then become your enemy by telling you the truth? 17 They make much of you, but for no good purpose. They want to shut

you out, that you may make much of them. 18 It is always good to be made much of for a good purpose, and not only when I am present with you, 19 my little children, for whom I am again in the anguish of childbirth until Christ is formed in you! 20 I wish I could be present with you now and change my tone, for I am perplexed about you.

KEY VERSE

But now that you have come to know God, or rather to be known by God, how can you turn back again to the weak and worthless elementary principles of the world, whose slaves you want to be once more? —**Galatians 4:9**

CREATION:
A DIVINE CYCLE

Unit 3: The Birthing of a New Community

LESSONS 10–13

LESSON AIMS

After participating in this lesson, each learner will be able to:

1. Identify the sole source of true freedom.

2. Explain how reliance on anything other than Christ represents a failure to receive God's message.

3. Write a prayer that thanks God for freedom in Christ.

LESSON OUTLINE

Introduction
    A. Freedom in Name Only
    B. Lesson Background
I. Wrong Focus (GALATIANS 4:8-11)
    A. Witless Slavery (v. 8)
    B. Willing Slavery (vv. 9, 10)
      Back-to-Egypt Syndrome?
    C. Wasted Work (v. 11)
II. Uncertain Status (GALATIANS 4:12-16)
    A. Welcomed in the Past (vv. 12-14)
    B. Doubted in the Present (vv. 15, 16)
      Second Impressions
III. Misplaced Eagerness (GALATIANS 4:17-20)
    A. Harmful Enthusiasm (v. 17)
    B. Healthy Zeal (v. 18)
    C. Heartfelt Longing (vv. 19, 20)
Conclusion
    A. Subtraction by Addition
    B. Prayer
    C. Thought to Remember

Introduction

A. Freedom in Name Only

A country is ruled oppressively. One day its people rise up and overthrow the oppressors. To mark a new beginning of freedom, they give their country a new name, perhaps beginning with something like "Democratic Republic of . . ."

But in time, oppression returns. The country's people are as bad off as they were before, if not worse. The country's new name endures, but only as a mockery of lost ideals. This tragic story has repeated itself too often.

Our text tells an even greater tragedy of lost freedom. It is the account of believers who gave up (or were on the verge of giving up) their freedom in Christ to return to the bondage they knew before having received the gospel.

B. Lesson Background

Our study picks up where last week's concluded at Galatians 4:7. The letter's critical tone continues. The crisis centered on this question: Should believers in Christ be required to adhere to the requirement of circumcision as set forth in the Law of Moses?

Paul's opponents answered this with a *yes*, to which Paul counterpunched with the emphatic *no* we saw last week. The stakes were high. If Paul's opponents prevailed on the issue of circumcision, then imposition of other stipulations in the Law of Moses (Sabbath-keeping, dietary restrictions, etc.) would not be far behind, further negating the sufficiency of Christ's work.

Judaizers is the term most often used to designate Paul's opponents in this regard. A Judaizer was someone who (1) adhered to the Jewish way of life and (2) intended to require Gentiles to adopt it as well. Judaizers thought it reasonable that the boundaries of the church should be defined by the rite of circumcision as given to Abraham and his descendants (see Genesis 17:9-14).

Some students propose that the Judaizers who were creating problems in Galatia were members of the church in Jerusalem, being "some believers who belonged to the party of the Pharisees" (Acts 15:5). Having gone on misguided missions to "the

Gentiles in Antioch and Syria and Cilicia," they "troubled [them] with words, unsettling" their minds (15:23, 24). They are conjectured to have done the same in Galatia.

Also worthy of consideration is the era of growing Jewish nationalism during which Paul ministered. That was a time when it may have been controversial for Jews to associate with non-Jews (Gentiles). Perhaps some Jews encouraged circumcision of Gentile Christians in order to make it easier for Jewish Christians to fellowship with them without being criticized by nationalists.

In any case, those who insisted on circumcision also presumed that their authority in the matter was greater than Paul's. This challenge is discerned from the lengthy defense Paul makes for his apostleship in Galatians 1:1–2:10. Paul referred to his opponents as those who "are trying to pervert the gospel of Christ" (1:7).

I. Wrong Focus
(Galatians 4:8-11)
A. Witless Slavery (v. 8)

8. Formerly, when you did not know God, you were enslaved to those that by nature are not gods.

Paul offers a reminder to the Galatian Christians of non-Jewish background what their previous lives really were. To have been *slaves to those who by nature are not gods* indicates that those believers had been followers of Greco-Roman religions. As such, they typically would have worshipped various fictitious gods, represented by idols, that were believed to hold power over aspects of the world (see Acts 17:22-29).

No one loves these gods. But many people fear them, believing they can cause problems for those

HOW TO SAY IT

Antioch	*An*-tee-ock.
Cilicia	Sih-*lish*-i-uh.
Galatians	Guh-*lay*-shunz.
Gentiles	*Jen*-tiles.
Judaizers	*Joo*-duh-*ize*-ers.
Pharisees	*Fair*-ih-seez.

who displease them. The worshippers' aim is to appease these gods with regular offerings, which function more as bribes than acts of heartfelt worship. This went hand in hand with being ignorant of the true God. It was a state of enslavement to falsehood. This was the life Gentiles left behind when they believed the gospel.

B. Willing Slavery (vv. 9, 10)

9. But now that you have come to know God, or rather to be known by God, how can you turn back again to the weak and worthless elementary principles of the world, whose slaves you want to be once more?

That life of ignorant *bondage* is now past. Galatians who had worshipped false gods now know the one true God through the good news of Jesus. But even better than knowing the true God is being *known by God*. Those formerly alienated from him now belong in truth to God's true people (compare 1 Corinthians 8:3).

To add circumcision to the gospel would be to return to the past (*turn back*). But how can that be true when the past for the Gentile Christians was not slavery to requirements to the Law of Moses, but to pagan gods? Here we must understand what Paul means by *weak and worthless elementary principles*.

In discussion of Galatians 4:3 in last week's lesson, we noted that the word *elementary* as Paul uses it in context means "something that is basic," such as learning one's ABCs. This points to something that one has while in an immature state to help bring him or her to the intended, fully mature state. Last week's commentary (lesson 10) offered the proposal that Paul refers to the Law of Moses as such a basic element (Galatians 4:3-5), something to be set aside when maturity comes.

But for Gentiles, Paul sees pagan worship as another kind of basic element. In its falsehood, such worship leaves the person anxious and hungry for the truth. So ironically enough, both the Law of Moses and idolatrous practices belong to the same category of "things followed in the past but now set aside by the good news of Jesus."

So for Gentile Christians to add circumcision to their faith in Christ is to return to a version of the past that must be left behind. For both Jew and Gentile, that past is not one of freedom and blessing, but of slavery and a curse (Galatians 3:10). For emphasis, Paul uses two words in the original language to signify *once more* in the last line of verse 9.

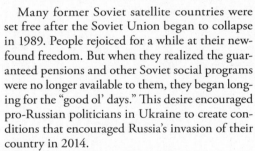

What Do You Think?
What "weak" things tempt Christians to return to past sin? How do you resist these personally?
Talking Points for Your Discussion
- Regarding issues of thoughts and attitudes
- Regarding issues of acceptable behavior
- Regarding manner of speech

◆ BACK-TO-EGYPT SYNDROME? ◆

Many former Soviet satellite countries were set free after the Soviet Union began to collapse in 1989. People rejoiced for a while at their newfound freedom. But when they realized the guaranteed pensions and other Soviet social programs were no longer available to them, they began longing for the "good ol' days." This desire encouraged pro-Russian politicians in Ukraine to create conditions that encouraged Russia's invasion of their country in 2014.

What happened in Ukraine illustrates the tendency to pine for the past when change comes, even if that change was once highly desired. We might dub this the *Back-to-Egypt Syndrome,* per the desires recorded in Numbers 14:1-4.

Some victims of the false teaching in Galatia (and perhaps even the false teachers themselves) seemed to have felt that way, uneasy with the radical change brought about by the gospel. The temptation to add stipulations from the "tried and true" Law of Moses was very appealing! But that law is analogous to the first stage of a multistage rocket: after that first stage serves its function, it drops away.   —C. R. B.

10. You observe days and months and seasons and years!

With circumcision comes the obligation to keep other elements of the Law of Moses. These include observances of the Jewish ritual calendar:

weekly Sabbaths, monthly new moon festivals, annual feasts like Passover, and special celebrations such as the year of jubilee. Paul mentions these as elements of the law that pointed to fulfillment in Christ (Colossians 2:16, 17, 20-22). To obligate oneself to obey these—as if they have something to do with one's relationship with God —is to reject Christ in favor of things designed to encourage people to look to him.

What Do You Think?
What are some telltale signs that a church's observances of special times of the year have become stumblingblocks? How do we keep that from happening?
Talking Points for Your Discussion
- Regarding observances that have a scriptural reference (Christmas, Easter, etc.)
- Regarding secular, cultural observances (Mother's Day, Independence Day, etc.)
- Regarding events unique to the congregation (anniversaries, etc.)

C. Wasted Work (v. 11)

11. I am afraid I may have labored over you in vain.

Paul notes how deeply the Galatian Christians' actions in this matter are affecting him. The Galatians are his work in the gospel. Their faith in Christ is the fruit of his ministry as a missionary. He is devoting his life to sharing the good news with them and others.

If Paul's audience, having already placed faith in Christ, make the wrong choice now, it will be as if he had never preached. The stakes are indeed high in the choice the Galatians must make!

What Do You Think?
What steps can you take to ensure that the work of your spiritual mentors will not be wasted?
Talking Points for Your Discussion
- In the self-discipline of memory recall
- In modeling aspects of the mentor's lifestyle
- In becoming a mentor in turn
- Other

II. Uncertain Status
(GALATIANS 4:12-16)
A. Welcomed in the Past (vv. 12-14)

12a. Brothers, I entreat you, become as I am, for I also have become as you are.

Persuasion by logic is one thing, and persuasion by example is another. Choosing the latter, Paul exhorts the Galatians to *become as I am.*

His personal example is that of one whose full faith in Christ has resulted in liberation from the strictures of the Law of Moses. In bringing the gospel's message of liberation to the Galatians, Paul had not parked himself in some seat of authority and insisted people meet various conditions before he would speak with them. Rather, he became as much like the Galatians as possible as he sought them out to tell of Jesus. Paul explains this evangelistic principle in more depth in 1 Corinthians 9:19-23.

As Paul has accepted fully God's freedom by faith in Jesus, so should the Galatians. They should not listen to false teachers who try to load on additional requirements such as circumcision.

12b, 13. You did me no wrong. You know it was because of a bodily ailment that I preached the gospel to you at first,

Paul refers to a specific experience of weakness when he preached among the Galatians. This passage, like 2 Corinthians 12:7, where Paul mentions his "thorn in the flesh," raises questions about his physical condition. Does his mention of *an illness* indicate that he suffers from some chronic condition?

Some have suggested that if Paul is writing to the southern Galatian region after his first missionary journey, then he may be referring to a case of malaria . Such a journey would have taken him though a mosquito-infested region where malaria could have been a danger. Others propose lingering effects from the stoning recorded in Acts 14:19. Yet another proposal is that of an eye disorder, which could be supported by Galatians 4:15; 6:11.

Though we do not know the specifics, we do know that Paul experienced some illness while he *preached the gospel* in Galatia *at first.*

14. and though my condition was a trial to you, you did scorn or despise me, but received me as an angel of God, as Christ Jesus.

The result of Paul's humble approach was to be welcomed by the Galatians. Paul refers to his illness as *a trial* to them, or an occasion of testing.

Paul speaks with warm exaggeration of the welcome he received during that testing, comparing their openness with the reception of a supernatural messenger from God. Even more, the Galatians had received Paul as if he were *Christ Jesus* himself! (We assume the welcome did not cross the line into being worship, as in Acts 14:11-18.)

Being now reminded of their joyous reception of the gospel, why would the Galatians even think about giving up the freedom they received in that wonderful moment?

B. Doubted in the Present (vv. 15, 16)

15. What then has become of your blessedness? For I testify to you that, if possible, you have gouged out your eyes and given them to me.

If the Galatians had received Paul so warmly despite his infirmity, why do they not extend to him the same blessing now? Paul urges the readers to think carefully about what he has meant and should mean to them as the messenger of freedom in Christ. Do the advocates of circumcision add anything to what the Galatians have already received? Certainly not! Adding circumcision

Visual for Lesson 11. *Start a discussion by pointing to this visual as you ask, "What U-turns does the Bible disallow after coming to Christ?"*

actually subtracts from the freedom they have received in the gospel.

The Galatians were at one time ready to make even the extreme sacrifice of their *own eyes* on Paul's behalf, because they recognized that he preached the message of true freedom. Why the change in attitude?

> **What Do You Think?**
> What sacrificial acts have you seen on the part of fellow Christians? How do these influence you to do likewise?
>
> *Talking Points for Your Discussion*
> - In making plans (2 Corinthians 1:15-17; etc.)
> - In changing a practice (Romans 14:21; etc.)
> - In monetary giving (2 Corinthians 8:1-4; etc.)
> - Other

16. Have I then become your enemy by telling you the truth?

Paul challenges the Galatians to decide where God's truth lies. Is Christ the fulfillment of what God promised Israel in the law, or is the law the means by which Gentiles join Israel in Christ? Does God bring his promised blessing to the world by receiving people of many nations through Christ, or by making them one nation through circumcision? If the latter are true in these two sets of questions, then Paul has indeed become the Galatians' enemy, for he has preached something false to them. But their experience should indicate the opposite.

◆ *Second Impressions* ◆

*You never get a second chance
to make a good first impression!*

The first-second logic of this axiom is airtight. Too often we draw wrong conclusions about people because of overreliance on first impressions. Later we may admit to ourselves that our negative first impression was because the other person reminds us of someone we do not like. Perhaps our negative impression was based on something minor, such as the other's use of filler phrases ("you know," "basically," "like," etc.) when speaking.

With the passage of time, however, we may discover the unfairly evaluated person to be "growing on us." We may realize that he or she has qualities that far outweigh whatever caused our initial dislike. The reverse may also be true at times. We may come to regret having formed a business partnership with someone if that partnership was the result of little more than initial positive vibes regarding his or her professional demeanor.

The Galatians accepted Paul warmly when he first brought the gospel. But their relationship with him cooled when his message was challenged by false teachers. Perhaps the Galatians relied too much on first impressions. Paul's letter to the Galatians is, in effect, an invitation to put both Paul and his opponents under the microscope of second, third, and fourth impressions. If they do, only Paul will pass inspection. Anyone can make truth claims, but few can pass truth tests.
—C. R. B.

III. Misplaced Eagerness
(Galatians 4:17-20)
A. Harmful Enthusiasm (v. 17)

17. They make much of you, but for no good purpose. They want to shut you out, that you may make much of them.

Those who advocate that the Galatian Christians be circumcised are quite enthusiastic. Their message is not complicated: take a painful but permanent step to truly become God's person.

As appealing as such a *zealous* message is, Paul warns that it is *for no good purpose*. Whether these teachers realize it or not, their teaching *would shut out* or separate the Galatians not merely from Paul himself but from God's people as a whole. To promote circumcision as a necessary religious rite is to reject the sufficiency of Jesus as the one who reconciles people and God. What Paul writes of unbelieving Israel in his letter to the Romans applies to the false teachers in Galatia: "They have a zeal for God, but not according to knowledge" (Romans 10:2).

B. Healthy Zeal (v. 18)

18. It is always good to be made much of for a good purpose, and not only when I am present with you,

Only one kind of enthusiasm is worthwhile: that of constant dedication to what is *good*. Of course, the good news of Jesus is the greatest good thing. The Galatians need to remember their initial enthusiasm for the gospel. The aim is not simply to recapture the emotion of that time but to refocus on the message that they received, remaining committed to its truth regardless. The Galatians demonstrated that enthusiasm when Paul was *present*. Now they need to do the same in his absence. God has provided them with what they need to remain faithful, whether or not Paul is present for their support.

> **What Do You Think?**
> What steps can you take to ensure that your zeal for Christ has scriptural truth as its basis?
> *Talking Points for Your Discussion*
> - Considering positive biblical precepts and examples (John 2:17; Romans 12:11; 2 Corinthians 7:7; 8:10-12; etc.)
> - Considering negative biblical precepts and examples (Ecclesiastes 7:16, 17; Romans 10:2; Philippians 3:6; etc.)

C. Heartfelt Longing (vv. 19, 20)

19. my little children, for whom I am again in the anguish of childbirth until Christ is formed in you!

The expression *my little children* stresses the close bond that Paul has with those who have come to faith through his ministry (compare 1 Corinthians 4:14, 15; etc.). Here he carries that figure of speech in a special direction. Paul's efforts in preaching to the Galatians, combined with the suffering that he experienced through his physical malady and otherwise, had been like labor pains that yielded the Galatian Christians' birth into God's family through faith in Christ.

Now the Galatian Christians are in a struggle to hold to that faith. To receive circumcision on the terms offered them would be to say that Christ was not enough to bring them into God's people. Paul's struggle to demonstrate this is like a second set of labor pains (*again in the anguish of childbirth*) to him. When his desire that *Christ be formed in* them is accomplished, their lives will be centered on and governed by the Savior, not the law's requirement for circumcision. His willingness to undergo such a struggle demonstrates the extent of his conviction about the sufficiency of the gospel and the depth of his commitment to them.

20. I wish I could be present with you now and change my tone, for I am perplexed about you.

Paul's letter to the Galatians represents his additional "travail in birth" on their behalf. But better still would be another personal visit. The goal of such a visit would be for Paul to be able *to change* his *tone* of *voice* to be softer than that of the letter. That could happen if face-to-face interaction reveals or results in the Galatians' rejection of the false teaching and teachers in view here. Whether Paul ever has the opportunity to make this desired personal visit depends on when this letter is dated.

Conclusion

A. Subtraction by Addition

We may look back on the Galatians' situation with bemusement. Why was circumcision so attractive to them? Why would they consider adding such a thing to their faith in Christ?

Those questions should make us ponder what we ourselves might add to faith in Christ as we consider what makes us God's people. In every place and age, some have sought to add to the gospel in ways that ultimately result in diminishing the freedom the gospel gives. If we are to be truly free in Christ, then he and he alone must be the object of our trust.

B. Prayer

Father, may we depend utterly on what your Son has done for us to free us from bondage. Teach us to rely on him and him alone. We pray this in his name, Jesus. Amen.

C. Thought to Remember

Adding requirements to the gospel always results in subtracting from the gospel.

INVOLVEMENT LEARNING

Enhance your lesson presentation with the reproducible activity page,
available as a free download at www.standardlesson.com.

Into the Lesson

On the board write, *"There ought to be a law against . . .*

Spend a few minutes allowing your class to create a list that finishes the statement. Encourage responses from the most serious to the silliest. Some examples might be:

. . . mowing one's lawn before 9 a.m. on Saturday.

. . . loud, personal cell phone calls in public.

. . . smoking where children are present.

. . . saying "There ought to be a law against . . ."

After creating the list, ask students to tell what problems might arise if there *were* a law such as one described on the list.

Alternative. Distribute copies of the "Would You Rather . . ." activity from the reproducible page, which you can download. Have students discuss their choices in pairs.

After either activity, lead into Bible study saying, "An interesting aspect of human nature is that we often want maximum freedom for ourselves, yet we want maximum control for others. But life does not work that way! We end up having to choose to sacrifice a part of our freedom for some degree of security. But when does freedom become anarchy or order become bondage? That is the big question Paul had for the church in Galatia."

Into the Word

Say, "The Socratic teaching method is named after the classical Greek philosopher Socrates. It is a teaching method based on asking and answering questions to stimulate critical thinking. Paul did not hesitate to ask some pointed, hard questions of the Galatian Christians."

Divide the class into three groups. Give each group a section of the Bible text. Instruct the groups to read their sections and write questions that would help people understand what Paul was saying about freedom and legalism in these verses.

The verse divisions and a few sample Socratic questions follow:

Group 1—Galatians 4:8-11.

What do people worship before they learn of the God of the Bible? Why would anyone who has tasted religious freedom return to legalism? How do people overemphasize special days and seasons in a religious sense?

Group 2—Galatians 4:12-16.

Why would Paul speak of his weakness rather than his authority in convincing the Galatians to be free in Jesus? In what way is accepting legalistic practices an insult to those who have taught us the gospel of grace?

Group 3—Galatians 4:17-20.

How do people let the personal characteristics and status of teachers influence their own faith and faithfulness? What is the risk of telling others of your faults of faith? How are learners sometimes fooled by the zealousness of false teachers?

Into Life

Say, "In 1941, President Franklin D. Roosevelt spoke of four freedoms that should belong to everyone in the world. He suggested that those freedoms could be obtained through political means." Those freedoms are:

Freedom of speech   Freedom from want

Freedom of worship   Freedom from fear

Video of Roosevelt listing those freedoms is available on video-sharing websites such as YouTube, should you wish to play it for the class.

Discuss whether or not class members agree that these four freedoms are basic and can be obtained. Ask, "What would Paul say? How do cultural views of the four differ from the biblical view?"

Alternative. Distribute copies of the "Four Freedoms" activity from the reproducible page. Since freedom in Christ is the theme of next week's lesson, you may encourage class members to take the page home and complete it in preparation for that lesson.

FREEDOM
IN CHRIST

DEVOTIONAL READING: Galatians 5:22-26
BACKGROUND SCRIPTURE: Galatians 5:1-17

GALATIANS 5:1-17

¹ For freedom Christ has set us free; stand firm therefore, and do not submit again to a yoke of slavery.

² Look: I, Paul, say to you that if you accept circumcision, Christ will be of no advantage to you. ³ I testify again to every man who accepts circumcision that he is obligated to keep the whole law. ⁴ You are severed from Christ, you who would be justified by the law; you have fallen away from grace. ⁵ For through the Spirit, by faith, we ourselves eagerly wait for the hope of righteousness. ⁶ For in Christ Jesus neither circumcision nor uncircumcision counts for anything, but only faith working through love.

⁷ You were running well. Who hindered you from obeying the truth? ⁸ This persuasion is not from him who calls you. ⁹ A little leaven leavens the whole lump. ¹⁰ I have confidence in the Lord that you will take no other view, and the one who is troubling you will bear the penalty, whoever he is. ¹¹ But if I, brothers, still preach circumcision, why am I still being persecuted? In that case the offense of the cross has been removed. ¹² I wish those who unsettle you would emasculate themselves!

¹³ For you were called to freedom, brothers. Only do not use your freedom as an opportunity for the flesh, but through love serve one another. ¹⁴ For the whole law is fulfilled in one word: "You shall love your neighbor as yourself." ¹⁵ But if you bite and devour one another, watch out that you are not consumed by one another.

¹⁶ But I say, walk by the Spirit, and you will not gratify the desires of the flesh. ¹⁷ For the desires of the flesh are against the Spirit, and the desires of the Spirit are against the flesh, for these are opposed to each other, to keep you from doing the things you want to do.

KEY VERSE

For you were called to freedom, brothers. Only do not use your freedom as an opportunity for the flesh, but through love serve one another. —**Galatians 5:13**

CREATION: A DIVINE CYCLE

Unit 3: The Birthing of a New Community

LESSON AIMS

After participating in this lesson, each learner will be able to:

1. Summarize Paul's concern regarding the status of the Galatians.

2. Contrast the life of freedom in Christ with the life of slavery to self.

3. Describe a guardrail that helps keep him or her from slipping back into the ways "of the flesh."

LESSON OUTLINE

Introduction

A. What Does a Free Person Look Like?

Occasionally we see newscasts of people experiencing political freedom for the first time. As totalitarian regimes fall, nations have to learn new habits. How can people live together in freedom without chaos? What does a free person look like?

Freedom in Christ raises the same questions, but with distinct answers. What keeps us from using our freedom to excuse the chaos of selfishness? What does a free person in Christ look like?

Today's text addresses these questions.

B. Lesson Background

Paul's letter to the Galatians addressed a struggle to come to terms with God's plan in history. The struggle involved deciding whether Gentile believers in Jesus had to adhere to the law that God gave to Israel. Some taught that Gentiles who accepted Christ had to be circumcised in order to become part of God's people; Gentiles had to receive the mark that distinguished Israel as having received God's covenant.

Paul's response is a lesson on the shape of God's work in history, which focuses on Christ's death and resurrection. Everything that came before was preparatory. God did not give Israel its law as the final expression of his purpose, but as a means of pointing to Christ (Galatians 3:24).

Part of that preparation had to do with what Israel's law did not accomplish. Even while God was giving the law to Israel, Israel was rejecting the God who gave it (Exodus 32:1-6). That pattern of rejection continued, as failure to keep God's law was the story of successive generations. This pattern demonstrated that if God's will was to be done on earth, it would take something more powerful than law.

Israel's Scriptures included promises that God would indeed do something greater: he would make a new covenant with his people, writing the law "on their hearts" (Jeremiah 31:31-34). He would replace stony hearts with new ones as his Spirit enabled them to obey (Ezekiel 36:22-32).

The cross of Christ signals the fulfillment of these promises. Now the people of God are defined not by the covenant of circumcision, but by faith in Christ who died for their sin. Because of Christ's death, God's Spirit is given to all Christians (Acts 2:38). The Galatian Christians needed to understand these truths.

I. Charter of Freedom
(Galatians 5:1)

1. For freedom Christ has set us free; stand firm therefore, and do not submit again to a yoke of slavery.

This verse both summarizes the message of Galatians to this point and begins application of that message to the Galatians' lives. Christ's mission was to give humanity true *freedom*, so there can be no going back to what formerly had caused people to be in *slavery*.

This means there is to be no return to the pagan practices that some followed before becoming Christians. But it also means no going back to rely on the Mosaic law to attempt to make oneself a member of God's people. Either path is a road back to slavery. To turn back would be to thwart God's plan and lose everything for which one submits to Christ.

II. Threat to Freedom
(Galatians 5:2-6)
A. Fall into Debt (vv. 2-4)

2. Look: I, Paul, say to you that if you accept circumcision, Christ will be of no advantage to you.

Christ came as the fulfillment of what Israel's law pointed toward but could not accomplish in and of itself. So for a Gentile Christian to receive circumcision would mean to turn back to the thing Christ came to fulfill! It would be to live as if God had not fulfilled his promises in Christ,

HOW TO SAY IT

Corinthians	Ko-*rin*-thee-unz (*th* as in *thin*).
Ezekiel	Ee-*zeek*-ee-ul or Ee-*zeek*-yul.
Jeremiah	Jair-uh-*my*-uh.
Mosaic	Mo-*zay*-ik.

as if Christ had accomplished nothing. Submission to circumcision threatens the very basis of the Galatians' relationship to God.

3. I testify again to every man who accepts circumcision that he is obligated to keep the whole law.

Circumcision signifies initiation into the people of God and intent to keep *the whole law* as God had given to his people. A *man who accepts circumcision* cannot claim to be part of Israel as the covenant people if he ignores the rest of the law!

Any attempt to keep the entirety of the law is, of course, a recipe for failure. Israel's history demonstrates inability to do so. To enter into that same covenant of obligation would be to repeat that same pattern of failure. God has fulfilled the promise of his law by supplying in Christ what humanity really needs: true forgiveness from sin and true power to overcome sin.

4. You are severed from Christ, you who would be justified by the law; you have fallen away from grace.

Circumcision has been offered to the Galatian Christians as the supreme sign of belonging to God. But where does that leave Christ? To *be justified* is to be acceptable to God. This requires that the conditions for a sinner to be acceptable to him have been satisfied. To attempt to *be justified by the law* through a rite of that law is to say that Christ does not accomplish our justification. It is to say *no* to the *grace* Christ offers in the gospel.

How high are the stakes? Eternally high! To accept circumcision as the sign of belonging to God is to reject the eternal freedom from sin's punishment that Christ purchased by his death.

B. Hope in Christ (vv. 5, 6)

5. For through the Spirit, by faith, we ourselves eagerly wait for the hope of righteousness.

A vital feature of the new covenant is the gift of the Holy Spirit (Acts 2:38; Galatians 3:14). Paul has already criticized his readers with the pointed question, "Did you receive the Spirit by works of the law or by hearing with faith?" (Galatians 3:2).

It's *either/or*, not *both/and*. As we noted in the Conclusion to lesson 11, attempts to add something to salvation in Christ actually result in subtracting. On the topic at hand, that which is subtracted is *the Spirit*. This is no small matter, since having the Spirit is a mark of a new covenant believer—a Christian (compare 2 Corinthians 1:22).

The appeal of adding or substituting circumcision as that mark may be that the future righteousness in view here is thought to be under human control. By works of the Law of Moses, a person may fantasize that he or she can achieve such righteousness on a personal timetable.

Paul squelches any such notion. It is *through the Spirit* that *the hope of righteousness* comes. Since such a hope comes about this way, we *wait* for it as we yield to the Spirit's timetable. Such expectant waiting can only happen *by faith*. It is when faith starts to wane that we are tempted to control the timing of things. Bad things happen when we yield to such temptation (example: Genesis 16).

What Do You Think?
How can we help one another be better at waiting "through the Spirit" for the stated hope?
Talking Points for Your Discussion
- Regarding help for preteens
- Regarding help for teenagers
- Regarding help for young adults
- Regarding help for middle-age adults
- Regarding help for older adults

---

6. For in Christ Jesus neither circumcision nor uncircumcision counts for anything, but only faith working through love.

Christ Jesus is at the center of everything God has done. So nothing else can matter as he does. Circumcision was a key part of God's unfolding plan, but circumcision is nothing compared with Christ. With the completion of his work, both Jew and Gentile come to God the same way: through faith in Christ.

Jesus Christ, the Son of God, embodied the fullest expression of the love God has for humanity (John 3:16). To put faith in him, therefore, means to have faith in God's *love*. Genuine faith in Christ must therefore reflect the same love that God showed in Christ. To pay lip service to the need for faith's outworking in love is to treat God's love for us in Christ with contempt.

III. Commitment to Freedom
(GALATIANS 5:7-12)
A. Run a Good Race (v. 7)

7. You were running well. Who hindered you from obeying the truth?

Paul likes to compare Christian experiences with athletic competitions (see 1 Corinthians 9:24-27; Galatians 2:2; Philippians 3:14; 2 Timothy 4:7). Runners who are focused on the finish line will have nothing to do with those who try to *hinder* them. In this case, those interfering oppose "*the truth* of the gospel" (Galatians 2:5, 14).

B. Avoid Ungodly Teaching (vv. 8-10)

8. This persuasion is not from him who calls you.

The opponents claim a godly purpose, but the opposite is the case. Their *persuasion* does not originate with God, the author of the gospel. To follow circumcision is to reverse his plan and to impede believers' progress to his promised future.

The word *persuasion* translates a Greek word so rare that it appears only here in the New Testament. Paul shows his brilliance in this choice because it forms a play on the Greek words translated "obeying" in verse 7, above, and "I have confidence" in verse 10, below, in that the three words originate from the same root. Anyone who thinks Paul is a lightweight needs to think again!

9. "A little leaven leavens the whole lump."

Leaven is yeast, the ingredient that makes bread rise. When used figuratively, the imagery of leaven is almost always in a negative or evil context (compare Matthew 16:6; 1 Corinthians 5:6-8; contrast Matthew 13:33). Only *a little* of this substance is required to make a loaf rise properly. And as leaven affects bread, so false teaching can affect a church. The circumcision advocates appear righteous. But to adopt their teaching will be to turn one's back on God's grace in Christ. This, the deadliest of things, will be the result if false teaching about circumcision is allowed to have a foothold.

10. I have confidence in the Lord that you will take no other view, and the one who is troubling you will bear the penalty, whoever he is.

Paul's harsh language to this point may leave the impression that he has little confidence in the Galatian Christians. Here he corrects potential misunderstanding in that regard as he expresses trust that his readers will decide for the gospel.

But a solemn warning remains to be offered. Those who advocate circumcision are potentially turning people away from God's grace. The fact that a righteous God judges rightly puts the false teachers on notice to repent.

> *What Do You Think?*
> What steps can our church take to express confidence in God's people while warning of God's judgment, as Paul did?
> *Talking Points for Your Discussion*
> - When gathered as a church
> - When gathered in mid-size groups
> - When gathered in small groups

C. Endure Persecution (v. 11)

11. But if I, brothers and sisters, still preach circumcision, why am I still being persecuted? In that case the offense of the cross has been removed.

Advocates of circumcision apparently insist that Paul himself continues to observe Jewish practices, even that of circumcision. The events recorded in Acts 16:3; 18:18; and 1 Corinthians 9:20 could serve as the false teachers' evidence, depending on when Galatians is written.

The contexts of those actions make clear, however, that Paul approaches the Law of Moses from the perspective of *the cross*. His continued observance of Jewish practices is always with the aim of sharing Jesus. So Paul's evangelistic technique among his fellow Israelites is to become "as a Jew" (1 Corinthians 9:20).

These are actions to extend grace, not to subvert it. The fact that Paul continues to be *persecuted* establishes that he does not insist on circumcision. Such persecution is part of the message of the cross. The idea that God should save human-

ity through the death of his Son is deeply offensive to so much in the human spirit. We want to believe that our lives are not so lost as to require something so extreme. The advocates of circumcision would like a different divine plan that makes salvation a matter of following the right laws. But the cross with all its *offense* offers the only way to the freedom that God has for his people.

> *What Do You Think?*
> How can we help each other appreciate freedom in Christ even while we are rejected because of the offense of the cross?
> *Talking Points for Your Discussion*
> - When one-on-one
> - When in small or mid-size groups
> - When gathered as a church
> - Other

D. Speak Boldly (v. 12)

12. I wish those who unsettle you would emasculate themselves!

With exasperated sarcasm, Paul expresses his disdain for the advocates of circumcision. They insist that commitment to God is defined by cutting off the foreskin. Well, Paul says, if they are so intent on showing commitment by cutting, let them cut off even more than the foreskin! Like Jesus' words about plucking out eyes or cutting off hands (Matthew 5:29, 30), Paul's expression is not literal. But it does indicate his strong feelings about the situation.

◆ *SPIRITUAL GANG CULTURE* ◆

A college professor entered the world of gangs in East Los Angeles a few years ago to study that subculture. He found that children who grew up in gang-controlled areas faced powerful incentives to join gangs. The threat of harm for not joining was a common enlistment tactic. Initiation rites could include being beaten by other gang members, committing a theft, etc. A common requirement for female initiates was to give sexual service to one or more gang members.

Religious groups have been known to be like gangs in their expectations regarding initiation and loyalty. This is especially true of groups that

Visual for Lesson 12. *Point to this visual as you ask, "Are the boundaries separating these three categories the same for everyone? Why, or why not?"*

tend toward cultish rules and practices. "True believers" are those who prove their loyalty by adhering to expectations that don't stand up to the light of Scripture or common sense. The simplicity of following Christ is lost in the excitement of establishing by personal effort one's worthiness for membership in the group.

This seems to be what was happening, or on the verge of happening, among the Galatian churches. I trust it is not happening in yours. —C. R. B.

IV. Responsibility of Freedom
(GALATIANS 5:13-17)
A. How to Use Liberty (vv. 13, 14)

13. For you were called to freedom, brothers. Only do not use your freedom as an opportunity for the flesh, but through love serve one another.

The good news of Jesus is a comprehensive call to *freedom*. To Jews it means (or should mean) being freed from the shackles of an unbearable system (Acts 15:10). To Gentiles it means freedom from the repeated pattern of devotion to things that are not of God.

Even so, Paul warns his readers against understanding liberty in Christ to mean they have a license to live as they please. This problem is what Paul refers to as *the flesh,* by which he means "selfish indulgence," life lived as if God were not in the picture at all.

To misuse Christian liberty can become *an opportunity for the flesh*—the Greek word translated *opportunity* referring to the staging ground from which an army launches operations. Freedom bought with Christ's blood is squandered if it merely serves as twisted reasoning for a new opportunity for sin.

But there is an alternative: *through love serve one another*. This is the very essence of the cross that bought our freedom: Christ in his love serving us, even though we are undeserving. To use our Christian liberty in this way is to live according to the gift God has given us. It is to let God replace our pattern of failure with the pattern of his own grace-filled, Christ-expressed love.

◆ *"HAPPY"* ◆

Roko Belic is a movie director known best for his 2011 documentary titled *Happy*. The filmmaker interviews people in various countries to see whether they are happy. Belic found that life circumstances have little to do with happiness. Instead, one's attitude about life and a spirit of serving others characterize the happiest people.

Christians do not love one another in order to be saved, but because we have been saved. Lest some consider such loving service to be a form of bondage, consider the alternative: slavery to self and to this world as someone or something other than Christ is enthroned as king of one's life. When happiness does not result, the pseudo king always has another rule to follow or a different path to self-improvement.

Faith in Christ sets us free from such a system. Any hard effort on our part comes because we are sure that Christ has already purchased our salvation. That's what releases us from the tyranny of a "trying hard, never sure" system. —C. R. B.

14. For the whole law is fulfilled in one word: "You shall love your neighbor as yourself."

As Jesus had emphasized the command to love one's neighbor (Leviticus 19:18; Matthew 19:19), so do Paul (Romans 13:9) and other New Testament writers (James 2:8). All emphasize that the entire Law of Moses comes to its focus *in one word*. God's purpose for us is that we should live in his world as he lives with us: in self-sacrificial, grace-filled love. All the commandments he gives are specific expressions of the honest, faithful, forgiving love that God himself demonstrates. This is how the gospel calls all people to the freedom that leads to the fulfillment of God's will.

> *What Do You Think?*
> What can we do to expand the ways in which we use our freedom in Christ to serve others?
> *Talking Points for Your Discussion*
> - In church programming
> - In personal sacrifice
> - Other

B. How Not to Use Liberty (vv. 15-17)

15. But if you bite and devour one other, watch out that you are not consumed by one another.

The circumcision controversy seems to be a point of bitter division in the Galatian churches. The time has come for all to remember the true message of Jesus, with the cross as its focus. God's love means God's people must love one another, even when they have been unlovely. To fail to live such love can mean the destruction of a church, to the ruin of God's purpose.

16. But I say, walk by the Spirit, and you will not gratify the desires of the flesh.

If the story of humanity is a story of failing to fulfill God's purpose, how can we possibly change that path? Through Christ we receive God's Holy Spirit, who empowers us to overcome the old mind-set and habits that work against the life for which God has freed us. Our objective is now to live moment by moment by the Spirit's power.

To do so is the opposite of the old life, which is rooted in self-centeredness. *The desires of the flesh* refer not just to physical desires but to all desires that put self on the throne. God's Holy Spirit empowers us to enthrone Christ instead. As we *walk by the Spirit*, we do not desire to return to the old, self-centered life.

17. For the desires of the flesh are against the Spirit, and the desires of the Spirit are against the flesh, for these are opposed to each other, to keep you from doing the things you want to do.

The two ways of life are always in conflict, battling for control as they are *opposed to each other*. Our frustrations with ourselves as Christ's followers stem from this conflict. When the old life seems to be winning, we become distrustful of ourselves as free people.

The answer to our problem is always in the gospel; the Holy Spirit is stronger than sinful selfishness. Trusting the sufficiency of Christ and the power of the Spirit, we can overcome the old patterns and learn the true life of freedom.

> *What Do You Think?*
> How can our church help her members recognize when they are hindering the Holy Spirit's battle against "the flesh"?
> *Talking Points for Your Discussion*
> - Regarding challenges various age groups are likely to face
> - Regarding gender-targeted challenges
> - Regarding Satan's tactics in general
> - Other

Conclusion
A. Set Free for What?

If you were free to become anything that you chose to be, what would you choose? To what use would you put such radical freedom?

We should all consider how our honest answer to such a question compares with what we confess as Christians. If we truly believe that Christ's cross saves us from the ruin of our lives, do we let the cross define what should become the purpose of our lives? For what has Christ set us free?

B. Prayer

God, we thank you for the freedom granted us in Christ! By the power of your Spirit, we ask that you enable us to use it in gratitude and praise to the one who gave it. In his name we pray. Amen.

C. Thought to Remember

Ours is not just freedom *from*.
It is also freedom *to*.

INVOLVEMENT LEARNING

Enhance your lesson presentation with the reproducible activity page,
available as a free download at www.standardlesson.com.

Into the Lesson

Before this session, gather 5–10 instrumental renditions of patriotic tunes. These will be used in a game of Name That Tune. You can obtain such compositions inexpensively from reputable music-download websites.

To begin the session, ask two members to volunteer to compete in this game. Proceed as follows:

1. The first contestant says, "I can name that tune in [a certain number of] seconds."

2. The second contestant has the chance to "underbid" the first by pledging to name the tune in fewer seconds.

3. Bidding continues until one player decides not to underbid and challenges, "Name that tune!"

4. You will then play the first song, carefully watching the counter on your player (or the second hand on a watch) to play the tune for exactly the amount of seconds bid.

A player gets a point for naming the tune, or the opponent gets the point if the player is unable to do so. Play as many rounds as time permits.

Alternative. Distribute copies of the "President or Poet?" activity from the reproducible page, which you can download. Have students work on it individually.

After either activity, lead into Bible study saying, "A lot of ideas are bound up in the word *freedom*. Paul helped the Galatian Christians understand the importance of being truly free."

Into the Word

Say, "Sometimes it is helpful to try to summarize a portion of Scripture in just a few words." Before class, cut some ordinary sheets of copy paper in thirds vertically to make bumper sticker–size strips. Have pencils, pens, and markers available.

Divide the class into four groups. Give each group a section of the Bible text as outlined in the commentary. Groups are to read their section of the text and create one or more bumper stickers with a slogan that summarizes that section. The verse divisions and sample Socratic slogans follow:

Group 1—Charter of Freedom (Galatians 5:1)
Get Free! Stay Free! Live Free!

Group 2—Threat to Freedom (Galatians 5:2-6)
Jesus did what we cannot.

Group 3—Commitment to Freedom (Galatians 5:7-12)
I want to be a slave to religious ritual. (Said no one ever!)

Group 4—Responsibility of Freedom (Galatians 5:13-17)
Freedom—It's about how you use it.

Alternative. Distribute copies of the "Prepositional Propositions" activity from the reproducible page. Assign each student a partner. Have students work on the activity individually and then talk about their responses with their partners.

Into Life

Give each learner a strip of paper resembling a highway guardrail. (Simple parallel lines on a strip with a label "guardrail" will do.) Say, "Driving along life's highway can be hazardous. Just over the side . . . way down below . . . is the Valley of the Way of the Flesh. The guardrail is in place to keep us from slipping off into the abyss. What is your 'guardrail'? What is it that keeps you from slipping off the road to Heaven?"

Allow time for learners to respond freely, suggesting that each listen and write some entries from the oral list onto their paper guardrails. Encourage students to tape their guardrails in a place where temptations to fleshly living abound (examples: on the television set or on the inside door of the car or near the handle of the refrigerator).

CHRIST CREATES HOLY LIVING

DEVOTIONAL READING: Romans 6:1-11
BACKGROUND SCRIPTURE: Galatians 5:18–6:10

GALATIANS 5:18-26

¹⁸ But if you are led by the Spirit, you are not under the law. ¹⁹ Now the works of the flesh are evident: sexual immorality, impurity, sensuality, ²⁰ idolatry, sorcery, enmity, strife, jealousy, fits of anger, rivalries, dissensions, divisions, ²¹ envy, drunkenness, orgies, and things like these. I warn you, as I warned you before, that those who do such things will not inherit the kingdom of God. ²² But the fruit of the Spirit is love, joy, peace, patience, kindness, goodness, faithfulness, ²³ gentleness, self-control; against such things there is no law. ²⁴ And those who belong to Christ Jesus have crucified the flesh with its passions and desires.

²⁵ If we live by the Spirit, let us also keep in step with the Spirit. ²⁶ Let us not become conceited, provoking one another, envying one another.

GALATIANS 6:1-10

¹ Brothers, if anyone is caught in any transgression, you who are spiritual should restore him in a spirit of gentleness. Keep watch on yourself, lest you too be tempted. ² Bear one another's burdens, and so fulfill the law of Christ. ³ For if anyone thinks he is something, when he is nothing, he deceives himself. ⁴ But let each one test his own work, and then his reason to boast will be in himself alone and not in his neighbor. ⁵ For each will have to bear his own load.

⁶ Let the one who is taught the word share all good things with the one who teaches. ⁷ Do not be deceived: God is not mocked, for whatever one sows, that will he also reap. ⁸ For the one who sows to his own flesh will from the flesh reap corruption, but the one who sows to the Spirit will from the Spirit reap eternal life. ⁹ And let us not grow weary of doing good, for in due season we will reap, if we do not give up. ¹⁰ So then, as we have opportunity, let us do good to everyone, and especially to those who are of the household of faith.

KEY VERSES

But the fruit of the Spirit is love, joy, peace, patience, kindness, goodness, faithfulness, gentleness, self-control; against such things there is no law. —**Galatians 5:22, 23**

Graphic: Kheng guan Toh / Hemera / Thinkstock

CREATION: A DIVINE CYCLE

Unit 3: The Birthing of a New Community

LESSON AIMS

After participating in this lesson, each learner will be able to:

1. Recite the key verses from memory.

2. Contrast the life reflecting God's grace with the life centered on serving self.

3. Identify the element of the fruit of the Spirit he or she models least and make a plan for change.

LESSON OUTLINE

Introduction

A. The Portrait of God's Person

If you happen to see a finely executed oil painting, not just a reproduction but the handiwork of an artist with a brush, look at it closely. From a distance, we see a singular image. But up close, we can see the many-layered colors that create the vivid image. The unity of a fine painting is the result of thousands of details.

So it is with lives transformed by the saving work of God. Such lives make a singular impression on us. They reflect how God saves undeserving sinners through faith in his Son. But that singular impression is the result of many fine details. God's grace reshapes every aspect of a saved sinner's life.

Our text provides an experience like close examination of a fine oil painting. In it Paul paints a word portrait of God's person. Closely examined, its details reveal a singular image of divine transformation.

B. Lesson Background

This is the final lesson of this unit's consideration of Paul's letter to the Galatians. At the risk of oversimplifying, *freedom* could be a one-word summary of Paul's emphasis up to the beginning of today's lesson. For former pagans, this meant freedom from slavery to falsehood. For those who came to faith in Christ from Judaism, it meant freedom from repeated failures to keep God's law.

But freedom can be a dangerous thing. Can we trust ourselves to do what is right if we are free from law or threat? That's the fundamental question Paul addressed as today's lesson picks up where the text of last week's concluded.

I. Charter of Life in the Spirit

(GALATIANS 5:18)

18. But if you are led by the Spirit, you are not under the law.

The Law of Moses marked Israel as God's people. But in Christ, we are marked as God's people in that we are *led by the Spirit*. The Spirit's power transforms us to reflect God's own character, displaying in our lives the grace by which God brought us into his family.

This has important implications. Not being *under the law* sounds to some like a license to do as one pleases, as if "anything goes." But in this law-free life, God's Spirit leads people to become like God, not to become more entangled in their own selfishness. In fact, it is by being led by God's Spirit that we actually fulfill the teaching found in God's law.

◆   NOT THE LETTER, BUT . . .   ◆

In Shakespeare's *The Merchant of Venice,* Antonio makes a deal with moneylender Shylock. If Antonio does not repay the debt, he will have to pay a literal "pound of flesh." When Antonio cannot repay, Shylock is ready to exact the punishment. But Portia, a wealthy heiress, appeals to Shylock to show mercy when she says, "The quality of mercy is not strain'd. . . . It is twice blest: It blesseth him that gives and him that takes."

Shylock is not moved by this appeal. So Portia quibbles with him about the precise wording of the agreement. Exacting a pound of flesh will cost Antonio blood as well as flesh. Since Shylock's threat did not mention blood, the "letter of the law" means he cannot get his pound of flesh.

Paul's appeal to be led by the Spirit rather than the law has the force of directing us to what God intends to happen as we follow him. Paul's opponents were interested first and foremost in a strict obedience to the Law of Moses. Paul challenged them to see, here and elsewhere, that "those who are led by the Spirit of God are the children of God" (Romans 8:14).   —C. R. B.

> *What Do You Think?*
>   What are some ways to help new Christians make the transition from life "under the law" to living the Spirit-led life?
> *Talking Points for Your Discussion*
>   - In speech patterns
>   - In behavioral habits
>   - In relationships
>   - In attitude
>   - Other

II. Details of the Self-Ruled Life
(GALATIANS 5:19-21)
A. Sexual Sin (v. 19)

19. Now the works of the flesh are evident: sexual immorality, impurity, sensuality,

For purposes of contrast, Paul reminds readers what life in *the flesh,* the self-ruled life, is like. His list of vices fall into four groupings across three verses. The verse before us has the first group: terms for sexual sin.

Sexual immorality is any sexual activity other than that between one woman and one man who are married to each other. *Impurity* suggests both sexual acts outside the marriage context and the effect that such acts have on those engaged in them. Sexual sin affects deeply . It involves physical dangers, but also it endangers heart and mind.

Sensuality translates a term that refers to behavior that is shocking to public decency. Even cultures far from godly standards uphold some standards of sexual propriety (1 Corinthians 5:1), but a life of selfishness will find a way to shock any society. Sometimes it seems there is no limit to extent sexual sin will take a person.

> *What Do You Think?*
>   What steps can we take to demonstrate that a life faithful to God's design for sex is superior to any other?
> *Talking Points for Your Discussion*
>   - In marriage
>   - In singleness
>   - In conversation
>   - Other

B. Occult Practices and Selfishness (v. 20)

20. idolatry, sorcery, enmity, strife, jealousy, fits of anger, rivalries, dissensions, divisions,

The two words at the beginning of this verse comprise the second group in Paul's list. *Idolatry* involves making gods in images chosen by humans (Isaiah 2:8; etc.). *Sorcery* is the attempt to use substances to manipulate the spirit world (compare 2 Chronicles 33:6).

The seven sins that follow the first two constitute Paul's third group. *Enmity* is the opposite of God's gracious love and the sure result of a selfish perspective. *Strife* translates a term meaning dissention among people. *Jealousy* is a strong passion that resents the success of others. *Fits of anger* are the strong expressions of wrath and conflict. *Rivalries* represent the forming of mutually hostile groups to advance one's own interests. *Dissensions* take that party spirit to higher conflict. *Division* suggests not just false belief but persistent, destructive factions.

C. Self-Destruction (v. 21)

21. envy, drunkenness, orgies, and things like these. I warn you, as I warned you before, that those who do such things will not inherit the kingdom of God.

Verse divisions in the New Testament were not created until about AD 1550, and *envy* fits better with the subgrouping in verse 20. It refers to the desire to deprive others of what they have.

Paul concludes with two terms that represent public display of the self-destructiveness produced by sinful selfishness. *Drunkenness,* intoxication from alcohol, suggests individual self-destruction. Drunkenness is part of the wild-party atmosphere of *orgies*, which includes unrestrained immorality (contrast Romans 13:13; 1 Peter 4:3). Since those who persist on this path live outside God's kingdom in the present, they can hardly claim to belong to it in the future.

III. Details of the Spirit-Led Life
(GALATIANS 5:22-24)

A. Foundational Characteristics (v. 22a)

22a. But the fruit of the Spirit is love, joy, peace,

The list of works of the flesh serves as a contrast to Paul's point: what the life controlled by the Holy Spirit produces. All the Spirit's work reflects God's character and actions. A hundred terms would not capture everything, but the short list that begins here provides a detailed portrait.

As with the previous list, this one groups similar characteristics. It begins with three foundational aspects of the Christ-follower's character: *love, joy,* and *peace.*

The kind of *love* Paul has in mind is not conditioned on how deserving of love the object is. Rather, the kind of love in view flows from grace that blesses the undeserving. It is the kind of love God demonstrates toward us (John 3:16). When God's Spirit creates the same kind of love in the heart of the Christian, we are impelled to love those who do not deserve it and can give nothing in return.

Joy is the outlook of celebration that flows from knowing what God has done. God's Spirit reminds us that God has triumphed through the work of Christ. This gives us reason to rejoice regardless of circumstances (Philippians 4:4).

Peace reminds us of Old Testament statements about the peace that God grants his people (Numbers 6:26; Psalm 29:11; Isaiah 9:6, 7; 55:12; etc.). More than the end of hostility, such peace means positive goodwill and fellowship (Luke 2:14). As God has made whole our relationship with him, his Spirit empowers us to make relationships whole with others.

B. Relational Characteristics (v. 22b)

22b. patience, kindness, goodness,

The second group consists of characteristics that undergird relationships. One who exhibits *patience* is tolerant of the failings of others. As God is patient with us, his Spirit empowers our patience toward others (compare Romans 2:4; 3:25).

Kindness names the attitude that seeks to do positive good to others in all circumstances. Again, because God treats his people in this way, his Spirit enables them to treat others likewise (Colossians 3:12).

Goodness further develops the idea of kindness, putting the attitude into action. Those empowered by the Spirit do not simply want the good; they actually do good things for others (Ephesians 5:9).

C. Devotional Characteristics (vv. 22c, 23)

22c, 23. faithfulness, gentleness, self-control; against such things there is no law.

The list concludes with three general characteristics that undergird all the believer's actions. *Faith-*

fulness in this context communicates a willingness to practice without fail what one believes. As God has been devoted and persistent to fulfill the promises he has made, so also his Spirit empowers us to be persistently devoted. We conduct ourselves just as faithfully as God has. We are dependably loyal to our Lord and to our fellow believers. We even dependably love our enemies.

A second general feature undergirding Spirit-filled action is *gentleness.* The gentle do not seek to assert rights or privileges. As Christ emptied himself of privilege in becoming human, so do those empowered by his Spirit (compare Ephesians 4:2).

Self-control is the ability to keep one's desires in check. This was a characteristic widely admired in Paul's time, but not widely practiced any more then than it is now. Coming at the end of Paul's list, this term reminds us that with the Spirit's many positive impulses, our desires no longer become the basis for selfish, destructive thoughts and actions (compare 2 Peter 1:5-7).

Those who exhibit the characteristics listed can be trusted to fulfill God's purpose, as expressed in his Word, in any situation. The Spirit-led require no threats of punishment. We serve God with a joyous freedom that wants nothing more than for his salvation to transform our lives.

Be a fruit inspector.

Sonkist

Visual for Lesson 13. *Point to this visual as you ask how the fruit of the Spirit relates to the need to be a fruit inspector (Matthew 7:20).*

> ### What Do You Think?
> How far along are you in each area of fruit production? How will you speed the process?
> *Talking Points for Your Discussion*
> - Areas in the germination phase: just sprouting
> - Areas maturing: taking in nutrients
> - Areas in the pollination phase: your fruit is an example to others

D. Victory in Life's Struggle (v. 24)

24. And those who belong to Christ Jesus have crucified the flesh with its passions and desires.

The fruit of the Spirit grows as the works of *the flesh* recede. That process has its decisive start at the beginning of the Christian life. Uniting with Christ in his death by faith at the time of baptism (Colossians 2:12), believers put to death the old, selfish life. What that life found attractive becomes repugnant in the new life. This does not imply instantaneous, complete victory over the old life. The struggle continues (Galatians 5:17), but Christ's victory at the cross assures our victory.

IV. Practicing the Spirit-Led Life
(GALATIANS 5:25–6:10)
A. In Community (5:25–6:6)

5:25. If we live by the Spirit, let us also keep in step with the Spirit.

The Christian follows the Spirit's empowerment and lives by the reality of the cross. To *keep in step with the Spirit* is to put into routine practice the fruit of the Spirit. It means really living what we confess to be true about God's saving grace.

26. Let us not become conceited, provoking one another, envying one another.

Being in step with the Spirit means seeking God's glory, not one's own. We encourage and support one another in this. Since Christ died for our brothers and sisters, his Spirit does not permit us to act in rivalry with them.

6:1. Brothers, if anyone is caught in any transgression, you who are spiritual should restore him in a spirit of gentleness. Keep watch on yourself, lest you too be tempted.

A genuinely spiritual person cannot have a superior attitude toward one who sins. *A spirit of gentleness* is called for instead. Spirit-led gentleness seeks what Christ sought: the restoration of the fallen, with constant awareness of one's own need for God's grace.

◆ FORGIVENESS TO RESTORATION ◆

Mary's 20-year-old son, Laramiun, was shot and killed in a fight at a party in 1993. The 16-year-old who pulled the trigger, Oshea Israel, was tried and convicted as an adult.

At the time, Mary called Oshea "an animal" that "deserved to be caged." But as a Christian, Mary finally decided that she had to forgive Oshea.

She visited him in prison, and when he was released after 17 years, she asked her landlord to invite Oshea to live next door to her. She says, "Unforgiveness is like cancer; it will eat you from the inside out." In the attempt to restore Oshea, one result was that Mary herself was restored!

We may never be called on to exercise the kind of forgiveness-to-restoration Mary demonstrated. But don't we like to think we could? —C. R. B.

2. Bear one another's burdens, and so fulfill the law of Christ.

By helping to restore one another, we are like fellow laborers who share one another's loads. Sometimes the only burden to be lifted is as simple as one of quenching thirst (Matthew 10:42). Restoring the fallen is, well, more burdensome. But Christ empowers us to do so. As we do, we join with Christ in fulfilling the purpose of the cross: forgiveness of sin.

> *What Do You Think?*
> What would a "mutual burden-bearing ministry" look like in a church? How will you help get one started?
> *Talking Points for Your Discussion*
> - In terms of establishing connections
> - In terms of developing empathy
> - In terms of cultivating openness
> - Other

3. For if anyone thinks he is something, when he is nothing, he deceives himself.

The opposite of the Spirit-led life that helps the fallen is the flesh-led life that builds up self. Pursuing personal glory denies the most essential truth of our salvation: the grace of God. In that denial we deceive no one but ourselves.

4. But let each one test his own work, and then his reason to boast will be in himself alone and not in his neighbor.

Life in the Spirit produces not self-promotion but self-testing. The cross-oriented person asks, "Does my life reflect the grace of God?" That is not a question of comparing ourselves to others. Compared with others, we realize merely that we are all sinners in need of grace. Seeing the work of grace in our lives, we rejoice in the Lord who is at work within us.

5. For each will have to bear his own load.

Paul speaks paradoxically. We bear one another's burdens, he says, when we seek to restore those fallen in sin. But others' failures or successes form no basis for one's perspective on one's own life. That question belongs only to the individual. By the Spirit's empowerment we both help one another and accept full responsibility for self.

> *What Do You Think?*
> What steps can we take to help people bear their own burdens?
> *Talking Points for Your Discussion*
> - Concerning financial issues
> - Concerning relationship issues
> - Concerning personalities that are chronically "needy"
> - Other

6. Let the one who is taught the word share all good things with the one who teaches.

In standing fully responsible before God, we do not think of ourselves as self-made people. We rely on Christ, and we rely on those who have taught us the gospel. To communicate with such a person is to share tangibly from God's good gifts with those who have shared God's greatest gift with us.

B. With Persistence (vv. 7-10)

7. Do not be deceived: God is not mocked, for whatever one sows, that will he also reap.

The Galatian Christians have already discovered how easy it is to forsake the gospel for old-life distortion when they added circumcision to faith in Jesus (Galatians 1:6-9). The same could happen again, should they again follow something rooted in the old life rather than in the grace God shows in Christ. God does not allow those who sow abandonment of grace to harvest grace. He will not allow his grace to be treated with hypocritical contempt.

8. For the one who sows to his own flesh will from the flesh reap corruption, but the one who sows to the Spirit will from the Spirit reap eternal life.

Following the old life yields a death-like result: *corruption* is the decay of death. But the life led by *the Spirit* means the opposite: *eternal life.* Christians are to persist in the good news of Christ as heard in its pure truth. Doing so will enable us to put into practice (sowing *to the Spirit*) the grace of God that makes us his people forever.

9. And let us not grow weary of doing good, for in due season we will reap, if we do not give up.

The grace-based, Spirit-empowered life is a life of constant challenge. As Christ endured the cross to bring God's grace, his people endure hardships as they live by God's grace, looking forward to the victory of God yet to come.

> ▶ **What Do You Think?**
> How do you defeat weariness personally? How can you help others do so as well?
> *Talking Points for Your Discussion*
> - In understanding the relationship between physical and spiritual weariness
> - In terms of overcoming "compassion fatigue"
> - Considering the role of the Holy Spirit
> - Other

---

10. So then, as we have opportunity, let us do good to everyone, and especially to those who are of the household of faith.

The grace-based life expresses God's grace by doing all kinds of good to all kinds of people. Our deepest kinship is with those who have received God's grace, our fellow Christians. To them we have first duty to express God's grace with our generous actions.

But we need never ask whether the call of grace stops at the doors of the church. Since Christ died for all and calls all to belong to him, then his people do good for all as well.

Conclusion
A. Grace and Power

Today's text sets forth key ideas. One is that God has a purpose for our existence. We are to be like him in his goodness, grace, and love. We find true satisfaction only when we fulfill that purpose.

A second key idea is that we fail to fulfill God's purpose when we pursue something that supplants God's grace. We too often prefer a life centered on selfishness instead of God's gracious love. Paul uses a single word to stand for this dark, universal tendency: *flesh.* By that he does not mean that our physical bodies or their desires are evil in and of themselves. Rather, he means that as a person lives by selfishness instead of God's grace, that person lives as if God were not in the picture. That person lives as if *flesh* is all that matters.

But there is an antidote to the life of the flesh: God's Holy Spirit. He empowers a person to overcome the old life that ignores God, adopting attitudes and behaviors that reflect what God has done. The Spirit's power is sure, but it requires our cooperation so that we fulfill God's purpose and reflect his grace.

Today's text gives us a huge task. But it gives us just as big a reason: the grace of God that grants eternal life by faith in Christ. And it gives us just as great a power: God's Holy Spirit, who enables us to overcome the old life to reflect God's grace.

B. Prayer

O God, may we always express your grace in who we are and what we do! We pray this in the name of the one who died for us. Amen.

C. Thought to Remember

Life in Christ is more than change of behavior.
It is a change in citizenship.

INVOLVEMENT LEARNING

Enhance your lesson presentation with the reproducible activity page,
available as a free download at www.standardlesson.com.

Into the Lesson

On the board write this infamous quote:

> *When the president does it,*
> *that means that it's not illegal.*
> —Richard Nixon to David Frost
> (April 1977 interview)

Ask, "What is meant by this statement? What was the context of the quote? Do you agree? Why or why not?"

Alternative. Distribute copies of the "Diplomatic Immunity" activity from the reproducible page, which you can download. Have students work on it in small groups.

After either activity, lead into Bible study saying, "Over the years, people in power have claimed to be above the law. In some cases, society has agreed that in order to do an important job, officials should not be required to answer to local laws. But this idea can certainly be misused.

"Today we will look at this question from a biblical perspective. As citizens of the kingdom of God, are believers somehow above the law in this world?"

Into the Word

Prepare 20 index cards on which you have written the first or second segments of the following 10 admonitions based on today's text, one segment per card: (1) "If one is led by the Spirit" / "he is not under the law"; (2) "The one who does the works of the flesh" / "will not inherit the kingdom of God"; (3) "The fruit of the Spirit is love, joy, peace, patience" / "kindness, goodness, faithfulness, gentleness, self-control"; (4) "Those who belong to Christ" / "have crucified the flesh"; (5) "If we live by the Spirit" / "let us keep in step with the Spirit"; (6) "We must not desire self-glory" / "provoking one another in envy"; (7) "If anyone is caught in a sin" / "those living in the Spirit should restore that person in a spirit of gentleness" (8) "If you bear one another's burdens" / "you will be fulfilling the law of Christ to love one another"; (9) "If a person thinks he is more than he really is" / "he is deceiving himself"; (10) "As we have opportunity, let us" / "do good to all, especially to fellow believers."

Shuffle the cards. Put these 20 cards, blank sides up, on a table. Say, "Today's text offers a challenging list of desirable attitudes and actions for the one who would follow Christ. I have on these 20 cards 10 verse ideas from today's text. Each idea is divided into two segments and on two cards. Find the matching pairs."

Have one learner turn over two cards and read them aloud. If the two cards do not complete one of the statements, they should be turned facedown again. Continue with other learners until all 10 statements are completed. At the end of the game, read the 10 statements aloud.

Into Life

The message of our lesson today is that we can choose to submit to the rule of the Holy Spirit or we can live as our own person, being ruled by our own wants.

Challenge students to look at the content of today's Bible lesson and create a pledge of allegiance to the kingdom of the Spirit. A sample pledge may read:

I pledge allegiance to the leading of the Spirit, rejecting the leading of my flesh. I choose love over lust, peace over conflict, and a life of service over a life of self-gratification.

Alternative. Distribute copies of the "Citizenship Test" activity from the reproducible page. Allow time for students to work on it in class or take it home to complete later.

GOD LOVES US

Special Features

Lessons

Unit 1: God's Eternal, Preserving, and Renewing Love

Unit 2: God's Caring, Saving, and Upholding Love

Unit 3: God's Pervasive and Sustaining Love

QUARTERLY QUIZ

Use these questions as a pretest or as a review. The answers are on page iv of This Quarter in the Word.

Lesson 1

1. The one who does not love does not know whom? (God, Paul, anyone?) *1 John 4:8*

2. John claimed to have seen God the Father personally. T/F. *1 John 4:12*

3. John affirmed that in love there is no what? (propitiation, perfection, fear?) *1 John 4:18*

Lesson 2

1. Before we became Christians, we followed "the course of this _____." *Ephesians 2:2*

2. Paul affirmed that we are saved by grace through _____. *Ephesians 2:8*

Lesson 3

1. Christ is the vine and we are the what? (root, branches, soil?) *John 15:5*

2. We abide in Christ's love if we keep his _____. *John 15:10*

Lesson 4

1. The Lord (through Joel) told people to rend their _____ to show repentance. *Joel 2:13*

2. What turns to blood before the day of the Lord? (sun, moon, stars?) *Joel 2:31*

Lesson 5

1. Even in the shadow of death, the psalmist said he would fear no _____. *Psalm 23:4*

2. God anointed the psalmist's head with what (wine, water, oil?) *Psalm 23:5*

Lesson 6

1. Nicodemus was a Sadducee. T/F. *John 3:1*

2. Jesus told Nicodemus that for people to enter the kingdom of God they had to be born of what? (pick two: water, oil, the Spirit, air, sin?) *John 3:5*

Lesson 7

1. Peter went into the tomb, but the disciple who accompanied him did not. T/F. *John 20:5-8*

2. Peter said that our faith is of greater worth than _____. *1 Peter 1:7*

Lesson 8

1. Paul affirmed that through Christ "we are more than _____." *Romans 8:37*

2. Experience teaches that only Satan can separate us from God's love. T/F. *Romans 8:38, 39*

Lesson 9

1. The one who does not enter the sheepfold by the door is a thief and a _____. *John 10:1*

2. The sheep will not follow a stranger. T/F. *John 10:5*

3. Jesus referred to himself as the _____ shepherd. *John 10:14*

Lesson 10

1. Jonah was identified as the cause of the storm at sea by the casting of lots. T/F. *Jonah 1:7*

2. Jonah told his shipmates he was fleeing from whom? (a king, the Lord, his wife?) *Jonah 1:10*

Lesson 11

1. After Jonah was swallowed by the great fish, he began to what? (pray, vomit, sleep?) *Jonah 2:1*

2. When Jonah was in the sea, what was wrapped around his head? _____ *Jonah 2:5*

Lesson 12

1. God sent Jonah to preach in the city of _____. *Jonah 3:2*

2. The king in the city where Jonah preached refused to believe his prophecies. T/F. *Jonah 3:6*

Lesson 13

1. Part of Jonah's complaint was that God was "slow to _____." *Jonah 4:2*

2. Jonah was so upset with God that he asked God to take away his what? (life, shade tree, leprosy?) *Jonah 4:3*

QUARTER AT A GLANCE

by Walter D. Zorn

I**S IT POSSIBLE** to spend too much time talking about the love of God? The inspired authors of both Old and New Testaments don't think so! This quarter offers a kaleidoscopic sampling.

Scratching the Surface

No greater truth has ever been uttered: "God is love" (1 John 4:8; lesson 1). The fact that he first loved us is what draws our love in return (v. 19). We were "dead in our trespasses" (Ephesians 2:5, lesson 2), and unless God in his love had taken the initiative to save us, we would be little more than walking dead people. Jesus, who embodied God's love, commands us to love one another as he has loved us (John 15:12, lesson 3). As a community of love abiding in Christ, we bear the fruit of love.

An important characteristic of divine love is that it keeps promises. This is demonstrated in God's promise to "pour out" his "Spirit on all flesh" (Joel 2:28, lesson 4). Promise became reality centuries later on the Day of Pentecost (Acts 2:17). Truly, we serve a God who is "gracious and merciful, slow to anger, and abounding in steadfast love" (Joel 2:13)! As profound as all this is, we're only beginning to scratch the surface on the nature of God's love.

Digging Deeper

Many of us memorized John 3:16 (lesson 6) as youngsters. Years or decades later, we can still quote its 23 words easily from memory. Even so, it continues to be difficult to comprehend its depths as it speaks of God's giving his utmost to redeem a world in rebellion against him.

God's love extends beyond our redemption. He does not redeem only to leave us to stand or fall by our own strength. We embrace this fact in the beloved Psalm 23 (lesson 5). The God who sent Jesus to purchase our salvation centuries ago is the God who comforts and provides for needs today. He is there in our fears and difficulties. We expe-rience the protecting love of God when we allow Jesus to be our shepherd (lesson 9). He cares for and protects us as a shepherd cares for and protects his sheep.

The depth of God's love is displayed magnificently in Christ's resurrection (lesson 7). The facts of Jesus' life, death, and resurrection establish that death cannot separate us from the love of God in Jesus Christ (lesson 8).

Getting Dirty

Perhaps the most difficult task for Christians is to love those we consider to be unlovable. Yet as God reached out to us through other people, we are to be his hands and feet in doing likewise. The book of Jonah offers us a fascinating contrast between the love God has for all people on the one hand and human bias on the other.

To ignore God's call is bad enough; to resist that call actively beggars description. The experiences of the prophet Jonah stand as a warning of

> **"God is love"** (1 John 4:8).

such rebellion. As the consequences of his decision to flee his call threatened the physical and spiritual lives of others (lessons 10 and 12), so may our similar decisions as well.

Sometimes it is only when we hit bottom that we come to our senses. As with Jonah, God may leave us in that rock-bottom state so we will realize our helplessness (lesson 11).

God's patience with Jonah resulted in citywide repentance in Nineveh, but that was not the end of the story. Jonah still had "anger management" problems regarding his own sense of justice and entitlement (lesson 13). There's a little bit (or a lot) of Jonah in each of us. What are we going to do about it?

GET THE SETTING

by Jim Eichenberger

A POP SONG of the 1980s asks, "What's Love Got to Do with It?" The lyrics express the singer's desire for a relationship, while at the same time revealing fear that the resulting vulnerability will lead only to pain. The question is an ancient one. Is love a flaw in the human psyche that leads only to broken hearts? Or can we experience a love that brings us closer together—not only to one another but also to God?

Greek Culture: Love Dominating

Love was personified in ancient Greece in the god Eros, the source of our word *erotic.* Love was usually thought of in sexual terms, one partner dominating the other. Marriage was for producing children, not for cultivating loving relationships. Men expressed this "eros of domination" outside of marriage. Sexual relationships with teenage boys were justified as a way for the lads to learn discipline and virtue.

Plato's Symposium (about 380 BC) records philosophers' speeches on the topic of love. Aristophanes' absurdly humorous view of the futility of love is that of a creation account in which people ended up with double bodies. When humans angered Zeus, he split them apart with a thunderbolt. Humans have searched for their other halves ever since. Socrates explored a love more transcendent in nature. While it is good to seek sexual satisfaction from a beautiful person, he proposed, men should grow into seeking wisdom in general.

Old Testament: Love Divided

In contrast with ancient pagan cultures, love as depicted in its best, godly sense in the Old Testament is not dehumanizing. Here, women are not mere vessels for childbirth and objects for sexual gratification. Rather, man and woman are incomplete without each other (Genesis 2:20b-24). Love in its ideal sense is not domineering, but seeks best for others. The Hebrew verb that indicates marital love in Genesis 24:67 is also used of proper parental love (Genesis 22:2) and the love one is to have for God (Deuteronomy 6:5). With regard to "things" to be loved, the godly love knowledge (Proverbs 12:1), God's Word (Psalm 119:97), etc.

The Old Testament is very realistic, however, in also depicting human tendency to distort the ideal. We see this where the Hebrew verb discussed above occurs in contexts where marital love is used to manipulate (Judges 14:16, 17), parental love is thinly veiled favoritism (Genesis 37:4), and love for God is redirected elsewhere (Hosea 9:1). With regard to "things," a love for "money will not be satisfied" (Ecclesiastes 5:10) and one who loves pleasure is destined for poverty (Proverbs 21:17).

That Hebrew verb is rarely used in descriptions of God's love for humankind, however. Instead, a Hebrew noun often translated "love" is found (example: 1 Kings 8:23). This kind of love assumes a hierarchy in which one in a higher position is merciful to one in a lower. The way the Old Testament uses these two major words reveals a divide between how God and humans exhibit love.

Jesus: Love Displayed

The New Testament reveals God's loving initiative (1 John 4:19). Abraham loved his son (again, Genesis 22:2), yet was willing to sacrifice him; God was willing to sacrifice his own Son as well. The expression of God's love as shepherd in Psalm 23 is fully illustrated in Jesus' selfdescription as the good shepherd who "lays down his life for the sheep" (John 10:11). The mercy of God that angered a prophet after an enemy's repentance (Jonah 4:2) is more fully understood in Jesus' sacrifice "while we were still sinners" (Romans 5:8).

"What's love got to do with it?" Everything! The ideal understanding of love that evaded the ancient Greeks and even the Israelites is now made available in the work of the mighty king of love!

THIS QUARTER IN THE WORD

Mon, May 15 — Destined to Prophesy to the Nations — Jeremiah 1:4-10
Tue, May 16 — "Return to Me," Says the Lord — Zechariah 1:1-6
Wed, May 17 — With Repentance Comes Joy — Luke 15:8-10
Thu, May 18 — Woes to the Unrepentant Communities — Matthew 11:20-24

Fri, May 19 — Proclaiming Repentance, Faith Lives — Acts 20:18b-24
Sat, May 20 — Gentiles Repent and Experience New Life — Acts 11:11-18

Sun, May 21 — Turn from Evil Ways — Jonah 3

Mon, May 22 — The Lord's Proclamation — Exodus 34:4-9
Tue, May 23 — The Lord Forgives Iniquity — Numbers 14:10b, 11, 17-20
Wed, May 24 — The Lord Did Not Forsake — Nehemiah 9:16-21
Thu, May 25 — Bless the Lord, O My Soul — Psalm 103:1-14
Fri, May 26 — A Prayer to the Lord for Help — Psalm 86:1-7
Sat, May 27 — Nations Will Bow Before the Lord — Psalm 86:8-13
Sun, May 28 — God's Compassion Endures — Jonah 4

Mon, Feb. 27 — Christ Died for Us — 1 John 3:11-17
Tue, Feb. 28 — Jesus and the Father's Love — John 14:18-24
Wed, Mar. 1 — Believe in Jesus; Love One Another — 1 John 3:18-24
Thu, Mar. 2 — The Spirit of God Confesses Jesus — 1 John 4:1-6
Fri, Mar. 3 — Loving God and Brothers and Sisters — 1 John 4:20–5:5
Sat, Mar. 4 — Thankful for God's Steadfast Love — Psalm 40:1-10
Sun, Mar. 5 — Dwelling in God's Love — 1 John 4:7-19

Mon, Mar. 6 — God Be Merciful to Us Sinners — Luke 18:9-14
Tue, Mar. 7 — Justified by Faith — Romans 3:21-31
Wed, Mar. 8 — Christ Died for Sinners — Romans 5:6-11
Thu, Mar. 9 — Raised with Christ — 1 Corinthians 15:12-25
Fri, Mar. 10 — Know the Love of Christ — Ephesians 3:14-21
Sat, Mar. 11 — Live Worthy of Your Calling — Ephesians 4:1-6
Sun, Mar. 12 — God's Overflowing Love — Ephesians 2:1-10

Mon, Mar. 13 — Restore Your Vine, O Lord — Psalm 80:8-19
Tue, Mar. 14 — Love, a New Commandment — John 13:31-35
Wed, Mar. 15 — Self-Discipline for Holy Living — 1 Peter 1:13-21
Thu, Mar. 16 — Walking in Truth and Love — 2 John 4-11
Fri, Mar. 17 — Becoming One in Christ — Ephesians 2:11-21
Sat, Mar. 18 — Abiding in God's Love — 1 John 4:16b-19
Sun, Mar. 19 — Love One Another and Bear Fruit — John 15:1-17

Answers to the Quarterly Quiz on page 226

Lesson 1—1. God. 2. false. 3. fear. Lesson 2—1. world. 2. faith. Lesson 3—1. branches. 2. commandments. Lesson 4—1. hearts. 2. moon. Lesson 5—1. evil. 2. oil. Lesson 6—1. false. 2. water, the Spirit. Lesson 7—1. false. 2. gold. Lesson 8—1. conquerors. 2. false. Lesson 9—1. robber. 2. true. 3. good. Lesson 10—1. true. 2. the Lord. Lesson 11—1. pray. 2. weeds. Lesson 12—1. Nineveh. 2. false. Lesson 13—1. anger. 2. life.

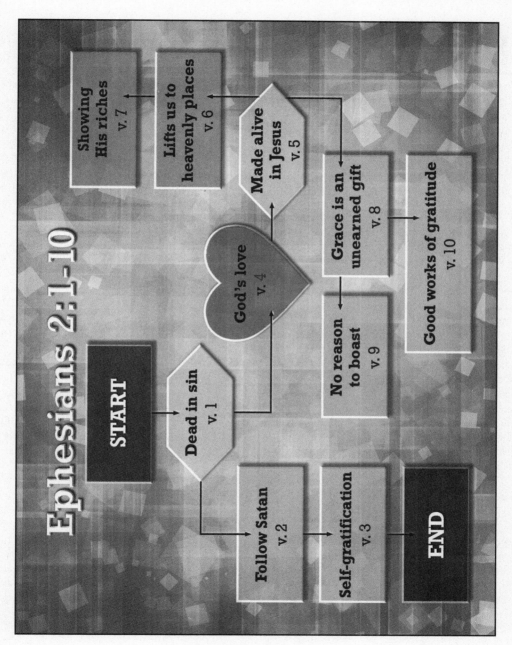

Ephesians 2:1-10

START → Dead in sin v.1

Dead in sin v.1 → Follow Satan v.2 → Self-gratification v.3 → END

Dead in sin v.1 → God's love v.4 → Made alive in Jesus v.5 → Lifts us to heavenly places v.6 → Showing His riches v.7

Made alive in Jesus v.5 → Grace is an unearned gift v.8 → No reason to boast v.9

Grace is an unearned gift v.8 → Good works of gratitude v.10

THE ALL-WOMEN CLASS

Teacher Tips by Holly Dainton

IF YOU HAD told me 20 years ago that some-day I would be teaching an all-women Sunday school class, I would have laughed out loud. But one day I found myself alone on a Sunday morning, not knowing where I fit, as my husband led worship. I tried classes for those my age, but they all consisted of couples, and I was alone. Further, many classes consisted of adults who were in phases of life that differed too much from my own. My quest to find a class (and now having taught for six years) resulted in some discoveries.

A Place to Be Known

Eventually, I and a few "fellow misfits" started a new, women-only class. We were in various walks of life—single, married, divorced, unwed mother—but all desired connection with protected vulnerability. The founding members of the class made that intention clear; it was a prerequisite for transparency with one another.

Along the way, we learned that the best classroom arrangement for achieving our goal was for class members to sit around a large table. That way each person could see all the others, which made it easier to gauge feelings as we shared. This, we discovered, was not for everyone. But as women came and went, we remained confident that God would send those who needed this format—and he did!

A Place for Authentic Relationships

We got closer as we shared. As a result, we connected with each other through common battles, experiences, and emotions. Our nonnegotiable rule to accomplish this level of authenticity was that *what was shared within the walls of our classroom stayed in the walls of our classroom.* A note about walls: our first classroom had retractable ones, and knowing we could be overheard was very inhibiting. But when we relocated to a room with solid walls, members felt safe about sharing. God shepherds his flock, and we became God's hands and feet in that regard as we shepherded one another through authentic relationships. Such relationships must have safety as their basis.

A Place for Supportive Challenge

Deep down, women have in common the need for supportive challenge. Iron sharpening iron (Proverbs 27:17) isn't comfortable, but a supportive environment makes the difficult easier! The women in our class support one another through hospital and bedside visitation, cooking and delivering meals, assisting with yard work, transporting each other's children, and cleaning and painting each other's houses.

We have prayed together, laughed and cried together, and dreamed together. There have been times of admonishment along the way as well. But given the climate God has created among us, godly confrontation is received more readily than it would be otherwise. It is through such mutual sharing that we become the church in action (Acts 2:42-47).

Bible study is an integral part of supportive challenge. As both teacher and fellow learner, I use a lot of open-ended questions to encourage discussion. I make sure that the lesson material is in the hands of every class member. The ultimate goal is always for each woman to make a practical application of biblical principles studied.

Conclusion: Common Ground

I mentioned at the outset my discouragement at not finding a class where members' phases of life were similar to my own. But women of all ages can find common ground in the model I suggest here. If you want to have a successful women's Sunday school class, then don't merely focus on having a good curriculum. Provide a place and a way for participants to be known, to have authentic relationships, and to be supportively challenged. If God is in it, they will come!

PERFECT LOVE

DEVOTIONAL READING: Psalm 40:1-10
BACKGROUND SCRIPTURE: 1 John 4:7-19

1 JOHN 4:7-19

7 Beloved, let us love one another, for love is from God, and whoever loves has been born of God and knows God. 8 Anyone who does not love does not know God, because God is love. 9 In this the love of God was made manifest among us, that God sent his only Son into the world, so that we might live through him. 10 In this is love, not that we have loved God but that he loved us and sent his Son to be the propitiation for our sins. 11 Beloved, if God so loved us, we also ought to love one another. 12 No one has ever seen God; if we love one another, God abides in us and his love is perfected in us.

13 By this we know that we abide in him and he in us, because he has given us of his Spirit.

14 And we have seen and testify that the Father has sent his Son to be the Savior of the world. 15 Whoever confesses that Jesus is the Son of God, God abides in him, and he in God. 16 So we have come to know and to believe the love that God has for us. God is love, and whoever abides in love abides in God, and God abides in him. 17 By this is love perfected with us, so that we may have confidence for the day of judgment, because as he is so also are we in this world. 18 There is no fear in love, but perfect love casts out fear. For fear has to do with punishment, and whoever fears has not been perfected in love. 19 We love because he first loved us.

KEY VERSE

Beloved, if God so loved us, we also ought to love one another. —**1 John 4:11**

GOD LOVES US

Unit 1: God's Eternal, Preserving, and Renewing Love

LESSONS 1–4

LESSON AIMS

After participating in this lesson, each learner will be able to:

1. Tell why the author (John) is known as "the apostle of love."

2. Explain why the fact that God is love does not exclude his also being wrathful.

3. Make a plan to participate in a ministry of his or her church that shows God's love in tangible ways.

LESSON OUTLINE

Introduction

A. First Love

Is there such a thing as mutual "love at first sight"? Psychologists debate the idea. Fans of romance endorse it. Filmmakers often employ the possibility as a plot device. Some happily married couples affirm it was true for them.

But relationships don't usually work this way. Far more common is for one person to be attracted to another and thereby begin a courtship to convince the other. One person loves first; the other person comes to love later.

In today's lesson, John uses this sequencing of love, but he is not writing about the romantic love that men and women have for each other. Rather, he is explaining our relationship with our loving God. He expresses this with one of the Bible's classic verses, "We love because he first loved us" (1 John 4:19).

We do not need to attract God's attention and convince him to love us. He has loved us from the start. God knows us before we are born (Psalm 139:13-16). That fact is more astonishing than even "love at first sight"!

B. Lesson Background

The three letters we call 1, 2, and 3 John name no author, but tradition attributes them to the apostle John. As he wrote those letters sometime after AD 90, he likely was the last of Jesus' original 12 disciples still living.

At some point, John relocated from the setting of his account of Jesus (the Gospel of John), which was mainly Judea and Jerusalem. Tradition tells us that he went to Ephesus, a large, prosperous city in the western part of what is now Turkey. John became involved in the daily lives of the Christians in the area. We might say he "ministered in the trenches" where people struggled to live.

Rivals in this arena contradicted the teachings of John despite his credentials. Experienced ministers know there will be factions within a church, and some will oppose them for various reasons. The reasons for such opposition may be valid or concocted, but the opposition is real. It can sometimes grow into outright animosity and divisiveness.

John's letters give evidence of such antagonism (3 John 9). Some of this was surely caused by false teachers whom John denounced (2 John 10), but there seems to have been other reasons too. Perhaps the aged apostle was seen as out of touch by other leaders who wanted to take the churches in new directions (note that the six churches of Revelation 2:8–3:22 are all within 120 miles of Ephesus and its church that is addressed in 2:1-7). Responding to such impatience is an underlying tone in 1 John, for the author repeatedly returns to the unchanging, ever loving, and always faithful God as the model for relationships within the church.

One caution: John likes to use absolute statements that may seem at odds at first glance. He can say both "God is light" (1 John 1:5) and "God is love" (4:8, 16) without logical contradiction. This is a technique of his writing, and we should realize that his absolute statements about people will sometimes present us with polar opposites for effect. John, being very experienced at ministry, knew that there are shades of gray when it comes to people—their mixed motives, inconsistencies, etc. We will see John's use of the absolute style in today's lesson.

I. Goal
(1 John 4:7-12)
A. Source of Love (vv. 7, 8)

7a. Beloved, let us love one another, for love is from God,

Beloved, used several times in this letter, is a favorite expression of affection of John for his readers. What follows affirms that the church is the fellowship of the beloved—people who recognize and accept God's love for them as they act in love for *one another.* This is John's heart on display. The apostle, who has decades of ministry experience, knows that the mutual love he and his readers share has God as its ultimate source.

HOW TO SAY IT

Ephesians	Ee-*fee*-zhunz.
Ephesus	*Ef*-uh-sus.
Judea	Joo-*dee*-uh.

7b. and whoever loves has been born of God and knows God.

This is one of John's absolute statements, so we should read with care. At first glance it may seem to say that *whoever* on earth demonstrates love has a personal relationship with the Lord, that loving behavior is proof that a person *knows God.* But we all have known people who demonstrate love toward others and yet have no relationship with God at all.

Instead, it's the other way around: all who have *been born of God* (that is, Christian believers) are to demonstrate the love of God in their lives and relationships. The further point is that a lack of love among those who claim to be Christian indicates that their relationship with the Lord is not what it should be.

> **What Do You Think?**
> How can we demonstrate to unbelievers the difference between the love shown by God and that shown by the world? Why should we?
> *Talking Points for Your Discussion*
> - With regard to motive
> - With regard to degree
> - With regard to limitations
> - With regard to recipients
> - With regard to methods

8. Anyone who does not love does not know God, because God is love.

John has sometimes been called "the apostle of love," because of his frequent use of that word and concept in his writings. Indeed, some form of the word *love* occurs about two dozen times in today's lesson text alone! But the churches in and around Ephesus seem to be lacking in love. John knows that love cannot be commanded, but it can be expected. His tone is not "I order you to love your brothers and sisters in Christ or else!" but rather "Why do you not love your fellow Christians?" This is a call for self-examination. To fail to be loving is to exclude God from one's life, *because God is love.*

Other religions speak of love and the love of God. For example, Islam speaks of God's mercy. But other religions would not agree with a state-

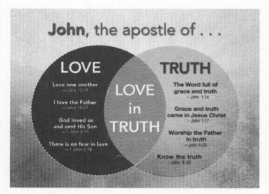

John, the apostle of . . .

LOVE

Love one another
—John 13:34

I love the Father
—John 14:31

God loved us
and sent His Son
—1 John 4:10

There is no fear in love
—1 John 4:18

LOVE
in
TRUTH

TRUTH

The Word full of
grace and truth
—John 1:14

Grace and truth
came in Jesus Christ
—John 1:17

Worship the Father
in truth
—John 4:23

Know the truth
—John 8:32

Visual for Lesson 1. *Start a discussion by point-*
ing to this visual as you ask, "What happens to
churches that get these two out of balance?"

ment as bold as *God is love* (also in v. 16). This
is not merely "God is loving" or "God is capable
of showing love." And especially, it is not "love is
God." John presents a doctrinal truth that there
is something essential and fundamental about the
nature of God that cannot fully be explained. God
did not learn how to love. God does not adopt love
as a practical good. God does not merely choose
to love. God *is* love! The implications of that statement should make our heads spin and our hearts
skip beats!

◆ *VISIBLE LOVE* ◆

Because of work-related relocations, our family has experienced many seasons of "church
shopping." But even when we made correct doctrine our main criterion, we sometimes ended up
in churches where biblical interpretations challenged those that we held. We have changed our
thinking due to some teachings, yet we have held
tightly to our understanding whenever we discovered an interpretive approach to the Bible to be
deficient. We grew in both cases because we con-
sulted God's Word to determine whether what we
held to be true matched his record of truth.

Today, we still seek sound doctrine when we
need to find a new church family due to relocation. But we have added two more criteria. One
considers how those of a particular church speak
the name *Jesus.* Do they speak of him as they
would of, say, Abraham Lincoln—as if discussing

any "good" historical figure? Or does the way they
say his name reflect the deep awe of love?

The other thing I look for is grace from those
who serve up front during worship. Do the folks
with the microphone speak about the love of God,
yet also express disdain for other people or, in particular, various Christian organizations? If so, it's
a red flag.

A stress on knowledge (correct doctrine) is a
good thing, but so is an emphasis on love. And
the two are related! Notice how the author connects doctrinal knowledge ("we know that") with
love in 1 John 3:14; 5:2.   —V. E.

> *What Do You Think?*
> What guardrails can we erect to ensure that we
> do not fail to show the love Christ desires?
> *Talking Points for Your Discussion*
> - At work or school
> - At home
> - When gathered with other Christians
> - Other

B. Demonstrator of Love (vv. 9, 10)

9. In this the love of God was made mani-
fest among us, that God sent his only Son into
the world, so that we might live through him.

We might imagine John's opponents asking
the questions skeptics ask today: "How do I know
that God loves me? What about all the pain in my
life?" Perhaps John's opponents try to explain the
apparent mismatch of continued suffering and the
doctrine of a loving God by teaching that claims
about God's loving nature are irrelevant.

We deduce from the letter that the false teachers are saying that the way to salvation is through
something other than faith in a God who loves.
They do not teach that Jesus came to die for our
sins, but to impart secret knowledge. What matters, they say, is being given secrets and insights
that allow membership in a fellowship of spiritual elites.

John's response is to pull the reader back to the
fact of history we see in the verse before us. How
do we know God loves us? Because he *sent his only*
Son on a mission to save the world (John 3:16).

John draws a direct connection between Jesus' life and God's love.

10. In this is love, not that we have loved God but that he loved us and sent his Son to be the propitiation for our sins.

John teaches, though, that it is not merely the life of Jesus, but his death that makes the difference. God did not send his Son just to teach us. He sent his Son to die for us, the great demonstration of God's eternal love (see Romans 5:8).

This was not God's response to people's overtures of love. God was not obligated to humanity because people loved him dearly. To the contrary, humans repeatedly demonstrate hostility to God by sin, becoming his enemies (Romans 5:10).

John describes the intervention of Jesus as being *the propitiation for our sins*. The word *propitiation* means "an offering that turns away wrath." That's how Christ's death takes care of our sins. The God of love is also "a consuming fire" (Hebrews 12:29). Jesus' willing death satisfied sin's penalty (see Romans 3:25, 26; 1 John 1:7; 2:2). What greater love could there be?

◆ *God's Anguish, and Ours* ◆

Sociologist Brené Brown shares about a crisis her community experienced when she was a child. A family in her neighborhood suffered the death of their toddler in a tragic in-home accident. Brown recalls that a speaker at the church memorial service for the child said those gathered shouldn't grieve—that it was a time to celebrate, because this child was with God.

Brown became furious. But when she experienced a personal crisis as an adult, she returned to church. She said she went back for the wrong reasons, hoping for something like an epidural to take away life's pain. But what she found instead was more like a midwife—someone who sits beside you through the pain.

We live with the question of how God can be love yet be in control of a world so wracked with pain. The answer has several elements; one is to realize that God himself is not unfamiliar with pain. His justice requires punishment for sin, punishment that his Son paid on the cross. In Jesus, we see God willingly entering this world

of pain to rescue us. We see yet more of the love of God when we realize that he stays with us and holds us through our grief. Jesus weeps with us, and that is what we are to do with each other (Romans 12:15). Love changes everything.

—V. E.

C. Perfecter of Love (vv. 11, 12)

11. Beloved, if God so loved us, we also ought to love one another.

John moves next to the application of this great truth about the love of God. When we become fully aware of the depth and magnitude of God's unmerited love for us, how can we fail to love our brothers and sisters in Christ?

Relationships among church members can be awkward. We all do stupid or silly things, and memories can be long. When we are unsure how to relate to each other, may we remember to lead with love. Don't fake love while harboring hate. Don't withhold your love to those you feel don't love you. Lead with love and you will be acting in a godly manner.

> *What Do You Think?*
> What are some ways to reflect to others the love that God shows to us?
> *Talking Points for Your Discussion*
> - To those sharing our faith and values
> - To those ambivalent to our faith and values
> - To those opposed to our faith and values

12. No one has ever seen God; if we love one another, God abides in us and his love is perfected in us.

Since *no one has ever seen God* (compare Exodus 33:20), how can people be sure he exists? There is more than one way to answer this, and the one John offers here is that when we lead with love, we embody a characteristic of God to others in a tangible, visible manner. People experience the loving presence of God when believers act in love.

A good goal is to turn the conditional *if we love* into a concrete *when we love*. As we do, we prove God's presence in our lives. On the idea of love's being perfected, see 1 John 2:5 and (below) 4:17, 18.

II. Results
(1 JOHN 4:13-19)
A. Gift (v. 13)

13. By this we know that we abide in him and he in us, because he has given us of his Spirit.

If we have doubts *that we abide in* God *and he in us*, John provides the certainty: we know we are truly in fellowship with God because of the presence *of his Spirit*. This gift comes from God himself. We don't knock on the door of God's heart and ask to be let in; rather, it's the other way around (see Revelation 3:20). One implication of this fact is that loving others is not solely a matter of our determination and strength. God's indwelling Spirit assists us in leading with love.

B. Testimony (v. 14)

14. And we have seen and testify that the Father has sent his Son to be the Savior of the world.

John and the other apostles saw God's Son in the flesh (1 John 1:1). Jesus is the focus of God's love, the expression of God's love to us. God proves his love to us by sending *his Son* to save the world (John 3:16). We prove our love to God by believing John's testimony and by replicating God's love to others.

C. Refuge (vv. 15, 16)

15, 16. Whoever confesses that Jesus is the Son of God, God abides in him, and he in God. So we have come to know and to believe the love that God has for us. God is love, and whoever abides in love abides in God, and God abides in him.

John now ties three things together: (1) our confessed belief *that Jesus is the Son of God*, (2) the mutual dwelling of God in us (through his Spirit) and we in God (through our faith), and (3) the uniting factor of *love*. To say *God is love* is not an abstract concept. It is the basis for our lives.

How do we get to know God better, to have a closer relationship with him? There may be more than one answer to this, but John is teaching here that our relationship with God grows deeper when we love others. Teresa of Calcutta, the tireless ser-

vant of the poor, said of the children she served, "Each one of them is Jesus in disguise." This outlook reflects Matthew 25:31-46, discussed below.

> *What Do You Think?*
> How can our church demonstrate love more effectively as a witness that Jesus is the Son of God?
> *Talking Points for Your Discussion*
> - With actions seen primarily by fellow believers
> - With actions seen primarily by unbelievers

D. Fearlessness (vv. 17, 18)

17a. By this is love perfected with us so that we may have confidence for the day of judgment,

John now gives a standard whereby we can test the validity of our faith: our fear of judgment from God (or lack of it). If we are living out the love of God, we will be bold on God's *day of judgment*. We have a confidence that comes from knowing we are loving like God. We will be bold rather than fearful, because we know our judgment will be positive.

John certainly remembers that Jesus gave his disciples a picture of final judgment that must have surprised them. Jesus taught that judgment would not be based on keeping the commandments of the law, but on loving actions that reveal faith in Christ (see Matthew 25:31-46). The Judgment Day questions "Did you love?" will trump "Did you keep my law?" although the two are interrelated (Matthew 22:36-40). If we do not love, we certainly should fear judgment, for it is coming and it is sure.

> *What Do You Think?*
> How do we evangelize those who have no fear of judgment but should?
> *Talking Points for Your Discussion*
> - Responding to statements that begin "Surely a loving God would not . . ."
> - Considering the role of our loving acts
> - Grappling with emotionally driven beliefs
> - Other

17b. because as he is so also are we in this world.

Jesus understood that he was sent to save a world that did not accept him (John 1:10, 11). We ourselves are only temporary citizens in this hostile world. As Peter wrote, we are "sojourners and exiles" (1 Peter 2:11) in a world that does not understand unselfish Christian love.

18. There is no fear in love, but perfect love casts out fear. For fear has to do with punishment, and whoever fears has not been perfected in love.

At this point in the line of thought, John does not see the opposite of *love* as hate, but *fear* (contrast 1 John 4:20). This resonates with us as we consider how often we fail to do the loving thing because we are afraid. How often do we look back on an encounter when we hesitated for fear of rejection or ridicule and see that an opportunity to show love was lost? True love is fearless. We do not fear God's judgment and we do not fear rejection of others if we are full of love. Love overcomes fear. The answer to fear in relationships is love.

As we contemplate this, we realize that we will always have some fear in our relationships in this life. We see here another one of John's absolute statements: *there is no fear in love*. We should not expect to be *perfect* in this life, but that's no reason to lower the standard. We are to move closer to that goal all the time (Matthew 5:48). Heaven will be a place of perfection, and that certainly means, among other things, there will be no more fear.

E. Love (v. 19)

19. We love because he first loved us.

John ends this section with a marvelously succinct summary. Love has a source for us. That source is God. We ourselves seem to be programmed for selfishness. True love begins with

VISUALS FOR THESE LESSONS

God. Our understanding of what love is depends on our understanding of God. When we understand the gospel story, the account of how God loved us so much that he gave his Son to save us, then we begin to fathom the true nature of love. Knowing God means knowing love. Loving God means loving others.

Conclusion
A. Hard Love

Some people are hard to love. A woman in a church where I ministered (I'll call her Diane) was consistently mean to my family and me. I do not know why. She said unnecessarily critical things about my wife. She spread untrue rumors about me. She never had a good word to say about my sermons, only condescending complaints.

Whenever I offered a kindness to her, Diane responded with suspicion. Any soft words said to her were rejected. She was hard to love. I wish I could say that eventually I wore down Diane with my love and we became friends, but that never happened. Yet I can say that I never returned her meanness with meanness of my own. While I tired of her behavior, I did not fear or hate her.

I think that God must feel that way toward us sometimes. We are hard to love. We are selfish. We are unfaithful. We act out of fear. Yet he still loves us. His love is never failing, perfect, and inexhaustible. May we not resist God's love, and instead, may we follow his example.

B. Prayer

Holy God, you are ever loving, but at times we are the opposite. We are selfish, bitter, jealous, petty. We are many things that would never be called "love." Teach us to be like you in loving others. Help us love even those friends and family who are very difficult to love. Make us more like you, the source and the goal of all our love. We pray this in the name of the greatest expression of your love, your Son, Jesus Christ. Amen.

C. Thought to Remember

Let God's love for you be
an endless source of your love for others.

INVOLVEMENT LEARNING

*Enhance your lesson presentation with the reproducible activity page,
available as a free download at www.standardlesson.com.*

Into the Lesson

Start class by dividing students into two groups for a mini debate. Say, "The proposition for the debate is: Two people often fall in love at first sight." *Group 1* will develop an argument for the proposition; *Group 2* will develop an argument against the proposition.

Allow each group a minute to present its argument, and then give each group 30 seconds to rebut the opposing group's argument.

Alternative. Distribute copies of the "Key Word" activity from the reproducible page, which you can download. Probably no learner will be familiar with every song title listed, but all will recognize that *love* is the word that is missing from each of the song titles. Briefly discuss what some of these titles say about love.

After either activity, lead into the Bible study, saying, "Everyone wants to be loved. People have very different opinions about love. But what is real love? How can we love others? What are the results of having real love in one's life? The apostle John addressed these questions in today's Bible text."

Into the Word

Draw a Venn diagram of three intersecting circles on the board. Label circles in this way:

We can KNOW what love is (1 John 4:7-10).

We can SHOW love to the world (vv. 11-15).

We can GROW in love (vv. 16-19).

In the intersection of all three circles write "*JESUS.*"

Divide the class into three groups, assign each group one of the three circles of the diagram. Have groups read their assigned text, summarize how the text supports the statement in their por-

tion of the diagram, and show how Jesus is key in fulfilling that statement.

After small-group discussion, ask a speaker from each group to share his or her group's findings.

Group 1—We can KNOW what love is—Love does not come from our nature, but comes from God. We can love by being reborn of God. This happens when we accept the ultimate demonstration of love—Jesus' dying to pay for our sins!

Group 2—We can SHOW love to the world—Though the world cannot see God, it can see us and how we love each other! We testify that we can love more completely because Jesus, God's Son, lives in us and empowers us through the Spirit.

Group 3—We can GROW in love—As our confidence grows in God's love, we can rely on that love. The more we love others in this world, the more we reflect Jesus' love for the world. Like Jesus, we give our lives away without fear, trusting God will grant us eternal life.

Into Life

Draw these three scales on the board:

< —————————————————— >
Selfish   Selfless

< —————————————————— >
In the world   In him

< —————————————————— >
Fearful   Fearless

Allow time for learners to evaluate themselves on each of these scales. Then have them gather with one or two other classmates to share their evaluations and to pray for one another.

Alternative. Distribute copies of the "Justice and Mercy" activity from the reproducible page. Have students work individually or in small groups to read the verses cited in this activity.

GREAT
LOVE

DEVOTIONAL READING: Ephesians 4:1-6
BACKGROUND SCRIPTURE: Ephesians 2:1-10

EPHESIANS 2:1-10

[1] And you were dead in the trespasses and sins [2] in which you once walked, following the course of this world, following the prince of the power of the air, the spirit that is now at work in the sons of disobedience— [3] among whom we all once lived in the passions of our flesh, carrying out the desires of the body and the mind, and were by nature children of wrath, like the rest of mankind. [4] But God, being rich in mercy, because of the great love with which he loved us, [5] even when we were dead in our trespasses, made us alive together with Christ—by grace you have been saved— [6] and raised us up with him and seated us with him in the heavenly places in Christ Jesus, [7] so that in the coming ages he might show the immeasurable riches of his grace in kindness toward us in Christ Jesus. [8] For by grace you have been saved through faith. And this is not your own doing; it is the gift of God, [9] not a result of works, so that no one may boast. [10] For we are his workmanship, created in Christ Jesus for good works, which God prepared beforehand, that we should walk in them.

KEY VERSE

Even when we were dead in our trespasses, [God] made us alive together with Christ—by grace you have been saved. —**Ephesians 2:5**

GOD LOVES US

Unit 1: God's Eternal, Preserving, and Renewing Love

LESSONS 1–4

LESSON AIMS

After participating in this lesson, each learner will be able to:

1. Summarize the basis of salvation.
2. Contrast salvation by works with salvation by grace.
3. Write a prayer of gratitude for the salvation available through grace.

LESSON OUTLINE

Introduction

A. Saving Ourselves

Some years ago, my father and I had a disagreement that was almost fatal. We were traveling together in a borrowed car across a high mountain pass in the dead of winter. It was a bright, blustery day, but the temperature was well below freezing, and there was lots of snow on the ground. Unbeknownst to us, the car we were driving had a defective fuel gauge, and we ran out of gas. There was no cell phone coverage in this remote place. We both knew we were in trouble, for the next town with services was miles away.

My father knew that the state patrol made regular rounds on this highway, so we would eventually be spotted, but I was impatient. After about 30 minutes, I decided to walk to a service station. My father protested, advising that I would freeze to death before I reached help, but I stubbornly refused to listen.

I had walked about 50 yards when I felt him bear-hug me from behind. When I turned and saw the look of panic in his eyes, I was persuaded to return to the car. Soon a truck driver with gas stopped, shared it, and followed us to the gas station. As we drove, I realized it was farther than I had thought. I doubt I would have made it.

People like me seem to be programmed to think we can always save ourselves, that we can fight our way out of any problems, that we don't need help. How foolish we are! When this is applied to our relationship with God, the foolishness is magnified manyfold. We are doomed to destruction if we seek to save ourselves. But God has made a way we can be saved from eternal destruction—a way that does not depend on our own efforts. Today's lesson looks at one of the great texts of the New Testament in that regard.

B. Lesson Background

Paul's letter to the Ephesians is considered one of his "prison epistles," because he speaks of physical confinement as he writes (see Ephesians 3:1; 4:1; 6:20). He does not mention the location of his imprisonment, but Rome is likely. This would be the house arrest situation where we find Paul at the end of Acts, awaiting his hearing before the Roman emperor (see Acts 28:16), and therefore dates the letter to about AD 63.

Ephesus in Paul's day was a commercial hub and a Roman government administrative center, one of the largest cities. It was (in)famous for its massive temple to the Greek goddess Artemis, known as Diana to the Romans. This temple was one of the so-called Seven Wonders of the Ancient World (see Acts 19:27). Ephesus had a synagogue where Paul preached successfully for a time (Acts 19:8-10). Paul's ministry in Ephesus was one of his longest (19:10; 20:31).

Jews of the day had a long history of despising Gentiles. But this fact didn't seem to be nearly the problem in Ephesus that it was in other places regarding church unity. Even so, Paul took care to show that Christ had removed any necessary division between Jew and Gentile, resulting in a single body of the people of God (see Ephesians 2:12-18; 3:6; 4:3-6). Salvation for neither Jew nor Gentile was earned through keeping the Jewish law, but found in the grace of God.

In Ephesians 1:15-23, which precedes today's text, Paul celebrated the implications of the resurrection of Christ. He reminded readers that the raising of Christ from the dead was a display of great power (1:19, 20) and that the risen Christ reigned in Heaven with his Father. Following that, he shifted the focus to the letter's readers.

I. Past Life: Living Death

(EPHESIANS 2:1-3)

A. Suicidal Sin (v. 1)

1. And you were dead in the trespasses and sins

With the opening *and you*, Paul moves from God's display of power in Christ to the results for humanity. As the dead Christ was brought back

HOW TO SAY IT

Artemis	*Ar*-teh-miss.
Ephesians	Ee-*fee*-zhunz.
Ephesus	*Ef*-uh-sus.
Gentiles	*Jen*-tiles.

to life by God, God has also given us a resurrection from death.

The immediate result of this transaction is not immunity to physical death (such death is overcome later; see 1 Corinthians 15). Rather, the new life at issue in the passage before us is spiritual in nature. Spiritual death is a consequence of our *trespasses and sins.*

Only here and in Romans 5:20, 21 (as "trespass" and "sin") do the Greek nouns behind this phrase occur in such proximity to one another. It's as if Paul is making sure the Ephesians don't miss the point: we are guilty of rebellion against God, deserving of death; therefore, we are without life spiritually (see Romans 6:23).

We may not want to admit it, but we are committing spiritual suicide when we sin. Those having been made alive in Christ should entertain no longing for that previous state.

> *What Do You Think?*
> What are some practical, specific ways for a Christian to demonstrate life in Christ?
> *Talking Points for Your Discussion*
> - In terms of doing, saying, and/or thinking what was not done, said, and/or thought before
> - In terms of not doing, saying, and/or thinking what was done, thought, and/or said before

B. Devilish Disobedience (v. 2)

2. in which you once walked, following the course of this world, following the prince of the power of the air, the spirit that is now at work in the sons of disobedience—

Before Christ became their love, Paul's readers may have believed themselves to be free. But such was not the case. Before Christ they actually were in bondage to three closely related influences.

First, they had been *following the course of this world.* That means they had chosen to act as if God's standards for living were not valid. Today we still hear voices that call us to selfish sin, to moral failure and dishonesty. The world wants to direct us by its standards. If we let it, we are neither free nor godly.

Paul connects this with serving *the prince of the power of the air.* Paul and his readers are acutely aware of the evil influences that attack them. The phrase *of the air* does not refer to a specific location, but to the spiritual nature of this evil. The letter to the Ephesians addresses this reality more than any other writing of Paul.

Even so, Paul is confident that Jesus has authority (and therefore victory) over all the spiritual forces that are in rebellion against God (see Ephesians 1:21). But this is an ongoing battle (see 6:12). *The prince* of these spiritual forces of evil is unnamed here, but identified as the devil later (6:11, 12). The spiritual beings who are in rebellion against God are not our friends, but seek to destroy us and keep us far from fellowship with the Lord. This leads to Paul's third element.

C. Rebellious Children (v. 3)

3a. among whom we all once lived in the passions of our flesh, carrying out the desires of the body and the mind,

The third element that promotes sin lies within us. *We all* (Paul includes himself) had been driven *once* by personal *passions of our flesh.* Paul clarifies by indicating that such behavior includes both *the body and the mind.* If one's body indicates that something feels good, the person may do it despite moral consequences. If one's mind wanders far from what is pure and holy, the person may excuse himself or herself by claiming privacy of thought life. As with the influences of the world and the devil, those mired in sinful desires think themselves to be in control, but they are not. They are slaves to passion and lust.

3b. and were by nature children of wrath, like the rest of mankind.

Paul's summary of that former life includes the fact that he and his readers had been *like the rest of mankind.* This refers to all who do not yield control of their lives to Christ. The characterization of unbelievers as being *by nature children of wrath* is quite striking, the phrase being seen as a landmark in the New Testament (compare Ephesians 5:6). What does Paul mean by this?

First, we should note that the phrase *the rest* is inclusive. It is not just pagan Gentiles who deserve

God's wrath. Jews outside of Christ do not get a pass. Without Christ, they too are children of wrath.

Second, Paul's use of the word *nature* indicates something fundamental about us. As a result of our inherent tendency to sin, "None is righteous, no, not one" (Romans 3:10). We need not debate the possibility of living a perfect life, thereby earning our salvation. It does not happen. It will not happen. Pride, part of "all that is in the world" (1 John 2:16), keeps us from admitting that we deserve God's wrath. Such was our former life: infatuated by the sinful world, beset by temptations from the evil one, and controlled by out-of-control passion for the forbidden fruits desired by body and mind.

> *What Do You Think?*
> How can we discuss God's wrath in such a way as to get a fair hearing?
> *Talking Points for Your Discussion*
> - With fellow believers, who accept the authority of the Bible
> - With unbelievers, who do not accept the authority of the Bible

II. Future Life: Exceeding Riches
(Ephesians 2:4-7)
A. Lavish Love (vv. 4, 5)

4. But God, being rich in mercy, because of the great love with which he loved us,

Having characterized one's pre-Christian past as consisting of infatuation with worldly influences, devil-driven disobedience, and indulgence in sinful passions, Paul now moves the discussion to his readers' future life. This shift is signaled by movement from the "and you" of verse 1 to the *but God* of the verse before us.

Any hope for us must begin with God's *mercy* and *love.* Even while deserving God's wrath, people still bear his image and likeness (Genesis 1:26, 27). God has gone to great effort to save his lost image-bearers (Luke 19:10; etc.).

Paul is given to large statements when it comes to the nature of God. We see a great example in the description here of God's attribute of being *rich in mercy*. This may bring to mind an image of wealth such as a pile of gold coins. God is an ultrabillionaire when it comes to mercy and compassion (compare Romans 2:4; also Ephesians 2:7 [below]).

Paul expands on this imagery by describing God's mercy as *the great love with which he loved us*. This may seem repetitive in English, but what is redundant to us is emphatic for Paul. He seems barely able to contain his excitement! God spends his inexhaustible supply of "golden mercy coins" on us freely and lovingly. "His steadfast love endures forever" is the repeated refrain of Psalms 118 and 136.

5. even when we were dead in our trespasses, made us alive together with Christ—by grace you have been saved—

Life before Christ was one of being *dead in our trespasses*. But as Christ has been raised from death to resurrected life, so too are we *made . . . alive* (also Colossians 2:13). We, the former children of wrath, have been given a new life, the children receiving God's great love.

The "afterthought" appearance of the statement *by grace you have been saved* may lead us to believe that this affirmation is somehow secondary to the thought at hand. But what is mentioned so briefly here serves two purposes: (1) it anticipates a fuller explanation of salvation by grace a bit later and (2) it helps paint the fuller picture of God's attitude toward his wayward children as his *grace* is considered alongside his mercy and love.

Since Paul had spent so much time with the believers in Ephesus, we can easily imagine that they hear his voice in the statement *by grace you have been saved*. Doubtless it is something he told them many times in person. This is a most fundamental thing. How salvation by grace is possible is summed up in this easily remembered acronym: Grace is **G**od's **r**iches **a**t **C**hrist's **e**xpense.

B. Prime Seats (v. 6)

6. and raised us up with him and seated us with him in the heavenly places in Christ Jesus,

Our spiritual resurrection from the death of sin is followed by an ascension. Christ ascended to

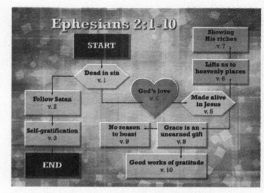

Visual for Lesson 2. *Use this chart as a "you are here" directory for today's lesson by pointing to it occasionally as you work through the text.*

Heaven after his resurrection (see Luke 24:50, 51; Acts 1:1-9; etc.), and following our resurrection from spiritual death we are positioned *in Christ Jesus* in *the heavenly places* (compare Colossians 3:1-3). Believers are even pictured on thrones in Revelation 20:4. Having front-row seats in the glorious light of the presence of Christ and his victories means we no longer fear the spiritual darkness.

◆ THE BEST SEAT ◆

Vertically challenged. Shorter than the average pygmy. Squatty body.

As one reaching the five-foot-nothin' mark on the measuring stick, I have heard all the jokes and jabs about short people.

Living at this "lower elevation" has its challenges, and if there is one thing I've learned over the years, it's the need to get a good seat. The experience of attending a performance or event is greatly diminished for me whenever I end up in a bad seat because I arrive late or pay less. Many times I have not been able to see the very thing I traveled to see.

An astonishing revelation in today's Scripture is the fact that we each have the best possible seat right now: in the heavenly realms! In Christ, the view is unobstructed, and we are spiritually able to see things from God's point of view. Now the question is, what are we going to do with this front-row seat?
—V. E.

C. Giant Grace (v. 7)

7. so that in the coming ages he might show the immeasurable riches of his grace in kindness toward us in Christ Jesus.

Paul gives an eternal reason for God's rescue of sinners from spiritual death: that we might serve as a demonstration of his marvelous grace forever. The era that begins with salvation through faith in Christ is not an intermediate stage in God's plan. Rather, it is for all time, a plan for *the coming ages*. Again, Paul pictures God's grace as inexhaustible wealth (*immeasurable riches*). To this is added the element of God's *kindness*, a word that implies essential goodness (compare Romans 2:4). *His grace in kindness toward us* is not God's response to anything meritorious we have done; rather, it is an offer that should draw a response from us.

III. Current Life: Saving Faith
(Ephesians 2:8-10)
A. God's Gift (v. 8)

8a. For by grace you have been saved through faith.

The concept of being saved *by grace*, introduced in verse 5, is now explored in greater depth. Salvation by grace expects and requires a response. The salvation God offers is of no effect unless accepted *through faith* on the part of the one who is dead in sins. Faith is often defined as "assent plus trust." In other words, assent is accepting the gospel facts as true. Trust, on the other hand, is surrendering control of one's life to Jesus on the basis of who he is and what he has done (John 3:16; Acts 10:43; 16:31; 1 Timothy 1:16).

8b. And this is not your own doing; it is the gift of God,

Paul wants to be sure his readers understand that there is something they have no right to take credit for. That "something" is signaled by the words *this* and *it*, which point back to verse 8a.

Here's where a technical issue of the original Greek must be considered, an issue that is not apparent in our English translation. Every Greek noun and pronoun has a grammatical gender: either masculine, feminine, or neuter. So the gender of one or both pronouns *this* and *it* in verse 8b must match the gender of one or both nouns *grace* and *faith* in verse 8a to determine the antecedent.

But there is no match. The nouns are both feminine, while the pronoun *this* is neuter. The pronoun *it* does not actually exist in the Greek text; it has been supplied in English for smooth reading.

We conclude, then, that verse 8b is not referring to any one particular element of verse 8a, but to God's system of salvation as a whole. Salvation is a *gift*; it cannot be earned. We are not partners with God in bringing salvation. We are recipients of this rich *gift of God*.

B. Excluded Bragging (v. 9)

9. not as a result of works, so that no one may boast.

If salvation resulted from our own efforts, we could be justifiably proud. Paul knows well the danger here. Before he met Christ, Paul's seemingly spotless life was a source of pride to him, evidence of his moral superiority (see Philippians 3:4-6).

But there are no *works*, no actions we can take, that make us worthy of being self-excused from our sins. The best of us still have lapses and failures; we still yield to self-centeredness and gratification of lusts. We have no room for boasting, only for humility.

C. Intended Purpose (v. 10)

10. For we are his workmanship, created in Christ Jesus for good works, which God prepared beforehand, that we should walk in them.

In the spiritual world of righteousness, then, there is no such thing as a self-made woman or man. Our spiritual resurrection is God's *workmanship.* To use another biblical image, he is the potter and we are the clay (Jeremiah 18:6).

Our new life has purpose, and this is part of God's design. We have been rescued from spiritual destruction so that we might be instruments of *good works.* Yet we must realize that living the life that pleases God is not how we are saved. Good works are not a condition of salvation; they are the result.

> *What Do You Think?*
> How do we identify the good works that God wants us to do right now?
> *Talking Points for Your Discussion*
> - In light of personal desires
> - In light of spiritual giftedness
> - In light of needs around us
> - Other

◆ *What I Get* ◆

Our young speaker said it—those words often heard from ministers and missionaries who share testimonies about God's work: "Of course, all the glory goes to God."

The Holy Spirit must have started working in me at that moment, for I was being very honest with myself as I thought *I want some glory, some credit for some of the things I do.* My mind lit on an accomplishment I was particularly pleased about. *Ha!* I thought. *I did that!*

Then it hit me: my success had come about through various circumstances that I did not control. There was my own contribution to be sure, but the skills I brought into play were given to me through God's design. He was the one who had set me up to succeed. The speaker was right—all the glory rightfully goes to God. Taking credit or glory for oneself is dangerous (compare Daniel 4:28-33; Acts 12:21-23).

But what do I get? I still wondered. At that moment a beautiful image came to mind that answered my question. I pictured the loving Father looking directly into my eyes with pleasure as in Matthew 25:21. I realized I was not equipped to handle glory. But in the end I will be lavished with something far more precious: the pleasure in his eyes.
　　　　　　　　　　　　　　　　　—V. E.

Conclusion

A. Living with Purpose

Having interacted with Bible college students for over 30 years, I often find them questioning their purpose in life. In counseling, we discuss life's big questions: *Who am I? Why am I here? What should I do?* All of these are wrapped up in purpose. Here are the Bible's answers:

Who am I? You are a beloved child of God who has disobeyed him through your sin. Yet you are now saved from the consequence of sin and from spiritual death by God's grace.

Why am I here? You are not an accident of genetics. You are created by God to serve him and glorify his name.

What should I do? Having made peace with God through Jesus, you are ready to give your life back to him in service and love.

Sin causes us to be spiritually dead. God's merciful grace gives us spiritual life in order that we might properly serve him in good works. If we submit to his will, he will use us in mighty ways, and our purpose in life will be clear. Is yours?

B. Prayer

God of grace and life, we are humbled when we realize that our part in our salvation is to accept it. We are amazed when we stop and contemplate your great love for us. We are excited when we anticipate your plans for us, both as instruments of your grace to others in this life and as participants in your glories in the future. In Christ's powerful name we pray all this. Amen.

C. Thought to Remember

Don't try to work for what God has already accomplished in Christ.

INVOLVEMENT LEARNING

*Enhance your lesson presentation with the reproducible activity page,
available as a free download at www.standardlesson.com.*

Into the Lesson

Before class, write on the board a list of things you can earn and things you can't (examples: paycheck, vacation, sunset, groceries, birthday presents, trust, forgiveness, dessert, an elected position, a job, family, friends, punishment). When learners arrive say, "Which items from this list are things you can earn?" Allow volunteers to make a case for why you can or can't earn the listed items. Circle "earnable" things as you go.

Alternative. Distribute copies of the "Big Change" activity from the reproducible page, which you can download. Have students work individually or in pairs.

After either activity, lead into the Bible study by saying, "We are familiar with working to earn something and with receiving an unearned gift. False religions teach that a god's favor must be earned by one's works. The Bible teaches that the one true God operates much differently! Let's look at that difference and the difference it makes."

Into the Word

Before class, write these words and phrases on separate index cards (without the verse references): Dead (v. 1). Disobedient (v. 2). Sinful Desires (v. 3). Alive by Love (vv. 4, 5). Front Row Seats (v. 6). Riches of Grace (v. 7). Unearned Salvation (v. 8). Nothing to Brag About (v. 9). Given Important Jobs (v. 10).

Say, "At the time Paul wrote this letter, there was a divide in the church of Ephesus between the law-abiding Jewish people and the Gentiles who'd come to follow Christ but hadn't grown up with the law. Paul, however, communicated that sin affected everyone, just as salvation was available to everyone—that no one was more worthy of God's grace than any other. Let's see what Paul has to say about both sin and salvation."

Arrange these three headings on the board in an outline style:

I. Valueless (Ephesians 2:1-3). II. Valued (Ephesians 2:4-7). III. Value Added (Ephesians 2:8-10).

Distribute your nine index cards to students. Have someone read today's Bible text one verse at a time. If a person holding a card believes that his or her card fits that verse, have the student come forward and attach the card under one of the three headings on the board with reusable adhesive. Continue, commenting as necessary when a card is placed, until the nine index cards have been placed on the board.

Into Life

Different religions propose different views of salvation. Read the following summaries of salvation, one at a time. Have the class respond to these ideas by referring to the main points of today's Bible lesson.

Universalism: The doctrine that all sinful and alienated human souls—because of divine love and mercy—will ultimately be reconciled to God.

Deism: Human nature is essentially good, and salvation is within reach of every person through faith and good works.

Hinduism: This world is unreal. The goal of a human being is to escape this world and become one with Brahman. This happens through enlightenment gained by ritual, study, meditation, and/or good works.

Alternative. Distribute copies of the "Heaven Bound?" activity from the reproducible page. Say, "Think of ways you would respond to each person giving a view of salvation on that page."

Close the session after either activity by challenging students to compare their own hopes of salvation to the Bible lesson. Do they think someone can be good enough without Jesus? Do they see good works as a way to make God love them?

MATCHLESS LOVE

DEVOTIONAL READING: 1 John 4:16b-21
BACKGROUND SCRIPTURE: John 15:1-17

JOHN 15:1-17

¹ "I am the true vine, and my Father is the vinedresser. ² Every branch in me that does not bear fruit he takes away, and every branch that does bear fruit he prunes, that it may bear more fruit. ³ Already you are clean because of the word that I have spoken to you. ⁴ Abide in me, and I in you. As the branch cannot bear fruit by itself, unless it abides in the vine, neither can you, unless you abide in me. ⁵ I am the vine; you are the branches. Whoever abides in me and I in him, he it is that bears much fruit, for apart from me you can do nothing. ⁶ If anyone does not abide in me he is thrown away like a branch and withers; and the branches are gathered, thrown into the fire, and burned. ⁷ If you abide in me, and my words abide in you, ask whatever you wish, and it will be done for you. ⁸ By this my Father is glorified, that you bear much fruit and so prove to be my disciples. ⁹ As the Father has loved me, so have I loved you. Abide in my love. ¹⁰ If you keep my commandments, you will abide in my love, just as I have kept my Father's commandments and abide in his love. ¹¹ These things I have spoken to you, that my joy may be in you, and that your joy may be full.

¹² "This is my commandment, that you love one another as I have loved you. ¹³ Greater love has no one than this, that someone lay down his life for his friends. ¹⁴ You are my friends if you do what I command you. ¹⁵ No longer do I call you servants, for the servant does not know what his master is doing; but I have called you friends, for all that I have heard from my Father I have made known to you. ¹⁶ You did not choose me, but I chose you and appointed you that you should go and bear fruit and that your fruit should abide, so that whatever you ask the Father in my name, he may give it to you. ¹⁷ These things I command you, so that you will love one another.

KEY VERSE

This is my commandment, that you love one another as I have loved you. —**John 15:12**

GOD LOVES US

Unit 1: God's Eternal, Preserving, and Renewing Love

LESSONS 1–4

LESSON AIMS

After participating in this lesson, each learner will be able to:

1. Identify the vine, the branches, and the fruit.

2. Explain how the Christian is able to bear "much fruit."

3. Make a list of God's "pruning" that often occurs in a Christian's life.

LESSON OUTLINE

Introduction

A. Thinning the Peaches

My brother used to work in a peach orchard. There, he and his fellow workers would climb ladders to remove enough tiny peaches so that the remaining ones were spaced every eight inches or so on the branch. This time-consuming task would eliminate more than half the peaches on some trees!

The rationale for this practice recognizes that a peach tree has access to a limited amount of nutrients. If the peaches are not thinned out, they will end up small and hard. If thinned, however, the peaches that remain will be robust and profitable.

Today's lesson involves an illustration of a different fruit-bearing flora: the grapevine. Orchard and vineyard are similar in at least one way: as peach trees need to have their produce thinned, grapevines need to be pruned in order to produce optimal fruit. But the pruning of which Jesus spoke has a different basis, as we shall see.

B. Lesson Background

The vineyard was a staple of agriculture in the ancient world. The fruit thereby produced became a source of sustenance year round, with many of the harvested grapes being converted into raisins and wine for later consumption (compare 2 Samuel 16:1). One of the enticing descriptions of the promised land was its productive vineyards (Deuteronomy 6:10, 11; 8:7-10). Indeed, a physical sign brought back by the ill-fated spying expedition into the promised land was a massive cluster of grapes (Numbers 13:23).

Vineyards were a common sight throughout Galilee, Samaria, and Judea in Jesus' day. Besides today's text, he also used vineyard imagery in his parables of the workers in the vineyard (Matthew 20:1-16), the two sons (21:28-32), the wicked tenants (21:33-39), and the barren fig tree (Luke 13:6-9). Some students consider today's text also to be a parable, but it's better thought of as an illustrative comparison or an extended metaphor without a plot. Everything depends on the definition of *parable*. Common experiences regarding vineyards are also assumed in 1 Corinthians 9:7.

Grapevines would be pruned severely at a certain time of the year, leaving little more than a leafless, branchless stump that would be propped up with a rock or two. All the old branches would be cut off and carried away, providing valuable fuel for home fires.

After new branches had grown, a second pruning would occur to remove the smaller branches. This allowed the larger branches to produce bigger clusters of larger grapes. Such pruning was part of the process known as cultivating the vines (Deuteronomy 28:39).

I. The True Vine
(JOHN 15:1-7)

Today's lesson is from a section in the Gospel of John known as the farewell discourses or the upper room discourses (John 13–17). These consist of Jesus' teachings on the night before his crucifixion as he spent time with his disciples. It was a time of solemn Passover observance with friends; the result was a rich deposit of Jesus' teachings that is invaluable for our spiritual health today.

Mark 14:15 and Luke 22:12 are the sources of the designation "upper room." Most of Jesus' teaching in this location is found only in John's Gospel.

A. Branches Bearing Fruit (vv. 1-3)
1a. "I am the true vine,

Jesus uses imagery of a vineyard as a familiar context for the vital teaching he is offering. From the outset, there is no doubt regarding whom the imagery represents. In referring to himself as *the true vine*, Jesus affirms that he is the one chosen by God for the task set forth in John 3:16.

God's covenant people of the Old Testament era are also pictured as a vine or vineyard (exam-

ples: Psalm 80:8; Isaiah 5:1, 2; Jeremiah 2:21). The Israelites failed to live up to the covenant, however (see Isaiah 5:7; Hosea 10:1). Therefore a new vine, one that is the ultimate true vine, is needed—Jesus.

1b. "and my Father is the vinedresser.

The second phrase at the beginning of this illustration is equally clear regarding identification. The word translated *vinedresser* is a general word for "farmer" (as in 2 Timothy 2:6; James 5:7). As such, it is not narrowly focused on someone who tends only vineyards. Yet the task of a vineyard worker can certainly be part of a farmer's capabilities.

2, 3. "Every branch in me that does not bear fruit he takes away, and every branch that does bear fruit he prunes, that it may bear more fruit. Already you are clean because of the word I have spoken to you.

The identification that should be obvious in these two verses will be explicitly clear in verse 5 (below): Jesus' disciples are the branches in this illustration. Lifeless branches need to be removed from the vine to allow for new growth. Regarding the disposition of unproductive branches that *he takes away*, see verse 6 (below).

The fruit-bearing branches are the new ones, budding off the vine in later spring. A bit later, these new branches will themselves receive the gardener's attention so they might be in the best possible state to produce robust fruit.

The action *he prunes* has the specific intent and result of the disciples' being *clean*. This is true of the 11 disciples who remain at this Passover celebration, the one "unclean" disciple already having departed (John 13:10, 11, 21-30). In the original language, the word behind the translation *prunes* is the verb form of the noun translated *clean*. The figurative pruning hook is *the word* of Jesus' teachings.

As vines are prepared for the final part of the growing season by a second pruning, so Jesus' disciples are prepared for their future ministry after he leaves them (John 16:5). This preparation will strengthen them to persist when persecution comes (16:1-4). Unlike the opening illustration in this lesson regarding peach trees, the pruning of which Jesus speaks is not because

HOW TO SAY IT

Canaan	*Kay*-nun.
Deuteronomy	Due-ter-*ahn*-uh-me.
Galilee	*Gal*-uh-lee.
Judea	Joo-*dee*-uh.
Samaria	Suh-*mare*-ee-uh.

the vines have access only to a limited amount of nutrients. God's resources are unlimited! The danger, rather, lies in worldly distractions and hindrances to the disciples' mission (compare Matthew 13:22). Another kind of distraction may be ministry opportunities that are valid in and of themselves, but siphon time away from a disciple's calling (example: Acts 6:2).

◆ NOW OR LATER? ◆

I once met a man who loved to grow pumpkins. The pumpkins he grew were BIG, weighing hundreds of pounds each. Two such pumpkins would fill the bed of a pickup truck!

His secret was to pull off every blossom on the pumpkin vine except the one at the end. He did this successfully year after year. You might say that his success resulted from having clean vines.

Jesus' disciples were clean because of what he had taught them. This fact should cause us to put ourselves in the spotlight of God's Word to reveal the deadwood in our own lives, deadwood that impedes our service to him. Which is better: to cut away the deadwood now at our own initiative or to wait until God does it himself?   —J. B. N.

> **What Do You Think?**
> How do you know whether a season of personal distress or retrenchment is to be interpreted as God's pruning?
> *Talking Points for Your Discussion*
> - Considering positive fruit-imagery in Scripture (Matthew 3:8; Romans 7:4; Galatians 5:22, 23; Ephesians 5:9; etc.)
> - Considering negative fruit-imagery in Scripture (Luke 13:6-9; Romans 7:5; Galatians 5:19-21; Ephesians 5:11; Jude 12; etc.)

B. Believers Abiding in Jesus (vv. 4-7)

4, 5. "Abide in me, and I in you. As the branch cannot bear fruit by itself, unless it abides in the vine, neither can you, unless you abide in me. I am the vine; you are the branches. Whoever abides in me and I in him, he it is that bears much fruit, for apart from me you can do nothing.

To *abide* can imply clinging to someone or something (compare John 8:31). In the context of the vine analogy, a branch that abides is one that is still attached to the main trunk of the vine.

Such is the relationship between Jesus (the main vine) and his disciples (the branches). When there is a strong, living connection, each disciple *bears much fruit*. Detached branches are not capable of producing fruit.

Jesus does not pause to define the fruit of the Spirit; the apostle Paul will do so in Galatians 5:22, 23. Rather, Jesus seems intent on keeping the disciples focused on the vital importance of remaining with him. What Jesus has to say in this regard applies not only to those gathered with him in the upper room, but to all Christians.

6. "If anyone does not abide in me he is thrown away like a branch and withers; and the branches are gathered, thrown into the fire, and burned.

If a branch is detached (*thrown away*) for any reason, it immediately begins to die. Its leaves wither. Any fruit that happens to be on it begins to rot (compare Matthew 7:15-20). Unless there is hope of being grafted back in (Romans 11:17-24), detached branches are used for fuel (compare Ezekiel 15).

Note that the act of detaching by "the vinedresser" (vv. 1, 2, above) happens because of a disciple's failure to *abide* in Christ. To withdraw from the Lord is to make oneself fit only for *the fire* of judgment and destruction (see Luke 3:8, 9).

> **What Do You Think?**
> What are signs a person is about to "get burned" in this life because he or she is not attached to the true vine?
> *Talking Points for Your Discussion*
> - Regarding causes/results of "burnout"
> - Regarding causes/results of "burning bridges"
> - Regarding causes/results of "burning with passion"

7. "If you abide in me, and my words abide in you, ask whatever you wish, and it will be done for you.

This verse clarifies how Jesus lives in us: it is due to the fact that his *words abide in* our hearts and minds. We have listened to his teachings and are following them.

This is a two-way relationship, however. For just as branches do not produce fruit without nutrients from the vine, so Jesus does not expect fruit from his disciples without his help. This he promises to give when asked (compare Mark 11:24; John 14:13; 16:23). The fact that his words abide in us helps ensure that we will pray in ways that are pointed toward producing fruit. When we do so, our thoughts will be aligned with the intentions of the one who will answer prayer: God.

II. The True Friend
(JOHN 15:8-17)

Verse 8 marks a transition as Jesus leaves the vineyard analogy behind in order to speak of the dynamics of friendship and love.

A. Disciples Glorifying God (vv. 8-11)

8. "By this my Father is glorified, that you bear much fruit and so prove to be my disciples.

The fruit-producing life of a sincere disciple brings glory to the Father (compare Matthew 5:16). For God to be *glorified* means that he is honored appropriately.

9, 10. "As the Father has loved me, so have I loved you. Abide in my love. If you keep my commandments, you will abide in my love, just as I have kept my Father's commandments and abide in his love.

The Father's love for his Son, Jesus, is a marvel to consider (see John 3:35; 10:17); it is eternal, existing "before the foundation of the world" (17:24). Also a marvel to consider is the fact that Jesus compares this eternal love of *the Father* for him with his (Jesus') love for the disciples!

An important distinction between the two loving relationships is that the first is unconditional while the second is conditional. The condition is clear: *If you keep my commandments, you will abide in my love.* The disciples should follow Jesus' example. As he has shown love for the Father by keeping the *Father's commandments,* so too the disciples can show their love for Jesus by keeping his *commandments* (John 14:15; 1 John 2:5; 5:3).

11. "These things I have spoken to you, that my joy may be in you, and that your joy may be full.

The time in the upper room—a time of confusion and uncertainty (John 13:22, 36, 37; 14:5, 22; 16:18)—is soon to give way to a time of great sorrow. That sorrow will result from the traumatic events of Jesus' arrest, trials, torture, crucifixion, and death, which are but a few hours away. But on the other side of this great sorrow will be *joy* (compare 16:22). Jesus promises joy that is *full* and complete (also 17:13). With our advantage of 20/20 hindsight today, how can it be otherwise?

> *What Do You Think?*
> What should others see in us that indicates the fullness of our joy in the Lord?
> *Talking Points for Your Discussion*
> - In times of want (Habakkuk 3:17, 18; 2 Corinthians 8:1-5; etc.)
> - In times of persecution (Acts 5:41; 1 Peter 1:3-9; etc.)
> - In times of blessing (Deuteronomy 16:15; Matthew 5:11, 12; etc.)
> - Other

B. Servants Becoming Friends (vv. 12-15)

12. "This is my commandment, that you love one another as I have loved you.

Jesus has just stressed the importance of keeping his commandments, but he does not state specifics such as what, when, where, etc. He has given the disciples no list like the Ten Commandments, no manual of discipline, no employee handbook. The reason why is clearer now in the fact that Jesus has in mind one central *commandment,* that they *love one another.* This is the "new commandment" Jesus introduced earlier in the evening (John 13:34).

John, the author of this Gospel, never forgets this imperative. He surely preaches it continually as the decades roll by, because he eventually refers to it as not new; it is one he has had "from the beginning" (1 John 3:11, 23; 2 John 5).

The disciples do not pick the type or intensity of the love they are to exhibit; those are established by Jesus as he teaches that their mutual love is to be on the order of how he has loved them.

13. "Greater love has no one than this, that someone lay down his life for his friends.

The significance of the qualifier "as I have loved you" in verse 12 is intensified yet cloaked by the prophetic word we see here. This is foreshadowing, a hint of what lies ahead (compare John 10:15). The greatest gift Jesus grants his friends is eternal life. That comes about through Jesus' death on the cross, which becomes reality in just a few hours from when Jesus speaks. What is cloaked in the upper room will remain so until understanding comes (Luke 9:44, 45; 24:25; John 20:9; etc.).

◆ *LAY DOWN YOUR TIME?* ◆

Years ago, a friend proposed that that we demonstrate John 15:13 love when we invest our time in others. That seems to minimize Jesus' intent or even miss it altogether. As valuable as spending time with others can be, doing so doesn't match the severity of the text's "lay down his life."

Jesus was emphasizing the need to love as he loves us. He demonstrated at the cross what he meant. The self-sacrifice on behalf of sinners of one who had no sin is the greatest example of love that can be imagined! The spirit and attitude of such willingness is what Jesus asks us to emulate. See 1 John 3:16.   —J. B. N.

> *What Do You Think?*
> What are some ways to emulate Jesus' self-sacrificial spirit?
> *Talking Points for Your Discussion*
> ▪ When among fellow believers
> ▪ When among unbelievers

14, 15. "You are my friends if you do what I command you. No longer do I call you servants, for the servant does not know what his master is doing; but I have called you friends, for all that I have heard from my Father I have made known to you.

A result of obeying Jesus' directive to love one another is that the disciples have a new status:

they are no longer called Jesus' *servants* but his *friends*. The word translated *servant* refers to a slave. The one-sided nature of the slave-master relationship is seen in Jesus' statement *the servant does not know what his master is doing*. The master never feels obligated to discuss his dealings with his slave.

In Jewish culture of Jesus' day, a disciple's status parallels that of a servant: "A disciple is not above his teacher, nor a servant above his master" (Matthew 10:24). But now Jesus frees his disciples from this model. The proof of their new status is Jesus' statement *all that I have heard from my Father I have made known to you*. Those gathered with Jesus in the upper room are, and will continue to be, privileged to have more information about God's plans than any believer prior to that time (John 14:26; 16:12-15; 1 Peter 1:10-12).

C. Jesus Charging Workers (vv. 16, 17)

16a. "You did not choose me, but I chose you and appointed you

The fact that Jesus has chosen those now gathered with him in the upper room (rather than the reverse) is documented in Matthew 4:18-22; Mark 1:16-20; 3:13-16; Luke 5:1-11; 6:13-16; John 1:35-51; 6:70. *Appointed* means Jesus has placed them in positions of authority, power, and purpose. The Gospels reveal the extraordinary nature of the authority and power Jesus grants his apostles (see Matthew 16:19; Luke 9:1; 10:19; John 20:23). They play a unique role in the founding of the church (Ephesians 2:19, 20; Revelation 21:14).

16b. "that you should go and bear fruit and that your fruit should abide,

Jesus qualifies his "bear much fruit" desire from verse 8, saying the fruit *should abide* (a form of the word *remain*). Believers exhibiting fruit of the Spirit produce enduring fruit in the form of new disciples. Evangelism becomes the primary fruit-bearing task (see Matthew 28:19, 20).

16c. "so that whatever you ask the Father in my name, he may give it to you.

We are considering verse 16 in three segments for convenience, but this third part must not be divorced from the other two in application. It is important that we understand that the *whatever* does not mean that Jesus is promising that any and all prayer requests will be granted. The larger context is that of fruit-bearing, and the construction of verse 16c is linked to that.

The wording and context of John 14:13, 14 are similar: Jesus' promise to do "whatever you ask" is tied to his statements regarding "the works" he has been doing and prophecy of the "greater works" to be manifested by "whoever believes in" him (14:12). The greater results to be achieved by Jesus' followers point to the expansion of Christianity, as growth in the number of converts accelerates after Jesus' ascension.

But what about all the other prayer concerns we may have? The author of this Gospel notes in one of his letters that "if we ask anything according to his will he hears us" (1 John 5:14). The power behind prayer is also noted in the statement "the prayer of faith will save the one who is sick, and the Lord will raise him up" (James 5:15). We like to claim this power, but all Christians have experiences when earnest, specific prayers are not answered in the way desired. We should never give up on prayer (Luke 18:1-8), but if our faith is based on an absolute reading of John 15:16 for us personally, we are in a danger zone.

> *What Do You Think?*
> How do we ensure that "in Jesus' name" is
>   more than words merely tacked on ritually to
>   the end of our prayers?
> *Talking Points for Your Discussion*
> - Cautions to be drawn from Exodus 20:7
> - Cautions to be drawn from Matthew 6:9
> - Cautions to be drawn from Acts 19:13-16
> - Cautions to be drawn from James 5:14, 15
> - Other

17. "These things I command you, so that you will love one another."

Yet again Jesus stresses the imperative to *love one another* (see John 13:34, 35; 15:12). To what extent should we take this? How far does this go? Remember that Jesus defined the greatest love for others as a willingness to die for them (John 15:13). This is a high standard, and frankly, we have a long way to go!

Visual for Lesson 3. *Start a discussion by pointing to this visual as you ask, "How does the theme you see here reflect today's lesson?"*

Conclusion
A. Limits on Love?

A common theme in advice about relationships is the need to set boundaries. Ministers, for whom demands on their time seem endless, are advised to learn how to say "no." Having been to Burn-out Land more than once in my four decades of ministry, I realize the dangers of overwork. But a friend recently advised me to learn how to say "yes." Find ways to help; don't be quick to limit your willingness to lend a hand.

This will work only if motivated by love. We must not serve others out of obligation or expectation, but out of love. This is particularly difficult for ministers who feel they are being paid to serve the members. In such cases, ministry becomes something like paying a plumber to fix a leaking pipe. But when love becomes our motive in serving, we may notice others following our example. Their love-motivated service will make our own burden of service lighter.

B. Prayer

Heavenly Father, may we produce fruit for you, fruit that is lasting, as we spread the message of your Son to the unbelieving world. We pray this in the name of the true vine, Jesus. Amen.

C. Thought to Remember
Love one another!

INVOLVEMENT LEARNING

Enhance your lesson presentation with the reproducible activity page,
available as a free download at www.standardlesson.com.

Into the Lesson

Say, "It will soon be time for backyard gardeners to begin preparing the soil." Start a discussion on gardening. Ask who is planning to have a garden, what they plan to raise, and talk about how much better homegrown vegetables taste. Have some of the home gardeners share some tips for producing the best garden favorites.

Alternative. Distribute copies of the "So You Think You Can Plant!" activity from the reproducible page, which you can download. Have students work in groups or use this as a whole-class activity.

After either activity, lead into the Bible study by saying, "Gardening is not only a great hobby, but it also puts some of our favorite foods on our tables! Grapes were an important crop in Israel. This made a gardening analogy a memorable way for Jesus to frame some final instructions for his disciples. Today we will look at this important lesson."

Into the Word

Say, "Jesus was teaching with metaphors in this passage. He spoke of familiar elements of his disciples' lives in order to illustrate more abstract truths." Read the lesson text aloud, and help the class understand what each item represents in Jesus' analogy: the vine (the part of the plant that remains from season to season), the vinedresser, the branches (the seasonal shoots and leaves growing from the vine each season), the harvest of grapes, the pruning, and the abiding in (remaining attached to) the vine.

Divide your class into three groups. Give each group paper and pen. Each group should be assigned a section of the lesson text. Each group should try to rewrite their text *without* using metaphor—that is, in plain, straightforward language. Assignments and our sample rewrites follow.

Group 1—Wise Vinedresser (vv. 1-3)

God wants the church to be faithful to him and make more faithful disciples. He will not allow empty piety or immorality to remain in the church for long. Doing so would only harm his people.

Group 2—Sturdy Vine and Fruitful Branches (vv. 4-8)

Every generation of disciples stays faithful to the church by being connected with the living Jesus. Ignoring Jesus' teaching and example will only cause unfaithful followers to be ineffective and useless.

Group 3—Plentiful Harvest (vv. 9-17)

A life connected to Jesus and to his church is the best possible life! It is a life of joy, love, and understanding that will draw more and more people to Jesus.

Allow time for the groups to share their summaries with the rest of the class.

Into Life

Say, "Pruning is not just a severing of the relationship between Christ and unfruitful disciples; it is also done to purge or cleanse those who do bear fruit. Therefore, we can expect some pruning in our lives."

Ask learners to make a list of events that they believe to be acts of pruning in their lives. These can be general or specific. For example, one might say, "God can use illness as pruning" (general), or "I believe God used my cancer diagnosis last year to call me back to what's really important" (specific).

Ask for volunteers to share from their list. (Be sure there is no pressure to share personal information; any such sharing ought to be purely voluntary.) Discuss the significance of these events. What is the proper response to such cleansing?

Alternative. Distribute copies of the "Rules of Gardening" activity from the reproducible page. Have students draw principles for spiritual growth from one or more of these rules.

Close either activity with prayer that each student can be a fruitful branch in God's vineyard.

RESTORING LOVE

DEVOTIONAL READING: 2 Peter 3:1-10
BACKGROUND SCRIPTURE: Joel 2

JOEL 2:12, 13, 18, 19, 28-32

12 "Yet even now," declares the LORD,
    "return to me with all your heart,
with fasting, with weeping, and with
        mourning;
13   and rend your hearts and not your
        garments."
Return to the LORD your God,
    for he is gracious and merciful,
slow to anger, and abounding in steadfast
        love;
    and he relents over disaster.

. . . .

18 Then the LORD became jealous for his land
        and had pity on his people.
19 The LORD answered and said to his people,
    "Behold, I am sending to you
        grain, wine, and oil,
        and you will be satisfied;
    and I will no more make you
        a reproach among the nations.

. . . .

28 "And it shall come to pass afterward,
    that I will pour out my Spirit on all
        flesh;

your sons and your daughters shall
        prophesy,
    your old men shall dream dreams,
    and your young men shall see visions.
29 Even on the male and female servants
    in those days I will pour out my Spirit.

30 "And I will show wonders in the heavens
and on the earth, blood and fire and columns
of smoke. 31 The sun shall be turned to darkness, and the moon to blood, before the great
and awesome day of the LORD comes. 32 And
it shall come to pass that everyone who calls
on the name of the LORD shall be saved. For
in Mount Zion and in Jerusalem there shall be
those who escape, as the LORD has said, and
among the survivors shall be those whom the
LORD calls.

KEY VERSE

*"Rend your heart, and not your garments." Return to the LORD your God, for he is gracious and merciful,
slow to anger, and abounding in steadfast love; and he relents over disaster.* —**Joel 2:13**

GOD LOVES US

Unit 1: God's Eternal, Preserving, and Renewing Love

LESSONS 1–4

LESSON AIMS

After participating in this lesson, each learner will be able to:

1. Identify the two places where portions of the lesson text are quoted in the New Testament.

2. Explain the difference between false repentance and true repentance.

3. Identify modern ways that people rend garments rather than hearts, and make a plan to avoid this hypocrisy.

LESSON OUTLINE

Introduction

A. Culture of Defiant Unrepentance

Deal with it. This seems to be the cry of many public figures whose lives fall far short of biblical standards. Caught committing adultery? Misusing public funds? Plagiarizing material? Just hire a public relations "spin doctor" to justify or explain away the behavior!

Moral and ethical failures happen so often that we are no longer shocked or even surprised. If anything does surprise us, it's a forthright admission of guilt that is accompanied by genuine repentance. Instead, we have come to expect excuses, finger pointing, etc. We live in a culture that is increasingly indifferent to accountability for misdeeds; it is a culture of defiant unrepentance. We are dismissed as "being judgmental" when we voice expectations for accountability and consequences. Culture wants us just to *deal with it.*

We see such an outlook in ancient times as well. But when people thought they could live above accountability, the Old Testament prophets responded to brazen sin in a most judgmental way: *repent or die!* The judgment of wrongdoing and consequences was not that of the human prophet, however; it was the judgment of Almighty God.

But how does God distinguish true repentance from false? The prophet Joel had God's answer to that question.

B. Lesson Background

The last 12 of the Old Testament's 39 books are known collectively as the Minor Prophets. The book of Joel is one of these. The word *minor* refers to the lengths of these books, not to their contents. The importance of the latter is seen in the 30 quotations from them that appear in the New Testament. The book of Joel is one of the eight Minor Prophets so quoted.

The name Joel means "the Lord is God." We don't know much about this man or when the book was written. Traditionally, the book is dated as early as 837 BC, making Joel a contemporary of King Joash (2 Chronicles 24). Joel's references to enemies are identified more readily with an earlier historical context (see Joel 3:4). Another viewpoint proposes a date several centuries later, partially because of reference to "Greeks" in Joel 3:6. The theory is that Joel would not have mentioned the Greek people until they had become internationally prominent.

The backdrop for the book is a cataclysmic locust infestation that had descended on Jerusalem and the surrounding area (see Joel 1:2-4). Locusts are voracious, grasshopper-like insects that multiply rapidly and swarm. The descent of a swarm on a small area may result in utter destruction of crops, trees, and other vegetation (1:7, 10). Such devastation could lead to famine, with starvation taking a great toll on both humans and animals. God used locusts as instruments of divine judgment on occasion (examples: Exodus 10:3-15; Psalms 78:46; 105:34; compare Revelation 9:3, 4).

For his part, the prophet Joel connected his horrific description of the locust plague by declaring the nearness of "the day of the Lord" (Joel 1:15; 2:1) and this challenge: "The day of the Lord is great and very awesome; who can endure it?" (2:11). The question was a warning with an obvious answer: no one can withstand that day. It is futile to resist the judgmental wrath of God. But there was another option.

I. Repentance
(Joel 2:12, 13)
A. Turning to the Lord (v. 12)
12. "Yet even now," declares the Lord,
   "return to me with all your heart,
   with fasting, with weeping, and with
   mourning;

The alternative to experiencing the judgment of "the day of the Lord" (Joel 2:11) is repentance. Repentance involves turning away from sin while turning back to *the Lord*.

But words and actions of repentance must match (compare Jeremiah 12:2), so the prophet goes on to list three characteristics of genuine repentance. *Fasting* is self-denial that indicates spiritual submission. *Weeping* indicates distress; it is a natural companion of *mourning*, a sign of profound grief (compare Esther 4:3). These are the basics of repentance for people reorienting their lives from sin to God.

> *What Do You Think?*
>   What should be the when, where, why, and how of fasting for Christians?
> *Talking Points for Your Discussion*
>   - Considering positive biblical examples (Matthew 6:17, 18; Acts 13:2, 3; 14:23; etc.)
>   - Considering negative biblical examples (Zechariah 7:5, 6; Matthew 6:16; Luke 18:12; etc.)

B. Tearing the Heart (v. 13)
13a. "and rend your hearts and not your
   garments."
   Return to the Lord your God,

Repentance is not a simple apology or an "I'm sorry" statement. It is a change of heart, a spiritual decision to reverse course. This change is based on recognizing that one's earlier decisions were wrong, self-destructive, and offensive to our holy God.

Joel describes this change as rending (meaning "tearing") our *hearts*. This contrasts with the common way of expressing personal anguish: tearing one's *garments* (examples: Genesis 37:34; 2 Samuel 3:31; Job 1:20). True repentance will rip one's heart wide open, break down any resistance to God's will, and lay bare our souls.

> *What Do You Think?*
>   What are some ways to rend one's heart in true repentance?
> *Talking Points for Your Discussion*
>   - In contrast with a halfhearted rending
>   - In terms of changed priorities
>   - In terms of how sin is viewed
>   - Other

13b. for he is gracious and merciful,
   slow to anger, and abounding in steadfast love;
   and he relents over disaster.

Joel gives the reason for genuine repentance: the compassionate nature of the Lord. Even when our punishment is deserved, he desires to forgive as we repent. Joel piles up the descriptions of this aspect of God's nature in a powerful and beautiful way. The Lord is *gracious and merciful*, not brutal and rigid. The Lord is *slow to anger*, not given

"Rend your heart...
not your garments" —Joel 2:13

Visual for Lesson 4. *Start a discussion by pointing to this visual as you ask the question associated with verse 13a, above.*

to knee-jerk bursts of rage. Unlike the fictitious gods of the pagans, the Lord's nature is *abounding in steadfast love*; this has the sense of "loyalty," love that does not give up easily.

Joel concludes his description of God's mercy with a statement that may strike us as curious: the Lord *relents over disaster*. The idea is that human repentance results in avoidance of deserved punishment from God (compare Jeremiah 18:8; Jonah 4:2). This is the forgiveness of God. When we repent sincerely, he is willing to forgive (compare Acts 5:31).

II. Rebuilding

(JOEL 2:18, 19)

A. Jealousy and Pity (v. 18)

**18. Then the LORD became jealous for his land
and had pity on his people.**

Joel does not leave us with a picture of irreversible devastation of God's *land* and *people*. He wants to restore the country stripped bare by voracious locusts. He cares deeply about the distress of those facing starvation. God indeed hears the cries of his people in distress (Exodus 3:7).

We should take care to understand what it means for the Lord to be *jealous*. God's jealousy is not like that of a boy who has a fit if he sees his girlfriend flirting with someone else. The biblical concept of jealousy when applied to God indicates a profound sense of caring and commitment. This is even more apparent where a word in the original language is translated "jealousy" in one passage but "zeal" in another.

For example, the Hebrew noun translated "jealousy" in Ezekiel 8:3, 5 and Zechariah 8:2 is rendered "zeal" in Isaiah 9:7; 37:32; 59:17; 63:15. In the New Testament, the Greek noun translated "jealousy" in 2 Corinthians 11:2 is the same one translated "zeal" in Philippians 3:6. Overlap in meaning is affirmed in English by a dictionary entry that offers one meaning of *jealousy* as "zealous vigilance." The common idea is one of fervency.

◆ JEALOUS GOD, ZEALOUS GOD ◆

As a university professor for over 40 years, I have seen student papers that have all but butchered the English language. One of my most startling experiences was when a graduate student turned in a three-page book review with 58 grammatical/spelling errors! I have seen sentences such as "He wanted to be untied with his friends." A spell checker won't catch this error, and the difference between *untied* and *united* is important!

I have always been interested in etymology, which is the study of word origins and how meanings change over time. For example, our word *hotel* comes from the French *hostel,* which in turn comes from the Latin *hospital.* Today these three words in English carry very different meanings. At the other end of the scale, some words undergo relatively fewer changes in meaning over time. The word *jealous* is an example, as we trace it back to thirteenth-century French, then further back through Latin and Greek.

We usually think of jealousy as a negative thing, but it can be positive when the fervency (zeal) is properly motivated and informed. We see the positive side in John 2:17 (quoting Psalm 69:9); we see the opposite in Philippians 3:6. For what are you jealous/zealous today?   —J. B. N.

B. Provision and Honor (v. 19)

**19. The LORD answered and said to his people,
"Behold, I am sending to you
grain, wine, and oil,**

and you will be satisfied;
and I will no more make you
a reproach among the nations."

The promise of Joel is that the locust-caused famine will soon be replaced by life-sustaining agriculture. There will be plenty, and the people *will be satisfied*. There will be no more want, as the famine conditions are replaced by the Lord's lavish provisions.

A further result is that God's covenant people will no longer be *a reproach among the nations*. This is an era when each nation is understood to have a patron god (1 Kings 11:33). Such nations will no longer be able to consider the people of the true God as abandoned by him (compare Joel 2:17). The Lord is always faithful (2:23). The locust plague was horrible, but the restoration will cause Joel's audience to truly know that the Lord is their God, the one who wants to bless them (2:27).

What Do You Think?
In what ways can churches be more attuned to God's will so that his blessings will serve to mute the reproach of secular culture?
Talking Points for Your Discussion
- Concerning charges of inconsistency
- Concerning charges of irrelevance
- Other

III. Revelation
(Joel 2:28-32)

A. Receiving the Spirit (vv. 28, 29)

28a. **"And it shall come to pass afterward,**
that I will pour out my Spirit on all
flesh;

Joel now describes a future beyond the restoration of Jerusalem and its people, a period he refers to as *afterward*. This passage is prophetic of the time when the old covenant gives way to the new. Centuries later, the apostle Peter will understand this as being fulfilled as the church is birthed on the Day of Pentecost (Acts 2:17-21).

We should understand this as Peter did: as a time that features the distribution of God's Spirit such as was never experienced by ancient Israel.

Joel's description as pouring is figurative language, of course, since the Holy Spirit is not liquid! But the figurative language is very powerful in painting an image of something coming from above *on all flesh* below. Such pouring indicates, among other things, that God's Spirit is not something inherent within ourselves; to receive the Spirit of God does not mean unlocking some hidden potential in our hearts. It is, rather, the introduction of a new presence in our lives: the comforting spiritual presence of the Lord himself.

The Spirit is said to come upon certain individuals at various times in the Old Testament era (example: Judges 6:34). But the availability of the Holy Spirit for everyone is not a reality until the New Testament era. Joel looks forward to that new reality, which we understand to be the established church. This is where all believers are given the Holy Spirit as a gift (Acts 2:38).

28b. **"your sons and your daughters shall**
prophesy,
your old men shall dream dreams,
and your young men shall see visions.

Joel describes the giving of God's Spirit as yielding spiritual results: the divinely given abilities to *prophesy*, to receive revelatory *dreams*, and to experience *visions* (compare Numbers 12:6). This is not the restoration of a previous state, but empowerment for something new. Joel is foreseeing the Holy Spirit's role in (at least) the founding of the church. Christians do not receive the Holy Spirit as a tool for their own pleasure, but as the presence of God to enable them for extraordinary activities as he chooses.

29. **"Even on the male and female servants**
in those days I will pour out my Spirit.

The phrasing here refers to both *male and female* slaves, and Joel prophesies that the Spirit will be poured on them as well. There will be no class or gender distinctions with regard to the gift of the Holy Spirit.

Addressing the topic of access to salvation in the New Testament era, the apostle Paul affirms, "There is neither Jew nor Greek, there is neither slave nor free, there is no male and female, for you are all one in Christ Jesus" (Galatians 3:28). Stated a little differently, in Christ we "are being built together into a dwelling place for God by the Spirit" (Ephesians 2:22).

◆   IT'S FOR EVERYONE   ◆

A student who was blind sued a music college to challenge its requirement for sight-reading music. A Christian university received negative media attention because the admission requirements included a weight limit. Overweight applicants claimed discrimination; school leadership believed that overweight applicants (we are talking *very* overweight here) were neglecting the Christian stewardship responsibilities for their bodies. Claims of discrimination regarding unequal access, overt or otherwise, are heard in many other contexts as well.

We live in an age when equal access is still a much-debated topic. Virtually everyone agrees that people should be treated fairly. But there is often disagreement on the boundary between reasonable and unreasonable accommodation. The fact that some organizations still attempt to achieve proportional representation by use of quotas indicates that society has not yet reached the point where it can take equal opportunity as a given.

But Joel points out that the pouring of the Spirit is to be "on all flesh." No discrimination here! Does the "targeted demographic" approach to church growth fit this category?   —J. B. N.

B. Seeing Wonders (vv. 30, 31)

30, 31. "And I will show wonders in the heavens and on the earth, blood and fire and columns of smoke. The sun shall be turned to darkness, and the moon to blood, before the great and awesome day of the LORD comes.

Joel's prophecy includes imagery that is commonly called apocalyptic. Just as God created *the heavens* and *the earth,* he can uncreate them as well. He can cause the "greater light" of *the sun* to go dark and/or the "lesser light" of *the moon* to appear any way he chooses (Genesis 1:16). These are signs of the great *day of the Lord* (compare Matthew 24:29-31; Mark 13:24-27; Luke 21:25-27; 2 Peter 3:10-12; Revelation 6:12-14). *Columns of smoke* seem similar to the "pillar of cloud" and "pillar of fire" that signified God's presence in Exodus 13:21, 22.

> **What Do You Think?**
>   What preparations can and should we make as we anticipate the day of which Joel speaks? What need we not bother with? Why?
> *Talking Points for Your Discussion*
>   ▪ Regarding personal preparations
>   ▪ Regarding preparations by our church as a whole
>   ▪ Other

Fire often refers to judgment (Jeremiah 21:12; etc.). But that does not seem to be the way Joel is using it here, since he has already used the locust plague as such an image. Instead, fire seems connected with the powerful spiritual movements of the Lord. This imagery is seen in Acts 2, where the Spirit descends upon the disciples with "tongues as of fire" (Acts 2:3).

C. Claiming Salvation (v. 32)

32. "And it shall come to pass that everyone who calls on the name of the LORD shall be saved. For in Mount Zion and in Jerusalem there shall be those who escape, as the LORD has said, and among the survivors shall be those whom the LORD calls."

What an exciting passage this has been! Spiritual indwelling that leads to powerful prophesying, divine dreaming, and revealing visioning! Visible displays of God's incredible power!

But let us not miss the climax of all of this, which is Joel's remarkable promise that *everyone who calls on the name of the Lord shall be saved.* This is more than a promise of earthly deliverance of ancient Israel. God is promising a salvation that Peter sees being fulfilled on Pentecost (Acts 2:21).

The apostle Paul clarifies in Romans 10 what it means to *call on the name of the Lord.* As a whole, Romans 10 is particularly concerned with the issue of righteousness that is based on faith vs. righteousness that is based on law as these apply to fellow Israelites. His quote of Joel 2:32 in Romans 10:13 is Romans 10:9 stated more succinctly. Within Romans 10:8-15 Paul confirms his argument by citing Old Testament passages that include Deuteronomy 30:14 and Isaiah 28:16; 52:7.

When we put all this together, we can only conclude with Paul that calling *on the name of the Lord* is the same as declaring "with your mouth that Jesus is Lord" (Romans 10:9) because it is "with the mouth one confesses and is saved" (10:10). To believe that Jesus is Lord is to submit to his lordship in following the plan of salvation as he established it (Acts 2:38; Ephesians 2:8, 9; etc.).

In quoting Joel 2:32, Paul is also clarifying what that prophecy means by the phrase *shall be saved*. Joel's picture is that of God's covenant people having been found guilty of sin, with the result of judgment in the form of a locust plague. The solution is for the guilty to turn, to rend hearts in true repentance and faith. Then God will bless their land again and restore them to a position of honor. But this second chapter of Joel also looks beyond this to the "afterward" time.

That time is about much more than abundant crops and national prestige. It is about our eternal relationship with our true Father, about accepting his restoring love with faith and loving him in return for his graciousness. The issues of what is required to be saved and what being saved entails are vital for us, so we take care to read Joel in the light of Paul's explanations.

> **What Do You Think?**
> What steps can we take to help others call on the name of the Lord for deliverance?
> *Talking Points for Your Discussion*
> - Concerning deliverance from unholy influence of certain people
> - Concerning deliverance from unholy influence of certain places
> - Concerning deliverance from unholy influence of certain things

Conclusion
A. Locusts of Life

I am writing this on a cold day. Winters are cold in Nebraska, but this is what one website described as "ridiculous cold." The high for the day will not be above 0°, and the windchill fac-

tor will hit –30°. All the schools are closed—in Nebraska! Although my wife and I moved here from California, we can put up with cold weather. But sometimes it just seems too much!

The old saw "When it rains it pours" seems to be true for all of us on a regular basis. Winter doesn't result in just one lingering episode of illness, but two; some months inflict not just one unexpected expense, but four; some summers witness not just one dear friend moving away, but three. These are the minor locust swarms of life, when one bad thing is piled upon another before we can recover from the previous.

What do we do? Although these may not be times when we have sinned to a greater extent than at others, we may take Joel as suggesting that such times are opportunities for spiritual examination. It would be presumptuous to think that all our misfortunes are God's judgments on us, but there is no wiser thing to do in times of distress than to turn to the Lord. There is no better thing to do than repent of being so busy that we have neglected prayer. There is no more comforting thing to do than to call on the Lord's name for his mercy.

When the locusts of life seem to swarm, remember that God's love is both restoring and sustaining. When those locusts devour your joy and peace, turn to God. He is gracious and merciful, slow to anger, and has a heart of great kindness.

B. Prayer

Heavenly Father, restore us where we are broken, love us when we are unlovable, rescue us when we have lost our way. We pray all this in the name of the Lord Jesus. Amen.

C. Thought to Remember
The Lord wants to restore us.

HOW TO SAY IT

apocalyptic	*uh*-paw-kuh-***lip***-tik.
etymology	*eh*-tuh-***mall***-luh-jee.
Ezekiel	Ee-*zeek*-ee-ul or Ee-*zeek*-yul.
Isaiah	Eye-*zay*-uh.
Pentecost	*Pent*-ih-kost.
Zechariah	Zek-uh-***rye***-uh.

INVOLVEMENT LEARNING

Enhance your lesson presentation with the reproducible activity page,
available as a free download at www.standardlesson.com.

Into the Lesson

Write "Crocodile Tears" on the board. Ask, "Who knows what the expression means?" Quickly you should get responses about insincere shows of sorrow or remorse.

Explain the origin of this strange phrase. Say, "It was an ancient (though inaccurate) belief that crocodiles wept while eating animals they killed. The image is of a predator appearing sorrowful for the death of an animal, but making a meal of its victim nonetheless!"

Spend a few minutes discussing ways people try to rebuild trust after damaging a relationship—a token gift, a promise to change, etc.

Alternative. Distribute copies of the "Sorry Apologies" activity from the reproducible page, which you can download. Have students work in pairs or small groups.

After either activity, lead into the Bible study by saying, "Time and time again in Bible history, the people of Israel and Judah rejected God's will and made messes of their lives. Too often, they offered insincere apologies and repeated bad behavior. The prophet Joel, however, instructed God's people about what it takes to rebuild a broken nation and broken lives."

Into the Word

Have a volunteer read the lesson text aloud. Then summarize the context of these words. Say, "Judah had sinned greatly, and the Lord sent a plague of locusts. The significance of a locust plague is that it totally devastated the agrarian economy of the nation. Judah tried to go it alone, and God showed how alone they were without him! Joel showed the path of restoration however."

Divide the class into three groups. Supply each group with pen, paper, and a Bible concordance. Each group will examine a key word from its passage, discovering the Hebrew word, meanings of the word, other passages using it, and its signifi-

cance in the context of restoring sinful people. The assignments and our responses follow.

Group 1—Rend (Joel 2:12, 13)
qara'—tear open, rip apart
Genesis 37:29; Isaiah 64:1; Hosea 13:8

God does not want rituals to show repentance, but honestly opening ourselves up to him, revealing our sin.

Group 2—Jealous (Joel 2:18, 19)
qana'—having a deep sense of commitment
Deuteronomy 4:24; Ezekiel 39:25

God cares so much for his people that he seeks to restore them, not destroy them.

Group 3—Call (Joel 2:28-32)
qara'—cry for help, proclaim
Psalm 4:1-3

God wants us to stop trying to go it alone but to accept his way and his help.

Allow time for groups to share and summarize their research.

Into Life

Before class, obtain small alphabet stickers from an office supply or craft store. Put aside all letters except for *R*s, *J*s, and *C*s.

Show the three letters to the class and remind them that they stand for the three key words from the Bible text—*R*end, *J*ealous, and *C*all. Ask them to think about which of these they most need to be reminded of regularly:

Rend: I need to be open and honest with God.
Jealous: I need to trust that God wants to help me be better, not just punish me.
Call: I need to commit myself to following God more consistently.

Invite students to take a sticker and put it someplace where they will see it daily.

Alternative. Distribute copies of the "Joel 2-Day" activity from the reproducible page. Students may discuss it in pairs, or you may decide to send it home as a devotional exercise.

SHEPHERDING LOVE

DEVOTIONAL READING: John 10:11-18
BACKGROUND SCRIPTURE: Psalm 23

PSALM 23

1 The LORD is my shepherd; I shall not want.
2 He makes me lie down in green
        pastures.
He leads me beside still waters.
3 He restores my soul.
He leads me in paths of righteousness
        for his name's sake.
4 Even though I walk through the valley of
        the shadow of death,
    I will fear no evil,

for you are with me;
        your rod and your staff,
        they comfort me.
5 You prepare a table before me
        in the presence of my enemies;
you anoint my head with oil;
        my cup overflows.
6 Surely goodness and mercy shall follow me
        all the days of my life,
and I shall dwell in the house of the LORD
        forever.

KEY VERSE

The LORD is my shepherd; I shall not want. —**Psalm 23:1**

GOD LOVES US

Unit 2: God's Caring, Saving, and Upholding Love

LESSONS 5–9

LESSON AIMS

After participating in this lesson, each learner will be able to:

1. Identify the shepherd and host metaphors.

2. Explain how the psalm's imagery brings comfort, goodness, and mercy to those who trust in the Lord.

3. Tell of a difficult life event when trust in the Lord as shepherd was essential for a God-honoring outcome.

LESSON OUTLINE

Introduction

A. An American Secular Icon—Psalm 23

William L. Holladay states that Psalm 23 became an American secular icon in the two decades after the American Civil War (1861–1865). Movement toward this status was sparked by Henry Ward Beecher's tribute to the psalm in the years just prior.

The tragic loss of life in that war plus the economic panics of 1873 and 1893 bolstered the popularity of Psalm 23. The general public gravitated toward the lines "the shadow of death" and "dwell in the house of the Lord forever" for comfort. The psalm's position as secular icon was finalized when funeral homes began to print it on the back of obituary handouts.

B. Lesson Background

Shepherding was a common occupation in ancient Israel through the centuries (Genesis 12:16; 26:14; 29:9; 30:31, 32; Jeremiah 33:12; Luke 2:8; etc.). It should not surprise us, then, that the Bible has scores of references to sheep and shepherds. Sheep were completely dependent on shepherds, making the job of shepherding what we would call 24/7 (note Luke 2:8, which has shepherds "keeping watch over their flock by night").

Since all this was so familiar to the ancient Israelites, the words *shepherd* and *sheep* became metaphors. Moses and David, two of Israel's greatest leaders, had been shepherds in the normal sense (Exodus 3:1; 1 Samuel 16:11) before they became figurative shepherds of God's people (compare Psalm 77:20; Isaiah 63:11; Ezekiel 34:23; etc.). The Old Testament describes God himself with the metaphor of shepherd (Psalm 78:52; 80:1; Isaiah 40:11). In the New Testament, it is Jesus who is "the great shepherd of the sheep" (Hebrews 13:20; compare John 10:1-16; 1 Peter 5:4).

The psalms are traditionally seen as five books, and Psalm 23 is in Book I. This psalm is part of an early collection of Davidic psalms, namely Psalms 3–41. A later Davidic collection, namely Psalms 51–65 and 68–70, is found in Book II. Our approach to Psalm 23 is in terms of two metaphors: shepherd (vv. 1-4) and host (vv. 5, 6).

I. Shepherd Metaphor

(PSALM 23:1-4)

This psalm's superscription attributes it to David. Those who have an electronic version of the Bible will note that such superscriptions are designated as "verse 0" of the particular psalm in view.

A. Identifications (v. 1)

1a. The LORD is my shepherd;

The profound nature of the opening statement comes to the fore when we remember that David himself had been a shepherd in his boyhood days (see 1 Samuel 17:34-36) and now he is the shepherd of the people of God (2 Samuel 5:1-5; 7:4-8; compare Psalm 79:13). In proclaiming *the Lord is my shepherd*, the twice-shepherd king of Israel therefore acknowledges that he himself has a shepherd.

That shepherd is none other than God. "For he is our God, and we are the people of his pasture, and the sheep of his hand" (Psalm 95:7; Hebrews 4:7 attributes this psalm to David). The king himself admits his own need for the divine shepherd. It is natural for the people of Israel to look to David as their chief earthly shepherd. David's identification of a shepherd higher yet should keep them from idolizing the king.

What Do You Think?

How do we resist idolizing those who would claim to guide (shepherd) us today?

Talking Points for Your Discussion

- Recognizing the danger before it happens
- Correcting the problem after it happens
- Other

1b. I shall not want.

David's next statement is a roundabout way of identifying himself as one of God's sheep. David's shepherding background reminds him that sheep

HOW TO SAY IT

Crimean	Kry-*mee*-un.
Davidic	Duh-*vid*-ick.
Yahweh (Hebrew)	*Yah*-weh.

want for nothing only when their shepherd provides for all their needs. He knows that the God of his ancestors supplied all their needs (Deuteronomy 2:7; etc.), and he will continue to do so.

B. Actions (vv. 2, 3)

2a. He makes me lie down in green pastures.

The phrase *green pastures* may bring up mental images of lush, rolling meadows that extend as far as the eye can see. But in reality the land in ancient and modern Israel often bears little resemblance to such an ideal. It is a semiarid climate that experiences little or no rainfall for five months each year. Shepherds lead nomadic lives as they move frequently from place to place in search of suitable grazing for the sheep (compare Genesis 37:12-17; 47:4).

So shepherds often have to settle for the scarce grass that is found on "the hills" and in "pastures of the wilderness" (Psalm 65:12; Joel 1:19, 20; 2:22; compare Job 39:8). The shepherd has to be skillful in finding adequate grazing in such places and be ready to move on when the likelihood of overgrazing presents itself (compare Genesis 13:5-9). But that's the point! God is able to provide sources of food that are more than adequate for the psalmist's needs.

The Old Testament sometimes describes God's ideal for the future in terms of abundant pastureland (Isaiah 49:9; Jeremiah 33:12; etc.; contrast Isaiah 13:20; Jeremiah 25:36; etc.). That abundance is accompanied by the blessing of allowed rest, the sense of *makes me lie down* (compare Isaiah 65:10; Ezekiel 34:14, 15).

◆ *NEW GREEN PASTURES* ◆

My husband's position was eliminated when the college where he taught downsized. To say we were devastated would be an understatement. We struggled with the stress of uncertainty. Realizing that a move was likely, we thought about the friends we would leave behind and the disruption to our children's lives. We pondered the unknown, about moving to a place where we knew no one.

We did it, though. Another teaching job became available at a Christian college halfway across the country, and we moved. We felt sure that God had opened that door for us, and so we followed him. Leaving loved ones took courage, and we mourned the loss of their constant company. But we believed that God would provide for us in our new area of ministry, our new pasture.

Two years later, I can say that stepping out in faith changed our family for the better. We love our new jobs and have much more family time than before. We have new friends we love, and we have been able to keep up with our old ones as well. Following God as sheep follow the shepherd can bring us to places where we can heal from hard times and experience God's presence anew.   —L. M. W.

> **What Do You Think?**
> How can we improve at recognizing when God is leading us toward "green pastures"? What can happen if we don't?
> **Talking Points for Your Discussion**
> - Regarding job relocations
> - Regarding spiritual nourishment
> - Regarding ministry service
> - Other

2b. He leads me beside still waters.

The importance of *still waters* is seen when we consider that the alternative of flowing streams introduces the elements of unreliability and danger in Palestine. A shepherd who seeks a flowing stream that was usable previously may find only a dry streambed on arrival (compare 1 Kings 17:7; Job 6:15-17; Jeremiah 15:18). At the opposite extreme, rainfall in the mountains or hills may turn dry streambeds or gently flowing water into deadly flash floods. Even today, tourists are warned about hiking through dry streambeds because of the possibility of being swept away should such a flood come (and tourist hikers have indeed drowned).

This distinction between nonflowing and flowing water should not be overemphasized, however, since positive images of the latter are to be found in many passages (examples: Deuteronomy 8:7; Psalm 1:3; 126:4). Such images sometimes occur in parallel with those of nonflowing water (Isaiah 41:18; etc.). Of greater importance is recognizing

that the *he leads me* phrase of the half-verse before us stands parallel with "he makes me" in verse 2a. Thus the image of rest is continued. The place of abundant food and water is not a place where one hastily washes down a doughnut with a cup of coffee before rushing to the next appointment. It is, rather, a place of repose and respite.

What a picture! Surely the Lord takes care of "his flock like a shepherd" (Isaiah 40:11)!

3a. He restores my soul.

A consideration of the word *soul* is in order for understanding what the psalmist says is restored. The Hebrew word behind our English translation *soul* occurs about 500 times in the original, and it signifies different things depending on context. It can refer to the "life" of a person (Genesis 32:30; 44:30); the "life" of an animal (Leviticus 17:14); "me" (Numbers 23:10); etc.

The word *soul* is therefore quite flexible! With all these potential choices of meaning, it can be difficult to know where to start. When we're stumped in such an instance, a safe approach is to begin by ruling things out; that is, start by determining what it *cannot* mean in the context at hand.

In that regard, we can be certain that the word *soul* as used here does not refer only to the spiritual side of the psalmist's being, with the physical side left out. The context of the psalm addresses the entirety of the psalmist as the object of the loving shepherd's restoring care. Many psalms plead for God's restoring favor (compare Psalm 6:4; 25:16; 31:2; 69:16; 71:2; 86:16; 88:2; 102:2; 119:132). This one, however, views that favor as an accomplished fact.

3b. He leads me in paths of righteousness for his name's sake.

Sheep by nature tend to act as a group rather than independently. This means that a herd of sheep will tend to follow a leader. But which leader? In 2005, nearly 1,500 sheep jumped off a cliff (with 450 dying) when they blindly followed the foolish path of a dominant member of the flock. All this happened while the Turkish shepherds, their usual leaders, were away at breakfast.

Traveling correct paths requires proper leadership. Different Hebrew words stand behind the two translations of *leads* in verses 2b and 3b, but the psalmist intends them to mirror each other. We see this also in Psalm 31:3 (also by David), where the same two Hebrew words are translated "lead" and "guide." Perhaps the wording of Exodus 15:13 is David's model.

Regarding the nature of *paths of righteousness* wherein the psalmist is led, compare Proverbs 8:20; 12:28; 16:31; Matthew 21:32; and 2 Peter 2:21. The phrase *for his name's sake* confirms the moral tone of the paths in view. Sometimes God takes action (or does not take action) specifically to protect the honor of his name. What David acknowledges in the verse before us he also acknowledges and/or requests outright in 2 Samuel 7:23-26; Psalm 25:11; 31:3; 109:21. Jesus, the good shepherd, always desires to lead us down the right path. But that becomes reality only as we choose to "hear his voice" (John 10:3).

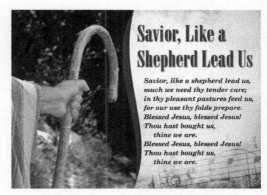

Savior, Like a Shepherd Lead Us

Savior, like a shepherd lead us,
much we need thy tender care;
in thy pleasant pastures feed us,
for our use thy folds prepare.
Blessed Jesus, blessed Jesus!
Thou hast bought us,
   thine we are.
Blessed Jesus, blessed Jesus!
Thou hast bought us,
   thine we are.

Visual for Lessons 5 & 9. *Use these lyrics as a lesson road-map by pointing to thoughts that reflect various points in the text as they are encountered.*

C. Confidence (v. 4)

4a. Even though I walk through the valley of the shadow of death, I will fear no evil,

The valley of the shadow of death is often thought to refer to situations where physical death is very possible or even likely. Although *shadow of death* can refer to danger that threatens one's physical life (compare Job 10:21, 22; Psalm 107:10-16), it also can be understood in a figurative sense (see Job 16:16; 34:22; Isaiah 9:2; Luke 1:79). Bible students who are confused by this ambiguity are not alone! Jesus' disciples often misunderstood his use of figurative language (Matthew 16:5-12; John 11:11-14; 16:25-29; etc.).

Metaphors function as figurative, symbolic language by stating or implying comparisons. In the context at hand, the psalmist compares himself with a sheep who is under the care of an expert shepherd. *The valley of the shadow of death* compares his life journey with the nature of terrain that actual sheep must enter to find sustenance. Whatever dangers lurk in these places, the expert shepherd knows how to avoid or neutralize them.

At first, we may think that the presence of the word *evil* tips the scale toward understanding *the valley* as standing for the spiritual dangers of living in a sinful world. Though the Hebrew word

is translated in a number of ways (examples: hurt, harm, wickedness, etc.), this word *evil* is best understood by its context. It can refer to physical harm or difficulties in some cases (examples: Genesis 26:29; 47:9; Exodus 32:14), while referring to issues of sin elsewhere (examples: Genesis 13:13; 39:9; Numbers 32:13).

Ultimately, it is the phrase "paths of righteousness" in verse 3b that leads us to think that the psalmist is using *the valley* to symbolize spiritual danger. Even so, the possibility of physical danger's inclusion in the reference cannot be dismissed (compare Jeremiah 2:6). We are at least aware that the phrase *the valley of the shadow of death* has a more than one possible meaning.

4b. for you are with me; your rod and your staff, they comfort me.

The word *for* marks the twenty-sixth Hebrew word of this fifty-word psalm. David does something interesting just after crossing this midpoint: he switches from addressing God with third person "he" to second person *you*. This change serves to heighten the closeness David has or wants with God: *you are with me*.

The *rod* in which the psalmist takes comfort is the shepherd's weapon to protect the flock (compare Job 21:9; Isaiah 10:5; etc.). The shepherd uses the crook of a *staff* for rescuing sheep that have wandered off and gotten themselves stuck in relatively inaccessible places.

II. Host Metaphor

(PSALM 23:5, 6)

Some students believe that the shepherd metaphor extends throughout Psalm 23. But the content of verses 5, 6 favors a shift to a host metaphor; it mirrors the shepherd metaphor but is more condensed.

A. Vindication (v. 5a)

5a. You prepare a table before me in the presence of my enemies;

Tables of food are prepared by those who host banquets, feasts, or other meals for visitors. To do so is part of one's obligation to extend hospitality in various contexts of the ancient world (Genesis 19:1-3; Judges 19:15-21; etc.). The meal is often an elaborate meal, with nothing but the best from the host (compare Genesis 18:3-8; 19:3; 24:31-33, 54; Proverbs 9:1, 2; Luke 15:23, 27, 30).

God is presented in the Old Testament as a gracious host to ungrateful people as they journeyed toward the promised land (Psalm 78:19). But David does not have such an attitude! He is secure enough in the divine shepherd to dine even while *enemies* are present. In writing another psalm, David prays against his enemies that "their own table before them become a snare; and when they are at peace, let it become a trap" (Psalm 69:22). The provision of food mirrors that in Psalm 23:2a, above.

◆ A TABLE PREPARED ◆

The Tatar people had lived in the Crimean Peninsula for generations before Stalin came to power. After World War II, he decided that they had collaborated with the Germans. To repay their supposed treason and to remove any ability for them to self-organize, his forces rounded up people at gunpoint and relocated them to central Asia. Following the dissolution of the Soviet Union in the 1990s, survivors moved back to Crimea and began to build villages.

One summer, I walked down their dusty streets. I noticed many times that entire families lived in one-room cinder-block buildings or even large tents. Women cooked and did laundry outside, exposed to the elements. Despite their circumstances, they almost always invited me to sit down for tea or coffee. Often they served me homemade cherry preserves and desserts. Think about it: people who had nothing, who had experienced trauma and despair, offering us such expensive hospitality! Like the host in Psalm 23, they prepared a table for us and treated us well.

God used the example of these hosts to teach me a lifelong lesson. What do you suppose that lesson was? —L. M. W.

B. Reward (vv. 5b, 5c)

5b. You anoint my head with oil;

The host honors the guest by anointing his *head with oil* (compare Psalm 45:7; 92:10). Given the fragrances that were available to add to olive oil (see Psalm 45:8; Proverbs 7:17), such anointing is a soothing and refreshing experience for a weary traveler. This anointing was not done for Jesus when Simon the Pharisee hosted him for dinner, an intentional oversight noted by Jesus (Luke 7:46).

David (the psalmist) possibly intends a double meaning: he may be recognizing his physical anointing to be king over Israel (1 Samuel 16:3, 12, 13; compare 2 Samuel 5:3) while acknowledging God's continual anointing in spirit.

5c. my cup overflows.

Presumably the host has given the guest a large cup of wine (compare Jeremiah 35:1-5), and the guest is well satisfied as a result. The Hebrew word translated *overflows* occurs elsewhere only in Psalm 66:12, there translated "place of abundance" in a context of being rescued by God. The host has given the guest more than enough to satisfy his thirst. This cup of satisfaction is equivalent to the waters of Psalm 23:2b, above.

C. Deliverance (v. 6)

6a. Surely goodness and mercy shall follow me all the days of my life,

Surely there is no doubt about the very characteristics of God that are *goodness* and *mercy*! Instead of worrying about any enemies who may be in temporary pursuit, the psalmist focuses on the goodness and love that follow him permanently. These two are equivalent to the rod and staff of verse 4b, above. God is the divine host who will always be there for his guest.

In numerous other places, the Hebrew verb translated *shall follow* is rendered in terms of pursuit or chasing after (examples: Genesis 14:15; Deuteronomy 11:4; 1 Kings 20:20). David knows what it's like to be both the pursuer (Psalm 18:37) and the pursued (1 Samuel 23:7-29). We will be pursued by God's goodness and mercy when we walk the "paths of righteousness" (Psalm 23:3b).

> *What Do You Think?*
> When was an occasion that God's goodness followed (even pursued) you, but you didn't recognize it at the time? How did you grow spiritually from the experience?
> *Talking Points for Your Discussion*
> • In your preteen years
> • In your teenage years
> • During various stages of adulthood

6b. and I shall dwell in the house of the LORD forever.

The shepherd and host metaphors mirror each other yet again in that the verb behind the translation *dwell* is from the same root as the one translated "restores" in Psalm 23:3a. The verb at issue is extremely common in the Old Testament; it is quite often used in the sense of returning (examples: Psalms 6:10; 18:37). But commonly used words are particularly subject to taking different meanings, depending on context (see discussion on *soul*, above). The old Greek version of the Old Testament affirms *dwell* to be a proper translation. Even without that version, we recognize that *return* better fits a context of a journey home, while *dwell* suggests a final destination.

As David expresses his conviction about where he *shall dwell,* we wonder if he is referring to an earthly location or a heavenly one. *The house of the Lord* is the same as the temple (note interchangeable terminology in Ezra 3:8-12), although that structure does not exist in David's lifetime. After it is built, people of that era view God as dwelling both in it and in Heaven (1 Kings 8:13, 27; Psalm 27:4; etc.). Therefore to try to determine with certainty which is meant here is probably to miss the main point: the psalmist desires to be in the presence of God, wherever that may be, *forever.*

> *What Do You Think?*
> What specific things can we do to prepare better to dwell with the Lord forever?
> *Talking Points for Your Discussion*
> • Regarding the imperative of holiness (1 Peter 1:15, 16; etc.)
> • Regarding the imperative to love (John 13:34; etc.)

Conclusion

A. Not an Icon, but a Test

The metaphors of shepherd and host remind us that God is our trustworthy provider. For all physical and spiritual needs, he is the source.

The ultimate question, then, does not concern God's trustworthiness, but ours. Do we yield to his shepherding leadership, or do we rebel? Do we accept his provisions with a sense of accountability, or with a sense of entitlement? Do we walk only in his paths of righteousness, or do we take little "side trips" occasionally? Think carefully—living eternally in his presence is at stake!

B. Prayer

Heavenly Father, refresh our lives with your Spirit as we gladly walk in the paths of righteousness you establish. Let us realize that those paths lead us to enter your presence and dwell with you forever. We pray this in the name of the good shepherd, Jesus. Amen.

C. Thought To Remember

The shepherd is trustworthy, but are the sheep?

INVOLVEMENT LEARNING

Enhance your lesson presentation with the reproducible activity page,
available as a free download at www.standardlesson.com.

Into the Lesson

Before class, create a list of songs about loneliness. Here are a few:

"Alone Again (Naturally)"—Gilbert O'Sullivan

"Are You Lonesome Tonight?"—Elvis Presley

"Heartbreak Hotel"—Elvis Presley

"Eleanor Rigby"—The Beatles

"I'm So Lonesome I Could Cry"
—Hank Williams

"Only the Lonely"—Roy Orbison

Play one or two of these songs to begin class. Discuss some thoughts and feelings about loneliness in these songs.

Alternative. Distribute copies of the "Puzzling" activity from the reproducible page, which you can download. Have students work individually or in pairs to discover a quote about loneliness from Teresa of Calcutta.

After either activity, lead into the Bible study saying, "Being truly alone is a frightening thought. Perhaps that is why a song in the Bible is probably the most widely known of all psalms. Let's see why it is so comforting."

Into the Word

Divide your class into three groups, and give each group paper and pen. Each group is assigned a section of the lesson text and should try to summarize the lesson text with a brief help-wanted ad as describing God's role found in its section of the Scripture. Assignments and sample help-wanted ads follow:

Group 1—Guide (Psalm 23:1-3)

Seeking a reliable guide to lead expeditions along routes that provide adequate places for rest, food, and water. A guide should have a reputation for choosing the best routes to lead his party safely and efficiently to a chosen destination.

Group 2—Protector (Psalm 23:4)

Seeking a fearless bodyguard. Qualified applicant should be able to protect and direct the cli-

ent in the most dangerous of situations, ensuring that no harm come to him or her.

Group 3—Host (Psalm 23:5, 6)

Seeking an experienced party planner. A qualified host must be able to ensure adequate provisions for the safety and comfort of his guests, regardless of the length of the event.

Allow time for groups to share their help-wanted ads and summarize their Scripture assignments.

Into Life

Close the class by having students brainstorm a list of ways that they can be, in a small way, a Psalm 23 shepherd to someone. That list may include mailing a postcard; visiting a home, hospital, or senior-care facility; sending a sympathy card; sending an encouraging e-mail; taking someone out to lunch or bringing food to an individual and his or her family.

When the list is complete, distribute index cards and pens. Ask each student to write the name of two or three individuals they know who need care of some sort. Have them write an item from the brainstorm-created list that would best serve each of those individual's needs.

Alternative. Distribute copies of the "Psalm 23 Mission" activity from the reproducible page. Have learners review the roles of God as a *guide*, *protector*, and *host*. Encourage them to think of someone they know in need of care and to write that person's initials in front of one or more of those tasks.

Close either activity with prayer. Say, "Lord, you want me to be a shepherd to others. I am thinking of the needs of _____."
[Allow students to bring a person's name to the Lord silently.] "Help me as I minister to _____ in this way." [Allow students to silently pray about an act of service they will undertake this week.]

SAVING
LOVE

DEVOTIONAL READING: Titus 3:1-7
BACKGROUND SCRIPTURE: John 3:1-21

JOHN 3:1-16

¹ Now there was a man of the Pharisees named Nicodemus, a ruler of the Jews. ² This man came to Jesus by night and said to him, "Rabbi, we know that you are a teacher come from God, for no one can do these signs that you do unless God is with him." ³ Jesus answered him, "Truly, truly, I say to you, unless one is born again he cannot see the kingdom of God." ⁴ Nicodemus said to him, "How can a man be born when he is old? Can he enter a second time into his mother's womb and be born?" ⁵ Jesus answered, "Truly, truly, I say to you, unless one is born of water and the Spirit, he cannot enter the kingdom of God. ⁶ That which is born of the flesh is flesh, and that which is born of the Spirit is spirit. ⁷ Do not marvel that I said to you, 'You must be born again.' ⁸ The wind blows where it wishes, and you hear its sound, but you do not know where it comes from or where it goes. So it is with everyone who is born of the Spirit."

⁹ Nicodemus said to him, "How can these things be?" ¹⁰ Jesus answered him, "Are you the teacher of Israel and yet you do not understand these things? ¹¹ Truly, truly, I say to you, we speak of what we know, and bear witness to what we have seen, but you do not receive our testimony. ¹² If I have told you earthly things and you do not believe, how can you believe if I tell you heavenly things? ¹³ No one has ascended into heaven except he who descended from heaven, the Son of Man. ¹⁴ And as Moses lifted up the serpent in the wilderness, so must the Son of Man be lifted up, ¹⁵ that whoever believes in him may have eternal life.

¹⁶ "For God so loved the world, that he gave his only Son, that whoever believes in him should not perish but have eternal life.

KEY VERSE

For God so loved the world, that he gave his only Son, that whoever believes in him should not perish but have eternal life. —**John 3:16**

GOD LOVES US

Unit 2: God's Caring, Saving, and Upholding Love

LESSONS 5–9

LESSON AIMS

After participating in this lesson, each learner will be able to:

1. Recite John 3:16 from memory.

2. Explain why Nicodemus had difficulty comprehending what Jesus said.

3. Write a prayer of commitment to love the world in the sense of John 3:16 while avoiding love for the world in the sense of 1 John 2:15.

LESSON OUTLINE

Introduction

A. A Mystery and a Love Story

One popular story type is the mystery. A foul deed is committed, clues are gathered, suspects are interviewed, and finally the perpetrator is revealed. Some readers prefer love stories. Two people meet, discover an unlikely attraction, and eventually overcome differences to form a lasting bond of love.

Today's lesson reflects on the good news of Jesus in a way that combines the mystery with the love story. The mystery is about how God acted to make his world right—a mystery revealed. The love story is about why God acted in such a self-sacrificial way on behalf of rebellious humans.

B. Lesson Background

Our text comes from one of the most beloved books in the Bible, the Gospel of John. In providing narratives of the life, death, and resurrection of Jesus, it is rather different from Matthew, Mark, and Luke. Those three (known as *the synoptic Gospels*) are notable for their similarities. John's Gospel, written later, assumes the reader knows the main points of the storyline found in the other Gospels as it provides different, additional material.

John likes to narrate Jesus' private, one-on-one conversations, including those he had with religious teachers. Today's text also belongs in this category: Jesus' interaction with Nicodemus, a Pharisee and leader of the Jewish people.

The Pharisees were a leading party of Jewish thought and practice in the New Testament period. They advocated careful adherence to the Law of Moses and to the traditions they had developed about the law. Their aim was to build a fence around the law. That is, they taught that if people followed their traditions (and thereby stayed outside the fence), then they wouldn't even come close to breaking God's law.

Though the Pharisees promoted a difficult form of Jewish observance, they were quite popular in Jesus' time and beyond. Their strictness was a channel for the zeal many felt for the God of Israel.

I. Nicodemus Meets Jesus
(JOHN 3:1-3)
A. Encounter at Night (vv. 1, 2)

1. Now there was a man of the Pharisees named Nicodemus, a ruler of the Jews.

John introduces an individual with whom Jesus will have a most significant conversation. As *a man of the Pharisees*, Nicodemus takes a strict view of the boundaries of God's people (see the Lesson Background). The fact that he is *a ruler of the Jews* means that he is part of the Sanhedrin. This council had come into being in the centuries between the Old and New Testaments. The high priest, who presides over the temple, appoints the 70 members of this council to assist him.

2a. This man came to Jesus by night

To come *to Jesus by night* is to come in secret. Is Nicodemus afraid to be seen with the controversial Jesus? Later John will contrast light and darkness as symbols of good and evil (John 3:19-21). Where does Nicodemus stand presently?

◆   *NIGHTTIME ADVENTURES*   ◆

When I was in college, my younger sister decided it was time for me to learn to drive a car with a manual transmission (a "stick shift," if you remember those!). She made this decision at 2:00 a.m. I was home on spring break, so there was no time like the present.

We crept outside and pushed the car down the driveway so the sound of the engine starting would not awaken our mother. We jumped in the car at the proper moment, then spent the next hour driving the back roads nearby. We laughed at my mistakes and had fun together, and I learned how to drive a stick shift that night. Our sneakiness aside, nighttime provided an ideal opportunity to learn before putting my

new skill into practice in the heavier traffic of daylight hours.

Something similar seems to have happened with Nicodemus. Perhaps he came to Jesus at night so his fellow council members wouldn't see them together. Whether or not that was the motive, it was an ideal time to learn, with no press of crowds to distract. Whatever he learned in private he could mull over later without being asked to take an immediate *agree* or *disagree* position.

Disciples who had accompanied Jesus openly for three years went into hiding after his death (John 20:19). But two other men, members of the council (Mark 15:43), did the opposite; Nicodemus was one of those two (John 19:38-42). People absorb information in different ways. We must give them a chance to do so.   —L. M. W.

2b. and said to him, "Rabbi, we know that you are a teacher come from God, for no one can do these signs that you do unless God is with him."

Nicodemus speaks highly of Jesus, since *Rabbi* is a title of great respect (compare John 1:38). Nicodemus affirms that Jesus' miraculous signs demonstrate decisively that *God is with him.* Jesus' miracles are polarizing: they cause some to believe in his divine identity (John 2:11, 23; 7:31; 9:16b) while not being persuasive to others (9:16a; 11:47; 12:37). The only right response to these signs is faith in Jesus as the Son of God sent to give life (John 20:30, 31).

> *What Do You Think?*
> How should we respond when people speak well of Jesus but don't acknowledge his full authority?
> *Talking Points for Your Discussion*
> • Regarding what we say and don't say
> • Regarding what we do and don't do

HOW TO SAY IT

Nicodemus	*Nick*-uh-***dee***-mus.
Pharisees	*Fair*-ih-seez.
Rabbi	*Rab*-eye.
Sanhedrin	*San*-huh-drun or San-*heed*-run.
synoptic	suh-*nawp*-tik.

B. Truth About Rebirth (v. 3)

3. Jesus answered him, "Truly, truly, I say to you, unless one is born again he cannot see the kingdom of God."

Jesus' response takes the form of a blunt and authoritative statement of what is required to *see the kingdom of God*—and Nicodemus hasn't even asked a question yet! At least, one is not recorded.

The succinct phrase *the kingdom of God* serves as a summary of the promises God gave to Israel about his making the world right again. Truth, justice, mercy, life—these are the blessings of God's kingdom, the ultimate fulfillment of his loving purpose for humanity.

As a religious teacher, Nicodemus understands that when God establishes his kingdom, his people will experience its blessings. Nicodemus further understands that belonging to God's people means being a faithful Jew, one who was born into the nation and who honors the Law of Moses.

But Jesus challenges all that. Birth into the 12 tribes of Israel does not confer automatic membership in the kingdom of God. To be a subject of this kingdom requires birth of a different kind.

In relaying Jesus' response, the Gospel writer uses a word in the Greek language that has two possible meanings for the context at hand: "again" and "from above." (Most Bibles have a footnote on this.) Which does Jesus mean? If "again," he means an experience separate from and after physical birth. If "from above," he means an action that God performs. Because both suit the context well, we may see a play on words here, as Jesus implies both meanings.

How big is God's love?

Visual for Lesson 6. *Point to this visual as you add this question to class discussion of John 3:16: "What are some ways to think globally as we act locally?"*

II. Nicodemus Engages Jesus
(JOHN 3:4-8)
A. Birth, Age, Womb (v. 4)

4. Nicodemus said to him, "How can a man be born when he is old? Can he enter a second time into his mother's womb and be born?"

Jesus' answer perplexes Nicodemus. Understanding "born again" in a physical sense, his questions serve to protest that a second such birth is impossible. As long as Nicodemus holds to his concept of what is required to be in God's kingdom, he will fail to understand Jesus.

B. Water, Wind, Spirit (vv. 5-8)

5. Jesus answered, "Truly, truly, I say to you, unless one is born of water and the Spirit, he cannot enter the kingdom of God.

Jesus continues to challenge the conventional understanding of membership in God's people. Like the previous challenge, this one compares entry into *the kingdom of God* with birth. This birth is *of water and the Spirit*. In the Greek text of John's Gospel, this phrase is constructed to show that the two items belong together, forming one idea. So *water* is not one kind of birth and *Spirit* another, but the two comprise a single event.

Interpretations vary, and one popular proposal is that *water* refers to baptism. This is natural to think, since the New Testament associates water baptism, in the context of faith in Christ, with becoming part of God's people and receiving the Spirit (Acts 2:38; 22:16; Romans 6:1-6; 1 Corinthians 12:13; Galatians 3:27; Colossians 2:11-14; Titus 3:5; 1 Peter 3:21). But if Christian baptism is what is meant, then John 3:10 (below) would have Jesus criticizing Nicodemus for not understanding something that will not come into being until the Day of Pentecost!

Jesus' point seems to be broader, with a good possibility that he is drawing on the Old Testament's depictions of water and Spirit in relation to each other. In that regard, most important for the case at hand is Ezekiel 36:25-27. There "water" indicates cleansing from impurity, while "new spirit" and "my Spirit" point to transformed hearts.

The previous chapter gives us a brief glimpse at the connection between water and ceremonial purification in first-century Judaism (John 2:6, 7). Taken in tandem with *the Spirit,* the reference is to cleansing performed by God. Therefore Nicodemus can *enter the kingdom of God* only if God cleanses him of what he cannot cleanse himself: the guilt of his sin. This is the very thing that Christian baptism will depict when it is instituted a few years after this conversation. So these two interpretations are not far apart.

6. "That which is born of the flesh is flesh, and that which is born of the Spirit is spirit.

Jesus emphasizes that God alone can accomplish the transformation. *Spirit* contrasts with *flesh* as the immortal God contrasts with mortal humanity. To receive God's blessing requires his action. Any status Nicodemus holds means nothing.

What Do You Think?
  What can we do to trust less in our own capabilities and more in the Holy Spirit's?
Talking Points for Your Discussion
  • As we respond to blessings (Job 1:1-5; etc.)
  • As we respond to hardships (Job 1:21; etc.)

---

7. "Do not marvel that I said to you, 'You must be born again.'

Repeating the thought of verse 3, the translation *again* can be "from above," with Jesus perhaps intending both. Either way, Jesus reaffirms that God's action is what gives a person the blessings of his kingdom.

8. "The wind blows where it wishes, and you hear its sound, but you do not know where it comes from or where it goes. So it is with everyone who is born of the Spirit."

Continuing to challenge Nicodemus's lack of understanding, Jesus makes a comparison between God's *Spirit* and *the wind.* That comparison is especially pointed because in Greek the same word can mean either *wind* or *Spirit.* Wind, Jesus says, blows as it wants, without influence of humans and without their understanding. God's Spirit is the same: the Holy Spirit does his work regardless of the approval or disapproval of religious leaders like Nicodemus.

That man's familiarity with Israel's Scriptures should help Nicodemus understand this point. God's actions often defy human expectation. He called aged, childless Abraham to be the father of a great nation. He called enslaved Israel to overcome mighty Egypt. He worked through unlikely prophets and kings against the most powerful human empires. Now in Jesus, God is doing the same.

◆   *THE UNCONTROLLABLE WIND*   ◆

Wind is a constant in Nebraska. No matter the season or the weather, the wind blows. Author Willa Cather described grassland under its influence: "There was so much motion in it; the whole country seemed, somehow, to be running."

Wind becomes dangerous during thunderstorms. Every year we hear of tornadoes destroying homes and even entire towns in our part of the country. I grew up in Indiana, so I was no stranger to tornado drills in school. At the signal, we would all hurry to the safest spot, crouch down, and wait for the "all clear" signal.

In time, however, I began to disregard the danger, since so many of the alarms proved false. But longtime Nebraska residents, many having had firsthand experience with damaging winds, take the warnings seriously.

Those who have experienced tornadic fury personally know all too well how true it is that "the wind blows where it wishes." We have no control over its course or its power. So it is with God's Spirit. We cannot control him. We cannot dictate our plans to him. Our response, rather, is that of respect and submission.   —L. M. W.

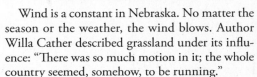

III. Jesus Critiques Nicodemus
(JOHN 3:9-16)

A. Contrast (vv. 9-13)

9. Nicodemus said to him, "How can these things be?"

Nicodemus remains perplexed. Jesus' words have defied the core of what Nicodemus believes about his relationship with God.

10. Jesus answered him, "Are you the teacher of Israel and yet you do not understand these things?

Jesus' reply now turns from the general to the personal. Nicodemus is a recognized authority among his fellow Jews, as the phrase *teacher of Israel* indicates (compare use of "teacher" in John 3:2). He believes that his position within God's people is secure. Yet he fails to understand Jesus' teaching.

If Nicodemus takes these words to heart, he will begin to discount his high position and surrender his cherished ideas (compare Philippians 3:4-11). Otherwise, he will have to deny Jesus' mighty deeds (John 3:2) and compelling teaching.

What Do You Think?

What should we contemplate before presuming to become teachers of the Bible?

Talking Points for Your Discussion

- Regarding what is to be taught (Titus 2:1-6, 9, 10; Hebrews 5:11–6:3; etc.)
- Regarding personal responsibility (Titus 2:7, 8; James 3:1; etc.)
- Regarding one's own teachability (Romans 2:21; Titus 2:12; etc.)
- Regarding spiritual giftedness and ability (Romans 12:7; 2 Timothy 2:24; etc.)
- Other

---

11. "Truly, truly, I say to you, we speak of what we know, and bear witness to what we have seen, but you do not receive our testimony.

A person can give *testimony* (not just opinion) about what the person knows as a witness. Jesus affirms that he and others are in such a position. Given that Nicodemus has already acknowledged the godly origin of Jesus' teaching and miracles (John 3:2), will he be inconsistent in daring to reject such witnesses?

12, 13. "If I have told you earthly things and you do not believe, how can you believe if I tell you heavenly things? No one has ascended into heaven except he who descended from heaven, the Son of Man.

Jesus knows of *heavenly things* because he is *from heaven* (compare John 8:23). But Nicodemus has had no such experience. So in speaking with him, Jesus has been using language and comparisons

that are accessible to that man, given his earthbound experiences: birth, water, and wind.

Yet Nicodemus does not understand. So Jesus calls on another Old Testament connection in referring to himself as *the Son of Man.* In Daniel 7:13, 14, "one like a son of man" receives authority from God to rule the earth, defeating the beastly empires. Jesus claims that role. He asserts that because God has authorized him and sent him down from Heaven, he speaks with unique knowledge and authority. The fulfillment of all God's promises is tied to Jesus (compare Proverbs 30:4).

What Do You Think?

How can we better show our need for the knowledge and help of one "from heaven"?

Talking Points for Your Discussion

- Before undertaking a project or ministry
- During a difficult situation
- After failing at something

B. Comparison (vv. 14, 15)

14. "And as Moses lifted up the serpent in the wilderness, so must the Son of Man be lifted up,

Jesus makes another connection with Israel's Scriptures. When God sent "fiery serpents" among the unfaithful Israelites *in the wilderness,* he instructed Moses to make a bronze serpent and lift it up on a pole. Those who looked at *the serpent* lived, their action being one of faith in God's mercy (Numbers 21:4-9). Jesus, *the Son of Man,* will also *be lifted up,* but on a cross (John 8:28; 12:32-34). Unlike the bronze serpent, Jesus is worthy of worship (compare 2 Kings 18:4).

15. "that whoever believes in him may have eternal life.

Like Moses' lifting of the bronze serpent for the stricken Israelites, Jesus' crucifixion will mean life. This will be life that is no longer plagued by the ancient serpent, the deceiver of humanity (Genesis 3:1-15). Daniel's triumphant "son of man" defeats the kingdoms of evil and establishes the reign of God (again, Daniel 7:13, 14).

We wonder how Nicodemus reacts to Jesus' declarations. The text does not say, but Jesus' words must seem to be an unsolvable riddle. The earth-shattering events of Jesus' death, resurrection, and ascension will be needed to make the meaning plain. For now, Nicodemus is challenged to set aside his own claim to authority and listen submissively to the one from Heaven.

C. Compassion (v. 16)

16. "For God so loved the world, that he gave his only Son, that whoever believes in him should not perish but have eternal life."

Jesus' discourse reaches its climax in what is probably the most famous verse of the New Testament. Having challenged Nicodemus with a new way of understanding God's plan, Jesus now focuses on the self-giving love of God for all humanity.

Such love transcends the kind that focuses on the attractiveness of the object or on one's connection to the object. This is more than the love of friendship, family, or romance. God loves humanity despite its unloveliness, failure, and open rebellion. *The world* that God loves is the world that refuses to listen to him (John 1:10, 11). For God's love to be effective, he must take the initiative—and he does.

God reaches out by sending *his only Son*. God had challenged Abraham to sacrifice Isaac, his unique son of promise (Genesis 22:2), and by faith Abraham had declared that God would provide the sacrifice (22:8). Now God provides that sacrifice to the world.

This gift, like all God's gifts, must be received by faith (Acts 10:43; 1 Corinthians 12:9; Ephesians 2:8; etc.). To believe in the one whom God sends is to affirm (1) that God has truly sent him, (2) that God truly saves through him, and (3) that one trusts persistently in what God has done through him. The promised blessing has two sides: escaping the eternal death we deserve and gaining the *eternal life* we do not deserve. Eternal life is life in the era of God's fulfilled promise. It is life restored to his ideal. It is life characterized by faith in the self-giving God. It is life in which believers in Jesus reflect God's self-giving love in their own self-giving service for one another (John 13:12-17, 34, 35).

Conclusion

A. The Mystery of God's Love

For Nicodemus, the story of God's love was a mystery for two reasons: it challenged his view of his own importance, and it was still unfolding before his eyes. For us the story may be a mystery as well. Though we might not think ourselves important, we still hold stubbornly to our independence. Though we know the story's climax, it may be so familiar to us that we find it commonplace.

Perhaps we need to reclaim the mysterious wonder of the Bible's storyline as it is summarized in today's text. The God who created us has acted time and again to undo the guilt and power of sin. Jesus predicted that such efforts would reach their climax in himself as the one who went on to be lifted up on the cross. The only Son of God surrendered to death so that undeserving humans would not have to.

You and I are those undeserving humans, the ones whom God so loved that he gave Jesus over to death (Romans 3:23-26). By his resurrection he claimed authority that belongs to God alone. By his authority alone can people enter God's promised kingdom, the full realization of his gracious love.

B. Prayer

God of unfathomable love, we thank you for your unspeakable gift in Christ! We commit ourselves again to trust in him and him alone, now and forever. We pray this in his name. Amen!

C. Thought to Remember

Only Christianity has a John 3:16.

INVOLVEMENT LEARNING

Enhance your lesson presentation with the reproducible activity page,
available as a free download at www.standardlesson.com.

Into the Lesson

As learners arrive, give each a piece of paper. Say, "Imagine being 10 years old and you have been asked, 'What do you want to be when you grow up?' Write down that occupation, but do not show it to anyone."

After all students have arrived and written their responses to the question, ask a volunteer to state, in any order, three occupations including the one on his or her paper. The class should try to guess the job written on that volunteer's paper. Continue this game with as many other volunteers as time and interest allows.

Alternative. Distribute copies of the "Here to Help" activity from the reproducible page, which you can download. Have students work individually or in pairs.

After either activity, lead into Bible study by saying, "There are many praiseworthy occupations. Many of us have chosen a job because we have a desire to help others and to make the world a better place. But as much as every job is necessary in some way, only one person came to do more than help. He came to save! Let's look at a very well-known passage of Scripture today."

Into the Word

Divide your class into three groups. Each group is to create a brief skit in which a Christian is responding to a non-Christian friend's idea about what will save the world. The ideas from the non-Christian and a relevant Scripture make up the assignments. Our suggested responses follow.

Group 1—The world doesn't need Jesus. We need education. When people know how the world works, everything will be better.

Respond with ideas from John 3:1-3 (focusing on v. 3).

We need more than learning what is right and wrong. We need a brand-new, born-again nature that will enable us to do right and not wrong.

Group 2—The world doesn't need Jesus. We need great social programs. When people have plenty of food and adequate health care, everything will be better.

Respond with ideas from John 3:4-9 (focusing on v. 6).

While it is great to make people healthy—even healthy people will eventually die. We need spiritual rebirth, not just physical maintenance.

Group 3—The world doesn't need Jesus. We need the wisest politicians possible. When the world is directed by truly learned people, everything will be better.

Respond with ideas from John 3:10-16 (focusing on vv. 11, 13).

Wise political leaders only know what they have experienced or studied about the world. We need authoritative answers from the Creator of the world.

Allow time for groups to perform their skits.

Into Life

Say, "John 3:16 is such a familiar verse that we may fail to consider how deeply profound it is."

Prepare to close the class by having a student read or recite John 3:16. Then look at that student and say, "So what!" You will probably get a shocked reaction, but continue to press, asking the class how those words should change our lives.

A few points that may emerge are: God loves the world, not just one nation, culture, or interest group. While God would have been justified giving people a death sentence, he sacrificed to give us life. Being saved means one no longer has to fear death. God made it possible to live for eternity, not just for this moment.

Alternative. Distribute copies of the "Applying John 3:16" activity from the reproducible page. Use it as a way to challenge learners to think of the tremendous change this precious statement can make in the lives of others.

VICTORIOUS LOVE

DEVOTIONAL READING: Luke 24:1-12
BACKGROUND SCRIPTURE: John 19:38-42; 20:1-10; 1 Peter 1:3-9

JOHN 20:1-10

¹ Now on the first day of the week Mary Magdalene came to the tomb early, while it was still dark, and saw that the stone had been taken away from the tomb. 2 So she ran and went to Simon Peter and the other disciple, the one whom Jesus loved, and said to them, "They have taken the LORD out of the tomb, and we do not know where they have laid him." ³ So Peter went out with the other disciple, and they were going toward the tomb. ⁴ Both of them were running together, but the other disciple outran Peter and reached the tomb first. ⁵ And stooping to look in, he saw the linen cloths lying there, but he did not go in. ⁶ Then Simon Peter came, following him, and went into the tomb. He saw the linen cloths lying there, ⁷ and the face cloth, which had been on Jesus'[a] head, not lying with the linen cloths but folded up in a place by itself. ⁸ Then the other disciple, who had reached the tomb first, also went in, and he saw and believed; ⁹ for as yet they did not understand the Scripture, that he must rise from the dead. ¹⁰ Then the disciples went back to their homes.

1 PETER 1:3-9

³ Blessed be the God and Father of our LORD Jesus Christ! According to his great mercy, he has caused us to be born again to a living hope through the resurrection of Jesus Christ from the dead, ⁴ to an inheritance that is imperishable, undefiled, and unfading, kept in heaven for you, ⁵ who by God's power are being guarded through faith for a salvation ready to be revealed in the last time. ⁶ In this you rejoice, though now for a little while, if necessary, you have been grieved by various trials, ⁷ so that the tested genuineness of your faith—more precious than gold that perishes though it is tested by fire—may be found to result

in praise and glory and honor at the revelation of Jesus Christ. ⁸ Though you have not seen him, you love him. Though you do not now see him, you believe in him and rejoice with joy that is inexpressible and filled with glory, ⁹ obtaining the outcome of your faith, the salvation of your souls.

KEY VERSE

The other disciple, who had reached the tomb first, also went in, and he saw and believed. —John 20:8

God Loves Us

Unit 2: God's Caring, Saving, and Upholding Love

LESSONS 5–9

LESSON AIMS

After participating in this lesson, each learner will be able to:

1. Summarize what happened on the first day of the week after Jesus' crucifixion.

2. Describe why Jesus' resurrection is the victory of God's love over death.

3. Explain to a new Christian or an unbeliever the importance of Christ's resurrection.

LESSON OUTLINE

Introduction

A. When Did the Victory Begin?

If you listen to the postgame analysis of a sports event, you are likely to hear discussed, in one form or another, this question: What was the key to the winning side's victory? The key may have been one particular play that shifted momentum decisively, the play in question becoming a turning point.

The same question can be modified to inquire of the grand storyline of our world. The question in that case is this: What event is key to God's victory in and over the world? The Bible's answer to that question is the resurrection of Jesus. In that event, God turned the tide of history decisively toward his goals. Jesus' resurrection fulfilled promises of the past, addresses the needs of the present, and anchors hope for the eternal future.

We study two texts today in that regard. The first concerns eyewitnesses of Jesus' empty tomb as recorded in the Gospel of John. There Jesus' resurrection serves as the greatest of his "signs." These are the events that proved him to be the divine Son of God, the events that provide yet today the impulse for the faith in him that gives life (John 20:30, 31).

The second text is from 1 Peter. This book, actually a letter, was addressed to several churches in regions of Asia Minor (modern Turkey) that faced social pressure and persecution because of faith in Christ. To readers living in fear and uncertainty, this book served to remind them that Jesus' resurrection meant that they were participants in Christ's life, his sufferings, his resurrection, and the eternal victory.

B. Lesson Background

We can appreciate that message better when we understand the background to belief in the New Testament's presentation of resurrection. Although the Old Testament ascribes to God the power of life and death, it is remarkably quiet about what lies beyond the universal human experience of death. Faithful people in the Old Testament era expressed confidence that God was reliable always, even as his people faced death (examples: Job 19:25; Psalm 56:13). Some of the prophets spoke briefly and mysteriously of God's raising the dead (Isaiah 26:19; Daniel 12:2). But their messages focused mostly on the restoration of Israel after exile.

Belief that God would one day raise the dead became stronger among the Jews during the centuries between the testaments. As they faced generations of disappointment, hardship, and persecution, people of faith came to understand that God would surely be faithful to *all* his people when he fulfills promises to remake the world. Those Jews reasoned that since many of God's people will be dead when he fulfills those end-time promises, then surely he will raise the dead at that time. As a result, all God's people—those who have already died and those still alive—will experience the fulfillment of God's blessings together.

Jesus, the New Testament writers, and some of Jesus' opponents affirmed belief that God will raise the dead (examples, respectively: Luke 20:35; 1 Thessalonians 4:16; Acts 23:6-8). But the New Testament describes something more radical yet: that God began to fulfill his end-time promises by raising the Messiah from the dead. No one anticipated this preparatory step (Luke 24:25-27; etc.). Jesus' resurrection means that God's promised gifts of the end time—truth, peace, justice, and mercy—were and are becoming reality.

I. The Risen Christ

(JOHN 20:1-10)

A. Empty Tomb Discovered (vv. 1, 2)

1. Now on the first day of the week Mary Magdalene came to the tomb early, while it was still dark, and saw that the stone had been taken away from the tomb.

Earlier in the text, readers are introduced to women who witness Jesus' death (John 19:25). Three of these are named *Mary*, so it's easy to get

HOW TO SAY IT

Magdalene	*Mag*-duh-leen or Mag-duh-*lee*-nee.
Messiah	Meh-*sigh*-uh.

confused. That's undoubtedly why John includes the designation *Magdalene* here. That is not her last name, as modern convention regarding surnames might tempt us to think. Rather, it indicates that she is from Magdala, a town on the western shore of the Sea of Galilee.

In Luke 8:2 "Mary, called Magdalene" is identified as one from whom Jesus cast out "seven demons." She and other women are coming to Jesus' tomb at dawn to complete the preparation of his body for burial (Luke 23:55–24:1, 10). That effort had been cut short by the beginning of the Sabbath at sundown on the day of the crucifixion (John 19:31).

The tomb's entrance had been sealed with a large, round, flat stone—very heavy and difficult to move. Mental alarm bells must go off for Mary Magdalene when she sees that this stone is now moved away from the tomb's entrance. Clearly something unusual has happened.

2a. So she ran and went to Simon Peter and the other disciple, the one whom Jesus loved, and said to them,

Alarmed, Mary returns hurriedly to report her discovery to two of Jesus' disciples. *Simon Peter* is often their spokesman, his name appearing first in all four listings of the Twelve in Matthew 10:2-4; Mark 3:16-19; Luke 6:13-16; and Acts 1:13.

References to this *other disciple* (though not always in those words) appear repeatedly in the latter part of this Gospel (John 13:23; 18:15, 16; 19:26, 27). Undoubtedly these refer to the author himself: John, whose name appears among the top four in the four listings above. Some see the phrase *the one whom Jesus loved* to indicate a close friendship between John and Jesus. Others believe that the phrase expresses the author's awe that he is personally loved by God's Son.

2b. "They have taken the Lord out of the tomb, and we do not know where they have laid him."

Mary reports what she has seen—or, rather, what she hasn't: Jesus' body. Grave robbery, common at the time, would be the first assumption. Regardless, Mary wants to retrieve the body of *the Lord* (compare John 20:15). That term reflects her deep devotion to him even after his death.

B. Empty Tomb Confirmed (vv. 3-7)

3, 4. So Peter went out with the other disciple, and they were going toward the tomb. Both of them were running together, but the other disciple outran Peter and reached the tomb first.

Peter and *the other disciple* react by rushing to *the tomb*. Given their continuing fear of later this day (John 20:19), they too have no expectation that an empty tomb means that Jesus has been raised to life.

The two men arrive at the tomb at different times, take different actions, and manifest different responses. The text supplies these details to challenge readers to move from the evidence of the story to faith in the one who is the subject of the story (John 20:30, 31).

5, 6. And stooping to look in, he saw the linen cloths lying there, but he did not go in. Then Simon Peter came, following him, and went into the tomb. He saw the linen cloths lying there,

The *he* of verse 5 is John, the "other disciple" per above. Without entering the tomb, he can see the pieces of fabric that had wrapped Jesus' body. These *linen cloths* must be those of Jesus, since the tomb has been otherwise unused (compare Luke 23:50-54).

Arriving after John, the characteristically bold (or rash) Peter steps past him and enters the tomb. Jesus' body has not been stolen by grave robbers, since thieves would not take the time to unwrap a body before making off with it. This is a mysterious matter indeed!

> **What Do You Think?**
> How do we know when a situation calls for the boldness of a Simon Peter rather than the caution of a John? How about the reverse?
> *Talking Points for Your Discussion*
> - "Fools rush in where angels fear to tread."
>   —Alexander Pope
> - "Sometimes the fool who rushes in gets the job done."   —Al Bernstein

7. and the face cloth, which had been on Jesus' head, not lying with the linen cloths but folded up in a place by itself.

Being closer to the scene than John, Peter sees the details noted here. Such details reinforce that we are reading the testimony of eyewitnesses. The tomb is undeniably empty, and not because of robbery, the story told by some of the opponents of Jesus (Matthew 28:11-15).

C. Empty Tomb Considered (vv. 8-10)

8. Then the other disciple, who had reached the tomb first, also went in, and he saw and believed;

Now John (*the other disciple*) enters. What he sees prompts him to believe. The text does not mention what he believes, because that is clear from the context: he believes that Jesus has risen from the dead. This final and greatest of Jesus' signs is having its divinely intended effect.

> **What Do You Think?**
> How should those who are quicker to believe respond to those who are slower to do so?
> *Talking Points for Your Discussion*
> - In attitudes
> - In words
> - In actions
> - Considering John 1:47-49 in relation to John 20:24-29

9. for as yet they did not understand the Scripture, that he must rise from the dead.

Although John now believes that Jesus has risen *from the dead*, John does not yet understand why this has taken place. With time to reflect, however, Jesus' followers will conclude that his death and resurrection were God's intention all along and therefore anticipated in *Scripture*.

That conclusion is based not on a single proof text, but drawn from numerous Old Testament passages (see Luke 24:27). Perhaps clearest of these is Isaiah 52:13–53:12, which depicts God's servant willingly giving his life for the guilty, yet being victoriously alive again.

10. Then the disciples went back to their homes.

As Peter and John exit the tomb, we are left with a sense of expectancy. Indeed, the verse before us serves as a transition. That which follows narrates Jesus' subsequent appearance to Mary Magdalene (John 20:11-18) and then to the gathered disciples on three occasions (20:19-23, 24-29; 21:1-23).

These appearances confirm what John, the disciple with Peter, has come to believe: that Jesus is victoriously alive again, even though he had been killed. God's promises are being fulfilled. The era of God's salvation has begun.

> What Do You Think?
> Which details of John's resurrection account most strengthen your faith? Why?
> Talking Points for Your Discussion
> - Regarding your Christian service now
> - Regarding your expectation of being with Christ for eternity

II. The Empowering Christ
(1 Peter 1:3-9)
A. Rejoicing in Resurrection Life (vv. 3-5)

3. Blessed be the God and Father of our Lord Jesus Christ! According to his great mercy, he has caused us to be born again to a living hope through the resurrection of Jesus Christ from the dead,

After the introductory greetings of verses 1 and 2, the verse before us marks the beginning of the thanksgiving section of 1 Peter. Most letters of this era include a brief statement thanking whatever god or gods the writer worships. New Testament letters turn this convention into an occasion for praise of the one true God.

The thanksgiving section opens here with a specific focus: thanks to God for the suffering Christian's relationship with the crucified and risen Jesus. Indeed, the letter as a whole emphasizes this relationship.

Similar to what Jesus says in John 3:3, Peter describes that relationship in terms of being "born again" (1 Peter 1:23). That points to the new beginning to life as brought about by *the resurrection of Jesus Christ from the dead.* Because he was raised from the dead, so are those who are united with him (Romans 6:3-11; Colossians

2:12; 1 Peter 3:21; etc.). In this new life, Christians have *a living hope*—a confident expectation about the future.

4. to an inheritance that is imperishable, undefiled, and unfading, kept in heaven for you,

Peter portrays the experience of the new life as *an inheritance.* That term reminds us of the Old Testament's description of God's gift of the promised land to Israel (Numbers 34:2). But the realization of the promise of which Peter writes is more certain than that one. Israel's disobedience meant exile from the land of promise; by contrast, the Christian's inheritance is assured.

Peter describes this assurance by piling up terms that stress its utter permanence (compare Matthew 6:19, 20). Unlike any earthly inheritance, it cannot fail because it is *kept in heaven.* That expression also indicates that the Christian's inheritance is to be experienced beyond the limits of life on earth. The hardships in the world cannot touch that blessing, for it is kept safe by God, who rules from Heaven. The gift of new life that Christians experience now, they shall have forever.

◆ *The Only Threat* ◆

Huguette Clark inherited her father's fortune, which he made in copper mining. When she died at age 104 in 2011, her last will and testament specified that 75 percent of her $300 million estate was to go to charity. The remaining 25 percent was to be divided among various nonrelatives and a foundation.

Then, of course, came the civil lawsuits and criminal investigations. When the dust had settled two years later, distant relatives ended up receiving substantial amounts. By contrast, someone originally designated to receive about $30 million ended up with nothing. No earthly inheritance can be considered totally sure!

By contrast, Peter assures us that our eternal inheritance *is* secure. We need not worry that others may steal it. No court action can revoke it. No power of darkness can prevent us from receiving it. Even so, Peter also warns of one threat to this certain inheritance. You can read about it in 2 Peter 3:17. —C. R. B.

He Lives

He lives, He lives,
Christ Jesus lives today!
He walks with me
and talks with me
along life's narrow way.
He lives, He lives,
salvation to bestow!
You ask me how I know
He lives?

The BIBLE tells me so.

Visual for Lesson 7. *Start a discussion by asking learners why the changed wording to the chorus of this familiar hymn is superior to the original.*

5. who by God's power are being guarded through faith for a salvation ready to be revealed in the last time.

Jesus' followers, though threatened on all sides, are nevertheless secure in every situation. Their security rests in *God's power*, which is greater than any force the hostile world can muster. Already experiencing God's salvation in the present (1 Peter 1:3), Christians look forward to that aspect of their *salvation ready to be revealed in the last time*—the time when God's victory will be completed at Christ's coming. Then the world will see what Christians already know: that God is victorious in Christ, and so are those who are united with Christ by faith.

B. Rejoicing in Fiery Trials (vv. 6-9)

6. In this you rejoice, though now for a little while, if necessary, you have been grieved by various trials,

The Christians' standing before God is in sharp contrast with their standing with the world. In a hostile world, they face many *trials*. These are tests of the Christian's faith in God's victory through Christ's resurrection.

Such testings come in many ways, each bringing a new challenge. They are no light matter: they cause deep sorrow, like the grief of death. Yet they do not overcome the joy that lives in the heart of the person who belongs to God in Christ. As Christ's resurrection has overturned his follow-

ers' grief at his death, so it empowers them in the midst of testings.

7. so that the tested genuineness of your faith—more precious than gold that perishes though it is tested by fire—may be found to result in praise and glory and honor at the revelation of Jesus Christ.

Put to the test, true *faith* witnesses to the power of God's victory in Christ (compare Psalm 66:10). As *gold* is *tested by fire*, separated from the less precious minerals mixed with it, so the faith of Christians is made purer and stronger by the challenges they experience (compare Zechariah 13:9; James 1:12; Revelation 2:2, 3, 13, 19; contrast Ezekiel 22:18; Matthew 13:20, 21).

God's plan reached its climax and his victory was secured as Christ underwent his own fiery trial. Believers whose faith is refined by trial show their unity with Christ in suffering and their empowerment by Christ's resurrection. *At the revelation of Jesus Christ*, when he returns to appear to all as the world's true king, the faithfulness of suffering believers will be testimony to his victory over evil. The result of that testing is ultimately God's glorification.

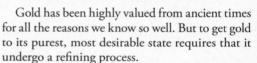

♦ *REFINING PROCESS AND RESULT* ♦

Gold has been highly valued from ancient times for all the reasons we know so well. But to get gold to its purest, most desirable state requires that it undergo a refining process.

When extracting gold from ore, smelting is the first step. This requires heat of about 1950° Fahrenheit. After successful extraction, impurities are removed by further melting. Borax and soda ash are added to the liquefied gold, which causes separation of gold from impurities.

Peter's comparison of faith with purified gold carries two vital truths. First, gold perishes. Think about how we tend to lose gold rings, etc., and how these are subject to theft. Even if a gold ring is never lost or stolen, it remains part of the physical world to be destroyed (2 Peter 3:10). Second, faith must be refined to be proven valid. That process comes in the crucible of a "fiery trial" (1 Peter 4:12-19). If you haven't had one (or more) yet, you will. Be ready.

—C. R. B.

What Do You Think?

In what ways have you seen God glorified through human trials? What have such experiences taught you?

Talking Points for Your Discussion

- Regarding trials you have experienced
- Regarding the trials of others

8. Though you have not seen him, you love him. Though you do not now see him, you believe in him and rejoice with joy that is inexpressible and filled with glory,

Peter is known to his readers as having been an eyewitness of Jesus' earthly ministry (2 Peter 1:16-18). But the readers are not eyewitnesses (*have not seen him*). Even so, they believe in Jesus because of the testimony of those who were there (compare John 20:29). Peter's audience trusts his testimony, so they put their confident trust in the invisible Christ. They express a deep, heartfelt joy that he has made them his and now rules over them.

Now these believers are under social pressure for their faith. This is pressure they experience firsthand. The question for them is whether what they see on earth will be more powerful than what they do not see, that is, Christ's triumphant rule from Heaven.

The day will come when they do indeed see Christ's rule, a day when all will see it. In the meantime, Christians express their belief in the unseen victory of Christ, present and future, with joy that is almost as difficult to express as Christ's glory is difficult to see.

What Do You Think?

What can we do to encourage others' faith in the risen Christ, whom we have not seen?

Talking Points for Your Discussion

- In face-to-face discussions
- When separated by great distance
- During a crisis
- Other

As they live this way and express this *joy that is inexpressible,* Christians are the "seen" manifestations of the "unseen" victorious power of Christ at work in our lives. Our joy while enduring suffering testifies to the world that the Christ who died is the Christ who rose and rules.

9. obtaining the outcome of your faith, the salvation of your souls.

This whole process—believing in the unseen, risen, glorified Christ and rejoicing in suffering because of him—naturally and inevitably accompanies the saving work that God is doing in our lives. *The outcome of your faith* speaks to the goal or purpose of our faith.

To receive that outcome does not speak merely of something that lies in the future. The sentence structure in the original language shows that this *obtaining* happens along with the believing and rejoicing of verse 8. *The salvation of your souls* is indeed life beyond the grave, but it is also the remaking of our lives in the present. Because God's love is victorious in Christ, you and I are already living in the salvation that God has for us forever. The blessed life we have now as God's people will only become greater when Christ appears.

Conclusion

A. The Christ of the Empty Tomb

Christ's resurrection is the turning point of all history. On that incomparable day, God defeated death for all time. He turned the tide of human life, bringing the evil one and those who serve him to their knees. He brought the fullness of his undeserved blessing to all who put their faith in the risen Christ.

Look to the empty tomb. Look to the lives of those who declare the Christ of that empty tomb to be Lord. As you do so, you will see God's victory.

B. Prayer

Lord, though we face many hardships that put us to the test, we rejoice in the new life we have through Jesus. Guide us so that we can live lives that express his glory. We pray this in Jesus' name. Amen.

C. Thought to Remember

See Christ's victory again for the first time.

INVOLVEMENT LEARNING

Enhance your lesson presentation with the reproducible activity page,
available as a free download at www.standardlesson.com.

Into the Lesson

Before class begins, write this list of historic turning points on the board or distribute as photocopied handouts:

1. President Truman orders atomic bombs dropped on Hiroshima and Nagasaki, Japan, ending World War II in the Pacific.

2. Martin Luther nails his 95 Theses to the door of the Castle Church of Wittenberg, providing the catalyst for the Protestant Reformation.

3. Gutenberg produces a Bible using movable type, starting the age of the printed book in the West.

4. Alexander the Great begins a 10-year campaign to conquer most of the civilized world, resulting in the spread of the Greek language and culture.

5. Christopher Columbus leads the first of four voyages to find Asia and lands in what is now the Bahamas. This opens the door to European colonization of what is now called the American continents.

Under the list of turning points, have these years: A. 336 BC. B. AD 1492. C. AD 1517. D. AD 1455. E. AD 1945.

Ask learners to match the events with the years. The answers are 1=E. 2=C. 3=D. 4=A. 5=B.

Lead into the Bible study by saying, "History has had noticeable turning points. But any turning points we can mention pale in comparison to an event that happened early on a Sunday morning in approximately AD 30. Let's explore this fact further."

Into the Word

Divide the class into two groups; give each group paper and pens. Each group should read its assigned text, looking for key words and phrases. Learners are to use the words to create an acrostic from the key word you gave them. Assignments and sample acrostics follow:

Group 1—DESPAIR (John 20:1-10)
> Still **D**ark
> Desecrat**E**d Grave
> Body **S**tolen
> **P**eter Investigates
> Gr**A**ve Clothes Left
> Lim**I**ted Understanding
> **R**eturn Home

Group 2—VICTORY (1 Peter 1:3-9)
> Li**V**ing Hope
> **I**nheritance
> **C**hrist's love
> Salva**T**ion
> P**O**wer of God's protection
> New Bi**R**th
> Jo**Y**

Allow time for groups to share their acrostics and summarize their assignments.

Alternative. Distribute copies of the "From Early Morning to the Late Show" activity from the reproducible page. Select volunteers to play Peter, John, Mary Magdalene, and a fictitious talk show host. Use this skit to help explain the Bible texts.

Into Life

Say, "You have a good friend who is a new Christian. Not growing up in the church, this person has a lot of questions and says, 'I understand why Christmas is so important, but why does the church make such a big deal about Easter? What makes this day extra special?'"

Have learners use today's lesson text as well as other passages (such as Romans 6:4; 8:11, 34; 1 Corinthians 15:54-57; 2 Corinthians 4:14) to explain the importance of the resurrection. Allow time for discussion, and close in group prayer.

RECONCILING LOVE

DEVOTIONAL READING: Romans 1:1-15
BACKGROUND SCRIPTURE: Romans 5:1-11; 8:31-39

ROMANS 5:6-11

[6] For while we were still weak, at the right time Christ died for the ungodly. [7] For one will scarcely die for a righteous person—though perhaps for a good person one would dare even to die— [8] but God shows his love for us in that while we were still sinners, Christ died for us. [9] Since, therefore, we have now been justified by his blood, much more shall we be saved by him from the wrath of God. [10] For if while we were enemies we were reconciled to God by the death of his Son, much more, now that we are reconciled, shall we be saved by his life. [11] More than that, we also rejoice in God through our LORD Jesus Christ, through whom we have now received reconciliation.

ROMANS 8:31-39

[31] What then shall we say to these things? If God is for us, who can be against us? [32] He who did not spare his own Son but gave him up for us all, how will he not also with him graciously give us all things? [33] Who shall bring any charge against God's elect? It is God who justifies. [34] Who is to condemn? Christ Jesus is the one who died—more than that, who was raised—who is at the right hand of God, who indeed is interceding for us. [35] Who shall separate us from the love of Christ? Shall tribulation, or distress, or persecution, or famine, or nakedness, or danger, or sword? [36] As it is written,

> "For your sake we are being killed all the
>   day long;
>   we are regarded as sheep to be
>   slaughtered."

[37] No, in all these things we are more than conquerors through him who loved us. [38] For I am sure that neither death nor life, nor angels nor rulers, nor things present nor things to come, nor powers, [39] nor height nor depth, nor anything else in all creation, will be able to separate us from the love of God in Christ Jesus our Lord.

KEY VERSE

I am sure that neither death nor life, nor angels nor rulers, nor things present nor things to come, nor powers, nor height nor depth, nor anything else in all creation, will be able to separate us from the love of God in Christ Jesus our Lord. —**Romans 8:38, 39**

GOD LOVES US

Unit 2: God's Caring, Saving, and Upholding Love

LESSONS 5–9

LESSON AIMS

After participating in this lesson, each learner will be able to:

1. List reasons why God's reconciliation in Christ is invincible.

2. Explain the connection between *being justified* and *being reconciled*.

3. Identify and implement one personal life change to make in order better to live out God's reconciling love.

LESSON OUTLINE

Introduction

A. Assuring Victory

We've just passed the time of year known in the sports world as March Madness. Media was saturated with coverage of this, the highlight of the year in college basketball. That coverage is certain to include analysis of the preparations that coaches and players undertake to assure victory. Such preparations cover a wide spectrum, from the eminently practical to the hilariously superstitious. But history tells us that there is no 100 percent assurance of victory, no matter what preparations are made. Upsets happen!

By contrast, the two text segments of today's lesson speak of that which is assured absolutely. God has done all the work through Christ to bring about this blessed assurance.

B. Lesson Background

Paul's letter to the church in Rome sets forth the grand scope of what he calls "my gospel" (Romans 2:16; 16:25). This scope includes how it addresses the deepest need of rebellious humanity, how it fulfills the foundational promises that God made to his people in history, and how it transforms death to life and slavery to freedom. The result is nothing less than fallen humanity's reconciliation with their Creator.

In laying out these truths, Paul was urging the Christians in Rome to renew their commitment not just to God but also to one another. Apparently the church had experienced a certain division between Christians of Jewish and non-Jewish backgrounds. Each group seemed to have been asserting a greater claim to God's forgiveness (compare Romans 2:17-29; 11:13-24). This tawdry game of one-upmanship was intolerable, so Paul demonstrated that no group can claim a privileged position; all people are rebels against God (3:9-18, 23).

But through Christ all can be reconciled to God (Romans 3:21-26). To be a Christian is to be one "whose lawless deeds are forgiven, and whose sins are covered" by the blood of Christ (4:7). This state of blessedness is available to both Jew and Gentile, without prejudice (4:9). These facts are preparatory for Paul's unfolding argument.

I. Enemies Become Children

(ROMANS 5:6-11)

The "therefore" of Romans 5:1 introduces the theme of assurance in terms of the peace the Christian has now and the hope he or she has for the future. When we reach verse 6, the apostle allows us to consider even greater proof of the assured peace and hope that Christians have as God's reconciled people.

A. Love and Death (vv. 6-8)

6. For while we were still weak, at the right time Christ died for the ungodly.

Regardless of who we are or what we have done, we are helpless to overcome the result of our rebellion against God. We can resolve to do better, and we may do so. But we can never go back and change what we have done. Paul has shown at this point in his letter that all are guilty of sin and without means of removing their own guilt.

But it is at this very point of weakness—our inability to reverse the guilt and power of our own sin—that Christ's saving work comes to bear. Christ came for those who are unable to help themselves, which is everyone. We are all members of *the ungodly* (compare Romans 4:5) before he rescues us. The ungodly have not shown God the honor that is his right and due.

Further yet, Christ did not simply come for the ungodly, as if merely to teach us how to live better. He *died* for us willingly. In his strength he gave himself over to utter weakness for the sake of the weak. In his goodness he gave his innocent life in place of our guilty lives. On his gracious love, demonstrated at the cross, stands the believer's confident assurance.

> *What Do You Think?*
> What convinces you most that you need daily what God offers in Christ?
> *Talking Points for Your Discussion*
> - Regarding physical challenges
> - Regarding spiritual challenges
> - Regarding relationship challenges
> - Other

7. For one will scarcely die for a righteous person—though perhaps for a good person one would dare even to die—

A person dying for another is most exceptional. Paul reminds us of this point to emphasize how extraordinary Christ's death is and how far beyond ordinary human experience God's love is.

Let us imagine, says Paul, *a righteous person*, someone who has been obedient to the laws and standards of society. Only in the rarest of cases can we imagine someone volunteering to die in the place of even such an honorable person. Then let us imagine *a good person*, one who "out of the good treasure of his heart produces good" (Luke 6:45). Certainly someone might voluntarily *dare even to die* on his behalf, but even that would be rare.

8. but God shows his love for us in that while we were still sinners, Christ died for us.

Christ did not die for righteous or good people. No, *while we were still sinners, Christ died for us*—for people who had rebelled against his authority as the divine king. This is well beyond even the outer bounds of human heroism!

The cross of Christ sets before the world the full demonstration of God's love. God loves not as humans do. We focus our love on those closest to us, but God's love is for everyone. It is boundless and utterly self-sacrificial. His love is for his enemies—and our sin makes us all his enemies at one time or another. The extent of God's love is seen in what he gives for the benefit of his enemies: the life of his Son.

Let there be no mistake here. God the Son, sinless himself (2 Corinthians 5:21) and sent by God the Father (John 3:16), physically died on a wooden cross to pay the penalty of the guilty (Romans 3:23-26). We will not be able to imagine a firmer foundation for confidence in our relationship with God than the cross of Christ. The death of the Son assures our peace and hope.

B. Justification and Reconciliation (vv. 9-11)

9. Since, therefore, we have now been justified by his blood, much more shall we be saved by him from the wrath of God.

The New Testament uses the language of salvation in different senses. Concerning time-based senses, which are seen here, we can think of salvation both in terms of what we possess right now and also as something that awaits realization in the future (Colossians 3:3, 4; 1 John 3:2).

By Christ's death (*his blood*) repentant sinners can be counted as righteous in the present (*have now been justified*; compare Romans 3:21-26). The fundamental truth is this: Christians stand justified before God—meaning treated as if not guilty of our sin—because of the righteousness imputed to us by Christ's work alone; being justified does not result from anything meritorious we have done. A marvelous result is that we enjoy God's blessings daily (Romans 4:6-8; etc.).

Regarding the future, we have no fear of Judgment Day. Being justified means to be *saved . . . from the wrath of God*. That future outpouring of anger will be his righteous, holy response to evil (Romans 2:5; Revelation 6:15-17; 11:18; etc.). Since God counts us as his people in the here and now, then certainly he will also save us from the wrath of judgment! His reconciling love assures our eternal future as long as we remain faithful (Romans 11:17-22; 1 Corinthians 15:1, 2; Colossians 1:21-23; Galatians 5:4).

> **What Do You Think?**
> What are some ways to express the confident assurance that Christ's death gives us?
> *Talking Points for Your Discussion*
> - In relationships
> - In priorities
> - In stewardship
> - In worship
> - Other

10. For if while we were enemies we were reconciled to God by the death of his Son, much more, now that we are reconciled, shall we be saved by his life.

This verse reveals parallels with verse 9 as Paul expands on his point about our present status in relation to our assured future. One parallel consists of the words *justified* (v. 9) and *reconciled* (here in v. 10). The former is from the language of the courtroom; the latter is from the language of relationships. Their use in parallel here may give Paul's readers an understanding that they might not otherwise have thought about. The parallel phrases *by his blood* (v. 9) and *by the death of his Son* (here in v. 10) help ensure that the readers don't miss this connection.

Looking back, we see that at one time *we were [God's] enemies*—the king's subjects who had mounted a rebellion against him. Not only were we hostile to him, he was hostile to us (Romans 1:18-32). God overcame that state of hostility, but it cost him dearly as the Father gave the Son over to death. Our penalty has been taken by another —the Son of God himself. Since God has paid such a high price to make possible the transforming of his enemies into his children (Romans 8:14-17), we can have utter confidence about the future (compare 2 Timothy 4:8).

◆ *Correct Sequence* ◆

In August 2014, a white policeman fatally shot a black man in Ferguson, Missouri, after a complicated chain of events. The result was a two-week wave of unrest. More unrest resulted in November when a grand jury declined to indict the officer.

Whether or not the grand jury's decision was proper in this particular incident, the U.S. Department of Justice subsequently determined that the practices of the Ferguson police department "violate the law and undermine community trust, especially among African Americans." This incident and its aftermath served to focus public attention yet again on issues of justice and reconciliation.

While some are quick to call for racial reconciliation, others say that justice must come first. How those two concepts interrelate can be complicated when they concern human-to-human relations! Part of the problem involves defining the terms *justice* and *reconciliation* to the satisfaction of all concerned.

But regarding our relationship with God, everything is quite straightforward: justice has already been served in the fact that the penalty for sin has been paid by Christ on the cross. This is the basis for our reconciliation with the one we once treated as an enemy—God.   —C. R. B.

11. More than that, we also rejoice in God through our Lord Jesus Christ, through whom we have now received reconciliation.

As our reconciliation in the present assures us of salvation in the future, so our future salvation transforms our present. Because we are justified, because we are reconciled, because we are saved —all *through our Lord Jesus Christ*—we have a triumphant declaration to make continually. *We also rejoice,* that is, we are victoriously joyful, about what God has accomplished in Christ. Love like this cannot be kept a secret.

II. Children Become Conquerors
(ROMANS 8:31-39)

Between the two segments of today's text, Paul further contrasts the readers' new status in Christ with their status before coming to him (Romans 5:12–7:6). This leads into thoughts on the purpose of the law in relation to sin (7:7-25) and implications of life in the Spirit (8:1-30). With those tasks completed, he is ready to summarize the "assurance section" of Romans, which extends from 5:1 through 8:39.

A. Invincible Advocate (vv. 31-34)

31. What then shall we say to these things? If God is for us, who can be against us?

In this section, Paul uses a series of questions to summarize the believer's status in God's love. The first question concerns the proper perspective to have in light of all that God has done. That question is answered with another, the answer to which is obvious. God is the greatest being, and what he has done to reconcile us is the greatest act of love we can imagine. So since God is our advocate—proven by what Jesus accomplished on the cross—then no opponent can prevail against us. Whatever hardships life brings, the cross speaks God's assurance to us.

32. He who did not spare his own Son but gave him up for us all, how will he not also with him graciously give us all things?

As he has done before, Paul reasons from God's past actions to his future actions. To reconcile us, God gave *his own Son* to suffer a tortuous, shameful death in our place. Christ put God's plan into action with great pain but greater determination (Luke 22:39-44).

In light of the cross, what will God do in the future? Surely he will affirm his Son's sacrifice by making him the world's king! But just as surely, he will affirm that sacrifice by making us to share in the Son's rule of the world (compare 1 Corinthians 15:25-28). Like a victorious army under an invincible general, God's people in Christ share with Christ the celebration of his victory.

33. Who shall bring any charge against God's elect? It is God who justifies.

No charge of guilt can be valid against those to whom Christ's blood has been applied—those whom God has made his *elect* because of their faith in his Son. Such people are in right standing with God, who has paid the penalty for their sin. No one can allege guilt where God pronounces innocence. "The accuser of our brothers has been thrown down" (Revelation 12:10).

34. Who is to condemn? Christ Jesus is the who died—more than that, who was raised— who is at the right hand of God, who indeed is interceding for us.

Should Jesus' followers worry that a charge of guilt will somehow slip through the forgiveness that God has provided? The answer is found in what Christ has accomplished. Christ's death was sufficient to pay the penalty of the sin of all humanity. His resurrection demonstrated his victory over the death that would have been our just punishment.

Jesus now rules in the position of supreme authority in Heaven. There he *is interceding for us* in the heavenly court of justice, an advocate who asserts authoritatively that our penalty is paid in full. There is no voice that speaks more authoritatively than his, nor any charge that is greater than the sacrificial price that he paid. As victor over death, Christ is the unanswerable advocate.

What Do You Think?
▶ In what specific ways can our church express in action that Christ was victorious in death?
Talking Points for Your Discussion
- Regarding outreach (evangelism, benevolence, etc.)
- Regarding upreach (worship, prayer, etc.)
- Regarding inreach (fellowship, nurture, etc.)

B. Insufficient Opponents (vv. 35-39)

35. Who shall separate us from the love of Christ? Shall tribulation, or distress, or persecution, or famine, or nakedness, or danger, or sword?

Having assessed our divine advocate, Paul now discusses various things that may threaten to *separate us from the love of Christ*. All are formidable. All are painful. But none measures up to God the Father or Christ the Son.

The listing is of the range of experiences that cause people to suffer. *Tribulation* is pressure or problems of any kind. *Distress* is similar: a term for pressured, painful trouble. *Persecution* is the distress wrought by people who deliberately oppose us.

The ancient world knows *famine* as a constant threat. The same is true for *nakedness,* when clothing is made by intensive manual labor and therefore very expensive. Paul uses the word *danger* eight times in 2 Corinthians 11:26 to refer to numerous perils he had faced to that point in his missionary travels. *Sword* reminds us specifically of human violence.

When faced with the difficulties of life, people ask, "Where is God? Does he no longer care about me?" But that's not what Paul asks. His preference is to ask whether anything can cancel the love of God that Christ has brought to us by his cross. Christ triumphed after he suffered. And in one way or another, we too will triumph after each and every suffering we endure. "If we endure, we will also reign with him" (2 Timothy 2:12).

What Do You Think?
▶ What guardrails can you erect to ensure that you do not separate yourself from the love of Christ during times of difficulty?
Talking Points for Your Discussion
- When unbelievers scorn your faith
- When you feel "not good enough"
- When negative circumstances pile up
- Other

36. As it is written:
"For your sake we are being killed all the day long;
we are regarded as sheep to be slaughtered."

The question of why God's people suffer is as old as humanity. Paul quotes an ancient biblical text to remind us of this, Psalm 44:22. There the faithful call out to God to deliver them as he had done for his people in the past. These words express the experience of God's people in every age, including those who can look back on the cross and therefore know the fulfillment of God's promises.

Human experiences are truly painful, as this quotation expresses. But as God's past deeds of deliverance provided assurance, so now Christ's victory provides even greater confidence.

◆ GOD'S LOVE IS GREATER ◆

American Christians have sometimes used the word *persecution* to describe their loss of a dominant role in American culture as values have changed. Often cited as evidence of this phenomenon are limits on Christian prayers at civic gatherings. But what's happening elsewhere in the world makes American "persecution" seem like a minor skin rash.

As Islamic militias expanded their violent control in the Middle East and Africa a few years ago, Christians there began to suffer severely. Many were beheaded publicly for the simple fact that they were Christians. Islamic radicals are the primary persecutors of the church in the Middle East, sub-Saharan Africa, Indonesia, and other parts of Asia. By one estimate, at least 180 Christians were killed each month for their faith in mid-2015.

It happened in the first century as well. Yet in writing to the Christians in Rome, Paul expressed his strong assurance of hope. Regardless of how much other people might hate them, God's love would be greater. Should martyrdom be their lot, God's love would still surround them (compare Acts 7:54-60). Do you know a "suffering someone" who needs your prayer that he or she continue to honor Christ? —C. R. B.

37. No, in all these things we are more than conquerors through him who loved us.

God's people experience a victory so great that Paul uses an intensified Greek word found nowhere else in the New Testament. In English it comes out as *we are more than conquerors*. Paul's confidence is not in his own strength, but in God's love-motivated victory in the work of Christ.

38, 39. For I am sure that neither death nor life, nor angels nor rulers, nor things present nor things to come, nor powers, nor height nor depth, nor anything else in all creation, will be able to separate us from the love of God that is in Christ Jesus our Lord.

To bring his point to a climax, Paul lists various threats to anticipate. He begins with *death*—the great fear of all people and the sentence that God pronounces on sin (Genesis 2:17; 6:3; Romans 5:12). Christ has overcome death by his resurrection (1 Corinthians 15:12-34). *Life* contrasts with death, but here it is named as a threat: anything that might befall as one lives. God's power is more than sufficient to overcome what life throws at us.

Angels and *rulers* are terms used in Paul's time for spirit beings. These threaten weak, mortal humans (Ephesians 6:12), but Christ stands supreme over all of them (Colossians 2:15). *Things present* and *things to come* suggest both our immediate circumstances and whatever may happen in the future. The terms *height* and *depth* encompass all that is above us and all that is below. The final category of *anything else in all creation* is an all-inclusive catchall to refer to any created thing imaginable.

Our relationship with God is secure because his love cannot be overcome by any external force. *Christ Jesus our Lord*, who reigns supreme, makes the ultimate outcome of God's love utterly certain.

Visual for Lesson 8. *Discuss this humorous visual as a preliminary to posing the serious question associated with verse 35.*

Conclusion
A. The Light of God's Love

Based as they are in the facts of Christ's death, resurrection, and ascension, today's texts paint a picture of enormous comfort: God's love reconciles us to him with utter certainty. Because our relationship to God is founded on his love in Christ and not on any goodness of ours, we can have complete confidence that we are now, and will always be, his saved and blessed people.

Even so, every believer has times of doubt as the turmoil of life raises questions about ourselves and our relationship to God. What transforms doubt into renewed faith is the good news of the cross and empty tomb. The divine Son of God gave his life for us to pay sin's price when we were his enemies. His resurrection assures our own. Even in our darkest moments, the light of God's love in Christ can shine brightly.

B. Prayer

O God, your love for us in Christ is indescribable! As we ponder how you reconciled us to yourself, may we be examples of people who are also reconciled to one another. We pray in Jesus' name. Amen.

C. Thought to Remember

When in doubt, remember the cross and the empty tomb.

INVOLVEMENT LEARNING

*Enhance your lesson presentation with the reproducible activity page,
available as a free download at www.standardlesson.com.*

Into the Lesson

Before class, write this phrase on the board:
You may be an egomaniac if . . .

As students arrive, have anyone who is willing go to the board and complete the sentence. You may wish to help your class along by starting the list with one or more of the following:

 . . . you have a special place in your heart for yourself!

 . . . you think a thunderclap is God giving you applause!

 . . . you believe you are too cool to be conceited!

 . . . you expect to get a gift on someone else's birthday!

Alternative. Distribute copies of the "Buy the Best!" activity from the reproducible page, which you can download. Have students work individually or in pairs to identify famous ad slogans.

After either activity, lead into the Bible study by saying, "Common wisdom tells us that we should be loved because we have great value. Today we will look at God's uncommon wisdom. The Bible says we have great value because we are loved!"

Into the Word

Divide your class into three groups. Give each group paper and pen, and assign each a section of the lesson text. Each group is to summarize its section with a couplet—two lines of rhyming poetry.

Assignments and sample couplets are as follows:

Photo: serdjophoto / iStock / Thinkstock

Group 1—Sure Hope (Romans 5:6-8)
  Though I declared war on the Deity,
  He willingly gave his Son for me!
Group 2—Divine Pardon (Romans 5:9-11)
  Jesus alone paid for my sin.
  I don't have to pay it again!

Group 3—Utter Victory (Romans 8:31-39)
  When next to God by Christ I stand,
  Victory is near at hand!

Allow time for the groups to share their couplet summaries.

Option. Write the Scripture assignments and the sample couplets on the board. Read each section of the text together as a class. Then discuss the content of each section, referring to the couplet and to the commentary.

Alternative. Distribute copies of the "Saying It Another Way" activity from the reproducible page. Have students work in small groups or pairs to complete the activity.

Into Life

Write these two headings on the board:
  Self-Esteem | God's Esteem

Ask, "How does today's lesson contrast these two types of evaluation?" Give one or more of these examples to get your class started:

Self-Esteem—I try to face God on my terms.
God's Esteem—I recognize that I am powerless to face God were it not for his grace.
Self-Esteem—I compare myself to others and conclude that I am better than most.
God's Esteem—I contrast myself to Jesus and see the depth of my sin.
Self-Esteem—I boast of my good work for others.
God's Esteem—I boast only of Christ's good work for me.
Self-Esteem—I am secretly afraid that I am not good enough for God.
God's Esteem—I openly acknowledge I am not good enough for God and accept Jesus' sacrifice as my own.
Self-Esteem—I try to prepare for the worst.
God's Esteem—I know that God is with me whatever comes.

Close with prayer that focuses on learners' embracing God's esteem above all.

PROTECTING LOVE

DEVOTIONAL READING: Matthew 18:1-5, 10-14
BACKGROUND SCRIPTURE: John 10:1-15

JOHN 10:1-15

[1] "Truly, truly, I say to you, he who does not enter the sheepfold by the door but climbs in by another way, that man is a thief and a robber. [2] But he who enters by the door is the shepherd of the sheep. [3] To him the gatekeeper opens. The sheep hear his voice, and he calls his own sheep by name and leads them out. [4] When he has brought out all his own, he goes before them, and the sheep follow him, for they know his voice. [5] A stranger they will not follow, but they will flee from him, for they do not know the voice of strangers." [6] This figure of speech Jesus used with them, but they did not understand what he was saying to them.

[7] So Jesus again said to them, "Truly, truly, I say to you, I am the door of the sheep. [8] All who came before me are thieves and robbers, but the sheep did not listen to them. [9] I am the door. If anyone enters by me, he will be saved and will go in and out and find pasture. [10] The thief comes only to steal and kill and destroy. I came that they may have life and have it abundantly. [11] I am the good shepherd. The good shepherd lays down his life for the sheep. [12] He who is a hired hand and not a shepherd, who does not own the sheep, sees the wolf coming and leaves the sheep and flees, and the wolf snatches them and scatters them. [13] He flees because he is a hired hand and cares nothing for the sheep. [14] I am the good shepherd. I know my own and my own know me, [15] just as the Father knows me and I know the Father; and I lay down my life for the sheep.

KEY VERSES

I am the good shepherd. I know my own and my own know me, just as the Father knows me and I know the Father; and I lay down my life for the sheep. —**John 10:14, 15**

GOD LOVES US

LESSON AIMS

After participating in this lesson, each learner will be able to:

1. Identify the good shepherd and the sheep.

2. Explain the metaphor of Jesus as the door or gate.

3. Suggest a twenty-first century, non-agrarian equivalent to the sheep-shepherd metaphor.

LESSON OUTLINE

Introduction

A. Mistaken Identity

Most of us have experienced the embarrassment of mistaken identity. We see someone across the room whom we think we recognize. We wave. That person waves back, but with a puzzled expression. We speak to someone standing behind us, thinking that person is a friend or family member. He or she responds uncertainly, if at all. Cases of mistaken identity cause confusion; those people are not who we think they are.

Today's text is about removing confusion regarding the identity of the one who leads, protects, and provides for God's people. Many claim to be God's designate for that role. But our text says that only one such claim is genuine. Only one individual can make us God's people and give us the life that God offers.

B. Lesson Background

Our text, from the middle of John's Gospel, records part of a series of conflict episodes between Jesus and his opponents. Important for context is the account of Jesus' healing of a man born blind (John 9), which occurs just before today's text. The healed man was confronted by religious leaders who were opposed to Jesus. But their opposition made the healed man all the more certain that Jesus had been sent by God (9:13-33).

The infuriated leaders threw the man out, effectively claiming that they had cut him off from fellowship with God's people (John 9:34). Subsequently, Jesus identified himself to the man as the one God had sent (9:35-38). The story closes with further confrontation between Jesus and the religious leaders (9:40, 41).

In providing the backdrop for today's text, that account addresses this question: Who truly governs God's people? In other words, do the religious leaders of Jesus' day decide who belongs in God's people and who is excluded, or does that authority lie elsewhere? The conflict between Jesus and his opponents concerning who Jesus is and what that means for God's people was accelerating.

Jesus' use of the phrase "I am the" occurs four times in today's text (John 10:7 9, 11, 14). These form part of the larger picture of Jesus' use of the phrase on other occasions in this Gospel (see John 6:35, 41, 48, 51; 8:12; 11:25; 14:6; 15:1, 5). The phrases serve as Jesus' claims regarding his unique role in God's plan to be the one who fulfills God's promises in finality.

But more than that, the phrase "I am" echoes God's statement to Moses that Moses should tell Israel that "I am" was the one sending him (Exodus 3:14; compare John 8:58). As Jesus used this expression, he was saying something about himself that implied that he was divine, God himself in human flesh. Jesus' opponents certainly didn't miss this implication, given their immediate attempts to stone him (John 8:59).

Our text focuses on shepherd imagery in regard to "I am the" statements. Keeping flocks of sheep and goats was a vital part of the economy of the biblical world. Shepherds often spent day and night with their animals to keep them nourished and safe (compare Luke 2:8).

The Old Testament frequently draws on these practices in depicting God as shepherd and his people as sheep (examples: Psalm 23:1; 80:1; Isaiah 40:11; Jeremiah 31:10). His faithful shepherding is contrasted with the harmful shepherding by others (Ezekiel 34; etc.). This history, familiar to Jesus' audience, is what he draws on as he delivers this discourse.

I. Jesus the Entryway
(JOHN 10:1-10)
A. Imagery (vv. 1-6)

1. "Truly, truly, I say to you, he who does not enter the sheepfold by the door but climbs in by another way, that man is a thief and a robber.

The Greek behind the translation *truly* is often transliterated as *amen* (example: Revelation 1:6). A

HOW TO SAY IT

Ezekiel	Ee-*zeek*-ee-ul or Ee-*zeek*-yul.
Hosea	Ho-*zay*-uh.
Isaiah	Eye-*zay*-uh.
Jeremiah	Jair-uh-*my*-uh.

word that is often used as a solemn finality, Jesus uses here to begin a statement. The intensified *truly, truly* stresses the importance and reliability of what he is about to say.

The image of *the door* of *the sheepfold* illustrates the difference between those who intend to harm the sheep and the one who cares for them. A sheepfold is an outdoor area bounded with a low stone wall. Sheep can be kept there overnight for safety. The door is the opening in the wall. It is guarded in such a way so that sheep do not wander out and predators do not enter. Any person or creature who enters by climbing over the wall is clearly not the sheep's protector.

We keep in mind that Jesus makes this point just after his rebuke of religious leaders in John 9:40, 41 (see the Lesson Background). His implication is clear: those leaders who claim to decide who belongs to God's people and who does not are the ones who come in over the wall.

What Do You Think?

What plans should a church have in place for dealing with "a thief and a robber" as Jesus uses that phrase?

Talking Points for Your Discussion
- In terms of advance recognition
- In terms of notifying leadership (sounding the alarm)
- In terms of leadership response
- In terms of repairing damage done
- In terms of preventing recurrence

---

2. "But he who enters by the door is the shepherd of the sheep.

We should note that Jesus' illustration is not an elaborate allegory. That is, each detail of the story is not intended to correspond with an event in reality. Jesus is probably not thinking of a particular event in his life when he speaks of *the shepherd* entering *by the door*. Rather, this detail is intended to contribute to the larger contrast between the shepherd and those who do not care for the flock as the shepherd does.

3. "To him the gatekeeper opens. The sheep hear his voice, and he calls his own sheep by name and leads them out.

The gatekeeper is the assistant shepherd who guards the opening to the sheepfold. He recognizes the true shepherd and gives him access. Likewise, *the sheep* recognize their shepherd's *voice*. Shepherds in the Middle East today reportedly use distinctive calls to which their sheep are conditioned to respond. Jesus seems to draw on a similar custom as he describes the sheep's response to the shepherd. Only the shepherd leads the sheep out to safe pasture (compare Psalm 23:2, lesson 5).

4. "When he has brought out all his own, he goes before them, and the sheep follow him, for they know his voice.

The depiction of the shepherd's care and the sheep's recognition continues. When daylight comes, it is time to exit the sheepfold for food and water. To get the sheep to the needed nourishment, shepherds of the biblical world do not drive their sheep from behind, but lead them from the front (*goes before them*). The sheep's recognition of the shepherd makes that possible; the word *voice* is used for the second time for emphasis in this regard (compare John 3:29; 5:25, 28; 18:37).

5. "A stranger they will not follow, but they will flee from him, for they do not know the voice of strangers."

This third use of the word *voice* contrasts the leading of the true shepherd with that of pretenders (*strangers*). The sheep do not recognize the voice of others, so they view them as a threat. These sheep are like the man healed of blindness. In contrast with his parents (John 9:18-23), he had refused to cower before the religious leaders but responded to Jesus instead (9:24-38). Bad things happen when wrong voices are heeded (2 Peter 2:1; etc.).

> *What Do You Think?*
> What are some things churches do to ensure that their teachers speak with the voice of Christ?
> *Talking Points for Your Discussion*
> - With regard to evaluating their track record in teaching (the past)
> - With regard to ongoing training (the present)
> - In terms of periodic monitoring (the future)
> - Other

6. This figure of speech Jesus used with them, but they did not understand what he was saying to them.

Jesus' opponents are nearby, listening to him teach. But as he has said before, they are blind to the truth because they claim that they can "see" (John 9:39-41). They cannot believe that God has authorized anyone other than themselves to speak for him and to lead his people. Thus, they refuse to listen as Jesus paints the portrait of the shepherd. They will not admit that instead of being shepherds who care for the sheep, they are more like thieves who fleece the flock.

B. Identity (vv. 7-10)

7. So Jesus again said to them, "Truly, truly, I say to you, I am the door of the sheep.

Again by use of *truly, truly,* Jesus solemnly emphasizes that he is speaking a vital truth. That emphasis is underlined by the use of *I am the,* with its implications as noted in the Lesson Background. Jesus' claim to be *the door of the sheep* may be surprising until we understand that shepherds often block entrances to sheepfolds with their bodies. They do so by lying across the opening at night so that nothing gets in or out without their consent.

In light of the controversy over the man healed of blindness, Jesus is making the audacious claim that he alone decides who belongs with God's people and who does not (contrast John 9:22, 34). The religious leaders do not make that determination. No one does but Jesus. And certainly no one truly decides who belongs to God except God himself. Thus, Jesus uses the suggestive *I am* to make this statement.

Taken with the earlier discourse, we understand Jesus' point: those who listen to and believe him are the sheep who listen to the true shepherd. They belong to the true flock. They are granted entry to the sheepfold. Jesus' followers are God's true people.

8. "All who came before me are thieves and robbers, but the sheep did not listen to them.

There can be only one chief shepherd. Anyone who pretends to be him is in the category of *thieves and robbers*. An example of how such false shepherds operate is found in Luke 19:45, 46, where worship acts of sacrifice are opportunities for profit. Most directly associated with the text before us is, again, the situation of the man healed of blindness. Note that the religious leaders would have preferred that the man not be healed rather than have it done on a Sabbath (John 9:14-16). This contrast makes clear that the shepherd stands alone and that there is no legitimate alternative to hearing his voice and following him.

◆ **SPIRITUAL CHARLATANS** ◆

Jim Jones (1931–1978) started his ministry career in Indianapolis. But it was after he moved his Peoples Temple to California in the late 1960s that he gained notoriety. His ministry focused on issues of social justice, and he developed a large following among society's downtrodden.

For a time, Jones was endorsed by many leading politicians. But following his exposure as a cult leader, he moved his congregation to "Jonestown" in Guyana. His little empire came crashing down in 1978 with the mass suicide and murder of over 900 people there, including Jones himself.

In retrospect, Jim Jones was merely one spiritual charlatan in a line stretching back centuries. God had to deal with such individuals even within the ranks of his chosen people (Isaiah 1:23; Jeremiah 7:9-11; Hosea 7:1-3; etc.). They stand in stark contrast with Jesus, who stands ever vigilant for the well-being of his flock. The saga of Jim Jones reminds us that only Jesus is worthy of unconditional trust. —C. R. B.

9. "I am the door. If anyone enters by me, he will be saved and will go in and out and find pasture.

Jesus repeats his claim to be *the door*—the only way to enter the flock of God's people. The one who enters Jesus' sheepfold *will be saved,* that is, be kept safe from harm.

As the sheep are led to and from the sheepfold, they *find pasture* needed to survive and thrive (compare John 4:13, 14; 6:27, 55). The shepherd's gift to them is life, and they have it only because of the shepherd.

> *What Do You Think?*
> What are some specific ways your church can better express the truth that Christ is the only means of access to eternal life?
>
> *Talking Points for Your Discussion*
> - In modification of tradition or routine
> - In special times of the year
> - In church discipline
> - In curriculum selection
> - Other

10. "The thief comes only to steal and kill and destroy. I came that they may have life and have it abundantly.

When we watch how *the thief* behaves toward the sheep, we see only self-interest. Thieves, by definition, do not act in the best interest of the sheep. Rather, they take advantage of the sheep. They bring death. Serving as examples are the religious leaders who seek to dissuade people from faith in Jesus (John 9:22-34). They are thieves who act out of self-interest, even at the expense of covering up the truth (11:48).

But the true shepherd does the opposite. He doesn't take, but gives. Jesus gives life where others give death. He protects and provides for his flock. And not just a little! Life from Jesus is abundant, like the overflowing cup in the Shepherd Psalm (Psalm 23:5). Jesus gives not just what is necessary for survival but what results in life in its divinely intended fullness.

> *What Do You Think?*
> In what specific ways can and should the nature of a Christian's abundant life in Christ be apparent to others?
>
> *Talking Points for Your Discussion*
> - Regarding what unbelievers see, considering 1 Corinthians 9:20; 10:27, 32; Philippians 1:13; Colossians 4:5; 1 Thessalonians 4:11, 12; 1 Timothy 3:7; 5:13; etc.
> - Regarding what fellow believers see, considering Matthew 6:1-18, 25; John 13:14-17; Romans 14:1, 13; 1 Corinthians 10:32; 11:1; Philippians 1:14; Hebrews 10:25; etc.

II. Jesus the Good Shepherd
(JOHN 10:11-15)
A. Giving and Caring (vv. 11-13)
11a. "I am the good shepherd.

Jesus now changes the metaphor slightly, making in the process a claim that is even more direct and audacious. As before, the phrase *I am the* carries the implications noted in the Lesson Background, particularly with the added descriptor *good*. The term *shepherd* is used in Israel's Scriptures for God or his promised messianic king. Jesus' claim of it for himself indicates fulfillment (see Genesis 49:24; Psalm 80:1; Ezekiel 34:23; 37:24; etc.).

11b. "The good shepherd lays down his life for the sheep.

Some Old Testament kings and priests were good at being shepherds of the people in a relative sense (example: Psalm 78:70-72). But Jesus is good in an exceptional way. Not only does he lead, feed, and protect the sheep, he also willingly *lays down his life for* them.

Certainly this description strikes Jesus' audience as astonishing! They know that a shepherd takes risks to protect the sheep, his most valuable possession. But dying for one's sheep is out of the question. The sheep live for the shepherd, not the other way around. But Jesus is a shepherd like no other.

Time will be needed for Jesus' meaning to be clear. When he is arrested, Jesus will insist that the soldiers let his followers go free as he surrenders himself willingly (John 18:3-9). His death will not be a case in which someone else takes his life; he will lay it down himself. It will be an act of sacrifice that serves as "a ransom for many" (Mark 10:45).

12, 13. "He who is a hired hand and not a shepherd, who does not own the sheep, sees the wolf coming and leaves the sheep and flees, and the wolf snatches them and scatters them. He flees because he is a hired hand and cares nothing for the sheep.

Again Jesus depicts figures to contrast with the shepherd. These figures serve to emphasize the shepherd's one-of-a-kind nature. Certainly we would expect a thief or robber (John 10:1) to have no concern for the sheep. But even a hired undershepherd—one who does not own the flock but is paid to care for it—lacks the shepherd's commitment. This *hired hand* is just there to do a job; he has no personal interest in the sheep.

As fine as other leaders of God's people may be, only Jesus is the good shepherd in an absolute sense. No one but he places the flock's well-being first. As the good shepherd, Jesus will give his very life for the sake of his people.

◆   WHO CARES?   ◆

A hallmark of the Great Recession that began in 2007 was home foreclosures. These resulted when many people allowed themselves to be lured into taking out larger mortgages than they could afford.

The unscrupulous lenders, mortgage brokers, etc., who did the luring were said to have engaged in predatory lending practices. These practices thrived in commission-driven environments that lacked accountability. Many, many home buyers trusted their assurances that housing prices would climb forever. No one seemed to have the client's best interest at heart, as self-interest ruled. The resulting foreclosures became a tidal wave across the stumbling economy—not just in America, but also in funds worldwide that had invested in mortgages.

Jesus' contrast between himself and those merely hired to do a job still applies. But where do we fit in that illustration? We are not the good shepherd himself, of course. But neither are we to be the hireling who runs away at the first sign of danger. It's impossible for us to know and care for Jesus' flock as he does. Peter received instructions in this regard (see John 21:15-17), and he has passed them along to us: "I exhort the elders among you, . . . shepherd the flock of God that is among you, exercising oversight" (1 Peter 5:1, 2).
—C. R. B.

B. Knows and Known (vv. 14, 15)
14. "I am the good shepherd. I know my own and my own know me,

A second time Jesus states that he is *the good shepherd*, again underlining the claim to be and do what only God is and does. The fact that he knows his sheep is a further implication of being able to call them by name (John 10:3, above).

The knowing is reciprocal: those whom Jesus knows as his sheep know him as shepherd in return. A precise example is the blind man just healed (John 9:35-38). Jesus knows the difference between true believers and those superficially impressed with him and his miracles (2:23-25). Those who know him as the shepherd are his true sheep, by his declaration, because they acknowledge him.

What Do You Think?
   What are some specific ways to exhibit confidence that Christ knows us as his sheep?
Talking Points for Your Discussion
   - In what we do routinely
   - In how we react to special opportunities
   - In what we think
   - In what we say
   - Other

15. "just as the Father knows me and I know the Father; and I lay down my life for the sheep."

The knowledge of the shepherd and the sheep for each other is mirrored in the knowledge of *the Father* for the Son. Jesus' reference to God as Father is noteworthy. In John's Gospel, this is one means by which Jesus affirms his knowledge of God.

That knowledge is based on something different than others' knowledge of God. Jesus knows God not by teaching, but by personal experience that no one else has (John 3:13; 7:28, 29; 8:14, 23, 54-58).

As a son knows his father, Jesus the Son knows God the Father. As the one who comes from Heaven, Jesus knows God the Father, the one who abides in Heaven. And as Jesus does and claims to be what only God can do and who he alone is, Jesus shows that he knows God because he *is* God. Jesus' authority is greater than that of any other, in his own time or in any other.

So—how awestruck are we with this one who is very God, the one who willingly surrenders his

Visual for Lessons 5 & 9. *Lead the class in singing this familiar hymn as a preliminary to posing the question associated with verse 14.*

life for the sake of his sheep? How different is he from any other shepherd—good or bad—of our experience? How far beyond our expectation is his love for us?

Conclusion
A. Follow the True Shepherd

Today's text is both disturbing and reassuring. It is disturbing because we prefer to think that there are many ways to find God. Yet Jesus says that he is the one who is the shepherd, the door to the sheepfold. Apart from him, there is no abundant life.

But that message is also reassuring. We do not need to discover our own path to God. We do not need to work a plan by which we find real life for ourselves. We need merely to listen to the true shepherd and follow him. He leads, provides, and protects. We follow, receive, and trust. That is the way of abundant life, the way for true sheep of the good shepherd.

B. Prayer

Father, we commit ourselves to follow your Son, to be secure in what he provides, to honor the life he gave for us as we give freely of ourselves for others. We pray this in Jesus' name. Amen.

C. Thought to Remember
Accept no substitute shepherd.

INVOLVEMENT LEARNING

Enhance your lesson presentation with the reproducible activity page,
available as a free download at www.standardlesson.com.

Into the Lesson

Write this phrase on the board: *You don't own a house; a house owns you.*

Ask, "How would you react to the statement on the board?" Students may want to share a story about the responsibilities of home ownership. Time permitting, you may substitute "car," "pet," or "business" for "house" to solicit more reactions.

Alternative. Distribute copies of the "Who's the Boss?" activity from the reproducible page, which you can download. Have students work individually or in pairs.

After either activity, lead into the Bible study by saying, "We take on big responsibilities when we own a business or buy a house. These things may bring the owner great joy, but having such a great responsibility requires a lot of work.

"The Bible uses another image to illustrate such responsibility and sacrifice. A shepherd in Jesus' day could not just let his sheep fend for themselves! The sheep needed the shepherd to provide constant care for them. This image pictures the kind of sheltering love Jesus has for those belonging to him."

Into the Word

Divide your class into groups of three to five students. Give each group paper and pens. Say, "Today most people live in urban or suburban settings and are therefore unfamiliar with sheep and shepherds. Think of other analogies that could be used today. Some examples are a good boss, teacher, babysitter, and coach. Then write a parable using that analogy. *Option*: Read one of the two examples that follow to get them started.

The Good Teacher

It's the truth. The teacher who is not dedicated to her class is no more than a bad substitute teacher. The good teacher knows her class. She calls each student by name. She knows their

personalities, problems, and potential. Those students follow because the good teacher has taken the time to really know them. A bad substitute teacher just sees a bunch of rowdy students. She doesn't take time to know them, so they don't bother to get to know her. After all, she'll be here today and gone tomorrow, so the class does not follow her leading.

The Good Babysitter

I am the good babysitter. The good babysitter puts her life on the line for the kids she watches. A poor babysitter only cares about the money she will earn—not the kids she watches. So if a robber breaks in or the house catches on fire during her watch, she's out of there! She might call 911 from somewhere down the road, but those kids are on their own! After all, she's not being paid enough to put herself in danger, is she?

Allow time for groups to share their revised parables.

Alternative. Distribute copies of the "How to Spot a Good Shepherd" activity from the reproducible page. Have students work individually or in pairs to pick out the main facts from the Bible text.

Into Life

Have a student read John 10:9 aloud. Ask, "In what ways does Jesus function as a door or gateway? Is it by giving access? by protecting? by providing a way out? by saving?"

Encourage students to make the connections between the functions of a door and Jesus' saying, "I am the door." Distribute index cards and markers to students. Instruct them to draw a picture of a door on one side of the index card. On the back of the card, instruct them to write, "Jesus is the doorway to Heaven for me." Encourage students to post the card somewhere at work or home as a reminder of today's lesson.

SUSTAINING
LOVE

DEVOTIONAL READING: Psalm 139:1-12
BACKGROUND SCRIPTURE: Jonah 1

JONAH 1:7-17

⁷ And they said to one another, "Come, let us cast lots, that we may know on whose account this evil has come upon us." So they cast lots, and the lot fell on Jonah. ⁸ Then they said to him, "Tell us on whose account this evil has come upon us. What is your occupation? And where do you come from? What is your country? And of what people are you?" ⁹ And he said to them, "I am a Hebrew, and I fear the LORD, the God of heaven, who made the sea and the dry land." ¹⁰ Then the men were exceedingly afraid and said to him, "What is this that you have done!" For the men knew that he was fleeing from the presence of the LORD, because he had told them.

¹¹ Then they said to him, "What shall we do to you, that the sea may quiet down for us?" For the sea grew more and more tempestuous. ¹² He said to them, "Pick me up and hurl me into the sea; then the sea will quiet down for you, for I know it is because of me that this great tempest has come upon you." ¹³ Nevertheless, the men rowed hard to get back to dry land, but they could not, for the sea grew more

and more tempestuous against them. ¹⁴ Therefore they called out to the LORD, "O LORD, let us not perish for this man's life, and lay not on us innocent blood, for you, O LORD, have done as it pleased you." ¹⁵ So they picked up Jonah and hurled him into the sea, and the sea ceased from its raging. ¹⁶ Then the men feared the LORD exceedingly, and they offered a sacrifice to the LORD and made vows.

¹⁷ And the LORD appointed a great fish to swallow up Jonah. And Jonah was in the belly of the fish three days and three nights.

KEY VERSE

The men were exceedingly afraid and said to him, "What is this that you have done!" —Jonah 1:10a

GOD LOVES US

LESSON AIMS

After participating in this lesson, each learner will be able to:

1. Describe the actions and attitudes of the sailors toward Jonah.

2. Compare and contrast the different ways that people react to someone who has confessed a wrongdoing.

3. List ways that people run from God today and write a prayer for divine help to avoid doing so personally.

LESSON OUTLINE

Introduction

A. Fleeing from Righteousness

He was one of three sons in the family, and he seemed to have all the advantages. His dark hair was naturally curly. He had sparkling blue eyes, and he had an infectious smile that disarmed others. He also brought the most grief to his mother.

His troubles began as a teenager. He was caught stealing, and his smile did not dissuade the arresting officer. He was now more than just a boy who was liked by all the neighbors. He had a criminal record, and he was sentenced to spend time at the expense of the taxpayers.

His parents went to see him in reform school. The mother came with the tears of tender love, but the father came with bewilderment. He was upset that his son had been disobedient to what he had been taught and to what had been modeled for him by family and friends.

The pattern was repeated several times, but the combination of tender love and civil discipline finally changed the young man. His mother's sustaining love persisted through the occasions when he was "testing the system" and God.

This lesson presents God's sustaining love for a disobedient prophet whose experiences toughened and shaped him for his mission.

B. Lesson Background

This lesson and the next three are taken from the book of Jonah. These studies will provide a better understanding of the man, his motivations, the message of the book, and the miracles contained in it.

Jonah's ministry, described in the book that bears his name, is difficult to date. The closest we can get is to recognize that he prophesied about events that occurred during the reign of Jeroboam II (2 Kings 14:25). That king ruled Israel from 793 to 753 BC. The designation Israel in this context refers to the northern kingdom after the original nation of Israel divided after King Solomon's death in about 930 BC (see 1 Kings 12). The southern nation became Judah.

The book of Jonah is probably the best known of the 12 in the section of the Old Testament designated as the Minor Prophets. The book of Jonah is different from the other 11 in that most of it is a narrative. It is therefore easier to read and to understand.

The printed text for this lesson begins at Jonah 1:7, but it is important that in the background the first six verses of the book be given. The word of the Lord had come to Jonah, and he was commanded to go to the city of Nineveh and preach against it. The reason is given in Jonah 1:2: its wickedness had come before the Lord.

Jonah decided to disobey the Lord's command, and he went west instead of east. He first traveled to Joppa, a city on the coast of the Mediterranean Sea. His plan was to sail in the opposite direction from what God had said. If he began his trip to Joppa from Israel's capital city, Samaria, the overland distance was about 30 miles. Jonah's hometown, however, was Gath-hepher (again, 2 Kings 14:25), which was a few miles north of Nazareth. The overland distance from there to Joppa was almost 60 miles.

Jonah found a ship that was ready to sail, and it was going to Tarshish (Jonah 1:3). The location of Tarshish is uncertain. Suggestions include Tartessus (a kingdom in Spain that was over 2,000 miles from Joppa) or Carthage in northern Africa (about 1,400 miles). Evidence in the last few years, however, suggests it was Sardinia, an island just west of Italy.

Jonah was trying to do something that was as impossible then as it is now: hide from God. About 250 years before the time of Jonah, David had declared the impossibility of such (Psalm 139:7-12).

Jonah's trip to Joppa, from either Samaria or Gath-hepher, wearied him. He paid his fare, boarded the ship, went down into the ship, and went to sleep (Jonah 1:5b). The ship set sail from Joppa, and the Lord sent a mighty storm to intercept it. The sailors reacted in the standard ways for such a situation: they lightened the ship by throwing its wares overboard (compare Acts 27:18). This storm was more than ordinary, however, and it also caused each man to pray to his god. The master of the ship awakened Jonah so that he could join them in the prayer meeting.

I. Storm's Cause
(Jonah 1:7-9)
A. Revealed by Lots (vv. 7, 8)

7. And they said to one another, "Come, let us cast lots, that we may know on whose account this evil has come upon us." So they cast lots, and the lot fell on Jonah.

The strength of the storm causes the sailors to conclude that someone on the ship has irritated a god. They react according to their customs: they *cast lots* to determine the guilty party. It is naturally assumed that no one will come forward to confess, so the practice of casting lots is used to determine who is guilty. This practice is frequently used in ancient times to determine guilt (compare 1 Samuel 14:41-45).

In such a situation, one marked object is placed in a container with other items that are similar. The marked item may be drawn by the guilty person or by someone who is drawing for the others. Proverbs 16:33 gives the view that it is the Lord who controls the outcome. In the case at hand, it is especially true that God controls the results. Jonah is correctly identified.

What Do You Think?
What should we do when we realize that a life storm of our own making is affecting others?
Talking Points for Your Discussion
- At home
- At work or school
- At church
- Other

B. Affirmed by Jonah (v. 9)

8. Then they said to him, "Tell us on whose account this evil has come upon us. What is your occupation? And where do you come from? What is your country? And of what people are you?"

The sailors rapidly ask a series of five questions. The first one seems unnecessary in view of the result of casting lots (and see v. 10). But a verbal confession will confirm what the casting of lots has indicated.

The other questions seek more information about Jonah himself. The sailors may believe that the answers will help identify the god involved. The ancients often associate a god with a particular nation (compare 2 Kings 23:13). Therefore the first order of business for escaping the storm is to ask the questions we see here.

9. And he said to them, "I am a Hebrew, and I fear the LORD, the God of heaven, who made the sea and the dry land."

These are Jonah's first spoken words in the book, and he tells the truth forthrightly. The word *Hebrew* as an identifier serves to contrast an Israelite from someone of another people group. It is used this way by both Israelites (Jeremiah 34:14) and others (1 Samuel 4:9) as a way of referring to the descendants of Jacob.

Jonah's affirmation that he serves *the Lord, the God of heaven* is followed with a jab at the fictitious gods of the sailors: Jonah's God is the one *who made the sea and the dry land*. Logic dictates that the God who has the power to create like this also has the power to cause and calm storms.

Jonah's answer is also a confession. Although he affirms that he fears the Lord, the storm indicates that he has been disobedient in some way. This is a self-indictment, for Jonah knows that his words and his actions are not in harmony with one another.

> *What Do You Think?*
> What evidence of repentance should others see when a Christian confesses personal failings?
> *Talking Points for Your Discussion*
> - In cases of public confessions
> - In cases of private confession

II. Sailors' Concerns
(JONAH 1:10, 11)
A. Regarding Jonah's Sin (v. 10)

10. Then the men were exceedingly afraid and said to him, "What is this that you have done!" For the men knew that he was fleeing from the presence of the LORD, because he had told them.

Jonah has said that he fears the Lord, and that prompts an even greater fear on the part of the sailors. They cannot comprehend any type of sin that could provoke the God of Jonah to send a storm of such magnitude. Through the noise of the raging wind, they ask another question.

The last half of the verse is not an answer. Rather, it stresses information that the sailors already know: Jonah *had told them* that *he was fleeing from the presence of the Lord* (compare Jonah 1:3).

◆ *THE STORMS OF LIFE* ◆

Heat waves, lengthy drought, violent tornadoes, hurricanes, and "polar express" blizzards seem more common in recent years. Some scientific data in the mid-twentieth century suggested the earth might be moving back into another ice age.

But thinking shifted in the 1980s toward the theory of global warming. Evidence was interpreted in different ways, resulting in significant debate. As a result, the terminology became that of *climate change*, which seemed (at least to some) to be a more neutral description.

Many factors contribute to the ongoing confusion, including the tendency of some scientists to change their minds from time to time, the news media's desire to sensationalize, and public distrust of government. "True believers" on both sides of the debate are so adamant in their views that many in the general public despair of ever knowing the truth.

Not so with the case of Jonah! Any debate about the cause of the violent storm that threatened his ship was settled when he confirmed the results of the cast lots. He was the undisputed cause of the change of weather causing them so much distress. That situation raises the possibility of a parallel: How many of life's storms are indisputably the result of our own actions? Are we as honest as Jonah in admitting as much?

—C. R. B.

B. Regarding a Solution (v. 11)

11. Then they said to him, "What shall we do to you, that the sea may quiet down for us?" For the sea grew more and more tempestuous.

The conversation between Jonah and the sailors is coming to an end. This is their final question to Jonah. The sailors know the following related to their plight: (1) since the intense storm is the fault of Jonah, then (2) something must be done to him. The last thing they want to do is make a move that will anger further the God who made the sea and the dry land! So they hope that Jonah has the answers, for their lives are in jeopardy.

III. Actions' Consequences
(JONAH 1:12-17)
A. Solution (vv. 12-14)

12. He said to them, "Pick me up and hurl me into the sea; then the sea will quiet down for you, for I know it is because of me that this great tempest has come upon you."

Jonah's response can be broken into four parts. The first two are what the sailors are to do. To follow Jonah's instruction *pick me up* would normally be fairly easy. But the tossing of the ship in the midst of *this great tempest* makes this much more difficult.

The second part of Jonah's response is the ultimate answer to the sailors' first question (Jonah 1:8). But it presents a problem, because *hurl me into the sea* involves the deliberate taking of Jonah's life (see next verse).

The third part is what the sailors really desire, that *the sea will quiet down*. The final section of Jonah's response reaffirms that the real cause of the storm is Jonah himself. One thing we can say about Jonah is that at least he's honest!

13. Nevertheless, the men rowed hard to get back to dry land, but they could not, for the sea grew more and more tempestuous against them.

HOW TO SAY IT

Gath-hepher	Gath-*hee*-fer.
Jeroboam	Jair-uh-*boe*-um.
Joppa	*Jop*-uh.
Nazareth	*Naz*-uh-reth.
Nineveh	*Nin*-uh-vuh.
Samaria	Suh-*mare*-ee-uh.

Visual for Lesson 10. *Point to this visual as you ask, "How do we avoid sinful* fight, flight, *or freeze reactions to God's ministry callings?"*

This verse provides a very interesting bit of information. The ship seems to be not far from *dry land*, for the sailors fervently desire to bring the ship to shore by rowing. It is customary at this time in history for ships to move along the coast if the captains cannot navigate by other means. This has been called "harbor hopping."

We may wonder how far the ship is from Joppa, the port of embarkation, when it encounters the storm. Is that the land that is in sight, or have they traveled a considerable distance along the coast? The only answer is that "the text does not say."

The rowing of a boat demands that oars come in contact with the water for the main stroke. It can be safely assumed that rowing is almost impossible given that the storm is tossing the ship from wave crest to wave trough, then back up again.

Ancient sailors do not enjoy a good reputation for noble character. But these men are honorable in their not wanting to hurl Jonah to a watery grave. They do their best to reach land, but they cannot. Their honorable effort is ultimately futile.

14. Therefore they called out to the LORD, "O LORD, let us not perish for this man's life, and lay not on us innocent blood, for you, O LORD, have done as it pleased you."

The first prayer in the book is *to the Lord*, but it is not prayed by Jonah. It is by the sailors, men who worship other gods. They are fully aware that killing an innocent man can result in great punishment. They are already experiencing plenty of God's wrath in the form of the storm. They do not want to experience more wrath for what they feel compelled to do: take the life of a man who has not committed any crime against them. Most religions of the ancient world have codes of law that prohibit the taking of human life without due process. The biblical restriction and mandate in this regard is given after the flood in Noah's time (Genesis 9:5, 6), and it was for all humanity in future civilizations (compare Acts 25:11; Romans 13:4).

Yet this is not their own judgment on Jonah, for this is the Lord's decree. Even so, they do not want to risk becoming guilty by expediting it without authorization.

> **What Do You Think?**
> What are appropriate ways for a Christian to respond to those who are caught in the effects of another person's sin?
> *Talking Points for Your Discussion*
> - Regarding victims who are adults
> - Regarding victims who are minors

B. Results (vv. 15-17)

15. So they picked up Jonah and hurled him into the sea, and the sea ceased from its raging.

The situation is desperate, so the men take the drastic measure that they have been resisting—casting Jonah into the tumultuous waters. It is dangerous to be close to the edge of the deck in such weather, but they have to do it.

The resulting calm leads some to think that a raging sea immediately becomes a tranquil body of water. Others propose that the tossing waves gradually subside, with normal wave action following. Either outcome can be directed easily by the God who made the heavens, the sea, and land (see v. 9). Note than when Jesus stilled the tempest, however, seasoned fishermen were awed that the wind and the waves ceased (Matthew 8:27; Mark 4:41).

For the case at hand, it is enough for us to know that when God directs, both water and wind obey. "You rule the raging of the sea; when its waves rise, you still them. . . . The world and all that is in it, you have founded them" (Psalm 89:9, 11).

◆ *LESSER OF TWO EVILS?* ◆

Many Iranians publicly protested what they saw as a rigged 2009 presidential election in their country. The government is said to have arrested and tortured opposition leaders. Mohsen Armin was an activist whose friends were arrested and forced to make scripted courtroom "confessions" of their alleged crimes against the government.

Armin assumed he would also be arrested and tortured, so he decided to act preemptively by issuing a retraction of any future televised confession he might make under duress. He said, "If the providence of God requires that I will be jailed as my brethren have been so far, and if, in jail and under pressure, I say something against what I have said, be sure that it is not my true belief and that I recanted under pressure."

Jonah urged his shipmates to throw him overboard. Prior to doing so, they admitted to God that they were about to kill Jonah and asked for advance forgiveness. They felt they had no other choice. Do we ever say, "God, I know what I am planning to do is a sin, but I'm going to do it anyway. Since there's no other choice, please forgive me"? Are there any circumstances when this line of thinking is acceptable for Christians? Why, or why not?
—C. R. B.

16. Then the men feared the LORD exceedingly, and they offered a sacrifice to the LORD and made vows.

The calming of the sea yields three reactions on the part of the sailors: they fear, sacrifice, and make vows. It would be interesting to know the rest of the story about these men. Do they abandon other gods? What is the nature of the vows they make? Do they keep those vows? Is the effect of their experience permanent?

God chose not to provide that information. But we can conclude that the three reactions are reasonable, given what the men have just endured and witnessed. They have to do *something* to express gratitude and thanksgiving for the fact that they are still alive after such a harrowing ordeal!

Jonah's deliberate sin has had powerful consequences for him, the sea, and the sailors. But it even causes good things to happen, as the sailors come to a rudimentary belief in the true God.

> **What Do You Think?**
> Which Scriptures are most helpful to you for seeing that God is greater than your failures?
> *Talking Points for Your Discussion*
> - Passages about his love
> - Passages about his power
> - Passages about his will
> - Other

17. And the LORD appointed a great fish to swallow up Jonah. And Jonah was in the belly of the fish three days and three nights.

It is not mere coincidence that *a great fish* is in the area at exactly this moment. God has allocated this creature for a special task, arranging for it to be in the right place at the right time. Some have suggested that the fish may be a type of whale (Matthew 12:40) or a shark. This detail is not essential. The important thing is that it does what God has directed it to do: *swallow up Jonah.*

The fact that Jonah is in the fish for *three days and three nights* is a key phrase in the book: it is cited by Jesus as the sign of the prophet Jonah that anticipates Jesus' burial for "three days and three nights in the heart of the earth" (Matthew 12:39, 40).

Some have wondered about the time factor that is mentioned. How can Jonah know the time involved, since he has no wristwatch and it is dark in the fish? The following possibilities are only conjectures: (1) God revealed the information to Jonah. (2) Jonah met some of the sailors when he was expelled from the fish, and they told him. (3) The given time factor is a figure of speech for one full, 24-hour day and parts of two others.

Several things in the book of Jonah are said to be provided or prepared by God. The lists may vary somewhat, but at this point there have been these two special things: a great storm and a great fish. The fact that a ship was just ready to sail may be more than a coincidence.

One sermon humorously suggested that since the Lord was the one who provided the fish, it could have had hot and cold running water, a luxurious bed, a color television in the corner so that Jonah could watch the news from Jerusalem, and air conditioning. It is more likely that it was dark, hot, smelly, and miserable.

One thing is certain: Jonah's experiences with the storm, the sailors, and the fish persuade him that when God says he should go to Nineveh, it is better to obey God.

> **What Do You Think?**
> How can you help your church prepare itself to be God's "great fish" in rescuing those whom he may send your way?
> *Talking Points for Your Discussion*
> - With regard to spiritual healing
> - With regard to physical need
> - With regard to confidentiality
> - With regard to remediation
> - Other

Conclusion

A. "Jonah Syndrome"

Slightly over 200 years ago, a certain man sensed a call to become a minister of the gospel. He felt that his first attempts at preaching were failures, so he gave up the idea. A lady heard of his decision and called him "a Jonah."

Her words were just the challenge that he needed to hear. He returned to his original goals, and he became an effective minister who influenced thousands for Christ.

Many today still repeat Jonah's error. Perhaps we can say they suffer from self-inflicted "Jonah Syndrome": they know full well what God expects in one or more areas of life, but they deliberately go in the opposite direction. How much better it is to heed God!

B. Prayer

O God, deliver us from "Jonah Syndrome"! May we be repentant when the storms of life are self-inflicted. Strengthen us to heed your calls. We pray in Jesus' name. Amen.

C. Thought for Today

Learn from Jonah, but imitate Jesus.

INVOLVEMENT LEARNING

*Enhance your lesson presentation with the reproducible activity page,
available as a free download at www.standardlesson.com.*

Into the Lesson

To begin class, read this famous news story:

On April 26, 2005, John Mason notified police that his fiancée was missing. Jennifer Wilbanks of Duluth, Georgia, did not return from her evening jog that night.

During the next few days, about 250 people searched for the missing woman, costing the city between $40,000 and $60,000. Police received many leads, all of which were false. The FBI joined the search, and Wilbanks's relatives offered a $100,000 reward for her return. The story dominated national news.

On April 29, Wilbanks called Mason from a pay phone, telling him that she had been kidnapped but was released. After she was found in New Mexico, Wilbanks admitted that she was not kidnapped, but had run away due to pressures of her upcoming wedding. A number of lawsuits were filed, and to this day, Wilbanks is best known as "the runaway bride."

Ask the class how much they remember about this story. Say, "Let's make a list of other reasons why people might run away from a person or situation."

Alternative. Distribute copies of the "Why Run Away?" activity from the reproducible page, which you can download. Ask students to complete it individually, and then discuss it as a class.

After either activity, lead into the Bible study saying, "History is full of stories of famous runaways. There is probably no more well-known fugitive than the one we will study today."

Into the Word

Ask for a volunteer to be Jonah, give him or her a copy of the lesson text, and direct your Jonah to a seat in the front of the room.

Ask the rest of the class to open their Bibles to Jonah 1:7-17. Say, "Read today's text and find questions that the sailors asked Jonah." Have the class play the part of the sailors and take turns asking your Jonah questions from the text. Jonah can find answers in the text, in Jonah 1, and in 2 Kings 14:25.

If your Jonah has trouble with a question, feel free to help him or her answer. After all questions are answered, summarize any other important aspects of the text, using the commentary.

Questions will be found in Jonah 1:8, 10, 11. The questions, loosely paraphrased are (1) Who are you/what is your name? (2) What is your occupation? (3) Where have you come from? (4) What is your native country? (5) Who are your native people? (6) Why did you disobey your God? (7) What can we do to you to appease your God and calm our seas?

Into Life

Bring a pair of running shoes for display. Say, "In the church's history, such items as hair shirts have been adopted to physically discourage one from yielding to temptation to do wrong and as penance for doing wrong. Think for a moment and tell me, how could we design these running shoes in such a way as to deter the temptation to run away from God?"

Suggest such strategies as painting "GOD" with an arrow pointing straight ahead on each toe. Or perhaps—to make running uncomfortable enough to deter it—put a rock in each shoe. Though you may have some fun with these responses, you will ultimately want to ask, "What specifically can you and I do to discourage any thought of running from God?"

To encourage response, ask these questions: "How do people try to run away from God today?" and "Why do people try to run away from God?"

Alternative. Distribute copies of the "A Servant of God with Flaws" activity from the reproducible page. Have students choose the flaws in the list that they might need to ask God to help them correct.

PRESERVING LOVE

DEVOTIONAL READING: Psalm 116:1-14
BACKGROUND SCRIPTURE: Jonah 2

JONAH 2

¹ Then Jonah prayed to the LORD his God from the belly of the fish, ² saying,

"I called out to the LORD, out of my distress,
  and he answered me;
out of the belly of Sheol I cried,
  and you heard my voice.
³ For you cast me into the deep,
  into the heart of the seas,
  and the flood surrounded me;
all your waves and your billows
  passed over me.
⁴ Then I said, 'I am driven away
  from your sight;
yet I shall again look
  upon your holy temple.'
⁵ The waters closed in over me to take my life;
  the deep surrounded me;

⁶ weeds were wrapped about my head
  at the roots of the mountains.
I went down to the land
  whose bars closed upon me forever;
yet you brought up my life from the pit,
  O LORD my God.
⁷ When my life was fainting away,
  I remembered the LORD,
and my prayer came to you,
  into your holy temple.
⁸ Those who pay regard to vain idols
  forsake their hope of steadfast love.
⁹ But I with the voice of thanksgiving
  will sacrifice to you;
what I have vowed I will pay.
  Salvation belongs to the LORD!"

¹⁰ And the LORD spoke to the fish, and it vomited Jonah out upon the dry land.

KEY VERSE

"I with the voice of thanksgiving will sacrifice to you; what I have vowed I will pay. Salvation belongs to the LORD!" —**Jonah 2:9**

GOD LOVES US

Unit 3: God's Pervasive and Sustaining Love

LESSONS 10–13

LESSON AIMS

After participating in this lesson, each learner will be able to:

1. Identify the circumstances that prompted a change in Jonah's thinking.

2. Explain how wrong decisions and their consequences may lead ultimately to a stronger faith.

3. Make a plan for his or her prayers and praises to be a part of everyday life, not just in crises.

LESSON OUTLINE

Introduction

Introduction

A. *Taking* Time, Not *Finding* Time

In 1884, the *American Christian Review* related a prayer experience between Jacob Creath Jr. and L. B. Wilkes that took place in 1854, as recounted by Wilkes. The location was Lagrange, Missouri, where Wilkes had come to preach. After breakfast, Creath invited Wilkes to take a walk into a nearby wooded area. Stopping by a fallen tree, Creath said, "Let us pray." According to Wilkes,

> My soul trembled with excitement. Brother Creath talked so to God that I voluntarily felt for the moment that if I should open my eyes I should certainly see Him upon whom no one can look and live. I never heard such a prayer before, and now thirty years have passed since that remarkable experience, and yet I have heard no such prayer since.

In today's world it is very difficult to have a quiet nook in the woods in which to pray. The important thing is to pray regardless. Busy schedules tend to squeeze prayer out of daily life. There is only one way to pray daily: *take time* to pray, for there is no such thing as "finding time." Don't be like Jonah, saving your most earnest prayer until a crisis forces it from you. Instead, "pray without ceasing" (1 Thessalonians 5:17).

B. Lesson Background

The background for this week's lesson is the same as last week's, so that information need not be repeated here. But lesson 10 may have made you wonder why—why was Jonah so determined to disobey God by not going to Nineveh, a major city in Assyria?

One definite reason is given in Jonah 4:2 (see lesson 13). Some students offer the further possibility that Jonah, as a prophet, did not want to associate with idol worshippers. Furthermore, there had been military conflicts between Israel and Assyria (of which Nineveh was the capital); this may have caused Jonah to dislike the Assyrians. That is speculation, but a review of the former campaigns between the two nations provides probable cause.

During the years of Jonah's ministry in the eighth century BC, Assyria was having internal problems and was not a threat to Israel. The actions of the past, however, were remembered. Some of the people involved in those wars could have been alive during Jonah's lifetime. The prophet's hometown of Gath-hepher was in northern Israel (2 Kings 14:25), a region more likely to have experienced conflict with the Assyrians. Jonah may have had relatives who fought against them.

In 853 BC, about 75 years before Jonah began his prophetic ministry, King Shalmaneser III (not mentioned in the Old Testament) had attacked a coalition of 11 or 12 kings that included King Ahab of Israel. Assyrian records proclaim Shalmaneser to have won the resulting Battle of Qarqar; the losses he claims to have inflicted on the coalition include 2,000 chariots and 10,000 men of Israel. Actually, it appears that the battle was indecisive, with the Assyrians advancing no farther that year. It is very possible that some of Jonah's relatives of a previous generation fought the brutal Assyrians in that battle.

In 841 BC, Shalmaneser III again flexed Assyrian power against Israel. His famous black obelisk shows Jehu of Israel bowing before him (although some think it is a representative who is bowing). Another king of Assyria reigned from 811 to 783 BC. He received tribute from Jehoash (Joash), father of Jeroboam II. Jonah prophesied about events in the reign of the latter (2 Kings 14:25). Considering all these factors, it is quite plausible that Jonah and his fellow Israelites had a great disdain, even hatred, for Assyria. Jonah would rather go anywhere than to those despised people!

HOW TO SAY IT

Ahab	*Ay*-hab.
Assyria	Uh-*sear*-ee-uh.
Assyrians	Uh-*sear*-e-unz.
Gath-hepher	Gath-*hee*-fer.
Jehoash	Jeh-*hoe*-ash.
Jehu	*Jay*-hew.
Jeroboam	Jair-uh-*boe*-um.
Joash	*Jo*-ash.
Nineveh	*Nin*-uh-vuh.
Shalmaneser	Shal-mun-*ee*-zer.
Sheol	*She*-ol.

I. Descriptions
(JONAH 2:1-3)
A. In the Fish (vv. 1, 2)

1. Then Jonah prayed to the LORD his God from the belly of the fish,

Jonah had been invited to the sailors' prayer meeting (Jonah 1:5, 6; last week's lesson), but there is no record that he participated by offering prayer himself. Also, it seems quite doubtful that Jonah prayed concerning his decision to go to Joppa to find a ship in his plan to flee from the Lord!

Therefore what we see in the verse before us is the first recorded prayer by Jonah in the book that bears his name. Jonah has had the "thrill" of being cast overboard into the raging sea, sinking into the water, and then being swallowed by a great fish. Only after all that do we find a record of him praying.

Here and 2 Chronicles 14:11 are the only two places in the Old Testament where the exact Hebrew wording translated *to the Lord his God* is found. In both cases, the prayer is offered by men in situations of life and death. Dire situations often compel prayer by people who do not have prayer as an ordinary part of their lives. They anticipate positive answers, and often they almost challenge God to hear and heed their prayers.

> **What Do You Think?**
> What steps can we take to avoid an "act now and pray later" mind-set?
> *Talking Points for Your Discussion*
> - To clarify the value of self-reliance
> - To distinguish boldness from rebellion
> - To better understand the power of prayer

2. saying,
"I called out to the LORD, out of my distress,
and he answered me;
out of the belly of Sheol I cried,
and you heard my voice.

Seeing *I called* and *I cried* may make us wonder if two prayers are involved, or if there is just one that is described twice. Behind the two translations *called* and *cried* stand different Hebrew words. The two words have a lot of overlap in meaning, but the one behind the translation of *cried* is more intense. This same pairing of Hebrew words occurs in Psalms 18:6; 28:1, 2; 119:146, 147; and Isaiah 58:9.

In all these cases, the reader detects (even with no knowledge of Hebrew) a heightening of intensity as the thought moves forward. We see this heightening here as Jonah's call in his *distress* is followed by his affirmation that he *cried* from *out of the belly of Sheol*—the second phrase obviously more pointed than the first. Sheol is a Hebrew word that the *English Standard Version* leaves untranslated in its dozens of occurrences in the Old Testament. Other Bible versions render it in various contexts as "grave," "hell," "realm of the dead," or in terms of various aspects of death.

The wording leads some to think that Jonah was actually dead when he uttered his prayer, and then he was resurrected when the fish expelled him (Jonah 2:10, below). Most, however, see the phrasing as Jonah's way of describing his circumstances as being very critical. The most important thing to Jonah is that God does indeed respond to the prayer.

B. In the Sea (v. 3)

3. **"For you cast me into the deep,**
   into the heart of the seas,
   and the flood surrounded me;
   all your waves and your billows
   passed over me.

As Jonah piles up descriptions of his ordeal, we see expressions set as parallels with one another:

into the deep —> *into the heart of the seas*
the flood surrounded —> *waves/billows passed over*

Not to be missed, however, is Jonah's acknowledgment of the ultimate power behind the prophet's ordeal: it is the Lord (*you*). The hands of the sailors had thrown Jonah overboard, but the hand of the Lord was behind theirs in doing so (Jonah 1:12, 15, last week's lesson). Jonah further affirms that the entirety of the watery environment that resulted belongs to God (*your*). To acknowledge God is a first step of repentance.

The poet Sam Walter Foss (1858–1911) is best known for works such as "The Coming American" and "The House by the Side of the Road." A lesser known poem is "The Prayer of Cyrus Brown."

In that work of 24 lines, a deacon, an elder, and two ministers give their opinions, in exalted language, regarding the best posture for prayer. The deacon advocates prayer while kneeling. A minister disagrees, contending that prayer should be offered while standing with arms outstretched and eyes lifted toward Heaven. The elder is adamant that praying with eyes closed and head bowed is the proper way. The second minister opines that prayer be offered with hands clasped in front, thumbs pointing downward.

Having heard all this, plainspoken Cyrus Brown offers an entirely different perspective: his own "prayingest prayer" occurred when he fell headfirst down a well and became stuck in that position! For both Cyrus Brown and Jonah, the desperation of their respective situations overruled issues such as posture when praying. But if situations of absolute desperation are the only times we pray . . . well, what do *you* think?   —C. R. B.

II. Despair
(JONAH 2:4-6a)
A. Away from God (v. 4)

4. **"Then I said, 'I am driven away**
   from your sight;
   yet I shall again look
   upon your holy temple.'

Jonah is fully aware that his own rebellion has caused him to be *driven away from [God's] sight* (compare Psalm 31:22; Jeremiah 7:15). As his strength fades, Jonah seems to despair, at least briefly, of ever again having fellowship with God.

Yet at some point Jonah expresses hope of someday looking again *upon [God's] holy temple*. We wonder if this refers to the temple in Jerusalem, even though Jonah is from the northern kingdom of Israel (2 Kings 14:25; note that 1 Kings 12:28-30 records Israel's worship centers to be elsewhere). The reference may even be to God's presence in Heaven (compare Psalm 18:6; Hebrews 8:2; 9:11, 24).

B. Covered by Water (v. 5)

5. **"The waters closed in over me to take my life;**

    the deep surrounded me;

    weeds were wrapped about my head

Jonah uses three vivid images to describe further the apparent hopelessness of his situation. The similarity to Psalm 69:1, 2 is noteworthy.

C. Down to the Lowest (v. 6a)

6a. **"at the roots of the mountains.**

    I went down to the land

    whose bars closed upon me forever;

Jonah's plight is described in language that reminds us of the mountain ranges and deep canyons that lie beneath the surface of the oceans. The people of Jonah's day have never seen such things, of course. So for Jonah to speak of being *at the roots of the mountains* and going *down to the land* may reflect his assumption that the lofty heights he sees on land continue their descent below sea level.

As Jonah looks back on this recent experience, things seemed hopeless at the time. The behavior of *the land* itself seemed to ensure his death. Finality is expressed in the time factor of *forever*. But then the impossible actually happened.

III. Declarations

(JONAH 2:6b-10)

A. By Jonah (vv. 6b-9)

6b. **"yet you brought up my life from the pit, O LORD my God.**

God rescued Jonah in a way that is beyond what anyone would have imagined, since this is believed to be the point at which the fish swallowed him. Thus he has a reprieve from death.

Is it possible for a huge fish to swallow a man? Many skeptics react to this event by saying that it is not only unbelievable, but impossible. Some question whether such a fish ever existed in the Mediterranean Sea. Fake stories of "modern-day Jonahs" do not help.

For example, a story circulated several decades ago about a man named James Bartley (1870–1909) who was swallowed by a whale near the Falkland Islands and lived for 18 hours before being rescued. But a researcher debunked this story in 1991. He discovered that the ship in question had not had anyone named James Bartley as a crew member. The wife of the ship's captain said this in a letter: "There is not one word of truth in the whale story. I was with my husband all the years he was in [the ship named] *The Star of the East*. There was never a man lost overboard while my husband was in her. The sailor has told a great sea yarn."

Given the decisive evidence for the bodily resurrection of Jesus, it is a very minor matter for God to have a fish swallow a man! Jesus even connects the two events (see Matthew 12:39, 40). We also note a connection with the very similar wording of Psalm 103:4: "who redeems your life from the pit."

7. **"When my life was fainting away, I remembered the LORD,**

    and my prayer came to you, into your holy temple.

What are one's final thoughts just before death? Jonah recalls his thoughts to have focused on remembering *the Lord*. Those thoughts had been in the form of a prayer that ascended into God's *holy temple*! Jonah can affirm this confidently because of the flow of events that follow, in which light he pens the verse before us.

We experience moments when it seems as if the whole world is conspiring against us, times when there is no relief in sight. Often, however, it's not the whole world conspiring against us, but a case of being our own worst enemy. Addictions to drugs and gambling are examples.

People with addictions may sound sincere about their desire to get on the road to recovery, but often that won't happen until they "hit rock bottom." This expression means that a person has reached the point where one's own coping mechanisms have proven insufficient. At such a point, the addict may realize that there is no hope for recovery without turning it all over to God.

At some point, Jonah realized that he had hit rock bottom. His coping mechanism of fleeing from God had failed. Stripped of the possibility of rescue, either by his own strength or by that of other people, Jonah realized there was only one source of help that remained: the God from whom he had tried to flee.

Most of us are not mired in addictions, nor are we in Jonah's predicament. But we can learn from his experience. The ironclad rule is this: *When God taps you on the shoulder for a task, turn to him for help right then and there.* Don't flee first and ask for help when things seem hopeless. To do so is to repeat Jonah's error. See 1 Corinthians 10:11, 12.

—C. R. B.

What Do You Think?
What are some ways a church can help those who have "hit rock bottom"?
Talking Points for Your Discussion
- Concerning Christians in such a state
- Concerning unbelievers in such a state

8. "Those who pay regard to vain idols forsake their hope of steadfast love.

Jonah has received a great act of love from God. In the midst of such a deliverance, the thoughts of the prophet turn to others. He has learned a great lesson, and he writes to warn against turning *to vain idols* (compare Psalm 31:6). To walk in one's own way instead of God's way is to forfeit God's love. Jonah still has the heart of a prophet in that he has concerns for others—especially, it seems, for those who worship fictitious gods. The only true source of love is the only true God.

What Do You Think?
What specific steps can we take to avoid the worthless idols that trap so many people?
Talking Points for Your Discussion
- Concerning temptations of power
- Concerning temptations of possessions
- Other

Comparisons have been made between Jonah's statement in the verse before us and the contest between Elijah and the prophets of Baal on Mount Carmel. Elijah was a prophet in Israel before the time of Jonah. In the Mount Carmel situation, the Lord demonstrated his power over the idolatrous Baal gods. That was a great vindication for the person and the preaching of Elijah (1 Kings 18:20-46).

Both events involved water, but in entirely different ways. Elijah had water poured over the sacrifice three times, and then he prayed. "Then the fire of the Lord fell and consumed the burnt offering and the wood and the stones and the dust, and licked up the water that was in the trench" (1 Kings 18:38). The backdrop to that contest was a three-year drought (18:1). In both cases God's answers to the prayers were dramatic.

9. "But I with the voice of thanksgiving will sacrifice to you; what I have vowed I will pay. Salvation belongs to the LORD!"

Jonah plans distinct responses in light of God's dramatic display of love toward him. The sailors had offered a sacrifice when they were delivered from the storm (Jonah 1:16), and Jonah intends to do so in light of his own deliverance, or salvation.

Sacrifices involve animals, however, and Jonah has none with him at the moment (except the great fish, which has *him* rather than the reverse!). The only material possession he likely has is the proverbial "shirt on his back." Therefore his sacrifice while inside the fish will take the form of the next best thing: his *voice of thanksgiving* (compare Psalms 50:14; 69:30; Hebrews 13:15).

Jonah affirms also that he intends to *pay* what he has *vowed*, but we don't know exactly what that vow is. While on the verge of drowning, Jonah may have made a promise to do something should God deliver him (Jonah 2:1-4). This is not a case of "foxhole religion" that wanes as soon as the battle is won or the crisis is over, however. As a prophet, Jonah is well aware that "if you make a vow to the Lord your God, you shall not delay fulfilling it, for the Lord your God will surely require it of you, and you will be guilty of sin" (Deuteronomy 23:21).

B. By the Lord (v. 10)

10. And the Lord spoke to the fish, and it vomited Jonah out upon the dry land.

The book of Jonah is different from other prophetic books in that it is largely a narrative. Most of Jonah 2 breaks this pattern, with the narrative resuming here at 2:10.

We are to understand that what *the fish* does is by God's control and direction. There is a certain irony here. When the Lord instructed Jonah to go to Nineveh, the prophet disobeyed and went in the opposite direction (Jonah 1:1-3); by contrast, the fish obeys God.

We normally associate vomiting with the body's natural rejection of something due to being sick, perhaps with a stomach flu or having consumed something indigestible or in excess (compare Proverbs 25:16; Isaiah 19:14). A long-standing humorous observation is that a fish can stomach a backslider for only three days before it becomes sick! However, the expulsion of *Jonah out upon the dry land* is by the Lord's direction, not natural bodily reactions of the fish.

Anyone who has experienced a storm on a lake or an ocean recalls the great sense of relief when reaching land safely. How much more Jonah must be relieved given the extreme nature of his experiences! Our sanctified imaginations tell us that this is the time for the prophet to offer his "sacrifice" of "thanksgiving" (Jonah 2:9, above).

Jonah's water tests are now behind him. The remainder of his tests will be on land.

Visual for Lesson 11. *Point to this as you compare and contrast Jonah's situation with the "be still" imperative of Psalm 46:10.*

Conclusion
A. Running to God

One outline of the book of Jonah is offered this way:

Chapter 1: Running from God
Chapter 2: Running to God
Chapter 3: Running with God
Chapter 4: Running Ahead of God

When we see this sequence in the life of Jonah, it can cause us to reflect on which of the four states we are in right now. At the midpoint in our four lessons from Jonah, we see that the prophet has learned the hard way that it's better to run *to* God than *from* him.

It's been said that there are two ways to learn things: either by wisdom or by experience. The former is learning from the mistakes of others; the latter is learning from our own mistakes. So which will it be? Shall we in wisdom learn from Jonah's error, or shall we by experience learn the same lesson the hard way?

B. Prayer

Almighty God, keep us attuned to your Word so that when you call, we will respond! We pray this in Jesus' name. Amen.

C. Thought to Remember

Run *to* God, not *from* him.

INVOLVEMENT LEARNING

Enhance your lesson presentation with the reproducible activity page,
available as a free download at www.standardlesson.com.

Into the Lesson

Many churches have signs on which new messages may be posted regularly. Sometimes those signs have clever messages to draw a passing motorist's attention.

Begin class by asking students if they remember any messages on church signs (or one that may be on your church's sign at the moment). Here are a few of those quips, just to get your conversation going:

7 days without prayer makes one weak.
The Bible prevents truth decay.
Can't sleep? Come hear a sermon.
Free life insurance! Details inside. Great benefits!
Sin burn is prevented by Son screen.

Discuss the effectiveness of such messages. Ask, "What does it take to get *your* attention?"

Alternative. Distribute copies of the "For a Reason" activity from the reproducible page, which you can download. Have students work individually or in pairs.

After either activity, lead into the Bible study by saying, "There are a number of ways to attract attention. Signs, sounds, and any variety of banners and billboards are calls to stop and receive a message. Last week we saw that God did something remarkable to get Jonah's attention. Today we will see if that message was received."

Into the Word

Say, "Prayers typically contain three primary elements: (1) praise to God for who he is and what he does, (2) penitence, as expressions of sorrow for sin, both one's own and that of others, and (3) petitions for pressing personal needs and the needs of others."

Have learners write these three elements of prayer on the top of a sheet of paper. Ask the learners to look at Jonah's prayer in Jonah 2 and write elements of the prayer into the appropriate columns. For example: verse 1, the fact that

"God hears and answers prayer," is an element of praise; or one could put it in the petition column. One might use verse 2 in the petition column since it speaks of calling to God because of Jonah's "distress." Verse 4 may be considered an element of penitence, as Jonah speaks of being cast out of God's sight; separation from God—a sense of guilt—is the key factor in motivating repentance. The end of verse 9 is another good example of praise, as it affirms the Lord is the one who saves. Allow five or six minutes for this activity. Have students share their placement choices and reasons with the class.

Ask, "Which verse or phrase in today's text best justifies the title of today's study, "Preserving Love"? Learners may offer several choices. Verse 6b, "You brought up my life from the pit," is one legitimate response.

Into Life

Write the phrase *Occasional Prayer* on the board. Say, "This does not refer to the frequency (or infrequency!) of prayer." Ask, "What then do you assume it indicates?" You are looking for a response indicating that occasions (or events) often elicit our prayers. Say, "Such prayers, all too often, become heavy on or even limited to petitions for help." Ask, "How do you keep your prayer life from falling into the 'Jonah Syndrome,' waiting for times of crisis to pray?" Allow learners to respond.

Suggest a one-week prayer journal in which each student notes the various occasions he or she "felt the urge" to pray. At the end of the week, suggest that they analyze their lists for occasions, motives, and elements of the prayers offered.

Alternative. Distribute copies of the "A Common Christian Resolution" activity page. It would make an effective homework assignment designed to elicit thought about different occasions for personal prayer.

FORGIVING
LOVE

DEVOTIONAL READING: Acts 11:11-18
BACKGROUND SCRIPTURE: Jonah 3; Nahum 1–3

JONAH 3

¹ Then the word of the LORD came to Jonah the second time, saying, ² "Arise, go to Nineveh, that great city, and call out against it the message that I tell you." ³ So Jonah arose and went to Nineveh, according to the word of the LORD. Now Nineveh was an exceedingly great city, three days' journey in breadth. ⁴ Jonah began to go into the city, going a day's journey. And he called out, "Yet forty days, and Nineveh shall be overthrown!" ⁵ And the people of Nineveh believed God. They called for a fast and put on sackcloth, from the greatest of them to the least of them.

⁶ The word reached the king of Nineveh, and he arose from his throne, removed his robe, covered himself with sackcloth, and sat in ashes. ⁷ And he issued a proclamation and published through Nineveh, "By the decree of the king and his nobles: Let neither man nor beast, herd nor flock, taste anything. Let them not feed or drink water, ⁸ but let man and

beast be covered with sackcloth, and let them call out mightily to God. Let everyone turn from his evil way and from the violence that is in his hands. ⁹ Who knows? God may turn and relent and turn from his fierce anger, so that we may not perish."

¹⁰ When God saw what they did, how they turned from their evil way, God relented of the disaster that he had said he would do to them, and he did not do it.

KEY VERSE

When God saw what they did, how they turned from their evil way, God relented of the disaster that he had said he would do to them, and he did not do it. —Jonah 3:10

GOD LOVES US

Unit 3: God's Pervasive and Sustaining Love

LESSONS 10–13

LESSON AIMS

After participating in this lesson, each learner will be able to:

1. Describe the reactions of the people and king of Nineveh to Jonah's message.

2. Explain God's reaction to the Ninevites' repentance.

3. Make a list of the actions and attitudes of repentance that he or she will model in the week ahead.

LESSON OUTLINE

Introduction
    A. Limited-Time Offer
    B. Lesson Background
  I. Repeating the Commission (JONAH 3:1-4)
    A. Mission Stated (vv. 1, 2)
    B. Mission Begins (vv. 3, 4)
  II. Reactions to the Message (JONAH 3:5-9)
    A. By the People (v. 5)
    B. By the King (vv. 6-9)
      Preacher to King and Commoner
  III. Response by God (JONAH 3:10)
    Burn . . . or Turn?
Conclusion
    A. The Need to be Forgiven
    B. Prayer
    C. Thought to Remember

Introduction

A. Limited-Time Offer

Some matters are easy to forgive. But occasionally a news report will tell of a person who forgives a killer who took the life of a family member. Most, however, find it impossible to forgive when a person kidnaps, tortures, or takes the life of a loved one.

Even so, there are examples of people who befriend the criminal in prison. Upon release, he or she is invited to share a meal or even live in the same house until a job and permanent housing are obtained. The emotions go from hatred to compassion to forgiveness.

Even given the absence of criminal behavior, people find it very difficult to request, offer, and/or receive forgiveness. When someone is offended, months or years may pass with no contact between parties. Eventually, one may extend an olive branch. Communication grows over a period of time, forgiveness is extended and accepted, and the parties eventually interact as if nothing ever happened. To seek forgiveness requires maturity. So does offering it.

Think about that from God's perspective as you imagine yourself sitting on a hillside overlooking a modern city at dusk. The sun goes down and lights appear. The city bustles in the darkness as hundreds or thousands engage in sin. When the accumulated impact of thousands of sinful acts is considered, you may wonder why God does not act to rid the world of all sin!

But God *has* acted: he sent his Son to redeem humanity from sin. This act is described in these well-known words: "For God so loved the world, that he gave his only Son, that whoever believes in him should not perish but have eternal life" (John 3:16).

God wants to forgive, and he does. But on a day known only to God, it will be too late either to seek or accept forgiveness because it will no longer be offered (see Acts 17:30, 31). The residents of Nineveh knew their time would be up in 40 days, and they repented. Since we do not know when Jesus will return, repentance is all the more imperative!

B. Lesson Background

The city of Nineveh is the place for the events considered in today's lesson. This city is first mentioned in the Bible when a descendant of Noah's son Ham built it (Genesis 10:11). It was a major city in the Assyrian Empire and became its capital about 700 BC. This is often misunderstood, for many think it was the capital in Jonah's day, but it was not. Jonah's time period was more than 50 years prior to the city's becoming the capital.

King Sennacherib was the Assyrian ruler who selected Nineveh as his capital. He is the one who greatly enlarged it and built a very large palace. He is also the one who lost 185,000 troops in a single night (see 2 Kings 19:35; Isaiah 37:36). The city was sited on the eastern side of the Tigris River; its ruins are across the river from the modern city of Mosul in Iraq.

Major cities often seem to be cesspools of sin. This was certainly true of Nineveh. The reason given for Jonah's mission to Nineveh was that the wickedness of the city had got God's attention (Jonah 1:2).

Sin and wickedness often produce feelings of guilt. When a city experiences a tragedy, conscientious people may wonder whether their sin is the cause. The nation of Assyria was in a period of temporary decline during Jonah's day. Provincial leaders acted as kings in their respective regions. This is normal in and of itself, but there were conflicts among them. These were exacerbated by famines. The area also experienced devastating plagues in 765 and 759 BC. The ancients considered eclipses to be bad omens, and a solar eclipse occurred on June 15, 763 BC, visible over much of Assyria. Jonah's message of impending doom may have had a greater impact because of some or all of these astronomical, economic, and political events.

I. Repeating the Commission
(JONAH 3:1-4)
A. Mission Stated (vv. 1, 2)

1, 2. **Then the word of the LORD came to Jonah the second time, saying, "Arise, go to Nineveh, that great city, and call out against it the message that I tell you."**

The command is very similar to the commission given in Jonah 1:2 (see the Lesson Background). That previous instruction was for Jonah to "call out against" the city; again, Jonah is informed that he must *call out* what God tells him to preach. Jonah is not to come up with his own set of sermons, but is to use those provided by God.

Jonah's location at the time of his second call is not revealed. We know the fish vomited him on "dry land" (Jonah 2:10, last week's lesson), perhaps on a beach in Samaria. Or time may have passed so that Jonah has already been walking toward Nineveh now for several days. Some propose that he has returned to his ancestral home in Gath-hepher (2 Kings 14:25). The possibilities are endless and speculative. A minority view is that the fish took Jonah on a wild ride of over 1,500 miles, traveling first west, then north around Asia Minor, then east into the Black Sea to be vomited on a beach north of Nineveh. But that would still leave 350 miles to travel.

B. Mission Begins (vv. 3, 4)

3. **So Jonah arose and went to Nineveh, according to the word of the LORD. Now Nineveh was an exceedingly great city, three days' journey in breadth.**

The distance from Samaria (the capital of Israel) to Nineveh is about 550 miles. Some believe Jonah to be an official prophet for King Jeroboam II (2 Kings 14:23-25). This would enable him to carry official credentials.

Jonah needs about six weeks for this overland trip. This assumes he can average at least 15 miles per day over varying terrain, with no travel on the Sabbath. The evidence suggests that he does not look forward to arriving at the destination, so he may travel at a slower pace.

The record of Nineveh's great size has been criticized on the supposition that there is no city in antiquity so large as to require *three days' journey* to traverse. This skepticism has drawn various responses. One response is that the three days include the time required for Jonah to stop and preach. Archaeological excavation reveals Nineveh to be at least 1,730 acres in size. Ancient cities have between 160 and 200 residents per acre; therefore the city's total population computes to between 276,800 and 346,000 (compare Jonah 4:11). That's huge for this era! For Jonah to preach neighborhood by neighborhood will easily require three days.

A second proposal is that the three days include the villages in the immediate vicinity of Nineveh. In such a case, Nineveh-plus-suburbs is an area with a 60-mile circumference. A third possibility is that a journey of three days is a figure of speech to describe an official visit to a major city. The first day is for exchange of greetings and getting settled. The purpose of the visit is carried out on the second day, and the guests depart on the third. These are all reasonable ways to interpret the language.

4. Jonah began to go into the city, going a day's journey. And he called out, "Yet forty days, and Nineveh shall be overthrown!"

The first half of this verse tends to confirm the first option given above. The message Jonah proclaims after passing through a huge city gate is very brief—just five words in Hebrew. He does not offer any hope—just words of doom.

Recent disasters (see the Lesson Background) probably have a significant effect on the superstitious audience. Jonah's prediction makes those disasters seem as mere previews of the major event that will come in *forty days*. Such precision enhances the effectiveness of Jonah's preaching.

> *What Do You Think?*
> How do we respond to the charge of "being judgmental" when we try to communicate the difficult message of God's judgment?
> *Talking Points for Your Discussion*
> - To fellow Christians
> - To unbelievers

II. Reactions to the Message
(JONAH 3:5-9)
A. By the People (v. 5)

5. And the people of Nineveh believed God. They called for a fast and put on sackcloth, from the greatest of them to the least of them.

Several startling events are recorded in the book of Jonah, but one of the greatest is the tremendous response to Jonah's pointed message. Jonah ends up being one of the most successful preachers of all time, as repentance is demonstrated at all levels of Ninevite society, *from the greatest of them to the least of them.*

The astonishing scope of the repentance is underlined when contrasted with the skepticism toward Jesus and his message. Jesus preached to fellow Israelites, and his ministry was accompanied by miracles; the resulting unbelief drew the divine denouncement of Matthew 11:20-24.

On the other hand, Jonah's preaching to foreigners was well received, and there is no record that he performed any miracles in Nineveh. Jesus himself drew the contrast: "The men of Nineveh will rise up at the judgment with this generation and condemn it, for they repented at the preaching of Jonah, and behold, something greater than Jonah is here" (Matthew 12:41).

Jonah's proclamation is followed by a proclamation by *the people of Nineveh* themselves. Fasting can indicate deep sorrow (example: Judges 20:26) as can the donning of *sackcloth*—a coarse, rough fabric (example: 2 Kings 19:1). Putting both together adds intensity to the picture (compare Psalm 35:13). The Ninevites have no assurance that their demonstration of repentance will result in the prophesied disaster's being averted. But they desperately want to do whatever it takes to preserve themselves.

B. By the King (vv. 6-9)

6. The word reached the king of Nineveh, and he rose from his throne, removed his robe, covered himself with sackcloth, and sat in ashes.

Usually people do as the king decrees or does. But here we have the reverse—another surprise!—

as *the king of Nineveh* exchanges his royal clothing for sackcloth. But since leaders lead, he takes the additional step of sitting *in ashes*. Ashes are associated with dust (Genesis 18:27; 1 Samuel 2:8; Job 30:19; 42:6; Psalm 113:7; Ezekiel 27:30), leading some to think that the king's use of dust/ashes connects with a conqueror's practice of burning enemy cities. Thus dust/ashes associate with death and destruction (compare Jeremiah 31:40).

This additional step by the king reinforces the actions of the people. A king with more pride may be tempted to execute the messenger in order to squash a disturbing message. Fasting, sackcloth, and ashes are mentioned together in Esther 4:3; Isaiah 58:5; and Daniel 9:3. "Earth" is used in Nehemiah 9:1-3. Repentance "in dust and ashes" is seen in Job 42:6.

Critics have questioned the accuracy of this account by charging that a king would not have lived in Nineveh during Jonah's day because the city did not become Assyria's capital until later. But Nineveh was a major city in the nation, and kings did reside there occasionally. Further, the hectic conditions in Assyria at the time may have caused some provincial leaders to assume titles of royalty. Earlier in the history of the Israelites, Joshua's forces defeated 31 kings (Joshua 12:7-24). Each was a king over what is called a city-state (compare "king of Jerusalem" in Joshua 10:1, 3; 12:10).

◆ PREACHER TO KING AND COMMONER ◆

Billy Graham was an unknown farm boy from North Carolina who eventually became a Christian evangelist known worldwide. His first evan-

HOW TO SAY IT

Assyria	Uh-*sear*-ee-uh.
Assyrian	Uh-*sear*-e-un.
Damascus	Duh-*mass*-kus.
Gath-hepher	Gath-*he*-fer.
Jeroboam	Jair-uh-*boe*-um.
Jonah	*Jo*-nuh.
Nineveh	*Nin*-uh-vuh.
Ninevites	*Nin*-uh-vites.
Samaria	Suh-*mare*-ee-uh.
Sennacherib	Sen-*nack*-er-ib.

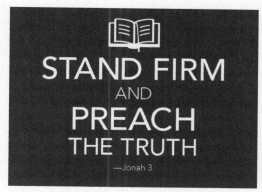

Visual for Lesson 12. *Point to this visual as you ask, "How can Christians who are not pulpit ministers by vocation accept this challenge?"*

gelistic crusade, in 1947, was the initial step to national recognition. His 1949 crusade, held in circus tents on a vacant lot in Los Angeles, was planned to last three weeks. But it went five more! One result was invitations to preach the gospel in many of the great cities of the world, including (eventually) Moscow.

Graham went on to become a spiritual adviser to American presidents, beginning with Harry S. Truman. For a time, Graham was considered America's conscience. His name has appeared dozens of times in the annual top-10 listings of most admired people—more than anyone else—as published by Gallup. If anyone could be considered to have been preacher to both king and commoner in the twentieth century, it was Billy Graham.

But Graham was not the first preacher able to reach all strata of society. Jonah found himself in that position some 28 centuries before Graham. If Jonah could be persuasive to king and commoner despite his own unwillingness, how effective might modern preachers be, were they to embrace God's calling with greater enthusiasm? How can we help them do so?   —C. R. B.

7. And he issued a proclamation and published through Nineveh, "By the decree of the king and his nobles: Let neither man nor beast, herd nor flock, taste anything. Let them not feed or drink water,

Kings don't always have the full support of those who serve in their courts (example: Jeremiah 38:24-27). But this one apparently does, and *the decree of the king* has extra weight, given that it is supported by *his nobles*. The Hebrew behind that designation is also translated "great men" in Nahum 3:10 in a prediction of Ninevites to be "bound in chains" when the city falls to enemies in 612 BC.

The actions of fasting decreed are unusual in that they apply also to livestock! Many households of the era include livestock of various kinds. Merchants in Nineveh have livestock for sale. Staples such as milk, meat, and eggs require nearby sources since there is no refrigeration. Therefore the fasting requirement will have a greater impact than what we may first think.

Noise! The fast prohibits both eating and drinking. This means that there will be great noise—from the crying of hungry children to the bellowing and complaining of the livestock. The noise will increase as expectations for food and water at customary times continue to go unmet.

What Do You Think?
What are some specific ways that leaders can encourage others to repent?
Talking Points for Your Discussion
- Regarding what to say
- Regarding personal transparency
- Regarding personal example
- Other

8. "but let man and beast be covered with sackcloth, and let them call out mightily to God. Let everyone turn from his evil way and from the violence that is in his hands.

For the decree to include a mandate that animals *be covered with sackcloth* seems strange! But adherence to this provision will further show that the repentance is genuine.

This requirement is sometimes cited to confirm that Jonah's preaching begins in the outer suburbs, where the larger flocks are pastured. But this supposition is unnecessary since it is customary to have animals in the towns.

The king strengthens the impact of the fast by further requiring that the people turn to God and

away from wickedness. By this the people will show that their repentance is more than fasting and wearing sackcloth. There must also be the actions that are the fruit of repentance.

What Do You Think?
What are some godly ways to respond after suffering violence at the hands of another?
Talking Points for Your Discussion
- Concerning requirements for forgiveness
- In how we desire the judicial system to treat the perpetrator
- In how we pray
- Other

9. "Who knows? God may turn and relent and turn from his fierce anger, so that we may not perish."

The king seriously reflects on whether all this will get God's attention. He certainly hopes so!

The word translated *relent* involves emotion. In this case, it carries the idea that God will look with compassion on those turning to him. As they do, perhaps God will *turn from his fierce anger*.

Self-preservation is basic for everyone. Each person wants to live at least another day. In this situation, the king reviews all that they have done and wonders whether it is enough. The ultimate purpose in all the self-depriving actions is *that we may not perish*. The primary motivation is obviously fear.

III. Response by God
(JONAH 3:10)

10. When God saw what they did, how they turned from their evil way, God relented of the disaster that he had said he would do to them, and he did not do it.

An important lesson about prophecies is illustrated here. Some prophecies are absolute; they will be fulfilled, no matter what (example: 2 Kings 24:1-4). Other prophecies are conditional; Jonah's prophecy falls into this category. When the various actions of the king, his nobles, and the people of Nineveh combine to demonstrate sincerity, God cancels his plan to visit judgment destruction on the city. But although the desired result is achieved, the king and people of Nineveh won't know it for sure until the 40 days elapse. (We don't know whether God reveals his decision to Jonah before the 40 days are up; opinions have been expressed both ways.) Showing sincere repentance for 40 days is much more difficult than showing it for 40 hours!

As we look back on our lives and the lives of biblical characters, we know that repentance even for 40 days doesn't guarantee repentance for a lifetime. That fact is demonstrated by the subsequent history of the nation of Assyria, with Nineveh as its capital, which becomes infamous for its atrocities on captured peoples.

In 655 BC, the prophet Nahum pronounces doom on Nineveh. This time there is no reprieve. Its demise becomes reality in 612 BC when a coalition totally destroys the city.

◆ *Burn . . . or Turn?* ◆

The Great Fire of London started in the bakery of Thomas Farriner just after midnight on September 2, 1666. The flames were soon out of control, and the fire raged through the city for four days. It consumed thousands of homes, dozens of church buildings, and a cathedral.

An eyewitness to the fire was Puritan preacher Thomas Vincent. It inspired him to write a book titled *Fire and Brimstone in Hell, to Burn the Wicked,* published in 1670. Some think the book became the touchstone for the "hellfire and brimstone" style of preaching that was to come in the decades ahead.

We would hope that practitioners of this style of preaching sincerely desired repentance on the part of those listening (compare Matthew 3:1, 2)! That is more than can be said for Jonah. He resisted and resented being called to warn Nineveh. Jonah 4:1, 2 (next week's lesson) reveals that he wanted his audience to ignore his warning. Often pointed out is that Jonah is perhaps the only preacher in history who was upset because people heeded his message! Now think of the most ungodly, murderous group of people currently being reported in the news. Do you want those people to "get theirs," or do you want them to repent? —C. R. B.

Conclusion
A. The Need to Be Forgiven

Fred had just become a Christian, and he was fully aware of God's forgiving love. Fred had a great memory, and he could recall things he had done that were wrong. His conscience would not let him brush them aside.

With thoughts of restitution, Fred decided to visit an acquaintance in the same town. After being invited in, Fred took some currency from his billfold, pushed it toward the other man, and said, "I owe you this." The offer was resisted with the protest, "Freddie, you don't owe me anything."

Fred then confessed to a time he had stolen a pig and sold it when he was running low on cash. He was sure that there were so many pigs in the herd that one would not be missed. He was right; it was not. Even so, Fred insisted on restitution, and the money was accepted. Fred also asked for forgiveness for taking advantage of a friend. The forgiveness was granted, and the forgiveness in love strengthened a friendship in Christ.

Repentance is demonstrated in its fruits. This was just as true of the ancient Ninevites as it was for Fred. Where's your fruit?

B. Prayer

Father, your love and desire to forgive are more than we can understand. Help us to model your example to forgive in love. We pray this in Jesus' name. Amen.

C. Thought to Remember

Repent for a lifetime to receive God's forgiving love for an eternity.

INVOLVEMENT LEARNING

Enhance your lesson presentation with the reproducible activity page,
available as a free download at www.standardlesson.com.

Into the Lesson

Begin class by asking students what they know about Orson Welles's famous *War of the Worlds* broadcast. If you have a smartphone or other mobile device, you may wish to play a short portion of it from a video-sharing website.

Here are the basic facts. On Halloween of 1938, Welles, a virtually unknown 23-year-old radio producer, directed and broadcast a radio adaptation of H. G. Wells's famous novel *War of the Worlds.* Although there were two clear announcements that the "invasion" was fictitious, the broadcast disturbed many people. Welles later apologized for any distress his broadcast caused, but the incident made him an instant celebrity.

Alternative. Distribute copies of the "It Must Be True! I Saw It on the Internet!" activity from the reproducible page, which you can download. Have students work individually or in pairs.

After either activity, lead into the Bible study by saying, "How do you know when people are taking you seriously? As we have learned, God sent Jonah to Nineveh with a message of judgment. Let's see how Jonah knew that the Ninevites took him seriously."

Into the Word

Divide the class into three groups. Give each paper and pen. Each group should be assigned a section of the lesson text. Each group should summarize the reaction to Jonah's preaching as a tabloid heading and subtitle.

Assignments and sample headings and subtitles follow:

Group 1—Inward Conviction (Jonah 3:1-5a)
Jewish Street Preacher Draws Record Crowds!
Hundreds believe Jonah's doomsday prediction!

Group 2—Visible Demonstration (vv. 5b, 6)
Sack Is the New Black!

Widespread religious revival breaks out!

Group 3—Urgent Communication (vv. 7-10)
Separation of Church and State Suspended!
King orders all citizens to appeal to God!

Allow time for the groups to share their headlines and subtitles with the rest of the class.

Alternative. Distribute copies of "Surprised or Expected?" from the reproducible page. Allow time for students to mark the statements, summarizing the content of Jonah 3 as something that surprised them or as something they expected. Ask students to defend their responses.

Into Life

Write this scrambled phrase, drawn from Romans 2:4, on the board:

**d'Gos deiknnss dhlosu adel
ouy ot aceeennprt!**

Unscramble the phrase. The thought is "God's kindness should lead you to repentance!"

Write this imperative from Luke 3:8 (by John the Baptist) on the board:

aBer firstu ni peeking thiw aceeennprt.

John's challenge was and is, "Bear fruits in keeping with repentance."

Say, "True repentance will result in action, even as it did in the time of Jonah." Ask, "How do you see yourself responding to God's kindness and his goodness, with behaviors in keeping with repentance? Do you see yourself making a literal turnaround in such choices as where to go (and invest your time), what confrontations to avoid, and what face-to-face meetings you should have?"

Say, "Repentance is always a matter of answering the question 'Which way will you go?' and answering it with God's direction!"

PERVASIVE LOVE

DEVOTIONAL READING: Psalm 86:8-13
BACKGROUND SCRIPTURE: Jonah 4

JONAH 4

¹ But it displeased Jonah exceedingly, and he was angry. ² And he prayed to the LORD and said, "O LORD, is not this what I said when I was yet in my country? That is why I made haste to flee to Tarshish; for I knew that you are a gracious God and merciful, slow to anger and abounding in steadfast love, and relenting from disaster. ³ Therefore now, O LORD, please take my life from me, for it is better for me to die than to live." ⁴ And the LORD said, "Do you do well to be angry?"

⁵ Jonah went out of the city and sat to the east of the city and made a booth for himself there. He sat under it in the shade, till he should see what would become of the city. ⁶ Now the LORD God appointed a plant and made it come up over Jonah, that it might be a shade over his head, to save him from his discomfort. So Jonah

was exceedingly glad because of the plant. ⁷ But when dawn came up the next day, God appointed a worm that attacked the plant, so that it withered. ⁸ When the sun rose, God appointed a scorching east wind, and the sun beat down on the head of Jonah so that he was faint. And he asked that he might die and said, "It is better for me to die than to live." ⁹ But God said to Jonah, "Do you do well to be angry for the plant?" And he said, "Yes, I do well to be angry, angry enough to die." ¹⁰ And the LORD said, "You pity the plant, for which you did not labor, nor did you make it grow, which came into being in a night and perished in a night. ¹¹ And should not I pity Nineveh, that great city, in which there are more than 120,000 persons who do not know their right hand from their left, and also much cattle?"

KEY VERSE

Should not I pity Nineveh, that great city, in which there are more than 120,000 persons who do not know their right hand from their left, and also much cattle? —**Jonah 4:11**

GOD LOVES US

Unit 3: God's Pervasive and Sustaining Love
LESSONS 10–13

LESSON AIMS

After participating in this lesson, each learner will be able to:

1. Summarize Jonah's reactions to God's sparing of Nineveh.

2. Explain why Jonah was not pleased at the success of his preaching.

3. Participate in a class project that reaches to a group having racial or cultural differences.

LESSON OUTLINE

Introduction

A. The Fighting Deacon

He said that in his younger days he was known as "the fighting deacon." This reputation was acquired by the fact that on two occasions in meetings of the church board he had "slugged" (his word) someone who disagreed with him. He no longer had such a violent temper, but he was almost proud of what he had done.

But anger can be a very toxic emotion. Mark Twain wrote that "anger is an acid that can do more harm to the vessel in which it is stored than to anything on which it is poured." Some have rationalized their outbursts of anger by saying that they lose their tempers quickly and then calm down almost immediately. Billy Sunday, a famous preacher of the past, once encountered a lady who said, "I blow up, and then it's all over." Sunday replied, "So does a shotgun, and look at the damage it leaves behind."

The Bible has much to say about anger (Proverbs 29:22; Ephesians 4:31; Colossians 3:8; James 1:19, 20; etc.). The words *anger* or *angry* occur several times in Jonah 4, the text for our lesson. Jonah had a problem with anger. As the Lord worked through him to bring the people of Nineveh to repentance, God also worked with Jonah to help him overcome this problem. Anger is not sinful in and of itself (note Jesus' anger in Mark 3:5). But irrational anger needs corrective action, and that's what God provides Jonah in today's lesson.

B. Lesson Background

Since the background material noted in the three previous lessons applies here as well, that information need not be repeated. Much of that material is very weighty, so we shall close this series with some "lighter side" distinctive facts that help to make the book of Jonah memorable.

1. Jonah is the only prophet recorded to have traveled on the Mediterranean Sea.

2. Jonah is the only prophet recorded to have outright refused to undertake a mission from God. Other prophets revealed doubt from time to time (example: 1 Kings 19:3, 14), but Jonah stands alone in his flagrant rebellion.

3. When Nicodemus attempted to defend Jesus during a discussion, he was rebuked with the observation that "no prophet arises from Galilee" (John 7:52). This overlooked the fact that Jonah was from Gath-hepher (2 Kings 14:25), which was less than three miles northwest of Nazareth.

4. The book of Jonah, being primarily a narrative about the man, records just one predictive prophecy—a prophecy of only five words in Hebrew (Jonah 3:4, last week's lesson).

5. The book of Jonah is the only prophetic book with miracles by God that involved the prophet personally—from the storm and the fish to the worm and the wind.

The traditional view of authorship for the book of Jonah is that Jonah himself wrote it. As he came to the end of it, he must have been greatly embarrassed about the prejudice and anger he had displayed so blatantly. Our lesson begins just after the point where God saw the repentance of the Ninevites and decided not to destroy the city (Jonah 3:10, last week's lesson).

I. Jonah's Pettiness
(JONAH 4:1-4)
A. Reaction and Reminder (vv. 1, 2)

1. But it displeased Jonah exceedingly, and he was angry.

The compassionate decision of God in Jonah 3:10 is not what the prophet wants to hear! He is angry that his preaching results in the city's being spared God's destructive wrath. This is not the way a preacher would normally react when his message brings repentance by the thousands! The Lesson Background of lesson 11 explains the possible basis of Jonah's anger.

As a bit of speculation, Jonah may wonder whether God will treat the people of his own nation (the northern kingdom of Israel) likewise, should they repent when under threat of similar judgment. Historically, however, the people of Israel do not repent, in spite of the preaching of prophets (see 2 Kings 17:13, 14, 23). The sparing of Nineveh will not be repeated for Samaria a few decades later. But neither will it be repeated for Nineveh itself, as the prophet Nahum and historical records make clear.

We may also wonder exactly when Jonah is informed of God's decision to spare Nineveh. Is it before the 40-day period of Jonah 3:4 is up, thereby implying that Jonah is angry and indignant for the remainder of that period? Or do it and the other events of Jonah 4 happen at the end of the 40-day period? Scholars disagree, but the last phrase of Jonah 4:5 may indicate that the 40 days are not yet completed.

2. And he prayed to the LORD and said, "O, LORD, is not this what I said when I was yet in my country? That is why I made haste to flee to Tarshish; for I knew that you are a gracious God and merciful, slow to anger and abounding in steadfast love, and relenting from disaster.

Jonah turns his anger into prayer, but his motivation is not to become compliant with what God has done. Instead, he seems to be trying to make God feel guilty for sending him on the mission trip to Nineveh.

Jonah's prayer includes an eloquent description of the great attributes of God. In that regard, the prayer mirrors Exodus 34:6 as Jonah affirms that God is *gracious . . . and merciful, slow to anger and abounding in steadfast love.* These were Jonah's conclusions before he *made haste to flee to Tarshish* (Jonah 1:3). Able to list God's outstanding characteristics, Jonah wants to be the one to decide to whom they will and will not apply. He had wanted to be saved when he was in the fish (Jonah 2:2),

HOW TO SAY IT

Assyria	Uh-*sear*-ee-uh.
Assyrian	Uh-*sear*-e-un.
Galilee	*Gal*-uh-lee.
Gath-hepher	Gath-*hee*-fer.
Jonah	*Jo*-nuh.
Mediterranean	*Med*-uh-tuh-*ray*-nee-un.
Nazareth	*Naz*-uh-reth.
Nicodemus	*Nick*-uh-*dee*-mus.
Nineveh	*Nin*-uh-vuh.
Ninevites	*Nin*-uh-vites.
Tarshish	*Tar*-shish.

but he does not want the Ninevites to be saved from the doom prophesied for them. He wants God to do things Jonah's way, not God's way.

A certain parallel can be seen in churches where people enjoy Christianity's benefits but are unwilling to support missionaries adequately. The sad result is to deny people in other lands and cultures the blessing of everlasting life through Jesus. After realizing how much the Lord has forgiven us, we should want others to know that there is a God who is willing to forgive them as well.

> **What Do You Think?**
> How can we avoid feeling resentful when God extends his mercy to others?
> **Talking Points for Your Discussion**
> - When extended to backslidden Christians
> - When extended to those who have heard and rejected the gospel
> - When extended to those who have never heard the gospel

B. Request and Question (vv. 3, 4)

3. "Therefore now, O LORD, please take my life from me, for it is better for me to die than to live."

Jonah's frustration with the flow of events overwhelms him—so much so that he expresses his preference for death over life. This contrasts with his attitude when he was inside the fish, for there he wanted to live and see God's temple again (Jonah 2:2, 4, lesson 11). Jonah has been spared from death himself, but now he is despondent and disappointed that the people of Nineveh have been spared from prophesied destruction. His inconsistent reasoning serves as a marvelous set-up for the memorable lesson God is about to teach him.

4. And the LORD said, "Do you do well to be angry?"

As with Job, *the Lord* responds with a question (compare Job 38:2). The fact that God's interrogation begins with the issue of anger implies that an adjustment is necessary in that regard, as Jonah is led to look at himself in a mirror. There are indeed legitimate reasons for being angry. Do any of these form the basis for Jonah's own anger?

We note that the Lord does not ask his question because he needs information—the Lord already knows everything. The question is designed to get Jonah to think. The fact that we see no response from him may indicate that he is compelled to do just that. On the other hand, a lack of response may indicate that Jonah is so aggravated that he cannot process the question.

> **What Do You Think?**
> What are some steps to take for moving from anger to mercy?
> **Talking Points for Your Discussion**
> - Considering how God himself does so
> - Considering how God has treated us
> - Considering our motives
> - Other

II. Jonah's Protection
(JONAH 4:5-8)
A. Hut and Plant (vv. 5, 6)

5. Jonah went out of the city and sat to the east of the city and made a booth for himself there. He sat under it in the shade, till he should see what would become of the city.

The previous verses reveal the emotional responses of Jonah. In this verse, physical actions take the spotlight.

If circumstances work against a person's desires in some way, he or she may not take it well! Physically, these reactions may cover the spectrum from becoming very active (from fear, as in 1 Kings 19:3; from anger, as in Acts 7:57, 58; etc.) to becoming completely inactive (1 Kings 19:4, 5; 21:4). Jonah ends up in the latter as he seems to adopt an attitude of denial. Surely God did not mean it when he said he wouldn't destroy Nineveh, did he? So Jonah takes the actions described here, a disposition we might call "watchful waiting."

Jonah's initial approach toward Nineveh would have been from the west. After crossing the Tigris River, he entered Nineveh to preach as he continued in an easterly direction. Today, some of the gates of ancient Nineveh have been restored in order to reflect the glory of the city's past. Archaeology and terrain suggest that Jonah likely makes his exit through a gate at the southeastern part of a wall after he finishes his preaching tour at a place *to the east of the city*.

After he is out of the city, he probably finds a mound or high point that gives him a better view. There he builds a crude hut for shade where he can wait to see what will happen to the city. His food and water sources are not given. This waiting reflects disbelief of the Lord's decision. This sequence may confirm that the 40-day period (Jonah 3:4) is not over, for Jonah does not want to be in the city when time is up—just in case. Most people who want to pout seem to prefer solitude.

◆ READY AND ACTING ◆

Benjamin Disraeli served Britain as prime minister from 1874–1880. He experienced many setbacks and once said, "I am prepared for the worst, but hope for the best." The saying has been adapted to read "I am expecting the worst, but hoping for the best." There seems to be no adaptation, however, for the saying to be "I am ready for the worst, but acting to bring about the best."

What Jonah saw as the worst case—the repentance of the Ninevites—was actually the best case from God's point of view. One would think that Jonah would have felt successful when his preaching brought about repentance. But his sinful attitudes blinded him to God's desired end.

What is our own outlook regarding what we consider to be a worst-case scenario to be ready for and a best-case scenario to act to bring about? Jesus' resurrection proved that God can take the worst the powers of this world can dish out and turn it into the best outcome possible. And Jesus described his forthcoming resurrection in terms of—of all things!—Jonah's time inside the fish (Matthew 12:38-41). —C. R. B.

6. Now the LORD God appointed a plant and made it come up over Jonah, that it might be a shade over his head, to save him from his discomfort. So Jonah was exceedingly glad because of the plant.

Five events or special objects are mentioned in the book of Jonah as being prepared by God:

a wind (Jonah 1:4), a fish (1:17), a plant (4:6), a worm (4:7), and an east wind (4:8). We are now at the third of these five as *the Lord God* temporarily supplements Jonah's protection from the sun by means of a rapidly growing plant. One possibility is that this is a castor-oil plant. It grows rapidly to a height of about eight feet, and it has very large leaves (see also v. 10, below).

> **What Do You Think?**
> What can we do to improve our helping skills in preparing to be God's instrument of comfort to others?
> *Talking Points for Your Discussion*
> - For counseling adults
> - For counseling teenagers
> - For counseling preteens

The double layer of shade for Jonah is better. He is *exceedingly glad* to have this additional blessing, which appears so suddenly and adds to his comfort. Jonah is certainly concerned for himself! But love for perceived enemies is still lacking. The teaching about loving your enemies is given by Jesus in Matthew 5:44; but Jonah has no excuse, even though he lives over 700 years before Jesus. By Jonah's day, the enemy-love principle has already been stated in Exodus 23:4, 5 and Proverbs 25:21.

B. Worm and Wind (vv. 7, 8)

7. But when dawn came up the next day, God appointed a worm that attacked the plant, so that it withered.

"Jonah and the Worm" is the title of one preacher's sermon on Jonah. This title is intended to pique curiosity, since sermons on Jonah are usually about "Jonah and the Whale." The latter is based on Matthew 12:40, which refers to "the whale's belly" in the *King James Version*.

God used a great sea creature to correct Jonah's attitude about a trip to Nineveh. Now he uses a small worm to teach his prophet a further lesson. First, the worm does what God programmed it to do: it begins eating the stalk of *the plant*. The speculation that "the plant" refers to a castor-oil plant fits well, since this plant withers very quickly if the main stalk is injured.

REACH OUT
AND
LOVE
THE UNLOVELY

—Jonah 4

Visual for Lesson 13. *Start a discussion by pointing to this visual as you ask, "What are some ways to meet this challenge in the week ahead?"*

8. When the sun rose, God appointed a scorching east wind, and the sun beat down on the head of Jonah so that he was faint. And he asked that he might die and said, "It would be better for me to die than to live."

With the plant now useless for shade, God increases Jonah's discomfort further by means of *a scorching east wind* (compare Jeremiah 18:17). As the sun rises, all this works together to cause Jonah to become light-headed and dizzy. He temporarily forgets his anger, but remains self-centered as he expresses his wish *to die*. He is physically and spiritually miserable while far from home, in the foreign land of an enemy. Exhaustion from a preaching tour he had not desired is now multiplied by the possibility of heat stroke.

God has to this point used a storm and a great fish to encourage Jonah to go to Nineveh. Now God uses a worm and an east wind to move Jonah to where he should be in his attitudes toward those who are different.

What Do You Think?
What can we do to prepare for times that will be difficult to endure?
Talking Points for Your Discussion
- Regarding emotional preparations
- Regarding spiritual preparations
- Regarding physical preparations
- Other

III. God's Pronouncements
(JONAH 4:9-11)
A. Question and Response (v. 9)

9a. But God said to Jonah, "Do you do well to be angry for the plant?"

God is not finished with his efforts to correct Jonah's thinking. Jonah is being challenged to think correctly about the mind-set a true prophet should have. The first seven words of God's question here are identical to the seven words of his initial question in Jonah 4:4. The added words *for the plant* here indicate God is probing deeper as he requires Jonah to think about something specific, something that is not associated with the city of Nineveh.

9b. And he said, "Yes, I do well to be angry, angry enough to die."

Jonah's answer is petty, defensive, and almost defiant. He attempts to bolster his position by asserting once again his preference for death.

Jonah's peevishness indicates confidence that he has done nothing wrong. Further, he cannot comprehend why he has to suffer the loss of the plant. Emotional people who learn to control their emotions can do well in telling others about the love of God. Jonah has not yet reached that point; he lacks any compassion for the Ninevites.

◆ *FLYING OFF THE HANDLE* ◆

In America's pioneer days, axheads were made in the industrialized East, then shipped to the frontier West for fitting with handles. The handles were often fashioned by unskilled handymen, yielding the deadly possibility that an axhead could fly off an ill-fitting handle when in use (compare Deuteronomy 19:5).

The suddenness of such an event became a metaphor for an outburst of anger: *flying off the handle.* Possibly the first such use of this figure of speech in print was in a satirical story by Thomas Haliburton in 1844. Haliburton was a Canadian who mocked human nature in general and American-Canadian relations in particular in essays in *The Nova Scotian.*

But the idea goes back much further than the year AD 1844! God's directive for Jonah to preach in Nineveh seemed to strike a deep vein of resentment in that prophet; thus we see him "flying off the handle" at God. Do you deal with your anger any better than did Jonah? See James 1:19, 20.

—C. R. B.

B. Rebuke and Reason (vv. 10, 11)

10. And the LORD said, "You pity the plant, for which you did not labor, nor did you make it grow, which came into being in a night and perished in a night.

God's second question (v. 9a) is designed to soften Jonah's attitude. But Jonah's response (v. 9b) indicates further work is needed. God's observations of fact challenge Jonah's thinking by reminding the prophet that he had no ownership of the plant, for he had neither planted nor tended it. These facts should compel the prophet to realize how absurd and small his defensive statements really are. But God has a bit more yet to say.

11. "And should not I pity Nineveh, that great city, in which there are more than 120,000 persons who do not know their right hand from their left, and also much cattle?"

The Lord's final question demands that Jonah contrast his thoughts about the plant with God's thoughts regarding Nineveh. Jonah should feel embarrassed, for it is obvious that the population of a large, *great city* is more important than a single, solitary plant! Jonah's self-centeredness is now so obvious that even he should see it.

The size and greatness of Nineveh is indicated by the number *120,000*. There are two main lines of interpretation regarding this number. Some propose that it is the total population of the city. A city of this acreage (see commentary on Jonah 3:3 in lesson 12) can accommodate twice that number easily.

Under this view, the declaration regarding the city's residents *who do not know their right hand from their left* has a spiritual dimension—that spiritually the Ninevites are somehow deficient in being able to distinguish good from evil. This viewpoint runs into trouble at Romans 1:20.

The other view is that the 120,000 refers to the number of children in Nineveh who are not yet old enough to tell right from left. That would

boost the total population significantly when estimates of the number of older children and adults are added in. The grand total may be too much according to our analysis of Jonah 3:3 in lesson 12, unless the villages in the immediate vicinity are included.

The reference to *much cattle* is a reminder that God is concerned for animals as well as people. The word translated *cattle* refers to livestock in general (Exodus 13:15; 22:19; etc.).

What Do You Think?
  What Christian ministries can your church offer to those of the nearest "great city"?
Talking Points for Your Discussion
  - Considering demographic factors
  - In terms of priorities
  - In terms of defining *ministry*
  - Other

Conclusion
A. Running Ahead of God

In general, there are two mistakes we can make in our relationship with God. First, we can lag behind him, failing to move as fast as he wants us to (example: Haggai 1:1-8). The other mistake is to run ahead of him. This may involve making plans that are not his (example: 2 Samuel 7:1-13) or anticipating what we think he "must" do, as in today's lesson.

It is so easy to run ahead of God and presume that he must do such and such! That presumption resulted in anger and pouting on Jonah's part, and it can do the same to us.

Don't run ahead of God!

B. Prayer

O God, may your Word ever remind us of your love for humanity! Enable us to do all we can to take the gospel to all, without bias or prejudice. We pray this in Jesus' name. Amen.

C. Thought to Remember

When God loves,
he loves the world!

INVOLVEMENT LEARNING

Enhance your lesson presentation with the reproducible activity page,
available as a free download at www.standardlesson.com.

Into the Lesson

Before class, write the following incomplete sentences on the board:

I switched cell phone plans to save money, but . . .
I thought I would cut calories by skipping breakfast, but . . .
I wanted to comfort a friend struggling in marriage, but . . .

Ask volunteers to complete the sentences. They probably will end up talking about some unintended consequence of an action. For example, a cheap cell-phone plan costs more because of hidden charges. Skipping a meal to cut calories was followed by indulging in high-calorie snacks. Helping a friend with marriage issues might put one in the middle of a heated domestic dispute! As time allows, ask students to add other situations that brought about unintended consequences.

Alternative. Distribute copies of the "Didn't See It Coming" reproducible page, which you can download. Have students work in pairs or as a class to complete the activity.

After either activity, lead into the Bible study by saying, "Sometimes things do not turn out as we planned. As we studied last week, Jonah obeyed God and preached a message of judgment. But things did not turn out as Jonah would have liked. Let's examine this further."

Into the Word

Say, "Text messaging has given birth to the *emoticon,* which is a grouping of keyboard characters to represent a facial expression when viewed sideways. For example, colon plus dash plus close parenthesis represents a happy, smiling face."

List the following emoticons on the board:

>:(	Angry
((+_+))	Confused
:-{	Depressed
:-O	Surprised
>:-/	Skeptical
(´-`)	Thoughtful

Divide the class into small groups. Make sure that each group has a copy of the lesson text and pen or pencil. Say, "Each group should read the lesson text and pencil in emoticons that represent how Jonah was or may have been feeling at a particular point of the text." Allow time for groups to share their markings.

Option. For a more active version of the above, reproduce the emoticons on sheets of paper, one emoticon each, with no duplications. Distribute the reproductions so that each student has one. Ask for a volunteer to read Jonah 4 slowly. While the text is being read, the student with the relevant emotion should raise it for all to see.

Into Life

Plan a group service project with your students. Seek to serve a group that does not share your class's racial and cultural heritage. The project could be mission related, for a distant people group. Or it could be for a ministry closer to home. Possibilities include a fellowship dinner for international students at a local university or simply providing funding and servers for an act of love for a needy group. An occasion providing personal contact will best parallel Jonah's experience of God's love.

Your class may well suggest a novel idea that will allow such exchange of faith and friendship. Take the opportunity to affirm to the group your class serves that God's love is pervasive and that you want yours to be also.

Alternative. Distribute copies of the "What Kind of Love?" activity from the reproducible page. It offers a good review and reinforcement of the quarter's theme and lesson series. Use it as a take-home puzzle.

GOD'S
URGENT CALL

Special Features

Lessons
Unit 1: Called to Be Strong

Unit 2: Calling of Prophets

Unit 3: Calls in the New Testament

QUARTERLY QUIZ

Use these questions as a pretest or as a review. The answers are on page iv of This Quarter in the Word.

Lesson 1
1. Deborah the judge was also a prophetess. T/F. *Judges 4:4*
2. Deborah sat under what kind of tree? (palm, oak, fig?) *Judges 4:5*

Lesson 2
1. How did the Lord first contact Gideon? (vision, voice, angel?) *Judges 6:12*
2. Gideon was a wealthy farmer from a prominent family. T/F. *Judges 6:15*

Lesson 3
1. After he attacked enemies and won, Jephthah demanded to be made chief. T/F. *Judges 11:9*
2. Jephthah made an unwise _____ before the battle. *Judges 11:30*

Lesson 4
1. The mother of Samson was told to drink no wine while pregnant. T/F. *Judges 13:7*
2. Samson was under a vow known as what? (Levite, Nazirite, Hittite?) *Judges 13:7*

Lesson 5
1. Who was the father-in-law of Moses? (Jedidiah, Rameses, Jethro?) *Exodus 3:1*
2. At the burning bush, Moses was required to put on special shoes. T/F. *Exodus 3:5*

Lesson 6
1. Isaiah had a vision of Heaven in the year that King _____ died. *Isaiah 6:1*
2. What cleansed Isaiah's lips? (holy oil, new snow, burning coal?) *Isaiah 6:6, 7*

Lesson 7
1. Jeremiah was chosen by the Lord on the day of his birth. T/F. *Jeremiah 1:5*
2. The Lord chose Jeremiah to be a prophet to what? (the nations, Israel, Assyria?) *Jeremiah 1:5*

Lesson 8
1. What advantage did Ezekiel have in speaking to Israel? (same language, loud voice, many friends?) *Ezekiel 3:5*
2. The Lord promised Ezekiel that the people of Israel would accept his message. T/F. *Ezekiel 3:7*

Lesson 9
1. Amos was forbidden to speak at the king's sanctuary at _____. *Amos 7:13*
2. Before the Lord called him to prophesy, Amos did what? (tended herds and fruit trees, made pottery, tanned leather?) *Amos 7:14*
3. The father of Amos was also a prophet. T/F. *Amos 7:14*

Lesson 10
1. How many men were chosen to serve food to the widows? (seven, ten, twelve?) *Acts 6:2, 3*
2. Stephen not only served tables but also did miracles. T/F. *Acts 6:8*

Lesson 11
1. The eunuch who met Philip was from where? (Egypt, Antioch, Ethiopia?) *Acts 8:27*
2. The eunuch was reading from the prophet _____ when Philip encountered him. *Acts 8:28*
3. Philip waited several days before baptizing the eunuch. T/F. *Acts 8:36*

Lesson 12
1. Saul (Paul) was healed from blindness in the city of _____. *Acts 9:10*
2. Ananias was told that Saul would bear God's name to both Israelites and Gentiles. T/F. *Acts 9:15*

Lesson 13
1. What position did Cornelius hold? (centurion, tribune, governor?) *Acts 10:22*
2. Cornelius resided in the city of Jerusalem. T/F. *Acts 10:24*

QUARTER AT A GLANCE

by Douglas Redford

ONE EVENING some years ago, I helped serve what was called a midnight breakfast at the college where I teach. It was scheduled during final exam week in order to provide a break for the students, and faculty and staff were asked to help fill the students' plates. Before we did so, we were told to put on a pair of plastic gloves in preparation for handling the food. "Do these come in different sizes?" asked one faculty member. "No," was the reply. "One size fits all." Our clumsy attempts to don the gloves revealed that that was not the case.

Neither does "one size fits all" apply to how God calls people to serve him—or for that matter, to how people respond to his call. Both are illustrated time and again in this series on "God's Urgent Call."

A Specific Call

Consider our first unit of lessons, drawn from the chaotic time of the judges in the Old Testament. God used the prophetess Deborah to call Barak to provide deliverance for God's people from their oppressors (lesson 1). An angel of the Lord challenged Gideon to face the Midianites in battle (lesson 2). Jephthah was called by elders of Gilead to save Israel from the Ammonites (lesson 3). Samson's "call" actually began with an announcement to a childless woman that she would give birth to a very special son who would deliver God's people from the Philistines (lesson 4).

The prophets of the Lord (whose calls are the focus of unit 2) also demonstrate a variety of "sizes" when it comes to being called to convey the Word of the Lord. Moses' experience at the burning bush is well-known (lesson 5). Isaiah, Jeremiah, and Ezekiel each received a vision of the Lord, but each setting was unique (lessons 6–8). Ezekiel's call included a command to eat a "scroll of a book" that was written on both sides (Ezekiel 2:9–3:3). This represented how thoroughly he was to be filled with the Lord's message so he could convey it to God's people in exile. Amos (lesson 9) referred to his being called by the Lord (Amos 7:14, 15), but no specific details of that call are provided in Scripture. It is clear, however, from the courage and passion Amos exhibited that he was a called man indeed!

As the calls were not uniform, neither were the responses to them. Usually the called person was quite hesitant about saying *yes* to what God had in mind. Barak, Gideon, Moses, and Jeremiah each offered an explanation of why he could not do what God commanded. The only eager respondent was Isaiah: "Here I am! Send me" (Isaiah 6:8).

A General Call

Our third unit draws from the book of Acts and illustrates the more general nature of God's call. These four lessons focus attention on what Christians are called to do in presenting Jesus to a broken world. At times we may wish for a call that is just as direct or intense as those in the Bible. However, Christians from all centuries have all been called to make a difference in whatever sphere of influence they live or work. Every follower of Jesus

> At times we may wish for a call that is just as direct or intense as those in the Bible.

can, by his or her lifestyle, witness, break down barriers, preach, and demonstrate the inclusive nature of the gospel (the themes for lessons 10–13). The means of delivering the gospel is not "one size fits all," since we are gifted differently.

Even so, we must remember that we speak for a Savior whose message does indeed "fit all," for he died for the sins of everyone. May our lives be a faithful testimony through which the call of that Savior to a lost world is clearly and lovingly heard.

GET THE SETTING

by Lloyd M. Pelfrey

INDIVIDUALS IN the Bible, both old and new covenant believers, experienced God's communication and calls in various ways (see Hebrews 1:1). But Satan counterfeits God's truth, and Satan uses a variety of methods to communicate his lies. People from antiquity to modern times have used Satan's methods in attempts to communicate with the supernatural. The choices literally range from A to Z—from abacomancy (examining patterns in dirt) to zygomancy (the use of weights in divination). Examples follow.

Egypt

The famous Oracle of Amun was located at the Siwa Oasis in ancient Egypt. There a priest served as an intermediary for a god. Alexander the Great is one of many who went there to have his questions answered. The ruins of the site reveal that a narrow chamber existed next to the place where people asked their questions. Thus the god Amun in the next chamber was able to provide intelligible answers because a hidden priest had overheard the questions.

Assyria

At the time that Jephthah was a judge in Israel (lesson 3), Tiglath-Pileser I was king in Assyria. In his royal archives he gave credit to Ashur and other gods for commanding him to expand the borders of the land. The king made sure to record that the gods placed their weapons in his hands; thus victory was assured. This same king also recorded this success:

> The gods Ninurta and Palil gave me their fierce weapons and their exalted bow for my lordly arms. By the command of the god Ninurta, who loves me, I slew four extraordinarily strong wild virile bulls in the desert.

Sargon II was the king of Assyria 722–705 BC. Samaria, the capital of the northern nation of Israel, fell to him; he states that he took 27,290 people captive (compare 2 Kings 17:6; Isaiah 20:1).

His annals describe another military action:

> In the second year of my reign, [Ilubidi of Hamath] . . . a vast [army] he collected in the town of Qarqar and the oath [of fidelity he forgot].
> . . . .
> By decree of the god Ashur, my lord, I inflicted a defeat upon [them]. I took away 9,033 people together with their numerous possessions.

Moab

The Moabite Stone confirms the rebellions of Mesha, a king of Moab, against the kings of Israel (see 2 Kings 1:1; 3:4-27). On this stone, Mesha credits his god Chemosh for successes.

> And Chemosh said to me, "Go, take Nebo from Israel." So I went by night and fought against it from the break of dawn until noon, taking it and slaying all: seven thousand men, boys, women, girls, and maid-servants, for I had devoted them to destruction for (the god) Ashtar-Chemosh. . . . And the king of Israel had built Jahaz, and he dwelt there while fighting against me, but Chemosh drove him out.

Babylon-Persia

Cyrus the Great captured Babylon in 539 BC. The famous Cyrus Cylinder attributes the rise of Cyrus to Marduk, the lord of the gods. Marduk was unhappy with Nabonidus, father of Belshazzar (Daniel 5:1-30; 7:1; 8:1). So Marduk

> called Cyrus, king of Anshan. He nominated him to be ruler over all. . . . [Marduk] gave orders that he go against his city Babylon. He made him take the road to Babylon, and he went at his side like a friend and comrade. . . . He got him into his city Babylon without fighting or battle. . . . He put an end to the power of Nabonidus the king who did not show him reverence.

Problem and Solution

It's easy to credit a false god for a victory when you do it after the fact! But proof of having received divine communication comes when prophecy is fulfilled. Isaiah 44:28–45:13 predicted the rise of Cyrus 150 years in advance. The Lord, not Marduk, enabled him to establish the Persian Empire!

Mon, May 29	Angel Rebukes Israel's Faithlessness	Judges 2:1-5
Tue, May 30	Joshua's Death Ends an Era	Judges 2:6-10
Wed, May 31	The People Lose God's Protection	Judges 2:16-23
Thu, June 1	Ode to Israel's Faithful Judges	Hebrews 11:29-40
Fri, June 2	Victory Song of the Divine Warrior	Judges 5:1-5
Sat, June 3	Jael Defeats the Enemy Leader, Sisera	Judges 5:24-27
Sun, June 4	Deborah: Prophetess, Judge, and Commander	Judges 4:1-10
Mon, June 5	Oppression Results from Disobedience	Judges 6:1-10
Tue, June 6	May God Judge Enemies Harshly	Psalm 83:1-12, 18
Wed, June 7	Gideon Sees the Angel of the Lord	Judges 6:19-24
Thu, June 8	Fleece Confirms Victory over Midianites	Judges 6:36-40
Fri, June 9	Midianites Defeated Without Weapons	Judges 7:19-23
Sat, June 10	Gideon Dies, Israel Forgets God's Ways	Judges 8:29-35
Sun, June 11	Gideon Answers Call to Deliver Israel	Judges 6:11-18
Mon, June 12	Jephthah, Rejected by His Family, Flees	Judges 11:1-3
Tue, June 13	Jephthah Tries Diplomacy	Judges 11:12-18
Wed, June 14	Jephthah Reveals God's Aid of Israel	Judges 11:19-22
Thu, June 15	Ammonite King Rejects Jephthah's Claims	Judges 11:23-28
Fri, June 16	Jephthah Fulfills Vow	Judges 11:34-40
Sat, June 17	Leaders Discern the Way Forward	Acts 15:6-21
Sun, June 18	Jephthah Called to Lead Israel	Judges 11:4-11

i

Mon, Aug. 14	Saul's Mandate to Capture Believers	Acts 22:1-5
Tue, Aug. 15	A Trustworthy Preacher/Teacher	Titus 1:5-9
Wed, Aug. 16	Saul Proclaims Jesus in Damascus	Acts 9:21-25
Thu, Aug. 17	Saul in Tarsus; Jerusalem at Peace	Acts 9:26-31
Fri, Aug. 18	Paralytic Aeneas Healed in Lydda	Acts 9:32-35
Sat, Aug. 19	Jesus Calls Saul on Damascus Road	Acts 9:1-9
Sun, Aug. 20	Ananias Confirms God's Call to Saul	Acts 9:10-20
Mon, Aug. 21	The Servant's Mission to All Nations	Isaiah 49:1-7
Tue, Aug. 22	Jesus Heals Centurion's Slave	Luke 7:1-10
Wed, Aug. 23	An Angel Meets Cornelius in a Vision	Acts 10:1-8
Thu, Aug. 24	People Are Neither Unclean nor Profane	Acts 10:9-18
Fri, Aug. 25	Gentiles Hear and Accept the Gospel	Acts 10:34-43
Sat, Aug. 26	Gentiles Included by Spirit and Water	Acts 10:44-48
Sun, Aug. 27	Peter and Cornelius Together in Christ	Acts 10:19-33

Answers to the Quarterly Quiz on page 338

Lesson 1—1. true. 2. palm. Lesson 2—1. angel. 2. false. Lesson 3—1. false. 2. vow. Lesson 4—1. true. 2. Nazirite. Lesson 5—1. Jethro. 2. false. Lesson 6—1. Uzziah. 2. burning coal. Lesson 7—1. false. 2. the nations. Lesson 8—1. same language. 2. false. Lesson 9—1. Bethel. 2. tended herds and fruit trees. 3. false. Lesson 10—1. seven. 2. true. Lesson 11—1. Ethiopia. 2. Isaiah. 3. false. Lesson 12—1. Damascus. 2. true. Lesson 13—1. centurion. 2. false.

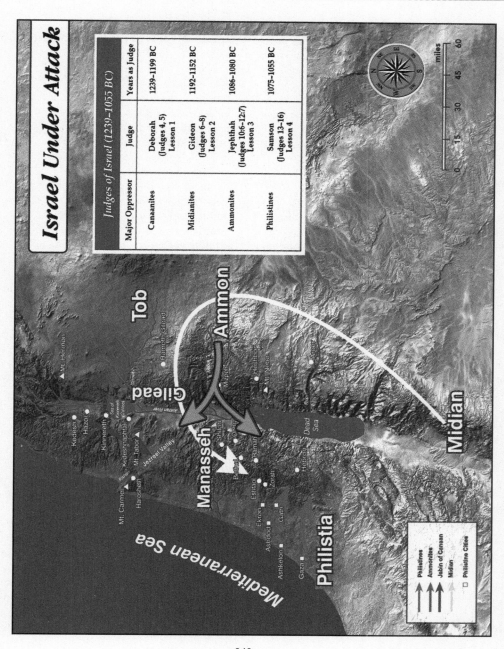

Israel Under Attack

Judges of Israel (1239–1055 BC)

Major Oppressor	Judge	Years as Judge
Canaanites	Deborah (Judges 4, 5) Lesson 1	1239–1199 BC
Midianites	Gideon (Judges 6–8) Lesson 2	1192–1152 BC
Ammonites	Jephthah (Judges 10:6–12:7) Lesson 3	1086–1080 BC
Philistines	Samson (Judges 13–16) Lesson 4	1075–1055 BC

THE INCURABLE HABIT

Teacher Tips by James B. North

I HAVE ALWAYS been a reader. One of my earliest memories in this regard was when my sister often made the mistake of bringing her first-grade reader home from school. She was two years ahead of me, but I soon began to read that book avidly. I just about had it memorized when I got to first grade, so they soon put me up in second grade. My sister was furious that I was now only one grade behind her.

Developing the Discipline

I attended three graduate schools after college, earning a Master of Arts (MA) degree in the first one. But because this school was not regionally accredited, the second graduate school put me through another MA. That was fine with me because I learned a lot there. Keeping track of my reading during one quarter of study, I discovered I was averaging 1,000 pages a week!

Both MA degrees I earned were in church history. But for my doctorate, I decided my studies would be in American history, political and secular. This meant I had to do a lot of reading to catch up with other students. As I was finishing up that degree, one of my professors said (in a casual conversation) that to keep up with the field I needed to "read, read, read." Even if I read a book on a topic I already knew, there would be additional information, he observed. And if it was a topic with which I was not familiar, everything would be new information and useful.

Reaping the Result

All that reading began to pay off when I finally finished school and began teaching at the college/university level. Because I had some expertise in both church and secular history, I often made associations between the two that illustrated points I was making. Having expertise "on both sides of the fence" meant that I often was able to answer students' questions that went beyond the immediate focus of the class presentations (not always, but often!).

Redeeming the Time

In my current city of residence, I rode the bus for almost 20 years to the college campus every day. I always had a book with me, and I averaged reading 30 books a year—just while riding the bus! Other riders spent the time gazing absently out the window. Not me.

Since I was, in fact, riding a bus, my reading was not that of technical textbooks that would require deep concentration, underlining, or marginal notes—a bumpy ride didn't lend itself to any of that! Rather, I often read biographies, novels, and similarly "light" material. But the result was the same: I was assimilating information that could be plugged into classroom presentations when unplanned issues or unexpected questions came up.

Choosing the Type

I strongly recommend that teachers develop "the incurable habit" of reading! But your reading doesn't have to be of biblical material only. Non-biblical material can provide illustrations to flesh out and enliven a Bible text.

Should you go for breadth or for depth in your reading? Obviously the more focused your reading program, the more in-depth you will become in the field you study. But don't feel you have to become a specialist. Every thought, every genre of literature, every subject can provide insight.

As you read, you will discover that most all information can be applied to the Christian life in one way or another. The world is full of information that can be used to illustrate God's creation, his grace, his providence, and his control. This is part of taking "every thought captive to obey Christ" (2 Corinthians 10:5). So as my professor said, "Read, read, read!"

DEBORAH AND BARAK

DEVOTIONAL READING: Hebrews 11:29-40
BACKGROUND SCRIPTURE: Judges 4, 5

JUDGES 4:1-10

¹ And the people of Israel again did what was evil in the sight of the LORD after Ehud died. ² And the LORD sold them into the hand of Jabin king of Canaan, who reigned in Hazor. The commander of his army was Sisera, who lived in Harosheth-hagoyim. ³ Then the people of Israel cried out to the LORD for help, for he had 900 chariots of iron and he oppressed the people of Israel cruelly for twenty years.

⁴ Now Deborah, a prophetess, the wife of Lappidoth, was judging Israel at that time. ⁵ She used to sit under the palm of Deborah between Ramah and Bethel in the hill country of Ephraim, and the people of Israel came up to her for judgment. ⁶ She sent and summoned Barak the son of Abinoam from Kedesh-naphtali and said to him, "Has not the Lord, the God of Israel, commanded you, 'Go, gather your men at Mount Tabor, taking 10,000 from the people of Naphtali and the people of Zebulun. ⁷ And I will draw out Sisera, the general of Jabin's army, to meet you by the river Kishon with his chariots and his troops, and I will give him into your hand'?" ⁸ Barak said to her, "If you will go with me, I will go, but if you will not go with me, I will not go." ⁹ And she said, "I will surely go with you. Nevertheless, the road on which you are going will not lead to your glory, for the LORD will sell Sisera into the hand of a woman." Then Deborah arose and went with Barak to Kedesh. ¹⁰ And Barak called out Zebulun and Naphtali to Kedesh. And 10,000 men went up at his heels, and Deborah went up with him.

KEY VERSE

"I will surely go with you. Nevertheless, the road on which you are going will not lead to your glory, for the LORD *will sell Sisera into the hand of a woman." Then Deborah arose and went with Barak to Kedesh.*

—**Judges 4:9**

GOD'S URGENT CALL

Unit 1: Called to Be Strong

LESSONS 1–4

LESSON AIMS

After participating in this lesson, each learner will be able to:

1. Describe the relationship between Deborah and Barak.

2. List possible reasons for doubts and fears on the part of Barak and evaluate their legitimacy.

3. Commit to helping one fellow believer overcome doubts regarding his or her leadership role in a ministry project.

LESSON OUTLINE

Introduction
  A. "Let's Ask Granny!"
  B. Lesson Background
 I. Cry to God (JUDGES 4:1-3)
  A. Sin and Subjugation (vv. 1, 2)
    What's Right in Whose Sight?
  B. Score of Suffering (v. 3)
 II. Challenge Others (JUDGES 4:4-7)
  A. Deborah's Role (vv. 4, 5)
  B. Barak's Call (vv. 6, 7)
    Prophets, True and False
 III. Collaborate as Needed (JUDGES 4:8-10)
  A. Barak Balks (v. 8)
  B. Barak Backed (vv. 9, 10)
Conclusion
  A. Pick Your Heroes Carefully!
  B. Prayer
  C. Thought to Remember

Introduction

A. "Let's Ask Granny!"

"Granny" was one of the sweetest, kindest, most humble persons in the congregation. "Let's ask Granny!" was frequently heard when the leaders of the church needed additional input on an issue.

Granny knew the Bible's precepts and principles better than many. Her wisdom had been accumulated through decades of Bible study, personal experience, and observations of the flow of events in her world. She held no official position of authority. But people willingly received her counsel, and she was willing to give it—especially when biblical concepts were involved.

Some are leaders by position. Others are leaders by their very natures. (And, of course, some are both.) A church's official leaders demonstrate wisdom when they recognize what has been called "leadership from below" and seek to learn from those such as Granny.

Today's lesson will help us better understand the importance of leadership skills as we examine how a leader of Israel, known as a judge, led her nation through a trying time.

B. Lesson Background

Joshua had been appointed by God and commissioned by Moses to lead Israel in conquering Canaan (Deuteronomy 31). But something was different when Joshua passed off the scene in about 1370 BC: no one was appointed to succeed him! The solution was very simple. God was in charge, and each tribe or unit would obey God and take care of its area.

In Joshua's farewell addresses (Joshua 23, 24), he warned the Israelites again, just as Moses had done, of what they would experience if they served other gods. But they did serve such gods, and Judges 2:10 explains why: "there arose another generation after them who did not know the Lord." What followed was disaster after disaster. If one generation does not teach the next generation about God, then tragedies follow.

The book of Judges is concerned primarily with the sin-cycles that Israel experienced during the period of the Judges. To date that era with precision is difficult. By one calculation, there were 330 years between the appearance of the first judge (Judges 3:9) and the passing of the last (1 Samuel 25:1). But depending on the interpretation of Acts 13:20 and other factors, some calculate the period to span 450 years.

Regarding the sin-cycles themselves, these have been summarized in terms of four stages: *sin, sorrow* (or *servitude*), *supplication,* and *salvation*. A different way of stating this cycle is *rebellion, retribution, repentance,* and *restoration*. When the Israelites worshipped other gods, they suffered. When the people eventually repented, the Lord would send a deliverer, known as a judge. Then the cycle repeated itself (see Judges 2:10-19).

The lessons of this unit are biographical studies of four of the 12 judges recorded in the book of Judges: Deborah, Gideon, Jephthah, and Samson. These four plus Othniel and Ehud are traditionally said to be the six "major judges" in light of all that is recorded about them. They were military deliverers; thus the word *judge* should not cause us to think exclusively in terms of civil magistrates.

The longest period of peace recorded within the book of Judges is the one of 80 years between Ehud and Deborah (Judges 3:30). Today's lesson takes us back to about 1225 BC as that period of peace comes to an end.

I. Cry to God

(JUDGES 4:1-3)

A. Sin and Subjugation (vv. 1, 2)

1. And the people of Israel again did what was evil in the sight of the LORD after Ehud died.

The phrasing *the people of Israel . . . did what was evil* occurs seven times in the book of Judges, and this is the fourth of those. Since the first occurrence in Judges 2:11 is a general reference (see the Lesson Background), the phrase's use here indicates the beginning of the third sin-cycle.

To consider what evil consists of in this context, we look to the use of this phrase in Judges 3:7, which introduces the first sin-cycle. The sin mentioned there is summed up with a single word: *idolatry*. The nations the Israelites had failed to destroy had become a snare to them in this regard

(Deuteronomy 7:16; 20:16-18; Joshua 23:12, 13; Judges 3:5, 6).

The exploits of *Ehud,* the second major judge, are noted in Judges 3:12-30. The non-major judge who follows him is accorded only a single-verse description (3:31) as the author hastens to move to the next sin-cycle.

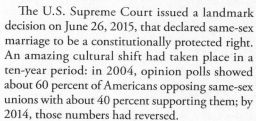

What Do You Think?

What are some ways to prevent negative things from happening during times of leadership vacuum in the church?

Talking Points for Your Discussion

- Regarding coverage of ministry tasks
- Regarding use of church resources
- Regarding political viewpoints
- Regarding teaching or leadership roles
- Other

◆   *WHAT'S RIGHT IN WHOSE SIGHT?*   ◆

The U.S. Supreme Court issued a landmark decision on June 26, 2015, that declared same-sex marriage to be a constitutionally protected right. An amazing cultural shift had taken place in a ten-year period: in 2004, opinion polls showed about 60 percent of Americans opposing same-sex unions with about 40 percent supporting them; by 2014, those numbers had reversed.

The five justices who created this decision seemed to hold to the theory that the U.S. Constitution is a "living document." This theory, known as *loose constructionism,* asserts that courts are free to interpret the Constitution in light of prevailing cultural winds. What's illegal in one decade can become a "right" in another.

We must recognize that God and humans often do not share the same conclusions regarding what is good and what is evil (compare Isaiah 5:20). This is true whether or not one embraces a loose-construction theory for interpreting a country's founding documents. The book of Judges offers this sobering observation twice: "everyone did what was right in his own eyes" (Judges 17:6; 21:25). The step from doing what is right in one's own eyes to doing "evil in the sight of the Lord" (4:1) is smaller than one may think!   —C. R. B.

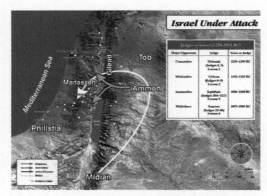

Visual for Lesson 1. *Keep this map posted through-out the first unit of this quarter's studies to give your learners a geographical perspective.*

2. And the LORD sold them into the hand of Jabin king of Canaan, who reigned in Hazor. The commander of his army was Sisera, who lived in Harosheth-hagoyim.

The oppression arises from northern *Canaan,* since the city of *Hazor* is located about eight miles north-northwest of the Sea of Galilee. Before 1400 BC, Joshua had destroyed Hazor utterly (Joshua 11:10-14). Mention of "Jabin, king of Hazor" occurs in conjunction with that military action of at least 175 years previous (11:1). There-fore we don't know if the word *Jabin* is a title that is passed along or is simply a favorite name for kings.

Despite Joshua's success, pockets of uncon-quered peoples remained by the time he had become elderly (Joshua 13:1-6). It was these people who rebuilt Hazor as a royal city. The mopping-up operations had been left to the individual tribes, but they did not follow through (Judges 1:27-34). In this particular case, it seems to have been the tribe of Naphtali that dropped the ball, since Hazor is in its tribal allotment (Joshua 19:32-39). Instead of obeying Joshua or the Lord, the tribes just became content with what they had.

Israel must confront *Sisera,* the military com-mander, not the king. Sisera's base of operations at *Harosheth-hagoyim,* near the Kishon River that flows into the Mediterranean, is perhaps 30 miles southwest of Hazor and 16 miles northwest of Megiddo. These factors become an important part of the battle plan that God designs.

B. Score of Suffering (v. 3)

3. Then the people of Israel cried out to the LORD for help, for he had 900 chariots of iron and he oppressed the people of Israel cruelly for twenty years.

The nature of the 20-year oppression isn't spec-ified. It may take the form of servitude (example: Joshua 16:10), a periodic taxation of gold and/or silver (example: 2 Kings 23:33), and/or a confis-cation of crops and livestock (examples: Deuter-onomy 28:51; 2 Kings 3:4). The latter could be collected as marauding groups go from place to place (example: Judges 6:2-6).

It is serious when oppressors take food that your family depends on to get through the rainy months of the winter season! Frustration and anger follow, as the Israelites watch the results of their labor snatched away. Prayers for deliverance undoubtedly begin far in advance of the 20-year point mentioned here. But it can take time for repentance to be joined with prayer. Even today, many people call upon the Lord in a crisis, but do not accompany that prayer with repentance.

A reason for the seeming hopelessness of Isra-el's situation is the *900 chariots* possessed by the enemy. The note that these are *of iron* is not a refer-ence to the entirety of their construction. Rather, the chariots are made of wood, with iron cover-ing strategic parts.

This is not the first time the issue of iron-reinforced chariots has come up; some Canaanites had them when Joshua divided the land among the 12 tribes in about 1400 BC (Joshua 17:16). The Iron Age is dated as beginning about 1200 BC, but some nations get technological advances later than others. Some Canaanites apparently know the techniques of processing iron ore that are yet unknown to the Israelites.

II. Challenge Others
(JUDGES 4:4-7)
A. Deborah's Role (vv. 4, 5)

4. Now Deborah, a prophetess, the wife of Lappidoth, was judging Israel at that time.

Deborah's position in the line of judges is noted in the Lesson Background. She seems to have abilities that are recognized by the people, resulting in her having become a leader in Israel in a twofold way: that of judge and prophetess. The latter means she is a spokesperson for the Lord. This passage is the only place in the Bible that mentions her husband, *Lappidoth*.

5. She used to sit under the palm of Deborah between Ramah and Bethel in the hill country of Ephraim, and the people of Israel came up to her for judgment.

Deborah's role as civil magistrate is revealed by the fact that Israelites seek *her for judgment* (compare Exodus 18:13). The phrase *hill country of Ephraim* refers to the central part of Israel (compare Joshua 17:15). The distance *between Ramah and Bethel* is about five miles, the towns lying about five and 10 miles, respectively, due north of Jerusalem.

The location of *the palm of Deborah* between the two towns probably places it within the tribal territory of Benjamin. We say "probably" because Bethel lies just outside the tribe's territorial boundary, in Ephraim (Joshua 18:13).

▶ **What Do You Think?**

How do we keep cultural expectations regarding gender roles from being a greater influence in the church than the Bible itself?

Talking Points for Your Discussion

- Before such influence occurs (preventive measures)
- After such influence occurs (curative measures)

B. Barak's Call (vv. 6, 7)

6a. She sent and summoned Barak the son of Abinoam from Kedesh-naphtali and said to him, "Has not the LORD, the God of Israel, commanded you,

Deborah fulfills her role as a prophet: having received a message from *the Lord, the God of Israel,* she delivers it to Barak as the one to lead Israel in battle. Barak is a popular name, so the man is further identified by the name of his father and his place of origin. *Abinoam* is mentioned only here and in Judges 5:12. The word *Kedesh-naphtali*

combines the name of the town Kedesh within the tribal territory of Naphtali. A bit of uncertainty exists regarding the location of this town. One proposal locates it on the southwestern shore of the Sea of Galilee; another proposal places it about 35 miles farther north (compare Joshua 12:22; 19:37; 20:7; 21:32; 2 Kings 15:29).

6b. "'Go, gather your men at Mount Tabor, taking 10,000 from the people of Naphtali and the people of Zebulun.

Barak receives his orders in terms of route of march and recruitment. Keeping in mind the current location of Deborah and Barak according to verse 5, *Mount Tabor* is roughly 50 miles to the north and about 11 miles east of the southern tip of the Sea of Galilee. This rounded mountain, which has been described as an upside-down teacup, lies just within the northern border of the tribe of Issachar, very close to where the border meets those of both *Naphtali* and *Zebulun*.

Men from these areas are likely to respond positively to a call to arms, for their families are likely to have suffered the most from two decades of oppression. The areas Naphtali and Zebulun form part of what is later called "Galilee of the Gentiles" in Matthew 4:15.

7. "'And I will draw out Sisera, the general of Jabin's army, to meet you by the river Kishon with his chariots and his troops, and I will give him into your hand'?"

HOW TO SAY IT

Abinoam	Uh-*bin*-o-am.
Canaan	*Kay*-nun.
Ephraim	*Ee*-fray-im.
Harosheth-hagoyim	Huh-*roe*-sheth-haw-goy-*em*.
Jephthah	*Jef*-thuh (*th* as in *thin*).
Kedesh-naphtali	*Kee*-desh-**naf**-tuh-lye.
Kishon	*Kye*-shon.
Lappidoth	Lap-*pih*-doth.
Manasseh	Muh-*nass*-uh.
Megiddo	Muh-*gid*-doe.
Naphtali	*Naf*-tuh-lye.
Sisera	*Sis*-er-uh.
Zebulun	*Zeb*-you-lun.

The Lord promises to do his part in the forthcoming battle: he will arrange for the enemy to gather near *the river Kishon,* which flows through the Jezreel Valley. The Israelite army at Mount Tabor will be several miles to the northeast. Once *Sisera, the general of Jabin's army,* hears that Israel has formed a fighting force, his natural reaction will be to muster *his chariots and his troops* for a showdown (Judges 4:12, 13).

The reason for Barak to have been instructed to take his force to Mount Tabor becomes clearer: his force of foot soldiers will have a great defensive position there against chariots. Wheeled conveyances don't function well in rugged, hilly terrain! But if Barak imagines the forthcoming battle to be defensive in nature, his thinking will change soon enough. The victory for his army is assured, but the manner of the victory will probably not be what Barak expects.

◆ *PROPHETS, TRUE AND FALSE* ◆

Yogi Berra (1925–2015), legendary baseball player, manager, and coach of the New York Yankees, was notable for his incongruous statements. One such is his purported lament that "it's tough to make predictions—especially about the future." Our laughter should not cause us to forget that false predictions have consequences. God's people of the old covenant were beset with false prophets (Jeremiah 14:14; Ezekiel 22:28; etc.); Jesus warned of the same for our era (Matthew 24:11).

How right he has been! In September 2013, a purportedly Christian blog prophesied an earthquake of magnitude 9.7—the largest in recorded history—to strike the California coast on October 3. As with all such failed predictions, the primary result was to make Christianity seem a little less credible.

In striking contrast, true biblical prophets were always right (compare Deuteronomy 18:22), and Deborah's prophecy of Israelite victory over the Canaanites came true just as she had relayed that assurance from the Lord (Judges 4:15). Jesus says we can recognize false prophets "by their fruits" (Matthew 7:15, 16). A track record of 90 percent accuracy isn't good enough. Would you be able to explain why to a friend?   —C. R. B.

III. Collaborate as Needed
(JUDGES 4:8-10)
A. Barak Balks (v. 8)

8. Barak said to her, "If you will go with me, I will go, but if you will not go with me, I will not go."

Although Barak knows the outcome that is promised, he voices the ultimatum we see here: he will go only if she will as well. His reasons are not given, so different ideas have been suggested. One theory is that Barak wants to have Deborah with him in case there are further instructions from God.

Another theory is that Barak lacks courage. Some object to this theory because Barak is listed as a man of faith in Hebrews 11:32 and is listed among other great leaders of the past in 1 Samuel 12:11. But courage can fail in even the greatest of leaders (example: just after his stunning victory at Mount Carmel, Elijah "was afraid, and he arose and ran for his life" when threatened by Queen Jezebel; 1 Kings 19:2, 3).

What Do You Think?
What are some ways to encourage others in their ministry tasks?
Talking Points for Your Discussion
- In contexts of doubt regarding spiritual giftedness
- In contexts of doubt regarding abilities
- In contexts of previous ministry failures
- Other

B. Barak Backed (vv. 9, 10)

9. And she said, "I will surely go with you. Nevertheless, the road on which you are going will not lead to your glory, for the LORD will sell Sisera into the hand of a woman." Then Deborah arose and went with Barak to Kedesh.

Deborah follows the Lord and has the ability to make good decisions quickly. This may explain why she is a recognized leader. She is also one who is prompt in encouraging others to fulfill their roles. This trait is a positive factor in the lives of the people who consult her.

What Do You Think?

What has to happen for Christians to exhibit the leadership qualities of Deborah?

Talking Points for Your Discussion

- In terms of supporting appointments of others to leadership positions
- In serving as an example to those already in leadership roles
- In preventing godly confidence (2 Thessalonians 3:4; etc.) from becoming overconfidence (1 Timothy 1:7; etc.)
- Other

Deborah gives an additional prophecy, and Barak probably misunderstands the meaning of *the Lord will sell Sisera into the hand of a woman*. He probably anticipates that it will be Deborah who brings an end to Sisera. However, the verses that follow the lesson text reveal that it will be Jael, the wife of Heber the Kenite, who ends Sisera's life (see Judges 4:11, 18-21).

10a. And Barak called out Zebulun and Naphtali to Kedesh.

The Kedesh that is located on the southwestern shore of the Sea of Galilee (see v. 6a, above) is an ideal place to muster troops from *Zebulun and Naphtali* before advancing to Mount Tabor. Men traveling in small groups toward Kedesh in answer to a call to arms will not attract much attention, since movement toward Kedesh is away from Sisera's base at Harosheth-hagoyim (v. 2, above).

10b. And ten thousand men went up at his heels, and Deborah went up with him.

As *ten thousand men* follow Barak with Deborah accompanying, they can think about the years of oppression that their families have endured. The thought of ridding themselves of such misery may be what attracts men of Ephraim, Benjamin, and Issachar to participate as well (Judges 5:13-15a). Members of other tribes, however, do not participate (5:15b-17). By and large, the latter are located in areas away from the oppression that originates from the north, so they may feel that it is not their fight. Even so, the result will be victory and 40 years of peace (4:23, 24; 5:31).

Conclusion

A. Pick Your Heroes Carefully!

A counselor asked his client to think of the people he knew whom he admired. Then he was asked to consider what those people had ever done that was worthwhile. The client replied, "As I think about it, all they have ever done is to complain. They never do anything else." He was advised to evaluate what he had said, and then to find some new heroes.

The account of Deborah and Barak illustrates that each respected the other. It also suggests that the soldiers in Barak's army trusted his leadership. The combination of interpersonal respect and God's help were the ingredients for success. And so it is yet today. Hebrews 11 encourages us to pick our heroes carefully! If their lives are not godly, how can they be our heroes?

What Do You Think?

What character traits do you look for in those whom you would accept as mentors? Why?

Talking Points for Your Discussion

- Regarding spiritual issues
- Regarding vocational proficiency
- Regarding consistency
- Other

B. Prayer

Almighty God, grant us the wisdom to select godly men or women as our heroes and mentors! But most of all, empower us by your Spirit to imitate Christ. We pray this in his name. Amen.

C. Thought to Remember

Who we follow today
shapes who we become tomorrow.

VISUALS FOR THESE LESSONS

The visual pictured in each lesson (example: page 348) is a small reproduction of a large, full-color poster included in the *Adult Resources* packet for the Summer Quarter. That packet also contains the very useful *Presentation Tools* CD for teacher use. Order No. 4629117 from your supplier.

INVOLVEMENT LEARNING

*Enhance your lesson presentation with the reproducible activity page,
available as a free download at www.standardlesson.com.*

Into the Lesson

Before class, write each of these names on a separate sheet of paper in large letters: *Bill Gates, Abraham Lincoln, Joan of Arc, Susan B. Anthony, Martin Luther, Winston Churchill, Cleopatra, George Washington, Harriet Tubman, Thomas Edison.* (Substitute other famous names for any you do not believe your group would recognize.)

To begin class, ask for 10 volunteers and tape one of the names to each of their backs. Have the volunteers move about the room while others talk to them as that person (without mentioning the name). As soon as a volunteer guesses his or her famous identity, that person can remove the label and take a seat.

Alternative. Distribute copies of the "Leading the Way" activity from the reproducible page, which you can download. Have students work individually or in pairs.

After either activity, discuss characteristics these leaders had that made them effective. Then lead into the Bible study by saying, "We can learn a lot from great leaders. Today we will examine how Deborah and Barak led their nation at a trying time."

Into the Word

Write this outline on the board with the title, *The Three Cs of a Leader*:

I. Crisis: God can prepare strong leaders during times of trouble (Judges 4:1-3).

II. Command: Good leaders not only identify problems but also identify solutions and those who can implement them (Judges 4:4-7).

III. Collaboration: No one person can do everything. Good leaders build and work with good teams (Judges 4:8-10).

Divide learners into groups and assign each group one of the three points of the outline. Give each group strips of paper (approximately 3" x 12")

and markers. Have groups read their assigned text and summarize it with one or more bumper-sticker slogans. After several minutes of small-group creativity, allow groups to share their slogans.

Some suggested bumper stickers follow.

Crisis

Troubles knock some down and raise others up.
Under Attack? Dial 1-800-CALL GOD

Command

Inspired Leaders Inspire Others
Looking for a Few Good Men
It Takes a Leader to Raise an Army

Collaboration

Surrender the ME for the WE
Together We Can
There are no limits when nobody cares who gets the credit

Into Life

Say, "Deborah seems to have been able to encourage Barak and help him believe in himself so he could accomplish the task God had given him. Has there ever been a person in your life who really believed in you and encouraged you during a difficult time?"

Ask students to pair off and tell their stories to a partner. Allow time for some students to share their stories. Then distribute an index card to each student.

Say, "Are there people you can encourage in their ministries? Write one person's name, the method you will use to communicate with him or her, and a date by when you will have completed this task."

Encourage your students to take these cards home with them and follow through on the task.

Alternative. Hand out copies of the "What's Holding You Back?" activity from the reproducible page. Allow students to share their fears; have other students give words of encouragement.

Close either activity with group prayer.

GIDEON

DEVOTIONAL READING: Psalm 83:1-12, 18
BACKGROUND SCRIPTURE: Judges 6–8

JUDGES 6:11-18

¹¹ Now the angel of the LORD came and sat under the terebinth at Ophrah, which belonged to Joash the Abiezrite, while his son Gideon was beating out wheat in the winepress to hide it from the Midianites. ¹² And the angel of the LORD appeared to him and said to him, "The LORD is with you, O mighty man of valor." ¹³ And Gideon said to him, "Please, sir, if the LORD is with us, why then has all this happened to us? And where are all his wonderful deeds that our fathers recounted to us, saying, 'Did not the LORD bring us up from Egypt?' But now the LORD has forsaken us and given us into the hand of Midian." ¹⁴ And the LORD turned to him and said, "Go in this might of yours and save Israel from the hand of Midian; do not I send you?" ¹⁵ And he said to him, "Please, Lord, how can I save Israel? Behold, my clan is the weakest in Manasseh, and I am the least in my father's house." ¹⁶ And the LORD said to him, "But I will be with you, and you shall strike the Midianites as one man." ¹⁷ And he said to him, "If now I have found favor in your eyes, then show me a sign that it is you who speak with me. ¹⁸ Please do not depart from here until I come to you and bring out my present and set it before you." And he said, "I will stay till you return."

KEY VERSE

The angel of the LORD appeared to him and said to him, "The LORD is with you, O mighty man of valor."

—**Judges 6:12**

GOD'S URGENT CALL

Unit 1: Called to Be Strong

LESSONS 1–4

LESSON AIMS

After participating in this lesson, each learner will be able to:

1. Describe the encounter between Gideon and the angel of the Lord.

2. Explain Gideon's three questions as they relate to their historical context.

3. Identify one struggle of life in which he or she views self as "the least" in being able to overcome it, and write a prayer for the Lord's strength to do so.

LESSON OUTLINE

Introduction

A. Against All Odds

The odds seemed to have been stacked against her, having been born into slavery in Maryland in 1822. As a child, she was often beaten and whipped by various masters. She received a head injury when a slave owner threw a heavy metal weight at another slave and hit her by mistake. The result was a lifelong struggle with epilepsy, dizziness, and pain.

Who would *not* expect such a person to live and die in obscurity? But that was not the case for Harriet Tubman! She escaped from slavery, but risked recapture as she returned to lead numerous missions to rescue approximately 70 enslaved family and friends. Against all odds and led by a strong Christian faith, Harriet Tubman overcame slavery, injury, abuse, and disability. History now knows her as an abolitionist, a humanitarian, and a Union spy who helped guide a raid that freed 700 slaves during the American Civil War.

Very few people who live in Western democracies will ever face the challenges of a Harriet Tubman. Even so, we all experience what it's like to have the odds stacked against us at one time or another. Today we will look at a judge of Israel who seemed to have little chance of success—until God stepped in!

B. Lesson Background

The lessons for this month feature four of the six major judges in the book of Judges. The previous lesson was about Deborah and Barak. This study moves directly to the next judge—Gideon, a member of the tribe of Manasseh. The final verse of Judges 5 states that Israel had rest for 40 years after Barak defeated Sisera and the Canaanites. During that time the memory of the previous oppression began to fade. A new generation arose and began to worship other gods.

Again God allowed others to oppress Israel—the Midianites, the Amalekites, etc. (Judges 6:3). The Midianites were descendants of Abraham and Keturah (Genesis 25:2). When Moses fled from Egypt, he settled in Midian and married a daughter of a priest in Midian (Exodus 2:15, 16, 21).

The Amalekites had Esau as their progenitor (Genesis 36:10, 16). The Amalekites attacked the Israelites after they left Egypt and as they were approaching Sinai (Exodus 17:8-16). That was the battle when Israel would prevail only when Moses raised his hands. After the battle Moses stated that there would be war against Amalek from generation to generation.

These two groups, plus "the people of the East" (a general name for eastern groups of Arabs), came against Israel in great numbers. For seven years they came and destroyed the crops and livestock of the Israelites (Judges 6:1-6).

After seven years the Israelites cried to the Lord (Judges 6:7). The Lord sent a prophet to remind Israel of what he had done for them when they came out of Egypt and to rebuke them for their disobedience (6:8-10). This condemnation by God's prophet is immediately before the text for today. God then moved to prepare another judge to deliver his penitent people.

It had been 47 years since Deborah and Barak, with God's help, subdued the Canaanites: 40 years of peace (Judges 5:31), followed by the 7 years of oppression (6:1). The approximate date for the events of this lesson has been determined to be about 1175 BC.

I. Big Trouble
(Judges 6:11-13)
A. Cowering Warrior (vv. 11, 12)

11a. Now the angel of the LORD came and sat under the terebinth at Ophrah,

The first verse of the lesson provides several facts. It contains three personalities, explanations about them, two helps to identify the place of the event, the strange action that one of them is doing, and why he is doing it.

The *angel of the Lord* is the first person mentioned. The word *angel* may also be given as *messenger*, so a messenger of the Lord comes and sits *under the terebinth* [tree] *at Ophrah*. This town is in the territory of Manasseh (Judges 6:15). Later information about it is very negative (8:27; 9:5).

There are dozens of references in the Old Testament to "the angel of the Lord" or "the angel of

God" (Judges 6:20). The first is Genesis 16:7, in the days of Abraham. This being makes the ground holy, as in Exodus 3:2-5 when Moses is first called to lead Israel from Egypt, or when he is called "the commander of the Lord's army" in Joshua 5:15. This being receives worship and sacrifices. The terminology may change to "commander of the army of the Lord" (Joshua 5:14). The "angel of the Lord" appearing in Exodus 3:2 says "I am . . . God" in Exodus 3:6. The angel of the Lord is mentioned in chapters 2, 5, 6, and 13 in the book of Judges.

Many have suggested that this is actually Jesus, God's divine messenger who appears as a man in the Old Testament era and then comes in the New Testament as one who experiences the totality of life in the flesh. In this regard, "messenger" would be intended, since angels do not receive worship (Revelation 22:8, 9; compare Hebrews 1:1-9).

11b. which belonged to Joash the Abiezrite, while his son Gideon was beating out wheat in the winepress to hide it from the Midianites.

Joash the Abiezrite and his family are of the tribe of Manasseh (Judges 6:15). Manasseh was the older son of Joseph in Egypt (Genesis 41:51), and Abiezer was a former leader in the tribe (see Joshua 17:2).

The third personality in this verse is Gideon, a son of Joash. Judges 8:19 indicates that Gideon had brothers and that they had been killed by the Midianites. This could have caused him to have differing emotions about the invaders—anger, vengeance, and a certain fear for what they could do to him and others.

In this verse Gideon's task is to thresh wheat. Threshing is usually accomplished by using a sledge pulled by animals. Gideon's method is different, for he is hiding. The word used means that he is using a stick to beat the wheat. The result is the same—the seed is separated from the chaff and straw.

His place of work is strange—a *winepress*. This type of winepress is made by excavating rock to form a recessed area where grapes could be smashed by walking on them. The juice then runs in a trough to a collecting vat. Gideon is hiding so that the Midianites will have difficulty seeing him. It may be imagined that he is muffling the sound as much as he can.

12. And the angel of the LORD appeared to him and said to him, "The LORD is with you, O mighty man of valor."

To say that *the angel of the Lord* appears means that he makes his presence known, not that he had been invisible for a while as he sat under the oak tree. Gideon is absorbed in his work, and the noise of his beating the grain stalks can drown out someone nearby.

The greeting to Gideon has two parts: a statement that *the Lord is with* him and that Gideon is *mighty*. Concerning the latter, the majority view is that he will become such a person because of what is about to happen. The minority opinion is that Gideon has already distinguished himself in combat, given that he is able to recruit a sizable army (Judges 7:3). The angel's statement carries with it a humorous contradiction—that a man of such courage is hiding.

> **What Do You Think?**
> What are some ways Christians send contradictory, mixed messages to the culture at large? How do we fix this problem?
> *Talking Points for Your Discussion*
> - Concerning mixed messages about Christianity in general
> - Concerning mixed messages about individual Christians

Two Midianite leaders affirm later that Gideon resembles a son of a king (Judges 8:18). He therefore has physical features that help him to be a leader among men.

B. Missing Miracles (v. 13)

13. And Gideon said to him, "Please, sir, if the LORD is with us, why then has all this happened to us? And where are all his wonderful deeds that our fathers recounted to us, saying, 'Did not the LORD bring us up from Egypt?' But now the LORD has forsaken us and given us into the hand of Midian."

Gideon begins to question the stranger. Little does Gideon know that he is trying to debate

God! This is indicated by his addressing him as *sir* rather than as Lord, with all capital letters. The same Hebrew word is translated "lord" in Genesis 43:20. By contrast, as Gideon uses the word *LORD* (all capital letters), he is referring to Yahweh (three times), the sacred name of God. This is explained more fully in the front matter of many Bibles.

Gideon's questions reveal that he is aware of the glorious history of Israel. In his family, these things are being told by the older generation to the younger. Gideon knows about the bondage in Egypt and the miraculous events that followed. This includes the 10 plagues, the crossing of the Red Sea, the giving of the Law, the 40 years in the wilderness, and the crossing of the Jordan when it was in flood stage.

After the questions, Gideon makes a statement that is really seeking an answer for the oppression that he, his family, and his people are enduring. Gideon has heard about the wonderful works of God in the past, but now it seems to him that God is no longer concerned about his people.

> **What Do You Think?**
> How can we resist thinking that God has abandoned us? What will happen if we don't?
> *Talking Points for Your Discussion*
> - In cases that affect you alone
> - When feelings of abandonment swirl around your group (family, Sunday school class, etc.)
> - When feelings of abandonment sweep across the nation

II. Weak Tribe
(JUDGES 6:14-16)
A. Promised Presence (v. 14)

14. And the LORD turned to him and said, "Go in this might of yours and save Israel from the hand of Midian; do not I send you?"

The speaker is now not referred to as an angel, but as *the Lord* (again, Yahweh). We notice immediately that the Lord does not answer Gideon's questions. Instead, he looks at Gideon and commands that he *go in this might of yours*. Gideon is the one who will *save Israel* from the Midianite oppressors.

Then God asks a question of his own: *Do not I send you?* This question has the force of a command. Obedience to this command is necessary, for the command is from the God of Israel, the only God there is.

> **What Do You Think?**
> What have you found to be the most reliable
>   indicators of God's will? Why?
> *Talking Points for Your Discussion*
> ▪ Regarding bigger "callings"
> ▪ Regarding smaller, daily activities
> ▪ Considering the cautions of Job 42:7;
>   Proverbs 15:22; James 4:13-17; 1 John 4:1;
>   Revelation 22:18, 19

B. Puny Pedigree (v. 15)

15. And he said to him, "Please, Lord, how can I save Israel? Behold, my clan is the weakest in Manasseh, and I am the least in my father's house."

Gideon does not like the oppression, but he does not think much of the idea of being the leader that lifts it either! So he responds with a question and statements about his unsuitability for such an important task. He suggests that he is a nobody. Gideon is not the first person to resist God's call to leadership. Moses had similar reactions when charged to deliver Israel from years of oppression in Egypt (see Exodus 3:10–4:17).

◆ *"I'm Not OK?"* ◆

The book *I'm OK, You're OK* hit the *New York Times* best-seller list in 1972 and remained there for two years. This was an early book promoting what became known as Transactional Analysis. The book's thesis is that relational problems can be addressed if we analyze our interactions with one another as transactions.

The author speaks of four life positions one takes in relationship transactions. They are (1) I'm not OK, You're OK, (2) I'm not OK, You're not OK, (3) I'm OK, You're not OK, and (4) I'm OK, You're OK. When God called Gideon to serve him,

Gideon responded in the *I'm not OK, You're OK* position. He listed reason after reason why he was not good enough to answer God's call. Although this may sound like humility, it showed that Gideon was leaving God out of the transaction.

In essence, God responded from the *I'm OK, You're OK* position. This position affirmed what Gideon could accomplish with divine help.

Most of us have areas in our self-perception in which we think *I'm not OK*. However, our relationship with God in Christ helps us realize that even though we are sinners, we have become new creatures. We are capable of doing whatever God calls us to do with him. He does not call us to service only to abandon us later! —C. R. B.

> **What Do You Think?**
> What are some ways to overcome feelings of
>   inadequacy when sensing God's call to a task?
> *Talking Points for Your Discussion*
> ▪ Regarding the content of prayer
> ▪ Regarding the counsel sought of others
> ▪ Regarding examples from Scripture
> ▪ Other

C. Sure Success (v. 16)

16. And the LORD said to him, "But I will be with you, and you shall strike the Midianites as one man."

The second promise has been interpreted to mean that the battle to come will seem as if Gideon is in combat against only *one man*. That is indeed a remarkable prediction! In the battle to come, it will appear as if Gideon is winning it all by himself! (The *you* in *you shall strike* is singular.) Assurance of victory is most welcome, but should there be some type of sign or proof that the source of this prediction is God?

III. Security Sought
(JUDGES 6:17, 18)
A. Asking for a Sign (v. 17)

17. And he said to him, "If now I have found favor in your eyes, then show me a sign that it is you who speak with me.

Gideon wants to know of a certainty that what he is concluding is true. Before he undertakes the difficult and dangerous task of gathering an army, he needs to know that what he is getting himself into has a good chance of succeeding. His politeness is shown in the phrase *if now I have found favor in your eyes* that prefaces his request for *a sign*.

Gideon's caution does not necessarily demonstrate a lack of faith. The somewhat aggressive nature of his responses thus far seems to indicate that the guest has the appearance of just an ordinary man (contrast Judges 13:6). Gideon may be assuming that the messenger is a prophet, but still he wants a sign. Even Moses expressed a concern that the people of Israel would not believe him, so God gave him signs that he could employ to show that the source of his commission was none other than God himself (Exodus 4:1-9).

◆   SEEING ANGELS AND SEEKING SIGNS   ◆

Many people testify that they have experienced the presence of so-called guardian angels. Some even claim to have video proof! An Internet search for "angel appearances," etc., will result in numerous hits. One video shows a figure with glowing hands appearing from nowhere to rescue a bicyclist who was hit broadside in an intersection by a truck. Immediately after the apparent collision, the figure and the victim disappear from the point of impact, only to be seen several yards away with the crash victim getting off a stretcher and limping to the curb. The figure that helped him is walking away.

Another site tells the story of a Christian man who survived a "10,000 pound truck axle" that crushed him while two angels came to his aid to save his life. He experienced what is said to be a "miraculous recovery." Of course, it is possible for digital footage to be faked. Yet however we explain such matters, numerous biblical passages confirm angelic appearances.

In Gideon's case, the angel's presence gave him the needed courage to go into battle for the Lord. But does that mean it's wise to anticipate, or even request, a visit of an angel? There is no indication that Gideon did either!

For those today seeking angelic visitation as a sign of some kind, the words of Jesus serve to remind that "a evil and adulterous generation seeks for a sign," but the only sign he offered the people was "the sign of Jonah" (Matthew 16:4). Our faith is strengthened by the ever-present reality of the indwelling presence of the Holy Spirit, not by a once-in-a-lifetime visit by an angel.

—C. R. B.

What Do You Think?
In addition to studying Scripture together, how would you counsel a fellow Christian who claims to receive signs from God?
Talking Points for Your Discussion
- When the claim involves receiving miraculous signs
- When the claim involves receiving non-miraculous signs

B. Receiving Assurance (v. 18)

18. "Please do not depart from here until I come to you and bring out my present and set it before you." And he said, "I will stay till you return."

Gideon seeks assurance that his unexpected visitor will not make an unexpected exit, and the request is honored. The messenger promises to remain until Gideon returns.

The word that Gideon uses for his special gift (*my present*) usually refers to a grain offering, similar to what is described in Leviticus 2. This may be a time of scarcity, but Gideon is still able to provide a meal for his unusual guest. Gideon probably anticipated that a miraculous sign of some sort after the meal will further credential the messenger and his message. Gideon wants to be certain that this is a commission from the Lord.

A sign is indeed given, but not in the way Gideon may anticipate. The verses that follow reveal that Gideon prepares a young goat, bread, and broth. The angel tells him to place the meat and unleavened bread on a rock (which is about to serve as an altar) and to pour out the broth. It is assumed that the broth is poured on the offerings. The angel then touches these gifts with the end of his staff. Fire erupts from the rock and consumes the gifts. The angel then vanishes from sight (compare Judges 13:20).

After Gideon recruits his army from four tribes, he asks for another sign to make certain that the Lord really will deliver Israel through him (see Judges 6:36-40). First, Gideon says he will place a fleece on the threshing floor. He wants the fleece to have dew on it the next morning, but the ground surrounding it to be dry. It happens.

But Gideon wants even more of these blessed assurances. It is natural for dew to evaporate more quickly from other surfaces, so he asks that the procedure be reversed on the next morning. That is, he desires that the fleece be dry, and that the ground be covered with dew.

But that is not the end of the story. If Gideon can ask for signs, then God himself can also make some unusual requests! After Gideon recruits 32,000 men (Judges 7:3) to go against 135,000 Midianites (8:10), God states that his army is too big! He instructs Gideon to reduce his fighting force to 10,000 and then to a mere 300. Thus the force ratio increases from more than 4-to-1 against Gideon's army to 450-to-1. But that is just right for God. The remainder of Judges 7 through 8:28 gives the account of Gideon's thrilling victory that results in 40 years of peace.

HOW TO SAY IT

Abiezer	Ay-buy-**ee**-zur.
Abiezrite	Ay-buy-**ez**-rite.
Amalek	Am-uh-lek.
Amalekites	Am-uh-leh-kites or Uh-**mal**-ih-kites.
Barak	Bair-uk.
Canaanites	Kay-nun-ites.
Esau	Ee-saw.
Keturah	Keh-too-ruh.
Manasseh	Muh-nass-uh.
Midian	Mid-ee-un.
Midianites	Mid-ee-un-ites.
Ophrah	Ahf-ruh.
Sinai	Sigh-nye or Sigh-nay-eye.
Sisera	Sis-er-uh.
Yahweh (Hebrew)	Yah-weh.

Visual for Lesson 2. *Start a discussion by pointing to this visual as you ask, "When was a time in your life that you found this to be true?"*

Conclusion
A. What's Your Excuse?

Gideon was called by God for a special task, and the man went to work to deliver his people. God had Gideon employ an unusual strategy (see Judges 7:16-25), and the sword of the Lord won a great victory.

If God were to tell you that he had special plans for you, how would you respond? Perhaps your excuses sound like some of these: *I'm too weak; I'm tired; I don't know what to say; I can't do it alone; Everyone is against me; Nobody cares about me; This world is changing so fast; Satan is making my life miserable; I just feel lost; I can't do anything right!*

Like Gideon, we may be tempted to answer a perceived call from God with excuses. But each of these excuses and more are answered in promises God gives to those who trust him. When God calls, he also provides the resources for us to answer.

B. Prayer

Thank you, O God, for the promise of your presence in the battles against sin and for giving the victory through our Lord Jesus Christ—regardless. We pray this in his name. Amen.

C. Thought to Remember
God plus one is a majority.

INVOLVEMENT LEARNING

Enhance your lesson presentation with the reproducible activity page,
available as a free download at www.standardlesson.com.

Into the Lesson

Read the following unlikely success story: "One of nine children, she was born a slave in Maryland in 1822. As a child she was often beaten and whipped by various masters. She received a head injury when a slave owner threw a heavy metal object at another slave and hit her by mistake, resulting in her lifelong struggle with epilepsy, dizziness, and pain. After escaping slavery, she returned many times to help other slaves to freedom along the Underground Railroad."

Ask students to identify this heroine who succeeded against all odds. The answer is Harriet Tubman. Mention that "she was a devout Christian who worked as an abolitionist, a humanitarian, and a spy for the North during the Civil War, helping guide a raid that freed 700 slaves."

Alternative. Distribute copies of the "What Are the Odds?" activity from the reproducible page, which you can download. Quickly go through this activity by letting the class call out guesses.

After either activity say, "We know what it's like for people to have the odds stacked against them. Today we will look at a judge of Israel who seemed to have little chance of success—until God stepped in!"

Into the Word

Divide students into small groups of four or five. Hand out the following interview questions, and ask the groups to use Judges 6:11-18 to help them prepare Gideon's responses to an investigative reporter. Each group should select one person to answer for Gideon. (1) "So, Gideon, what exactly were you doing when the angel of the Lord appeared and called you a 'mighty man of valor'?" (6:12). (2) "It seems like your first words to the angel were to complain that God wasn't taking very good care of you and your people. Why is that?" (3) "There's some confusion about who was

speaking to you: was it an angel or the Lord himself?" (4) "What did the Lord want you to do?" (5) "It seems like you were less than eager to obey. What excuse did you use?" (6) "Were you reassured by what the Lord told you? Why?" (7) "And yet you asked him for a sign. What sign did he give you?" (See Judges 6:19-21.) Rotate between the various groups as you ask the questions to the selected "Gideons."

Use the following Scripture references to lead a discussion of the questions that Gideon asked of the Lord. Have someone read Judges 6:1, 2, then say, "Gideon's first question seems to imply that God wasn't taking good care of them. But why were they in such a mess?" *(They did evil in God's sight.)* Then read Judges 6:8-10, 13 and ask, "How did Gideon use God's past help to further his complaint?" *(He wasn't showing them mighty miracles as he did in Egypt.)* Just like Gideon, what other great leader tried to make excuses for himself? *(Moses; see Exodus 3:11.)* Say, "Gideon may have remembered the signs that God gave Moses when he asked for a sign. Do you remember the three signs?" *(changed rod to a snake, made his hand leprous, and turned water to blood).*

Conclude by asking, "What was it about Gideon's situation that explains why he needed so much convincing?"

Into Life

Divide the class in pairs and have partners ask each other these two questions:

1. What excuses have you been using for not serving God in some area?

2. How can the promises God made to Gideon help you overcome this excuse?

Alternative. Distribute copies of the "What's Your Excuse?" activity from the reproducible page. Allow students time to consider it individually and then take it home with a challenge to memorize one of the verses there.

JEPHTHAH

DEVOTIONAL READING: Acts 15:6-21
BACKGROUND SCRIPTURE: Judges 11

JUDGES 11:4-11, 29-31

⁴ After a time the Ammonites made war against Israel. ⁵ And when the Ammonites made war against Israel, the elders of Gilead went to bring Jephthah from the land of Tob. ⁶ And they said to Jephthah, "Come and be our leader, that we may fight against the Ammonites." ⁷ But Jephthah said to the elders of Gilead, "Did you not hate me and drive me out of my father's house? Why have you come to me now when you are in distress?" ⁸ And the elders of Gilead said to Jephthah, "That is why we have turned to you now, that you may go

with us and fight against the Ammonites and be our head over all the inhabitants of Gilead." ⁹ Jephthah said to the elders of Gilead, "If you bring me home again to fight against the Ammonites, and the LORD gives them over to me, I will be your head." ¹⁰ And the elders of Gilead said to Jephthah, "The LORD will be witness between us, if we do not do as you say." ¹¹ So Jephthah went with the elders of Gilead, and the people made him head and leader over them. And Jephthah spoke all his words before the LORD at Mizpah.

. . . .

²⁹ Then the Spirit of the LORD was upon Jephthah, and he passed through Gilead and Manasseh and passed on to Mizpah of Gilead, and from Mizpah of Gilead he passed on to the Ammonites. ³⁰ And Jephthah made a vow to the LORD and said, "If you will give the Ammonites into my hand, ³¹ then whatever comes out from the doors of my house to meet me when I return in peace from the Ammonites shall be the LORD's, and I will offer it up for a burnt offering."

KEY VERSE

Jephthah said to the elders of Gilead, "If you bring me home again to fight against the Ammonites, and the LORD gives them over to me, I will be your head." —**Judges 11:9**

GOD'S URGENT CALL

LESSON AIMS

After participating in this lesson, each learner will be able to:

1. Summarize the conditions of the agreements made between Jephthah and the elders of Gilead.

2. Compare and contrast the vow of the elders of Gilead with the vow of Jephthah.

3. Dramatize a situation in which participants work to overcome suspicion of one another.

LESSON OUTLINE

Introduction

A. Imperfect Leaders

Who are the greatest leaders you can name? Chances are, even though those on your list accomplished great things, some parts of their lives were far from virtuous.

Abraham Lincoln is known as the Great Emancipator. Nevertheless, he once wrote, "If I could save the Union without freeing any slave I would do it." Mahatma Gandhi led India to independence. Yet, he opposed the adoption of modern technology that would have helped his nation become more prosperous, freeing them from decades of poverty. Henry Ford was a pioneer in automotive engineering. But Ford also sponsored a weekly newspaper that published anti-Semitic views. Steve Jobs was undoubtedly a tech genius responsible for many innovations that changed the way we receive, store, and interact with information. But he was known for eccentricities such as odd diets and a refusal to bathe!

It is obvious that no human leader is perfect. Even the most popular and most effective leaders have flaws. Today we will look at a judge in Israel who was used by God in spite of the man's huge imperfections.

B. Lesson Background

The land of Israel was undisturbed for 40 years after Gideon defeated the Midianites (Judges 8:28). That is the last period of peace mentioned in the book of Judges.

Peace came to an end after Gideon died when Abimelech, one of Gideon's 70 sons, attempted to kill all of his brothers (Judges 9). He had a three-year reign, but it was more as a ruler of a city-state, not over all Israel.

At the conclusion of a rebellion, Abimelech captured a nearby city where people had taken refuge in a fortified tower. But he ventured too close to the tower and died after being hit in the head by a millstone (Judges 9:50-55; compare 2 Samuel 11:21).

The judges Tola and Jair came next, with their services lasting 23 and 22 years, respectively (Judges 10:1-3). It is generally concluded that the two men were judges at about the same time, but in different parts of Israel.

The axiom "The only thing learned from history is that no one learns from history" was verified in Israel time after time. Israel's sin-cycle repeated itself anew as the Israelites again embraced idolatry (Judges 10:6). Consequently, the Lord sold them into the hands of the Ammonites and the Philistines for 18 years (10:7, 8). This is estimated as having been on both sides of 1100 BC. When the Israelites cried out for deliverance, the Lord challenged them to cry out to the gods that they had chosen (10:14). The people eventually repented and appealed to God again (10:15, 16).

The Ammonites had come from the east and oppressed the Israelites on both sides of the Jordan River (Judges 10:7-9). The people had repented, but they needed someone to organize them and lead in the effort to expel the Ammonites. That man was Jephthah, the delivering judge in this lesson.

The opening verses of Judges 11 provide background information about Jephthah himself. His father, Gilead, had sons by his wife, but Jephthah had a different mother. This factor caused his brothers to drive him from home. Jephthah went north to the land of Tob. He had the ability to lead, and soon other men came to him. They are called "worthless" in Judges 11:3, which may speak to their being of low character. It is usually assumed that Jephthah's guerilla force raided nearby areas, even in Ammon itself.

I. Reluctant Ally
(JUDGES 11:4-7)
A. Present Need (vv. 4-6)

4. After a time the Ammonites made war against Israel.

The historical review was a reminder about what was given early in Judges 10:7-9—that idolatry in Israel has consequences. Israel is attacked by people immediately to the east. These raiders are intent on looting, and they often commit atrocities against anyone who resists.

5. And when the Ammonites made war against Israel, the elders of Gilead went to bring Jephthah from the land of Tob.

Gilead, located east of the Jordan River, is territory allocated to tribes Reuben and Gad plus the half-tribe of Manasseh of Israel's 12 tribes (Deuteronomy 3:12-17). *The elders of Gilead* apparently can find no one locally who is willing and able to lead a military resistance. So in desperation and shame, they travel northeast as a group to *the land of Tob* to ask Jephthah to return. Conjectures have been made that he knows some of these men personally. He may have looked up to them in his youth. But in figurative terms, they are crawling to him for help.

What Do You Think?
How should we deal with people who come to us only because they need our help?
Talking Points for Your Discussion
- Regarding fellow believers
- Regarding unbelievers

6. And they said to Jephthah, "Come and be our leader, that we may fight against the Ammonites."

The elders of Gilead make their offer to Jephthah, and the task that they have for him is very specific. They do not ask him to become a fellow elder, etc. The request to *be our leader* is that Jephthah serve as a military commander.

As that leader *against the Ammonites*, Jephthah is aware that he and his men will have the spoils of war if they are the victors (compare Numbers 31:9-12, 25-47). Jephthah, however, has no assurance of victory. His situation is different from that of Gideon in the previous lesson. Gideon was called by the Lord. Jephthah is being called by men.

◆ HOW DO WE RESPOND? ◆

The war in Vietnam was one of the more troublesome military ventures in American history. It was a proxy war, with North Vietnam supported by Communist China and the Soviet Union, and South Vietnam backed by America and its allies. American involvement was significant by the mid-1960s, and the country became deeply divided over the war. Protests sprang up all over the country. Many believed the government had lied to them about the reason for the war, the need to escalate it, the number of casualties, and the chances for victory. The military draft became increasingly unpopular, and many thousands were accused of draft dodging.

Providentially for Israel, Jephthah was willing to serve! (Apparently Israel had men willing to fight as soldiers, but no one qualified to lead them.) Most of us never have had to face the danger of armed warfare. But we are called to demonstrate spiritual courage now, as our country struggles through another wrenching time of cultural decline. This applies to both spiritual leader and "foot soldier." When the challenge comes to engage in spiritual battle, do you respond "Here I am! Send me" (Isaiah 6:8)?   —C. R. B.

> ### What Do You Think?
> Under what circumstances, if any, would you refuse to serve in your country's armed forces? Why?
> *Talking Points for Your Discussion*
> - Considering cases of armed intervention on behalf of another country (rescue)
> - Considering cases of self-defense after being attacked
> - Considering service as a noncombatant

B. Past Abuse (v. 7)

7. But Jephthah said to the elders of Gilead, "Did you not hate me and drive me out of my father's house? Why have you come to me now when you are in distress?"

Jephthah responds to the invitation with two rhetorical questions. The first one confirms that at least some of these leaders were involved in his being sent into personal exile. Jephthah makes the accusation that they had hated him, and that they had at least concurred with the decision of his brothers when they drove him from home. He rebukes *the elders of Gilead* for their part in his expulsion from the area many years before.

Jephthah's second question serves as a reprimand. Since they are congenial toward him only in their hour of need, their hypocrisy is clear.

Comparisons have been made with the occasion in Egypt centuries prior to this event when Joseph's brothers appeared before him. That family situation also involved more than one mother, but that factor was not as important as it is here (see the Lesson Background).

> ### What Do You Think?
> In what circumstances, if any, should past mistreatment be considered in making decisions?
> *Talking Points for Your Discussion*
> - In issues involving only family members
> - In issues involving governmental power structures
> - In issues involving only unbelievers
> - Other

II. Leadership Contract
(JUDGES 11:8-11, 29)
A. Position Promised (vv. 8-10)

8. And the elders of Gilead said to Jephthah, "That is why we have turned to you now, that you may go with us and fight against the Ammonites and be our head over all the inhabitants of Gilead."

Jephthah's rhetorical questions result in the conditional promise we see here. We notice that *the elders of Gilead* are using a negotiating tactic that is still used today. These leaders had decided beforehand that whoever leads the *fight against the Ammonites* will be *head over all the inhabitants of Gilead* (see Judges 10:18). But the initial offer in Judges 11:6 is only the position of "leader." Getting resistance to that, the elders now make their best and final offer, an offer decided in advance.

9. Jephthah said to the elders of Gilead, "If you bring me home again to fight against the Ammonites, and the LORD gives them over to me, I will be your head."

The new offer to be head gets Jephthah's attention! If the Lord enables him to be victorious, are they definitely saying that that will happen? The last phrase in this verse can be translated as a question, but can also be taken as an affirmation: *I will be your head.* A subtle change has taken place. In the previous verse it was the elders who gave the conditions for Jephthah's becoming their head. In this verse the same conditions are repeated and become Jephthah's conditions to them.

10. And the elders of Gilead said to Jephthah, "The LORD will be witness between us, if we do not do as you say."

In verses 9-11, Jephthah seems to take a little revenge against his own people as they swear an oath to make him their head as well as commander over the fighting forces. It is either all or nothing! The sting of illegitimacy now becomes tolerable as Jephthah contemplates his change in circumstances.

It is a serious thing to incorporate the name of *the Lord* into a vow, and that is what *the elders of Gilead* do when they say that *the Lord will be* their *witness*. The leaders of Gilead understand that Jephthah may not believe them, so they say that with the Lord as their witness, they will keep their word. This type of oath is done in special situations. When Ruth made her pledge to Naomi, she incorporated the name of the Lord into her statement (Ruth 1:17). The high priest put Christ under oath when he commanded Jesus to say whether or not he was the Christ (Matthew 26:63, 64). Normally, however, the Christian is not to swear oaths in the name of the Lord (Matthew 5:33-37; James 5:12), although Paul takes a vow on at least one occasion (Acts 18:18). Christians are to be seen as trustworthy when they speak.

What Do You Think?
How should we respond when faced with the opportunity to take an oath or vow that is expected by culture?
Talking Points for Your Discussion
- Regarding legal, courtroom situations
- Regarding oaths of office
- Regarding wedding vows
- Other

B. Commitment Confirmed (v. 11)

11. So Jephthah went with the elders of Gilead, and the people made him head and leader over them. And Jephthah spoke all his words before the LORD at Mizpah.

The scene changes as Jephthah accompanies *the elders of Gilead* to a place named *Mizpah,* also spelled Mizpeh. There is more than one town of this name; one view identifies the location as being on the east side of the Jordan River. Another Mizpeh is situated about six miles due north of Jerusalem (Joshua 18:26; also known as Jebus per Judges 19:11), between Ramah and Bethel (see Judges 4:5, lesson 1).

It was the elders who gave the original invitation to Jephthah, but now it is *the people* who have the final confirmation on his being their *head and leader.* The same two words that were used in verses 6 and 8 are used in reverse order. It is logical that Jephthah wants immediate authority to organize the people for the pending military campaign.

But first, Jephthah tries diplomacy. Judges 11:12-28 (not in today's lesson text) informs us that he sends messengers to the king of Ammon to discover the nature of that man's grievance against Israel. The king responds with the charge that the Israelites had taken his land when they came out of Egypt. Jephthah's reply shows that he know the facts of history better than does the king of Ammon! Ultimately, however, that king reveals that he is not interested in the facts of history, as he refuses a peaceful solution that is based on those facts.

C. Spirit Strengthens (v. 29)

29a. Then the Spirit of the LORD was upon Jephthah,

Verse 6 of our text indicates that it is men who call Jephthah to serve, not the Lord. In the verse before us, God sanctifies that decision, given that *the Spirit of the Lord* comes on Jephthah.

In Old Testament times, the Spirit of the Lord comes on select individuals to empower them for specific tasks. An example is Bezalel, who received the Spirit of God to lead in the construction of the tabernacle (Exodus 35:30, 31). In the book of Judges, there are four judges who receive this special gift: Othniel (Judges 3:9, 10), Gideon (6:34, lesson 2), Jephthah, and Samson (14:6, 19; 15:14). The fact that the Spirit comes three times on Samson indicates that the gift is not permanent.

29b. and he passed through Gilead and Manasseh and passed on to Mizpah of Gilead, and from Mizpah of Gilead he passed on to the Ammonites.

Jephthah needs more men in his fighting force. (Contrast the Lord's systematic reduction of Gideon's army from 32,000 to a mere 300 in Judges 7:2-8.) It may be that the Spirit led him to go on a recruiting tour throughout Gilead, and then north into the tribal territory of Manasseh. He would have been well-known to the people of that area, for it was not far from Tob, where he had lived. He returned to his starting point, organized his forces, and began his advance to the east to make contact with the foe.

III. Rash Vow

(JUDGES 11:30, 31)

A. The "If . . ." Clause (v. 30)

30. And Jephthah made a vow to the LORD and said, "If you will give the Ammonites into my hand,

Previously a vow was made by the men of Gilead, who asked Jephthah to return. This time it is Jephthah who makes *a vow*. He is doing something that he has not done before. He is ready to lead an army into battle, and he may feel insecure. He might have made raids on these people in the past, but this was an entirely different type of operation. This was not Jephthah's method—until now.

Jephthah's vow is more than a wish, and it goes beyond a simple prayer. This is a vow made to the Lord with the condition of what he wants to accomplish in the impending battle. His desire is to have victory, and he uses a figure of speech to

express it—that he wants the oppressors delivered into his hands.

B. The "Then . . ." Clause (v. 31)

31. "then whatever comes out from the doors of my house to meet me when I return in peace from the Ammonites shall be the LORD's, and I will offer it up for a burnt offering."

This verse is the famous vow of Jephthah. There are different opinions on what he actually intended to say, and what he did as a result.

The verses that follow reveal that Jephthah's army was successful. When he comes home, it is his daughter who comes out to meet him with tambourines and dancing—his only daughter. Jephthah is grief stricken. The middle part of verse 39 reads this way in Hebrew: "he did to her his vow that he vowed." Therefore it is certain that he kept his promise. It is also certain that the Spirit of the Lord had come on him earlier (v. 9), and it is certain that he is listed in Hebrews 11:32 as a person of faith.

The older view about Jephthah is that he actually sacrificed his daughter when she returned from bewailing her virginity. The rationale for this interpretation includes these major considerations: (1) actual sacrifice is the natural sense of the text; (2) actual sacrifice was the interpretation for 2,000 years; (3) the old Greek translation of the Old Testament has "whoever" comes from his house, not whatsoever; and (4) neighboring people groups regularly sacrificed their children to their gods. The list could continue, but these are the major points.

In about AD 1200, Rabbi Kimchi proposed a different interpretation: Jephthah gave his daughter to the Lord to serve at the tabernacle (see 1 Samuel 1:23-28). Support for this theory is based on (1) translating the final phrase of verse 31 as "or I will offer it up for a burnt offering"; (2) the fact that the Hebrews are not to imitate their neighbors' practices, including human sacrifice (Deuteronomy 12:30, 31; 18:10); (3) the daughter bewailed her virginity, not her death; and (4) Jephthah's inclusion in Hebrews 11 argues against his actually sacrificing his daughter.

Jephthah was faithful. He knew the history of his people. He was not crushed by rejection or adversity, but rose above it. He could overlook the bad behavior of his brothers in order to help people in need. He received a special gift of the Holy Spirit, and he kept his word—especially to God.

◆ **RASH PROMISES** ◆

Remember as a youngster when you made a hasty promise "not to tell," but you ended up doing so anyway? Perhaps it involved a pledge to keep a secret, but you couldn't resist gossiping about such juicy information. Perhaps someone told you not to tell anyone of a prank he or she committed, but you violated trust and did so anyway. There are all kinds of rash promises people make; the promise "not to tell" is just one of them.

There's a lot of overlap in meaning of the words *promises, oaths,* and *vows.* All involve the making of a commitment, and God takes such commitments seriously (see Deuteronomy 23:21-23; Matthew 5:33-37; James 5:12; etc.). Jephthah, Saul (1 Samuel 14:24, 43-45), and others did so as well. The ungodly King Herod found himself trapped in a rash promise he had made (Matthew 14:6-11).

Before committing ourselves too quickly to certain paths in our service for Jesus, it's important to count the cost of doing so (Luke 14:28-33). The more significant the opportunity seems to be, the greater should be the depth of prayer about it (Colossians 4:3-5; etc.). The godly counsel of the spiritually mature can also keep us from making rash commitments (Proverbs 15:22).

—C. R. B.

HOW TO SAY IT

Abimelech	Uh-*bim*-eh-lek.
Ammon	*Am*-mun.
Ammonites	*Am*-un-ites.
Bezaleel	Bih-*zal*-ih-el.
Gilead	*Gil*-ee-ud (*G* as in *get*).
Jephthah	*Jef*-thuh (*th* as in *thin*).
Mahatma Gandhi	Muh-*hot*-muh *Gon*-dee.
Manasseh	Muh-*nass*-uh.
Midianites	*Mid*-ee-un-ites.
Mizpah	*Miz*-pah.
Philistines	Fuh-*liss*-teenz
	or *Fill*-us-teenz.

Lead on, O King Eternal

Lead on, O King eternal,
Till sin's fierce war shall cease,
And holiness shall whisper
The sweet amen of peace.
For not with swords'
loud clashing,
Nor roll of stirring drums;
With deeds of love and mercy
The heavenly kingdom comes.

Visual for Lesson 3. *Use this visual in conjunction with Judges 11:8, 9 to open a discussion of how God is our ultimate leader in all situations.*

Conclusion

A. On the Lookout for Leadership

There is no such thing as a perfect leader. And if the elders of Gilead were looking for one, they certainly did not find him in Jephthah! Yet God used that man for his purposes in his time.

There is a fine line to walk here when it comes to looking for church leaders. If the leadership values in 1 Timothy 3:1-13; Titus 1:6-9; etc., are taken as absolute qualifications, then the church may end up with no elders and deacons! There are no perfect church leaders. On the other hand, to view these characteristics as *qualities* rather than *qualifications* may put one on the path to "explaining away" a potential leader's shortcomings—with disaster looming.

The solution is to be on the lookout for diamonds in the rough, potential leaders who are open to mentoring. Paul trained Timothy and Titus for years to assume leadership roles; tomorrow's leaders need today's training.

B. Prayer

We ask, O God, that you help us find, train, and follow leaders who will accomplish your will among us. We pray this in Jesus' name. Amen.

C. Thought to Remember

The God who makes a lump of coal a diamond can create faithful leaders from imperfect people.

INVOLVEMENT LEARNING

Enhance your lesson presentation with the reproducible activity page,
available as a free download at www.standardlesson.com.

Into the Lesson

To begin class, write the following names and numbers on the board:

Barack Obama—69, 57
George W. Bush—90, 71
Bill Clinton—73, 54
George H. W. Bush—89, 60
Ronald Reagan—68, 56

Ask the class if they can guess what the two numbers after each name indicate. (They are the highest approval rating received by the president during a certain point in his administration followed by the highest disapproval rating received by the same president during another point in his administration.) After a few guesses, reveal the answer, noting that at a certain point in time, more than half of the American public disapproved of the job their president was doing!

Alternative. Distribute copies of the "Imperfect Leaders" activity from the reproducible page, which you can download. Have students work in groups or use as a whole-class activity.

After either activity lead into the Bible study by saying, "It is obvious that no human leader is perfect. Even the most popular and most effective leaders have flaws. Today we will look at a judge in Israel who was used by God even though he had huge imperfections."

Into the Word

Divide your class into three groups. Each group will prepare to act out a fictitious job interview for Jephthah.

Assignments and sample interview questions follow.

Group 1—Candidate's Background (vv. 4-7, refer to vv. 1-3, if needed)

Tell us about your family background.
What qualifies you for this job?

Group 2—Job Desired (vv. 8-11)
What do you see as your job responsibilities?

What would you expect from us if you perform your duties to our satisfaction?

Group 3—Spiritual Background (vv. 29-31)

How would you describe your relationship with the God of Israel?

How will you ensure that God will help you succeed?

Allow time for the groups to perform their portions of the interview.

Alternative. Distribute copies of the "All Is in Order" activity from the reproducible page. Have students work in small groups to put the key events of Judges 11:4-11, 29-31 in chronological order.

Close either activity by saying, "Jephthah would not be someone we would expect to be a leader of God's people. He had a rough background, was not well-liked by the people he would lead, and had a rather manipulative view of God. Yet God saw fit to use him! How can we ensure that those who are chosen for church leadership today get the preparation they need to do the best job possible?"

Into Life

To close, turn with the class to 1 Timothy 3:1-13. Have the class call out qualifications for church leaders found in these verses. Write them on the board as they are mentioned.

With that list before the class, ask the following questions:

How can we go about finding leaders with these qualifications?

What specific behaviors do you think would disqualify a person from leadership?

What part would the time frame of such behavior and whether or not it is habitual play in your consideration?

What types of training would help prepare people to meet some of these qualifications?

What other steps can a church take to prepare people for future positions of leadership?

SAMSON

DEVOTIONAL READING: Judges 13:19-23
BACKGROUND SCRIPTURE: Judges 13–16

JUDGES 13:1-7, 24, 25

¹ And the people of Israel again did what was evil in the sight of the LORD, so the LORD gave them into the hand of the Philistines for forty years.

² There was a certain man of Zorah, of the tribe of the Danites, whose name was Manoah. And his wife was barren and had no children. ³ And the angel of the LORD appeared to the woman and said to her, "Behold, you are barren and have not borne children, but you shall conceive and bear a son. ⁴ Therefore be careful and drink no wine or strong drink, and eat nothing unclean, ⁵ for behold, you shall conceive and bear a son. No razor shall come upon his head, for the child shall be a Nazirite to God from the womb, and he shall begin to save Israel from the hand of the Philistines." ⁶ Then the woman came and told her husband,

"A man of God came to me, and his appearance was like the appearance of the angel of God, very awesome. I did not ask him where he was from, and he did not tell me his name, ⁷ but he said to me, 'Behold, you shall conceive and bear a son. So then drink no wine or strong drink, and eat nothing unclean, for the child shall be a Nazirite to God from the womb to the day of his death.'"

· ·

²⁴ And the woman bore a son and called his name Samson. And the young man grew, and the LORD blessed him. ²⁵ And the Spirit of the LORD began to stir him in Mahaneh-dan, between Zorah and Eshtaol.

KEY VERSE

"Behold, you shall conceive and bear a son. No razor shall come upon his head, for the child shall be a Nazirite to God from the womb, and he shall begin to save Israel from the hand of the Philistines.

—Judges 13:5

GOD'S URGENT CALL

Unit 1: Called to Be Strong

LESSONS 1–4

LESSON AIMS

After participating in this lesson, each learner will be able to:

1. List factors and conditions intended to shape Samson's spiritual development.

2. Evaluate how expectations may have shaped Samson's attitudes and actions as he grew up.

3. Describe a parental or community expectation that has shaped his or her life in a positive way.

LESSON OUTLINE

Introduction

A. Childhood Memories

When you reflect on your childhood, what memories come to mind? Is it that family outing to the beach during which you were first taught to swim? Is it the aroma of your favorite meal being lovingly prepared? Is it a favorite family tradition that was always practiced during holiday times?

But maybe it is a curfew that you had to follow that was an hour earlier than the curfew of your friends. Perhaps it is your parents' insistence that you not go to a movie that everyone was talking about, because it celebrated ungodly behavior. Possibly it is going to church every Sunday, even when you didn't *want* to!

Good parents make a real difference in the lives of children. Some parental actions are pleasant and affirming. But some will seem unpleasant and even unreasonable in the mind of a child. Yet both are necessary to bring a youngster to maturity. Today we will conclude our look at some famous judges of Israel, not by looking at the judge himself, but at this judge's parents.

B. Lesson Background

This is the last of the studies on four delivering judges in the book of Judges, the seventh book of the Old Testament. There were two other major judges (Othniel and Ehud) and six judges who seem only to have served as magistrates in different parts of Israel.

In the previous lesson Jephthah defeated the Ammonites that had oppressed the central portions of the land for 18 years. Judges 12 gives the details on another problem that confronted Jephthah: Ephraimites from the western side of the Jordan came to complain that he had not called them when he led the battle against the Ammonites. Jephthah's reply was that he had called them and they had not come (Judges 12:2, 3). It could be surmised that after Jephthah's situation with his daughter (see last week's lesson), he did not feel like trying to appease men who wait until the battle is over before they choose sides.

The outcome was a battle between two groups of Israelites. Jephthah and his Gileadites defeated the Ephraimites from the western side of the Jordan (toward the Mediterranean Sea).

As the Ephraimites retreated, Jephthah's men gained control of the fords where the Ephraimites would cross the Jordan River. Each Ephraimite who attempted to cross the Jordan was asked to say a certain word. Anyone who pronounced the word a certain way was recognized as being an Ephraimite and therefore executed (Judges 12:6). Tribes had conquered the promised land some 300 years previously (11:26), which provided time for regional dialects to develop.

The last verses of Judges 12 give basic facts of three men who seem to have served only as magistrates in their areas: one in the south, one in the north, and one in the middle section of Israel.

I. Childless Couple
(JUDGES 13:1-3)
A. Dark Days (v. 1)

1. Again the people of Israel again did what was evil in the sight of the LORD, so the LORD gave them into the hand of the Philistines for forty years.

Each generation of God's people seems to have been determined to make its own mistakes, especially as it involved doing evil. To do evil is defined in Judges 10:6 as serving the gods of five nations that bordered parts of Israel.

The result of this idolatry is given in Judges 10:7: *the Lord* "sold *them into the hand of the Philistines* and . . . Ammonites." Ammonite oppression (previous lesson) lasted 18 years. The Ammonites had spread across the Jordan River into Judah and Benjamin (Judges 10:9). Jephthah was selected to crush the Ammonites, and he did so.

The Philistine oppression of *forty years* is the longest of any in the book of Judges. Both Abraham and Isaac had dealings with individuals who were Philistines (Genesis 21 and 26), but they were not a threat at that time. They are not mentioned as one of the nations that the Israelites were to drive from Canaan.

It is generally thought that they came from islands in the Mediterranean or Aegean Sea. Overpopulation may have contributed to their migrating in larger numbers and, finally, settling along the coast of Canaan about 1200 BC. One of the early judges had a conflict with them (Shamgar in Judges 3:31). Soon they became a major factor in oppressing Israel. The ark of the covenant was captured by the Philistines in the days of Eli (a mentor for Samuel). Conflicts continued into the days of Samuel, Saul, and David.

The 40-year oppression has been dated as starting at approximately 1115 BC. This may be about the time that Samson is born. In the middle of that oppression, Samson will become a one-man army who regularly embarrasses the Philistines with his physical strength.

◆ *EMBRACING EVIL . . . AGAIN?!* ◆

Addictions to alcohol and drugs involve millions of people. But there are addictive behaviors as well as addictive substances. For example, involvement in social media is becoming increasingly common as an obsessive-compulsive behavior. A similarly addictive behavior is computer gaming. This compulsion may take the form of competing with one's self, always trying for a higher score or lower time of completion.

The declaration of today's text that "the people of Israel again did what was evil in the sight of the Lord" is evidence that the nation was addicted to sin in general and idolatry in particular. But this isn't just dusty history of a bygone era! No, it is "written down for our instruction, on whom the end of the ages has come" (1 Corinthians 10:11). Psychologist Dr. Phil has said, "The best predictor of future behavior is past behavior." We prove we have learned from history when we do not repeat it.   —C. R. B.

What Do You Think?
What are some things we can do to resist joining the larger culture in its pursuit of evil?
Talking Points for Your Discussion
- In terms of accountability practices
- In terms of environments we put ourselves in
- In terms of which Scripture passages to memorize for instant guidance
- Other

B. Brighter Tomorrow (vv. 2, 3)

2. There was a certain man of Zorah, of the tribe of the Danites, whose name was Manoah. And his wife was barren and had no children.

There is a very special announcement for a couple in Israel who are Danites. The tribal territory for Dan is immediately to the north of the areas where the Philistines had settled. This proximity provides us geographical context for Samson's temptations, his feats of strength, and his death.

Manoah is the name of the husband; the name of his wife is not given. They have not been able to have children, but that is about to change. They live in the town of *Zorah,* some 14 or 15 miles west of Jerusalem, near the border between Dan and Judah. The town of Zorah is mentioned as being involved in a Danite migration to a region north of the Sea of Galilee (see Judges 18:1-29). The tribal members who moved gave the name Dan to the leading town of the region. This is a tribute to their progenitor, Dan, one of the 12 sons of Jacob.

Other couples in the Bible are described as being childless, and special announcements from the Lord promised that they would have sons. These include Abraham and Sarah, who became the parents of Isaac (Genesis 21:1-3) when Abraham was 100 years old and Sarah was 90 (17:17).

Isaac married Rebekah when he was 40 years old (Genesis 25:20). The first 20 years of this marriage did not produce an heir. When Isaac was 60 (25:26), Rebekah gave birth to twins—Esau and Jacob.

Another special birth involves Hannah. A priest named Eli states his hope that the Lord grant Hannah her desire, and the Lord does so (1 Samuel 1:9-20). Angelic announcements precede the births of John the Baptist (Luke 1:8-25) and Jesus (Luke 1:26-38).

3. And the angel of the LORD appeared to the woman and said to her, "Behold, you are barren and have not borne children, but you shall conceive and bear a son.

The angel of the Lord seems to appear suddenly. He wastes no time in getting to the point, just as when he spoke to Gideon (Judges 6:12).

This unexpected event makes a vivid impression on Manoah's wife. In verse 6 the appearance of the heavenly messenger is described as creating awe or terror. The other factor is the declaration itself. The angel of the Lord knows all about her status of being barren.

Through the years she has probably tried to be with child by using every remedy that anyone suggests. All to no avail. Now a total stranger factually announces that her hopes will be fulfilled, and she will *bear a son* of her own!

II. Conditions Given
(JUDGES 13:4-7)
A. Child Set Apart (vv. 4, 5)

4, 5a. "Therefore be careful and drink no wine or strong drink, and eat nothing unclean, for behold, you shall conceive and bear a son. No razor shall come upon his head, for the child shall be a Nazirite to God from the womb,

The next statement introduces a caution. She is to be on guard and *drink no wine* or other beverage that is known to cause drunkenness. The reason for this is that the one to be born is to be *a Nazirite to God from the womb.* In this situation it may be that the restrictions that are on a Nazirite are also to be on the mother from the time of conception, for she is supplying the nutrition to the son.

The word *Nazirite* means "consecrated," or "dedicated." The guidelines for a Nazirite are given in Numbers 6:1-8. Any Israelite, male or female, could be a Nazirite, and for any length of time. Samson is to be a perpetual Nazirite. Such a person is to have no wine, strong drink, grape juice, fresh grapes, dried grapes, grape seeds, or grape skins—nothing from a grapevine. Grapes have sugar, and they are highly desired. It will be a challenge for a Nazirite to watch others eat things that he or she cannot have.

Samson's mother not only receives restrictions on what she may drink but also on what she may eat. Mrs. Manoah lived during the Mosaic dispensation, so clean foods for her are to conform to the guidelines that Moses gave in the law. In Leviticus 11 (see also Deuteronomy 14) the details are provided for what an Israelite is permitted to eat. Four categories are given:

1. Quadrupeds must have a hoof that is split and must chew the cud.

2. Animals in the water must have fins and scales.

3. Birds that are carnivorous or eat carrion are forbidden; others are permitted.

4. Insects must have four jointed legs for jumping—primarily various kinds of locusts (similar to grasshoppers).

HOW TO SAY IT

Aegean	Uh-*jee*-un.
Ammonites	*Am*-un-ites.
Canaan	*Kay*-nun.
Eli	*Ee*-lye.
Ephraimites	*Ee*-fray-im-ites.
Esau	*Ee*-saw.
Eshtaol	*Esh*-tuh-oll.
Gaza	*Gay*-zuh.
Gileadites	**Gil**-ee-uhd-ites (*G* as in *get*).
Isaac	*Eye*-zuk.
Jephthah	*Jef*-thuh (*th* as in *thin*).
Mahaneh-dan	*May*-hah-neh-dan.
Manoah	Muh-*no*-uh.
Mediterranean	*Med*-uh-tuh-**ray**-nee-un.
Nazirite	*Naz*-ih-rite.
Othniel	*Oth*-ni-el.
Philistines	Fuh-*liss*-teenz or *Fill*-us-teenz.
Shamgar	*Sham*-gar.
Zachariah	Zack-uh-*rye*-uh.
Zorah	*Zo*-ruh.

The ordinary restrictions prohibit anything from grapes, cutting the hair, or going near a dead person. Samson's physical appearance to others must have been frightening with his long hair and long beard.

Samson is the only person in the Bible who is actually said to be a Nazirite. Samuel is thought to have been a Nazirite, because his mother vowed that no razor would come on his head (1 Samuel 1:11). The same conclusion is made about John the Baptist, but for a different reason. The angel who appears to Zechariah says that his son is not to drink wine or strong drink (Luke 1:15).

◆ *SELF-DENIAL OR SELF-INDULGENCE?* ◆

The Nazirite vow that God commanded for Samson's mother—and later, Samson himself—involved abstaining from things that were part of an Israelite's normal life. Even today we may choose to give up something such as eating chocolate or watching TV as temporary self-denial. Self-denial reminds the participant that the Son of God gave up much more to make salvation possible.

The call to self-denial is a difficult one to hear in a self-indulgent culture. Missionaries report that self-denial is accepted more readily in parts of the world with lower standards of living. Perhaps the higher one's standard of living, the more one realizes how much self-denial really costs.

But consider the one who had the highest standard of living imaginable, the one who gave it all up for us: Jesus. Philippians 2:7, 8 bears frequent reading: "[He] emptied himself, by taking the form of a servant, being born in the likeness of men. And being found in human form, he humbled himself by becoming obedient to the point of death, even death on a cross."   —C. R. B.

5b. "and he shall begin to save Israel from the hand of the Philistines."

The final revelation of the heavenly messenger perhaps gives Manoah's wife the idea that Samson will be like others in the past who led armies against the enemies of God's people. That will not be the case.

Instead, Samson will act more as a free agent than a team leader of thousands. Feats of strength

I will make known God's faithfulness to all generations.
(see Psalm 89)

Visual for Lesson 4. *Point to this visual as you ask, "In what ways does God make his faithfulness known to our generation today?"*

His *very awesome* appearance is almost beyond description. One of the first things to be done for a visitor is to ask where he is from. But she had not done so, perhaps due to being speechless. Nor did he tell her *his name* (contrast Genesis 32:29).

Each statement by the angel is that of a bold, if not shocking, promise. Manoah's wife is overwhelmed. This is so much the case that she had not thought to attend to the common courtesies of the day.

> *What Do You Think?*
> Under what circumstances should we seek the input of others on spiritual matters? Why?
> *Talking Points for Your Discussion*
> - Circumstances when input of family members is wise or not wise
> - Circumstances when input of nonfamily members is wise or not wise

such as killing a lion with his bare hands (Judges 14:5, 6), killing 1,000 Philistines with the jawbone of a donkey (15:15), and lifting the city gates of Gaza and carrying them toward Hebron (16:3) will be done without assistance.

His task is to use his great strength to keep the Philistines off balance, to keep them concerned and confused, and to do things that cause them to realize that their gods are nothing. The judges that led organized armies against enemies include Deborah in accompanying Barak (lesson 1), Gideon (lesson 2), and Jephthah (lesson 3). Samson's role is different.

B. Parents United (vv. 6, 7)

6. Then the woman came and told her husband, "A man of God came to me, and his appearance was like the appearance of the angel of God, very awesome. I did not ask him where he was from, and he did not tell me his name,

The words in the biblical text say nothing about the manner by which the woman tells her husband what she has just experienced, but we imagine that it is with great excitement. She first describes her special visitor as *a man of God*. This was the ordinary way to refer to a special servant of the Lord (see Joshua 14:6; 1 Samuel 2:27; 9:6, 7).

She is very perceptive, however, for she continues the description by saying that *the appearance* of this special guest *was like . . . the angel of God*.

7. "but he said to me, 'Behold, you shall conceive and bear a son. So then drink no wine or strong drink, and eat nothing unclean, for the child shall be a Nazirite to God from the womb to the day of his death.'"

Manoah's wife faithfully repeats the instructions that were given to her by the angel of the Lord. But she makes two changes. First, she adds *to the day of his death* as the extent of the Nazirite requirement. It is possible that the messenger actually said this. Second, she does not mention that the son will begin delivering Israel from the hands of the Philistines. Again, she may have relayed it to her husband, but that is not recorded.

III. Blessings Bestowed
(Judges 13:24, 25)
A. For Manoah's Wife (v. 24)

24. And the woman bore a boy and called his name Samson. And the young man grew, and the LORD blessed him.

In the verses between the designated verses for this lesson, Manoah prayed for the Lord to let the man of God return. He wants to know what they should do for this special son. Manoah is to be commended for his faith—and perhaps his curiosity, for he believes what has been said.

The angel of the Lord returns, and Manoah asks questions about the future vocation and manner of life for the promised son. Manoah invites his visitor to remain for a meal, for he does not comprehend that this is the special angel of the Lord. Instead, Manoah is instructed to prepare a burnt offering. As the flames of the fire ascend, the angel of the Lord also ascends in the flame.

It is an exciting nine months for Mr. and Mrs. Manoah and their friends as they await the arrival of their son. He is called Samson, which is similar to the word meaning "sun."

The descriptions about his growth and his being blessed by the Lord are similar to the phrases that are used for future sons of promise—Samuel (1 Samuel 2:26; 3:19) and Jesus (Luke 2:40, 52).

> *What Do You Think?*
> What indicators should make us confident that a leader of a ministry project has God's approval?
> *Talking Points for Your Discussion*
> • Regarding indicators established in Scripture
> • Regarding indicators not established in Scripture

B. For Israel (v. 25)

25. And the Spirit of the LORD began to stir him in Mahaneh-dan, between Zorah and Eshtaol.

The context implies that Samson is coming of age. He is no longer apathetic or passively resigned to the oppression by the Philistines, for *the Spirit of the Lord* begins to prompt him to action. The designation *Mahaneh-dan* means "Dan's camp" (see Judges 18:12).

The action of the Spirit of the Lord is what empowers judges Othniel (Judges 3:9, 10), Gideon (6:34), and Jephthah (11:29). "Rushed upon" characterizes the Spirit's empowerment of Samson three times (14:6, 19; 15:14); that action may be functionally equivalent to the phrasing *the Spirit of the Lord began to stir him* that we see here. This phrase is unique to Samson.

Samson's parents have done their part in rearing him according to the divine mandates. Samson is ready to begin what the angel of the Lord has said: to deliver the Israelites from the Philistines. Others will also have roles to play in this task at various times. They primarily include Samuel, Saul, and David. God is protecting his people as he focuses on preparing the world to receive the Messiah. He will arrive to deliver people from the ultimate enemy: sin.

> *What Do You Think?*
> What practices can help us remember the divine source of all our strength today?
> *Talking Points for Your Discussion*
> • Considering aids offered by technology
> • Considering interpersonal accountability
> • Other

Conclusion

A. Parenting Manual

In 1946, Dr. Benjamin Spock published *The Common Sense Book of Baby and Child Care*. For more than half a century, this book was a consistent best seller, selling more than 50 million copies and being translated into about 40 languages. Mothers were encouraged by a basic message: *you know more than you think you do!*

Samson's parents lived well before Dr. Spock. They received direction, not from a popular author, but from God himself. Child-rearing experts have some value, but we can encourage parents to this day with the words of God, who knows more than all of us combined!

B. Prayer

Almighty God, as Samson had a way to serve, give me strength to fulfill my place in God's kingdom in the different segments of my life, and always in a way that is pleasing to you. In Jesus' name we pray. Amen.

C. Thought to Remember

It is never to late to offer a prayer of thanks for godly parents.

INVOLVEMENT LEARNING

Enhance your lesson presentation with the reproducible activity page,
available as a free download at www.standardlesson.com.

Into the Lesson

Divide the class into groups of three to five students. Give each group a pen and paper and ask them to list characteristics of good parents.

After a few minutes of group discussion, ask one group to read its list, one item at a time. As the characteristics are read, ask the other groups if that characteristic appeared on their list. If half or more of the groups had the same characteristic, write it on the board. Allow time for all groups to share, and continue to create a master list of characteristics of good parents.

Alternative. Distribute copies of the "Childhood Memories" activity from the reproducible page, which you can download. Have students work individually for a minute or two and then share a response with the entire class.

Lead into the Bible study by saying, "Good parents make a real difference in the lives of children. No parent is perfect; nor does every child of a good parent live a trouble-free life. Today we will conclude our study on judges of Israel, not by looking at a judge himself, but at his parents."

Into the Word

Dialogical reading of a narrative is a good way to focus a class on the facts in a text. Assign readers for these four parts:

Part 1—The words of Manoah's wife
Part 2—The words of Manoah
Part 3—The words of the angel of the Lord
Part 4—All other words

Instruct your readers to read all of Judges 13, each reading his or her own part. When a character quotes another character (see v. 7), the character who originally spoke the words should speak.

Then reinforce the facts of this chapter by reading the following questions aloud, asking class members to fill in the blanks correctly.

Distribute a handout for students to complete as a closed book test, or divide the class into two

teams and alternate the statements between them. If there is a tie, use the seventh question as a tie-breaker for the first team to call out the answer.

1. The oppression by the Philistines had lasted _____ years. *(40)*

2. Manoah and his wife had no children because she was _____. *(barren)*

3. The angel _____ appeared to the woman and told her that she would have a son. *(of the Lord)*

4. She was told not to drink wine or _____ and to avoid eating anything unclean. *(strong drink)*

5. No razor was to be used to cut the child's hair, since he would be a _____ from birth. *(Nazirite)*

6. The woman told her husband that _____ had appeared to her and told her she would have a son. *(a man of God)*

7. During the years when Samson was growing up, the Lord _____ him. *(blessed)*

Alternative. Distribute copies of the "Childhood Rules" activity from the reproducible page. Students may complete it individually, or you may decide to use it as a take-home exercise.

Into Life

Write this question on the board: *On which of the following areas did your parents place the most emphasis as you were growing up?* Underneath it list these categories:

1. Personal appearance
2. Academic achievement
3. Sports or other physical activities
4. Morality and behavior
5. Spiritual growth and church involvement

After a time of discussion, ask for volunteers to share how their parents' expectations affected them. For those on whom expectation had a negative effect, ask if they did things differently with their children in the area of expectations as a result.

MOSES

DEVOTIONAL READING: 2 Chronicles 19:4-7
BACKGROUND SCRIPTURE: Exodus 3

EXODUS 3:1-12

¹ Now Moses was keeping the flock of his father-in-law, Jethro, the priest of Midian, and he led his flock to the west side of the wilderness and came to Horeb, the mountain of God. ² And the angel of the LORD appeared to him in a flame of fire out of the midst of a bush. He looked, and behold, the bush was burning, yet it was not consumed. ³ And Moses said, "I will turn aside to see this great sight, why the bush is not burned." ⁴ When the LORD saw that he turned aside to see, God called to him out of the bush, "Moses, Moses!" And he said, "Here I am." ⁵ Then he said, "Do not come near; take your sandals off your feet, for the place on which you are standing is holy ground." ⁶ And he said, "I am the God of your father, the God of Abraham, the God of Isaac, and the God of Jacob." And Moses hid his face, for he was afraid to look at God.

⁷ Then the LORD said, "I have surely seen the affliction of my people who are in Egypt and have heard their cry because of their taskmasters. I know their sufferings, ⁸ and I have come down to deliver them out of the hand of the Egyptians and to bring them up out of that land to a good and broad land, a land flowing with milk and honey, to the place of the Canaanites, the Hittites, the Amorites, the Perizzites, the Hivites, and the Jebusites. ⁹ And now, behold, the cry of the people of Israel has come to me, and I have also seen the oppression with which the Egyptians oppress them. ¹⁰ Come, I will send you to Pharaoh that you may bring my people, the children of Israel, out of Egypt." ¹¹ But Moses said to God, "Who am I that I should go to Pharaoh and bring the children of Israel out of Egypt?" ¹² He said, "But I will be with you, and this shall be the sign for you, that I have sent you: when you have brought the people out of Egypt, you shall serve God on this mountain."

KEY VERSES

"Now, behold, the cry of the people of Israel has come to me, and I have also seen the oppression with which the Egyptians oppress them. Come, I will send you to Pharaoh that you may bring my people, the children of Israel, out of Egypt." —**Exodus 3:9, 10**

GOD'S URGENT CALL

Unit 2: Calling of Prophets

LESSON AIMS

After participating in this lesson, each learner will be able to:

1. List the who, what, where, when, and why of God's call of Moses.

2. Compare and contrast Moses' reaction to God's call with that of Gideon's (lesson 2).

3. Personalize Moses' question "Who am I, that I should [perform a specific mission]," and give an answer considering the difference God's presence makes.

LESSON OUTLINE

Introduction

A. Agony or Victory?

Years before ESPN became the primary sports network, there was ABC's *Wide World of Sports*. On Saturday afternoon one could tune in as announcer Jim McKay introduced this sports anthology. McKay would remind viewers that attempting to achieve greatness in sporting events led to both "the thrill of victory and the agony of defeat."

Such a phrase aptly describes the experience of the Lord's servants throughout the years. Serving the Lord in a broken, sin-cursed world can be the source of some of life's greatest joys, but it can also produce some agonizing moments. Perhaps no group of individuals in Scripture exemplifies this battle better than the Old Testament prophets, who are the focus of our next unit of studies. The first of this group to be considered is Moses.

B. Lesson Background

One could use the letters in the word *prophet* in an acrostic to define the Old Testament prophets as **p**assionate **r**epresentatives **o**bediently **p**roclaiming **h**eaven's **e**ternal **t**ruth. The prophets were God's spokespersons who proclaimed his message (usually but not always) fearlessly.

Some people view a prophet as one who predicts the future. That is certainly part of what the Old Testament prophets did, but their task was by no means limited to that. It is helpful to see the prophets as both *foretellers* (those who predicted the future accurately) and *forth-tellers* (those who declared God's truth). Prophets were often subject to verbal and/or physical abuse because they spoke unpleasant truth boldly and plainly. They often did so without regard for the consequences.

Some look at Moses' role as that of a lawgiver more than a prophet. But the Scriptures clearly refer to him as a prophet (Deuteronomy 18:15). The same book concludes with these words of tribute to Moses: "And there has not arisen a prophet since in Israel like Moses, whom the Lord knew face to face" (34:10).

Moses began his service to the Lord in need of his own prophet or spokesman, his brother Aaron

(Exodus 4:14-16; 7:1, 2). But in time Moses would learn an important lesson: the key to answering God's call is found not in who the human servant is but in who God is. That principle still holds true.

In his defense before the Sanhedrin, Stephen related that Moses had killed an Egyptian whom he saw beating one of "his brothers, the children of Israel" (Acts 7:23, 24; compare Exodus 2:11, 12). According to Stephen, Moses assumed that his fellow Israelites would acknowledge him as their deliverer and rally around his efforts; "but they did not understand" (Acts 7:25). When Moses realized that his murderous act was known by others and that he had been rejected as a deliverer, he fled Egypt. He ended up in Midian, where he married Zipporah, one of seven daughters of Jethro. We find Moses in that situation as today's text opens.

I. Incredible Meeting
(Exodus 3:1-5)
A. Fire on the Mountain (vv. 1-3)

1. Now Moses was keeping the flock of his father-in-law, Jethro, the priest of Midian, and he led his flock to the west side of the wilderness and came to Horeb, the mountain of God.

Jethro is first introduced in Exodus 2:18 as Reuel. Some suggest that Reuel (meaning "friend of God") is this man's given name, while Jethro (meaning something like "his excellency") is a title. The verse before us describes him as *the priest of Midian.* The nature of Jethro's priesthood is a bit uncertain, since the Bible does not specifi-

HOW TO SAY IT

Aaron	*Air*-un.
Amorites	*Am*-uh-rites.
Amram	*Am*-ram.
Aqaba	*Ock*-uh-buh.
Canaanites	*Kay*-nun-ites.
Damascus	Duh-*mass*-kus.
Gideon	*Gid*-e-un (*G* as in *get*).
Hittites	*Hit*-ites or *Hit*-tites.
Hivites	*Hi*-vites.
Horeb	*Ho*-reb.
Immanuel	Ih-*man*-you-el. (continued)

cally say that he is a priest of the Lord. Originally Midian was one of the sons of Abraham born to him through Keturah, whom he married following Sarah's death (Genesis 25:1, 2). Whether Abraham's faith in the true God was eventually passed on to the Midianites or how many of them embraced it is difficult to know.

In Jethro's case, he may have at one time worshipped the true God alongside other gods. This theory is supported by Jethro's declaration "Now I know that the Lord is greater than all gods" (Exodus 18:11) after learning what the Lord had done for the Israelites.

Midianite territory includes a vast desert area. As Moses tends *the flock of . . . Jethro,* he leads it (perhaps in an effort to find sufficient grazing) *to the west side of the wilderness* (the more distant side). This area around Horeb likely includes the land west of what is known today as the Gulf of Aqaba. Such land is part of the Sinai Peninsula. The traditional site of Horeb is at the peninsula's southern end.

The term *Horeb* is generally believed to be either (1) another name for Mount Sinai, (2) another peak in the region of the Sinai Peninsula, or (3) the entire range of mountains, with the word *Sinai* designating a specific mountain in that range. (Compare Exodus 33:6; Deuteronomy 1:6.) Horeb may be called *the mountain of God* because here is where he speaks to Moses and later gives his law. Or perhaps the Midianites have already given the mountain that name for reasons unknown to us.

2. And the angel of the Lord appeared to him in a flame of fire out of the midst of a bush. He looked, and behold, the bush was burning, yet it was not consumed.

The angel of the Lord coming to Moses *in a flame of fire* is echoed in Psalm 104:4. That verse tells us that the Lord "makes his messengers winds, his ministers a flaming fire." Such a fiery manifestation may point to the later association of God's presence and fire on this same mountain in the sight of the Israelites. At that time the fire will be much more intense (Exodus 19:18).

3. And Moses said, "I will turn aside to see this great sight, why the bush is not burned."

Moses is captivated by a bush aflame yet not consumed. Clearly something out of the ordinary is happening before his very eyes—it is a *great sight*. Who wouldn't *turn aside* to take a closer look?

> ### What Do You Think?
> What are some ways to turn our church into a "burning bush" that draws people to Jesus?
>
> *Talking Points for Your Discussion*
> - Regarding how mutual love is demonstrated
> - Regarding building and grounds appearance
> - Regarding the nature of preached and taught messages
> - Other

B. Voice from the Flames (vv. 4, 5)

4. When the Lord saw that he turned aside to see, God called to him out of the bush, "Moses, Moses!" And he said, "Here I am."

Verse 2 of our text speaks of "the angel of the Lord," but the verse before us speaks of the presence of the Lord himself from within *the bush*. Some believe the angel of the Lord to be a pre-incarnate appearance of Jesus.

Moses' sight has been captured by the burning bush; now his ears hear a voice. His name is called twice, which occurs on some other notable occasions in Scripture: with Abraham just before he offers up Isaac as a sacrifice (Genesis 22:11), Jacob (Genesis 46:1-4), young Samuel (1 Samuel 3:10), and Saul of Tarsus on the road to Damas-

HOW TO SAY IT (CONT.)

Jebusites	*Jeb*-yuh-sites.
Jethro	*Jeth*-ro.
Keturah	Keh-*too*-ruh.
Levi	*Lee*-vye.
Midian	*Mid*-ee-un.
Midianites	*Mid*-ee-un-ites.
Perizzites	*Pair*-ih-zites.
Pharaoh	*Fair*-o or *Fay*-roe.
Reuel	*Roo*-el.
Sanhedrin	San-huh-drun or San-*heed*-run.
Sinai	*Sigh*-nye or *Sigh*-nay-eye.
Zipporah	Zih-*po*-ruh.

cus (Acts 9:4). Moses responds with a simple *Here I am,* even though he does not yet know who is calling to him.

5. Then he said, "Do not come near; take your sandals off your feet, for the place on which you are standing is holy ground."

The order to remove *sandals* because of *holy ground* is not unique to this verse. A similar command will be given to Joshua when the Lord prepares him for the task of conquering the promised land (Joshua 5:13-15).

> ### What Do You Think?
> What actions on our part can acknowledge our awareness of being in the presence of the God of all holiness (1 Peter 1:15, 16)?
>
> *Talking Points for Your Discussion*
> - Within the context of marriage and family
> - During worship on the Lord's Day
> - During private devotions
> - Other

II. Divine Awareness
(Exodus 3:6-10)
A. Who God Is (v. 6)

6a. And he said, "I am the God of your father, the God of Abraham, the God of Isaac, and the God of Jacob."

Moses learns the reason why the ground on which he stands is holy: it is God who is speaking to him. In so doing, God first identifies himself with Moses' father, Amram, of the tribe of Levi (Exodus 2:1; 6:20). Of even greater significance is God's lordship with regard to Moses' ancestors. We refer to *Abraham, Isaac,* and *Jacob* as *the patriarchs*. It is the covenant that God made with them that now moves him to come to the rescue of his enslaved people (Exodus 2:24).

6b. And Moses hid his face, for he was afraid to look at God.

Moses' reaction of fear is immediate. He had been eager to "see this great sight" before him (v. 3); now he shields *his face* from it as he learns who is speaking to him. Moses may well recall his ancestor Jacob's surprise at being still alive after having "seen God face to face" on a particular occasion (Genesis 32:30).

B. What God Knows (v. 7)

7. Then the Lord said, "I have surely seen the affliction of my people who are in Egypt and have heard their cry because of their taskmasters. I know their sufferings,

God's people—the descendants of Abraham, Isaac, and Jacob—have been in bondage *in Egypt* some 400 years at this point in time (Genesis 15:13; Acts 7:6). That God knows the sorrows of his people provides consolation for us today. We know that in Jesus we see a "man of sorrows" who "carried our sorrows" at the cross (Isaiah 53:3, 4).

Even so, for God to note at this point that he knows of *the affliction* of his people in Egypt raises an immediate and obvious question: Why has he waited so long to come to their aid? Questions concerning God's timetable or scheduling of events are not addressed in most cases in Scripture. Rather, the Scripture's focus is more on learning to trust that the Lord will keep the promises he has made—and leaving the timing up to him.

Centuries later, Jesus' inquisitive disciples will ask, "Lord, will you at this time restore the kingdom to Israel?" (Acts 1:6). His blunt response at that time will serve as something of a thump on the head: "It is not for you to know times or seasons that the Father has fixed by his own authority" (1:7). God's servants are to focus on their duties, and predicting dates of the Lord's return, etc., is not one of them (1 Thessalonians 5:1, 2; 1 Timothy 6:14, 15).

> **What Do You Think?**
> How do we eliminate hindrances that cause us to neglect relieving the suffering of others?
> *Talking Points for Your Discussion*
> - Regarding emotional suffering
> - Regarding physical suffering
> - Regarding spiritual suffering

C. What God Intends (vv. 8-10)

8a. "and I have come down to deliver them out of the hand of the Egyptians and to bring them up out of that land to a good and broad land, a land flowing with milk and honey,

The Lord is moving from awareness to action. He is committed to delivering his people from Egyptian servitude. God is pictured as doing that by means of his own "strong/mighty hand" in Exodus 13:9; Deuteronomy 4:34; 5:15; 6:21.

But the pending deliverance is not just *from* something but *to* something. God intends to bring his people to much different surroundings: *a good and broad land, a land flowing with milk and honey.* This is a fulfillment of God's earlier promise to Abraham in Genesis 15:13, 14. The metaphor *milk and honey* speaks to the productivity and abundance awaiting the Israelites when they arrive in the new land. It will be a striking contrast to what came to be called the "iron furnace" known as Egypt (Deuteronomy 4:20; 1 Kings 8:51).

8b. "to the place of the Canaanites, the Hittites, the Amorites, the Perizzites, the Hivites, and the Jebusites.

The most comprehensive list of the promised land's inhabitants is found in Genesis 15:19-21. The presence of these competing people groups in an area about the size of the state of Vermont highlights both the instability of the area and the challenge the Israelites have ahead of them. These are peoples whom God will want the Israelites to eliminate. In so doing, the Israelites will be carrying out his judgment against them because of their extreme depravity (Deuteronomy 7:1, 2).

9. "And now, behold, the cry of the people of Israel has come to me, and I have seen the oppression with which the Egyptians oppress them.

The Lord repeats the fact of his awareness. The all-knowing God is about to teach both his people and the Egyptians that he is no mere tribal or territorial deity. *The people of Israel* will eventually learn that their God is the God of all nations; the oppressive wickedness of Egypt draws God's attention just as much as the well-being of Israel does.

◆ WHAT GOD STILL SEES ◆

A wave of fear cascaded across America on December 7, 1941. Two months after the attack on Pearl Harbor, President Roosevelt signed Executive Order 9066, which authorized his Secretary of War to designate areas as "military zones." One result was the forcible relocation of more than 100,000 people of Japanese ancestry living on the West Coast. Of the internees, 62 percent were American citizens.

Those held captive were released after the war, but it took decades for America to admit the injustice. In 1988, President Reagan signed a reparations act that acknowledged that "race prejudice, war hysteria, and a failure of political leadership" all played a role in what had been done.

Jacob's family had gone willingly to Egypt to escape a famine. But 400 years later, they had become the victims of racial prejudice. The Egyptians feared that so many Israelites were a threat. So they enslaved the Hebrews to keep them under control (Exodus 1). These two episodes of history, separated by millennia, witness to the evil result of ungodly fear. But God is watching.   —C. R. B.

10. "Come, I will send you to Pharaoh that you may bring my people, the children of Israel, out of Egypt."

No doubt Moses is grateful to hear about the Lord's concern for his people in bondage. Now, however, God is recruiting Moses to implement the plan!

III. Supernatural Provision
(EXODUS 3:11, 12)
A. Moses' Reluctance (v. 11)

11. But Moses said to God, "Who am I that I should go to Pharaoh and bring the children of Israel out of Egypt?"

Moses may have been more than willing to lead the people out of Egypt when he killed the Egyptian (Exodus 2:11-15). But that was 40 years ago, when he held some clout as the son of Pharaoh's daughter (Acts 7:21-29; Hebrews 11:24). Now at age 80 (Exodus 7:7), he is but a lowly shepherd. Given his present status and age, surely he is not the kind of man whom God will send to confront the mighty Pharaoh and lead the Israelites to freedom, is he?

The vast majority of those who run for elected office do so quite willingly. But that was not the case for Dwight D. Eisenhower following his success as Supreme Commander of Allied forces in Europe in World War II.

Before the 1948 presidential election, both major parties mounted "draft Eisenhower" movements, trying to persuade him to run. President Truman even offered to serve as vice president if Eisenhower would accept the Democratic nomination for president.

What convinced Eisenhower that he should run was the announcement by Senator Robert A. Taft of his own candidacy. Taft was an isolationist, but Eisenhower believed America needed to combat communism actively. Eisenhower finally affirmed, "I do not believe that you or I or anyone else has the right to state, categorically, that he will not perform any duty that his country might demand of him."

Moses was also reluctant: he tried to fend off God's "draft Moses" call by focusing on his own lack of ability, even disability (see Exodus 3:13–4:13). But God would not take *no* for an answer. He still doesn't.   —C. R. B.

> **What Do You Think?**
> How do we recognize the difference between humble, honest self-doubt and mere lack of desire to "get involved"—or worse?
> *Talking Points for Your Discussion*
> - In circumstances that cry out for a leader
> - In circumstances that desperately need more follower-participants

B. God's Reassurance (v. 12)

12. He said, "But I will be with you, and this shall be the sign for you, that I have sent you: when you have brought the people out of Egypt, you shall serve God on this mountain."

Like many people in the pages of Scripture (including individuals we are studying this quarter such as Gideon and Jeremiah), Moses comes to learn that his sense of unworthiness does not disqualify him from the Lord's service; if anything, it makes him just right for God's holy purpose. Moses asks, "Who am I that I should go to Pharaoh?" Therein lies the basis of Moses' state of readiness. The key to delivering the Israelites from their bondage is not in who Moses is but in who God is and the certainty of his promise to be with Moses.

Gideon (Judges 6:16) and Jeremiah (Jeremiah 1:8) both receive similar assurances from God before they embark on their respective ministries. The promise of God to be with his people is one of the most significant in all of Scripture. It reminds us that our God is not a far-removed, unfeeling, fickle deity who leaves his people to fend for themselves in a world suffering from the ravages of sin.

Ultimately this is demonstrated most powerfully in the birth of Jesus, who is Immanuel, meaning "God with us" (Matthew 1:23). This same Jesus will, by his own suffering at the cross, deliver humanity from the ravages of sin to allow us to enter the ultimate "promised land" of Heaven. There God will declare, "Behold, the dwelling place of God is with man. He will dwell with them, and they will be his people, and God himself will be with them as their God" (Revelation 21:3).

God also provides Moses with a sign as part of his assurance: *When you have brought the people out of Egypt, you shall serve God on this mountain.* Indeed, Horeb (or Mount Sinai) will be the place where God assembles his people to establish his covenant with them and give them his laws (Exodus 19:2-5) The intent is that they might be "a holy nation" (19:6) fit to usher in Immanuel.

Visual for Lesson 5. *Start a discussion by pointing to this visual as you ask, "In what circumstance did you realize most powerfully that God was with you?"*

Conclusion

A. The With-ness in Our Witness

When God chose Moses for leadership, did Moses anticipate the thrill of victory or the agony of defeat? Confronting the leader of a great empire was quite a task! Like Moses, we too can be intimidated by the seeming impossibility of our tasks. We can be intimidated into silence by peer pressure, social media, our workplace atmosphere, and other sources of opposition. But before we ask *Who am I?* let us remember who God is.

Jesus concluded his commission to his disciples with these words: "Behold, I am with you always, to the end of the age" (Matthew 28:20). Moses was called to lead Israel from physical bondage to freedom. The church is called to lead people from spiritual bondage to eternal life. The God who assured Moses of his presence with him assures us of the same thing now. Jesus has done the hardest work; we point others to him.

B. Prayer

Father, let us take courage from knowing that your presence sustains us. May we never be so intimidated by troubled times that we lose sight of the one who is above us. We pray this in Jesus' name. Amen.

C. Thought to Remember

God's promise to be with us still applies!

INVOLVEMENT LEARNING

Enhance your lesson presentation with the reproducible activity page,
available as a free download at www.standardlesson.com.

Into the Lesson

As class begins, ask learners to engage in a quick game of Simon Says. Acting as Simon, give learners a series of simple commands (example: lift your right arm, nod your head). Precede some with "Simon says!"

As learners accidentally complete commands for which you didn't specify "Simon says," disqualify them from the game. When the game has dwindled to two or three learners, give an impossible command, such as "Simon says 'fly,'" or "Simon says, 'end world hunger!'"

Allow learners a moment to object to or puzzle over this. Then say, "Obviously, I know you aren't able to do these things! But what if instead of Simon, God asked you to do the impossible?"

Alternative. Distribute copies of the "It'll Never Happen" quiz from the reproducible page, which you can download. Have students work in pairs or small groups.

After either activity, lead into the Bible study by saying, "We have all faced situations in which we felt we were being asked to do the impossible. In today's lesson, we will see Moses face this dilemma when God asked him to lead the enslaved Israelites to freedom. Let's see how Moses reacted."

Into the Word

Divide your class into three groups, giving each one paper and pens. Each group will be assigned a section of the lesson text and should quickly draw a sketch that summarizes its contents.

Scripture assignments and some suggestions concerning sketches follow:

Group 1—Incredible Meeting (Exodus 3:1-5)

Sketch ideas: a flock of sheep, since Moses was called to be a shepherd of another sort; a mountain, since this event took place on or near Mount Horeb; a burning bush, since that was used to indicate God's presence.

Group 2—Impossible Demand (Exodus 3:6-10)

Sketch ideas: eyes wide open, indicating God's seeing the condition of his people; eyes crying, indicating the suffering of God's people; milk and honey, indicating where God wanted Moses to lead Israel; pyramids, indicating from where God wanted Moses to lead his people.

Group 3—Supernatural Provision (Exodus 3:11, 12)

Sketch ideas: a hand held up in refusal, since Moses did not feel qualified to perform the task; two sets of footprints, one large and one small, indicating that God would go with Moses; an altar, indicating that Israel was to come out of Egypt and worship God.

After groups finish, reassemble the class and have groups share their sketches and summaries of their Scripture assignments.

Into Life

Close the class by giving each group member a few slips of paper and a pen. On each slip, ask students to write a word beginning with the letters *UN* that gives a reason why they cannot do what God asks (examples: feeling *UN*qualified, *UN*willing, *UN*able, *UN*talented, and/or *UN*available to serve).

Remind students that God's answer to those excuses is his promise to be with them. Have students carefully tear the UN from their slips of paper, revealing what they are with God's presence.

Alternative. Distribute copies of the "Who Am I That . . . ?" activity from the reproducible page. Have students review the common excuses people make for not serving God. Challenge them to check two or three items on the list, committing to no longer use those excuses.

ISAIAH

DEVOTIONAL READING: Isaiah 66:18-23
BACKGROUND SCRIPTURE: Isaiah 6

ISAIAH 6:1-8

¹ In the year that King Uzziah died I saw the Lord sitting upon a throne, high and lifted up; and the train of his robe filled the temple. ² Above him stood the seraphim. Each had six wings: with two he covered his face, and with two he covered his feet, and with two he flew. ³ And one called to another and said:

"Holy, holy, holy is the LORD of hosts;
the whole earth is full of his glory!"

⁴ And the foundations of the thresholds shook at the voice of him who called, and the house was filled with smoke. ⁵ And I said: "Woe is me! For I am lost; for I am a man of unclean lips, and I dwell in the midst of a people of unclean lips; for my eyes have seen the King, the LORD of hosts!"

⁶ Then one of the seraphim flew to me, having in his hand a burning coal that he had taken with tongs from the altar. ⁷ And he touched my mouth and said: "Behold, this has touched your lips; your guilt is taken away, and your sin atoned for."

⁸ And I heard the voice of the Lord saying, "Whom shall I send, and who will go for us?" Then I said, "Here I am! Send me."

KEY VERSE

I heard the voice of the Lord saying, "Whom shall I send, and who will go for us?" Then I said, "Here I am! Send me." —**Isaiah 6:8**

GOD'S URGENT CALL

Unit 2: Calling of Prophets
LESSONS 5–9

LESSON AIMS

After participating in this lesson, each learner will be able to:

1. List the circumstances of Isaiah's call.

2. Explain Isaiah's initial reaction to what he saw and heard at his call.

3. Write a letter of appreciation and encouragement to a missionary for answering the Lord's call as he or she has.

LESSON OUTLINE

Introduction

A. Wash Up!

What do you expect of a cook at your favorite restaurant? Should the person have experience as a cook, know the basics of food preparation, and follow recipes? Of course. But there is an even more basic expectation you have of your chef: clean hands!

Any business that deals with preparing food must be extremely conscientious about maintaining high standards of cleanliness. For example, no one would want to eat at a restaurant if news surfaced that a customer there found evidence that such standards had in some way been violated. In restrooms at restaurants, one will see the omnipresent sign that reads, "Employees must wash hands before returning to work."

Almost any job requires a person to be qualified in some way to do it. But what qualifies a person to be a prophet of the Most High God? One might conclude that such a servant of God would need to meet a long list of qualifications. As we consider Isaiah's call to be a prophet, we may be surprised to learn that a standard that applied to him as a deliverer of spiritual food is similar to what we expect of those who prepare physical food: cleanliness. Let's review the call of this great prophet.

B. Lesson Background

Isaiah received his call to be a prophet approximately 200 years after the nation of Israel separated into two kingdoms in 931 BC: Israel (the northern kingdom) and Judah (the southern kingdom). Isaiah was living when the northern kingdom fell to the Assyrians in 722 BC, but his primary ministry was to the southern kingdom of Judah. (The kings mentioned in Isaiah 1:1 are all kings of Judah.)

The life of Isaiah illustrates the wide range of circumstances in which a prophet of the Lord could find himself as he carried out his mission. He served the Lord during the reign of one of Judah's most wicked kings (Ahaz) as well as during the reign of one of Judah's best (Ahaz's godly son, Hezekiah). In fact, Isaiah's counsel guided Hezekiah during an Assyrian invasion that threatened the southern kingdom in 701 BC (Isaiah 37:5-7, 21-35). Hezekiah prayed to the Lord in trusting faith (37:14-20), and Judah was spared the onslaught that had befallen the northern kingdom of Israel 21 years earlier.

The fact that the call of Isaiah is not found until Isaiah 6 causes some to wonder why it is not recorded closer to the book's beginning, as is the case with Jeremiah (Jeremiah 1:4-19) and Ezekiel (Ezekiel 1:1–3:15). Some suggest that Isaiah's call actually did precede his messages, but the account of the call is placed in chapter 6 to make a specific and important point. The messages in the first five chapters explain why a prophet like Isaiah was so desperately needed to confront God's people. The fifth chapter in particular elaborates on what has happened to a people originally called by God to be "a kingdom of priests and a holy nation" (Exodus 19:6). Isaiah 5 features a word picture of a vineyard to describe both the Lord's care for his people and his disappointment that they had not produced the desired crop (Isaiah 5:1-7).

A Jewish tradition says that Isaiah suffered a cruel death of martyrdom by being sawn in two during the wicked reign of Hezekiah's son, Manasseh. This incident may be referred to in Hebrews 11:37.

HOW TO SAY IT

Ahaz	*Ay*-haz.
Assyrians	Uh-*sear*-e-unz.
Azariah	Az-uh-*rye*-uh.
Babel	*Bay*-bul.
cherubim	*chair*-uh-bim.
Elijah	Ee-*lye*-juh.
Ezekiel	Ee-*zeek*-ee-ul or Ee-*zeek*-yul.
Hezekiah	Hez-ih-*kye*-uh.
hypocrisy	hih-*pah*-kruh-see
Isaiah	Eye-*zay*-uh.
Jeremiah	Jair-uh-*my*-uh.
Judah	*Joo*-duh.
leprosy	*leh*-pruh-see.
Manasseh	Muh-*nass*-uh.
seraphim	*sair*-uh-fim.
Sinai	*Sigh*-nye or *Sigh*-nay-eye.
Uzziah	Uh-*zye*-uh.

I. So High
(Isaiah 6:1-3)
A. Exalted Lord (v. 1)
1a. In the year that King Uzziah died

The year that king Uzziah died was 740 BC. He had been one of Judah's more godly kings. But he did not finish well because at one point he defiantly entered the temple to offer incense, an act reserved only for the priests. When he reacted angrily to the priests who confronted him, he was immediately stricken with leprosy and had to be quarantined for the remainder of his life (2 Chronicles 26:16-21).

Uzziah's reign was one of the longest during the divided monarchy, covering a span of 52 years (792–740 BC). Note that Uzziah is sometimes called Azariah (2 Kings 14:21; 15:1).

> *What Do You Think?*
> How should Christians react to transitions in political leadership, if at all? Why?
> *Talking Points for Your Discussion*
> ▪ In the form and content of prayers
> ▪ In discussions with fellow believers
> ▪ In discussions with unbelievers

1b. I saw the Lord sitting upon a throne, high and lifted up; and the train of his robe filled the temple.

Deaths of national leaders are accompanied by varying degree of uncertainty about the future. What follows in our text shows that any such concerns are unnecessary regarding Judah's future. Judah's ultimate king is still in control, as Isaiah declares in the verse before us.

Some individuals in the Old Testament are privileged to see the Lord or a limited revelation of his glory (Exodus 24:9-11; 33:17-23; etc.). The Lord himself determines to what extent and by what means he allows himself to be experienced by humans. In the case of the prophet Elijah, he came in "a low whisper" (1 Kings 19:12); in the case of Job, he presented himself "out of the whirlwind" (Job 38:1). Isaiah's experience of the Lord is likely by means of a vision since the word *saw* is used.

The manner in which Isaiah sees the Lord is similar to John's description of one who is "seated on" *a throne* (Revelation 4:2). John speaks of himself as being "in the Spirit" on that occasion; perhaps something akin to this occurred with Isaiah (note also Ezekiel's testimony in Ezekiel 2:2; 3:12-15, where "the Spirit" can be understood as the Holy Spirit). *The train* refers to the hem of the Lord's robe (compare Revelation 1:13). The fact that it fills *the temple* conveys an image of the Lord's majesty and splendor.

It is difficult to say whether the temple Isaiah sees is the earthly temple of Solomon in Jerusalem or the heavenly temple. Clearly John's vision in Revelation is one of Heaven (Revelation 4:1, 2). In Isaiah's case, one should keep in mind how King Uzziah had violated the sanctity of the Jerusalem temple by offering incense when he was unauthorized to do so. Perhaps Isaiah's vision is of this earthly temple in order to show him (and in turn, the nation of Judah) that the Lord has not departed from the temple (contrast Ezekiel 11:22, 23).

B. Heralds of the Holy (vv. 2, 3)
2a. Above him stood the seraphim.
Seraphim are mentioned in the Bible only here and in verse 6 (see below). The term comes from a Hebrew word meaning "fiery." For the seraphim to have such an appearance would certainly be fitting, since fire is indicative of God's presence as noted in last week's study of Moses and the burning bush (Exodus 3:1-6; compare Exodus 24:17; Revelation 4:5).

2b. Each had six wings: with two he covered his face, and with two he covered his feet, and with two he flew.
We are not told how many seraphim Isaiah sees, but we are told that each has *six wings*. This characteristic highlights another similarity to John's vision where the four living creatures "around the throne" each have six wings (Revelation 4:6-8). The covering of both *face* and *feet* may represent complete submission to the one seated on the throne. One might say that "from head to toe" the seraphim recognize his authority.

3a. And one called to another and said: "Holy, holy, holy is the LORD of hosts;
The cry of the seraphim is similar to that of the four creatures in Revelation 4:8. The threefold repetition of the word *holy* serves to emphasize that quality.

The concept of holiness implies "separation" or "distinctiveness." Such separation is primarily ethical or moral and only secondarily positional or geographical. This is why Isaiah becomes so distraught at being in the Lord's presence (Isaiah 6:5, below); he knows how unholy, how sinful, he and his people are.

> **What Do You Think?**
> What are some ways to manifest personal holiness as befitting our holy God?
> *Talking Points for Your Discussion*
> - As the holy temple of the church at worship
> - As the holy temple of the church meets needs
> - Other

3b. "the whole earth is full of his glory!"
Isaiah is seeing God's glory in the temple (whether earthly or heavenly), but his glory cannot be confined to any structure. Solomon acknowledged this same truth at the dedication of the temple he constructed in Jerusalem: "Heaven and the highest heaven cannot contain you; how much less this house that I have built!" (1 Kings 8:27).

The whole earth, God's creation, is a testament to his glory. This theme is echoed often in Psalms (examples: Psalms 8:1; 72:19).

II. So Unworthy
(ISAIAH 6:4, 5)
A. Overwhelming Scene (v. 4)
4. And the foundations of the thresholds shook at the voice of him who called, and the house was filled with smoke.

Isaiah has heard the proclamation of God's glory from the seraphim; now he begins to experience it in an intensely personal way. The shaking and the presence of smoke remind one of what the Israelites witnessed at Mount Sinai (Exodus 19:18). They were terrified by such a demonstration of holy power. The stage is set for Isaiah to express similar anxiety.

B. Overcome with Guilt (v. 5)

5. And I said: "Woe is me!" For I am lost; for I am a man of unclean lips, and I dwell in the midst of a people of unclean lips; for my eyes have seen the King, the LORD of hosts!"

Just as the Israelites trembled at the presence of God at Mount Sinai (Exodus 19:16), Isaiah is overcome with a sense of his unworthiness to be in such sacred surroundings. His sense of feeling terribly out of place reminds us of how Adam and Eve attempted to hide from God after breaking his commandment (Genesis 3:8).

Isaiah finds himself gasping for breath in a spiritual sense. He is painfully aware of the immeasurable gap between himself and the holy God into whose presence he has been ushered. He knows he has no business seeing what he does. King Uzziah may have died, but Judah's real and ultimate *King, the Lord of hosts,* still rules!

Isaiah's mention of his *unclean lips* and the fact that he dwells *in the midst of a people of unclean lips* seems to focus on speech. Perhaps Isaiah initially desired to join the seraphim in their praise of God, but now he realizes that to do so would be the height (or depth) of hypocrisy. How can holy words be spoken by an unholy person?

What Do You Think?
In what ways can and should we acknowledge our own accountability for having and being among "unclean lips"?

Talking Points for Your Discussion
- Regarding sins of commission
- Regarding sins of omission

In the previous chapter, the prophet pronounced a series of six woes on the people (Isaiah 5:8, 11, 18, 20, 21, 22) and then stated this indictment: "Therefore the anger of the Lord was kindled against his people, and he stretched out his hand against them and struck them" (5:25). Isaiah's seventh *woe,* directed at himself in the verse before us, completes the sequence. (The number seven often represents "completeness" or "totality" in Scripture.) Perhaps he fears that the hand of the Lord will also be stretched angrily against him as well.

III. So Fitting
(ISAIAH 6:6-8)

A. Action and Result (vv. 6, 7)

6. Then one of the seraphim flew to me, having in his hand a burning coal that he had taken with tongs from the altar.

As if in response to Isaiah's admission in the previous verse, *one of the seraphim* goes into action on Isaiah's behalf. The altar from which he takes *a burning coal* possibly refers to the altar in the temple Solomon built. But an altar in a temple of the heavenly environs cannot be ruled out because an altar is present there as well (Revelation 6:9).

Isaiah must be watching the unfolding scene with great apprehension. Having just confessed his own sinful unworthiness, is he about to be punished?

7. And he touched my mouth and said, "Behold, this has touched your lips; your guilt is taken away, and your sin atoned for."

It is not unusual for prophetic visions to appeal to the senses. This helps the recipient understand that what is happening is real (compare Jeremiah 1:9-13; Ezekiel 1:4-28). Regarding Isaiah, four of his five senses have informed his experience thus far. By sight he beholds the Lord (Isaiah 6:1); by hearing he perceives the declaration of the seraphim (v. 3); by sight and smell (assumed) he is aware of smoke (v. 4); and now touch comes into play.

We do not know if Isaiah feels any sting or pain from the red-hot coal that is touched to his *lips.* If so, it must be temporary, as the words *your guilt is taken away, and your sin atoned for* speak not of judgment, but of forgiveness.

The association of fire with the presence of God bears revisiting. While God is indeed a "consuming fire" (Hebrews 12:29), what Isaiah experiences is the fire of cleansing or purging, as fire removes impurities from metals (see 1 Peter 1:7). Isaiah is not "lost" as he had earlier feared (Isaiah 6:5). Instead, he has received a great work of grace.

◆ DESTROYED? TESTED? PURIFIED? ◆

The horror of destruction by fire was realized to a massive degree in World War II. Germany was the first to firebomb cities, doing so in night-time terror raids. Allied forces eventually did the same in return. The morality of the firebombings of Dresden, Tokyo, and other cities is still debated.

Fire changes things. Biblically, such changes can be seen in at least three contexts: judgmental destruction, testing, and purification. Judgmental fire is depicted throughout the Bible, from Genesis 19:24 to Revelation 20:14. Fiery testing is seen in 1 Corinthians 3:12-15 and 1 Peter 4:12. Purification by fire is described in Numbers 31:22, 23.

Not infrequently, these concepts overlap. For example, testing and purification overlap in cases when the former results in the latter, as in Zechariah 13:9. We also see overlap between testing and purification in today's text as the prophet experienced a "burning coal" placed on his lips. But the overlap seems to be in the reverse direction: purification came first; then the testing of Isaiah's resolve came later as he preached judgment to a hostile audience that God foresaw would not listen (Isaiah 6:9-13). Since God states that fact *after* Isaiah accepted his call, we wonder if the man would have volunteered had he heard the prediction of "mission failure" first!

That question is relevant today, since Jesus described his own mission by quoting Isaiah 6:9, 10 in Matthew 13:14, 15. Before we "go" (Matthew 28:19, 20), we must recognize our own sin and the need for having had it purified (Hebrews 1:3). But all our preparation will not equip us for the testing of sorrow that comes as we encounter cold, unrepentant hearts. We are Isaiah.   —R. L. N.

What Do You Think?
   What are some ways our church can audibly and visually stress the reality of sin taken away by Christ?
Talking Points for Your Discussion
   ▪ During baptisms
   ▪ In observances of the Lord's Supper
   ▪ Other

B. Challenge and Acceptance (v. 8)
8a. And I heard the voice of the Lord saying, "Whom shall I send? And who will go for us?"

To this point, Isaiah has not heard the Lord speak—only the seraphim. Given what happens when they speak (see v. 4, above), what must Isaiah think will happen as the Lord himself does so? Elsewhere in Scripture *the voice of the Lord* produces utter terror in those who hear it (Exodus 20:18, 19; Deuteronomy 5:25). It is described as "powerful" and "full of majesty," with awe-inducing results (Psalm 29:4-9).

Yet when Isaiah hears the voice of the Lord, the tone is not terrifying. Instead, the tone appears to be that of pleading for assistance. The Lord is fully aware of the "people of unclean lips" whom Isaiah has mentioned (Isaiah 6:5). He needs someone to go to them, so he asks *who will go for us?*

The use of the pronoun *us* is similar to the language used in the creation of human beings and in response to the building of the Tower of Babel (Genesis 1:26; 11:6, 7). The plural pronoun may refer to God plus the seraphim who have been present throughout Isaiah's vision. Or it may refer to the persons of the Trinity. It is interesting to consider how much Isaiah has to say about the persons of the Trinity in his prophetic messages (see Isaiah 11:1-3; 32:15; 42:1; 44:3; 48:16; 52:13–53:12; 59:21; 61:1-4; 63:10-14).

◆   *DISCERNING GOD'S CALL*   ◆

Charles Spurgeon, the famous nineteenth-century preacher, had no formal theological education. Yet he preached to thousands every Sunday for more than 40 years!

How did God call him to such a task? Once when describing his call to ministry, Spurgeon said it was "an intense, all-absorbing desire for the work." Those who like neat logical categories may be unsatisfied with that description. They may desire to have the idea of God's calls examined in specific terms of form, content, etc.

Perhaps we may discern a more practical approach in the New Testament, where God's calls seem to come about as character and spiritual giftedness are observed. The first-century church chose "seven men of good repute, full of the Spirit and of wisdom" to serve in a certain capacity (Acts 6:3-5). Can we not conclude that they answered God's call to do so? Barnabas seems initially to have simply grown into his leadership role, having been recognized by others as a "son of encouragement" (4:36) who led by example (4:37) and spoke up on behalf of others (9:27; compare 15:37-39). These traits were evident before he was set apart for missionary travels by specific directive of the Holy Spirit (13:2).

Martin Luther was on target when he described his call as "God's voice heard by faith." When our aptitudes, spiritual gifts, circumstances, and opportunities come together, let us make sure we are not overlooking God's call. —C. R. B.

8b. Then I said, "Here I am! Send me."

Isaiah has just declared his own lips to be "unclean" (v. 5, above). But since these have now been touched by the burning coal and purged (v. 7), he is free to speak words of commitment to service on behalf of the holy God: *Here I am! Send me.* Isaiah's unholiness came to be corrected through the cleansing action taken by one of the seraphim—but the prophet's own admission of unholiness had to come first.

It is interesting to contrast Moses' hesitant reaction of "Who am I?" in response to God's call (Exodus 3:11) with Isaiah's seeming eagerness to respond. Whereas Moses' reply could be summarized as "Why me?" Isaiah's may be restated as "Why *not* me?"

Consider how each man experienced a powerful, unforgettable demonstration of God's presence. Yet each reacted to God's call quite differently! Even so, God is able to take each man as he is and shape him into the man he needs to be. Both Moses and Isaiah learned an important lesson that is still true: in the Lord's training ground, surrender is the key to victory.

What Do You Think?

What should others see in Christians who claim to be answering God's call?

Talking Points for Your Discussion

- In use of our time
- In use of money
- In relationships
- Other

Visual for Lesson 6. *Point to this visual as you ask, "Who in your personal experience has responded to God's call with Isaiah's willingness?"*

Conclusion

A. Surprised by Holiness

The edge that spiritual words are meant to possess can be dulled with misuse. Without thinking, we may utter insipid interjections such as "Holy mackerel!" We may refer to a misbehaving child as "a holy terror," etc.

Isaiah's vision of the holy God had an intensity that we will probably never experience in this earthly life. The intensity of his experience will be further diminished for us as we misuse the word *holy.* The holiness of God must be understood in an absolute sense. That understanding was what caused Isaiah to be utterly dismayed by his own lack of holiness.

To take a nonchalant view of one's own unholiness probably indicates a failure to understand what it means to be holy. We know that "God is love" (1 John 4:8, 16). Do we also know that God is "holy, holy, holy"?

B. Prayer

Father, help us each day to examine ourselves for unholiness that may interfere with saying, "Here I am! Send me." We pray this in the name of the Lord of all holiness. Amen.

C. Thought to Remember

May Isaiah's vision of a holy God leave us wholly committed to him.

INVOLVEMENT LEARNING

Enhance your lesson presentation with the reproducible activity page,
available as a free download at www.standardlesson.com.

Into the Lesson

Read the following pairs of jobs one at a time:

Organize a blood drive or hold a garage sale?

Help a friend balance a checkbook or help a friend with marriage problems?

Read to kids at the library or sit quietly with ill patients in the hospital?

Ask for a show of hands from students to indicate which of the two tasks in each pair of jobs they would feel more qualified to perform. You may ask volunteers to briefly explain their responses.

Alternative. Distribute copies of the "Alphabet Soup" activity from the reproducible page, which you can download. Have students work individually or in pairs.

After either activity, lead into the Bible study saying, "Almost any job that we can consider takes a person qualified in some way to do it."

What do you think qualifies a person to be a prophet of the most high God? When Isaiah was called to be a prophet, we get a glimpse as to what is required from a person assuming that role.

Into the Word

Divide your class into three groups. Each group is to read its assigned portion of the text and summarize ideas from it as directed. The assignments and some anticipated responses follow.

Group 1—So High (Isaiah 6:1-3).

List ideas from these verses that show that God's presence was overwhelming.

God is shown as being in an elevated position demonstrating his position of great power. He is so large that only the bottom part of his robe would fit in the massive temple. The fact that even the holiest of angels hid behind their own wings in his presence shows God's great holiness. The voices of the seraphim heralding God's presence both in his holy temple and in the world he created described God as being far beyond anything in this world.

Group 2—So Unworthy (Isaiah 6:4, 5).

List ideas from these verses that show that Isaiah felt unworthy and insignificant in God's presence.

God's presence was accompanied by smoke and the shaking of the temple to its very foundations. The feeling of being trapped in a fire and earthquake surely would have caused Isaiah to feel helpless. Knowing that a mere mortal had no right to stand before a holy God made Isaiah especially aware of his sinful state.

Group 3—So Fitting (Isaiah 6:6-8).

List ideas from these verses that show how a human being can be made right with God.

Fire is a common image in the Bible for judgment and cleansing. The idea of a hot coal on the lips would be painful. Only through this ordeal was Isaiah qualified to be God's prophet.

Allow time for groups to explain their findings. Comment as necessary, referring to the commentary.

Into Life

Say, "Today, the word *holy* is used so commonly that it's lost some of its punch; but even at that time, *holy* was not strong enough to describe the scene revealed to Isaiah. As he witnessed the angels' worship of the Lord, Isaiah went through fear, then guilt, and finally after his cleansing, worshipful answering of God's call."

Write the words *eyes, ears, nose, hands,* and *mouth* across the top of the board. Ask the class to brainstorm ways they might keep their respective *sense* clean, and ways they might worship God with it as well.

Alternative. Distribute copies of the "Keeping It Clean" activity from the reproducible page. Use the first part of the activity by soliciting answers from the class as a whole.

Challenge students to take the page home and consider the final questions throughout the week.

JEREMIAH

DEVOTIONAL READING: Psalm 75
BACKGROUND SCRIPTURE: Jeremiah 1

JEREMIAH 1:4-10

4 Now the word of the LORD came to me, saying,

5 "Before I formed you in the womb I knew you,
and before you were born I consecrated you;
I appointed you a prophet to the nations."

6 Then I said, "Ah, Lord GOD! Behold, I do not know how to speak, for I am only a youth."
7 But the LORD said to me,
"Do not say, 'I am only a youth';
for to all to whom I send you, you shall go,
and whatever I command you, you shall speak.

8 Do not be afraid of them,
for I am with you to deliver you,
declares the LORD."

9 Then the LORD put out his hand and touched my mouth. And the LORD said to me,

"Behold, I have put my words in your mouth.
10 See, I have set you this day over nations and over kingdoms,
to pluck up and to break down,
to destroy and to overthrow,
to build and to plant."

KEY VERSE

"Do not be afraid of them, for I am with you to deliver you, declares the LORD." —**Jeremiah 1:8**

Photo: Krasimira Nevenova / iStock / Thinkstock

GOD'S URGENT CALL

Unit 2: Calling of Prophets
LESSONS 5–9

LESSON AIMS

After participating in this lesson, each learner will be able to:

1. Describe the Lord's intent for Jeremiah's prophetic ministry.

2. Explain how the gospel accomplishes the objectives given to the prophet in Jeremiah 1:10.

3. Propose a strategy for presenting the gospel to one or more people groups that are especially hostile to its message.

LESSON OUTLINE

Introduction

A. When I Grow Up . . .

"What do you want to be when you grow up?"

When children are asked that question, their answers are remarkably consistent. Occupations such as doctor, athlete, teacher, dancer, police officer, firefighter, scientist, musician, actor, and nurse are common responses.

Regional differences also affect the choices. A child growing up in Silicon Valley might want to be a video-game designer while a child from rural Wisconsin may aspire to be a dairy farmer. Of course, childhood fantasy becomes a consideration with the appearance of such goals as becoming a princess, a superhero, a dinosaur, a mermaid, etc. As people grow older, we expect the answers to that question to become more realistic and not grounded in fantasy. We would look with more than a little surprise at a 19-year-old who still wants to be a superhero!

We probably can recall being asked this same question many times as children, and our responses became more realistic as the years passed. But how many who are reading this now were ever told specifically and honestly, "When you reach adulthood, your career will be that of a ____"? As far-fetched as this may sound, something of the sort *did* happen to a young man named Jeremiah. He was not asked what he wanted to be; he was *told*! Jeremiah came from a priestly background (Jeremiah 1:1), but God had other plans for him.

B. Lesson Background

The prophet Jeremiah began his ministry "in the days of Josiah the son of Amon, king of Judah, in the thirteenth year of his reign" (Jeremiah 1:2). By modern reckoning, that was about 626 BC. These times were increasingly chaotic in the southern kingdom of Judah. Although the Assyrian threat—which resulted in the fall of the northern kingdom of Israel in 722 BC (2 Kings 17:18)—no longer existed, it was being replaced by Babylonian aggression.

Godliness and holiness on the part of the Judeans, not military might, was the key to staving off disaster. Only reliance on and dedication to the true God would turn aside the threat of foreign invasion. In that regard, things may have looked hopeful for a time because of godly King Josiah's dedication to the Lord (2 Chronicles 34:1–35:19). But the spiritual condition of Judah took a quick and fatal turn for the worse after he died in 609 BC.

Four ungodly kings followed him, the final one being his son Zedekiah. It was he who was on the throne when the Babylonians sacked Jerusalem and destroyed Solomon's great temple in 586 BC (2 Kings 24:18–25:7; Jeremiah 1:3).

Another issue of background is Jeremiah's hometown of Anathoth (Jeremiah 1:1). This village was located in the tribal territory of Benjamin, about three miles north-northeast of Jerusalem. Anathoth was a Levite town, a convenient residence for workers in the Jerusalem temple. As a resident of this town, Jeremiah undoubtedly thought he would follow in his father's footsteps in terms of career. But God had other plans.

I. God's Plan
(JEREMIAH 1:4, 5)
A. Jeremiah Foreknown (vv. 4, 5a)

4. Now the word of the LORD came to me, saying,

The first three verses of the book are written in the third person; now the text switches to first person (*me*). Although we're only four verses into the book at this point, this is not the first mention of *the word of the Lord* coming to Jeremiah.

HOW TO SAY IT

Anathoth	*An*-uh-thoth.
Assyrian	Uh-*sear*-e-un.
Babylonian	Bab-ih-*low*-nee-un.
Goliath	Go-*lye*-uth.
Hananiah	Han-uh-*nye*-uh.
Jehoiakim	Jeh-*hoy*-uh-kim.
Josiah	Jo-*sigh*-uh.
Leviticus	Leh-*vit*-ih-kus.
seraphim	*sair*-uh-fim.
Zedekiah	Zed-uh-*kye*-uh.

The previous two verses indicate that *the word of the Lord* begins to come to him during the reign of Josiah and continues to do so through the reign of Zedekiah (see the Lesson Background). This is a total of about 40 years (626–586 BC).

5a. "Before I formed you in the womb I knew you,

The Lord has been active on Jeremiah's behalf long before this moment. The four verbs used of the Lord in the three segments of verse 5 reveal the intimacy of his care for Jeremiah.

First, we note that the word *formed* translates a Hebrew verb that is similarly rendered in Isaiah 29:16. There it refers to a potter's creative activity in making functional and decorative objects from clay. Jeremiah will later be commanded by the Lord to go to a potter's house and learn a lesson from watching the potter work with the clay (compare Jeremiah 18:1-11).

In the Old Testament, the Hebrew word translated *womb* is used of a person's belly (Judges 3:21, 22), the stomach of a person or an animal (Job 20:15; 40:15, 16), as well as of a woman's womb, as here (also Genesis 25:23, 24; 38:27). The intent is clear: God's creative activity includes the life in the womb, a point underlined by David in Psalm 139:13.

The verb in the phrase *I knew you* implies intimacy. It is often used to portray sexual intimacy between a man and his wife (Genesis 4:1, 17; 1 Samuel 1:19), but that is not the case here, of course. David conveys in Psalm 139:1, 2 a similar message about God's knowledge of the present ("O Lord, you have searched me and known me! You know when I sit down and when I rise up; you discern my thoughts from afar"), connecting it with God's knowledge in 139:16.

♦ *OWNERSHIP* ♦

Pottery making is a very old art, still practiced around the world. In developed countries it tends to be done for artistic reasons more than practical ones.

In few places is this more evident than in the one-stoplight town of Seagrove, North Carolina. More than 100 potters call it home, and Seagrove is one of the oldest and largest pottery-making centers in the nation. The town's pottery businesses are housed in old homes, log cabins, and former stores and gas stations.

Deposits of natural clay in the region make the abundance of pottery possible. Even so, no tourist thinks, *I have a right to take any pottery with me for free because the stuff it's made from is little more than abundant dirt.* The potters' work in forming and shaping creates the value!

God used the language of forming pottery in calling Jeremiah to be a prophet. This reminded Jeremiah of the divine claim on him that existed before his birth. It is the same claim that God has on us today (Romans 9:20, 21). *He* formed *us*, not we him (Acts 17:29). —C. R. B.

B. Jeremiah Foreordained (vv. 5b, c)
5b. "and before you were born I consecrated you;

To be *consecrated* is to be sanctified or set apart. It is applied in the Old Testament to both people (such as the Israelites in Leviticus 20:26, who are described as "separated") and objects (such as altars and their accessories in Exodus 40:10).

For Jeremiah this setting apart will become much more than just ritual or ceremony. It will also define the (sometimes harsh) reality of his prophetic ministry. Jeremiah's uncompromising message of judgment will set him apart from rebellious kings (like Zedekiah), fraudulent priests (like Pashhur in Jeremiah 20:1, 2), false prophets (like Hananiah in chapter 28), and those of the general populace who believe that the mere presence of the temple will guarantee safety from any foreign oppressor (7:1-15). Even the people of his hometown will command him to stop prophesying or face death (11:21-23).

What Do You Think?
How does the fact that God knows people even before their birth affect your worldview?
Talking Points for Your Discussion
- Concerning life-purpose
- Concerning sanctity of life
- Concerning personal accountability
- Other

5c. "I appointed you a prophet to the nations."

The Lord reaches the climax of his initial message to Jeremiah and gets specific as to what the man is being set apart to do. The fact that he is to be *a prophet to the nations* implies a ministry that extends beyond the borders of Judah (see Jeremiah 1:10; 25:15-26). The particular construction of the Hebrew phrase translated *I appointed you* is also used in describing roles given by God to Abraham (Genesis 17:5), Moses (Exodus 7:1), the servant of the Lord (Isaiah 49:6), and Ezekiel (Ezekiel 3:17).

Does God set us apart in a similar way—even before birth? One should be cautious in expecting a "call" similar to that of Jeremiah. His call is recorded not so much to give us a specific example to follow, but to tell us why we need to heed the words that we are about to read. The primary call that we are to answer today is that of the gospel to call on the Lord and be saved (Acts 2:21; Romans 10:13). After that we are to pursue the Lord's will and use our talents and spiritual gifts in his service. For some, that may involve full-time service in the church; for others, it may entail ministry in a more secular setting.

II. God's Corrective
(Jeremiah 1:6, 7)
A. Human Self-Doubt (v. 6)
6. Then I said, "Ah, Lord God! Behold, I do not know how to speak, for I am only a youth."

Jeremiah's initial response to the Lord's call is as hesitant as Moses' was (Exodus 3:11, lesson 5). Jeremiah claims a weakness in the area of his speech due to lack of age. One may find it somewhat ironic that Jeremiah is speaking while claiming an inability to speak. But he is likely thinking in terms of lacking the more polished or trained speaking ability that comes with the experience of years. Perhaps like Amos (lesson 9), Jeremiah is concluding that he is "no prophet, nor a prophet's son" (Amos 7:14).

The Hebrew word rendered *only a youth* can describe a wide range of ages from an infant (Exodus 2:6) to a man old enough to marry (Genesis 34:19). Thus it is difficult to know Jeremiah's age at this point. He seems to fear that his age could be a hindrance to addressing others, since youths are generally expected to remain quiet and respect those who are older (Job 32:6, 7).

B. Divine Reassurance (v. 7)

**7. But the LORD said to me,
"Do not say, 'I am only a youth';
for to all to whom I send you, you shall go,
and whatever I command you, you shall
speak."**

The Lord does not deny that Jeremiah is *a youth* (whatever age he may be). Rather, the Lord is telling him that he must not allow that to be an excuse for why he cannot answer the Lord's call. The key to Jeremiah's fulfillment of his ministry will not lie in who he is but in who the Lord is and in Jeremiah's obedience to the Lord's directions. Both audience and message are to be determined by the Lord: *For to all to whom I send you, you shall go, and whatever I command you, you shall speak.*

Given the hostile responses Jeremiah will receive to his message, he may be tempted to give in to fear or intimidation, altering his message to avoid conflict. But the prophet must remember who is calling him and to whom he is accountable. To use Paul's words, Jeremiah must "look not to the things that are seen but to the things that are unseen" (2 Corinthians 4:18).

III. God's Provision
(JEREMIAH 1:8-10)
A. Deliverance (v. 8)

**8. "Do not be afraid of them,
for I am with you to deliver you,
declares the LORD."**

Ezekiel will also be told during the Lord's call to him to *not be afraid* of those who are in his audience (Ezekiel 3:9). Those people will be in Babylon, where the prophet is among those taken captive (1:1). The ones who threaten Jeremiah, on the other hand, are in Jerusalem. They will also include those in his hometown of Anathoth, who will threaten him with death if he does not cease prophesying (Jeremiah 11:21).

I am with you is one of the most frequent assurances from the Lord in Scripture. It is the same assurance that was offered to timid Moses (Exodus 3:12, lesson 5). It is the same assurance given to followers of Jesus today as they carry his gospel to the nations (Matthew 28:18-20).

The Hebrew word translated *deliver* is used of the Israelites' rescue from their oppression in Egypt (Exodus 3:8; 18:10) and of David's deliverance from the lion, the bear, and Goliath (1 Samuel 17:37). Jeremiah will require such divine rescue from the enemies that oppress and harass him throughout his ministry.

B. Message (v. 9)

9. Then the LORD put out his hand and touched my mouth. And the LORD said to me, "Behold, I have put my words in your mouth.

Now comes a visual aid intended to offer additional support to Jeremiah. The Lord's action is reminiscent of what happens to Isaiah, only with Isaiah one of the seraphim comes to him and touches his lips with a burning coal taken from an altar (Isaiah 6:5-7, lesson 6). Here it is the Lord who reaches *out his hand* and touches Jeremiah's *mouth.*

By adding *I have put my words in your mouth* to this action, the Lord specifically addresses

Jeremiah's earlier objection that he does "not know how to speak" (v. 6, above). Now, having received the Lord's words, he must speak! Or as Amos puts it, "The Lord God has spoken; who can but prophesy?" (Amos 3:8).

The Lord's declaration of putting his words in Jeremiah's mouth calls to mind the Lord's promise to Moses in Deuteronomy 18:18: "I will raise up for them a prophet like you from among their brothers. And I will put my words in his mouth, and he shall speak to them all that I command him." While this prophecy is said to be fulfilled in Jesus (Acts 3:22, 23), perhaps it can also be applied to God's provision of the prophetic ministry to his people, as illustrated by Jeremiah.

God also says through Moses that "whoever will not listen to my words that he shall speak in my name, I myself will require it of him" (Deuteronomy 18:19). This too comes to pass through Jeremiah; when the people of Judah to heed his words, they pay the price through their country being conquered and the citizens taken captive.

> ### What Do You Think?
> What are some specific steps to take to ensure that the words we utter are consistent with God's Word (Psalm 39:1; 119:13)?
> *Talking Points for Your Discussion*
> - In steps of personal devotion (Psalm 119:148; Matthew 6:6-15; etc.)
> - In steps to seeking godly counsel and teaching (2 Chronicles 25:16; Hebrews 13:7; etc.)
> - In steps to gain understanding of the times (1 Chronicles 12:32; Matthew 16:3; etc.)

C. Mission (v. 10)

10. "See, I have set you over this day over nations and over kingdoms, to pluck up and to break down, to destroy and to overthrow, to build and to plant."

Jeremiah will spend most of his life in Judah (chapters 41–44 of the book of Jeremiah record his journey to Egypt after the fall of Jerusalem). But his prophetic ministry will have an impact far beyond Judah. God will set him *over nations and over kingdoms*, but not due to any of Jeremiah's own achievements or merit. This will occur only because the Lord has placed his words in Jeremiah's mouth. The authority is from the Lord alone. Chapters 46–51 of the book of Jeremiah include the prophet's oracles directed against various nations and kingdoms of his day, including a particularly lengthy one against Babylon in chapters 50 and 51.

The nature of Jeremiah's ministry to the nations is then pictured through a series of verbs: *to pluck up and to break down, to destroy and to overthrow, to build and to plant.* The first four are negative; the final two are more hopeful and promising. This may indicate that Jeremiah's ministry will be more negative than positive, but it will conclude on a positive note: hope will prevail beyond the current tragic circumstances in Judah that will culminate in divine judgment. Jeremiah does offer hope—of a future king who will "execute justice and righteousness in the land" (Jeremiah 23:5, 6) and of a new covenant (31:31-34).

The language of the verse before us is used elsewhere in the book of Jeremiah to highlight God's activity in fulfilling Jeremiah's prophetic words (Jeremiah 18:7-10; 24:6; 31:28; 32:41; 42:10; 45:4). This is a way of affirming that the Lord makes certain that Jeremiah's ministry will accomplish exactly what the Lord has intended it to do.

◆ WORD POWER ◆

The source of the adage "The pen is mightier than the sword"—the wording if not the concept itself—is the 1839 play *Richelieu*, by English playwright Edward Bulwer-Lytton. The idea is that communication gets things done more effectively than does the violence of armed confrontation.

But it's not always a simple either-or choice, since written and spoken communication can lead and has led to use of the sword. The twisted words of Adolf Hitler persuaded his country and its allies to launch a world war; the candid words of Winston Churchill galvanized his country and its allies to meet violence with violence to defeat that threat.

Twisted communication seems almost to be an art form these days, designed to influence behavior rather than to communicate truth. George Orwell, writing in 1949, predicted as much (and worse) in his novel *1984*: "If thought corrupts language, language can also corrupt thought." Since the year he wrote that, the world has seen no fewer than 17 countries include the wording or idea of *Democratic Republic* in their designations; yet the citizens in the majority of these countries enjoy few of the freedoms available in Western democracies.

None of this should come as a surprise to readers of the Bible. The Scriptures record numerous instances in which human communication results in violence being avoided, as well as violence being initiated or intensified. (Contrast the results of Gideon's tactful response to the angry Ephraimites in Judges 8:1-3 with those of Jephthah's confrontational response in 12:1-6.)

Given how much power human words have to incite violence and to quell it, to hurt and to heal, to depress and to encourage, how much more must the same be true of the Word of the living God! He still seeks those who will take his Word to build so that he does not have to destroy (compare Ezekiel 22:30). What will be your response to his invitation?   —C. R. B.

Visual for Lesson 7. *Point to this visual as you ask how the objection of age in verse 6 can relate to Paul's admonition in 1 Timothy 4:12.*

> **What Do You Think?**
> What is God calling you to do on a daily basis?
> *Talking Points for Your Discussion*
> - Regarding things "to destroy"
> - Regarding things "to build and to plant"

Conclusion

A. No Solos

With certain tasks, one's ability to go it alone without any assistance is the measure of success. A would-be pilot must fly his or her plane solo. A young driver takes great pride in being able to drive to and from school or work without Mom or Dad riding along. From youth, it seems, to do something "all by myself" becomes the standard of success in many areas of life.

In contrast, God said that his presence, his words, and his purpose were to identify Jeremiah's ministry. Never would there be a time when he would have to go solo, even as he suffered perhaps more persecution and harassment than any other prophet in the Old Testament. "No solos" can be a difficult concept to accept and apply in many areas of one's life, but it is absolutely vital to apply in our service for the Lord.

Let us remember that there was never a self-made prophet or a self-made apostle. And there are no self-made servants of Jesus in the twenty-first century. We must draw our strength from the Lord! It was a go-it-alone philosophy that led humanity into the tragedy of sin in the Garden of Eden, the consequences of which still reverberate. If the temptation to "fly solo" spiritually grows as you gain skills and knowledge with the passing years, remember: "Not by might, nor by power, but by my Spirit, says the Lord of hosts" (Zechariah 4:6).

B. Prayer

Father, help us avoid the extremes of fearful silence and go-it-alone arrogance! Let us rather be always and only your instruments to speak the words of confrontation and comfort as you enable us. We pray this in Jesus' name. Amen.

C. Thought to Remember

A child of God is no mere child!

INVOLVEMENT LEARNING

Enhance your lesson presentation with the reproducible activity page,
available as a free download at www.standardlesson.com.

Into the Lesson

Make arrangements ahead of time for a class of elementary-age children to visit your class. Begin class by pointing to a specific child at random and asking what he or she wants to be when grown up. Repeat the question for each child, jotting responses on the board as you go.

After all children have answered, thank them and their teacher as you release them to return to their own class. (If you have a computer or mobile devise, you may wish to play a prerecorded clip from the Internet of children being asked that question.)

Alternative. Distribute copies of the "When I Grow Up" activity from the reproducible page, which you can download. Have students work this puzzle in small groups or as a class activity.

After either activity lead into Bible study by saying, "We probably can recall being asked that same question many times when we were children. We probably gave some of the same or similar answers. Today we will look at a variation of this scenario in the call of a Bible prophet. God did not ask Jeremiah what he wanted to be. He *told* him!"

Into the Word

Divide the class into three groups, and give each group paper, pens, and one of the following Bible research assignments. Suggested responses are listed under each assignment.

Group 1—God's Plan (Jeremiah 1:4, 5)

Find statements about what God had already done.

"I formed you."

"I knew you."

"I consecrated you."

"I appointed you."

Group 2—God's Command (Jeremiah 1:6-8a)

Find statements about what God was commanding Jeremiah to do or not do.

"Do not say, 'I am only a youth.'"

"To all to whom I send you, you shall go."

"Whatever I command you, you shall speak."

"Do not be afraid of them."

Group 3—God's Provision (Jeremiah 1:8b-10)

Find statements about how God would provide for Jeremiah and his mission.

"I am with you to deliver you."

"I have put my words in your mouth."

"I have set you . . . over kingdoms."

Allow time for groups to share and summarize their Scripture assignments with the rest of the class.

Into Life

Say, "Jeremiah protested that he was not mature enough to be God's servant. That seems like a protest we could all make. Note, however, God's solution—God put his words in Jeremiah's mouth! That solution is also ours. God's Word can be in our mouths when we study it daily."

To help your students see how God's Word aided Jeremiah in the most trying of circumstances, give them the following schedule for devotional reading this week:

Sunday—Death threats (Jeremiah 11:18-20)

Monday—Betrayal (Jeremiah 12:5-13)

Tuesday—Beatings (Jeremiah 20:1-6)

Wednesday—His message censored (Jeremiah 36:1-26)

Thursday—Left to die (Jeremiah 38:1-13)

Friday—Taken to Egypt (Jeremiah 43:1-13)

Saturday—Witnessed the destruction of Jerusalem (Jeremiah 52:1-30)

Alternative. Distribute copies of the "I Want to Be . . ." activity from the reproducible page. This exercise will help students choose areas in which they need to mature and to memorize Scripture that will remind them of God's will in that specific area of their lives.

EZEKIEL

DEVOTIONAL READING: Ezekiel 17:22-24
BACKGROUND SCRIPTURE: Ezekiel 1–3

EZEKIEL 3:1-11

¹ And he said to me, "Son of man, eat whatever you find here. Eat this scroll, and go, speak to the house of Israel." ² So I opened my mouth, and he gave me this scroll to eat. ³ And he said to me, "Son of man, feed your belly with this scroll that I give you and fill your stomach with it." Then I ate it, and it was in my mouth as sweet as honey.

⁴ And he said to me, "Son of man, go to the house of Israel and speak with my words to them. ⁵ For you are not sent to a people of foreign speech and a hard language, but to the house of Israel— ⁶ not to many peoples of foreign speech and a hard language, whose words you cannot understand. Surely, if I sent you to such, they would listen to you. ⁷ But the house of Israel will not be willing to listen to you, for they are not willing to listen to me: because all the house of Israel have a hard forehead and a stubborn heart. ⁸ Behold, I have made your face as hard as their faces, and your forehead as hard as their foreheads. ⁹ Like emery harder than flint have I made your forehead. Fear them not, nor be dismayed at their looks, for they are a rebellious house." ¹⁰ Moreover,

he said to me, "Son of man, all my words that I shall speak to you receive in your heart, and hear with your ears. ¹¹ And go to the exiles, to your people, and speak to them and say to them, 'Thus says the Lord GOD,' whether they hear or refuse to hear."

KEY VERSES

[The Lord] said to me, "Son of man, all my words that I shall speak to you receive in your heart, and hear with your ears. And go to the exiles, to your people, and speak to them and say to them, 'Thus says the Lord GOD,' whether they hear or refuse to hear." —Ezekiel 3:10, 11

GOD'S
URGENT CALL

Unit 2: Calling of Prophets
LESSONS 5–9

LESSON AIMS

After participating in this lesson, each learner will be able to:

1. Describe the context of Ezekiel's call.

2. Contrast the difficulty of correcting those who don't know better with the difficulty of correcting those who should and/or do know better.

3. Identify situations in modern churches about which one should be "hardheaded."

LESSON OUTLINE

Introduction

A. Gourmet or Garbage?

Foods considered delicacies in some parts of the world may turn stomachs in others. For example, in Mexico City you may be offered a dish called *escamoles*. At first glance it may look like some sort of cooked grain. Don't ask, or you will be told that escamoles are ant larvae!

Casa marzu is a traditional Sardinian cheese. You may balk when you learn that the Italian name for it is *formaggio marcio*, meaning "rotten cheese." If it seems to you that it is moving, it is. This "delicacy" is a sheep-milk cheese filled with live maggots!

Coffee lovers may be tempted to try *kopi luwak*, the most expensive coffee money can buy. Some specialty coffee shops sell the brew for $80 per cup. The reason this Indonesian delicacy is rare is that the coffee beans are first eaten by a type of wild cat, then collected after the beans have made their way through the animal's digestive system!

At one time or another, our reluctance to eat a certain food was met by someone saying, "Just try it!" The call of Ezekiel held forth a similar challenge. Ezekiel was commissioned to prophesy to people who found God's Word unappetizing. Therefore God offered Ezekiel a taste test.

B. Lesson Background

The prophet Ezekiel was a contemporary of the prophet Jeremiah (see lesson 7). Both were living at the time Jerusalem fell to the Babylonians in 586 BC. Jeremiah was likely some years older than Ezekiel since (1) Jeremiah saw himself as "only a youth" when he received his call from the Lord (Jeremiah 1:6) in 626 BC and (2) Ezekiel was 30 years old (if that's the correct reference of the text) in "the fifth year of the exile of King Jehoiachin" (Ezekiel 1:1, 2), which was the year 592 BC. Thus Ezekiel would have been born in 622 BC. Perhaps there was some personal contact between Ezekiel and Jeremiah prior to Ezekiel's captivity. But the Scriptures are silent on that.

Ezekiel is introduced as "the priest" (Ezekiel 1:3). And that is what he would have been had it not been for the tragic turn of events in the southern kingdom of Judah. The first stage in these events came in 605 BC, when Daniel and his friends were taken captive to Babylon (2 Kings 24:1, 2; Daniel 1:1-6). Ezekiel's relocation to Babylon was a part of the second stage of exile; he was among the 10,000 of the elite citizenry taken in 597 BC (2 Kings 24:12-14).

Daniel and other Jews were taken to serve "in the king's palace" (Daniel 1:4), while Ezekiel found himself in a completely different setting: "among the exiles by the Chebar canal" (Ezekiel 1:1). Even so, "the hand of the Lord was upon him" (1:3). It was there that the Lord proceeded to call the priest to a task he undoubtedly did not anticipate.

The call began with an intense display of what Ezekiel describes as "the appearance of the likeness of the glory of the Lord," which caused Ezekiel to fall facedown (Ezekiel 1:28). Then followed this command: "Son of man, stand on your feet, and I will speak with you" (2:1). As with other call accounts in this unit, Ezekiel's included both sounds and sights. The sound was the voice of the Lord. The sight was, first, the awe-inspiring glory of the Lord, then an outstretched hand that held "a scroll of a book" (2:9). As we recall from lesson 6, taste was the one bodily sense of five that Isaiah did not experience in his call. The situation was different with Ezekiel, however!

Visual for Lesson 8. *Point to this visual as you ask, "In what ways does resistance to the Word of God manifest itself today? How should we respond?"*

I. Tasted Words
(Ezekiel 3:1-4)
A. Command to Eat, Part 1 (vv. 1, 2)
1a. And he said to me, "Son of man,

The designation *Son of man* occurs over 90 times in the book of Ezekiel, always when the Lord is addressing the prophet. We recognize this phrase as a self-designation of Jesus in the New Testament, a title of messianic significance as it reflects Daniel 7:13, 14. However, the phrase does not appear to have any messianic significance when applied to Ezekiel. *Son of man* simply draws attention to the humanity and mortality of Ezekiel in contrast with the eternal God who calls him.

1b. "eat whatever you find here. Eat this scroll,

The *scroll* that Ezekiel is commanded to eat is the one written "on the front and on the back" with "words of lamentation and mourning and woe" in Ezekiel 2:10. Language such as this points to the visionary nature of Ezekiel's call. It is similar to John's dietary experience in Revelation 10:8-11, though the aftereffect in each case is quite different, as later noted.

1c. "and go, speak to the house of Israel."

It is important that Ezekiel first receives the message within himself. Only then is he qualified to carry out the command we see here. God's Word must become a part of the messenger before the messenger can impart it to others.

2. So I opened my mouth, and he gave me this scroll to eat.

Ezekiel complies. Those who preach on the importance of obedience to the Lord must first be obedient to him themselves.

B. Command to Eat, Part 2 (vv. 3, 4)
3a. And he said to me, "Son of man, feed your belly with this scroll that I give you and fill your stomach with it." Then I ate it,

For Ezekiel to eat the scroll signifies that God's message is to become the prophet's source of spiritual nourishment. The comparison of God's Word with food is found elsewhere in the Bible (Psalm 119:103; Hebrews 5:12-14; 1 Peter 2:2, 3).

The phrasing *fill your stomach with it* points to the thoroughness with which Ezekiel is to receive

God's message that is written on the scroll. The word translated *stomach* is used figuratively in the Old Testament to describe an individual's inner self—the place of understanding and/or emotion. Other translations are "heart" (Psalm 40:8) and "inmost self" (Isaiah 16:11).

3b. and it was in my mouth as sweet as honey.

The sweet taste that follows Ezekiel's eating of the scroll may seem odd since its contents consist only of "lamentation and mourning and woe" (Ezekiel 2:10). Most likely the sweetness is linked to Ezekiel's faithfulness to his appointed task. Even though his message will not be pleasant to hear and the audience will be resistant and hostile (a point the Lord will make shortly), Ezekiel's fulfillment will come from his faithful delivery of the words given by the one who has called him (compare Jeremiah 15:16).

We must grasp the significance of honey in this era to get the full impact. Today we tend to view honey as one sweetener among many that are readily available (cane sugar, corn syrup, etc.). But the people of Ezekiel's time and place do not have all these options. Honey is a delicacy (compare Proverbs 25:16). Psalm 19:9-11 places it alongside gold in a comparison with "the rules of the Lord" by which "your servant [is] warned." God's decrees can be sweet, because "in keeping them there is great reward."

However, we note a certain contrast when the apostle John ingests "the scroll" in his heavenly vision in Revelation. It is "sweet as honey" at first, but turns bitter in his stomach (Revelation 10:8-10). Perhaps that is because the judgments John bears witness to are the harshest in Scripture, eternal in their scope.

4. And he said to me, "Son of man, go to the house of Israel and speak with my words to them.

Here are the three essentials in conveying God's message in any era. First, we must take the initiative and *go*. Second, we must have an audience. Third, we must have a message from God.

II. Tested People
(Ezekiel 3:5-7)
A. Same Language (vv. 5, 6)

5. "For you are not sent to a people of foreign speech and a hard language, but to the house of Israel—

The prophet Daniel's concurrent ministry is with *a people of foreign speech*, a language he and his friends are expected to learn (Daniel 1:4). Ezekiel, on the other hand, is to speak to people who share his identity and heritage: *the house of Israel*. One would think this would be a plus for communicating the Lord's message. But such will not be the case, as the Lord proceeds to explain.

6. "not to many peoples of foreign speech and a hard language, whose words you cannot understand. Surely, if I sent you to such, they would listen to you.

Language barriers can be difficult to overcome. But here the Lord tells Ezekiel that those of other lands and of *foreign speech and a hard language* would have welcomed the prophet's message. Those in Nineveh, for example, heeded Jonah's preaching and turned to God in a national expression of repentance (Jonah 3:4, 5). Jesus cites that incident in an indictment of those in his day who refuse to repent in response to his preaching (Matthew 12:41; compare 11:20-24).

B. Same Result (v. 7)

7. "But the house of Israel will not be willing to listen to you, for they are not willing to listen to me: because all the house of Israel have a hard forehead and a stubborn heart.

By contrast, *the house of Israel* (God's covenant people) *will not be willing to listen to* Ezekiel. Of course, ultimately it is not Ezekiel-the-spokesman who is rejected, but God. The prediction reminds us of what God told Samuel when the elders of Israel demanded a king: "They have not rejected you, but they have rejected me" (1 Samuel 8:7). Centuries later, Jesus will speak in similar terms to his disciples: "the one who rejects you rejects me, and the one who rejects me rejects him who sent me" (Luke 10:16).

God uses highly unflattering terms to portray his people: *hard* and *stubborn.* One would think that a people in captivity as a result of God's judgment on them would be more sensitive to spiritual matters and willing to heed his prophet! Some will be willing to give the prophet a hearing and will encourage others to do so as well (Ezekiel 33:30). But Ezekiel's audience ultimately sees him as an entertainer (33:32) and as one whose message is obscure (20:49). Their response ends up being nothing more than lip service (33:31, 32).

◆ *WAVELENGTH* ◆

Living in Ukraine, another American and I were spending several weeks in intense language training. There were many chances for miscommunication. One problem stemmed from Russian words that sounded or looked like English words.

One day our teacher was drilling us with flash cards that featured Russian words for common objects. The drill required that we point to pictures of the objects, and the word *krovat* kept tripping us up. We thought it was a type of necktie, but there was no such picture. We tried to describe it to the instructor, but she could not understand. Finally she pointed to the correct picture: *krovat* meant "bed."

We found that hilarious. Before long the teacher was laughing with us. Something that started as a communication gap ended as a bonding experience. Although we didn't speak the

same language, we did indeed end up on the same wavelength.

Ezekiel's problem was the exact opposite. Sent to people who spoke his language, his message ended up being rejected because his fellow Israelites were not on God's spiritual wavelength. It's bad enough to face misunderstandings; it's worse to be understood but rejected anyway. May we have the strength God gave Ezekiel to face such opposition when it comes. —L. M. W.

> **What Do You Think?**
> What are some ways for Christians to prepare themselves for negative reactions that may come when sin is confronted within a church?
> *Talking Points for Your Discussion*
> - For reactions that hide behind Matthew 7:1
> - For reactions that hide behind John 8:7
> - For reactions that hide behind cultural concepts of "privacy"
> - Other

III. Toughened Prophet
(EZEKIEL 3:8-11)

A. Unyielding Messenger (vv. 8, 9)

8. "Behold, I have made your face as hard as their faces, and your forehead as hard as their foreheads.

God will not change the prophet's message to make it less offensive to the hostile crowd, but he will change his prophet. In that light, God makes Ezekiel's *face* and *forehead* as hard as theirs.

The language pictures intense resistance toward the prophet, but also sufficient resources to counter it. Anyone who tries to "butt heads" with Ezekiel will meet his or her match and then some! The Lord's promise to Ezekiel is similar to that which he gives to Jeremiah (Jeremiah 1:17-19) and to Moses (Exodus 7:1-5). The name Ezekiel means "God strengthens" or "God hardens" in Hebrew. God is promising his messenger the power to live up to his name.

9. "Like emery harder than flint have I made your forehead. Fear them not, nor be dismayed at their looks, for they are a rebellious house."

The word translated *like emery* is an adjective meaning "firm" or "unyielding." But it can also describe any substance, such as *flint*, of extreme hardness. Because of such preparation, Ezekiel is to *fear them not, nor be dismayed* by his opposition.

Fear seems to be a common initial reaction of those called by God, so God reassures those he calls with various promises of his sustaining power. Ezekiel must not give in to his fears, though the opposition he is to face is likened to "briers and thorns" and "scorpions" (Ezekiel 2:6).

◆ *STUBBORNNESS AS A GO(O)D THING* ◆

My children love computers. So for the first week of summer break, we let them have unlimited time on the home computer.

After a week of bloodshot eyes and disengaged children, we initiated a strict time limit. The first few days we saw rebellion. They stubbornly insisted that they couldn't do any of their summer projects without online video instructions. They extolled the merits of learning correct keyboarding and keeping up with their generation by participating in online games.

We stood firm, however, and took them on bike rides to the park. We had family game time or group reading time. We invited neighborhood kids over to play. We baked cookies and made dinner together. Within a few days, the powerful habit of continuous computer usage was broken.

HOW TO SAY IT

Babylon	*Bab*-uh-lun.
Babylonians	Bab-ih-*low*-nee-unz.
casa marzu	*caw*-zoo **marh**-zoo.
Chebar	*Kee*-bar.
escamoles	ess-kuh-*mow*-less.
Ezekiel	Ee-*zeek*-ee-ul or Ee-*zeek*-yul.
formaggio marcio	fohr-*mod*-djoh *mar*-choh.
kopi luwak	co-*pea* lu-*wah*.
krovat	*craw*-vawht.
messianic	mess-ee-*an*-ick.
Moab	*Mo*-ab.
Nebuchadnezzar	*Neb*-yuh-kud-**nez**-er.
Nineveh	*Nin*-uh-vuh.
Solomon	*Sol*-o-mun.

Children can be stubbornly persistent in using childish logic to persuade parents to give them their hearts' desires! But when those desires threaten their development, parents must be more stubborn than their children. They must make rules and stick with them until the children themselves see the value of those rules.

Ezekiel faced what amounted to a nation of spiritual children. In that regard, they stubbornly insisted on following the ungodly way of their ancestors, "a stubborn and rebellious generation" (Psalm 78:8). Ezekiel had to match their stubborn hardheadedness with his own, since he was right and they were wrong.

We must cling to the truth. This does not give us license to hurt those who disagree, since our hardheadedness is based in the softheartedness of John 3:16. But the exercise of softhearted compassion must not result in our spiritual compass pointing anywhere but to God alone.

—L. M. W.

B. Unyielding Message (vv. 10, 11)

10. Moreover, he said to me, "Son of man, all my words that I shall speak to you receive in your heart, and hear with your ears.

The Lord desires that Ezekiel *receive in* his *heart* what he is now hearing. The prophet has already had to "stomach" these words (Ezekiel 3:3, above), and the inclusion of *heart* stresses how complete Ezekiel's reception of the Lord's message must be.

The words of Psalm 119:11 are applicable: "I have stored up your word in my heart, that I might not sin against you." Ezekiel may be in captivity on foreign soil, but God's Word is in no way held captive (see 2 Timothy 2:9).

11. "And go to the exiles, to your people, and speak to them and say to them, 'Thus says the Lord GOD,' whether they hear or refuse to hear."

The Lord has spoken of Ezekiel's audience as "hard," "stubborn," "rebellious," and "not willing to listen" in today's text. These add to their depiction as "briers and thorns" and "scorpions" in Ezekiel 2:6. Now, however, as the Lord's commission to Ezekiel comes to its conclusion, he describes the exiles in somewhat softer terms as *your people.*

This phrasing indicates that Ezekiel is in the same situation as his fellow Israelites. It is a situation of servitude to a foreign power in a foreign land. They suffer with Ezekiel the same result of God's judgment. Because of their stubborn disobedience and refusal to heed prophetic warnings, the people deserve to be where they are. But they are still Ezekiel's kin; he shares with them a common identity as part of the covenant people.

Ezekiel undoubtedly views his fellow Israelites with the same compassion that moves the apostle Paul to say centuries later, "For I could wish that I myself were accursed and cut off from Christ for the sake of my brothers, my kinsmen according to the flesh" (Romans 9:3).

At the same time, Ezekiel's compassion must not be allowed to alter the Lord's message. Ezekiel still must declare, *"Thus says the Lord God."* Resistance to the message must not influence the prophet's delivery of it. *Whether they hear or refuse to hear* makes no difference in that regard. Ezekiel's primary duty is to remain faithful to the Lord's message. His listeners must decide for themselves whether they will do the same.

The Lord will expand on this point in Ezekiel 3:16-27, where the prophet's work is compared with that of a watchman. The watchman can only sound the alarm when an enemy approaches; it is up to the residents of a city or town to take appropriate action. If Ezekiel is faithful to his duties as a watchman yet his listeners scorn his warnings, then they will have no one to blame but themselves when disaster comes.

Conclusion
A. Balancing Act

God called Ezekiel to walk a prophetic tightrope. On one hand, he was given a message that was filled with mourning and woe. On the other hand, he noted that the message was nourishing and sweet. God's harshest rebukes are given for the eternal good of the hearer.

Christians today are faced with a similar balancing act. Some complain that Christianity is a religion of *no* and that we are defined only by what we are against. On the other hand, some look at positive, affirming messages and then grumble that the church does not take sin seriously anymore! How do we preach the sweetness of the gospel without compromising what the Bible says about the seriousness of sin?

The prophecies of Ezekiel contain some of the bleakest words in Scripture regarding the fate of those who resist the truth of God's Word. But the same prophecies contain great words of hope and conclude with the promise, "The Lord Is There" (Ezekiel 48:35). May we seek to offer that same balanced message today.

B. Prayer

Father, harden us against whatever opposition we may encounter; but keep our hearts soft with your compassion for a lost world. We pray this in Jesus' name. Amen.

C. Thought to Remember

A message of judgment without grace
is no gospel at all.

INVOLVEMENT LEARNING

Enhance your lesson presentation with the reproducible activity page,
available as a free download at www.standardlesson.com.

Into the Lesson

Begin the class by playing a game of "Would You Rather?" Read from the list of food pairs below, asking class members to stand if they would rather eat the first item of the pair and remain seated if they would prefer the second food item. Encourage students to decide quickly.

Ask, "Would you rather eat . . ."
. . . spinach or brussels sprouts?
. . . tofu or cottage cheese?
. . . mushrooms or turnips?
. . . black licorice or cotton candy?
. . . anchovies or oysters?
. . . mayonnaise or sour cream?
. . . liver or Spam®?
. . . pea soup or lima beans?

Alternative. Distribute copies of the "Gourmet or Garbage" activity from the reproducible page, which you can download. You may do this as a class or as a small-group activity.

After either activity, lead into the Bible study by saying, "Some foods seem extremely unappetizing to us. At some time or another, our reluctance to eat a certain food was met by someone saying, 'Just try it!' The call of Ezekiel held a similar challenge. Ezekiel was commissioned to prophesy to people who found God's Word unappetizing. For that reason, God offered Ezekiel a taste test."

Into the Word

Divide your class into three groups, and give each group paper and pens. Each group should be assigned a section of the lesson text with a key image from that section. Each group is to summarize the lesson text as instructions to someone who wants to share the gospel today. They are to use straightforward language, not using the main image they are given.

Scripture assignments and sample instructions follow:

Group 1—The Scroll (Ezekiel 3:1-4)
Before you share God's Word, you must experience it for yourself. It should become a part of you, and you must be convinced of its goodness.

Group 2—House of Israel (Ezekiel 3:5-7)
The most difficult people to reach are not those who know nothing about God. It is those who should know better! Stubborn people are resistant people.

Group 3—Hard Head (Ezekiel 3:8-11)
Those who bring the gospel must be tough. You will be tempted to back down or compromise for acceptance. Don't do it! Be firm and stand strong!

Allow time for groups to share their instructions and summarize their Scripture assignments.

Into Life

Write this on the board: *Ezekiel was challenged to present the sweetness of God's message without sugarcoating it.* Ask the class to explain this statement.

Write each of the challenges below on separate index cards. Divide the class into three groups, and give each group one of the cards. Have groups discuss how they would present the sweetness of the gospel without backing away from truth for the challenges they are given.

Group 1—Unloving Christians
Christians today only say what they are against. They are such haters!

Group 2—Silent God
I believed when I was a child. I prayed and prayed that my parents would not divorce, but God ignored my prayers. I ignore him now!

Group 3—Living Life
I may consider following God later in life. I have too much living to do now!

Alternative. Distribute copies of the "Rock Solid" activity from the reproducible page. Use it in class or as a take-home exercise.

AMOS

DEVOTIONAL READING: Psalm 119:1-8
BACKGROUND SCRIPTURE: Amos 7

AMOS 7:10-17

¹⁰ Then Amaziah the priest of Bethel sent to Jeroboam king of Israel, saying, "Amos has conspired against you in the midst of the house of Israel. The land is not able to bear all his words. ¹¹ For thus Amos has said,

"'Jeroboam shall die by the sword,
    and Israel must go into exile
    away from his land.'"

¹² And Amaziah said to Amos, "O seer, go, flee away to the land of Judah, and eat bread there, and prophesy there, ¹³ but never again prophesy at Bethel, for it is the king's sanctuary, and it is a temple of the kingdom." ¹⁴ Then Amos answered and said to Amaziah, "I was no prophet, nor a prophet's son, but I was a herdsman and a dresser of sycamore figs. ¹⁵ But the LORD took me from following the flock, and the LORD said to me, 'Go, prophesy to my people Israel.' ¹⁶ Now therefore hear the word of the LORD.

"You say, 'Do not prophesy against Israel,
    and do not preach against the house of
    Isaac.'

¹⁷ Therefore thus says the LORD:

"'Your wife shall be a prostitute in the city,
    and your sons and your daughters shall
    fall by the sword,
    and your land shall be divided up with
    a measuring line;
you yourself shall die in an unclean land,
    and Israel shall surely go into exile away
    from its land.'"

KEY VERSES

Amos answered and said to Amaziah, "I was no prophet, nor a prophet's son, but I was a herdsman and a dresser of sycamore figs. But the LORD took me from following the flock, and the LORD said to me, 'Go, prophesy to my people Israel.'" —**Amos 7:14, 15**

GOD'S URGENT CALL

Unit 2: Calling of Prophets
LESSONS 5–9

LESSON AIMS

After participating in this lesson, each learner will be able to:

1. Summarize the nature of the resistance to Amos's message and his response to that resistance.

2. Compare and contrast that resistance with modern resistance to the gospel.

3. Write a short "letter to the editor" that contrasts a biblical view of a current controversy with the prevailing secular view.

LESSON OUTLINE

Introduction

A. What's My Profession?

A young man in seminary was very talented. So talented that he believed that it was only fair that he offer his services as a minister of the gospel to the highest bidder. He spent time poring over data to discover which denomination offered the highest average salary. He was more than willing to tailor his doctrine to the beliefs of those willing to pay him for it!

In contrast, we all know individuals who serve faithfully in full-time ministry as a vocation. There is certainly nothing wrong with a preacher's being paid a living wage as compensation for his work (1 Corinthians 9:7-14). There need be no conflict between earning a living and being an obedient servant of God. Although we would hope that the attitude of the man above is rare, those who choose vocational ministry struggle with a difficult question: *Is there a difference between a **professing** and a **professional** follower of Christ?*

During his task of proclaiming judgment, the prophet Amos was confronted by a man who was paid for being a priest but who did not profess God's truth faithfully. Their conflict is insightful.

B. Lesson Background: Israel in General

Amos was one of the many prophets whom God raised up during the period of the divided monarchy (931–722 BC) in Old Testament history. His ministry took place during the reigns of Uzziah as king of Judah and Jeroboam as king of Israel (Amos 1:1). Commentators generally refer to this Jeroboam as Jeroboam II to distinguish him from the Jeroboam who was the first king of northern Israel after the nation divided.

Both Uzziah and Jeroboam II experienced lengthy reigns: Uzziah (also known as Azariah) from 792 to 740 BC and Jeroboam from 793 to 753 BC (dates are approximate). Spiritually, however, the kings were quite different. The Scriptures record that Uzziah "did what was right in the eyes of the Lord" (2 Chronicles 26:4; an exception being the incident noted in 26:16-21). Jeroboam, by contrast, "did what was evil in the sight of the Lord" (2 Kings 14:24).

In fact, no kings of the northern nation of Israel were considered good or godly. This is an important reason the northern kingdom fell under God's judgment much sooner than did the southern kingdom of Judah. Prophets like Amos came on the scene to sound the alarm and warn of coming judgment. Many Bible students date the start of his ministry around 755 BC, toward the conclusions of the reigns of Uzziah and Jeroboam.

Amos himself seemed an unlikely candidate for the prophetic task. He was a simple shepherd and fruit farmer from a village in Judah (Amos 7:14, part of today's text), but God sent him to shepherd his wayward people of northern Israel. In the warnings prior to today's text, Amos prophesied God's condemnation of various locations around Israel, including the southern kingdom of Judah (1:3–2:5). That was followed by a long, scathing indictment of Israel. Injustice was rampant there, and God intended to correct that problem (4:1; 5:7, 10-12; etc.).

C. Lesson Background: Bethel in Particular

A major factor in the spiritual decline of northern Israel was the idolatry encouraged by Jeroboam I when he set up golden calves to be worshipped in the towns of Bethel and Dan. He did so to keep his residents of the northern kingdom from traveling to Jerusalem, worshipping at

HOW TO SAY IT

Ahab	*Ay*-hab.
Amaziah	Am-uh-*zye*-uh.
Azariah	Az-uh-*rye*-uh.
Amos	*Ay*-mus.
Assyrians	Uh-*sear*-e-unz.
Bethel	*Beth*-ul.
Elijah	Ee-*lye*-juh.
Elisha	Ee-*lye*-shuh.
Ezekiel	Ee-*zeek*-ee-ul or Ee-*zeek*-yul.
Jeroboam	Jair-uh-*boe*-um.
Mosaic	Mo-*zay*-ik.
Rehoboam	Ree-huh-*boe*-um.
Samaria	Suh-*mare*-ee-uh.
Uzziah	Uh-*zye*-uh.
Zion	*Zi*-un.

the temple, and reaffirming their allegiance to the house of David (1 Kings 12:26-30).

Bethel was still quite active as a pagan shrine in Amos's day, nearly 200 years later (Amos 3:14; 7:13). The spiritual danger posed by that center of idolatry, only 11 miles due north of Jerusalem, was immense. The danger was underlined by the fact of Bethel's association by reputation with Gilgal, another center of idolatry (4:4; 5:5). The prophet Hosea mocks Bethel (which means "house of God") by referring to it as "Beth-aven" (which means "house of wickedness"), associating it with Gilgal in the process (Hosea 4:15).

Bethel is mentioned by name seven times in the book of Amos. The text of today's lesson features the last two of those seven.

I. Professional Priest
(Amos 7:10-13)
A. Report to the King (vv. 10, 11)

10a. Then Amaziah the priest of Bethel sent to Jeroboam king of Israel, saying, "Amos has conspired against you in the midst of the house of Israel.

Amaziah the priest is no servant of God and neither is *Jeroboam king of Israel*. The vested interest those two men share is the town of *Bethel*, described by Amaziah as "the king's sanctuary" and "a temple of the kingdom," the town where Amos is preaching (Amos 7:13, below; also see the Lesson Background). Should that which Amos prophesies about the town and its altars come to pass, both king and priest will be out of a job (Amos 3:14; 5:5, 6; compare John 11:48).

So Amaziah sends word to Jeroboam of a conspiracy against him, a conspiracy fomented by Amos. It is noteworthy that Amaziah sends this report only after Amos prophesies against Jeroboam by name in Amos 7:9.

10b. "The land is not able to bear all his words.

This part of the report points to the effectiveness of Amos's message. He is not compromising the Lord's righteous standards or watering down his content just to curry favor with leaders such as Jeroboam and Amaziah. He is definitely getting people's attention! But for someone like Amaziah, Amos is nothing but a troublemaker (compare the label attached to the prophet Elijah by wicked King Ahab in 1 Kings 18:17).

11. "For thus Amos has said,
'Jeroboam shall die by the sword,
and Israel must go into exile
away from his land.'"

One should note that Amaziah's quotation of Amos begins with *thus Amos has said.* The usual way to preface a prophet's message is with the phrase "thus says the Lord" or some variation of it (that is how Amos responds to Amaziah in verse 17, below). Clearly, Amaziah sees nothing authoritative in Amos's message; he's just spouting his own words, not the Lord's.

Though Amos's message as we see it recorded has little to say about Jeroboam specifically, the prophet *does* have much to say about Israel's going *into exile away from his land* (Amos 3:12; 5:27; 6:7, 8; 7:17; 9:4). Sadly, that's just what happens. The Assyrians will conquer Samaria, the capital of the northern kingdom, as the prophecy is fulfilled (2 Kings 17).

> *What Do You Think?*
> How do we know when our message should primarily be one of dire warning?
> *Talking Points for Your Discussion*
> ▪ Regarding nations and their policies
> ▪ Regarding other religions
> ▪ Regarding individual people

B. Rebuke for the Prophet (vv. 12, 13)

12. And Amaziah said to Amos, "O seer, go, flee away to the land of Judah, and eat bread there, and prophesy there,

Amaziah follows his message to the king with a blunt directive to Amos: Go home! He is from *the land of Judah*, and the northern kingdom of Israel has no use for this interloper. If Amos wants to make people's lives miserable, then let him do it to his own countrymen!

To *eat bread there* in Judah may imply that Amos will be fed or paid better in his homeland than he currently is in the northern kingdom. Per-

haps Amaziah believes that prophets are interested in nothing more than earning a livelihood.

Seer was the term commonly used before the designation *prophet* replaced it (1 Samuel 9:9). The older term reflects how a prophet is empowered by the Lord to "see" what others cannot, whether in a spiritual sense or by means of visions. In Amos's case, Amaziah seems to use the term *seer* sarcastically; else he would not demand that Amos stop prophesying in northern Israel.

> *What Do You Think?*
> How should we react when others try to restrict our message?
> *Talking Points for Your Discussion*
> ▪ When access to an audience is restricted
> ▪ When topics on which we may speak are restricted
> ▪ When threats are expressed or implied

◆ OUTSIDERS ◆

While traveling, my husband and I stopped at a store. Not finding what we wanted, we approached a woman in the parking lot and asked if a Walmart was nearby. She looked at us for a moment before loudly proclaiming, "You don't know where Walmart is?" She started laughing.

"Hey, Joann! They don't know where Walmart is!" she called to her companion. The women then got the attention of someone else they knew across the parking lot. "Hey, Charlie!" they hollered. "They don't know where Walmart is!" All three laughed.

At that point, we began to back away from these strangers who were taking such joy in our lack of knowledge. Finally one woman informed us that Walmart was just around the corner, very easy to find.

Outsiders draw attention, often in a negative way. By definition, outsiders do not share the common, personal history of the insiders—those of the immediate culture. The locals may treat outsiders dismissively simply because of their outsider status. Viewing Amos as a threat, Amaziah had a choice to make: neutralize the threat either by discrediting the message or by discrediting the messenger. Amaziah chose the latter path, his tactic being an attack on Amos's outsider status. When we hear a person/message we don't like—whether that message be spiritual or secular in nature—do we do the same? Examples in Numbers 23; Jonah 3; and Mark 9:38-41 caution us in that regard.   —L. M. W.

13. "but never again prophesy at Bethel, for it is the king's sanctuary, and it is a temple of the kingdom."

Amos's preaching is especially unwelcome *at Bethel,* which implies his current location. The word translated *sanctuary* can also be found elsewhere (example: Ezekiel 45:3), while the word translated *temple* is commonly rendered *house* when referring to a dwelling place of either God or people (examples: Zechariah 14:20 and 13:6, respectively). Taken together, these may imply that King Jeroboam II has a residence in Bethel in addition to the one he would have in the capital city of Samaria (compare 1 Kings 16:23, 24; 22:37; Amos 3:15). Alternatively, this may be just Amaziah's way of emphasizing that Bethel is Jeroboam's turf. Either way, Amos is viewed as having no business whatsoever trespassing on the king's domain.

But Amos cares nothing about the reactions or feelings of any earthly authority who opposes him. The prophet answers to a far greater king, the one who resides in a heavenly sanctuary. His words and actions will be reflected centuries later by the apostle Peter when he squares off with the religious leadership in Jerusalem: "We must obey God rather than men" (Acts 5:29). Decades earlier, King Jeroboam I had been confronted by an anonymous man of God from Judah who came to Bethel while the king was offering a sacrifice on the altar he had built (1 Kings 13:1-4). Now King Jeroboam II is being challenged by another man of God from Judah.

II. Professing Prophet
(Amos 7:14-17)
A. Source of Authority (vv. 14-16)

14. Then Amos answered and said to Amaziah, "I was no prophet, nor a prophet's son, but I was a herdsman and a dresser of sycamore figs.

Visual for Lesson 9. *Point to this visual as you ask, "How do you relate the calls of Jesus' disciples in Mark 1:16, 17 and of Amos to your own life?"*

The response by Amos may be understood one of two ways. First, he may simply be stating a fact of heredity: there is nothing about his earthly lineage that suggests he should be a prophet. No one in his family has ever held that responsibility.

The second possibility turns on the meaning of the phrase *a prophet's son,* since it may refer to the group known as "the sons of the prophets." Its members appear to have been undergoing training of some kind in order to be ready for the Lord's call to serve him in that way. The prophet Elisha, whose ministry ended about a half century before Amos's began, had frequent contact with this group (2 Kings 2:1-15; 4:1, 38; 6:1, 2; 9:1).

If the second of the two possibilities is intended by Amos, then he is openly admitting that he has none of the credentials or official training of other prophets. That would help explain at least some of the contempt Amaziah has shown toward him. Like Peter and John, Amos may be seen as "uneducated" and "common" (Acts 4:13). But also like them, Amos has the one credential that matters most: the Lord's calling.

15. "But the LORD took me from following the flock, and the LORD said to me, 'Go, prophesy to my people Israel.'

Amos twice highlights the source of his calling and prophetic authority: *the Lord.* Like Moses and David, who also tended flocks (Exodus 3:1; 1 Samuel 16:11-13), Amos has been called to a ministry of shepherding people (compare Psalms

77:20; 78:70-72; Isaiah 63:11). Amos's response to Amaziah's intimidation therefore yields not an inch of ground. The prophet from Judah answers to no earthly priest or king—only to the Lord God who took him from his accustomed life on the farm to be a proclaimer of his Word.

What Do You Think?
What are some deciding factors when considering a change in vocation?
Talking Points for Your Discussion
- If changing from secular to ministerial
- If changing from ministerial to secular

◆ **CREDENTIALS** ◆

In the winter of 2015, a 17-year-old boy wandered the halls of a medical center in West Palm Beach, Florida. He wore a white lab coat with the hospital's logo, carried a stethoscope, and even donned a surgical mask at times. People working in the center assumed he was a doctor. They assumed wrongly; he had no medical credentials.

This type of thing happens more often than one would like to think. A few years earlier, another 17-year-old boy impersonated a doctor at a different medical center in Florida. For five days, he examined patients, provided care, and accessed patient information. Suspicions grew as he repeatedly attempted to gain access to restricted areas. He was caught when staff in the Emergency Department reported him.

Credentials were important in antiquity too. And the only valid "accrediting agency" for prophetic work was God. The credentials for Amos came straight from him. Some who would lead us astray today may appear outwardly well qualified, yet still be "ravenous wolves" on the inside (Matthew 7:15). Amos's experience in evaluating sycamore figs may have helped him in examining spiritual fruit. That is a quality we are to have as well. See Matthew 7:16-20.   —L. M. W.

16. "Now therefore hear the word of the Lord. "You say, 'Do not prophesy against Israel, and do not preach against the house of Isaac.'

Amos continues his rebuttal by quoting Amaziah's demand back to him. An important purpose in doing so is to make certain that Amaziah realizes he has been heard loud and clear. Amos is leaving himself no room to escape persecution by later claiming he misunderstood Amaziah's directive.

Double meanings in one language are often very difficult to translate smoothly, and that is the case with the demand *do not preach.* Elsewhere the underlying Hebrew speaks of rain as it drops or pours down (Judges 5:4; Psalm 68:8). The same Hebrew is rendered "preach" and "preacher" sarcastically in Micah 2:6, 11, and that may be the intent here as Amaziah speaks mockingly of Amos as one who speaks drivel. By repeating it back to Amaziah, Amos is establishing part of the basis for his prophecy of judgment in the verse to follow.

Of interest is the rare expression *house of Isaac* (only here in the Old Testament) with "high places of Isaac" in Amos 7:9, rather than "house of Jacob" (used 22 times) or "people of Israel" (over 500 times). As a bit of conjecture, perhaps Amos is changing the word Amaziah actually utters in order to inject irony: the meaning of the Hebrew word *Isaac* is "to laugh" (Genesis 18:11-15; 21:3), and the people of the northern kingdom who are laughing it up at the moment (Amos 6:1, 4-6) will experience the exact opposite soon enough.

What Do You Think?
What are some steps to take when our message is rejected?
Talking Points for Your Discussion
- When our motives are misrepresented
- When our words are misquoted
- When our character is questioned
- Other

B. Essence of the Message (v. 17)

17a. "Therefore thus says the Lord:
"'Your wife shall be a prostitute in the city,
and your sons and your daughters shall
fall by the sword,

The consequences of attempting to silence a prophet of the Lord are severe indeed! Since the word *your* (three times) is singular, this prophecy is aimed at Amaziah's family. What could be more agonizing to a husband and father than to watch his family members suffer what is being prophesied here? Amos has already prophesied that the Lord says, "I will rise against the house of Jeroboam with the sword" (Amos 7:9). Now the fuller prophecy includes the violent end of Amaziah's lineage.

17b. "'and your land shall be divided up with a measuring line;

Amaziah will not be able to leave family property to descendants because (1) no descendants will remain to inherit it and (2) no property will remain to bequeath anyway. For Amaziah's land to *be divided up with a measuring line* means it will be parceled out to others by its conquerors. This will be something of a reversal of the process of land allotment to the Israelites during the time of Joshua (Joshua 14:1-5; 18:1-10). Amaziah claims that "the land is not able to bear all" the words of Amos (Amos 7:10). But the truth is that the land is not able to bear the sins of the people of the northern kingdom (compare Leviticus 18:28).

17c. "'you yourself shall die in an unclean land,
and Israel shall surely go into exile away from its land.'"

We come to the sentence pronounced on Amaziah himself. An unclean land is a defiled land (compare Jeremiah 19:13). It is in such areas that pagan gods are worshipped. Such places are profane, polluted, and impure in contrast with the holiness required by the Mosaic law (compare Ezra 9:11).

That Amaziah *shall die* in such a land can imply that he will be taken captive after witnessing what is to befall his wife, sons, and daughters. To accompany others who are also taken *into exile* also signifies that Amaziah will witness the destruction of "the high places of Isaac . . . and the sanctuaries of Israel" prophesied in Amos 7:9. What, then, will he think of the gods he worshipped in those places —gods powerless to save him?

The Scriptures provide no record of the fulfillment of this prophecy against Amaziah. Even so, we can be sure it was fulfilled, since it is "the word of the Lord" (Amos 7:16). History records the fate of Israel when it falls to Assyria in 722 BC (2 Kings 17:6). The fact that the line *and Israel shall surely go into exile away from its land* repeats word for word (in the original Hebrew) the prophecy in Amos 7:11 means that Amaziah's attempts to intimidate the Lord's prophet have utterly failed.

> *What Do You Think?*
> What are some ways to respond if a necessarily harsh message is rejected as "unloving"?
> *Talking Points for Your Discussion*
> • Considering the agenda of those voicing objection
> • Considering validity of the objection

Conclusion
A. True to the Call

Amos was under intense pressure to modify or silence his message rather than risk offending the high officials in the northern kingdom; the pressure the church faces today is similar (compare Matthew 15:12-14; Acts 4:18-21). The pressure may tempt us to ask ourselves, "Who am I to judge another's conduct?"

Amos shows how to meet such a challenge: it is a matter of *calling.* When Amaziah asked, in effect, "Who do you think you are?" Amos had a ready answer. We must be prepared to do the same (1 Peter 3:15). Amos knew who he was, and he knew his task. God expects the same of us (Matthew 28:19, 20; 2 Timothy 2:15). A simple review of how God has worked and desires to work in your life may result in your becoming an Amos to the lost of your community.

B. Prayer

Father, grant us the conviction that comes from the study of your Word so that we may profess boldly the grace of your Son by whose blood the coming judgment may be escaped. We pray for this in his name. Amen.

C. Thought to Remember

True profession overcomes oppression.

INVOLVEMENT LEARNING

Enhance your lesson presentation with the reproducible activity page,
available as a free download at www.standardlesson.com.

Into the Lesson

Before class write the following statements on the board:

> "I am a pro athlete."
> "I am pro athletics."

Point out the differences in the two statements. "The first is saying that he gets paid for being an athlete. The second is saying that he believes that athletic activity is good."

Then ask, "Is there a difference between someone who claims to be a professing follower of God and one who claims to be a professional follower of God?"

Alternative. Distribute copies of the "Sort of" activity from the reproducible page, which you can download. Allow students to work individually or in small groups.

After either activity, lead into Bible study saying, "We know ministers of the gospel who are paid for faithfully professing the gospel. There are many examples in Scripture of people doing just that. The prophet Amos was in a different situation, however. He was called to confront a man who was paid for being a priest but who did not profess God's truth faithfully. Let's look at the conflict between Amos and Amaziah."

Into the Word

Divide your class into groups of three to five students. Give each group paper, pen, and one of the two assignments below, but *without* the sample entries listed below the passage reference in parentheses. Each group is to read its portion of today's text and write a job description for either Amaziah or Amos as indicated. Mention one or more sample entries if learners seem stuck.

Assignment 1—Amaziah the Professional Priest
(Amos 7:10-13)

The priest must recognize he is employed by the king of Israel.

The priest must view any activity opposing his employer as treason and report it at once.

The priest must do everything in his power to suppress messages seen as treasonous.

Assignment 2—Amos the Professing Prophet
(Amos 7:14-17)

The prophet must place loyalty to God above financial gain.

The prophet must go whenever and wherever God directs.

The prophet must speak the truth, even if it means confronting the powerful.

After groups have finished, reassemble the class and have a spokesperson from each group share its job descriptions and summarize its assigned passage of Scripture as basis for conflict between the two men.

Into Life

Say, "Speaking out for God will always put a believer on the spot! In our text today, we see Amos experiencing such a confrontation. He responded by giving what is commonly called his testimony."

Give class members paper and pens. Ask them to quickly outline their personal testimonies using the following outline:

I. My life before knowing Jesus.

II. How I became a Christian (include specifics).

III. The change Jesus has made and is continuing to make in my life.

Allow time for a couple students to share their testimony with the rest of the class.

Alternative. Distribute copies of the "Prophet and Profit" activity from the reproducible page. Have students work on this activity individually. If you prefer, use this as a take-home activity.

CALLED TO WITNESS

DEVOTIONAL READING: Acts 2:14-28
BACKGROUND SCRIPTURE: Acts 1, 6, 7

ACTS 6:1-8

¹ Now in these days when the disciples were increasing in number, a complaint by the Hellenists arose against the Hebrews because their widows were being neglected in the daily distribution. ² And the twelve summoned the full number of the disciples and said, "It is not right that we should give up preaching the word of God to serve tables. ³ Therefore, brothers, pick out from among you seven men of good repute, full of the Spirit and of wisdom, whom we will appoint to this duty. ⁴ But we will devote ourselves to prayer and to the ministry of the word." ⁵ And what they said pleased the whole gathering, and they chose Stephen, a man full of faith and of the Holy Spirit, and Philip, and Prochorus, and Nicanor, and Timon, and Parmenas, and Nicolaus, a proselyte of Antioch. ⁶ These they set before the apostles, and they prayed and laid their hands on them.

⁷ And the word of God continued to increase, and the number of the disciples multiplied greatly in Jerusalem, and a great many of the priests became obedient to the faith.

⁸ And Stephen, full of grace and power, was doing great wonders and signs among the people.

KEY VERSE

Therefore, brothers, pick out from among you seven men of good repute, full of the Spirit and of wisdom, whom we will appoint to this duty. —**Acts 6:3**

Photo: Aquir / iStock / Thinkstock

GOD'S URGENT CALL

Unit 3: Calls in the New Testament

LESSONS 10–13

LESSON AIMS

After participating in this lesson, each learner will be able to:

1. Summarize how the Twelve addressed the issue of food distribution in terms of ministry priorities.

2. Diagram a problem-solving approach for churches desiring to use the principles found in this account.

3. Make a plan to recruit, train, and commission new workers for ministries in his or her church.

LESSON OUTLINE

Introduction

A. Waiting On . . . What?

When dining at restaurants in Los Angeles, I would often hear a young server say, "I'm an actor. I'm just waiting tables between acting gigs."

Some of them made good livings by serving tables, but they did not see themselves as waiters. The outer self waited tables while the inner self waited for a big break into stardom. By contrast, I never met a person who had a successful acting career but was biding his time until he got his "big break" to get into waiting tables! This reveals something about cultural values.

Today's lesson is also about values. The apostles, the primary leaders of the first-century church, had been taught a value of the kingdom of God: that serving others was not beneath them (Mark 9:33-35; 10:35-45; John 13:14; compare Philippians 2:5-8; etc.). But there was more than one value at issue in the situation addressed by today's text. The apostles' handling of it has been seen as marvelously insightful through the centuries, and still is.

B. Lesson Background

Today's lesson focuses on the earliest days of the Jerusalem church, when the memory of Jesus was still vividly strong. Acts 6, from which our text is drawn, reflects a time when the church consisted of Christians from a Jewish background only, since the gospel had yet to be extended to Gentiles (compare Acts 10:1–11:18).

A common religious background did not mean uniformity in doctrine and practice, however. The Judaism of Jesus' day had divided itself into four sects: Pharisees, Sadducees, Essenes, and Zealots, as described by the first-century Jewish historian Josephus. As Jews accepted Jesus as the promised Messiah, they brought into the church their various (and sometimes contradictory) expectations. Some had to be modified or abandoned altogether.

For example, the Scriptures clearly stated God's desire that widows and other needy people be cared for (Isaiah 1:17; etc.). But there was not a uniform understanding on how benevolence programs were to be funded and who was eligible to receive aid. Regarding funding, Josephus interpreted Deuteronomy 14:28, 29; 26:12 to mean that support was to be funded by a third tithe brought every third year (*Antiquities* 4.240). Jesus had harsh words for a tradition that allowed one to redirect a gift to avoid supporting a needy parent (Mark 7:9-13). The lack of consensus on eligibility could have been one aspect of Paul's need to address the topic later (1 Timothy 5:3-16).

The first-century church in Jerusalem recognized its obligation to provide food daily to its widows. That was quite an undertaking for a church that numbered in the thousands (Acts 4:4), and direct oversight of this complex ministry was shouldered by the leaders of the congregation, the apostles. But complaints were being heard, and the nature of this important task consumed their time. Something had to be done.

I. Growing Pain
(ACTS 6:1-4)
A. The Thorny Problem (v. 1)

1. Now in these days when the disciples were increasing in number, a complaint by the Hellenists arose against the Hebrews because their widows were being neglected in the daily distribution.

It is easy to misunderstand the nature of this conflict of *the Hellenists . . . against the Hebrews.* All are of Jewish background (see the Lesson Background). The distinction is that some identify themselves secondarily with the Greek language and culture that predominates outside the borders of Israel, while others identify more with the Hebrew language and culture that predominates within Israel proper. (The issue at hand is therefore not the same as Peter's problem in Galatians 2:11-13, which involves Jews and Gentiles.)

Jerusalem is a magnet for Jews all over the Roman world, and many come for extended stays. For example, Barnabas, a Levite from the Greek-speaking island of Cyprus (Acts 4:36), resides in Jerusalem at this time. The apostles in Jerusalem from Galilee have at least some ability to speak the Greek language, but they probably identify more with the Hebrew group. A charge of bias on the part of the Hebrews (or Hebraic Jews) regarding

the daily ministration of food to widows therefore lands in their laps. Something must be done, and quickly! Some issues may resolve themselves over time, but this is not one of them.

B. The Wrong Solution (v. 2)

2. And the twelve summoned the full number of the disciples and said, "It is not right that we should give up preaching the word of God to serve tables.

The twelve are the apostles chosen by Jesus, minus Judas, plus his replacement (Acts 1:15-26). Acts gives us the picture that these men have assumed the role of leaders for the congregation in all things since the beginning of the church on the Day of Pentecost (chap. 2). These leaders recognize a brewing crisis that can divide the church. Disaster looms unless something changes.

Some preliminary observations are in order. First, whether the neglect of certain widows is an issue of objective fact or an issue of subjective perception, something must be done. Second, any charge of intentional bias on the part of the apostles is surely untrue, since they are honorable, godly men (compare James 2:1-10).

Even if the complaint has a factual basis, the cause for the unequal treatment may simply be a lack of adequate time and manpower as the apostles both *serve tables* and attend to *the word of God.* (The latter refers to the ministry of teaching and preaching; see Acts 5:42.) The apostles are the best qualified to preach and teach; others can manage the food distribution.

So a congregational meeting ensues as the apostles call *the full number of the disciples* together. While Acts 2:41 and 4:4 indicate that thousands of people have believed and been baptized, those actually responding to the summons may be a core group of a few hundred. The place of assembly is undoubtedly outdoors, perhaps in a public meeting area such as Solomon's Portico (Acts 5:12).

No mention is given of the complaint of the Grecian Jews that has precipitated the crisis. Rather than frame this as a need for avoiding factional strife in the congregation, the Twelve realize the root problem is their inability to perform this food ministry well, given their other responsibilities. We might say they wisely want to treat the disease (inadequate manpower for food distribution) rather than the symptom (complaints of bias).

> **What Do You Think?**
> What are some ways for church leaders to keep a volatile issue from becoming more so?
> *Talking Points for Your Discussion*
> - Considering the nature of the issue
> - Regarding initial reaction to a complaint
> - Regarding how perceptions are managed
> - Regarding response to misinformation
> - Regarding the role of prayer
> - Other

C. The Right Solution (vv. 3, 4)

3. "Therefore, brothers, pick out from among you seven men of good repute, full of the Spirit and of wisdom, whom we will appoint to this duty.

The apostles do not ask for a strategy to resolve the problem. They have already decided what they themselves need to do: focus on preaching and teaching. What they ask of those gathered is that they select men from among them to be appointed *to this duty* of food distribution to widows. Realizing that those chosen will be important functionaries in the church, the apostles specify several criteria for the selection process.

First, the number is set at *seven*. Seven is an important symbolic number in the Bible, the number of perfection or completion (example: Revelation 15). Whether or not symbolism is present here, the apostles know—either by analysis or divine inspiration—that seven is the right number.

We should note that the text does not say that the seven will be the only ones involved in distrib-

uting food to widows, since the wording *appoint to this duty* may imply that the seven will have the authority to exercise full control of this ministry. Thus the seven might supervise others they choose to assist.

> **What Do You Think?**
> How do we know how many people should be appointed to a given ministry task?
> *Talking Points for Your Discussion*
> - Considering "many hands make light work"
> - Considering "too many cooks spoil the broth"
> - Considering, if relevant, Exodus 18:21; Joshua 4:4-7; Ezra 8:24; Nehemiah 11:1; Mark 3:14; Luke 10:1; Acts 1:21-26; 15:2; 2 Corinthians 8:18-21; Titus 1:5

The men must have positive reputations, their character evident to all. They are not unknown quantities, but are to be men acknowledged as being *full of the Spirit and of wisdom*. These men are being authorized to assume duties in which a considerable amount of money may be involved, and the church has recently experienced a troubling incident of deceit with regard to money (5:1-

HOW TO SAY IT

Antioch	*An*-tee-ock.
apostolic	ap-uh-*stahl*-ick.
Aramaic	*Air*-uh-**may**-ik.
Barnabas	*Bar*-nuh-bus.
Cyprus	*Sigh*-prus.
diakonos *(Greek)*	dee-*ah*-ko-nawss.
Gentiles	*Jen*-tiles.
Grecian	*Gree*-shun.
Hebrews	*Hee*-brews.
Nicanor	Nye-*cay*-nor.
Nicolaus	*Nick*-uh-lus.
Parmenas	*Par*-meh-nas.
Pentecost	*Pent*-ih-kost.
Prochorus	*Prock*-uh-rus.
proselyte	*prahss*-uh-light.
Sadducees	*Sad*-you-seez.
synagogue	*sin*-uh-gog.
Tarsus	*Tar*-sus.
Timon	*Ty*-mon.

11). A high degree of accountability along with proven spiritual and life-experience maturity are musts (compare 1 Timothy 3:6, 7). All this will help them be spiritually attuned to the needs of the widows while remaining above reproach in administrating a large operation.

Finally, the word *appoint* establishes that the apostles retain for themselves the final stamp of approval regarding congregational selections. How that approval is communicated is the subject of Acts 6:6, below.

> **What Do You Think?**
> When is it better to ask select individuals privately to serve rather than putting an appeal for volunteers in the church newsletter? Why?
> *Talking Points for Your Discussion*
> - Considering the spiritual giftedness needed
> - Considering the confidentiality required
> - Considering the nature of the task in terms of visibility, etc.
> - Other

4. "But we will devote ourselves to prayer and to the ministry of the word."

Not only do the apostles need time for *the ministry of the word* (their teaching and preaching of Acts 5:42), but also time for *prayer*. Mention of the latter introduces a topic thus far unaddressed in Acts: proper attention to prayer requires time.

We assume that our church leaders are people of prayer. But would we think highly of a minister who declined to help with a project (like feeding widows) because he was booked for prayer all morning? The ministry of prayer can and does take time and planning.

This episode in Acts is often seen as the origin of the office of deacon in the church. Our term *deacon* comes from the Greek word *diakonos,* which is not used in Acts 6. Therefore the seven men are "deacons" only by inference. However, a form of the word *diakonos* is behind the translation *ministry,* which describes the functions the apostles have chosen to focus on.

In effect, the apostles are saying, "Let us focus on serving as deacons/ministers of the Word, and let the seven serve as deacons/ministers of the

tables." Titles in the New Testament describe functions more than offices. The question should be "Who will serve as a deacon?" more than "Who will be a deacon?"

II. Pleasing Consensus
(Acts 6:5, 6)
A. The Candidates (v. 5)

5. And what they said pleased the whole gathering, and they chose Stephen, a man full of faith and of the Holy Spirit, and Philip, and Prochorus, and Nicanor, and Timon, and Parmenas, and Nicolaus, a proselyte of Antioch.

Of the seven chosen, all but Philip have distinctively Greek names. This is likely a deliberate effort to assure everyone that the Grecian widows will receive adequate food.

Two of the names become more prominent as the storyline of Acts unfolds. The ministry of *Stephen* is the focus of the rest of chapter 6 and all of chapter 7. The ministry of *Philip* is discussed throughout chapter 8. (He is "Philip the evangelist" [Acts 21:8], not the apostle Philip.)

For the man named *Nicolaus* to be identified as *a proselyte of Antioch* means he is a Gentile who has converted to the Jewish faith. His mention foreshadows the expansion of the church to Gentiles and to the important city of Antioch (see Acts 13:1-3). No additional information exists regarding the other four men named.

Delegating the oversight of feeding widows is easy to see in today's lesson. But we should not fail to notice that the apostles also delegate the task of choosing the seven men to head up the program. This serves to create a sense of ownership by *the whole gathering.* Wise leaders know the importance of delegating (compare Exodus 18:13-26).

◆ **DELEGATING AS TRUST** ◆

A small group was no longer "small," and the associate minister of pastoral care had delegated to group leaders the authority to split oversized groups. But before exercising that authority, the leader of the group in question discussed the need with both the group and the associate minister. The group leader then decided to split the group.

One member objected loudly to the change. The group leader informed the associate minister to expect a call from the disgruntled member. The minister supported the group leader's decision, but also discussed the matter with the person who was upset.

Delegation requires a certain "hands-off" trust. A leader who delegates a task to a team member must not be quick to micromanage that person later. But that does not mean remaining so distant as to be unavailable to help resolve conflict. The associate minister demonstrated a delicate balance of authority and trust.

In deciding to delegate an important task to seven others, the apostles were prepared to trust the decisions of those seven. But in so doing, the apostles did not adopt an attitude of "don't bother us with this any further," given their decision to confirm the selections personally.

The apostle Paul walked a similar leadership tightrope later (2 Corinthians 8:16-21). In what ways can we better model the balance that they struck when it comes to delegating?   —D. C. S.

B. The Consecration (v. 6)

6. These they set before the apostles, and they prayed and laid their hands on them.

The men chosen are presented to *the apostles* for a ceremony to inaugurate their ministry. This is a time of prayer for the men, accompanied by the apostles laying *their hands on* the seven. This act of praying while hands are on the shoulders and heads of the men is a way of granting them authority and giving them a commission for their work (compare Acts 13:3; 1 Timothy 4:14). This public event takes place in the presence of the whole body of believers. The commissioning is presented as something done with dignity and reverence.

Although the word *ordain* is not used here, we often see Acts 6:6 as a model for the church's practice of ordaining ministers, elders, and/or deacons. Ordination is the church's way of setting chosen individuals apart for a designated area of ministry. Ordination should be done with the approval of the congregation and the blessing of the church leadership. It should be a time of solemn dedica-

tion, yet also a joyous time of commissioning people for the service of Christ's church.

> **What Do You Think?**
> In what instances should appointment to a task be public rather than private, if any? How about the reverse? Why?
> *Talking Points for Your Discussion*
> - Considering the nature of the task itself
> - Considering the personality traits of the individuals appointed
> - Considering the visibility desired for the congregation as a whole
> - Other

III. Marvelous Result
(ACTS 6:7, 8)
A. The Multiplication (v. 7)

7. And the word of God continued to increase, and the number of the disciples multiplied greatly in Jerusalem, and a great many of the priests became obedient to the faith.

We come to three summary statements regarding the progress of the church after the seven are chosen (compare Acts 2:47). First, the fact that *the word of God continued to increase* indicates that the apostles are indeed able to dedicate their time to preaching and teaching. Second, the result of that focus is a significant growth in *the number of the disciples*; but so far this growth happens only *in Jerusalem*. Persecution will soon push the gospel beyond the environs of the city (Acts 8:1b, 4).

Third, the growth includes *a great many of the priests* (compare John 12:42). These are likely Sadducees, the elites of Jerusalem: wealthy, educated, and cultured. This party of the Jews is known for its denial of the possibility of resurrection from the dead (Luke 20:27; Acts 23:8). To become *obedient to the faith* includes dropping this skepticism about life after death, for there is no gospel without the resurrection of Jesus (see 1 Corinthians 15:16, 17).

An implication of these summary statements is that the growth of the church, stalled by the widow controversy, has now resumed. Unity and harmony in a congregation do not ensure it will grow. But disunity and division form a reliable recipe for a church to decline. Our energies should be pointed at increasing the ministry of the Word and making disciples (Matthew 28:19, 20).

◆ IT'S ALWAYS SOMETHING ◆

Comedienne Gilda Radner popularized the expression above in the 1970s through her character Roseanne Roseannadanna. The long version of the observation is "It just goes to show you, it's always something—if it ain't one thing, it's another."

How we react to the truth of that observation about daily life depends on the context in which it is stated. When spoken as dry comedy, it may make us smile. When uttered while pondering a series of problems that never seems to end, it can be a tacit admission of defeat.

If the churches that were led by the apostles themselves had problems, then our churches today will not be exempt. Solutions begin with outlook. A despairing cry of "it's always something" merely highlights our inadequacy to cope. On the other hand, a confident cry of "it's always Jesus" looks beyond the problem to the one who is always ready, willing, and able to help.   —R. L. N.

B. The Miracles (v. 8)

8. And Stephen, full of grace and power, was doing great wonders and signs among the people.

Stephen is described in Acts 6:5 as "a man full of faith and of the Holy Spirit." Here the description is reworded: he is a man *of grace and power.* The power he has is that of the Holy Spirit.

Stephen seems to move quickly from overseeing distributions of food to something more like the apostles' ministry of the word. He is now out *among the people* where the *great wonders and signs* he does can be witnessed by many. This parallels Stephen's ministry with those of Jesus (Acts 2:22) and the apostles in general (5:12). The parallels cause us to realize that primary among the miracles are healings.

The story about Stephen that follows offers further parallels between him and Jesus (compare Acts 6:11, 13, 14; 7:60 with Matthew 26:59-61, 65; Luke 23:34).

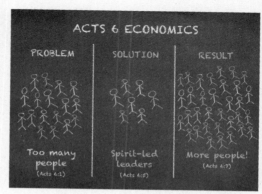

Visual for Lesson 10. *Close the lesson by pointing to this visual as you ask, "How can we improve the summary statements at the bottom?"*

Conclusion
A. Needed: A Culture of Change

A growing church is like a living organism. Difficulties encountered must be addressed before they become crippling crises. Adaptation may result in unforeseen consequences, both good and bad. People may be given chances to serve in modest roles, and some (like Stephen) rise to this challenge and go beyond. But this also implies meeting the challenge of filling the modest role that is vacated as a result. There are always problems to address, but also potential new leaders whom God is preparing to help do so.

Within scriptural boundaries, methods for ministry are subject to change. Consider how the benevolence ministry of the first-century church changed as we trace it from Acts 2:45 to Acts 4:34, 35 to Acts 6:1-6 to 2 Corinthians 8:13–9:15 to 1 Timothy 5:3-16. A church willing to change may be a church poised for growth.

B. Prayer

Father, grant us wisdom to see when changes in methods are necessary and courage to implement them so our church can fulfill the Great Commission. We pray this in Jesus' name. Amen.

C. Thought to Remember
A successful church cannot be
a one-person endeavor.

INVOLVEMENT LEARNING

Enhance your lesson presentation with the reproducible activity page, available as a free download at www.standardlesson.com.

Into the Lesson

To begin class, read this famous news story:

Ray was a middle-aged salesman for a company in decline. Fewer and fewer people were buying Prince Castle Multi-Mixers, preferring the lower cost products produced by another company. Noticing a small restaurant ordered not one, but five of his mixers, Ray investigated. He discovered that the restaurant had an assembly-line method of producing hamburgers they called the "Speedee Service System."

Because hamburgers were produced quickly and inexpensively this way, customers streamed in, buying not only burgers, but milkshakes as well. Ray Kroc saw the possibilities ahead for the McDonald brothers and joined their enterprise. McDonald's restaurants were born because a struggling salesman was having difficulty selling mixers.

Discuss this story by asking your students whether they have experienced an unexpected success in the midst of what seemed to be failure.

Alternative. Distribute copies of the "Invented by Accident" activity from the reproducible page, which you can download. Use it as a class activity.

After either activity, lead into the Bible study saying, "Sometimes failures, problems, and crises turn out to be disguised opportunities. The early church faced a problem of disgruntled believers and division. A solution to that problem birthed a new group of leaders, making the church more effective than ever."

Into the Word

Divide your class into three groups. Give each group one of the assignments that follow. Each group will read their assigned portion of the text and act out a meeting that may have happened between the lines of today's text.

Group 1— Acts 6:1
  Meeting of Greek-Speaking Jewish Christians
    Questions to be addressed:
      What is the problem?
      Who is to blame?
      What should we do?
Group 2— Acts 6:2-4
  Meeting of Apostles
    Questions to be addressed:
      What is the problem?
      What are our priorities?
      What should we do?
Group 3—Acts 6:5-8
  Meeting of New Leaders
    Questions to be addressed:
      How is this plan working?
      What more can we do?
Allow time for groups to share their findings.

Alternative. Distribute copies of the "Put Them in Order" from the reproducible page. Use it as a small-group or a class activity.

Into Life

Divide the class into groups of three to five students. Have each group choose one of the following scenarios. Each group will propose a solution using principles from today's Bible lesson.

Scenario 1—A small group has grown to an attendance of 20 adults and meets in a space that barely fits everyone. The group wants to continue to maintain these relationships but also wants to be able to invite others to join them.

Scenario 2—A group in the congregation desires to start a food pantry while another group wants to start a clothing closet to help resource people in the community. The church facilities only have one space available and cannot host both ministry opportunities.

Scenario 3—The number of senior adults continues to grow due to the aging population of the community. The ministry staff is no longer able to address the needs of this demographic.

Allow time for groups to share and explain their solutions.

CALLED TO BREAK DOWN BARRIERS

DEVOTIONAL READING: Romans 10:9-15
BACKGROUND SCRIPTURE: Acts 8

ACTS 8:26-39

26 Now an angel of the Lord said to Philip, "Rise and go toward the south to the road that goes down from Jerusalem to Gaza." This is a desert place. 27 And he rose and went. And there was an Ethiopian, a eunuch, a court official of Candace, queen of the Ethiopians, who was in charge of all her treasure. He had come to Jerusalem to worship 28 and was returning, seated in his chariot, and he was reading the prophet Isaiah. 29 And the Spirit said to Philip, "Go over and join this chariot." 30 So Philip ran to him and heard him reading Isaiah the prophet and asked, "Do you understand what you are reading?" 31 And he said, "How can I, unless someone guides me?" And he invited Philip to come up and sit with him. 32 Now the passage of the Scripture that he was reading was this:

"Like a sheep he was led to the slaughter
  and like a lamb before its shearer is
    silent,
  so he opens not his mouth.

33 In his humiliation justice was denied him.
    Who can describe his generation?
  For his life is taken away from the earth."

34 And the eunuch said to Philip, "About whom, I ask you, does the prophet say this, about himself or about someone else?" 35 Then Philip opened his mouth, and beginning with this Scripture he told him the good news about Jesus. 36 And as they were going along the road they came to some water, and the eunuch said, "See, here is water! What prevents me from being baptized?" 38 And he commanded the chariot to stop, and they both went down into the water, Philip and the eunuch, and he baptized him. 39 And when they came up out of the water, the Spirit of the Lord carried Philip away, and the eunuch saw him no more, and went on his way rejoicing.

KEY VERSE

Philip opened his mouth, and beginning with this Scripture he told him the good news about Jesus.

—Acts 8:35

GOD'S URGENT CALL

Unit 3: Calls in the New Testament

LESSONS 10–13

LESSON AIMS

After participating in this lesson, each learner will be able to:

1. Identify the cultural factors that separated Philip from the Ethiopian.

2. Explain why it was important for Luke, the author, to note the cross-cultural issues and context of Philip's encounter with the Ethiopian.

3. Research some questions that those of another culture have about Jesus and make a plan to answer them.

LESSON OUTLINE

Introduction

A. Crossing Cultures

Approximately 8,500 Sudanese live in Omaha. Most have immigrated since 1995 because of warfare in their nation. The number of Somalis who live in Minneapolis is estimated to exceed 60,000. Louisville has about 80,000 immigrant refugees from Bhutan, Burma, Iraq, and Somalia.

Your nearest city likely has its own population of new immigrants whose culture is very different from the traditions of that city. How do we effectively understand and communicate with people having languages and customs different from our own? Our lesson today reveals how Philip reached across cultural lines for Christ.

B. Lesson Background

Acts 8 records two episodes in which Philip, a Jewish Christian from Jerusalem, was pressed to cross cultural lines. First, he found himself in Samaria after persecution broke out in Jerusalem (Acts 8:1b, 4-8). The Samaritans of a certain city had for years been under the sway of a sorcerer named Simon (8:9-11). This was a people invested in the occult—surely not how Philip was accustomed to living! But despite crossing two cultural lines, Philip preached boldly, and many Samaritans came to faith in Christ (8:12).

Dealing with those cultural distinctives was a stretch for Philip, but at least he did not have to deal with barriers such as language difference or economic status. Yet the second episode (today's lesson) challenged Philip to cross even more cultural lines. As we consider his success in this, we take care to remember that he is "Philip the evangelist" of Acts 21:8, not the apostle Philip of Mark 3:18; etc.

I. Obedience

(ACTS 8:26-29)

A. Road (vv. 26, 27a)

26, 27a. Now an angel of the Lord said to Philip, "Rise and go toward the south to the road that goes down from Jerusalem to Gaza." This is a desert place. And he rose and went.

In Old Testament times, the city of *Gaza* was in Philistine territory (1 Samuel 6:17; etc.). Gaza in the first century is on the important commercial roadway that connects Egypt with cities such as Jerusalem, Antioch, and Damascus. To travel the approximately 50 miles *from Jerusalem to Gaza*, one has to cross a semiarid coastal plain described here as *desert*. This indicates an unpopulated place.

The movements of Philip are not devised by his own planning but directed by God through *an angel of the Lord*. In obedience, he travels through the countryside to be where God wants him at the precise time God intends.

◆　**WHOSE PLANS?**　◆

An elderly gentleman collapsed in the store aisle where my friend happened to be. As she called for help and rushed to steady him, she observed people avoiding the scene and looking away.

When we have the opportunity to assist someone else, will we decline because of schedule or inconvenience (compare Luke 10:30-32)? Will we argue with ourselves whether helping is a good idea (compare Acts 9:13, 14)?

Philip was a busy man, already occupied with an astonishingly successful ministry in Samaria (Acts 8:9-13). He could have objected to the angel's call with something like, "You want me to leave a successful ministry here and go to the des-

ert?" But the text reveals no such reluctance, no such objection.

Will we self-justify our plans over God's? Will we argue with him, or will we go willingly where he sends?　　　　　　　　　　—C. M. W.

B. Read (vv. 27b, 28)

27b. And there was an Ethiopian, a eunuch, a court official of Candace, queen of the Ethiopians, who was in charge of all her treasure. He had come to Jerusalem to worship

Philip meets an exotic character whom he would have seen only from afar prior to this encounter. We learn five things about this man that create cultural separation from Philip. First, he is *an Ethiopian,* coming from a kingdom in Africa south of Egypt. While it is likely that he speaks Greek, that is not his primary language.

Second, he is *a eunuch.* Eunuchs originally served kings who had harems. Having been emasculated, eunuchs do not pose a threat in looking after the king's wives and concubines. Since this man serves a queen, his duties do not include harem management.

Third, he is a servant to royalty. In particular, he serves the *queen of the Ethiopians*, known as *Candace.* This is not a personal name, but a dynastic title. This title functions much like the Roman title *Caesar* or the Egyptian title *Pharaoh.* The text implies that this man is under the direct command of the queen, making him one of the top half dozen officials of the realm.

Fourth, this man serves specifically as the treasurer for the queen. Not only is this a position of great responsibility and influence, but also one that probably makes him quite wealthy. Evidence of his wealth is seen in the fact that he is

HOW TO SAY IT

Antioch	*An*-tee-ock.
Caesar	*See*-zer.
Caesarea	Sess-uh-*ree*-uh.
Candace	*Can*-duh-see.
Damascus	Duh-*mass*-kus.
Esaias	Ee-*zay*-us.
Ethiopia	Ee-thee-*o*-pea-uh (*th* as in *thin*).
Ethiopians	Ee-thee-*o*-pea-unz (*th* as in *thin*).
eunuch	*you*-nick.
Gaza	*Gay*-zuh.
Pharaoh	*Fair*-o or *Fay*-roe.
rabbi	*rab*-eye.
Samaria	Suh-*mare*-ee-uh.
Samaritans	Suh-*mare*-uh-tunz.

traveling by chariot rather than by foot, camel, etc. It's almost certain that he is accompanied by servants and bodyguards, but the text gives no details on this.

Fifth, the man's awareness of the much larger world beyond Israel is evident in the fact that he is even here. A trip from Ethiopia to Jerusalem and back is an arduous one exceeding 1,000 miles. It is for him the trip of a lifetime, a treasured experience.

The reason for the Ethiopian's having traveled to Jerusalem is *worship*. The man may be Jewish by lineage, having Jewish parents in Ethiopia. Or he may have converted to Judaism at some point; this is a possibility since a Gentile convert to Judaism is mentioned in Acts 6:5, which is prior to God's extension of the gospel to Gentiles in Acts 10. The fact that the man has invested so much time, money, and effort to make such a trip allows us to conclude that he is quite devout in his faith.

> **What Do You Think?**
> Which of the ways the man is described would be the most helpful to know if you were to share the gospel with him today? Why?
> *Talking Points for Your Discussion*
> - Country of origin (Ethiopia)
> - Physical condition or limitations (eunuch)
> - Status in life (important official)

28. and was returning, seated in his chariot, and he was reading the prophet Isaiah.

The Ethiopian is returning home in a manner befitting his position. The chariot is a mode of travel that allows him to sit, not stand as a chariot warrior would. Someone else is driving.

The man has what is probably a souvenir of his trip to Jerusalem: a copy of the book of *Isaiah*. This is a confirmation of his great wealth, for the cost of such a handwritten scroll is out of the reach of most people. This is likely a copy of Isaiah in the Greek language. The fact that he is able to read any language is a testimony to his high level of education. As with many details of this story, these factors do not seem to be accidental,

but somehow prepared by the Lord. Isaiah, of all the Old Testament books, has the greatest witness to the coming Messiah. So the stage is now set for Philip to talk with the Ethiopian about Jesus as being that Messiah.

C. Ride (v. 29)

29. And the Spirit said to Philip, "Go over and join this chariot."

A common man like Philip does not have the status to accost a rich and regal person such as the Ethiopian in this scenario. It is a "don't speak unless spoken to" situation.

Furthermore, the Ethiopian and his crew might see Philip as a threat. A lonely road is a perfect haunt of bandits, so for Philip to appear and run toward (see the next verse) the Ethiopian is risky. But the Lord nonetheless directs Philip through *the Spirit* to approach *this chariot*. That prodding gives Philip both direction and confidence.

> **What Do You Think?**
> What are some ways to overcome hesitancies to share the gospel?
> *Talking Points for Your Discussion*
> - Hesitancies tied to cross-cultural issues
> - Hesitancies tied to a generational divide
> - Hesitancies rooted in "beneath me" or "above me" economic distinctions
> - Other

II. Observation
(Acts 8:30-35)

A. Investigation to Invitation (vv. 30-34)

30. So Philip ran to him and heard him reading Isaiah the prophet and asked, "Do you understand what you are reading?"

Reading is done aloud in the ancient world, so Philip is able to hear the Ethiopian and recognize which text he is working through. Philip takes the risk of speaking first, but the Lord has given him the perfect question: *Do you understand what you are reading?* Philip's Spirit-given insight likely provides him the answer before the question is even asked.

31. And he said, "How can I, unless someone guides me?" And he invited Philip to come up and sit with him.

The Ethiopian's response is almost as if he is saying, "I bought this scroll, and I should have hired someone in Jerusalem to come with me and explain it." The Ethiopian sees no threat in Philip, so he invites him to *come up and sit with him* on the bench seat of the chariot. This highly educated man is not ashamed to admit his lack of understanding. He welcomes Philip's assistance.

32. Now the passage of the Scripture that he was reading was this:

"Like a sheep he was led to the slaughter
and like a lamb before its shearer is silent,

so he opens not his mouth.

Again, we see the providential hand of the Lord working in preparation for this encounter. The Ethiopian is reading from Isaiah 53 and is stuck on verses 7 and 8. Being at that point means he is about 80 percent through the scroll.

Surely by this point he has encountered texts such as the prediction of a virgin conceiving a son to be named "Immanuel" (Isaiah 7:14) and the prophecy of a coming one who would be the "Everlasting Father" (9:6). Such texts also must be inexplicable to him. He likewise would have read by this point the marvelous inspirational passage of Isaiah 40:31, which promises strength to those who trust in the Lord.

Isaiah 53 is one of several Servant Songs of the book of Isaiah. These all speak of a coming servant of the Lord who will be called as a leader of the people but suffer many abuses and much pain for his service. For Christians today, these are obvious prophecies about the coming Messiah that have been fulfilled in Jesus. But for Jews of Philip's day (and even today), the Servant Songs are very difficult to understand, because they portray a coming leader who is humiliated rather than victorious.

Isaiah 53:7, quoted here, pictures something Jewish people have at least a yearly experience with: slaughtering a lamb. The Passover lamb submits silently to being killed; not expecting death, it yields passively. Although quite aware of the cross ahead, Jesus remained silent before his accusers (Mark 14:61).

33. "In his humiliation justice was denied him.
Who can describe his generation?
For his life is taken from the earth."

This "death without a fight" is a great *humiliation* for the servant of the Lord. To say *justice was denied him* means he is not given due process of a legal system. No one stops his unjust death. Just as the lamb is silent during its preparation for slaughter, so is the servant of the Lord. The fact that no one *can describe his generation* means that his death will be the end of his family line.

34. And the eunuch said to Philip, "About whom, I ask you, does the prophet say this, about himself or about someone else?"

The Ethiopian realizes the paradox in the verses. Why would the mighty Lord of the people of Israel send a sheep-like leader to end up humiliated and deprived of justice? Isn't the God of the Jews both powerful and just?

The man reasons that Isaiah must be talking about a specific and identifiable person—either *himself or . . . someone else*. The first option is possible given that Isaiah sometimes speaks of his own experiences (compare Isaiah 6). But the Ethiopian probably realizes the passage under consideration does not quite fit the prophet. Therefore he likely suspects *someone else* to be in view. His careful reading of Scripture has brought him to the place where he is open to hearing about Jesus.

B. Invitation to Interpretation (v. 35)

35. Then Philip opened his mouth, and beginning with this Scripture he told him the good news about Jesus.

Philip does not miss this great opportunity, orchestrated by the Spirit and made possible by Scripture. Sometimes the most effective sharing about Jesus is done in one-on-one situations. In Samaria, Philip had preached to crowds (Acts 8:5, 6). Here, his target audience is a single man (and perhaps his retinue of servants and guards).

◆ LIFE-GIVING COMMUNICATION ◆

Three ships crossed the Atlantic to help establish Jamestown colony in May of 1607. Preparedness was essential for the colony to survive and thrive. Supply ships from the other side of the Atlantic arrived irregularly, leaving the colonists responsible to ensure they had provisions.

Key to this was achieving good cross-cultural communication and relations with the local Powhatan Indians. When the colonists reached across cultural divides to establish and maintain communication, many problems were averted.

Tragically, communication broke down a couple of years after the colony was established. The result was the "starving time" winter of 1609–1610. Indians laid siege, and about 80 percent of the colony's 300 settlers died before spring arrived.

Successful cross-cultural communication is also a vital part of taking the gospel to "all nations" (Matthew 28:19, 20). Not making the effort to reach across cultural divides is to deny the gospel to those who may otherwise be open to it.

Many of us do not need to travel far in order to witness to people of other cultures and subcultures. They are all around us! Expect opportunities to share the gospel with someone whom the Holy Spirit puts in your path. Are you prepared for "the Ethiopian" you may encounter today?

—C. M. W.

III. Outcome
(ACTS 8:36-39)
A. Belief and Baptism (vv. 36-38)

36. And as they were going along the road they came to some water, and the eunuch said, "See, here is water! What prevents me from being baptized?"

Although the Gaza road goes through a sparsely populated and semiarid landscape, there are nevertheless several places for water. It is impossible to pinpoint the site of the *some water* that is *along the road,* since courses and sources of water change over the years. Some research suggests the location to be an ancient spring near what is today the archaeological site of Tell el-Hesi, which is about 15 miles east of Gaza.

Although the specific elements of Philip's gospel presentation are not recorded, the man understands his need for faith in Jesus, repentance of sin, and *being baptized*, for this is the New Testament pattern (Acts 2:36-39; etc.). Jewish customs of the day involve ritual cleansings with water (compare John 2:6), so the Ethiopian probably already has some idea about what his pending baptism involves. Because of his physical situation, he may not have been allowed to experience Jewish ceremonial cleansings during his Jerusalem visit (see Leviticus 21:18-20; Deuteronomy 23:1). But he eagerly desires baptism now, and his physical condition cannot disqualify him if he has faith (compare Isaiah 56:3).

> *What Do You Think?*
> When, if ever, would it be unwise to agree to a request for immediate baptism?
> *Talking Points for Your Discussion*
> - Considering need to count the cost (Luke 14:25-33)
> - Considering degree of conviction (Acts 2:36-41)
> - Considering ability to understand baptism's significance (Galatians 3:27, 28; Colossians 2:12; 1 Peter 3:21; etc.)
> - Considering precedents (Acts 10:47, 48; 11:17; 16:31-33)

37, Footnote. [And Philip said, "If you believe with all your heart, you may." And he replied, "I believe that Jesus Christ is the Son of God."]

This verse does not appear in the oldest manuscripts of the New Testament. But the fact that it repeats teaching on confessing Christ as found elsewhere indicates that it is genuine. (See Matthew 16:16; John 6:69; 9:35-38; 11:27; 1 John 4:15; 5:5.) And before baptizing the Ethiopian, it only makes sense for Philip to check the man's faith situation with regard to Jesus, whether or not that inquiry is recorded in the text. Baptism without faith is meaningless.

38. And he commanded the chariot to stop, and they both went down into the water, Philip and the eunuch, and he baptized him.

The description of the baptism is simple and beautiful. The fact that they both go *down into the water* implies baptism by full immersion, the practice of the church in its earliest days.

B. Rejoicing and Relocation (v. 39)

39. And when they were come up out of the water, the Spirit of the Lord carried Philip away, and the eunuch saw him no more, and went on his way rejoicing.

As they leave the pool of baptism, a most surprising thing happens. We may have preconceived notions about how *the Spirit of the Lord* removes Philip from the scene (science fiction dematerializations, etc.). In the ancient world, however, this more likely is understood in terms of Philip's body being carried into the sky as if by an unseen hand. The main thing is that Philip is gone. The Ethiopian is surely astonished, but his reaction is not one of puzzled paralysis. Instead, he continues his journey home with joy in his heart and on his lips.

We might ask why Philip is not allowed to accompany the eunuch to Ethiopia, where there may be a ready audience for the gospel. We are not told, but we must assume that Christ has more things for Philip to do in Palestine. That his name appears later in Acts 21:8 as "Philip the evangelist" hints at many successes in preaching the gospel over the coming years.

Conclusion

A. Divine Appointments

Philip was prepared for this encounter because he knew not just the book of Isaiah, but the gospel as well. The exposition of Scripture is a powerful way to present the gospel to those who seek

Visual for Lesson 11. *Start a discussion by pointing to the caption on this visual as you ask, "When was a time you found this to be true?"*

truth. We can fumble our own divine appointments if we cannot answer basic questions. A Christian should love the Bible not just for the marvelous encouragement it is personally, but as the true sword of the Spirit to be used in fighting unbelief among those who need the gospel (Ephesians 6:17; Hebrews 4:12).

There is no mention in the text of Philip's being a trained rabbi or scribe; he probably was quite ordinary, not unlike Peter and John (Acts 4:13). Lacking a formal theological education is no excuse for us today! Having been chosen as one "full of the Spirit and of wisdom" (6:3) implies Philip's love for Scripture, since it is the ultimate source of wisdom (Psalm 119:105; etc.).

God used Philip's self-preparedness to good effect—and that preparedness was likely the reason the Lord selected him for the divine appointment with a foreigner in the first place. And it took place on Philip's home turf! Opportunities to cross cultural lines with the gospel are all around.

B. Prayer

O God, give us divine appointments to share Jesus. May you use our preparation to say the right things at the right time in the right way. We pray for this in Jesus' name. Amen.

C. Thought to Remember

People of all cultures need Jesus.

INVOLVEMENT LEARNING

*Enhance your lesson presentation with the reproducible activity page,
available as a free download at www.standardlesson.com.*

Into the Lesson

Begin class by telling this joke:

Q: What do you call a person who speaks three languages?
A: Trilingual.
Q: What do you call a person who speaks two languages?
A: Bilingual.
Q: What do you call a person who speaks one language?
A: American.

Discuss this joke briefly, asking if class members see truth in it. What might be some reasons for Americans speaking fewer languages than people in many other countries? What problems might this present?

Alternative. Distribute copies of the "Take a Guess!" activity from the reproducible page, which you can download. Allow students to work individually or in pairs.

After either activity, lead into the Bible study saying, "Cultures around the world differ in so many ways. How do we effectively understand and communicate with people with languages and customs different from our own? Our Bible lesson today shows how Philip reached across cultural barriers for Christ."

Into the Word

Divide the class into three research groups. Give each group one of these assignments:

Assignment 1—Why would this powerful, wealthy Ethiopian eunuch be seen as someone unlikely to follow Jesus? Acts 8:26-29; Deuteronomy 23:1; Matthew 19:23; James 2:6; Zephaniah 2:12.

Assignment 2—How could Philip teach about Jesus by using only the Old Testament book of Isaiah? Acts 8:30-35; Isaiah 42:1-4; Isaiah 49:1-6; Isaiah 50:4-9; Isaiah 52:13-15.

Assignment 3—Why was baptism a part of Philip's message? Acts 8:36-40; Acts 2:37-39; Romans 6:3, 4; Galatians 3:27; 1 Peter 3:18-22.

Allow time for each group to share its report with the class. Add information as necessary from the commentary to ensure questions are answered as completely as possible.

Into Life

Provide some demographic information about your own area. Some data to consider would be socioeconomic level, race, age groups, religion, etc. If you have students with mobile devices in the class, you can have them access such information directly from various sites that offer it; be prepared to direct students to specific sites you have researched in advance.

From this information, identify groups that are not represented to any great degree in your congregation. Select a group or two and discuss ways of learning more about their subcultures. Valuable information may be gained as students ask themselves the following questions:

Are there particular public places where members of this group are likely to frequent (ethnic restaurants, shopping centers, entertainment venues, etc.)? Are there ways we can help members of this group during important personal events (births, weddings, funerals, etc.)? What is a typical family structure for members of the group? Are there ways we can help meet family needs?

Use this information to consider ways of increasing your congregation's influence in this mission field that is so close to home.

Alternative. Distribute copies of the "Peace Child" activity from the reproducible page. It could be the beginning of a class or church-wide outreach project. Discuss this famous missionary story and look for ways to address a resistant subculture close to home with the message of the gospel.

CALLED
TO PREACH

DEVOTIONAL READING: 1 Timothy 4:6-16
BACKGROUND SCRIPTURE: Acts 9:1-31

ACTS 9:10-20

¹⁰ Now there was a disciple at Damascus named Ananias. The Lord said to him in a vision, "Ananias." And he said, "Here I am, Lord." ¹¹ And the Lord said to him, "Rise and go to the street called Straight, and at the house of Judas look for a man of Tarsus named Saul, for behold, he is praying, ¹² and he has seen in a vision a man named Ananias come in and lay his hands on him so that he might regain his sight." ¹³ But Ananias answered, "Lord, I have heard from many about this man, how much evil he has done to your saints at Jerusalem. ¹⁴ And here he has authority from the chief priests to bind all who call on your name." ¹⁵ But the Lord said to him, "Go, for he is a chosen instrument of mine to carry my name before the Gentiles and kings and the children of Israel. ¹⁶ For I will show him how much he must suffer for the sake of my name." ¹⁷ So Ananias departed and entered the house. And laying his hands on him he said, "Brother Saul, the Lord Jesus who appeared to you on the road by which you came has sent me so that you may regain your sight and be filled with the Holy Spirit." ¹⁸ And immediately something like scales fell from his eyes, and he regained his sight. Then he rose and was baptized; ¹⁹ and taking food, he was strengthened.

For some days he was with the disciples at Damascus. ²⁰ And immediately he proclaimed Jesus in the synagogues, saying, "He is the Son of God."

KEY VERSE

Now there was a disciple at Damascus named Ananias. The Lord said to him in a vision, "Ananias." And he said, "Here I am, Lord." —**Acts 9:10**

GOD'S URGENT CALL

Unit 3: Calls in the New Testament

LESSONS 10–13

LESSON AIMS

After participating in this lesson, each learner will be able to:

1. Describe the interactions of Ananias with God and Saul.

2. Explain the fear Ananias expressed when directed to meet with Saul.

3. Evaluate how much of an "Ananias" he or she is when responding to God's call and formulate a plan to change shortcomings identified.

LESSON OUTLINE

Introduction

A. Physicist Becomes a Preacher

John Polkinghorne was one of the greatest British physicists of the twentieth century. He finished a doctorate at Cambridge University at age 25 and was invited to return to Cambridge to teach when he was 27. He participated in formulating the theory of the quark, a particle that is one of the building blocks of matter. He was one of the most brilliant men of his age. Yet after 25 years of this spectacular career in science, Polkinghorne left it all to train for the priesthood in the Church of England. He was ordained and eventually returned to Cambridge University in 1986 to serve as chaplain for Trinity Hall, one of the colleges of the university. The physicist became a preacher.

This week's lesson is about an even more dramatic career change.

B. Lesson Background: Saul

Saul, a Jew from Tarsus, had been trained as a rabbi by the best teachers in Jerusalem (compare Acts 22:3). His education in the law would have been the ancient equivalent of a doctoral degree today. When the Jewish leadership began to persecute Christians, Saul was their point man. We first see this in his leadership role in this regard in the stoning of Stephen (7:58).

Saul went on to terrorize the church by conducting house-to-house searches for Christians (Acts 8:3; 22:4). His persecuting zeal reached a fever pitch when he took the initiative to ask the high priest for authority to extend the persecution to Damascus, about 150 miles to the north of Jerusalem. His plan was to find Christians in the Jewish population there and bring them back to Jerusalem by force (9:1, 2). His encounter with the risen Christ is the immediate backdrop for today's lesson (9:3-9). Saul's ambitions and zeal had not gone unnoticed by the Lord of the church!

C. Lesson Background: Damascus

The site of today's lesson is the city of Damascus. In the Old Testament, this city is identified with the kingdom of Syria (or Aram), the sometime ally but often foe of ancient Israel (see 1 Kings 15:18). Some claim that Damascus is the oldest continually inhabited site in the world. Indeed, the Bible notes its existence in the time of Abraham (see Genesis 15:2), and archaeological data extends back even further.

Damascus was important in the first century AD as a trading hub for caravan routes. It was a multiethnic city with a substantial Jewish population. These facts highlight the perceived need to extend persecution against Jewish Christians there. Threats to the "purity" of synagogues in Damascus could not be tolerated.

Saul's mission to this city changed, however, before he arrived there. As today's lesson opens, Saul is in his third day of blindness as a result of his encounter with Christ.

I. Disturbing Vision
(ACTS 9:10-16)

A. Saul Waits (vv. 10-12)

10. Now there was a disciple at Damascus named Ananias. The Lord said to him in a vision, "Ananias." And he said, "Here I am, Lord."

We gain a bit more information about this *disciple . . . named Ananias* by consulting Acts 22:12, where Paul (formerly the Saul of today's lesson) says that Ananias was "a devout man according to the law, well spoken of by all the Jews who lived there." We take care, of course, not to confuse him with two others by the same name in Acts 5:1 and 24:1.

Luke, the author of the Gospel of Luke and the book of Acts, uses the word *disciple* dozens of times in his two works. In his Gospel, a disciple is a dedicated student of Jesus the teacher. In Acts, a disciple is a committed follower of the risen Lord. In that regard, Ananias may be much like many Christians today: serving the Lord faithfully in relative anonymity. How surprised Ananias must be, then, to experience *a vision* in which *the Lord* communicates with him personally!

The word *vision* implies seeing things not normally seen, but may also consist of hearing things not normally heard. The Lord's communication with Samuel in 1 Samuel 3 is instructive. Verse

15 calls the episode "the vision," although Samuel apparently sees nothing (but hears plenty). The same seems to be the case here. Further, both instances involve the Lord's calling the name of the one being spoken to. But unlike young Samuel, Ananias recognizes what is happening immediately. So he answers, *"Here I am, Lord."*

What Do You Think?

How can you show appreciation for the behind-the-scenes, nearly anonymous people who have influenced you for Christ?

Talking Points for Your Discussion
- Sunday school teachers from your early years
- Someone who showed you unusual kindness
- Someone who provided wise counsel during a difficult period

---

11. And the Lord said to him, "Rise and go to the street called Straight, and at the house of Judas look for a man of Tarsus named Saul, for behold, he is praying,

The divine communication with Ananias bears similarities to and differences from the divine communication with Cornelius in Acts 10:1-6 (next week's lesson). Both visions name the individual being addressed, name the person to be sought, and provide location of the latter. They are different in that Ananias is directed personally to *go*, while Cornelius is directed to "send men" to accomplish the assignment at hand.

When we consider the verse before us in light of Acts 9:9, we realize that Saul's "time-out" for prayer and fasting (while blind!) is in its third day.

What Do You Think?

What steps can we take to ensure we do not stagnate while in a "time-out" of life?

Talking Points for Your Discussion
- During a lengthy recovery from an injury
- During an unpaid furlough from work
- While on military deployment
- While spending much time providing end-of-life care for another

---

The street called Straight is a major east-west thoroughfare in Damascus. It is some 50 feet wide, with impressive gates at each end. It would be equivalent to the Broadway or High Street of some cities today, and a house on such a boulevard would be prestigious.

The Bible records no other facts about the particular *Judas* mentioned here. It is very unlikely that he is a Christian, but rather is one of the Jews in the city who expects to receive Saul and support his assignment from the high priest (see the Lesson Background). Ananias, as a Christian of Jewish background, likely knows of *the house of Judas* since the location of the man's house on an important street is likely an indicator of his prominence and wealth. Judas is not an uncommon name at the time; therefore giving his address clarifies his identity.

12. "and he has seen in a vision a man named Ananias come in and lay his hands on him that he might regain his sight."

The Lord reveals to Ananias that a parallel vision has taken place. Saul is proceeding as instructed (Acts 9:6), and we notice irony in the fact that the blind Saul is privileged to have *seen in a vision* the pending arrival of Ananias for the purpose of restoring Saul's eyesight.

The irony should not distract us from the crucial issue of Saul's blindness. This trauma surely prompts deep soul searching on his part! The vital nature of his experience on the road to Damascus is seen in that its facts are recorded in three places in the book of Acts: chapters 9, 22, and 26. The crucial nature of what is taking place surely

is not lost on Saul, even at this early point. Saul's vision of Ananias undoubtedly gives hope. But on another level, it also deepens the mystery for the time being.

Before moving on, we should note that the fact that Ananias is designated by name in Saul's vision is important for at least a couple of reasons. First, the arrival of a man with that very name will be evidence for the divine source of the vision. Second, Saul will be able to inform the owner of the house of the pending arrival of Ananias so that the visitor will not be denied entrance.

◆ *VISION, MIRAGE, OR HINDSIGHT?* ◆

Constantine the Great was the Roman emperor from AD 306 to 337. During a time of unrest and civil war, he found himself leading an army against a larger force that had occupied Rome. The climactic battle, fought at Milvian Bridge on October 28, 312, was a decisive victory for Constantine, putting him firmly on the path to being uncontested as emperor.

The victory also led the pagan Constantine to be the first emperor of the Roman Empire to embrace Christianity. According to church historian Eusebius of Caesarea, this came about because of a vision Constantine allegedly had from Christ on the day before the battle. The claimed vision was that of the *Chi-Rho*, the first two letters of the word *Christ* in Greek, superimposed. This "trophy of a cross of light in the heavens" bore the inscription "Conquer by this." Constantine did just that, after putting the *Chi-Rho* on the banners of his army.

Did the vision actually occur, or was it made up later to fit the facts of the battle's outcome? It's impossible to say. The Bible clearly establishes that God has used visions and dreams to communicate (Genesis 41:15; Numbers 12:6; etc.). But Scripture is equally clear regarding the problem of false visions (Jeremiah 14:14; 23:16; Ezekiel 13:6-9; etc.; compare Deuteronomy 18:22). Our lesson text—interesting in that God uses a vision of one man (Acts 9:10) to explain the vision of another man—records ironclad facts of history. Even so, Hebrews 1:1, 2 sets forth a vital caution regarding

HOW TO SAY IT

Ananias	An-uh-*nye*-us.
Cornelius	Cor-*neel*-yus.
Damascus	Duh-*mass*-kus.
Eusebius	You-*see*-be-us.
Gentiles	*Jen*-tiles.
Judas	*Joo*-dus.
Messiah	Meh-*sigh*-uh.
Nazareth	*Naz*-uh-reth.
Pentecost	*Pent*-ih-kost.
Tarsus	*Tar*-sus.

claims of visions today: "Long ago, at many times and in many ways, God spoke . . . but in these last days he has spoken to us by his Son."   —J. B. N.

B. Ananias Fears (vv. 13, 14)

13. But Ananias answered, "Lord, I have heard from many about this man, how much evil he has done to your saints at Jerusalem.

Like others called, Ananias does not immediately accept his assignment (compare Exodus 4:10-13). He wants nothing to do with Saul, having heard two disturbing things about the man.

First, Saul's reputation has preceded him, since Ananias knows that this man has already done *much evil* to the believers back in Jerusalem. The nature of this harm is outlined by the perpetrator himself years later: "I not only locked up many of the saints in prison . . . , but when they were put to death I cast my vote against them. And I punished them often in all the synagogues" (Acts 26:10, 11).

Ananias is saying that he knows that Saul has been a persecutor of the church. Implied in this is knowledge of Saul's complicity in the death of Stephen (see Acts 7:58). This too the repentant perpetrator admits to in due time (see 22:20).

14. "And here he has authority from the chief priests to bind all who call on your name."

Second, Ananias also knows that Saul intends to do in Damascus what he has done in Jerusalem. The *authority from the chief priests* under which Saul operates does not result in an undercover endeavor. Rather, Saul's intentions seem to be a matter of common knowledge (compare Acts 9:1, 2; 22:5; 26:12). The concern of Ananias is understandable, given this man's track record.

C. The Lord Insists (vv. 15, 16)

15. But the Lord said to him, "Go, for he is a chosen instrument of mine to carry my name before the Gentiles and kings and to the children of Israel.

The Lord does not allow fear to alter the assignment. Instead, Ananias is privileged to be made aware of the broad contours of the plan. And as history reveals, Saul (as Paul) does indeed end up presenting Christ *before the Gentiles* (example: Acts 18:6-11), *and kings* (example: 26:1-29), *and to the children of Israel* (example: 17:1-3). The zeal with which Saul serves the high priest (see Philippians 3:6) is being redirected for the Lord's service.

Surely this prophetic word is an eye-opener for Ananias. Preaching Christ to the Israelites is understandable according to Jesus' own model (Matthew 15:24; etc.), but by Saul of all people! Further, there is apparently no expectation of extending the gospel to Gentiles at this point in time (compare Acts 11:18, 19). The idea of witnessing to political rulers seems farfetched if Daniel 2 is not called to mind.

16. "For I will show him how much he must suffer for the sake of my name."

The man who has caused more suffering among Christians than any other will join their ranks as one who endures persecution (compare 2 Corinthians 11:23-28). No more letters from high priests, but a commission from the Lord of the church (also Acts 22:10; 26:15-18). No more well-funded expeditions to arrest believers, but shoestring-budgeted missions to cities to make believers (see 1 Corinthians 9:7-12). No more threats of murder for Jews who have become Christian, but plots against his own life (see Acts 9:23-25; 23:12-22).

What Do You Think?
What are some ways to respond to excuses for resisting God?
Talking Points for Your Discussion
- Concerning the "I don't have time" excuse
- Concerning the "I'm not qualified" excuse
- Concerning the "It's too dangerous" excuse
- Other

What Do You Think?
In what ways have you seen Christians put aside fears and follow the will of God?
Talking Points for Your Discussion
- In dealing with a family issue
- In dealing with an abusive coworker
- In dealing with a financial crisis
- In dealing with a crisis in the church

II. Dramatic Visit

(ACTS 9:17-20)

A. Ananias Obeys (v. 17)

17. So Ananias departed and entered the house. And laying his hands on him he said, "Brother Saul, the Lord Jesus who appeared to you on the road by which you came has sent me so that you may regain your sight and be filled with the Holy Spirit."

As Ananias encounters Saul, we should remember that Saul cannot see him. There is no indication that the two have ever met, so Ananias's voice is not familiar to Saul. We have to imagine that Saul is just as fearful as Ananias, if not more so! Saul may be doubting everything he has been taught and has believed to this point. His world is turned upside down. He has been waiting sightless for three days without eating or drinking anything (Acts 9:9).

No idle chitchat is recorded as Ananias seems to get immediately to the point of the visit. His willingness to touch Saul while addressing him as *Brother* seems to indicate that Ananias's fear has been at least partially allayed. We do not have to be completely without fear in order to obey. Fear grows when we sit and stew about what might happen. Fear is overcome by faith as faith is put into action.

What Do You Think?

Under what circumstances should physical contact with someone in distress be encouraged or discouraged? Why?

Talking Points for Your Discussion

- Regarding private, one-to-one counseling sessions
- In light of cultural expectations or dictates
- Other

The Lord Jesus is the focus of Ananias's pronouncement to Saul. It is Jesus who has granted the parallel visions of Ananias and Saul. This supernatural knowledge confirms again for Saul that the Lord is active in all of this. This is not demonic deception. The fact that the risen Jesus has sent Ananias to restore Saul's eyesight as predicted establishes that the man has not been abandoned.

But Ananias has also been sent for Saul to *be filled with the Holy Spirit*, something not recorded to have been made known to that man (see v. 12, above). Only Luke of the New Testament authors uses the phrases "filled with the Holy Spirit" or "full of the Holy Spirit." In Luke's Gospel, this status is applied to John the Baptist (Luke 1:15), his parents (1:41, 67), and Jesus (4:1).

In the book of Acts, the same status characterizes the disciples on the Day of Pentecost (Acts 2:4), Peter on a later occasion (4:8), believers gathered for prayer (4:31), Stephen (6:5; 7:55), Barnabas (11:24), Saul (here and 13:9), and unnamed disciples (13:52). The second of the two passages applied to Saul is accompanied by his name change from Saul to Paul. Further, there is significant irony in the fact that the context has the previously blinded Paul pronouncing blindness on an enemy of Christ (13:9-11).

B. Saul Sees (vv. 18, 19a)

18, 19a. And immediately something like scales fell from his eyes, and he regained his sight. Then he rose and was baptized; and taking food, he was strengthened.

As Saul's blindness had been imposed instantaneously, so now is restoration of *his sight*. The word for what drops *from his eyes* is translated *scales*, indicating something like the scales of a fish. This does not mean that Saul has grown a fish-like skin over his eyes. The sense is of something that can be peeled off like the scales of a fish. It is as if a layer of skin that has covered his eyes is miraculously peeled away by the hand of God and falls to Saul's lap. This may indicate that Saul's eyesight was not damaged in and of itself, but has been blocked in a physical way as a result of his encounter with Christ on the Damascus road.

With this disabling condition removed, Saul wastes no time in receiving baptism. This likely is administered by Ananias, perhaps in the nearby Brada River. Saul is ready to go! The weakness that results from a three-day fast is quickly reversed by a meal. But we notice that the thing of greater spiritual significance (baptism) comes first.

C. Synagogues Hear (vv. 19b, 20)

19b, 20. For some days he was with the disciples at Damascus. And immediately he proclaimed Jesus in the synagogues, saying, "He is the Son of God."

The Jews of Damascus had expected Saul to come from Jerusalem and condemn those of their fellow Israelites who had embraced Christ. Instead, Saul begins to advocate the Christian message, that Jesus *is the Son of God*. So begins Saul's career as a preacher.

◆ *THE FOUNDATION OF PREACHING* ◆

Walter Scott (1796–1861) was a highly effective evangelist and author. Over a lifetime of ministry, he developed an emphasis on Jesus as the Son of God, the Christ. His book *The Messiahship,* of nearly 400 pages, documented his thought and study in this regard.

By analyzing the preaching of the apostles, Scott concluded that they preached only about Christ—that he was the Son of God, the promised Messiah. The apostles supported their assertion by pointing to Jesus' miracles, to the fulfillment of Old Testament prophecies, and to the testimony of eyewitnesses. Scott argued that this was a matter-of-fact conclusion, one that anyone with normal intelligence could accept, based on the factual support.

Much of Scott's gospel preaching drew from a simple outline regarding things a person must do and things God promised to do for someone to receive salvation. Some parts of that outline are worded better than others, given the advance of biblical understanding since Scott's day. But the outline as a whole rested on the foundational premise of Paul's preaching: Jesus is the Son of God. And so it should remain.   —J. B. N.

Conclusion

A. Faith and Obedience in Two Men

The dramatic events of Acts 9 record how extreme God's action had to be for Saul to turn his attention to God's call. Saul was so obsessed with climbing the ladder of favor within the Jewish leadership (Galatians 1:14) that he did not rec-

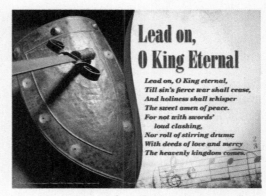

Visual for Lessons 3 & 12. *Point to the last two lines of this hymn as you ask, "What has to happen for us to be aware of the deeds God expects of us?"*

ognize the legitimacy of the Christian message. He was spiritually blind to the fact that he was persecuting Jesus Christ, the risen Son of God.

Saul, as Paul, went on to become the great apostle to the Gentiles. Christians of non-Jewish background owe him a great debt of gratitude, for he fought a somewhat lonely battle to gain an equal place in the church for people of all backgrounds. Even so, let us not forget the key role of the nearly anonymous Ananias, who was called by God to overcome his fears and minister to the church's greatest enemy at just the right time.

The voice of Ananias was part of the call of God for the one who came to be known as the apostle Paul. Nearly 30 years later, Paul mentioned this man by name (Acts 22:12). He never forgot this man of faith, a faith that overcame fear.

Acts 9 is not intended as a pattern for how God brings people to faith, and the role of Paul as apostle was unique. Even so, God expects us at times to be his hands and feet, as was Ananias. May we overcome our fears as we answer that call.

B. Prayer

Lord, tune our spiritual eyes and ears to perceive the tasks you have for us. Grant us humility with courage as we embrace those tasks. We pray this in Jesus' name. Amen.

C. Thought to Remember

God's call is insistent and persistent.

INVOLVEMENT LEARNING

Enhance your lesson presentation with the reproducible activity page,
available as a free download at www.standardlesson.com.

Into the Lesson

Before class, write this incomplete sentence on the board: *"One household chore I try to avoid doing is _____."*

As students arrive, draw their attention to the sentence on the board. To begin class, ask for volunteers to complete the sentence and give reasons for their feelings about the chore named.

Alternative. Distribute copies of the "Not My Job!" activity from the reproducible page, which you can download. Have students discuss it in pairs or small groups.

After either activity, lead into Bible study saying, "Some jobs are not pleasant, but they need to be done nonetheless. In the early days of the church, Ananias of Damascus was given a job to do by God himself. Let's see how he reacted to the job and the difference that was made because of it."

Into the Word

Divide your class into three groups. Give each group paper and pens. Each group should be assigned a section of the lesson text. Each group should try to title their section of the text four times—once in four words, once in three words, once in two words, and once in a single word.

Scripture assignments and sample titles follow:

Group 1—Acts 9:10-14
Nightmare on Straight Street
Mutiny in Damascus
Impossible Mission
Fear

Group 2—Acts 9:15-17
From Fear to Eternity
The Reborn Identity
Mission Possible
Chosen

Group 3—Acts 9:18-20
Guess Who's a Christian!
God in Charge

Altered Fates
Transformer

Allow time for groups to share their titles and summarize their Scripture assignments.

Option. Write each title on a separate slip of paper and distribute them to different class members. Read the sections of the text aloud one at a time, asking the class if anyone has a slip of paper with a good title for that particular section.

Into Life

Ask the class to create a list of fears that are common in our society. List them on the board. Here are some fears that students will probably mention:

Fear of death
Fear of the dark
Fear of public speaking
Fear of losing a job
Fear of failure
Fear of rejection
Fear of being alone
Fear of crime

Divide the class into small groups. Provide each group with a concordance and have them look for Bible verses that can strengthen their faith and overcome specific fears.

For example, they may find Psalm 23:4 helpful in confronting fear of death or darkness. God's promise to always be with us in Deuteronomy 31:6 can comfort those who fear rejection or being alone. Matthew 10:28 might comfort those who fear crime, because of Jesus' statement that we have no reason to fear those who might harm our bodies.

Alternative. Distribute copies of the "Faith Greater Than Fear" activity from the reproducible page. Have students work on this individually, and have volunteers report. If you prefer, use this as a take-home activity.

CALLED TO BE INCLUSIVE

DEVOTIONAL READING: Psalm 15
BACKGROUND SCRIPTURE: Acts 10

ACTS 10:19-33

¹⁹ And while Peter was pondering the vision, the Spirit said to him, "Behold, three men are looking for you. ²⁰ Rise and go down and accompany them without hesitation, for I have sent them." ²¹ And Peter went down to the men and said, "I am the one you are looking for. What is the reason for your coming?" ²² And they said, "Cornelius, a centurion, an upright and God-fearing man, who is well spoken of by the whole Jewish nation, was directed by a holy angel to send for you to come to his house and to hear what you have to say." ²³ So he invited them in to be his guests.

The next day he rose and went away with them, and some of the brothers from Joppa accompanied him. ²⁴ And on the following day they entered Caesarea. Cornelius was expecting them and had called together his relatives and close friends. ²⁵ When Peter entered, Cornelius met him and fell down at his feet and worshiped him. ²⁶ But Peter lifted him up, saying, "Stand up; I too am a man." ²⁷ And as he talked with him, he went in and found many persons gathered. ²⁸ And he said to them, "You yourselves know how unlawful it is for a Jew to associate with or to visit anyone of another nation, but God has shown me that I should not call any person common or unclean. ²⁹ So when I was sent for, I came without objection. I ask then why you sent for me."

³⁰ And Cornelius said, "Four days ago, about this hour, I was praying in my house at the ninth hour, and behold, a man stood before me in bright clothing ³¹ and said, 'Cornelius, your prayer has been heard and your alms have been remembered before God. ³² Send therefore to Joppa and ask for Simon who is called Peter. He is lodging in the house of Simon, a tanner, by the sea.' ³³ So I sent for you at once, and you have been kind enough to come. Now therefore we are all here in the presence of God to hear all that you have been commanded by the Lord."

KEY VERSE

[Peter] said to them, "You yourselves know how unlawful it is for a Jew to associate with or to visit anyone of another nation, but God has shown me that I should not call any person common or unclean. —Acts 10:28

GOD'S URGENT CALL

Unit 3: Calls in the New Testament

LESSONS 10–13

LESSON AIMS

After participating in this lesson, each learner will be able to:

1. Identify the "clean" and "unclean" references in Peter's vision and his reaction thereto.

2. Evaluate Peter's resistance to interacting with Gentiles in light of his declaration on Pentecost that the gospel is for everyone (Acts 2:39).

3. Pray for an opportunity to present the gospel cross-culturally.

LESSON OUTLINE

Introduction

A. Steadfast or Stubborn?

What are the nonnegotiables of your congregation, spoken or unspoken? A set order of service? A particular style of worship music? A certain Bible translation? A specific time for services? The mode of baptism? Home small groups? Type of clothing? Leadership qualifications?

Nonnegotiables that involve Bible doctrines we can call *matters of the faith* (with "the faith" referring to the body of doctrine to be believed; compare Titus 1:13; Jude 3). The things some may consider to be nonnegotiable but which have no basis in Scripture can be called *matters of expediency.* Typically, these are changeable methods of making ministry happen.

The matters-of-the-faith list is, of course, the more important. As we ponder our lists, we should ask this question: *When is "standing firm" valid and when it is merely lifeless legalism?* Being steadfast in following God's will is one thing; stubbornly insisting on our own will, which we think to be God's will too, is another. Let's look at how Peter dealt with this dilemma.

B. Lesson Background

Following the account of Saul's conversion, the focus of the book of Acts shifts back to Peter. Persecution had subsided, and Peter enjoyed freedom of movement (Acts 9:31, 32). He healed a bedridden man in Lydda, which resulted in mass conversion to Christianity (9:33-35).

Called hurriedly to nearby Joppa, Peter encountered the grief of those whose friend Tabitha had died. Mass conversion resulted yet again, as God brought the dead woman back to life through Peter's ministry (9:36-42). A welcome reception resulted in his staying "for many days with one Simon, a tanner" (9:43). The fact that Peter would stay there for any length of time is interesting given that tanners were regularly "unclean" because of contact with animal carcasses (Leviticus 11:26-28).

Joppa is a coastal city of central Palestine, situated on a bluff overlooking a small natural harbor. It is about 35 miles northwest of Jerusalem. A well-traveled thoroughfare connected the two cities, for Joppa effectively had served as the Mediterranean port city for Jerusalem since the time of Solomon (see 2 Chronicles 2:16).

About 30 miles north of Joppa was the newer city of Caesarea Maritima (Caesarea by the sea), rebuilt by Herod the Great and named for his patron and friend Caesar Augustus. Herod created Caesarea according to the pattern of grand Roman cities, with broad streets, landmark temples, an aqueduct water supply, and a spacious theater. These features made Caesarea Maritima (not to be confused with Caesarea Philippi [Mark 8:27]) the preferred residence for Roman officials stationed in Palestine. When compared with hot, dusty, and trouble-prone Jerusalem, we can see why!

Centurions, one of whom Peter encountered in Caesarea, were professional, career soldiers. A centurion commanded a unit known as a century, which consisted of 100 soldiers and support personnel. There were six centuries in a band (or cohort), and 10 bands in a Roman battle legion.

The centurion Peter encountered in today's lesson is said to have been part of "the Italian Cohort" (Acts 10:1). The designation *Italian* indicates that the unit's constituents were men primarily from Rome and its surrounding regions. The men were not provincial auxiliaries from allies or conquered territories. This was an elite group, as Roman as Roman could be. The word *Cohort* may indicate that the troop strength in Caesarea was at least 600 soldiers.

HOW TO SAY IT

Caesar Augustus	*See*-zer Aw-*gus*-tus.
Caesarea Maritima	Sess-uh-*ree*-uh Mar-uh-*tee*-muh.
centurion	sen-*ture*-ee-un.
Cornelius	Cor-*neel*-yus.
Galilee	*Gal*-uh-lee.
Gentiles	*Jen*-tiles.
Joppa	*Jop*-uh.
Judea	Joo-*dee*-uh.
Lydda	*Lid*-uh.
Mediterranean	Med-uh-tuh-*ray*-nee-un.
Samaritan	Suh-*mare*-uh-tun.
Solomon	*Sol*-o-mun.

Acts 10:1 also tells us that the name of the centurion Peter encountered was Cornelius. He seems to have been a most unusual Roman! Rather than despising the Jews of Palestine (as most Romans did; contrast Luke 7:1-5), he is attracted to them and their religion. He is described as devout: one who feared God, gave to the poor, and prayed (Acts 10:2). His lifestyle and attitude had not gone unnoticed either by God (10:4) or by the Jewish people (10:22).

I. Peter Responds
(ACTS 10:19-24)

Just before today's lesson text opens, Peter experiences a three-part vision in which he sees many animals that are "unclean" by Jewish law, and yet he is commanded three times to kill and eat them. Peter protests the directive each time, claiming that he has never violated the law by eating what is considered unclean (Acts 10:10-16).

This is a side of Peter we have not really seen before as recorded by the author Luke (who wrote Luke and Acts). He has been presented as a self-confessed sinful man (Luke 5:8). His sinfulness lies in areas other than keeping the dietary laws, though, and he cannot conceive of eating pork or lizard meat.

Yet the voice in the vision tells him, "What God has made clean, do not call common" (Acts 10:15). This points to a coming need for Peter to move beyond his long-held understanding of Jewish purity and Gentile uncleanness.

A. Listening to God (vv. 19, 20)

19, 20. And while Peter was pondering the vision, the Spirit said to him, "Behold, three men are looking for you. Rise and go down and accompany them without hesitation, for I have sent them."

A stunned Peter is sorting it out when *the Spirit* interrupts with instructions. The *three men* who are outside looking for Peter consist of two household servants and a trusted soldier sent by Cornelius (Acts 10:7). The ultimate sender though is God, for the Spirit tells Peter, *I have sent them.* God is orchestrating the meetings of key people according to his plan. What is being arranged is the most startling of divine appointments: a Jewish fisherman with a Gentile army officer!

> **What Do You Think?**
> How do we know when hesitating is a good thing or a bad thing?
> *Talking Points for Your Discussion*
> - In Christian contexts (new ministries, etc.)
> - In secular contexts (job offers, etc.)
> - "He who hesitates is lost" vs. "Look before you leap"

B. Receiving Others (vv. 21-24)

21. And Peter went down to the men and said, "I am the one you are looking for. What is the reason for your coming?"

Peter may be puzzled, but he obeys the urging of the Spirit without delay. The three men are Gentiles, so greeting and meeting them is not normal procedure for one such as Peter, who keeps the Law of Moses.

Peter doesn't play hard to get as he immediately identifies himself and pushes the visitors to disclose their mission. He wants to make sense out of all this. How do three strangers at the door relate to a vision of eating forbidden food?

22. And they said, "Cornelius, a centurion, an upright and God-fearing man, who is well spoken of by the whole Jewish nation, was directed by a holy angel to send for you to come to his house and to hear what you have to say."

Imagine the conflicting thoughts in Peter's mind as he listens. *Another* centurion *like the one I met earlier? [Luke 7:1-10] An arrogant occupier of my homeland?* An upright and God-fearing man? *Is there any such thing among the brutal Romans? How can he fear the one true God, since the Romans worship many gods?* Well spoken of by the whole Jewish nation? *A holy angel* has spoken to an unholy Gentile?

Peter's head must be spinning with all this startling information—information that ends with an invitation. But it is presented in a way that makes it hard to sustain his doubts.

> **What Do You Think?**
> How should Christians respond to those who fear God but have not yielded to Jesus?
> *Talking Points for Your Discussion*
> - Ways to respond relationally
> - Ways to respond doctrinally
> - Ways to respond emotionally
> - Other

23. So he invited them in to be his guests.

The next day he rose and went away with them, and some of the brothers from Joppa accompanied him.

Peter welcomes the men into Simon's house. Simon himself is regularly "unclean" (see the Lesson Background), and now more uncleanness is added as Gentiles are provided lodging. But this indicates that Peter is agreeing to accompany them the next day. *The brothers from Joppa* who join Peter on the trip number six (Acts 11:12). Adding those six to the three from Cornelius plus Peter himself yields a traveling group of 10. A 30-mile trek by foot to Caesarea means a journey requiring more than a single day of dawn-to-dusk walking.

24. And on the following day they entered Caesarea. Cornelius was expecting them and had called together his relatives and close friends.

The time required for the envoys of Cornelius to travel to Joppa and back allows the centurion time to assemble *his relatives and close friends*. This gives the impression that he has been stationed in Caesarea for some time, having brought family along on the deployment. Caesarea is a Gentile enclave, making it unlikely that a Jewish fisherman from Galilee has been there before.

> **What Do You Think?**
> In what unusual ways have you seen God open doors for the gospel?
> *Talking Points for Your Discussion*
> - Among neighbors
> - Within families
> - Among your colleagues at work or school
> - Other

II. Peter Clarifies

(ACTS 10:25-29)

Before we consider what Peter has to say to those gathered, we can pause to realize that he has already spent more than a day walking and talking with the three men Cornelius sent. The text does not record the content of those conversations, but their substance is easy to imagine!

A. Shared Humanity (vv. 25-27)

25, 26. When Peter entered, Cornelius met him and fell down at his feet and worshiped him. But Peter lifted him up, saying, "Stand up; I too am a man."

The surprises continue for Peter as *Cornelius,* a centurion who is quickly recognizable as such by his attire, falls down in a posture of worship toward the apostle! This is both unexpected and unpleasant for Peter. It unexpected because if anyone is to show deference toward another in that culture, it would be Peter's deference toward the Roman centurion. Moreover, Peter knows that worship is to be directed toward God alone (Exodus 20:3; etc.).

Therefore Peter cannot allow this false worship to continue. In affirming their common humanity, Peter implies that mortals are not to be worshipped (compare Acts 14:11-18).

◆ *ON BEING NOT GOD* ◆

I once met a man who had been a radio operator in the Russian army in 1953. When he sent out word that Stalin had died, his commander threatened to shoot him for spreading a falsehood. "Stalin cannot die," the commander declared.

History is filled with accounts of people who think more highly of themselves than they ought (compare Romans 12:3). Roman emperors considered themselves to be at least semi-divine (compare Acts 12:21-23). Medieval kings were often thought to have miraculous healing powers. The disciples themselves needed correction in their self-evaluations (Mark 9:33-37; 10:35-45).

Today's text reveals that Peter rejected any divine prestige for himself. While no genuine Christian would dare claim to be deity, we skirt

the edges of that danger when we take credit that belongs to God (see Daniel 4:29-32). The best way to handle such temptation? Listen to Jesus: "When you have done all that you were commanded, say, 'We are unworthy servants; we have only done what was our duty'" (Luke 17:10).

—J. B. N.

27. And as he talked with him, he went in and found many persons gathered.

A potential surprise for Peter: this is not to be a private discussion. There is a houseful of men and woman, likely all Gentiles, who have assembled to hear what Peter has to say.

B. Divisive Differences (vv. 28, 29)

28. And he said to them, "You yourselves know how unlawful it is for a Jew to associate with or to visit anyone of another nation, but God has shown me that I should not call any person common or unclean.

Peter is processing his conflicting thoughts out loud. On the one hand, he believes strongly that Jews are to have no contact with *anyone of another nation.* This is what he has been taught from childhood. His view of Gentiles is culturally ingrained and is supported by Scripture applicable to the old covenant (Leviticus 20:23, 24, 26; etc.).

On the other hand, Peter has just had a troubling vision that has challenged his most cherished taboo: eating the flesh of an animal forbidden as unclean (see the Lesson Background). This has served to remind him that the Lord is the master of his own laws.

God's laws are purposeful. He set boundaries on what the nation of Israel should eat and with whom they should associate for their benefit. But as Peter hears himself say *I should not call any person common or unclean,* he seems to realize that these ancient laws are passing away. He must let the Lord's leading overcome long-held beliefs that cause him to shun Gentiles.

◆ *WHEN TO OBEY, AND WHEN NOT TO* ◆

The Fugitive Slave Act of 1850 required that authorities and citizens in America's "free" states had to assist in the capture and return of runaway slaves. This unjust law caused political upheaval across much of the United States, and the law was often disobeyed. Given our need to respect governing authority (Romans 13:1-7), this question arose: Under what circumstances can or should a law be disobeyed?

At least three situations present themselves. A given law should be disobeyed if (1) it contravenes universal principles of morality and justice or (2) following it would result in breaking a more important law or (3) it has been superseded or set aside by appropriate authority. The first situation fits that of disobeying the Fugitive Slave Act. The second concern stands behind the dialogue in Mark 12:28-34. The third is illustrated by today's text.

The Law of Moses required separation from that which was unholy (Leviticus 11:44, 45; 19:2). Therefore there was to be no friendship with the unholy pagans (Deuteronomy 7:1-6). Various traditions developed over the centuries to ensure enforcement, lest sins of the past be repeated. But Peter realized that something had changed!

The holiness mandate still applied, as Peter himself later wrote (1 Peter 1:15, 16). But he was not to allow old-covenant mandates for maintaining holiness to keep him from interacting with those who need the gospel. It took time for Peter to conduct himself consistently in this regard (Galatians 2:11-14). May it not take us as long!

—J. B. N.

Visual for Lesson 13. *Create a multiple-choice test with these four topics as the potential responses to each question. Use the test as a unit review.*

29. "So when I was sent for, I came without objection. I ask then why you sent for me."

While Peter has come *without objection,* he does not know exactly why God has put him in this position. Peter is ready to do God's will and assumes that Cornelius can provide details that will help him understand. Peter is already aware that Cornelius has also had a vision from God (Acts 10:3, 22).

III. Cornelius Explains
(ACTS 10:30-33)

Recalling the information in the Lesson Background enriches our understanding of what happens next as Peter yields the floor to Cornelius.

A. Prepared Host (vv. 30-32)

30. And Cornelius said: "Four days ago, about this hour, I was praying in my house at the ninth hour, and behold, a man stood before me in bright clothing

Cornelius begins by recounting the facts of the angelic visitation of Acts 10:3-6. *Four days* may seem like a long time for us, but it shows the immediacy of these events to the first-century readers. Considering the time it takes to walk to and from Joppa, there is no delay. A clue to the devoutness of Cornelius is seen in the fact that *the ninth hour* (about 3:00 p.m.) is "the hour of prayer" for Jews (Acts 3:1).

31. "and said, 'Cornelius, your prayer has been heard and your alms have been remembered before God.

We are not told the exact content of the prayer of Cornelius, but that is not the point here. The angel reveals to him that God has been hearing his prayers and noting his kindness toward the poor. *Alms* means, in awkward English, something like "compassionateness." This may refer specifically to monetary gifts (as in Acts 3:1-6) or to acts of compassion in a general sense (as in Matthew 6:1).

A very important thing to learn from this verse is that God may indeed hear the prayers of non-Christians. Cornelius is neither a Jew nor a Christian at this point, yet his prayers have been heard. It is God who decides whose prayers are heard, not we or our doctrinal positions.

32. "'Send therefore to Joppa and ask for Simon who is called Peter. He is lodging in the house of Simon, a tanner, by the sea.'

The detail of Cornelius's vision must startle Peter. The centurion has been made aware of the details of Peter's name and given the apostle's exact location! It is also important that Peter come to Cornelius rather than the other way around, because full acceptance of Gentiles is best brought about in a Gentile home.

B. Eager Audience (v. 33)

33. "So I sent for you at once, and you have been kind enough to come. Now therefore we are all here in the presence of God to hear all that you have been commanded by the Lord."

By means of the last sentence of this verse, Cornelius yields the floor back to Peter. History is about to be made, and Cornelius seems to know it. The stage is set for a great leap of inclusion, the moment when the church expands beyond its Jewish foundations. The barrier between Jew and Gentile is about to fall.

God does not leave this to chance or accident. He has chosen Cornelius to be the launching point for Gentile inclusion in the church because that man's heart is receptive to God's leading. Cornelius surely has his own baggage of bias against Jews. He surely is tainted with his own history of pagan practices as any Roman of the day is. But the Lord sees into his heart. God knows he is the right person at this pivotal moment in history.

The vital nature of this moment is underlined and highlighted by the outpouring of the Holy Spirit (Acts 10:44) and Peter's lengthy defense of his actions later in Jerusalem (11:1-18). That section ends with Peter's critics saying, "Then to the Gentiles also God has granted repentance that leads to life." God's activities are truly remarkable!

> **What Do You Think?**
> What can your church do to make its outreach more inclusive? What limits to inclusiveness, if any, should be maintained in the process?
> *Talking Points for Your Discussion*
> - In reaching across racial divides
> - In reaching across generational divides
> - In reaching across doctrinal divides
> - Other

Conclusion
A. Just for You

There is an insurance company commercial in which the spokesperson offers a great deal to a customer. The grateful response is, "You'd do that just for me?" The spokesperson replies, "Just for you . . . and everyone else." A turning point in history occurred when God revealed to Peter that Jesus was just for him . . . and everyone else.

The Christian faith is intended to be universal. The church Jesus established is to stand apart from the ethnic or national ties that characterize so many other religions, whether in the first century or in the twenty-first. The church is not just for those who dress as we do or share our taste in worship music. The church has no second-class citizens. The church is not just for those of a "targeted demographic." Jesus expects us to invite everyone from everywhere. See Matthew 28:19, 20.

B. Prayer

Father of all, we thank you for including us in the church your Son established. May the Spirit empower us to ensure that others are included as well. We pray this in Jesus' name. Amen.

C. Thought to Remember

May we heed God as he teaches us where to stand and where to stretch.

INVOLVEMENT LEARNING

Enhance your lesson presentation with the reproducible activity page,
available as a free download at www.standardlesson.com.

Into the Lesson

Divide the board into two columns, with *Practices of the church that should NEVER change* heading one column and *Practices of the church that COULD be changed* heading the other.

Spend a few moments asking students to suggest practices that could go into either one of these columns. After making these lists, discuss how we decide which practices go into which column. Ask, "When is standing firm guarding the purity of the church and when is it lifeless legalism? When is change simply making accommodation to the needs of others and when is it a compromise of core values?"

Alternative. As students arrive, distribute copies of the "Positive or Negative?" reproducible page, which you can download. Students can begin working on it immediately. Discuss the activity briefly after all students have arrived.

After either activity, lead into Bible study saying, "We have identified a question with which the church has wrestled from the very beginning. While being steadfast in following God's will is one thing, stubbornly insisting on our own will is another. Let's look at how Peter dealt with this problem."

Into the Word

Divide your class into three groups. Give each group paper and pens. Each group should be assigned a section of the lesson text and should summarize its portion of the lesson text as a tabloid heading and subtitle.

Scripture assignments and sample headlines follow:

Group 1—Be Available (Acts 10:19-25)
  Delegation Sent to Jewish Teacher!
  Peter Welcomes Cornelius's Emissaries
Group 2—Clarify the Situation (Acts 10:26-29)
  Unlikely Summit
  Jew Meets with Roman Military Leader

Group 3—Accept Opportunities (Acts 10:30-33)
  Commander or Crazy Man?
  Cornelius Claims to Have Had a Religious Vision

Allow time for groups to share their headlines and summarize their Scripture assignments.

Alternative. Distribute copies of the "Surprised or Expected" activity from the reproducible page. Give students a chance to mark the statements summarizing the content of the lesson text as something that surprised them or as something they expected. Ask students to defend their responses.

Into Life

Move to the closing of the class by saying, "Cornelius was a person many would have seen as unlikely to believe in Jesus. Over the course of history, many more unlikely converts have become Christians." Then read the following list.

Leif Erikson—Viking explorer who turned from Norse paganism to Christ. He was given the mission of introducing Greenland to Jesus.

Wernher von Braun—This German aerospace engineer, considered the "father of rocket science," accepted Jesus after visiting a church in Texas.

Chuck Colson—Once known as President Nixon's "hatchet man," Colson went to prison due to his part in the Watergate scandal. After accepting Jesus, he became an influential Christian leader and author.

Lee Strobel—This former atheist and journalist for the *Chicago Tribune* sought to disprove Christianity, but his research convinced him to accept Christ.

Dr. Rosaria Champagne Butterfield—A professor of English and Queer Theory (a form of gay and lesbian studies) once despised Christianity. She is now a Christian and a minister's wife.

Close class by praying with students that God will bring unlikely converts into their lives.